WALKING IN THE ALPS

The attractive alp hamlet of Jungen, with the Dom beyond
the great trench of the Mattertal

WALKING IN
THE ALPS

by

Kev Reynolds

CICERONE PRESS
MILNTHORPE, CUMBRIA, ENGLAND

ISBN 1 85284 261 X
A catalogue record for this book is available from the British Library.

ACKNOWLEDGEMENTS

This book owes much to a great number of people whose knowledge, enthusiasm, companionship and/or practical assistance has been drawn upon and so readily given. I am indebted to the willingness of all who participated in this project, and to those who gave permission to quote from copyright material. First among these must be Ernst Sondheimer who from the very start has been feeding information, lending maps and books, and urging me to visit specific remote glens where the magic of the past is still a part of the present. His lasting encouragement has added much to pleasures gained in the hills. Other mountain friends have given welcome advice which I readily acknowledge; in particular Martin Collins, Andrew Harper, Roland Hiss and Anne Shipley; Brian Evans and Walt Unsworth at Cicerone, and Cecil Davies who spontaneously sent me a preview of a new edition of his Austria guide to study. Heidi Reisz at the Swiss National Tourist Office, and Marion Telsnig at the Austrian National Tourist Office, were both extremely generous with their assistance. I am also indebted to Air U.K., Ken Rawlinson of Phoenix Mountaineering, David Brown at Zamberlan U.K. and Clive Allen at Lowe Alpine. Hamish Brown, Janet Carleton (formerly Janet Adam Smith), Cecil Davies, Brian Evans, Anne Shipley and Walt Unsworth kindly allowed me to use quotations from their letters, books or magazine articles which add quality to the text. Despite my searches I have failed to locate the owners of copyright of several quotations used, and apologise to them for this. Finally, as ever, my wife shared some truly magical days in the Alps, and has provided the all-important back-up at home to enable me to concentrate on this book. My thanks to her, and all the above, is greater than I can adequately express.

Kev Reynolds
Spring, 1998

Cicerone guides by the same author:

Walks in the Engadine - Switzerland
The Bernese Alps
Ticino - Switzerland
Chamonix to Zermatt - the Walker's Haute Route
Tour of the Vanoise
Langtang, Gosainkund & Helambu
Walks & Climbs in the Pyrenees
The Wealdway & Vanguard Way
The South Downs Way & The Downs Link

The Valais
Central Switzerland
The Jura (with R.B. Evans)
Alpine Pass Route
Annapurna - a Trekker's Guide
Everest - a Trekker's Guide
Walking in Kent Vols I & II
The Cotswold Way

Front cover: Above Saas Fee, the Gemsweg (Route 27) looks to the Mischabel peaks (The Pennine Alps)

CONTENTS

INTRODUCTION

E xtending in a huge arc from the Mediterranean coast near Nice to the low
wooded hills on the outskirts of Vienna, the Alps are the world's best known
mountains. Over the past two centuries every peak, ridge and valley has
been mapped and explored, every glacier measured, every natural beauty described,
advertised and, in some way or other, exploited. Library shelves groan beneath the
weight of books that record the range's history, detail its geology, or recount tales
of adventure on rockface and icefall illustrated with stunning coloured photographs,
while guidebooks by the hundred, in who knows how many languages, provide all
the detail required to move with a degree of confidence and safety from valley bed
to snow-capped summit.

Nearly fifty years ago J. Hubert Walker published his classic *Walking in the Alps*.
This finely crafted book was directed at the British hill walker and mountaineer 'of
modest attainment' who had not yet grown familiar with the greater heights of the
Alps. It was a selective book, of course, both in the Alpine groups described and
in the routes suggested, but it succeeded in everything the author set out to achieve.
With the most elegant prose Walker unfolded the Alpine landscape so that it
became as clear as if one were studying a series of photographs, and with
instinctive skill led his reader into some of the loveliest of all valleys, onto hillsides
that would display the finest views, and over passes that gave the greatest
contrasts. Without preaching, and without stressing his own accomplishments,
Walker gently advised where the best walks and climbs were to be had, and then
made suggestions for filling a holiday of a week or more in a round that would
provide a sense of achievement and enough memories to last a lifetime.

For three decades Walker's book has been my Alpine bible. It has been, and still
is, a constant source of inspiration and pleasure; there's not a dull paragraph in it.
But of course, in half a century the Alps have changed - by this I mean some of the
mountains as well as valleys and villages. Some of the glens much loved by Walker
have been flooded for hydro-electricity schemes. Once remote hillsides are now
adorned with chairlift and cable-car, and bulldozed pistes scar mountain flanks
where before only the chamois strayed. And with an explosion of interest in all
manner of mountain activities, footpaths have multiplied and at times the busiest
of them all now better resemble shopping malls in the run-up to Christmas. That is
not to suggest the Alps are finished, played out, or 'destroyed' in their wild and
pristine sense, as claimed by some activists at the sharp end of the climbing world,
but there are certainly more honeypot regions now than Walker himself would
have known. Penned a century and more ago, the description, 'the Playground of
Europe' was never more apt than it is today. There are still wonderlands left,
though, thank heaven; still a few permanently inhabited villages where no roads
lead and where the only means of approach is by walking for a couple of hours or
more. There are walkers' passes and lonely alps virtually unvisited from one year-
end to the next - yes, even in Switzerland - and trails to follow in mid-summer where
you can find as much solitude as you wish. And the glory of the high Alps remains
as fresh as it always has been. If you know where to look.

Walker's book continues to feed dreams. However, in order to make those dreams come true it needs updating to fit the Alps as they are in reality today. For several years I'd been assembling notes in order to do just that, when I received a phone call one day from Walt Unsworth at Cicerone. "Do you know Hubert Walker's *Walking in the Alps*?" he asked. "We'd like to publish something along those lines, bringing Walker up-to-date but with wider coverage, and hope you'll take it on." This, then, is the result. It's a volume that, in trying to cover virtually the whole complex Alpine chain, attempts the impossible. From the start I acknowledge its failings for I know that before the ink is dry on the page, the occasional passage contained in this book will be obsolete, thanks to the evolution of Alpine development. I offer my apologies and beg the reader's understanding.

Like its namesake this book sets out to describe some of the loveliest Alpine regions from the point of view of the walker who is, after all, in the most favoured position to witness and enjoy mountain scenery in all its abundant variety. The motorist is divorced from all that is best in the Alps by being restricted to the highway. The non-active tourist is confined to mechanised means of uplift, the climber's attention is for the most part taken up with the intricacies of his chosen route, while the downhill skier needs full concentration in the rush to get to the foot of the slope without accident. Only the mountain walker, the individual with good general fitness, a modicum of scrambling experience and an eye for the hills, can move far enough and at the right pace to enjoy the full range of wonders that the Alps so generously offer. This is the person for whom this book is written. It attempts to reveal the multitude of opportunities available. Not with precise route descriptions, a number of which may be found within available guidebooks mentioned in each chapter's summary, but by giving a nudge in the right direction. Happily, detailed guidebooks do not exist for each and every individual district described, and I have specifically avoided giving too much information about some of my favourite areas about which little has been published, for it is good to retain that element of surprise that may only be experienced when you make a 'discovery' of your own. Hints will be found within these pages as to where some of these special places lie, but you'll have to work them out for yourself, while other routes and multi-day treks are treated to rather more detail.

In the early days of the Alpine Club there was a kind of division between those who saw themselves as 'centrists' and those who claimed to be 'ex-centrists'. The first class of mountaineer based himself in Grindelwald, Chamonix or Zermatt, say, and from there struck out to climb the local peaks, after which he would always return to the same valley hotel. The 'ex-centrist' on the other hand (and first-rate examples of this class were F.F. Tuckett and W.M. Conway), would travel from one region to the other across passes and glaciers on their way to climb. The same could be said today of the mountain walker. One chooses a particular valley base and goes out day by day to wander the local trails, the other fills his rucksack and sets out from hut to hut or camp to camp on a tour lasting anything from a few days to a month or more. There's much to be said in favour of both methods of approach, and lucky the man who has the opportunity to enjoy each one! In this book I've taken account of both the 'centrist' and 'ex-centrist' point of view, for the Alps are big enough to encompass both, and to reward in generous fashion.

An attempt has been made to define the topography of each Alpine group in turn, for in order to work out a tour of any region it is first necessary to understand what features will confuse the onward route. Major valleys and their feeder glens are looked at with an eye to spending a day or so enjoying their tarns, ridges, meadows and distant views. Where huts exist these are often mentioned as an overnight base or as the goal for a walk which returns to the valley at the end of the day. Later, when multi-day tours are considered, these huts will often form the only lodgings. Mostly I have avoided routes that stray onto crevassed glaciers, the assumption being made here that equipment such as ice-axe, rope and crampons will not automatically be carried on a walking holiday. Some of the summits visited by Walker are similarly dismissed from this present book for much the same reason, although I have included certain peaks that demand little more technical skill than would be required to gain modest summits in lesser ranges. I have also outlined one glacier tour in the Bernese Alps as a sample illustration of the delights to be had in such travel - once the necessary skills have been acquired and equipment carried.

As suggested at the beginning of this Introduction, the mountaineer's library is a rich one, and following Walker's lead I have chosen to quote here and there passages that to me sum up the essence of most districts under review. The reason for this is twofold. Firstly we can hold a mirror to the Alps known by those who preceded us, and learn from their experience. And secondly by so doing I hope to introduce newcomers to the Alps to writers of the past, for they have much to offer. At the end of each chapter I've given a list of books from which further enjoyment may be gained.

The Alps of course is a vast subject, and the more we walk and the more we read, so the chain seems to grow in extent; but as was once pointed out by R.L.G. Irving, its very size increases the possibility of my having added something new to those whose experience of the range is greater than my own. With each valley traversed and each successive pass gained, so I become more aware of how much there is yet to see - such are human limitations in a world so full of scenic goodness. I cannot claim to have explored every corner of these mountains whilst undertaking research for this book; nor is one lifetime sufficient to do more than scratch the surface. But it has been an immensely satisfying project, built on the back of dozens of active seasons stretching back to the mid-sixties. What a marvellous excuse to revisit mountains and valleys first wandered years ago! And what an opportunity to explore other parts of the Alps that I'd never managed to see before! Yet still there remain enough tours untrod to last another three lifetimes...

In this book I make no claim to match Walker's erudition, only his enthusiasm for these peaks, passes and valleys. His was the initial inspiration. May this present volume serve to inspire you to dream, and then lead you among the mountains where I fervently hope you will harvest as much pleasure as I have gained whilst walking in the Alps.

THE MARITIME ALPS

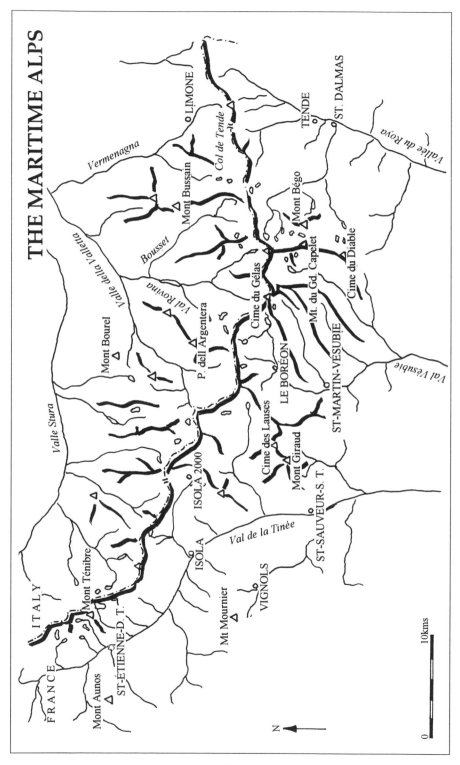

ITALY

FRANCE

Mont Aunos

ST-ÉTIENNE-D. T.

Mont Ténibre

Valle Stura

Mont Bourel

Valle della Valletta

Vermenagna

LIMONE

Col de Tende

Mont Bussain

Bousset

Val Rovina

P. dell' Argentera

Cime du Gélas

Mont Bégo

TENDE

ST. DALMAS

Vallée du Roya

Mt. du Gd. Capelet

Cime du Diable

LE BORÉON

ST-MARTIN-VÉSUBIE

Val Vésubie

Cime des Lauses

Mont Giraud

ST-SAUVEUR-S. T.

ISOLA 2000

ISOLA

Val de la Tinée

VIGNOLS

Mt Mournier

N

0   10kms

Rocky peaks, typical of the Maritime Alps, surround Madone de Fenestre

1: THE MARITIME ALPS

There is a wild sense of remoteness about the southernmost group of the Alpine chain that belies its proximity to the Mediterranean. In little more than an hour's drive from the hotels and palm trees of Nice, for example, it is possible to be wandering through uninhabited valleys as rough and rocky as any in Europe, where the skyline is stark and uncompromising and where trails can so easily vanish in a low drifting mist.

Moulded against the grain the Maritime Alps spread across the general alignment later developed by the South-West Alps, their configuration here running from north-west to south-east and with the Franco-Italian border being such as to tilt the French side toward the south, thus providing Riviera resorts with a protective wall. Hot air drifts up from the Mediterranean to be confronted now and then by cooler airstreams flowing south from snow peaks of Dauphiné. Where the two meet frequent thunderstorms occur, and as the first of the loftier mountains, Mont Bégo (2872m) in the Merveilles attracts more than its fair share. Being a ferritic peak lightning strikes are commonplace, and it is this high incidence of lightning activity that is put forward as one possible theory to explain the huge number of Bronze Age rock engravings discovered nearby - the engravers being intent on placating the mountain gods.

By comparison with ranges farther north, the Maritime are not high mountains, for none of the summits reaches three and a half thousand metres - the highest being Punta (or Cima) dell'Argentera at 3297 metres. The lower valleys are sub-tropical, the upper regions a wilderness of stone. There are few glaciers of any extent, snowfields are relatively insignificant and many of the more notable peaks are accessible to walkers with some mountain experience, without calling on technical climbing skills. Yet the Maritime Alps are truly Alpine for all that, with numerous jade-green tarns, great screes and boulder-choked corries, and spiky, rugged little rock peaks that not only provide sport for the climber drawn by the promise of a favourable climate and the odd day spent festering by the sea, but also create a backcloth of considerable charm to a wilderness camp adopted by the walker seeking somewhere a little different, a rarely-publicised region (outside of France, that is) that is not without its challenge.

The group is a geological hotch-potch. In places limestone dominates. Elsewhere gneiss, sandstone, metamorphic schist and outcrops of granite form the base materials of which the mountains are composed. Of wildlife chamois are the most numerous and on the Italian flank alone there are estimated to be somewhere in the region of 3500 individuals. The Italian Alpi Marittime also claims some 650 ibex, thanks to a programme of reintroduction from the Gran Paradiso area that began in 1920. Alpine marmots abound, and under the protection of the Mercantour National Park, mouflons - a form of wild mountain sheep - have been introduced from Corsica. Wild boar, now rare in most other regions of the Alps, are said still to inhabit some of the lower valleys on the Italian side of the border, while the birdlife is also rich and varied. But it is the flora of the region that is so outstanding. The three small reserves of Argentera, Palanfré and Alta Valle Pèsio claim more than three thousand species of plants, many of which are extremely rare, while the Mercantour heartland contains half the native flowers of France, and around forty that are unique to the area.

The official designation of the range gives Col de Tende as its south-eastern limit and Col de Larche forming the northern link with the Cottian Alps. In truth, however, the mountains extend eastward from Col de Tende as the Ligurian Alps, a definition not always recognised on maps of the area, and dismissed by Coolidge (whose classification of the Alpine chain in the nineteenth century largely stands today) for their lack of Alpine characteristics. The heart of the range contains the highest summits and probably the best walking opportunities, and is neatly concentrated on the adjoining Parco Naturale dell'Argentera on the Italian slope, and Parc National du Mercantour on the French side, the latter being the most recently designated Alpine park in France, established in 1979 against a great deal of locally-generated opposition.

Parc National du Mercantour

Within the 68,500 hectares of the park no building is permitted, hence the controversy that surrounded its formation, for plans had been proposed to create a downhill ski area there. So it is that walkers and climbers may roam today among uncluttered landscapes and enjoy a degree of solitude the more remarkable for its absence in some of the better-known ranges further north.

Between the Mercantour and the sea the Provençale countryside is characteristically cleft by narrow gorges scoured out by tributaries of the Var, and through which minor roads provide access from Nice. St-Martin-Vésubie, with a goodly assortment of hotels, pensions, gîtes d'étape and campsites, holds the key to exploration of the eastern Mercantour; St-Sauveur-sur-Tinée and St-Étienne-de-Tinée do likewise for the central and north-western sections. We'll take the Haute Vésubie first, since most of the highest mountains are located here along the Italian border.

Several tributary glens feed into the main Vésubie: the Vallon de la Gordolasque which spills down to Roquebillière, Vallon de la Madone de Fenestre which drains westward and enters the Vésubie by St-Martin, and the Vallée du Boréon to the north of St-Martin. At the head of the first of these glens stands the Cime du Gélas (3143m), highest of the Mercantour peaks and second highest of all the Maritime Alps - Punta dell'Argentera being located entirely on the Italian side of the border. Several lakes lie under the frontier ridge, and Refuge de Nice, a hut belonging to the French Alpine Club (CAF), provides a suitable base with accommodation and meals available in the main summer season. A narrow road projects for some way through the Vallon de la Gordolasque, and when this ends at Pont du Countet a trail continues, climbing between Mont Neiglier and Cime de Roche Garbière, to reach the dammed Lac de la Fous and the hut about two hours or so from the roadhead. Mont Clapier (3045m) dominates the scene above the hut to the north-east.

From Refuge de Nice (2232m) a number of opportunities present themselves for cross-country walking tours and single-day outings, including the ascent of neighbouring peaks, or the possibility of crossing into Italy where the Italian Alpine Club (CAI) has a few huts too. The ascent of Mont Clapier on the frontier ridge is a great attraction here, its summit providing a quite incredible panorama whose extent in good visibility is said to include the Matterhorn and Monte Rosa in one direction, the outline of Corsica in the other.

West of Mont Clapier lies the old smugglers' way into Italy via Pas de Pagari (2798m), which leads to the Rifugio Pagari in a little under three hours, while to the east of the Nice hut several small tarns linked by clear streams are passed by the GR52 which makes a multi-day tour of the district. South-east of the hut Lac Autier is trapped in an old glacial cirque overlooked by Mont du Grand Capelet, a peak whose ridges form part of the wall dividing the Vallon de la Gordolasque from the Vallée des Merveilles.

The Vallée des Merveilles is more easily reached from the Vallée du Roya to the east, where the road from Nice passes into Italy via the tunnel under Col de Tende, and a minor road breaks off at St-Dalmas-de-Tende to provide access by way of either the Vallon de la Minière or Vallée de Valmasque. However, walkers who have spent time at the Refuge de Nice are able to make a direct approach by following the GR52 over the 2693 metre Baisse du Basto towards Mont Bégo, then either crossing the Baisse de Valmasque (2549m) and descending to the Merveilles hut, or heading north alongside three lakes to stay in the Refuge de Valmasque.

This is a fascinating area and a justifiably popular one too on account of the rock engravings, said to number more than 100,000, that are scattered over a landscape of boulders, tarns and slabs. Archaeologists believe that the primitive agricultural race responsible for all these pictographs made special journeys to the area round Mont Bégo to carve out images and symbols - all of which are found above the two thousand metre contour. Since so many are oriented towards Mont Bégo, it is thought that the mountain was looked upon as having particular religious significance. The engravings are now protected under French law; it is forbidden to deface or stand upon them, and wardens patrol the main sites. Guided tours are arranged during the height of the summer season from Refuge des Merveilles, and explanatory booklets are on sale at both the Merveilles and Valmasque huts.

West of Refuge des Merveilles a well-marked route crosses Pas de l'Arpette (2511m) to allow walkers to return to the Vallon de la Gordolasque, thus giving an opportunity to create a circular tour before moving on to the next valley worth exploring from a general base at St-Martin-Vésubie.

This is the Vallon de la Madone de Fenestre which drains roughly east to west from another tarn-dashed headwall topped by Cime du Gélas, the distinctive peak which also looks down on the upper Gordolasque valley. The GR52 suggests an obvious link with Refuge de Nice by way of the Pas du Mont Colomb, and walkers who have been based there would be better served by crossing that pass instead of making a very long valley detour. Those with their own transport may have other plans. In which case a road invites motorists through the Fenestre glen from St-Martin to the Refuge de la Madone de Fenestre set among a group of buildings at 1903 metres, a distance of about twelve kilometres from St-Martin. By virtue of the easy access (minibus service from St-Martin) it is the busiest of all huts in the area, and there's no shortage of ideas for walkers spending a few nights of a holiday there. Above the Madone hut the little Lac de Fenestre lies under the frontier ridge below Col de Fenestre (2474m), an easy and popular destination for walkers. The pass, from which views stretch beyond the Piedmont plain to Monte Rosa and the Matterhorn, carried a Roman road from St-Martin to Entracque - which proves its strategic importance. Walkers can now use this as an obvious way down to the Rifugio Dado Soria on the Italian flank.

The ascent of Cime du Gélas is popular, especially by the *voie normale*. So too is that of the neighbouring Cime St-Robert when tackled from the south. But there are lots of little tarns to visit too. Not only those that sparkle among crags walling the upper glen over which lies the Gordolasque valley, but south-east of the hut where the five Lacs de Prals are found in a large grassy basin on the far side of Mont Caval. A circuit of Mont Caval could easily be made whilst visiting these tarns from the Madone hut.

Both ridge systems that defend the Fenestre valley have walking routes along and across them. At the western end of the southern crest stands the peaklet of Cime de la Palu (2132m), a noted local viewpoint. From Madone de Fenestre a trail climbs up to the saddle of Baisse de Ferisson, then follows the ridge westward over Mont Lapassé and several other tops, before reaching Cime de la Palu and descending then through woodland to St-Martin at the end of a memorable five hour walk. The north wall of the valley has a matching route on which Cime de Piagu (2338m) is the highpoint. Both routes could be used by walkers on their way out of the glen.

However, those who are planning to move on in order to make further explorations of the district should note that another CAF hut is easily reached from the Refuge de la Madone de Fenestre. Situated near the head of the Vallée du Boréon and backed by a girdle of cliffs, Refuge de Cougourde is gained by way of Pas des Ladres (2448m). An alternative approach is by way of the hamlet of Le Boréon in about three hours.

Le Boréon is a small cross-country ski centre with hotel and refuge accommodation located at the mouth of the wooded Vallon de Salèse, about eight kilometres from St-Martin. This tributary glen is of interest for its access to more walking country, while the main valley here, the Vallée du Boréon, is the third of those named above which converge on St-Martin. Non-motorised visitors should be able to reach Le Boréon by minibus from St-Martin, while those who walked over Pas des Ladres to the Cougourde hut may well be drawn to the frontier ridge which makes a headwall above it, for yet again there are ways over into Italy where Punta dell'Argentera looms above the upper Valletta valley. But those who choose Le Boréon as a base in preference to the hut have frontier crossings to consider too, at Col de Cerise (2543m) and Col de Frémamorte (2615m), both of which descend on the north side with plenty of scenic interest to the Valle della Valletta in the Parco Naturale dell'Argentera. Alternatively a recommended there and back outing leads to the turquoise Lac Nègre by a trail from the jeep road at Col de Salèse.

The next major valley system to the west of Vésubie is that of the Tinée river which rises near the north-western limits of the Mercantour National Park in a mountain cirque topped by the Rocher des Trois Évêques. Val de la Tinée is deep and narrow, in places dwarfed by huge overhanging cliffs. Above St-Sauveur Vallon de Mollières is a tributary whose upper reaches form a link with Le Boréon via Col de Salèse. At Isola, halfway between St-Sauveur and St-Étienne, a road breaks out of the main valley and twists its way in a sinuous journey to the hideous, purpose-built ski resort of Isola 2000, and continues from there over Col de la Lombarde into Italy. But the main Tinée valley draws the motorist on to St-Étienne-de-Tinée where there are hotels, gîtes d'étape and a campsite, sufficient to prove tempting as a base for a few days. The ultra long-distance GR5 route, which makes a traverse of the French Alps from Lake Geneva to the Mediterranean, comes through here, while more local trails climb the frontier side of the valley where numerous tarns lie cradled among wild and stony corries. Refuge de Rabuons is perched up by one of these tarns at an altitude of 2500 metres. Refuge de Vens is another, located further north at 2360 metres. Both have trails leading from them that stray over the border into Italy where other rifugios may tempt the enterprising walker into devising a hut to hut tour in the hills above the Valle Stura, from whose lower reaches access is given to the Parco Naturale dell'Argentera.

✻   ✻   ✻

Parco Naturale dell'Argentera

The Italian Alpi Marittime boasts a few small glaciers draped among the north-facing slopes of the highest peaks. Like their French counterparts the upper valleys display a chaos of rocks, boulders and screes, but alpine meadows abound too, fringed here and there with stunted mountain pines. Outside the Argentera park, and located to the east of Col de Tende (Colle di Tenda), the dolomitic Marguareis (2651m) soars above the karst plateau of Conca delle Carsene which is honeycombed with vast sink-holes - a stark contrast to the granite of the Argentera where streams dash silver streaks from slope to slope and dozens of tarns rival those of the French side of the border.

The key to access to the Parco Naturale dell'Argentera is Cuneo, the first town of note on the Italian side of the mountains if coming from France via Col de Tende. A minor road breaks away from the Tende road at Roccavione, south of Cuneo, and heads south-west along the Valle della Valletta. Beyond Valdieri this divides and subdivides again with southern branches delving deep into the park through the Vallone della Rovina and the glens watered by the Gesso di Barra and the Bousset. Wild camping is prohibited in the Argentera park, but there's an official campsite in Valdieri, and hotel accommodation in Valdieri, Sant'Anna di Valdieri and Terme di Valdieri.

With Punta dell'Argentera spreading itself in a large imposing mass between Valle della Valletta and Vallone della Rovina it is natural that this should be the focus of attention here. The mountain consists of four main tops rising from an extensive ridge system thrusting forward from the main frontier crest in a south to north alignment, and there are four huts scattered on or near its various slopes: Rifugios Remondino, Genova, Bozano and Morelli. All, apart from the Genova hut which is reached from the Rovina glen, are approached by way of the Valle della Valletta or one of its tributaries, while Rifugio Franco Remondino (2430m) is also accessible by a tough cross-border route from Le Boréon by way of Col Guilié - on this route an ice axe may be deemed an essential piece of equipment due to extensive snowfields on the north side of the frontier ridge.

Without being drawn into activity on the highest peaks though, the walker will still find much to occupy his (or her) time here. From Terme di Valdieri where the Valletta forks, for example, a mule track laid during the mid-nineteenth century when the whole area was declared a hunting reserve for King Vittorio Emanuel II, leads through forests and rocky outcrops, up to a region of lakes trapped in the stony wilderness of the frontier ridge: Lagos di Valscura, del Claus and delle Portette. An unguarded hut (Rifugio di Questa) stands on the north shore of this last lake at an altitude of 2388 metres. The three lakes are linked by a rough path that may be followed down to a fourth tarn, and beyond this into the lonely Freddo valley which eventually feeds into the Valle Stura near Ruviera.

Other tarns are accessible from the Valle della Valletta roadhead. Consider, for example, those which are lodged on a broad terrace under the frontier ridge near Cime de Frémamorte; a charming string of tarns and with a one-time military route enticing over the border into France to Col de Salèse. Instead of crossing that border at Col de Frémamorte, however, the Cime itself might appeal - there is a track which crosses screes below the south-east ridge and goes to the summit without difficulty.

*   *   *

Having treated the heart of the Maritime Alps to a rather selective introduction, pointing out just a few of the opportunities that exist for walkers among some of the finest valleys, it seems opportune here to devise a tour of the region from hut to hut using the GR52 as a rough guide, but with a few diversions thrown in as a way of illustrating the district's appeal. It will be a challenging route in places, and depending on one's ambition for peak-bagging along the way, it might be useful to carry an ice axe. If a straight hut to hut route is envisaged during the summer months, such equipment can be left at home.

HUT TO HUT IN THE ALPES MARITIME

Our route makes an east to west traverse, mostly on the French side of the border, and begins at St-Dalmas-de-Tende in the Vallée du Roya. St-Dalmas can be reached by train from Nice, and the first day will be spent walking up the Vallon de la Minière to Refuge des Merveilles. A minimum of two nights should be spent here in order to visit some of the pictograph sites, and to climb Mont Bégo or Cime du Diable (2685m). An alternative to spending two nights at the Merveilles hut would be to spend the second night at Refuge de Valmasque. This would still allow time to see some of the rock engravings, and to climb Mont Bégo.

Moving on cross the saddle of Baisse du Basto to Refuge de Nice, passing on the way some of the finest accessible rock engravings of the Merveilles region. Good visibility is needed for this crossing, for in mist the way is not obvious. Once there time should be spent exploring the area round the Nice hut, Mont Clapier may be climbed by enterprising walkers with a little scrambling experience, and it may also be tempting to cross the border by Pas de Pagari in order to spend a night in the Rifugio Pagari. Much will depend, of course, on the amount of time available.

To continue the route westward go round Lac de la Fous, then climb up the west flank of the valley to Pas du Mont Colomb (2548m), and there make a diversion to the right for the ascent of the easy 2816 metre Mont Colomb which rewards with some splendid views. On the descent from the pass take caution if snow is still lying. An ice axe may be useful here in the early part of the summer. The trail leads down to Madone de Fenestre and the refuge, and once again there are plenty of distractions to delay further progress on the hut to hut traverse. Among the excuses to delay are possible ascents of Cime St-Robert and Cime du Gélas, and the temptation to stray across Col de Fenestre to visit Rifugio Dado Soria. It would also be feasible for strong walkers to descend in Italy after a night at the Dado Soria hut, and head through the valley of the Gesso di Barra to its junction with the Rovina glen, then return towards the frontier ridge via the Vallone della Rovina, spend a night in the Genova hut, and next day return to France by way of Col de la Ruine above Refuge de Cougourde. This would give a brief introduction to the north flank of the mountains.

A more straightforward route across the mountains to Refuge de Cougourde resumes along GR52 from the Madone de Fenestre hut. The crossing here is made at the Pas des Ladres, but beyond the Lac de Trecolpas GR52 is abandoned in favour of an alternative trail which leads to the hut, while the waymarked route descends to the Vallée du Boréon. Since this is the last hut on our basic traverse it will be worth booking a bed for two or three nights in order to take advantage of the peak-bagging opportunities that abound. Rock climbers will be attracted to the quartet of Cougourde peaks that are thrust above the hut to the north-east, while mountain walkers with no pretensions towards climbing agility could find entertainment on the Cime Guilié or the Tête de Ruine. The two Lacs Bessons on the way to the Tête are also worth a visit in their own right, even if you have no interest in collecting summits. The big diversion here though, for experienced Alpine walkers, is to cross the border at Col Guilié and make for the Rifugio Franco Remondino, and there spend the night. Next day climb Punta dell'Argentera and return to the Cougourde hut. The West Col guide, *Mercantour Park,* gives the necessary route descriptions.

Finally descend to Le Boréon and on to St-Martin-Vésubie where a bus may be caught back to Nice.

HUT TO HUT IN THE ALPES MARITIME - ROUTE SUMMARY

Day 1:	St-Dalmas-de-Tende - Refuge des Merveilles
Day 2:	Refuge des Merveilles - Mont Bégo (or Cime du Diable) - Refuge des Merveilles
or:	Refuge des Merveilles - Mont Bégo - Refuge de Valmasque
Day 3:	Refuge des Merveilles (or Refuge de Valmasque) - Baisse du Basto - Refuge de Nice
Day 4:	Refuge de Nice - Mont Clapier - Refuge de Nice
or:	Refuge de Nice - Pas de Pagari - Rifugio Pagari
Day 5:	Refuge de Nice - Pas du Mont Colomb - Mont Colomb (optional) - Refuge de la Madone de Fenestre
or:	Rifugio Pagari - Pas de Pagari - Pas du Mont Colomb - Refuge de la Madone de Fenestre
Day 6:	Refuge de la Madone de Fenestre - Cime St-Robert or Cime du Gélas (optional) - Refuge de la Madone de Fenestre
or:	Refuge de la Madone de Fenestre - Col de Fenestre - Rifugio Dado Soria
	Refugio Dado Soria - Gesso di Barra - Vallone della Rovina - Rifugio Genova
	Rifugio Genova - Col de la Ruine - Refuge de Cougourde
Day 7:	Refuge de la Madone de Fenestre - Pas des Ladres - Refuge de Cougourde
Day 8:	Refuge de Cougourde - Cime Guilié or Tête de Ruine - Refuge de Cougourde
or:	Refuge de Cougourde - Col Guilié - Rifugio Franco Remondino
	Rifugio Remondino - Punta dell'Argentera - Refuge de Cougourde
Day 9:	Refuge de Cougourde - Le Boréon - St-Martin-Vésubie

THE MARITIME ALPS

Location:
Astride the Franco-Italian border north of Nice. The range extends from Col de Larche in the north-west to Col de Tende in the south-east. In the heart of the region lie the Parco Naturale dell'Argentera and Parc National du Mercantour. The Maritime Alps form the southern limit of the Alpine chain.

Principal valleys:
On the Italian side these are Valle della Valletta, Vallone della Rovina and Gesso di Barra. Of the French valleys the main ones are the Tinée and Vésubie, with Vallée du Boréon, Vallon de la Madone de Fenestre and Vallon de la Gordolasque. Also Vallée des Merveilles, Vallon de la Minière and Vallée de Valmasque. The Vallée du Roya is important for access.

Principal peaks:
Punta dell'Argentera (3297m), Cime du Gélas (3143m), Mont Clapier (3045m), Mont Bégo (2872m)

Centres:
Valdieri and Terme di Valdieri on the Italian slope, St-Martin-Vésubie and St-Étienne-de-Tinée on the French side.

Huts:
A fair selection of huts exists on both sides of the range in the main areas of interest. Owned by either the CAF or CAI.

Access:
In Italy the best way is by train from Turin to Cuneo, and bus from there to Valdieri (for the Argentera). Train from Cuneo to Vernante (for the Palanfrè). Trains also run from Nice to Cuneo. Nearest international airport is Turin. On the French side by plane or train to Nice. Train from Nice to St-Dalmas-de-Tende for the eastern Mercantour. Buses serve St-Martin-Vésubie from Nice and minibuses feed into selected tributary valleys.

Maps:
IGC sheet number 8, *Alpi Marittime e Liguri* for the Italian side of the mountains, at a scale of 1:50,000. The Didier Richard sheet 9, *Mercantour massif et parc national* - also at 1:50,000 has huts and the main walking routes clearly outlined for the French half of the range.

Guidebooks:
Mercantour Park - Maritime Alps by Robin Collomb (West Col) is very useful for the main valleys and highest peaks in the national park. It also strays over the border for selected routes.
Walking the Alpine Parks of France & Northwest Italy by Marcia R. Lieberman (Cordee/The Mountaineers) describes a number of moderate walks in the Mercantour region.

Other reading:
Wild Italy by Tim Jepson (Sheldrake Press/Aurum Press, 1994) is a natural history guide that includes a short chapter on the Alpi Marittime with some useful information.
The Outdoor Traveler's Guide to the Alps by Marcia R. Lieberman (Stewart, Tabori & Chang; New York, 1991) has a brief chapter devoted to a small part of the Mercantour park.

✳   ✳   ✳

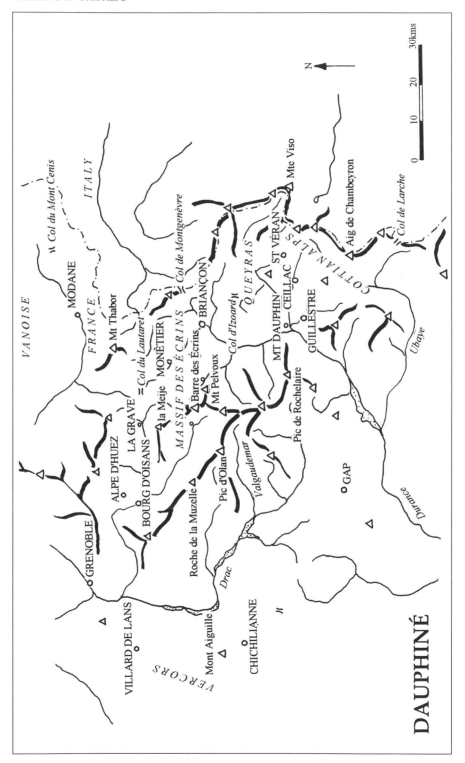

N

30kms

20

10

0

Col du Mont Cenis

ITALY

VANOISE

MODANE

FRANCE

Mt Thabor

Col du Lautaret

LA GRAVE

ALPE D'HUEZ

BOURG D'OISANS

la Meije

MONÊTIER

Col de Montgenèvre

BRIANÇON

MASSIF DES ÉCRINS

Barre des Écrins

Mt Pelvoux

Col d'Izoard

QUEYRAS

ST VÉRAN

CEILLAC

MT DAUPHIN

GUILLESTRE

Mte Viso

Aig de Chambeyron

Col de Larche

COTTIAN ALPS

Ubaye

GRENOBLE

Roche de la Muzelle

Pic d'Olan

Valgaudemar

Pic de Rochelaire

GAP

Durance

VILLARD DE LANS

Mont Aiguille

CHICHILIANNE

VERCORS

Drac

DAUPHINÉ

Lac Lérie, with la Meije and glacier-draped Rateau

2: DAUPHINÉ
Including the Cottian Alps, Queyras, Massif des Écrins & the Pre-Alps of Vercors

The mountains of Dauphiné contain the highest and most important summits, in terms of mountaineering appeal, of all the South-West Alps, and the various groups offer an unrivalled diversity of landscapes for the enterprising walker. There is a world of difference, for example, between the soaring, glacier-etched scenery of the Massif des Écrins and the vast limestone plateaux of the Vercors, but both provide a wealth of walking opportunities as, of course, does the more remote Queyras in the Cottian Alps with its small, rugged peaks reflected in dozens of little tarns.

Dauphiné consists of the French départements of Isère, Drôme and Hautes-Alpes. Here the green hills of the Pre-Alpes, including the Vercors, create a long wall running north-south parallel to the Isère which flows down the western side, while the higher mountains stand in great blocks towards the Italian border. The Cottian Alps spread over both sides of that border, but only those that lie within France are included in the Queyras massif. North-west of the Queyras, across the Durance, Central Dauphiné is the largest and most attractive mountain block; the group known as either the Massif des Écrins, l'Oisans, or Massif du Pelvoux, which has the distinction of hosting the most southerly four thousand metre summit of the Alpine chain. Beyond the large and complex peaks of the Écrins several comparatively minor massifs continue the appeal of Dauphiné. These include the Chartreuse massif, the Chaine de Belledonne which culminates in the Grand Pic de Belledonne, the Grandes Rousses massif, and Les Aiguilles d'Arve.

*   *   *

QUEYRAS

The Cottian Alps, of which the Queyras forms a small, yet important part, stretch from the road pass of Col de Larche northwards to Col du Mont Cenis, effectively running in a narrow strip along the Franco-Italian border which acts as the watershed between the Po and the Rhône. The highest, and without question the most distinctive, of its peaks is that of Monte Viso (3841m), first climbed in 1861 by the Victorian pioneers William Mathews and F.W. Jacomb, with their guides, M and J.B. Croz. But apart from this notable peak, the district holds little of mountaineering interest beyond the attention of local activists, although there are a good many summits attainable by strong mountain walkers, offering extensive views as their reward.

Col de Larche (1991m) takes traffic from the French valley of the Ubayette, flanked on the south by the Réserve Naturelle du Lauzanier, into the Italian Valle Stura. From St Paul on the French side another low pass, Col de Vars, crosses the mountain rim that marks the boundary between the départements of Hautes-Alpes and Alps-de-Haute-Provence, on the north side of which access by road is made possible to the Queyras district.

With the Massif des Écrins rising to the north-west, the Queyras lies fully within the old administrative region of Dauphiné, and presses like an elbow of mountains against the Italian frontier which curves round it in a protective wall on three sides. Monte Viso has a dominating influence on much of the region, but since it stands just across the frontier it is thereby not counted as one of the Queyras peaks. Of these the major summits are Pic de Rochebrune (3320m), Grand Glaiza (3293m), Le Pain de Sucre (3208m), Tête des Toillies (3175m) and Le Grand Queyras (3114m). There are no glaciers, although evidence of past glaciation is abundantly clear in many valleys and the rugged scenery reflects its Alpine pedigree.

It is an isolated district, tucked quietly away in a seeming back-of-beyond with only one year-round road of access. In 1977 the Parc Naturel Régional du Queyras was established in order to reconcile the demands of ecology and local economy, to check a steady population drift away from the harsh demands of mountain life, while at the same time protecting the quality of the environment. With an area of some six hundred and fifty square kilometres, the boundaries of the park extend from the Gorges du Guil in the west to the Tête du Pelvas in the east, and from Col Girardin in the south to Col des Thures in the north. The classic approach from Briançon is via the spectacular road pass of Col d'Izoard, which is open for only a few weeks in mid-summer, and which links the valley of the Durance with that of the Guil, the main Queyras river whose valley is the major geographical feature.

Draining the west flank of Monte Viso and those frontier peaks grouped around it, the Guil cuts right through the Queyras from north-east to south-west, its major tributaries flowing from attractive valleys on the southern side, while the northern half is drained by a few short glens. At first the Guil flows north-west, collecting a few early tributaries on the way, then curves south-westward at Abriès, which sits at the confluence of the Guil and the Bouchet flowing from the north. Beyond Abriès the river passes Aiguilles, the so-called capital of the valley, before rushing below the medieval, fortified Château-Queyras (with the inevitable Vauban additions) perched on an outcrop, and soon after enters the deep and narrow Combe du Queyras. A hundred years ago the only ways out of the valley below Château-Queyras were along paths that climbed hillsides high above the river. "Now a remarkable road traverses the gorges," announced one commentator just before the last war, "crossing and recrossing the torrent and often gouged out of the perpendicular sides of the immense cleft which it has cut." Above the left bank the lovely village of Montbardon sits amid flower-rich meadows dotted with pine and fir trees. Further down, near Guillestre, the Guil washes into the Durance, the river that drains the eastern slopes of the Écrins.

Set in an open basin surrounded by low mountains Guillestre, with its attractive medieval streets and sixteenth century church guarded by marble lions, is very much the entry point to the central Queyras. A four-kilometre branch road off the N94 Gap-Briançon highway is an important link with the rest of Dauphiné, while the Col de Vars route also comes down to that little market town. Visitors coming by train should aim for Montdauphin-Guillestre in the Durance valley. Buses from there serve the main Queyras valleys.

In these southerly mountains the climate is heavily influenced by the Mediterranean and is therefore more amenable for active walking or climbing holidays than almost anywhere in the Alps. The peaks, though not as high nor as dramatic as those of the Écrins, are certainly no less attractive than that neighbouring range, and have an appealing, rugged charm. East of Château-Queyras the Haut Queyras are largely formed of mica-schist, while in the Bas Queyras limestone is also evident. On the way to the Col d'Izoard the lunar landscape of the Casse Déserte reveals numerous rocky pinnacles, curious eroded formations of limestone, dolomite and gypsum sprouting from a mountainside of grey screes. Large forests of larch and pine edge meadows noted for their spring flowers. Marmots are numerous; so too are chamois. There are many small lakes, the gift of long-departed glaciers, and mountain streams tumbling in waterfalls from bare cliffs and snow-clad peaks. So far the region has been spared any major ski development, and the walking is excellent.

In order to give some idea of the district's charm, and its appeal for walkers, the following summary of opportunities will serve as an introduction before we outline the route of the multi-day GR58, otherwise known as the Tour du Queyras.

Vallons du Mélezet, d'Albert and Cristillan

These glens lie to the east of the Guil and may be reached from Guillestre by bus as far as Ceillac, a low-key cross-country ski centre where two valley systems merge, the upper reaches of the Cristillan which flows from the north-east, Vallon du Mélezet from the south-east. Built on a sloping terrace Ceillac has hotel and gîte accommodation, and there's a campsite in the Mélezet valley. The village makes a fine base for a few days of a walking holiday, as there are several high cols accessible from it by reasonable trails, among them: Col Girardin, Col Albert, Col des Estronques, Col de Bramousse and Col Fromage. In addition to these walkers may be tempted by a few modest summits that provide superb viewpoints, while' there are valley-based walks to the popular lakes of Ste-Anne and Mirroir, and less-trod trails in the wild upper valleys of the Cristillan and d'Albert.

Reached by way of the Vallon du Mélezet Lac Ste-Anne, or rather the tiny chapel on its shore, is the focus of a pilgrimage that takes place each year on 26 July by villagers from Ceillac and Maurin. The route of that pilgrimage is a short one from the roadhead at Chaurionde, but an alternative approach may be made via the Lac Mirroir (also known as Lac des Prés-Sebeyrand) following the trail of the GR5 which, sadly, is rather devalued for a short stretch by the presence of a ski-lift. However, above this the turquoise Lac Ste-Anne is a gem cupped among soaring, wild-looking peaks. Rarely, on a fine summer's day, will you enjoy it in solitude.

Of the walkers' cols accessible from Ceillac, Col Girardin (2699m) is an obvious saddle in the cirque wall that curves behind Lac Ste-Anne, from which it may be gained in an hour over rough ground of rock and fairly steep scree. The col marks the border between the départements of Hautes-Alpes and Alpes-de-Haute-Provence, and is crossed by the GR5 on the way to the valley of Ubaye. From it views to the north-west show the snowy mass of the Écrins with the Pelvoux massif looking especially fine, while the Aiguille de Chambeyron is seen to the south-east. The tiny chapel-adorned summit of Tête de Girardin (2876m) rises above the col to the east, and makes a tempting destination for enterprising walkers, while in the bed of the Ubaye, a little under two hours from the col, the stone-built Refuge Maljasset (CAF owned) provides an opportunity for walkers to explore yet another valley system, returning perhaps by way of Col Tronchet (2658m) which rewards with still more grand views.

Although the Ubaye valley lies outside the Queyras district proper and flows down to St Paul, it has some good walking opportunities amid wonderful high mountain scenery. The upper reaches are hemmed in by big peaks, including the Aiguille and Brec de Chambeyron, and near the head of the valley a collection of little tarns lies just beneath the frontier ridge.

Vallon d'Albert branches off the Mélezet glen to the south-east behind the hamlet of La Riaille and has about it a singularly wild appeal. It's a short glen, uncompromising both in the nature of its trails and the beauty of its upper meadows. At its head Col Albert (2846m), again overlooking the Ubaye, is an obvious destination for a walk, but it's a strenuous one on a trail that is not always clear.

As for the Vallée du Cristillan, it is the glaciated upper valley that is of particular appeal for walkers based in Ceillac, for there are numerous possible routes to follow with varying degrees of waymarking. Some trails apparently begin promisingly enough, only to fade and disappear. Others are blazed with paint marks and appear to be well-trodden. Among the many destinations, either signposted, or hinted at from the map, the following selection provides an idea of what is in store: Lac de Clausis, Col du Cristillan and Col Nord du Cristillan, Col Ceillac and Col Longet. There's also Col de la Cula and the 3121 metre summit of

Tête de la Cula immediately above it that provide excellent views of the high peaks of the Ubaye.

Ceillac, of course, occupies a prime site in the Cristillan valley, and is on the route not only of GR5, but also that of GR58 and one of its variantes. Between them, these multi-day routes cross three cols above the village: Col de Bramousse (2251m) to the north, the grassy Col Fromage (2301m) to the east of that, and Col des Estronques (2651m) south-east of Col Fromage. By linking Col de Bramousse and neighbouring Col Fromage, for example, an enjoyable day's circuit could be achieved. Between the two cols the Crête des Chambrettes is exposed in places, but the trail along it should be good enough for all but those with a tendency towards vertigo. As for Col des Estronques, this is overlooked by the Tête de Jacquette (2757m), a superb viewpoint that should be on the list of all walkers spending time in Ceillac.

Vallées de l'Aigue Blanche & l'Aigue Agnelle

These two valleys come together as one near the old settlement of Molines-en-Queyras and then flow roughly northward as the Aigue Agnelle to enter the main Guil valley at Ville-Vielle, a short distance upstream of Château-Queyras. Of the two, the Vallée de l'Aigue Agnelle carries an unpaved road over the frontier ridge at Col Agnel where, it is thought, Hannibal crossed on his epic trans-Alpine journey with his thirty-seven elephants in 218 BC (another conjectured crossing place is Col de la Traversette further east by Monte Viso), while the highlight for many in the Aigue Blanche valley is the rather commercialised, yet still-charming village of St-Véran which lays claim to being the highest community in Europe. However, despite the fact that St-Véran is perched on a steep, south-facing slope at an altitude of 2040 metres, this claim is a little wide of the mark since the village is still some eighty-six metres lower than Juf in the Averstal in Switzerland. Be that as it may, St-Véran has a heavy, old-fashioned air about it, with many of its stone and timber buildings dating from the seventeenth or eighteenth centuries hugging narrow streets overhung with massive eaves and wide balconies. Walkers planning to use it as a base for a few days will find there are two gîtes d'étape and a choice of hotels, and the village is reached by an infrequent bus service from Guillestre.

Among the many walking possibilities in the Vallée de l'Aigue Blanche, one of the most popular leads to the easy Col de St-Véran (2844m) which is on the Franco-Italian border. This is taken as an alternative by the GR58 and is recommended for the quality of the scenery experienced from the ridge. East of the col the small peak of Pic de Caramantran (3025m) with views of Monte Viso and Pain de Sucre, is easily gained in about thirty minutes, and by continuing down to the north you come to Col de Chamoussière where the 'official' GR58 comes up from St-Véran. A combination of these two cols allows a loop-trip to be made using St-Véran as a base.

Another day-long loop from St-Véran makes a circuit of the Tête des Toillies (3175m; also known as Tête Noire). Three cols are used on this tour: Col de la Noire, which overlooks the Ubaye district, Col de Longet and Col Blanchet, the last two being on the international border. It's a fine, energetic walk with lots of dazzling mountain tarns in view, and counts as one of the best days out in this part of the

Queyras. But good clear conditions are essential.

Molines-en-Queyras gives access to the upper valley of the Aigue Agnelle, in which a trio of small villages, Pierre Grosse, Le Coin and Fontgillarde, remain pretty much unspoiled despite their use as cross-country ski centres. Walkers will find a choice of routes to attempt in the vicinity.

The Upper Guil Valley

Above Abriès the narrow upper reaches of the Guil taper towards Monte Viso. A road projects into the valley, passing Ristolas, La Monta and L'Echalp, and then becomes wild and uninhabited as it rises to the Belvédère du Cirque (or Belvédère du Viso) which, as its name suggests, gazes at a tremendous amphitheatre of mountains. Monte Viso soars above a saddle in the centre of this crowd of peaks, a crowd all in excess of three thousand metres and which includes Monte Granero, Pointe de Marte, Pointe Gastaldi and Mont Aiguillette (otherwise known as L'Asti). In the cirque, on a site that enjoys glorious views and the alpenglow on Monte Viso's summit snows, stands the Refuge du Balif-Viso (2460m), built by the CAF in 1976.

The valley provides plenty of walking possibilities; some short and popular, others quite arduous. There are tarns to visit, cols to cross, summits to reach and a few circuits that could be achieved by the fit and enterprising, which stray over the border into Italy. One of these is the three-day Tour of Monte Viso, a scenic route achieved by way of a trio of passes and with no less than three huts and a mountain inn providing accommodation along the way. The Tour du Queyras also comes down the valley of the Guil, and the route of that classic multi-day circuit will be outlined later. But for our walker who wants to focus on the Guil valley for a few days, accommodation may be had in Abriès, where there are hotels, a dortoir and gîte d'étape, Ristolas (hotel and gîte d'étape), and La Monta (gîte d'étape), as well as the CAF refuge already mentioned.

Vallon de Bouchet

Flowing from the north, the Torrent de Bouchet drains the second of Abriès' valleys. This forks near the hamlet of Le Roux, and forks again a little higher. All the tributary streams come down from the Italian border which arcs around the head of the valley. Le Roux has a gîte d'étape, but no shops, and there's a campsite at Valpreveyre. Visitors planning to spend a few days here may need to stock up with provisions in Abriès. Once again the Tour du Queyras passes through on its way from La Monta via a high ridge crossing, and next day leaves to cross Col des Thures and Col du Malrif. There are, of course, plenty of other trails worth exploring, including routes from Valpreveyre up to the cols of Bouchet and Malaure, both of which mark the frontier ridge.

The Brunissard Valley

Coming down from the Col d'Izoard, this is the largest of the northern valleys in the Queyras and, accessible by road all the way from Château-Queyras, offers a choice of walking routes. On the way to the col there's accommodation to be had at Arvieux; the hamlet of La Chalp has a hotel with lower-priced dortoir beds, while

Brunissard, at 1746 metres the highest village below the hairpins that lead into the Casse Déserte, has a gîte d'étape and a campsite nearby.

Brunissard is sited at the confluence of two streams. The Torrent de la Rivière flows from the north-west, while the Izoard squeezes through a gorge below the road to the col. Two major walking routes converge on the village, GR5 and GR58. The first, having come from Briançon, crosses the blocking ridge at Col des Ayes which, when reversed from Brunissard, would make an interesting excursion, as indeed would a visit to the Col de Néal (2509m), south-west of Col des Ayes. To reach Col de Néal from Brunissard entails following GR5 to the Chalets de l'Eychaillon, then along a gravel road to a second collection of houses shown as Chalets de Clapeyto on the map. Above these you come to some splendid high meadows littered with tarns, beyond which you climb easily to the col and look down on another, larger tarn, Lac de Néal nestling on the far side.

By following GR58 north of Brunissard, one gains good views of the spiky formations of the Casse Déserte before reaching Col du Tronchet, a 2347 metre pass in the dividing ridge that separates the main Brunissard valley from a glen that drains down to Château-Queyras. Midway down that glen the hamlet of Souliers has a gîte d'étape used by trekkers on the Tour du Queyras. Instead of, or before, crossing Col du Tronchet and descending to Souliers, it would be worth bearing left along a footpath spur that leads to Lac de Souliers. This tarn enjoys a superb situation below Pic Ouest and the craggy Crête des Oules. Pic Ouest itself is accessible to any fit walker with a head for heights. From the summit a full circular panorama includes Monte Viso, of course, a maze of peak, ridge and hinted valley of the Écrins and, farther away, La Grande Casse in the Vanoise.

This brief summary of valleys has done little more than scratch the surface of possibilities available for keen mountain walkers. It will be evident that much awaits those who are drawn by country that has seldom been fashionable, whose villages, glens, peaks and ridges are largely unknown outside a small circle of enthusiasts, yet whose landscape quality is as rich and varied as almost anywhere in the Alps. If there's one sure way of having that variety unfolded day after day, it will be by following that multi-day route already referred to several times in the preceding paragraphs, the GR58, better known as the Tour du Queyras.

* * *

TOUR DU QUEYRAS

The standard circuit of about eight days is a fine one which remains entirely within France and is thus parochially contained by the boundaries of the Queyras district, but there are assorted variations available that stray beyond these boundaries and even follow a short section of the Italian Tour of Monte Viso. Since it is my intention in this book to offer the best walking and most spectacular scenic viewpoints throughout the Alpine ranges, the following outline tour will include some of these variations, thereby increasing the length to one of twelve stages. It's a route that would appeal to first-time trekkers in the Alps since some of the stages are rather modest in length. Accommodation is available at the end of every stage, with meals provided during the main summer season. But as there are few shops along the way there will be many sections where food will need to be carried for several days at a time to provide refreshment along the trail.

The 'official' start of the Tour du Queyras is made in Ceillac, but Alan Castle, author of the English-language guidebook to the circuit on which the following outline is largely based, suggests Montdauphin-Guillestre in the Durance valley as being more appropriate, since most trekkers will approach the district by rail. His guide, therefore, begins the route at the railway station and makes as his destination of this initial stage, the Refuge de Furfande set in a verdant pastoral basin below Col St-Antoine on the west flank of the Guil valley, not far from the Chalets de Furfande, the only mountain farms in the district not accessible by road. For a first day of a multi-day walking circuit it's quite demanding, with almost twenty kilometres of distance to cover and two cols to cross, Col de Moussière (2354m) and Col St-Antoine (2458m). The ascent to Col de Moussière is long and will, no doubt, be fairly punishing to those who are not yet in full mountain-fitness. But the change of landscape on reaching the col will be reward enough, for there's a transformation from forest and pasture to true mountain austerity marked by craggy crests rising from apparently barren screes. It should be noted that there are no accommodation alternatives between Montdauphin-Guillestre and Refuge de Furfande, and that a full day's walking of about eight hours should be allowed for this stage.

Having begun the tour by heading roughly eastward, the second stage joins the GR58 proper and follows it southward, across the main Guil valley to Ceillac along what is normally taken as the final section of the 'official' Tour du Queyras. Should our walker prefer to follow the standard tour, however, the first day's route outlined in the preceding paragraph should be ignored, and instead Ceillac reached from Montdauphin-Guillestre railway station by bus, there to begin the walk in earnest.

Coming as we are though from Refuge de Furfande the day begins with a descent to Les Escoyères, a hamlet overlooking the gorges of Combe du Queyras. The route goes down to the main valley road and crosses the river by footbridge. There follows a steady climb, much of it through woodland, to the Col de Bramousse (2251m), but an alternative to this crossing exists, being the one adopted as a GR58 variante as well as by the GR5 later on. The variante leaves the main trail at the hamlet of Bramousse, which is reached by road from the Combe de Queyras, then skirts eastward through the Bois de Riou Vert into the glen of the same name, through which the trail climbs to Col Fromage, there to join GR5. Col Fromage (2301m) lies to the east of Col de Bramousse along the Crête des Chambrettes. As noted earlier, there's a fine linking trail along this ridge, although as our route is quite long enough in itself, few trekkers will be tempted by this diversion.

Col de Bramousse, with its fine view south to the Pics de la Font Sancte at the head of the Vallon du Mélezet, makes an obvious passage over the wall of mountains that hems the north flank of the Cristillan valley. From it a 600 metre descent leads directly to Ceillac nestling at the confluence of the Cristillan and Mélezet rivers.

The next stage, Ceillac to St-Véran, is normally tackled on the first day of the standard circuit. Although it makes the highest crossing so far (Col des Estronques;

2651m), it is the shortest of our three days, a factor which may encourage the additional ascent of Tête de Jacquette that is easily accessible from the col. Col des Estronques neighbours Col Fromage, and is gained from Ceillac by way of a series of steep zig-zags enlivened by gradually expanding views. An undemanding path strikes away from the col to ascend the nearby Tête de Jacquette, an excellent viewpoint from which Monte Viso appears in the east for the first time. The summit here is marked by trenches and barbed wire, presumably relics of the last war - barbed wire is also a feature of some of the cols on the Franco-Italian border. Over the col the trail descends, steeply at first to a natural terrace, then down a ravine before coming to woodland. Through this the well-marked trail crosses the Aigue Blanche stream at the Pont de Moulin, goes up to Le Raux (dortoir accommodation), then on a road which climbs to St-Véran where there are several hotels, two gîtes d'étape and foodstores, the latter being rather important as the next opportunity to buy food does not occur for a further four days until we reach Abriès.

Stage four leads to Refuge Agnel, a popular GTA hut situated high in the Aigue Agnelle valley with tremendous views out to the Écrins. The GR58 standard route crosses Col de Chamoussière in the ridge which divides the valleys of Aigue Blanche and Aigue Agnelle, but an alternative fine-weather option goes first to Col de St-Véran on the border with Italy, then climbs over Pic de Caramantran (3025m) and descends to join the standard trail at Col de Chamoussière. Should conditions be favourable, this is the recommended route to take. Views will certainly reward the extra effort involved. Among the mountains in view is Pain de Sucre (3208m), a very popular summit tackled by numerous walkers staying at Refuge Agnel. A Scottish friend who scrambled up this on a day off whilst walking the Tour du Queyras described it as: "...a bit like Union Street on a Saturday afternoon...We didn't linger long on the summit [but] dropped down to Lac Foréant, then back up to Lac de l'Eychassier and on to Pic de Foréant, a much better summit in my opinion, with not a soul in sight and an equally magnificent view." Trekkers planning a second night at Refuge Agnel might find one or other of these peaks worth considering, but only if conditions allow. The ascent of Le Pain de Sucre may be quite energetic for some, and the way could be tricky in mist, but the route is waymarked to the summit.

Walkers determined to stick to the 'official' Tour du Queyras will leave Refuge Agnel and cross Col Vieux (2806m) on the way to La Monta in the upper Guil valley. This makes an entertaining stage, but the alternative offered here strays out of the Parc Naturel Régional du Queyras by trespassing into Italy, where the tremendous peak of Monte Viso dominates the landscape. The supremacy of this mountain is undeniable. Whether it is viewed from a distant summit, from one of the many walkers' passes accessible on three sides, or from the plains round Turin, Monte Viso's grand signature is unmistakable. From the Agnel refuge a short walk of about forty minutes leads to Col Agnel (2744m). Over this the way descends into the Italian Vallone dell Agnello which yields lovely views to the Maritime Alps in the south. Then you turn into the Valle de Soustre through flower meadows raucous with the shrill call of marmots. At the head of this a stiff climb brings you onto the Passo della Losetta (2870m), from where a scenically-spectacular belvedere trail leads to Col de Valante (2815m), Monte Viso looming magnificent nearby. Before tackling this belvedere trail, however, the nearby Pointe Joanne (3052m) beckons. It only needs thirty minutes of effort from the Losetta Pass, but the summit vista is incredible - given good conditions, that is. Of course, Monte Viso looks impressive as ever, but the extensive panorama also includes the Écrins, Vanoise, Mont Blanc and even the sharp tip of the Matterhorn far off. Much depends on your planned destination for the day whether you linger on the summit. Should you intend to cross back into France and descend to Refuge du Balif-Viso, then you'll need about two and a half hours to achieve this from the summit of Pointe Joanne. If, however, your plans are to remain in Italy and spend the night at the Rifugio Vallanta, you should have a little longer to enjoy summit views.

The guidebook tour of the Queyras crosses Col de Valante (Passo di Vallanta) and descends a tight little ravine, then screes, before reaching a tarn (Lac Lestio) from where a trail leads directly to Refuge du Balif-Viso. An alternative to this, as hinted above, adds an extra day to the tour by remaining for two nights in Italian huts. The first, Rifugio Vallanta, the second Rifugio Sella beside a little lake, the latter an extremely popular hut used as a base for climbers tackling Monte Viso, and normally reached by trail from the Valle del Po. Gazing across the lake one sees Monte Viso's east face soaring in a great shaft, the summit actually hidden, but a tower on the east ridge providing much of the drama in this view. The day's route between these two huts goes down the Vallone di Vallante, then crosses Passo Gallarino. On the following day the return to French soil is by way of Col de la Traversette (2947m) and down to the Balif-Viso hut. Below the Traversette col a tunnel, the so-called Buco di Viso, was forced in the fifteenth century as an aid to the transportation of salt from Provence. It is still possible to pass through this, thus avoiding the final climb to the col proper, although anyone carrying a large rucksack may find it a bit of a squeeze.

When the standard Tour du Queyras left Refuge Agnel for the gîte d'étape in La Monta it made a direct crossing via Col Vieux and the Lacs Foréant and Egorgeou. Our suggested route from the Balif-Viso hut to the same destination is a devious one that crosses back into Italy again - despite the fact that La Monta is, of course, easily accessible by a straightforward downhill stroll through the upper glen of the Guil. On our route there are two cols to cross (Col Sellière; 2834m and Col Lacroix; 2299m), with two Italian huts between them. These are Rifugio Granero and Rifugio Jervis. Above Rifugio Granero the 3166 metre Monte Granero makes a tempting diversion, but since it will entail about four hours for the ascent and descent with some scrambling involved, this would be better attempted from an intermediate overnight base at either the Granero or Jervis hut - which is fine if you have the time and energy to devote to it. Once again, a tremendous panorama of mountain and valley is spread out from the summit.

Without the ascent of Monte Granero it will take about six and a half hours to reach La Monta. If, however, this climb is added to the route and you decide to overnight at Rifugio Jervis, the better plan next day will be to cross back into France by the unfortunately-named Col d'Urine (2525m), adding the summit of Tête du Pelvas (2929m; excellent views) to your tally of peaks, and then descend either to Le Roux or Abriès. Once again the ascent of Tête du Pelvas involves some scrambling and danger of stonefall, and should not be attempted unless you have

Above:
The Refuge de Vallonpierre in Dauphiné (Ch 2)

Left:
Mont Aiguille in the Vercors
(*R.B. Evans.* Ch 2)

Above:
Lac des Vaches below
La Grande Casse in
Vanoise (Ch 3)

Left:
The trail linking the
Chabod and Vittorio
Emanuel huts passes
below the beautiful
Herbetet-Gran Paradiso
ridge (Ch 3)

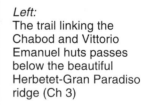

Left:
The ever-popular
Rifugio Vittorio Sella,
Gran Paradiso (Ch 3)

a degree of experience. The route is cairned from the col. Since our suggested Tour du Queyras also crosses Col d'Urine on the stage leading from La Monta to Le Roux or Abriès, those who chose the Italian alternative will have caught up with the outline tour described here.

Assuming Abriès is chosen as the finishing point for stage seven, the next day begins with a decision to be made as to which route should be adopted for the crossing of Col du Malrif, by which the gîte d'étape at the summer-only hamlet of Les Fonds de Cervières is reached at the head of the Cervières glen. There are two ways; the shorter of course is the more direct and goes by way of a good waymarked trail to the deserted hamlet of Malrif and via the charming Lac du Grand Laus. The longer alternative heads north up the Bouchet glen first and will be favoured by walkers who chose Le Roux for their previous overnight accommodation. From Le Roux continue upvalley a little farther, before breaking away on a two and a half hour climb to Col des Thures (2797m) on the frontier ridge. Thereafter there's some pretty rough country to trek through, at first along the frontier crest to Col de Rasis (2921m), then down to a tarn and over wild, barren hillsides before coming to the Crête aux Eaux Pendantes leading to Col du Malrif (2866m). Yet again views of an impressive nature greet the eye, particularly of the central block of snow and ice mountains of the Écrins, while much of the Tour du Queyras so far trekked will be on display. An even broader view may be obtained from the summit of Pic du Malrif nearby.

Both routes having joined at the col the way now descends into a surprisingly lush glen with trees, meadows and streams softening the landscape after the pseudo-wilderness experienced a little earlier. In this haven of peace sits the little hamlet of Les Fonds de Cervières and its gîte.

Stage nine is a short one, requiring little more than a morning's walk to reach Souliers across the 2629 metre Col de Péas, and it would be quite feasible to continue as far as Brunissard the same day should you be running short of time. But the occasional short and easy stage slipped into a multi-day circuit such as this, is no bad thing and will have a value all its own. Those with an abundance of energy and enthusiasm will not be short of ideas to fill the day, either on this or tomorrow's stage.

Between Souliers and Brunissard a diversion to Lac de Souliers and Pic Ouest is recommended, although you'll need good weather to make a visit worthwhile. Without straying to these stage ten becomes an even shorter one than yesterday's, and again, for those running short of time, it could be added to the next stage which leads for a second visit to Refuge de Furfande, albeit the approach is from a different direction.

A possible alternative to the GR58 route from Brunissard to Refuge de Furfande would be to follow the GR5 north from Brunissard over the rim of the Queyras district at Col des Ayes, and down from there to Briançon, from whose railway station trains depart for Lyon or Vallence. Remaining true to the spirit of the Tour du Queyras, however, for this penultimate stage we take the trail heading down-valley along the steep right flank (west side) along a forest track. Much of this stage is among trees, but the final climb to Col de Furfande (2500m) is through open country above the Bois du Devez. A dirt road also leads to the col which is marked by a large wooden cross. From it you look directly down into the lovely basin of Furfande, and on the descent it is important to bear left at a junction of trails, the alternative here being GR541, the route used on stage one from Montdauphin-Guillestre.

For the final day's walking on this tour a number of options are available. The first is to wander the main GR58 to Ceillac, and take the bus from there to Montdauphin-Guillestre for the journey home - but this would mean walking a section already followed on day two. The second option would reverse our initial stage one across Col St-Antoine and Col du Moussière - no bad thing since views would be quite different to those experienced on the way in. But the third alternative is that which the guidebook recommends. It returns to Montdauphin-Guillestre by way of the grassy Col Garnier (2279m), then down to woodland overlooking the Combe de Queyras before coming to the ruins of Les Girards and the hamlet of Gros on the way to the Durance valley; a mostly downhill walk of about six hours with the sun in your face.

TOUR DU QUEYRAS - ROUTE SUMMARY

Day 1: Montdauphin-Guillestre - Col de Moussière - Col St-Antoine - Refuge de Furfande

Day 2: Refuge de Furfande - Col de Bramousse - Ceillac

Day 3: Ceillac - Col des Estronques - St-Véran

Day 4: St-Véran - Col de St-Véran - Pic de Caramantran - Col de Chamoussière - Refuge Agnel
 or: St-Véran - Col de Chamoussière - Refuge Agnel

Day 5: Refuge Agnel - Col Agnel - Passo della Losetta - Pointe Joanne - Col de Valante - Refuge du Balif-Viso
 or: Refuge Agnel - Col Agnel - Passo della Losetta - Pointe Joanne - Rifugio Vallanta

Day 6: Refuge du Balif-Viso - Col Sellière - Col Lacroix - La Monta
 or: Refuge du Balif-Viso - Col Sellière - Monte Granero - Rifugio Jervis
 or: Rifugio Vallanta - Passo Gallarino - Rifugio Sella

Day 7: La Monta - Collette de Gilly - Col d'Urine - Abriès
 or: Rifugio Jervis - Tête du Pelvas - Col d'Urine - Abriès
 or: Rifugio Sella - Col de la Traversette - Refuge du Balif-Viso

Day 8: Abriès - Col du Malrif - Les Fonds de Cervières
 or: Abriès - Le Roux - Col des Thures - Col de Rasis - Col du Malrif - Les Fonds de Cervières

Day 9: Les Fonds de Cervières - Col de Péas - Souliers

Day 10: Souliers - Col du Tronchet - Lac de Souliers - Pic Ouest - Brunissard

Day 11: Brunissard - Col de Furfande - Refuge de Furfande

Day 12: Refuge de Furfande - Col Garnier - Montdauphin-Guillestre

MASSIF DES ÉCRINS

At the very hub of Dauphiné, midway between the Queyras and Vercors, rise the mountains of the Massif des Écrins, variously known as the Massif du Pelvoux or l'Oisans, a relatively compact, yet complex region, much of which is protected by national park status. On its periphery a few hideous ski centres have been built, but elsewhere the peaks, passes and valleys represent a wild and seemingly little-developed refuge of Alpine beauty. Rich in wild flowers this wonderland of savage, shapely mountains and extensive ridge systems contains steep little glens with an undeniable charm all their own. High passes, some of which are accessible to walkers, cross these ridges to link the glens and the valleys they feed, while in those valleys few villages provide more than the most basic of amenities. Those that do have largely managed to avoid compromising their intrinsic character.

The two highest mountains are the Barre des Écrins (4102m), the most southerly four thousand metre summit in the Alps, which lends its name to the whole area, and the famous Meije (3982m), the last major Alpine peak to be climbed. Although they may be only about ten kilometres apart, between them a chaos of glaciers and snowfields forms a girdle round a group of attendant peaks, such as Roche Faurio, La Grande Ruine, Pic Gaspard, Le Pave and the western extension of the Meije's bold profile, Le Rateau. Their glaciers may not be quite as extensive as those of the Pennine or Bernese Alps, nor as well-known to the general tourist as some of the ice-sheets of the Mont Blanc range, but their significance to the quality of the scenery is considerable.

Writing about the area in his *Histoire des Hautes-Alpes*, J.C.F. Ladoucette found it difficult to contain his enthusiasm:

> "Filled with high mountains, rearing their heads as if to reach to heaven, crowned with glaciers, and fissured with immense chasms, where lie the eternal snows guarded by bare and rugged cliffs; offering the most varied sights, and enjoying all temperatures; and containing everything that is most curious and interesting, the most simple and the most sublime, the most smiling and the most severe, the most beautiful and the most awful; such is the department of the High Alps."

La Meije towers above the village of La Grave near the northern edge of the massif, with the Barre des Écrins not far away to the south-south-east. Then in a block to the south of this, beyond Pic Coolidge, rise Mont Pelvoux (3943m) and the region's third highest, L'Ailefroide (3954m). Between these last two Pic Sans Nom and Pic du Coup de Sabre are close neighbours, while a little farther south-west, Les Bans (3669m) throws out a ridge that effectively separates two fine valleys: Val Gaudémar to the west and the valley of Entre les Aygues that flows eastward to Vallouise. In addition, Les Bans blocks the upper Vallée du Vénéon with its glacier-plastered cirque, and makes a north-south division as well as an east-west divide.

South of this line only the group headed by Pic de Bonvoisin, Pointe de Verdonne and Le Sirac still hang onto their glaciers, while elsewhere within the boundaries of the Parc National des Écrins isolated peaks and groups of peaks, such as L'Olan and Les Rouies, shine their little napkin icefields from afar. That is not to suggest that other mountains fanning out from the central core fail to attract through a lack of ice or snow, for the whole region is one of generous proportions. But the overall effect is of a great mountain mass whose bare outer rim serves to protect a cluster of inner peaks upon whose flanks the development of mountaineering interest has been concentrated.

Great names from the Golden Age, and even earlier, made their mark here: Forbes and Bonney, F.F. Tuckett, William Mathews, Edward Whymper - who climbed the Barre des Écrins in 1864 with A.W. Moore, Horace Walker and the guides Christian Almer and Michel Croz - and W.A.B. Coolidge (the 'Boswell of the Alps'), who made the first ascent of L'Ailefroide in 1870, also with Almer as his guide. In the early 1870s it was Coolidge and his indomitable aunt, Miss Meta Brevoort, who concentrated on a systematic exploration of the range, and who subsequently made more than two hundred and fifty ascents - a number of which were new. Often Coolidge was accompanied by his dog Tschingel, which also reached the summits of Le Rateau and La Grande Ruine, among others. "I am not quite sure what it was that made us choose Dauphiné as our battleground," he wrote, "but I believe it was ambition. There was a whole world to explore there and that was enough for us."

For the modern mountain walker, exploration remains a personal journey of discovery, and it does not matter how many others might have crossed a pass, photographed a view or given directions in a guidebook, each 'new' valley, tarn or col visited becomes a 'first' to be celebrated and enjoyed to the full. The Massif des Écrins will surely not disappoint in this respect.

✳   ✳   ✳

Vallée du Vénéon

Taking the Barre des Écrins as the pivot in our mountain hub, the two main glaciers that drain its western flanks flow into the Vallée du Vénéon, the head of which is not the Barre des Écrins itself, but Les Bans whose dramatic glacial cirque faces almost due north. Here the Glacier de la Pilatte is an unevenly textured plaster spreading from one side of the cirque to the other, broken here and there by ribs of dark rock that project through the snow and ice. On the left bank of the glacier, not far from its snout, stands the Refuge de la Pilatte, reached by a delightful walk through the valley from La Bérarde.

The upper Vallée du Vénéon drains northward, then curves round the flank of the Tête du Chéret. On the right bank of the stream a path climbs steeply to the Refuge du Temple Écrins, above which soars Pic Coolidge and the uncomfortably-named Pointe des Avalanches. There's yet another hut nearby, in the bed of the valley, that is well patronised by walkers since it may be reached in only an hour's walk from La Bérarde. Refuge du Plan du Carrelet gazes on some savage mountain scenery from its position opposite a tributary glen with the narrow tongue of the Chardon glacier straining down from Col des Rouies. The Chardon is a narrow glen, typically wild as are so many that feed the Vénéon.

La Bérarde stands at the roadhead in the midst of some of the finest scenery in the French Alps. When T.G. Bonney made his first visit in August 1860 he thought it a miserable hamlet. "Fowls and goats, pigs and people, occupy harmoniously the squalid huts, and the cows are as well lodged as their masters." *(Outline Sketches in the High Alps of Dauphiné)*

Well over a hundred years later, and despite its having become a Mecca for active mountain enthusiasts, La Bérarde remains little more than a small hamlet, deserted and closed to the outside world during winter. Its reputation as a superb walking and mountaineering base is well justified, for there are some tremendous mountains and mountain tours accessible from it. Served by infrequent buses along an exciting road that used to be known as the first obstacle in reaching the village, it has campsites, a couple of hotels, a CAF refuge, modest shop - and a variety of trails that lead to viewpoints of splendour.

Two valleys converge on La Bérarde. The Vénéon, as has already been mentioned, comes in from the south-east and is dominated by Les Bans, L'Ailefroide and the Barre des Écrins. Departing the hamlet it then veers westward as a deep and narrow gorge-like valley. To the north the Étancons glen entices with its mystery, and as you wander into it from La Bérarde so a huge rock wall topped by a ragged spine is seen to rise directly from the Étancons glacier. This is the south face of La Meije, so different to the northern side which looks down upon La Grave. Whymper wrote disparagingly of this glen after descending through it from the Brèche de la Meije in 1864. He called it "a howling wilderness, the abomination of desolation; destitute alike of animal or vegetable life...suggestive of chaos, but of little else." Nowadays it is generally viewed more favourably and with greater appreciation for its wild grandeur.

Above La Bérarde the dome-like Tête de la Maye (2581m) guards the entrance to the Vallon des Étancons, and its easily-accessible summit provides a wonderful panorama of all the neighbouring high peaks, including La Meije and Barre des Écrins. An orientation table aids identification of the main points in that view. A path climbs from the hamlet, and near the top fixed cables safeguard a few rocky sections, while south of La Bérarde a similar path climbs to Les Clots (2529m) for more fine views.

The main trail north of the hamlet crosses to the eastern side of the Étancons torrent and rises gently upvalley towards the south face of La Meije and its flanking peaks of Le Rateau and Pic Gaspard, and goes directly to the CAF's Refuge du Châtelleret (2232m) in the very heart of big mountain country. Surprisingly, in the mid 1950's this refuge was described as being little more than a broken-down, three-walled hovel built against a huge boulder. It had a stone floor covered with leaves, a pot-bellied stove and rudimentary furniture. In fact little had changed since it was inaugurated in 1882. How different it all is now!

About three kilometres downstream from La Bérarde, Les Étages, with its impressive view to the Écrins, squats at the junction of the Vallon des Étages, another tributary glen which flows from the south. A path projects part-way into that valley, while another climbs steeply behind the hamlet to confront an astonishing triangular granite spear, the Aiguille Dibona. Like something transported from Chamonix, this is very much a rock-climber's playground. A small hut, Refuge du Soreiller, provides overnight accommodation with views south across the Vallée du Vénéon.

Still flowing westward the Vénéon alternates between being very narrow and then somewhat wider; the road that traces its northern bank is a marvel of engineering and demands full concentration of all who drive along it. There are many tales from the past of vehicles negotiating this route with one or two wheels overhanging a precipice, or of the road disappearing overnight into the torrent.

Midway between Les Étages and St-Christophe-en-Oisans another tributary glen drains from the south, with the bulk of L'Olan at its head. The Muande actually takes the melt of the little glaciers of Les Rouies, caught in a shelf of a hanging valley near the head of the cirque under the Glaciers de la Lavey. Halfway along the glen Refuge de la Lavey is reached by a footpath spur off the main valley path that links St-Christophe with La Bérarde.

A road snakes above St-Christophe towards the hinted Vallée de la Selle that effectively cuts east to west through the mountains behind the village. While the road itself does not project far, a path climbs through the glen alongside the Torrent du Diable to reach the Refuge de la Selle at the head of the valley, with Le Rateau rising in a tease of ice to the north-east, and the Massif du Soreiller opposite, to the south. The path continues from the hut to the edge of the Selle glacier where, for those with the necessary equipment and expertise, a crossing could be made of Col de la Selle (3201m) in the eastern ridge, and a subsequent descent to Refuge du Châtelleret in the Étancons glen above La Bérarde.

The trail through Vallée de la Selle is not the only one worth considering from St-Christophe, for another mounts the Tête de la Toura (2885m) which acts as the glen's northern gatepost. There a broad panorama enables a fresh perspective to be gained of this part of the region. North of the Tête cableways string the mountains from Les Deux-Alpes, a major ski resort occupying a high terrace midway between the valleys of Vénéon and Romanche. As the name implies Les Deux-Alpes comprises two resorts that have merged into one; Alpe de Vénosc and Alpe de Mont-de-Lans. Almost entirely devoted to the whims of the ski industry, one of the cableway systems links the resort with the glaciers of Le Rateau at the western end of the crest spreading from La Meije. Les Deux-Alpes may be reached by walkers along a variant of the GR54, or by cableway from Venosc just outside Bourg d'Arud.

Bourg d'Arud is another small village astride the road that makes its tortuous way along the valley to La Bérarde. It boasts a couple of hotels, a gîte and a large campsite, while just to the south, on the opposite bank of the Vénéon, the neighbouring hamlet of l'Alleau also offers camping facilities at the foot of a pathway that climbs steeply to the Refuge, Lac and Col de la Muzelle on the route of the GR54, Tour de l'Oisans. The lake is a particular favourite with walkers based in the valley, as is the beautiful Lac Lauvitel in the neighbouring glen to the west. A waymarked footpath links these two by way of Col du Vallon (2531m), and an excellent two-day circuit could thereby be achieved using Refuge de la Muzelle as the overnight base. Strong walkers could manage the circuit in a single day, no doubt, but the two adjacent glens are so delightful that they ought to be treated with the respect they deserve. On a one-day circuit there would be little time available to enjoy them both at leisure, and some landscapes are just too good to race through.

Bourg d'Arud is served by bus from Bourg d'Oisans, and the little village would make an admirable base for several days of a walking holiday, as would the smaller hamlet of La Danchère nearby. La Danchère does not have the main valley road passing through, for it sits on a spur of wooded land above the Vénéon and below the entrance to the Lauvitel glen. As such it is a quieter place, attractive and with hotel accommodation. Walkers with their own transport might find it worth considering as a short-stay base in preference to some of the valley-bed villages. Lac Lauvitel is reached in an hour and a half by one of two paths. Above the lake Brèche du Périer (2491m) makes it possible to achieve a crossing to a choice of valley systems lying west and south of the mountain barrier walling the lake, with a very fine circuit of two or three days' duration being an obvious challenge.

Another trail, much less strenuous than that to Lac Lauvitel, descends among lush vegetation to Les Gauchoirs, then continues on the left bank of the Vénéon heading south-west through the steadily-broadening valley. Five kilometres before reaching Bourg d'Oisans, just after passing the Cascade de la Pisse, the Vénéon is swollen by the lesser flow of the Romanche which enters from the right and gives its name to the valley thereafter.

For a small town Bourg d'Oisans is a busy place on a site very much seen as the gateway to the Écrins massif, for it serves as a funnel linking the rest of France with the National Park. Downstream the Romanche swings in a south-westerly arc before correcting its course and joining forces with the Isère in Grenoble, the city from which fan out all routes of access to the various corners of Dauphiné. Buses ply the route from Grenoble to Bourg d'Oisans, and from there a brutal twist of hairpins takes a road to the ski resort of Alpe d'Huez on the edge of the Grandes Rousses, which still carry a covering of snow throughout the summer. Another heads upstream into the Romanche valley proper by way of the Gorges de l'Infernet, Le Freney d'Oisans, the dammed Lac du Chambon, La Grave and Villar d'Arène, and finally departs by way of the Col du Lautaret (2057m). While views from the col are very fine, especially to Pic Gaspard and La Meije, the higher Col du Galibier (2642m) provides additional interest as from it, not only can many of the major peaks of the Écrins be seen to advantage, but northward rise the Vanoise mountains, and far off even Mont Blanc is evident on the proverbial clear day.

The Romanche Valley

The Romanche forms the most northerly moat to the central block of the Écrins massif, and may be considered one of the most important of the whole region. It does not rise at Col du Lautaret, but in a glen further south below the Glacier de la Plate des Agneaux and between the peaks of La Grande Ruine and Roche Faurio. Soon after its birth it is joined in the Plan de Valfourche by the first of its many tributaries, the Torrent du Clot des Cavales. This stream comes out of its own lovely glen carved between the block of La Grande Ruine and the southern flanks of La Meije, here given additional character by the summits of Le Pavé and the tower of Pic Gaspard.

Both glens are accessible to walkers by way of the Refuge de l'Alpe de Villar Arène, recently rebuilt and enlarged and set in buckled pastures an hour and a half's walk from the roadhead. From the hut a trail rises south-westward and forks in the Plan de Valfourche. The left-hand option follows the infant Romanche to its source, then climbs steeply for 850 metres to Refuge Planchard (3169m) on the eastern slopes of La Grande Ruine overlooking the curving Glacier de la Plate des Agneaux. The alternative trail heads west into the glen below Pic Gaspard. A privately-owned refuge, Cabane des Pichettes, is found there beside the Cavales stream, but higher on the flanks of Pic Gaspard, Refuge du Pavé hugs a knoll at the southern end of a small tarn with a very lonely outlook.

In the pastures below Refuge de l'Alpe de Villar Arêne a wooden post marks another junction of paths, with one cutting round the north-eastern hillside to gain the unseen Col du Lautaret road pass, while the main trail either climbs past the hut to cross Col d'Arsine (2340m), or descends in tight zig-zags to the gravel beds of the upper Romanche valley. La Meije is badly foreshortened above and to the west of this part of the valley, where its great bulk looms overall.

At the roadhead a campsite on the right bank of the river is backed by pines in an open situation, with a hint of good things up towards Col d'Arsine, and more gentle, pastoral country curving away Down valley. No more than three kilometres downstream the Lautaret road enters Villar d'Arène, a village with gîte and hotel accommodation, rather less developed for tourism than is La Grave, the main mountain base in the valley and one of the massif's three centres for mountaineering; the others being La Bérarde and the hamlet of Ailefroide below Mont Pelvoux.

Much of La Grave stands above the road, a huddle of stone-built houses with narrow alleyways between, happily safe from the worst excesses of modern architectural blight that goes under the name of sophistication and which has afflicted certain other resorts in mountain France. There are old-fashioned hotels in the original part of the village, more modern lower down, and two campsites by the river. Alongside the main road the *Bureau des Guides* is found not far from the Meije cable-car which, despite its name, does not rise to that mountain, but instead deposits tourists, climbers and skiers onto a high point near Col des Ruillans overlooking the Glacier de la Girose which spreads from Le Rateau.

The north face of La Meije soars gracefully above La Grave for more than 2500 metres, a face climbed first in 1898 and one that dominates this part of the valley. "The view of this mountain from the village of La Grave can hardly be spoken of too highly," commented Whymper. "It is one of the finest road-views in the Alps...But from La Grave one can no more appreciate the noble proportions and the towering height of the Meije, than understand the symmetry of the dome of St Paul's by gazing upon it from the churchyard. To see it fairly, one must be placed at a greater distance and at a greater height."

Walkers are able to do just that by climbing a waymarked footpath to the hillside villages of Les Terraces and Le Chazelet. But even better views of La Meije and Le Rateau are won from the shores of either Lac Lérié or the slightly higher Lac Noir well to the west of Le Chazelet on the Plateau de Paris. These tarns provide sparkling foregrounds to some of the loveliest mid-height views in the Écrins range. Between tarn and mountain the deep valley of the Romanche lies hidden as a shadow-filled trough out of which snow-gilded peaks challenge the clouds.

The Romanche continues to flow westward with only one other hamlet to note on the twelve-kilometre journey from La Grave to the dam at the end of Lac du

Chambon. Les Fréaux lies in the valley immediately below Le Chazelet. From it a trail rears up the southern flank of the valley to gain Refuge Chancel perched above a tarn in a horseshoe scoop of mountainside below Le Rateau. One fairly level path, which links the hut with the intermediate station on the Meije cableway, passes the end of Lac du Puy Vachier, while a more strenuous trail rises to the upper terminus.

Beyond the dam at the western end of Lac de Chambon another tributary stream flows down from the north to join that of the Romanche. Mizöen guards the entrance to this northern valley through which a minor road forces passage to the small, unsophisticated hamlets of Clavans-le-Bas and Clavans-le-Haut, then crosses Col de Sarenne for a rough approach to Alpe d'Huez. Another road branches north-eastward from just below Clavans-le-Bas and wriggles up the hillside to the handsome village of Besse-en-Oisans. Not much more than a kilometre beyond Besse the tarmac ends, yet the continuing dirt road twists and turns agonisingly to reach an enchanting high pastureland basin with distant views of the Meije. Of more interest, however, is the footpath route which claims right to those same views, and better.

Adopted as a variant stage on the classic Tour de l'Oisans, the path makes an exposed rising traverse above Lac du Chambon before cutting up broad verdant hillsides, gazing on waterfalls and seemingly endless rolling hills, along another dirt road, passing an occasional gîte, then heading into that enormous grassland basin between Col Bichet and Col du Souchet. By taking GR54 to Col du Souchet a better view of La Meije is won, while an even more delightful panorama is that seen from the shores of Lac Noir and Lac Lérié - the tarns mentioned above as providing a better opportunity to study La Meije than was possible from La Grave. A vague trail leads directly to them from Col du Souchet.

This vast region of undulating pastureland on the edge of the Maurienne north of the Romanche valley offers tremendous possibilities for walkers. There are easy flower-covered passes to cross, broad ridges to wander along, modest summits to aim for. Though not among mountains of the first order, these walks provide scintillating views to a distant coronet of peaks farther south. Also in view are the glacial dustings of Les Grandes Rousses to the west, the horn-like Aiguilles de la Saussaz and du Goléon, and the Aiguilles d'Arves off to the east. In between, a soft scoop of grass and marshland, with gentle streams meandering through and a scattering of small chalets that provide the human touch. Accommodation is available in Refuge du Rif Tor, a few minutes' walk from Col Bichet.

Valley of the Guisane

Third of our valleys that encircle the Écrins massif is that of the Guisane which links Col du Lautaret with Briançon.

Col du Lautaret was used by the Romans who built a small temple there. No sign of that remains today, but views from the col are quite lovely as one gazes over a foreground of sweeping green hillsides to the shapely Meije and neighbouring Pic Gaspard. East of the Lautaret, and walling the upper valley, the limestone Massif des Cerces is criss-crossed with paths, making this area something of a treat for walkers. GR57 and its variants make a thorough exploration of the mountains and glens that lie rucked between the loftier Écrins and the Italian border, and GR5 creeps through too, edging the district on its way to Briançon.

The valley of the Guisane flows south-eastward with the National Park boundary tracing the right bank almost as far as the attractive small village of Le Casset; perhaps the valley's best base for walkers content with gîte accommodation. Thereafter the ski industry has carved pistes and strung mechanical hoists up the north- and east-facing hillsides, making it necessary to delve deeper into tributary glens in order to regain nature's tranquillity.

Coming down the valley, here a flat-bedded, broadening trough, Monte Viso can be seen far-off - that cone-shaped, pre-eminent mountain of the Cottian Alps already studied from the Queyras. Forest clothes the lower hillsides, and meadows spread across the valley, while between Le Casset and Monêtier-les-Bains tents and caravans stand almost camouflaged by riverside scrub. Monêtier is a large village with ambitions to be taken seriously as a ski-station. It consists of an assortment of traditional dwellings and modern apartments, with hotels, restaurants and enough shops to be of use to backpackers passing through. Walks up through the forests and into wooded glens nearby can be delightful, but there have been some harsh things done to the upper slopes in the cause of downhill skiing that make one scurry away in search of wilder country.

Below Monêtier several villages gather in close proximity, ski-slopes to the right, unfussed hills to the left. Along the upper left-hand flank of the valley a linking of trails makes it possible to avoid all habitation in a long and sunny belvedere walk from just below the Col du Lautaret to Briançon. At Briançon the Guisane loses its identity. Thereafter it is the Durance which forms the far-eastern boundary of the Massif des Écrins, collecting the waters of several fine mountain valleys as it works southward to Argentière-la-Bessée, Embrun and Savines-le-Lac where it relinquishes all claim to the range of l'Oisans.

Fortified by Vauban in the late seventeenth century, and reckoned to be the highest town in Europe, Briançon holds much of interest and is worth retreating to in the event of bad weather forcing escape from high cols and ridges. It also has an important railway link with Paris, and road access via Col d'Izoard with the Queyras massif, but its valley is too busy, too fussy, to make it worth using as a base for a walking holiday.

Downstream, Argentière-la-Bessée also has a railway station, and with easy access to the Vallouise and a clutch of splendid glens, is perhaps a better place to aim for if the plan is to concentrate a walking holiday in this south-eastern corner of the range where some of the loveliest high mountain scenery is on show.

Vallouise and Val de l'Entre-les-Aygues

Midway along the Vallouise, at a junction of glens with some tremendous high mountains nearby, is its main village, a busy little resort that shares the same name as the valley itself. The old village of Vallouise faces south, its back to the mountains and with more recent development spread out below. It has a choice of hotels, two gîtes and a municipal campsite. There are a few shops and bars, a summer bus service into neighbourhood glens, and an atmosphere of excited anticipation with so much dramatic scenery close at hand. Mont Pelvoux dominates as you approach from the south, although it cannot be seen from Vallouise itself due to intervening ridges.

The main valley here drains from the north, while another, Val de l'Entre-les-Aygues, flows from the west. Both of these divide again to collect the melt from assorted glacier systems. The first we need to consider is the Vallon de Chambran which runs roughly north to south, with a westward kink in its uppermost reaches. It is formed in a little glacial cirque under the Crête des Grangettes, east of Pointe des Arcas, which is itself merely part of a long ridge extending south of Montagne des Agneaux. In that cirque Lac de l'Eychauda makes a popular goal for walkers on day trips from the Vallouise, and in summer a bus service daily journeys as far as the *buvette* at Chambran midway through the main part of the valley. Chambran is not even a hamlet, but several rough buildings with a lovely outlook.

This glen is itself subdivided above Chambran, for the Crête de l'Yret, which extends below Lac de l'Eychauda, effectively contains a little hanging valley on its eastern side that has now been exploited for skiing. Walkers heading south from Monêtier-les-Bans on GR54 cross Col de l'Eychauda and descend through that wasted hanging valley before dropping in steep zig-zags to the Vallon de Chambran upstream of the *buvette*. Above Chambran the Eychauda stream glides in silver braidings, then gathers into a semblance of order to dance through a steepening cleft among masses of wild flowers and the raucous summer sound of the cicadas. Wandering down the pathway that accompanies this stream is to be reminded of the southerly nature of these mountains. While snow and ice may coat the upper peaks, deep valleys embrace the light, fragrance and flavour of the Mediterranean.

St-Antoine and neighbouring Les Claux stand either side of the confluence of the Eychauda torrent with that of the Ailefroide. The road from Vallouise curves leftward through rocky narrows with woods on the lower slopes, and all eyes are eager to catch the first exciting views of Mont Pelvoux that rises directly ahead. Close to Ailefroide the valley forks yet again; the western glen is watered by the glaciers of l'Ailefroide and Pointe du Sélé, the northern glen by the Glacier Noir and Glacier Blanc; the first coming from Mont Pelvoux, the second from Barre des Écrins.

Like La Bérarde, Ailefroide is a summer-only hamlet, a magnet for climbers and with opportunities for outstanding walks to the very edge of the glaciers. There are campsites, two hotels and a gîte, and meadows thick with flowers in early summer. Not surprisingly it is extremely busy during the high season. Above the hamlet the road continues below the huge walls of Pelvoux as far as the drab boulderfield of Pré de Madame Carle, for Refuge Cézanne. There the scene is typically Alpine, being one of big mountains and glacial moraines. The summit of Pelvoux is more than 2000 metres above the road and the Glacier Noir has carved a highway round its northern buttresses; ahead Glacier Blanc appears from behind the Barre des Écrins. A short, almost level, walk leads to a junction of paths. One veers left to follow the north bank of the Glacier Noir on a narrow moraine crest, while the other climbs to the snout of Glacier Blanc and a CAF refuge at 2543 metres. While the Glacier Noir trail passes beneath the southern wall of the Barre des Écrins and overlooks the rubble-strewn glacier to the north face of Mont Pelvoux, that which climbs to Glacier Blanc shows even more grandeur. Just below Refuge du Glacier Blanc it passes the first hut to be built in the region, Refuge Tuckett. Views from here are absolutely stunning, for the hut gazes on an incredible seven-kilometre spread of crusty peaks, glaciers, buttresses and ice-choked couloirs, with Mont Pelvoux regal-looking to the south across a foreground brightened by a small tarn.

The western glen cutting away from Ailefroide is deep and narrow, and was once described as a "cheerless and desolate valley [which] contains miles of boulders, débris, stones, sand and mud." A path heads into it from Ailefroide and then divides. The right-hand trail continues directly beneath the south face of Pelvoux to reach a pair of climbers' huts provided by the CAF, Refuge Pelvoux and Refuge du Sélé, while the left-hand option enters another sub-glen, Vallon de Clapous, with a scrambly col at its head by which Entre les Aygues may be reached.

The Val de l'Entre-les-Aygues is another lovely narrow valley that begins beneath the mass of Les Bans and flows eastward, soon among patches of meadowland, then splendid forests that lead nearly all the way down to Vallouise. Part-way along the glen there's a camping area on the right bank of the river at Pont des Places, otherwise there's no accommodation to be had except for two huts; one in the cirque at the upper end of the valley, the other in its tributary glen, Vallon de la Selle. The roadhead is about nine kilometres upstream from Vallouise, at Entre les Aygues itself, where there is a buvette and space to park cars. There the valley divides. The continuing, western branch, is that which leads to a cirque topped by Les Bans. The south-west branch, the Vallon de la Selle, is longer and rises to a curious, though strangely attractive, amphitheatre rimmed with a crest of bare rock from which extensive screes and slopes of black grit fan to rough pastures. At the head of that crest Col de l'Aup Martin (2761m) provides access to a secondary valley that plunges eastward and is drained by the Fournel to join the Durance at Argentière-la-Bessée.

The upper, western, extent of Val de l'Entre-les-Aygues is closed at its head by a bold-looking group of mountains. Pic de Bonvoisin forms the southern limit of this cirque, then come Pic Jocelme, Pic des Aupillous, Les Bans, Pointe des Boeufs Rouges and Pointe Guyard, each one well in excess of 3000 metres, but appearing even higher. In the ridge linking Les Bans and Pointe des Boeufs Rouges two cols suggest strenuous possibilities for achieving a crossing to the upper Vénéon. Whymper's party made the first crossing of one of these in 1864 (he called it Col de la Pilatte, although his description better fits that of Col des Bans), but that and its neighbour lie outside the scope of this book, for one need only look at the Glacier de la Pilatte which hangs on the other side of the ridge to know that considerable mountaineering skill is a prerequisite for anyone toying with such a proposition.

South of Les Bans, between Pic des Aupillous and Pic Jocelme, Col du Sellar (3084m) provides another challenging route over the mountains, not to the Vallée du Vénéon, but to the upper Val Gaudémar. This pass also has a small glacier to negotiate on its western side, but Whymper claims that local peasants told him sheep and goats could easily be taken across. The Didier and Richard map, however, marks this col as being both difficult and dangerous, so caution is advised should the route be chosen.

Below the cirque walls east of the col Refuge des Bans serves as a climber's base; it's also a popular destination for short walks from the roadhead on a good footpath that sticks to the true left bank of the Torrent des Bans. At the Entre les Aygues roadhead an alternative footpath is directed by signpost across the multi-stranded river and into the Vallon de la Selle, in which the small Cabane du Jas Lacroix stands above the left bank among grassy hummocks and lichen-patterned boulders and with Pointe de Verdonne rising nearby. It is through this glen and over Col de l'Aup Martin and its neighbouring Pas de la Cavale, that the easiest, though certainly not the most direct, route for walkers leads from the Vallouise to the south-western valleys of the Oisans region.

Val Gaudémar and Vallonpierre

Val Gaudémar is the principal, though by no means the only, one of these. Beginning in the shadow of Les Bans it drains westward at first, then flows south-west below the small village of Villar-Loubière along the outlying flanks of the range, before its river curves in a great northerly sweep towards Grenoble. Approach from Grenoble by road is first made along the N85, then south of Corps and the Lac du Sautet a minor road (D985) breaks away north-eastward. Its upper limit is reached about eight kilometres upstream of La Chapelle-en-Valgaudémar at the Chalet-Hotel du Gioberney in the tributary glen of Muande Bellone below the west face of Les Bans. From there a number of trails climb to vantage points on the slopes of the surrounding mountains; that which visits Lac du Lauzon on the flank of Les Rouies provides especially fine views.

Les Bans once again shows itself to be a pivotal mountain, for here it offers a generous outstretch of ridges that effectively create a long wall to close off the end of Val Gaudémar; a knuckle of rock, scree and steeply-plunging grass. The southern limit of that knuckle wall is marked by the block of Le Sirac (3440m) that sends out a dark, slender schistose arête roughly westward to Pic de Vallonpierre and the higher Aiguille de Morges. From the latter, or rather from a subsidiary of it, another ridge extends northwards, thereby containing a steep but extravagently beautiful glen, the Vallonpierre, which counter balances the Muande Bellone glen opposite.

Vallonpierre is a true gem, its small tarn below the screes of Le Sirac blocked above the north bank by a low ridge of boulders, its eastern shoreline being a broad grassy meadow as level as a bowling green. The CAF has provided a small, mottled, stone-built hut in this idyllic setting. Refuge de Vallonpierre attracts, not only for the romance of its setting, but by being on the route of the Tour de l'Oisans, as well as having ease of access to Le Sirac and some safe but airy ridges. The main walking interest in the glen is focused on the crossing of Col de Vallonpierre (2607m), by which Vallouise may be reached by a linking of four other walkers' passes. But for experienced trekkers coming clockwise from the direction of Vallouise an alternative to the direct descent to Val Gaudémar is worth considering. From the hut a minor trail curves round the mid-height slopes of Le Sirac and Pointe de Verdonne to gain Refuge de Chabournéou in an intimate cirque topped by Pic de Bonvoisin. A continuing high-level path remains well above the valley bed and curves northward along that knuckle wall, eventually zig-zagging into the glen of Muande Bellone at Chalet-Hotel du Gioberney. That route requires some care, while the main path through the glen is by no means uninteresting but faces some very steep sections below Refuge de Vallonpierre, with streams and cascades and a steady change of vegetation being evident the deeper it goes.

The Torrent de Muande Bellone joins that which drains the Vallonpierre to boost the Séveraisse at the head of Val Gaudémar. On the right bank, among groves of silver birch and boulders partly covered with vegetation, squats yet another hut, Refuge du Clot (or Xavier Blanc), easily reached by a short footpath spur descending from the valley road. Between this hut and La Chapelle the valley descends in steps and with little habitation other than a huddle of farm buildings and the hamlets of Le Bourg and Le Casset. Waterfalls spray from narrow cleaves while the mountain walls soar steeply both to the north and the south. Few trails assault these soaring walls, but the valley path is a delight of insect jungles, wild blackberries and raspberries hanging heavy on either side. There's camping to be had on the right bank of the river opposite Le Bourg, and gîte accommodation at Le Casset. But at La Chapelle there's plenty of both as well as modest hotels, a good store and a restaurant or two. Although it's only a small village, La Chapelle makes a reasonable base from which to explore the surrounding mountains and their little glens. The boundary of the Parc National des Écrins runs through the valley and cuts across the southern flank of L'Olan, a huge mountain block to the north. From Les Portes, a hamlet just to the south of La Chapelle, a good view is to be had of that mountain block opposite.

From the northern outskirts of La Chapelle a fine invigorating walk leads up to Refuge de l'Olan (2344m), crosses Pas de l'Olan another two hundred metres higher, then heads westward to Col de Colombes (2423m) and Lac de Lautier before descending to Refuge des Souffles by way of Col des Clochettes. The hut is set upon a sun-trap of hillside way above Villar-Loubière where the Val Gaudémar makes its leftward curve. To the west, across a vast green bowl of hillside, another path can be seen snaking up to the Col de la Vaurze, by which access is provided to Le Désert from Val Gaudémar.

Val Jouffrey

While the southern slopes of L'Olan fall into Val Gaudémar, its western side drains to a narrow glen that becomes the Val Jouffrey. This glen, with the waters of the Bonne river flowing through, turns distinctly pastoral lower down around Le Désert, a hamlet that, despite providing basic dortoir accommodation for walkers passing through, retains its traditional farming values with haybarns and cattle byres crowding the alleyways. Below the hamlet the valley slopes off to Les Faures, La Chalp and La Chapelle-en-Valjouffrey where the Béranger glen enters from the north, but upstream a farm road continues beyond Le Désert as far as the Cascade de la Pisse. A walker's trail continues from there, following the stream all the way to the CAF hut, Refuge de Fond Turbat, built in a wild combe below L'Olan.

The valley of the Béranger torrent that joins the Bonne at La Chapelle-en-Valjouffrey is shorter than its neighbour, but it is every bit as charming, and well protected under the auspices of both the National Park and its own Réserve Naturelle du Béranger. There's only one very small village in that glen. Valsenestre is a pretty little summer-only hamlet whose houses are almost clinically neat, with troughs of geraniums and petunias at every window and water gushing from fountains at practically every corner. There's a gîte in the village with overflow accommodation in a nearby building. The head of its valley is formed by a cirque topped by Pointe Swan, seen through a screen of pine and larchwoods not far away to the east, while a lesser corrie invites interest to the north, the Vallon de Valsenestre. Trails give an opportunity to study both from close quarters. In addition there's a path that climbs into the Combe Guyon north-west of Valsenestre, to Lac Labarre, eleven hundred metres above the village, with a continuation that goes up to a col with a spur path tracing a ridge to the summit of Tête de Rame. It's an undeniably attractive yet challenging patch of country.

The road which serves Valsenestre breaks away from that which goes to Le Désert at La Chapelle. Down valley it reaches Entraigues at another junction of valleys. Here the Bonne cuts away to the south-west, eventually to link up with the Severaisse on its way to Grenoble, while from the north flows the Maisanne. The D526 road heads along the latter valley and, crossing Col d'Ornon, twists into the Romanche valley a short distance downstream of Bourg d'Oisans.

That route, of course, is for the motorist. Our walker meanwhile has a choice of mountain paths that will link Le Désert, Valsenestre and Bourg d'Oisans by more strenuous but far more rewarding ways, and in so doing provide a series of tremendous panoramas to enjoy hour after hour. The following outline circuit of the massif provides the key to this western edge of the Écrins, as to the rest of the district. It is the GR54, widely known as the Tour de l'Oisans.

✳ ✳ ✳

TOUR DE L'OISANS

This is not a mountain tour to dismiss lightly. Although of similar scale and distance to the better-known Tour du Mont Blanc, and being possible to walk in nine or ten days, as is the TMB, similarities end there. GR54 is more strenuous, more demanding and with a much greater sense of remoteness than will be experienced around Mont Blanc. Routes to and from some of the passes are extremely steep and on occasion severe, and a few of the ridges crossed by these passes are so narrow that one could easily sit astride them with legs hanging on either side. It's a wild district, with many inner glens that are seductively untamed, uninhabited and where the mists of morning and evening spin webs of enchantment.

But mountain walkers with experience of multi-day journeys in other Alpine regions will find in the Écrins massif as much scenic variety and diversity of landscape as they could possibly wish. Huts, gîtes d'étape or modest hotels will be found at the end of every stage, and in almost every valley and glen visited there will be temptations to stray from the waymarked route in order to explore further. For surely to walk round the Tour de l'Oisans will be enough to deepen one's love of the district and to ensure that a return visit becomes a subsconscious demand. The challenge and rewards of such a walk, and the dreams conjured for the future, are met in equal measure.

As the western gateway to the Oisans, the little town of Bourg d'Oisans makes an obvious and convenient base from which to begin the tour. Served by bus from Grenoble its shops can supply guidebooks and maps of the region, as well as foodstuffs to fill a rucksack for several days on the trail. Not that such provisioning is necessary, other than for the determined backpacker, for most of the early stages, at least, have an opportunity to buy a few basic items of food to eat on the hoof, while meals will be supplied at each overnight lodging.

The Tour de l'Oisans is usually tackled in a clockwise direction, and on this, as on most long mountain treks, it is advisable to make an early start to each stage of the walk, especially as summer temperatures in this southerly range can soar through the day. By setting out early it's possible to make height and distance before the day grows too warm. And nowhere on the Tour de l'Oisans is this advice more apt than on the very first stage, for having crossed the Romanche from Bourg, waymarks lead the 'trail' up a steep slab wall from one narrow shelf to the next, at such an angle as to have you gasping from the sudden exertion.

It's not all like that, of course, and before long the gradient eases, but then the way heads up through forest ankle deep in pine cones and the dried needles of past decades, and the sweat starts running again. There is some road walking here and there, but at the hamlet of Le Rosay a narrow trail strikes off across rough meadows with views to Alpe d'Huez, then plunges steeply to the Sarenne, here a clear stream dancing through forest in a tight wedge of a valley. Some walkers tackling the Tour de l'Oisans choose to avoid the exertions of this initial stage by taking bus or taxi to Alpe d'Huez, then walking along the GR549 which follows a dirt road into the valley of the Sarenne to join the main route of GR54. But by doing so they miss an old Roman bridge, moss-cushioned walls of a one-time mill, and the pleasures (as well as the pains) of the first stretch of the trail.

The first two days are spent high above the Romanche valley heading roughly west to east across minor spurs that seem anything but minor to the walker fresh into the mountains after a lowland winter. They're long days too and it's important to settle to an even pace that gently devours both time and distance before coming to the big country that will challenge your fitness in no uncertain manner. The map shows this initial stage as crossing Col de Sarenne, more than twelve hundred metres higher than Bourg d'Oisans. That crossing, however, is straightforward, for there's a metalled road over it and the approach is made through the easy valley of the Sarenne stream on a dirt track that allows progress to be made without undue effort. Once over the col a path breaks away for a steep descent to the twin villages of Clavans-le-Haut and Clavans-le-Bas caught in a knuckle of valley tilted to drain south-south-west into the Romanche. Instead of descending with the valley, however, our route drops to the river (the Ferrand) immediately below Clavans-le-Bas, then climbs steeply on the eastern side to gain a spur beyond which the charming village of Besse-en-Oisans faces south from a sunny slope of pasture. At the end of a nine-hour walking day its charms are more than welcome.

Besse has a reasonable amount of accommodation, a couple of small foodstores, and a campsite about one kilometre beyond the village. The scenery is hardly Alpine. Groves of silver birch line the stream. Grass slopes rise behind the village, and sweep below it too, and the next day's stage spends the first two hours on an ascent of big green hills east of Besse-en-Oisans. Once Col Bichet (2245m) is reached, though, real mountains are in view and the landscape grows not only in stature but in grandeur too.

Col Bichet is unmarked as such on the Didier and Richard map, but is found a little south-west of Refuge du Rif Tor with a large wooden cross nearby. All around spreads a scene of pastoral ease, but these pasturelands form a marked contrast to the upthrust of La Meije and Le Rateau whose glaciers dazzle out to the south-east, while to the north-east the Aiguilles de la Soussaz and du Goléon show brazen horns, and north-west Les Grandes Rousses provide a distant barrier of snow above more grass-bound hillsides.

Given time it would be worth diverting here from the Tour de l'Oisans in order to explore country north and east of Col Bichet. Trails entice from the map and assorted tours of a day or more could so easily be created. It's all good walking country, and from high viewpoints major peaks of the Écrins can be seen as crenellations of rock and ice and snow on the southern horizon.

On the eastern side of the pastureland bowl Col du Souchet (2365m) guards the entrance to the so-called Plateau de Paris which plunges from its southern lip into the depths of the Romanche valley. The GR54 crosses the grassland to it, and midway between Col Bichet and Col du Souchet is met by a variant path that has made a twelve hundred metre climb from Mizöen. The official Tour de l'Oisans skirts the northern edge of the Plateau de Paris, but two tarns (Lacs Noir and Lérié) lie south of the trail in such exquisite country and with such lovely views, that given decent weather conditions no walker should be so devoted to the main GR54 as to miss an opportunity to stray to them. The diversion is not a lengthy one, but the drawing power of the scenes offered from both lake shores is such that an hour or more could easily be devoted to enjoyment of each. Both are as rich in alpine flowers as they are in visual stimulation, while the tarns provide double value with a mirror image of Meije and Rateau whenever the breeze dies and the waters still to a sheen.

The continuing route of GR54 descends interminably to Le Chazelet, a village perched on a hillside shelf above a tributary glen, then swings steeply down to Les Terraces and at last to La Grave in the Romanche valley below the north face of La Meije. With its hotels and campsites La Grave makes an obvious overnight halt, although being on a major road that comes down from Col du Lautaret makes for a noisy contrast to the peace of the hills experienced thus far.

Above La Grave the upper Romanche valley is explored by the Tour de l'Oisans after an initial crossing of a wooded spur on the left bank. Crossing that spur involves a three hundred metre climb followed by a descent to the river opposite Villar d'Arène. Thereafter the way traces the river among silver birch and thickets of alder along the very boundaries of the National Park. The Park boundaries then desert the valley bed, while the GR54 continues now on the true right bank as the valley itself is squeezed by converging walls to east and west.

Tighter and tighter the valley is squeezed to a narrow defile, and all mountain views are foreshortened to a grey looming presence. The path now begins to climb; there's a cascade pouring from the left, a stream surging through another defile off to the right, and zig-zags mount to a sudden open pastureland in a secretive upper valley whose mountain walls now lean back and appear far more friendly and approachable. In these pastures, where the valley forks, Refuge de l'Alpe de Villar d'Arène offers welcome refreshment after a good morning's exercise, and with temptations to call a halt in order to explore the two glens accessible from it. One has been carved out between Pic Gaspard and La Grande Ruine, the other between La Grande Ruine and Roche Faurio; a land of rock, ice and glacial moraines.

South-east of the refuge the trail meanders over more ruffled pastures before mounting the final short stretch below a huge wall of terminal moraine to reach Col d'Arsine (2340m), a broad saddle, drab and desolate with the Glacier d'Arsine above to the right and a limited funnel view ahead. That funnel view allows no hint of the joys of the descent to come. But on the way down to the Guisane valley the path leads beside milky glacial streams, over flower-rich hillsides, a steep plunge to Lac de la Douche followed by forest shade; pleasures in almost every step.

The valley is reached at the small village of Le Casset where there's gîte accommodation, while less than an hour further downstream Monêtier-les-Bains offers more choice with a variety of hotels. Making a broad moat along the north-eastern side of the Écrins massif, the Guisane valley is only briefly touched upon by the Tour de l'Oisans, although its devotion to the ski industry makes sure its presence is felt even when you've turned your back to it. The waymarked trail heads south out of Monêtier, climbing through forest, then in a narrow glen drained by the Torrent de la Selle whose simple delights are rudely interrupted by ski tows and bulldozed pistes on the way to Col de l'Eychauda. Once at the col there's still no imminent means of escape, for this barren spot merely shows a continuation of broad scarred pistes, and in the desolate hanging valley just below on the south side more mechanical hoists litter the upper bowl.

But there are better things to come, and after scooting down the left-hand side of a great open bowl of mountainside you pass through a narrow cleft and enter a lower level devoid of ski clutter. Marmots shriek from boulder-rough slopes, big mountains tease from a distance, and gazing south the soft light of Mediterranean France floods every deep-cut valley. In numerous zig-zags the path drops to the Vallon de Chambran, a flat-bottomed glen served by narrow road from the Vallouise. At its head the glen climbs in a curve to Lac de l'Eychauda, and walkers bound upon the Tour de l'Oisans will surely note how tempting that upper glen appears and lay plans for a return visit to explore it in more detail.

Below Chambran with its *buvette*, few rough buildings and a tiny unadorned chapel, a narrow path descends alongside the Eychauda stream, then forks. The main trail continues south and eventually gains the growing resort village of Vallouise, while an alternative swings back towards the north-west to the mountaineering hamlet of Ailefroide. The Vallouise trail is that adopted by GR54, but it would be a shame to miss the opportunity to enjoy a near view of Mont Pelvoux and Barre des Écrins, having come so close, and with a day or two to spare there's majestic Alpine country to explore above Ailefroide; a wild and glorious land of soaring rock walls daubed with snow and with glaciers carving from them.

Ailefroide has two hotels, a gîte d'étape and campsites, while those walkers with energy to spare could push on further upvalley to Refuge Cézanne below the terminal moraines of Glacier Noir and Glacier Blanc in readiness for deeper investigation next day before returning down valley to Vallouise from where the Tour de l'Oisans can be resumed.

Vallouise has character, despite the obvious intrusion of tourism. It has dormitory, as well as hotel, accommodation, a few shops and restaurants and bureaux de change. And it has access to big mountains. Below the village the rivers l'Onde and Ailefroide combine their mountain torrents and flow south-east to join the Durance. The Tour de l'Oisans, of course, declines the temptation to go with the flow down valley, and turns westward along the Val de l'Entre-les-Aygues (the valley of the Onde torrent) for about nine kilometres to the roadhead. Most of the valley is forested, and charmingly so. It's a narrow shaft, but because of its configuration, is early lit by the morning sun. A third of the way upvalley from Vallouise a semi-official camping area is found on the right bank at Pont des Places; a convenient site for backpackers touring GR54, it is also used by white-water kayak enthusiasts and car-bound walkers making day-long forays into the surrounding mountains.

The roadhead at Entre les Aygues overlooks gravel beds at the confluence of the Torrent des Bans and Torrent de la Selle. Our route crosses these gravel beds among slender trees and bushes, then mounts along the true left bank of the Vallon de la Selle, passes the Cabane (or Refuge) du Jas Lacroix and continues on a gentle gradient towards Pointe de Verdonne towering over the upper corrie. A short distance beyond the Jas Lacroix hut the trail bears left, crosses a stream and then climbs into a high basin of pastureland rimmed with jagged peaklets from which great aprons of scree fan out. Climbing from one natural step to the next the landscape becomes more stony and wild, and the final ascent to Col de l'Aup Martin (2761m) consists of an exposed rising traverse of a slope of shifting black shale and grit. But the col, the highest point on the Tour de l'Oisans, produces some fine views, not only of the Vallon de la Selle and its walling peaks, but southward too, across the head of another glen whose amphitheatre mountains display broad bands of strata, and south-south-west where Pas de la Cavale marks the next immediate goal to be won.

A continuing narrow path edges round the steep mountainside on more scree and grit, crosses a ledge showered by a small cascade, and soon after comes to Pas de la Cavale to be followed by a long and wearisome descent of some nine hundred and fifty metres to the splendid Refuge du Pré de la Chaumette. Set in extensive pastures at a junction of valleys, the Chaumette refuge is a welcoming place at the end of a strenuous day's trekking. It also marks the southern-most point of the Oisans circuit. Behind the hut to the north is a short glen into which the GR54 climbs next day, a stage with three high passes to cross in order to reach the Val Gaudémar. First of these is Col de la Vallette (2668m), a bare windswept saddle, narrow but interestingly gained and with dramatic views on the final approach. From it the second col can be clearly seen just below Puy des Agneaux a little north of west from Col de la Vallette, and it only takes forty minutes to walk from one to the other. The initial descent from the col, however, demands some care, but potential danger is soon passed and it just leaves an easy stroll on a good, clear trail over a neat grassland with a small pool in its midst, then a sharp twist up to Col de Gouiran (2597m).

It takes a little longer to gain the third pass from the second, than it did to gain Col de Gouiran from the first, but it should still be accomplished in less than an hour. Col de Vallonpierre (2607m) is a dip in a sharp ridge sweeping west of Le

Sirac, the dominant mountain hereabouts, and is probably the narrowest pass of all those encountered on the tour, with excessively steep slopes plunging to north and south. In dry, snow-free conditions the descent from it is not as bad as at first appears, and you work a way down to the idyllically-situated Refuge de Vallonpierre without too much trouble.

The Vallonpierre refuge is perched on the north shore of a small tarn, and gazes up at the soaring mass of Le Sirac. It's a spellbinding situation for a refuge, with a contrast of smooth meadows, boulder slopes and gaunt mountains peering over all. Regrettably, walkers who spent the previous night at the Chaumette hut will reach Vallonpierre too early in the day to consider stopping - unless, that is, they have several days in hand.

Behind the hut the trail continues to descend in numerous tight windings, views consistently fine, and at the foot of the zig-zags passes the entrance to a corrie on the right headed by Pic Jocelme, Pic de Bonvoisin and Pointe de Verdonne. There follows a gentle, fairly level stretch alongside the Severaisse with bilberries growing thick beside the trail, and two hours from Vallonpierre you come to the farmlike building of Refuge Xavier Blanc set in a glade of trees, boulders and shrubs near the head of the Val Gaudémar. A further hour and half, or two hours at most of easy valley walking - past farms being strangled by rampant vegetation, through the little turf-roofed hamlet of Le Bourg and by-passing Le Casset (gîte d'étape) - will bring you to the village of La Chapelle-en-Valgaudémar where there are campsites, hotels, another gîte and foodstores - and temptations to delay progress in order to explore the neighbourhood. The map feeds that temptation with several side trails to follow and remote mountain huts to visit.

Down valley from La Chapelle, where the Val Gaudémar begins its south-westerly curve, the attractive huddle of Villar-Loubière marks another northerly turn for GR54. There is, however, an alternative route which goes almost due north from La Chapelle into a glen drained by the Torrent du Clot, curves left to cross Col de Colombes (2423m) and Col des Clochettes (2183m), and joins the main Tour de l'Oisans at Refuge des Souffles. The GR54 path from Villar-Loubière is a demanding one; not difficult or dangerous, but steep in places where it picks a route up the side of a ravine.

Beyond the refuge the trail swings north-west to cross an amphitheatre topped by Pic des Souffles. At first the path makes a belvedere across the steep flank of the mountain, then enters a broad pastureland basin before turning to the serious business of climbing the western side to Col de la Vaurze (2500m). This is another narrow pass, a brief gap in the south-west ridge of Pic des Souffles before it rises to Tête du Clotonnet, and a huge panorama provides ample reward for the effort of gaining it. Far off and way below, La Chapelle-en-Valgaudémar may be seen huddled in its deep green valley. Above that Le Sirac aids identification of Col de Vallonpierre, while to the east L'Olan, big and handsome, dominates with its bulk. The northern side of the pass appears somewhat forbidding, but more than 1200 metres below Le Désert lies in a cleft of a valley, with the next pass on the list, Col de Côte-Belle, almost due north of Le Désert's rooftops.

It's an unrelentingly steep descent to Le Désert, the few houses in sight almost all the way. But it's an interesting route and the hamlet itself, on arrival, charms with its determination to remain a quintessential mountain-farm community. Its situation makes it an important staging-post on the Tour de l'Oisans, so there's gîte accommodation, a small restaurant and modest foodstore to satisfy the needs of mountain walkers, but beyond that the hamlet is tied very much to the land with small fields outlined upvalley and hay meadows on both sides of the river.

The stage from Le Désert to Valsenestre is a short one. The two hamlets are similar in size and situation, and separated by Pic de Valsenestre, their streams coming together below La Chapelle-en-Valjouffrey. Whilst the crossing of Col de Côte-Belle is not unduly arduous, it's no place to be caught by storm so, almost unique on the Tour de l'Oisans, in inclement weather it would be possible to walk from one to the other by a valley route all the way. Col de Côte-Belle is, however, a broad and grassy saddle and quite unlike most other passes on this circuit. From it the next pass, Col de la Muzelle, is seen ahead slightly east of north, and the descent to Valsenestre made memorable by an amazing variety of alpine flowers and aromatic herbs reminiscent more of Mediterranean regions than of the Alps. The final valley stroll into the hamlet goes through forest of larch, pine and fir, fragrant on a hot summer's afternoon.

After Valsenestre only one pass remains to be crossed on the Tour de l'Oisans. Though high, at 2613 metres Col de la Muzelle is not as high as some of those previously tackled, yet it has a character all its own. Little more than a gash in the ridge spreading west from Roche de la Muzelle, it retains its secrets until the very last. With more than 1300 metres to climb from Valsenestre, it also has the reputation of being the most difficult of all those tackled on GR54; the French guide warns about the dangers of attempting it in wet conditions, and the map uses symbols to indicate a 'hazardous Alpine route'. Such a reputation may be well-founded under certain conditions, but most walkers on the Oisans circuit who have coped with all the previous passes should take this in their stride - unless snow is lying or a storm brewing, that is. It will take three hours or so to reach from the Valsenestre gîte on an approach that begins with a gently rising track through forest, but which then breaks away to tackle steep grass slopes that lead into a neat hanging valley flowing at right-angles to that which you've just left.

The ascent is straightforward until about forty minutes below the col when a steep cone of black shale and grit has to be negotiated. There are faint signs of a path (or paths) working up this cone, and it should be possible to simply stomp and kick your way up it, emerging into a blast of wind, no doubt, that funnels through the narrow gap of the col itself. Behind to the south a grand vista clearly displays the cols of Côte-Belle and Vaurze, and provides a true indication of the helter-skelter nature of the route thus far. Northward the green tarn of Lac de la Muzelle glimmers below a clutter of screes, while far-off Les Grandes Rousses shine their snows, with the mid-distance laced in cableways from Les Deux Alpes.

From the col Refuge de la Muzelle is reached in little over an hour. Set on a slope of grassland overlooking its tarn, the hut has the appearance of a timber- and stone-built chalet, bright with flower boxes on its balcony, and with a simple shepherd's hut nearby. Its position is quite charming. From it the standard descent to Bourg d'Arud in the Vallée du Vénéon is a delightful two-hour jog down a series of tight zig-zags, passing several cascades, then alongside a good clear stream before forest marks the final descent to l'Alleau on the opposite bank of the Vénéon to Bourg d'Arud.

But there is an alternative, longer route to the Vénéon that may be worth considering. This involves a climb of four hundred metres or so to gain Col du Vallon just west of Refuge de la Muzelle. From the col a rocky landscape is negotiated in order to reach the northern shore of Lac Lauvitel - a magnificent tarn trapped in a deep well gouged out by a long-vanished glacier. From its northern shore the descent to La Danchère can be made by one of two paths, both of which are steep but uncomplicated. La Danchère has hotel accommodation, while Bourg d'Arud has a gîte d'étape and campsite, as well as hotel beds.

In order to complete the circuit of the Oisans region, a final easy valley walk remains. This leads along the left bank of the Vénéon all the way to Bourg d'Oisans, partly in forest, sometimes over open pastureland, through one or two small village communities, and only on tarmac towards the very end. A fine circuit indeed.

TOUR DE L'OISANS - SUMMARY OF CIRCUIT

Day 1:   Bourg d'Oisans - Col de Sarenne - Clavans-le-Haut - Clavans-le-Bas - Besse-en-Oisans

Day 2:   Besse-en-Oisans - Col Bichet - Col du Souchet - Lacs Noir & Lérié - Le Chazelet - La Grave

Day 3:   La Grave - Refuge de l'Alpe de Villar d'Arêne - Col d'Arsine - Le Casset - Monêtier-les-Bains

Day 4:   Monêtier - Col de l'Eychauda - Chambran - Ailefroide

Day 5:   Ailefroide - Vallouise

Day 6:   Vallouise - Cabane du Jas Lacroix - Col de l'Aup Martin - Pas de la Cavale - Refuge du Pré de la Chaumette

Day 7:   Refuge Chaumette - Col de la Vallette - Col de Gouiran - Col de Vallonpierre - Refuge de Vallonpierre - Refuge Xavier Blanc - La Chapelle-en-Valgaudémar

Day 8:   La Chapelle - Villar-Loubière - Refuge des Souffles (or La Chapelle - Col de Colombes - Col des Clochettes - Refuge des Souffles) - Col de la Vaurze - Le Désert

Day 9:   Le Désert - Col de Côte-Belle - Valsenestre

Day 10: Valsenestre - Col de la Muzelle - Refuge de la Muzelle - Bourg d'Arud (or Refuge de la Muzelle - Col du Vallon - Lac Lauvitel - La Danchère)

Day 11: Bourg d'Arud (or La Danchère) - Les Gauchoirs - Bourg d'Oisans

The basic tour is reasonably well waymarked on mostly clear trails. Strong, fit walkers could achieve the circuit in about nine days, but there are many tempting options that would easily fill a fortnight's holiday. Some crossings are high, remote and demanding, and should be not be attempted in adverse weather conditions. The best time to tackle it is from mid-July to October, but some huts can become very crowded during the French school holiday period.

VERCORS

"It is one of the most terrible and gruesome paths which I or any member of our party has ever trodden. There is a half-league of ladders to climb up and a league beside, but the summit is the most glorious place you ever saw. To give you a picture of the mountain, the summit has a circumference of nearly a league. It is a quarter of a league in length and a cross-bow shot in breadth, and is covered with beautiful pasture. Here we found a preserve of chamois which are destined to remain for eternity. With them were new-born young, of which we killed one by accident."

So wrote Antoine de Ville in a letter to the President of Grenoble after reaching the great flat crown of Mont Aiguille on 25 June 1492, the same year in which Columbus 'discovered' America. It was a remarkable achievement for the time, and even more astonishing that anyone should even dream of attempting to climb it, for Mont Aiguille, considered then to be one of the Seven Wonders of Dauphiné, looks impregnable, the summit bounded on all sides by near-vertical cliffs. No wonder it was known as Mont Inaccessible throughout the Middle Ages. Of course, today such walls provide a challenge to climbers, but five hundred years ago there was no such sport as rock climbing, and mountains in general were looked upon with fear and dread. Be that as it may, de Ville, who was ordered by Charles VIII to climb it, was obviously not deterred, and with ten companions including one of the king's ladder-men, a professor of theology, two lawyers and a carpenter, not only scaled the mountain "by subtle means and engines", but clearly loved what he found on top. The official report describes the meadow there as being larger than forty men could mow in a day, and in addition to the chamois herd, they saw red-legged choughs and released some tame rabbits in the high pastures.

Mont Aiguille (2086m) was not climbed again until 1834 when Jean Liotard, a local shepherd, made the ascent solo and bare-footed after he found his nailed shoes made the climbing somewhat perilous. In 1878 the French Alpine Club secured what was thought to be the de Ville route with metal wires and pegs. Though it may have thus been partially tamed, the route remains impressive - as does the sight of this great table mountain rising from forest, pasture and scree in a series of gleaming limestone walls.

For many, Mont Aiguille has become the symbol of the Vercors. Although it is not the highest of the district (Le Grand Veymont, 2341m, claims that distinction), it is truly an astonishing sight, yet these attractive little mountains of the Pre-Alps are humble by comparison with the rugged peaks of the Écrins, for example, from whom they are separated by the Romanche and the Drac, and of course the great Mont Blanc massif whose snowfields are seen like a distant floating cloud from most of the higher summits.

The northern chain of the Pre-Alps, of which the Vercors marks the southern extent, are predominantly limestone massifs that form a western line of defence to the Alps proper, and were produced by the same earth movements that gave birth to the Jura. Characterised by rocky obelisks, spires and molars, the Vercors is also deeply riven by impressive gorges and surrounded on all sides by steep, fortress-like crags. A large portion is protected as a Parc Régional, while the uninhabited Haut Plateau is a special nature reserve.

Roughly triangular in shape, with Grenoble at its north-eastern apex, the Vercors is enclosed by the Isère, the Drôme and the Drac. A high-level valley drained by the Vernaison and Romayère rivers makes a neat north-south divide through the centre of the massif, while the deep Gorges de la Bourne slice the countryside between Villard-de-Lans and Pont-en-Royans with vast crags that appear so metimes gold-coloured, sometimes white, ochre, steel grey or even black. The remainder of the Vercors consists of a complex series of plateaux with precipitous limestone escarpments, the dense woodland cover thinning to open grassland grazed by large flocks of sheep as height is gained. In the east the landscape is tilted, with peaks rising in a wave-like crest that terminates in an almost unbroken line of cliffs stretching for something like eighty kilometres from the outskirts of Grenoble to the Col de Menée.

Walking in the Vercors has its own special appeal. Brian Evans, who has made a number of tours there in winter as well as in summer, enumerated some of the attractions in a chapter published in *Classic Walks in the Alps*. He wrote of "...broad views over roll upon roll of forest and clearing. Snow-covered Alpine giants sparkle to the east, whilst here is dry limestone with rocky paths which twist among tiny tangled pines." Elsewhere he described "paths [which] traverse their length at different levels, amongst forest or higher on more open crests. White ribbons of limestone crags dance along for miles. It is still possible to find solitude and the best areas are not ruined by commercialism." Being limestone and riddled with pits, much of the high land is dry in summer; some of the water sources are sporadic, some distinctly feeble, and anyone making a multi-day traverse or circuit will find their routes influenced by the availability of drinking water. The 1:25,000 maps of the area indicate sources with a small symbol. June and July are said to be the best months, while September (often a good month in the high Alps) can be very difficult in the Vercors following a long dry summer. Camping is forbidden in the Hauts Plateaux nature reserve, but a chain of rather simple huts has been established for backpackers - although potential users should expect no more than the most basic of facilities.

Compared to most other areas described in this book, walking in the Vercors is quite modest, for instead of a constant steep switchback from valley to col and back to valley again, once up on the plateau there are large sections where gentle gradients and almost level walking can be enjoyed. There are walkers' ways onto the plateau from a choice of villages, and day trips are easily arranged. Longer, waymarked *grandes randonnées* routes exist such as GR9, and the GR91 which makes a traverse of the high plateau, or the north-south traverse by the Balcon Est which provides a marvellous opportunity to understand the true nature of the Vercors. This latter route is said to offer "a sporting challenge" for it contains several exposed sections, especially where steep and awkward ravines are crossed, and if tackled early in the season carrying an ice-axe is recommended. On such multi-day routes walkers will need to carry supplies as there are few opportunities to drop down to a village with a foodstore.

* * *

DAUPHINÉ

Location:
Entirely in France. North of the Maritime Alps, and to the south of the Graian Alps. The Pre-Alps range of the Vercors is on the western edge; Queyras on the south-east, and Massif des Écrins midway between the Queyras and Vanoise.

Principal valleys:
In the Écrins, these are Vallées du Vénéon, Romanche, Guisane and Durance, Vallouise and Val Gaudémar. The main Queyras valleys are those of the Guil, Bouchet, Cristillan and Mélezet, while those of the Vernaison, Romayère and Bourne represent the Vercors.

Principal peaks:
Barre des Écrins (4102m), La Meije (3982m), L'Ailefroide (3954m), Mont Pelvoux (3943m) are the major peaks of the Écrins; Monte Viso (3841m) in the Cottian Alps; Pic de Rochebrune (3320m), Grand Glaiza (3293m) and Le Pain de Sucre (3208m) in the Queyras; Le Grand Veymont (2341m) and Mont Aiguille (2086m) in the Vercors.

Centres:
Bourg d'Oisans, La Grave, Vallouise, Ailefroide, La Chapelle-en-Valgaudémar, Bourg d'Arud, La Bérarde in the Massif des Écrins. Guillestre, Ceillac, St Véran and Abriès in the Queyras. Grenoble, Villard-de-Lans and Pont-en-Royans for the Vercors.

Huts:
Plenty of huts in the Queyras and Écrins for walkers and climbers, mostly run by the CAF, but others privately owned. A number of valley bases have gîtes d'étape that are useful. In the Vercors refuges built by the PRV are very simple and provide only basic facilities.

Access:
By rail or bus to Grenoble. Buses run from Grenoble into the Écrins region via Bourg d'Oisans, and to the Vercors via Villard-de-Lans. The Queyras region is best approached by train to Montdauphin-Guillestre (on the Briançon line) from where buses serve the central Queyras. Nearest airport - Lyon.

Maps:
Massif & Parc National des Écrins, and *Massifs du Queyras & Haut Ubaye* at 1:50,000 published by Didier & Richard, but for the Vercors, three sheets at 1:25,000 published by IGN are probably best for walkers since they show water sources. These are: *Vercors Nord, Hauts Plateaux Nord* and *Hauts Plateaux Sud*.

Guidebooks:
Tour of the Oisans by Andrew Harper (Cicerone Press) is a detailed walking guide to GR54, with optional extras.
Tour of the Queyras by Alan Castle (Cicerone Press) describes this circular route.
Walking the Alpine Parks of France & Northwest Italy by Marcia R. Lieberman (Cordee/The Mountaineers) includes a number of walks in the Écrins and Queyras.

Other reading:
The Outdoor Traveler's Guide to The Alps by Marcia R. Lieberman (Stewart, Tabori & Chang; New York, 1991) provides an up-to-date view of selected valleys in the Queyras and Écrins.
The Alps by R.L.G. Irving (Batsford, 1939) contains a brief sample of the region.

Scrambles Amongst the Alps by Edward Whymper (John Murray - various editions) for a pioneer's perspective.

Outline Sketches in the High Alps of Dauphiné by T.G. Bonney (Longmans, 1865). Illustrated by his own sketches, in this book Bonney provides an interesting historical view of the region in the mid-nineteenth century.

Mountaineering Holiday by F.S. Smythe (Hodder & Stoughton, 1940) describes a number of pre-war climbs in the Dauphiné.

Classic Walks in Europe edited by Walt Unsworth (Oxford Illustrated Press, 1987) has a chapter by Andrew Harper on the Tour de l'Oisans, and another by Brian Evans which describes a traverse of the Vercors by the Balcon Est.

Classic Walks in the Alps by Kev Reynolds (Oxford Illustrated Press, 1991) contains a chapter on a winter traverse of the Vercors high plateau, also written by Brian Evans.

Walking & Climbing in the Alps by Stefano Ardito (Swan Hill Press, 1995) describes a traverse of the Vercors similar to the Evans route mentioned above.

The Mountains of Europe by Kev Reynolds (Oxford Illustrated Press, 1990) contains a good background chapter by John Brailsford.

✳   ✳   ✳

La Grande Casse (left) and Grande Motte, from the lip of the Doron gorge

3: THE GRAIAN ALPS

Including the mountains of Beaufortain, Vanoise and Gran Paradiso.

"They cannot compete with the Dauphiné Alps for the favour of men in their prime who want to test their climbing powers," wrote R.L.G. Irving. "The Graians will be the choice of those who prefer beauty that is less invariably severe."

From Col de la Seigne on the southern edge of the Mont Blanc massif, to the road pass of Col du Mont Cenis which links the Haute-Maurienne with the Valle di Susa, the Graian Alps spread across a complex region of high mountains coated here and there with glaciers and fields of permanent snow. Though its loftiest peaks are not as high as principal summits of either the neighbouring Écrins or Mont Blanc ranges, the quality of this Alpine landscape is of the very best. It's all splendid country that will appeal to a wide variety of outdoor interests, from hard rock climbing to comparatively easy ascents of big snow peaks, and from downhill skiing with all the paraphernalia of mechanical hoists and cableways, to hut to hut trekking, the study of a rich alpine flora and, within the sanctuary of two national parks (Parc National de la Vanoise, and Parco Nazionale del Gran Paradiso), abundant opportunities for observing wildlife.

Until the mid-19th century Savoie was included in the kingdom of Piedmont-Sardinia, but in 1860 the western part was ceded to France, and the following year

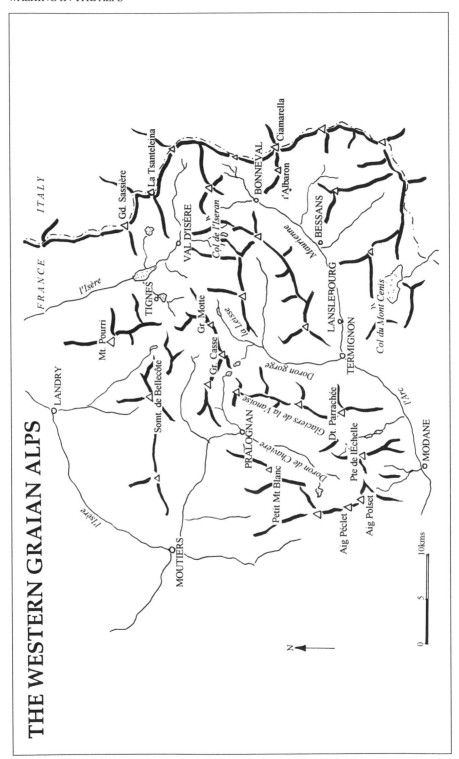

THE WESTERN GRAIAN ALPS

the emerging nation of Italy annexed the eastern section, thereby splitting the Graians into separate political units. With the frontier between France and Italy now making an uneven divide, a frontier breached by no less than seven passes that may be crossed on foot, as well as the 2188 metre road pass of Col du Petit St Bernard (known to the Romans as Col Alpis Graia), the range is broken into two distinct regions, west and east.

✳   ✳   ✳

THE WESTERN GRAIANS

Two major rivers flow roughly westward through the French Graians, thereby subdividing these mountains into the districts of Beaufortain and Vanoise. The rivers, l'Isère and l'Arc, rise just a few kilometres from each other separated only by a ridge crossed by the Col de l'Iseran, and actually bear different names to the valleys they water. The valley of l'Isère, for example, is uniformly known as the Tarentaise, while that of l'Arc is the Maurienne.

North of the general trend of l'Isère the modest heights of Beaufortain stretch off to outliers of the Mont Blanc massif, while to the south the best-known feature is the Vanoise National Park whose farthest boundary is drawn by the valley of l'Arc.

In the Tarentaise the towns of Moutiers, Landry and Bourg St Maurice are not only connected by the N90 via Albertville, but are also served by rail, thus providing ease of access to some of the best walking country in Beaufortain and the northern Vanoise. The valley itself has several important tributaries flowing into it, especially from the south where the mountains offer arguably the finest and most comprehensive opportunities for skiing in all France. By contrast with this winter playground, communities on the northern flank of the Tarentaise bask in what's become known as le Versant du Soleil, the 'Hillside of the Sun' - named from the sheltered, south-facing aspect that denies them long-lasting snow conditions.

Although it contains some wild and rocky peaks and several artificial lakes, Beaufortain has no glaciers, it has a distinctly pastoral character and its forests are among the finest in all Savoie. The Tour du Mont Blanc links Beaufortain with the immensely popular range to the north whose gleaming snows tend to dominate almost every high view, while the GR5 (La Grande Traversée des Alpes) explores the central part of the district on its way south from Col de la Croix du Bonhomme. Despite the presence of these major routes and, to a certain extent, the Tour of the Beaufortain (outlined in J.W. Akitt's guide to Walking in the Tarentaise & Beaufortain Alps), the hills and glens remain perhaps the least-known of all the Western Graians.

South of the Tarentaise, on the other hand, the bigger, more impressive mountains of the Vanoise provide a lure that is hard to resist. By contrast with Beaufortain the district has a plentiful covering of ice, especially in the Glaciers de la Vanoise which run in an extensive block between La Dent Parrachée and Col de la Vanoise. In effect the range consists of a high plateau cut by a few deep valleys, out of which rise rock crests capped with ice and snow. Many of its peaks rise well above 3500 metres in height. La Grande Casse (3855m), Mont Pourri (3779m) and La Grande Motte (3653m) are the three highest, but there are many others either with strikingly individual characteristics, or combined with neighbours in a tracery of glacier and snowfield, that demand attention, while south of the Maurienne the lofty Pointe de Charbonnel (3752m) signals another group of high mountains ranged along the border with Italy.

The Vanoise National Park was established in 1963 as the first in France, and was twinned with that of the nearby Gran Paradiso nine years later, thereby creating the largest nature reserve in western Europe. On its own the Vanoise park covers an area of 53,000 hectares, ranging in altitude from 1250 to 3855 metres. It boasts 107 summits above 3000 metres, and a network of around 500 kilometres of footpaths - many of which are snow-free from mid-June to late October. Catering for an influx of summer visitors the park contains some forty-two mountain huts within the central and peripheral zones, while outlying villages supplement these with a variety of campsites, modest hotels and gîtes d'étape.

The establishment of the National Park not only provides protection for around 700 ibex (bouquetin) and 4500 chamois, but it has effectively saved some of the most spectacular mountain scenery from the worst excesses of the downhill ski industry. On its very rim the winter playgrounds of Courchevel, Méribel, Val Claret, Tignes and Val d'Isère have brutalised huge areas with their pylons, cableways and insensitive architecture, yet a relatively short stroll across an easy col will reveal nature in the raw, seemingly untouched glens where streams dance, wild flowers dazzle each early summer's day, and chamois, marmot and ibex roam undisturbed. While a number of roads penetrate its outer limits, the heart of the Vanoise retains a semi-wild purity of immense appeal to the mountain walker.

The park's western limits edge the vast Courchevel and Méribel ski grounds, with a short buffer zone of the Réserve Naturelle du Plan de Tueda running up to the summit of Mont du Borgne. A high ridge, nowhere dropping below 2989 metres, projects south from there to Aiguille de Péclet (3561m) which, with the neighbouring Aiguille de Polset (3531m), looms over the Chavière and Gébroulaz glaciers. A CAF hut (Refuge de Péclet-Polset) occupies a very wild landscape on the eastern side of this ridge, with Col de Chavière (2796m) a short distance to the south providing a link for walkers between the Tarentaise and Maurienne. Crossed by GR55, Col de Chavière is the highest point reached by any Grande Randonnée trail.

The Maurienne

A gentle glen, wild and rough in its upper reaches, but more homely lower down, drains the south side of Col de Chavière with the Ruisseau de St Bernard easing beyond the park's southern boundary into steep forests that clothe hillsides walling the Maurienne above Modane. The Maurienne, or valley of l'Arc, effectively forms the southern limit of the Parc National de la Vanoise. It's a fine valley, and one which provides rail access with the rest of France by way of Chambéry and, via a tunnel above Modane, with Turin. Modane, therefore, acts as a useful gateway to the southern Vanoise. It has a handful of modest hotels and a campsite. From it buses serve a string of villages further upstream; villages and hamlets like Aussois,

Termignon, Bessans and Bonneval-sur-Arc that provide accommodation (including gîtes d'étape in some cases) and access to glens which form knuckle indents to the main Vanoise massif.

One such glen directly above Modane is that of Orgère which flows parallel with, and to the east of, the Ruisseau de St Bernard from which it is separated by the block of Tête Noire. At the entrance to the glen is a comfortable refuge, or *porte du parc*, provided by the National Park authority. Overlooking Refuge de l'Orgère is the attractive Aiguille Doran (3041m), a towering rock peak that is a prominent feature of the view north from Modane itself. The northern end of the glen is effectively blocked by this aiguille, but trails climb to either side; that which forces a route along the flank of Tête Noire heads for Col de Chavière, while the path which veers to the east of Aiguille Doran crosses Col de la Masse (2923m) as a challenging route across the mountains to Plan d'Amont in the next glen to the east.

Walkers based for a day or two at Refuge de l'Orgère have several options open to them. There's a pleasant nature trail that eases along the eastern flank of the valley, beginning just below the hut where a track rises from the few stone chalets of l'Orgère hamlet, and heads north towards Aiguille Doran, crosses just below it and returns down the western side of the glen. A longer and more rewarding day's outing could be won by climbing immediately above the hut on a steep forest trail that eventually shafts right and makes a splendid belvedere working north to a high plateau below Col de Chavière. From this plateau, with the little Lac de la Partie tucked in a scooped basin to the right, another trail cuts off left. This is the GR55 which is then followed southward, descending through the St Bernard glen to Polset where a narrow service road is joined. This leads directly back to Refuge de l'Orgère.

A third day's outing is rather more demanding than those previously outlined, for it crosses Col de la Masse north-east of Aiguille Doran, descends very wild terrain to the next glen to the east, then returns to l'Orgère by way of the GR5 trail that crosses the grassy Col du Barbier (2287m) high above the Maurienne. This makes for a magnificent day's mountain walking, with some very fine scenery to enjoy throughout.

Refuge de l'Orgère is not the only accommodation available here, for an alternative, privately-owned refuge exists on a shelf of meadowland just south of the Orgère chalets. Refuge de l'Aiguille Doran has forty places and, being situated just outside the National Park boundary, allows camping in its grounds (camping is forbidden by the park authorities, other than at selected huts where lightweight tents are permitted on a transitory overnight basis only, and between 7.00pm and 7.00am).

The village of Aussois is found, not astride the main N6 that links most of the Maurienne communities, but north of it and below a delightful glen containing two artificial lakes, Plan d'Amont and the lower Plan d'Aval overlooked by La Dent Parrachée (3697m). Aussois is a minor resort with modest opportunities for skiing in winter and, through road access to the two dammed lakes, popular for walking in summer. As for accommodation, an eighteenth century fortress just outside the village, one of the five Forts de l'Esseillon, has been converted as another *porte du parc*. With a cobble-stone courtyard, double walls and surrounding moat, Fort

Marie-Christine has an atmosphere all its own.

Within the Aussois glen three mountain huts provide lodgings for climbers and walkers in rather more remote settings than that of Fort Marie-Christine. Refuge du Fond d'Aussois and Refuge de la Dent Parrachée are both owned by the CAF. The first lies deep within the glen beside a stream, while the second is located on a spur of hillside at 2511 metres, and is patronised by climbers tackling the *voie normale* on the Dent Parrachée which ascends through the Vallon de Fournache. The third hut is a converted farm which, with outhouses turned into dormitory accommodation, is situated on a hillside shelf on the east side of the glen overlooking the two lakes which lie several hundred metres below. Refuge du Plan Sec is privately-owned and is very popular with walkers tackling the Tour des Glaciers de la Vanoise, Tour of the Vanoise and the GR5.

Short day walks are available from the roadhead below the upper lake, while longer routes are possible from a base in one of the above-mentioned huts. At the head of the glen Col d'Aussois (2916m) offers a way over the mountains to the Chavière valley which flows down to Pralognan-la-Vanoise (this col is crossed in the opposite direction by one of the options on the Tour des Glaciers de la Vanoise), while the rocky little Pointe de l'Observatoire which juts above the col to the west, is a fine viewpoint reached in about thirty minutes, and is worth tackling for itself alone.

A clockwise circuit of the glen is another option worth considering. When taken from Aussois a steep climb becomes inevitable from the start in order to gain the GR5 just north of Col du Barbier. The trail heading along the west flank of the glen is narrow and stony in places, but there are no major difficulties to contend with under normal summer conditions, and views are consistently fine. Midway along the glen the route climbs to a high point, then levels across an open moorland cut by numerous streams. Continuing northward the way climbs again to a junction with the path that heads west to Col de la Masse and Orgère. At this point the GR5 swings to the right following a few low cairns where the path is thin on the ground, then descends among alpenroses to a track at the northern end of Plan d'Amont. Off to the left here the glen continues towards its head, but to complete the circuit involves crossing a stream and following a narrow trail eastward. This eventually joins another track, or dirt road, which heads south past Refuge du Plan Sec to a few ski tows, then drops steeply to Plan d'Aval and Aussois.

Upvalley from Aussois the little village of Sardières is set among meadows below the ninety-three metre tooth of rock known as the Monolithe de Sardières, which juts from the forest and attracts both climbers and general tourists alike. A gîte d'étape in the village provides another accommodation option in this part of the Maurienne.

Termignon sits in a loop of the Arc river by its confluence with the Doron. The Doron flows from the north, its valley having cut a deep trench in the main Vanoise massif - the most profound tributary valley carved in the southern flank of these mountains. Termignon has one or two modest hotels, a gîte d'étape and campsite and, of considerable use to walkers, a shuttle bus service (the *navette*) which maintains a daily schedule throughout the summer along the east flank of the valley between Termignon and Entre Deux Eaux, with stops at a large parking area

Aiguille Verte, Drus and Mont Blanc seen from the Col de Balme on the famous
TMB walk (Ch 4)

The Chamonix Aiguilles
(*R.B. Evans.* Ch 4)

The Trient Glacier
(Ch 4)

The Dents du Midi from Planachaux, a
scene on the GR5
(*W. Unsworth*. Ch 4)

In the Chablais Alps
(*W. Unsworth*. Ch 4)

Walkers on the Dents du Midi (*W. Unsworth*. Ch 4)

(Bellecombe) from which a number of walks begin, and Refuge du Plan du Lac with its glorious panorama of high mountains, glaciers and snowfields. The road along which the *navette* journeys is closed to private vehicles beyond Bellecombe, thus preserving a certain aura of peace in the high pasturelands of Plan du Lac.

This is magnificent walking country. Trails explore both sides of the valley, but not the bed of the valley itself which, upstream of le Villard, is a wild and narrow gorge - the upper end with a brief track marked on the map as *itinéraire dangereux*.

Refuge du Plan du Lac is a modern, comfortable hut built by the PNV (Parc National de la Vanoise). The view west across the Doron gorge is breathtaking, while to the north the great rock wall of the Grande Casse looks most impressive. A short walk south leads to the beautiful tarn which gives Plan du Lac its name, and trails north and north-east lead to other mountain huts; to the privately-owned Refuge d'Entre Deux Eaux, and to Refuge de la Femma (PNV). Entre Deux Eaux is another converted dairy farm open in summer only, while La Femma is a three-storey timber building standing near the head of the pastoral Vallon de la Rocheure. This vallon, or glen, cuts back to the east of Entre Deux Eaux and offers good walking prospects; easy valley strolls with charming views, prospects of exploring tempting cirques gouged from the south flank of the valley, and more demanding treks across the walling mountains - via Col de Pierre Blanche (2842m) to Refuge de la Leisse, or by way of Col de la Rocheure (2911m) for a choice of several distant and moderately challenging destinations. As with almost all other huts in the Vanoise region, a winter room is permanently open when the main accommodation at La Femma is closed.

High on the west bank, set upon a shelf of rock and grass below the Glacier de l'Arpont, Refuge de l'Arpont is a PNV hut with ninety-five dormitory places and a small space for camping. Nearby cascades shower from the Glaciers de la Vanoise. Ibex are often seen grazing near the hut and the shrill whistle of marmots pierces the stillness. A small tarn is lodged on the mountainside about 350 metres above the hut, and this makes an interesting and scenic destination for a short walk. The Arpont hut is used by walkers on the Tour des Glaciers de la Vanoise, as well as by those tackling the longer Tour of the Vanoise and the classic GR5. But it makes a first-class destination in its own right when approached either directly from Termignon, or by way of Plan du Lac. A short hut to hut tour of the Doron valley would be worth considering by walkers with only limited time at their disposal, for the mountain scenery hereabouts is second to none, and the trails linking each of these huts provide all the variety a walker needs.

Continuing eastward from Termignon there are no more major glens flowing into the Maurienne from the Vanoise massif until you come to Bonneval-sur-Arc, some twenty-odd kilometres upstream. However, there's still plenty of good walking country on mid-height trails that make a steady traverse of the valley's north wall, with three mountain huts (Refuges du Cuchet, Vallonbrun and Molard) that provide essential accommodation in comparatively remote country linked by those trails. Above, the mountains rise as stark, bony projections; below them forests and steep meadows of grass and flowers. Between Refuge du Cuchet and Refuge du Vallonbrun a minor path breaks away north of the GR5 at Pla de la Cha in a combe below the Grand Roc Noir, and climbs to a large block of schist known as the Pierre-aux-Pieds. This rock is something of a mystery, for carved in its east side are about fifty small feet thought to date back to Neolithic times.

Refuge du Cuchet stands on a small spur of hillside high above the valley, an unmanned hut belonging to the PNV, and with good views south across the valley to the Col du Mont Cenis, which is crossed by a road leading into Italy. Far below, in the bed of the valley where the Mont Cenis route breaks away from the main valley road, Lanslebourg-Mont-Cenis is a useful restocking point for long-distance walkers choosing the GR5E variant known as the Sentier du Petit Bonheur, which links a number of fine Haute-Maurienne villages noted for their vernacular architecture. A trail climbs steeply from Lanslebourg to Refuge du Cuchet, nearly 800 metres above the village, while the Chemin de la Ramasse breaks away to the south, climbs to the Col du Mont Cenis and makes a circuit of the dammed lake which fills the valley south of the col, and offers further walking possibilities among the frontier mountains.

Refuge du Vallonbrun, by contrast with the rather exposed position of the Cuchet hut, is snug within a secret pastoral glen that runs parallel with the Maurienne (though high above it), from which it is hidden by a grassy bluff whose crown reveals the Glacier de l'Arcelle Neuve seen hanging from the face of Signal du Grand Mont Cenis and Pointe de Ronce opposite. A short distance upvalley stands the little Chapelle St-Antoine and a handful of chalets and farms at the hamlet of La Fesse d'en Haut. High above the hamlet Col du Vallonbrun is a climber's (and ski-mountaineer's) route over the walling mountains that separate the Maurienne from Vallon de la Rocheure.

Beside the Chapelle St-Antoine a footpath descends to the Col de la Madeleine, site of a major landslip that once completely blocked the valley of l'Arc midway between Lanslevillard (the next village upstream of Lanslebourg) and Bessans. This is the route chosen by the Tour of the Vanoise. Bessans, a short walk upvalley from Col de la Madeleine, offers accommodation, refreshments and opportunities for reprovisioning. There's a campsite downstream, and a gîte d'étape about half an hour's walk upstream at the charming hamlet of Le Villaron, tucked on the right bank of the Arc between the river and the steep forested hillside.

The south wall of the valley here is cut by two important tributaries, Vallée du Ribon and Vallée d'Avérole. The first is long and straight with a tempting trail that projects far into it for challenging routes by way of the Glacier de Rochemelon into Italy (Rifugio Tazzetti is lodged on the south side of the Col de la Resta), or via Glacier de Derriere le Clapier, a difficult route that leads into a remote upper glen feeding into Vallée d'Avérole. This latter valley is another wild and atmospheric place containing three tiny villages, a CAF hut (Refuge d'Avérole) and some rugged mountain scenery. Only mountain walkers experienced in scrambling, and with essential equipment and knowledge to deal with glacier travel, should attempt to tackle some of the high routes here. But there are some tremendous challenges to be won among these very fine but little-sung mountains, crossing and recrossing the international frontier.

Back along the Maurienne's northern wall, a fine combe, or minor glen, is accessible from the small unmanned PNV hut, Refuge du Molard. Through the glen a stream drains the Glacier de Méan Martin, and in early summer the pastures are a-dazzle with countless alpine flowers. Across the mouth of this glen the GR5 invites walkers north-eastward to the charming Vallon de la Lenta, a superb little valley edged by the Iseran road. Happily that road makes little impact on the glen itself for it climbs high above it, leaving the pastures with their huddled chalets, waterfall and clear dancing streams to the natural peace of the mountains. At the upper end of the vallon a narrow rocky gorge has a wild impact, but stand on the rim of this gorge and gaze south and south-east and your heart will be lifted by a truly spectacular view of glacier-clad mountains that create part of the frontier with Italy - the Ciamarella group whose grace of form, and whose elegant waves of snow and ice tilted above dark walls holding shadow, are all a lover of grand mountain scenery could ask for. Between the glen and those mountains, but hidden from sight, lies the much-loved village of Bonneval-sur-Arc.

Bonneval is the finest of all Haute-Maurienne villages, its handsome medieval stone houses huddling one against another as if for mutual protection at the foot of a steeply sloping hillside on the right bank of the Arc. Varnished balconies are bright with geraniums and petunias, the rooftops a puzzle of lichened stone slabs, the narrow alleyways full of charm. In neighbouring Tralenta, a modern hamlet 'suburb' where planning constrictions are not as evident as in preserved Bonneval, there are several hotels, and the CAF-owned Chalet-Refuge de Bonneval standing only a few paces from the Office de Tourisme. Another refuge, privately owned and situated on the hillside above and to the south-east of Tralenta, gives access to more walking possibilities on the slopes of Ouille du Midi below Pic Regaud and l'Albaron. Refuge du Criou is also linked by a belvedere trail with Refuge des Évettes, a CAF hut used by climbers tackling a number of those peaks on the international frontier noted above, the best of which is the lovely Ciamarella (3676m). This latter hut is reached also by a footpath that climbs from the recently-restored hamlet of l'Écot, highest in the Maurienne, from which some more delightful country may be explored by walkers who are lured by the little-known. The scenery in this back-of-beyond is glorious, and a brief glance at the map is sufficient to have one reaching for the boots. One of several options here leads to the Refuge du Carro (CAF owned) set in a grassy basin containing a pair of tarns, Lac Noir and the larger Lac Blanc. An alternative path leading to the same hut begins at a parking area on the Iseran road, and leads by way of the Sentier Balcon, a long traverse of wide appeal that is almost always in full view of a vast panorama of high peaks heavily draped with snowfields, and the impressive Glacier des Sources de l'Arc.

The Tarentaise

North of Bonneval Col de l'Iseran (opened in 1936) provides vehicular access between the Haute-Maurienne and the upper valley of l'Isère. At 2764 metres it's the highest major road pass in the Alps. Marked by a huge cairn, a chapel, and the inevitable sturdy stone bar/souvenir building described by Janet Adam Smith (in *Mountain Holidays*) as being "rather like a gaunt Highland shooting-lodge", the col is not the place where lovers of wild mountain scenery will wish to linger, although evening views to the "pointed Albaron, the dark mass of the Charbonel, and the tent-shaped Ciamarella, startlingly white above the darkening valley of the Arc" provide a sober contrast to the immediate surroundings. On the northern side of the col, despite designation as a nature reserve, the hillsides are laced with cables and ski tows. If one were able to visualize the mountains without these encumbrances, no doubt the landscape would hold appeal, but that's not easy.

Descend to the valley proper and visual quality is restored in part. The upper Isère remains unmarked, and through the Gorge du Malpasset leads to lovely alpine meadows where marmots play. Under glacial napkins draped below the frontier ridge, which here briefly runs north-south, Refuge de Prariond sits at a junction of streams in a cirque at the very head of the valley. Col de la Galise (2987m) immediately above it offers a high crossing into Italy where a counterpart to the French hut is the Rifugio Plan della Ballotta above Lago Serru in the Parco Nazionale del Gran Paradiso. But walkers who have no desire to cross into Italy here have an opportunity to gain the modest rounded summit of the Grand Cocor (3034m) just to the south of the col on the frontier ridge. Ibex are often to be seen between the hut and the ridge crest.

The valley flows roughly westward, and below the Gorge du Malpasset the Iseran road snakes along the right bank of the stream through Le Fornet as far as the outskirts of Val d'Isère. Val d'Isère has grown from a small mountain village into one of the most popular of all French ski resorts. Unlike many ski resorts, however, it does not die in summer, but continues to flourish with steady business, and its hotels mostly remaining open. In 1939 Irving predicted many of the changes that have come to this once-peaceful backwater, when he wrote: "Now that the road runs through, and not only up to Val d'Isère, that village will develop rapidly the things that motorists require." But he went on to add: "At the same time it will continue to provide for the visitor who wants them, places where he can enjoy upland pastures and summits fairly easy to attain, without fear of disturbance from a tourist crowd." Of course, he didn't imagine a plethora of cableways, but as J.W. Akitt points out in his guide to the area, there is still a great deal of unspoiled countryside where the mountain walker can find inspiration.

Due south of the resort, for example, a Y-shaped glen, sliced by the Ruisseau de la Calabourdane, leads to some interesting walking possibilities. By taking the road through the glen as far as Le Manchet at the upper stem of the Y, a trail can then be joined which leads through the south-eastern branch to Refuge du Fond des Fours, a PNV hut at 2537 metres overlooked from the south by Pointe de Méan Martin, the Glacier des Fours draped across its upper north face. Above the hut Col des Fours provides a way over the eastern ridge to Pont de la Neige on the Iseran road - from where one could join the GR5 and descend to Bonneval in the Haute-Maurienne, or instead follow the same path north to Col de l'Iseran and down to Val d'Isère. An alternative route from Refuge du Fond des Fours continues upvalley, then crosses to the western side and up to a col with close views of cliff, glacier, moraine, and mountain peak, then over scree and sometimes snow, to Col de la Rocheure (2911m) with its small tarn and lovely views west to the dazzling Glaciers de la Vanoise at the far end of the Rocheure glen. Instead of crossing the col, descend north-west over more scree to a good path which heads back to Le Manchet to conclude a pleasant day's circuit of between five and six hours.

For an easy three or four-day circuit from Val d'Isère it would be worth following the route outlined above by way of Refuge du Fond des Fours and Col de la Rocheure, from which you descend south-west to Refuge de la Femma, set on the right bank of the Torrent de la Rocheure, and there spend the night. Next day either cross Col de Pierre Blanche to Refuge de la Leisse, or have an easy day reaching that hut by way of a gentle down valley walk to Refuge d'Entre Deux Eaux, where a good trail works north and north-east into the Vallon de la Leisse. Leaving the Leisse hut climb through the glen to cross Col de la Leisse on the route of GR55, go down to Lac de Tignes and continue over Pas de la Tovière in order to return to Val d'Isère.

North of Val d'Isère, and hidden from view by a steep mountain wall, the Réserve Naturelle de la Grande Sassière protects a corrie that is very popular with walkers. The normal access to this is by way of a road that writhes up from the eastern shore of the dammed Lac du Chevril, but there are two rather strenuous walkers' routes that lead directly from Val d'Isère itself. The steepest and most direct of these is the crossing of Passage de Picheru in the ridge north-west of the Aiguille du Dôme. This demands a climb of almost a thousand metres, and on the north side of the ridge drops to Lac de la Sassière. On the descent the big wall of the Grande Sassière opposite makes an imposing sight, the glaciers that flank the Tsanteleina clearly seen on the blocking wall of the cirque to the right.

The alternative walkers' route into the Sassière corrie first makes an eastward traverse of hillside from Val d'Isère to beyond Le Fornet, before climbing sharply to the little Lac de la Bailletta and the col above that which makes an obvious crossing point just east of Pointe de la Bailletta. The descent to Lac de la Sassière is a slanting north-west trend which joins the Picheru trail just above the barrage at the end of the lake.

To the west of Val d'Isère hillsides have been systematically developed for the downhill ski industry, a usage which proves incompatible with those landscapes of natural harmony most often sought by mountain walkers. It is not impossible, however, to escape the mechanical hoists and piste scars, even though one may be compelled to spend a morning wearing metaphorical blinkers. The route of GR5 links Val d'Isère with ugly Lac de Tignes, but in between explores the green and gentle Vallon de la Tovière whose north-western end is crossed at an easy flower-starred col, from which a lovely view reveals the south side of Mont Blanc far off at the end of a long tunnel-like valley.

Lac de Tignes and neighbouring Val Claret are visual eyesores, yet escape can be found quite easily by following walkers' routes that return to the unscarred sanctuary of the National Park; routes that cross Col du Palet (GR5) to a PNV hut and a charming valley draining north to Landry in the Tarentaise; or by way of Col de la Leisse (GR55) in the shadow of La Grande Motte, and down into the Vallon de la Leisse which leads to the wonderful Doron gorge, to a choice of fine huts, or by way of Col de la Vanoise to Pralognan on the route of the Tour of the Vanoise. On such routes stimulating scenery and an all-embracing peace can once more be found. In the heartland of the Vanoise there is no shortage of either.

Below Val d'Isère the Isère river enters the dammed Lac du Chevril, then continues roughly northward as the eastern moat of Dôme de la Sache and Mont Pourri, whose long glacial fingers are valley-bound between dividing spurs and ribs, the National Park boundary tracing just below them. The eastern, or right-hand walling mountains, form the border with Italy in an extensive north-south ridge system topped by a number of fine peaks culminating in the "beautiful gleaming sickle" of the Aiguille de la Grande Sassière (3747m). Trails lead up to these frontier mountains, to the glaciers of the Grande Sassière, to Col du Rocher Blanc and nearby Col du Lac Noir (both of which cross to Rifugio Mario Bezzi high in the Val Grisenche), to Col du Mont and Col de la Sassière (the last a long way north of the peak of the same name), both of which again provide crossing points into Italy.

There are few villages of any noteworthy size in this stretch of the Isère, but Ste-Foy-Tarentaise sits at a junction of roads, one of which provides access to a cluster of glens worthy of exploration between the main valley and the frontier ridge, where projecting spurs create magnificent cirques, some of which have tempting trails that link huts in neighbouring glens. Refuge du Ruitor in the Sassière glen, and Refuge de l'Archeboc (or la Motte) in the Vallon de Mercuel, for example, are joined by a trail that crosses the Arête de Montseti. The CAF's Refuge du Ruitor is particularly well situated for routes onto the crusty frontier ridge, on the eastern side of which the extensive Glacier du Ruitor makes an impressive sight. Avoiding this glacier a choice of crossings (some trackless and requiring good visibility) may be made into Italy from a base at the Ruitor hut, via such cols as du Tachuy (2673m) and de la Louie Blanche (2567m), where continuing routes descend over wild country to Rifugio A. Deffeyes and a series of spectacular cascades that drain the Ruitor glacier above La Thuile.

✳   ✳   ✳

TOUR DU MONT POURRI

On the west side of the Tarentaise Mont Pourri dominates the lower valley with its ponderous mass of snow and ice. In 1829 William Brockedon travelled from Bourg St-Maurice to Val d'Isère, describing the mountain thus: "Towering over this sombre valley, rises one of the grandest mountains in the Alps from its magnitude, and one of the most beautiful from its form - its vast mass of snow and glaciers surmounted by a triangular pyramid of pure white." Walkers understandably drawn to this mountain will find local publicity for a three-day tour around it, a tour that is growing in popularity. Two nights are spent in mountain huts (Refuge du Mont Pourri and Refuge de la Martin), but since the Martin hut has no meals provision, food will need to be carried for at least one night. The recommended start and finish of this tour is the purpose-built ski resort of Arc 2000, reached by a tortuous road from the Isère valley near Villaroger, or more directly from Bourg St-Maurice.

From Arc 2000 the way leads south initially among ski lifts to Plan de l'Homme and Col de la Chal (2457m) and continues below Aiguille du St-Esprit to the CAF-owned Refuge du Mont Pourri situated just inside the boundary of the Vanoise National Park at 2370 metres, and reached in little more than three hours from Arc 2000. An alternative approach comes from Les Lanches in the valley of the Ponturin through which GR5 makes its way from Landry.

The second stage continues southward along the west flank of Mont Pourri towards the head of the Ponturin valley, but then slants left at the Chalets de la Plagne to begin the ascent to Col de la Sachette (2713m). The upper part of the climb goes through a wild and rocky landscape, and the terrain on the initial descent is every bit as rough as that on the ascent. The col is situated on a ridge carrying the PNV boundary south from Dôme de la Sache, and just below and to the north of Rochers Rouges (3002m). The view east shows the Aiguille de la Grande Sassière and other frontier mountains across the depths of the Isère valley, and the first part of the descent is a little exposed and demands care. However, although the route maintains its rough character and is steep for quite some way, the path itself improves and eases through the Vallon de la Sachette where there are several little tarns. Veering left below the Vallon de la Sache where the path forks, the way passes below glaciers that drape unseen down the face of Dôme de la Sache, and eventually reaches the PNV-owned Refuge de la Martin. At the end of this stage there should still be time, energy permitting, to wander up a good trail from the hut to gain a close view of the Glacier de la Savinaz in an austere setting.

For the final stage of the Tour du Mont Pourri follow a trail that descends northwards to la Gurraz, then rise on a track that becomes a footpath leading to another PNV hut, the unguarded Refuge de Turia which takes its name from Mont Turia, a summit just to the north of Mont Pourri to which it is joined by a splendid crest. The Arc 2000 trail continues beyond the hut and crosses a ravine, passes below the Aiguille Rouge and Signal de l'Aiguille Rouge, then descends steeply to a junction of paths. The way now veers left along the mountainside with Mont Blanc in view ahead to the north, and joins a track leading to a chairlift. Rounding the northern flank of Aiguille Rouge the buildings of Arc 2000 are soon visible and completion of the tour in sight.

TOUR DU MONT POURRI - SUMMARY

Day 1:   Arc 2000 - Col de la Chal - Refuge du Mont Pourri

Day 2:   Refuge du Mont Pourri - Col de la Sachette - Refuge de la Martin

Day 3:   Refuge de la Martin - Refuge de Turia - Arc 2000

✳   ✳   ✳

Vallée du Ponturin

Flanked by the Sommet (or Dôme) de Bellecôte (3417m) on the west, and Mont Pourri to the east, the Ponturin flows from just below the Col du Palet to Landry where it joins l'Isère. In its upper reaches the valley's glacial origins are obvious, but lower down it is river cut, the steep hillsides clothed with mixed forests. Landry is an obvious point of entry, for it has a railway station on the line which goes to Bourg St-Maurice, and a bus service to Peisey-Nancroix a few kilometres inside the Ponturin valley. Landry village, for a village is what it remains, has hotel accommodation and a campsite. The GR5 passes through after having crossed the Beaufortain Alps from Mont Blanc, and then strikes southward along the Ponturin valley on its way to the Vanoise massif. The GR5 therefore gives the valley the mountain walker's seal of approval. The small but sophisticated resort of Peisey-Nancroix, noted for its slender, handsome church, sits on the right flank and provides some winter appeal with cross-country ski facilities, while three huts (four if you count Refuge du Mont Pourri) effectively underline the opportunities that abound here for the exploration of some fine mountain country. Apart from Landry, Peisey-Nancroix and these huts, overnight facilities are available in the hamlets of Le Moulin and Nancroix. The valley also has a campsite and gîte d'étape.

As for the huts, these are the PNV's *porte du parc*, Chalet-Refuge de Rosuel which is accessible by road; the privately-owned Refuge d'Entre le Lac above the Lac de la Plagne; and Refuge du Col du Palet situated, as its name implies, just below Col du Palet across which GR5 briefly leaves the National Park to descend to Lac de Tignes. Refuge du Mont Pourri has already been mentioned, and is accessible from the valley by a trail which climbs from Les Lanches.

Walking routes abound, and with accessible cols providing opportunities to cross the walling ridges to east and west, a variety of hut-to-hut tours are possible. Beginning in the lower part of the Ponturin, one such option sets out from Le Moulin and enters the tributary glen of the Nant Benin which flows from the south. Sections of this glen have been sacrificed to the ski industry, but there's still some worthwhile country to wander through. At its head Col de Frête (2492m) is a dip in the ridge linking Roche de Mio and the Sommet de Bellecôte, and from it a way leads down the south side to Champagny-le-Haut and another *porte du parc*, Refuge du Bois.

Upvalley from Le Moulin, Chalet-Refuge de Rosuel has an unusual appearance in that its turfed roof has a wave-like shape designed to reduce the impact of avalanches. Situated near the roadhead, and with car parking facilities, it is obviously very busy throughout the summer. Refuge du Mont Pourri is easily accessible from Rosuel either by the trail from Les Lanches a short way downstream, or from another path which cuts back from the GR5 upvalley towards the Chalets de la Plagne. Another route breaking away left (east) from the chalets is that which was adopted by the Tour du Mont Pourri and which climbs to Col de la Sachette on the way to Refuge de la Martin.

But the most popular walk from Rosuel is that which leads in around three hours to Lac de la Plagne and Refuge d'Entre le Lac. It's a fine, scenically interesting route that crosses meadows with grand views left to Mont Pourri and a series of cliffs down which a cascade and numerous streams drain the glaciers. From Entre le Lac a trail continues south-west and climbs, quite steeply in places, to Col du Plan Séry. Descent on the western side of the col passes eroded limestone pillars, crosses high meadowland, then drops in zig-zags to Refuge de Plaisance, about 600 metres above the Vallée du Doron de Champagny. The continuing route descends into that valley, where there's a gîte d'étape at Laisonnay d'en Haut, or breaks away upstream to the small, privately-owned Refuge de la Glière.

On the way to Col du Plan Séry from Refuge d'Entre le Lac the trail forks. The left-hand option here is an alternative route to Refuge du Col du Palet, which joins the main GR5 near another trail junction at the upper end of Plan de la Grassaz. The south-west option at this junction leads to what may be regarded as one of the finest of all mountain panoramas enjoyed by walkers in the Graian Alps, but in order to gain that you have to climb to Col de la Grassaz (2637m). The path is not too demanding though, for it ascends gradually through a broad glen, wild yet enchanting with the little Lac Verdet tucked below the austere Aiguille des Aimes. But on emerging at the col a scene of astonishing beauty is the reward. Dominating the view to the south is the north wall of the Grande Casse flanked by numerous glaciers, the largest of them all being a vast sheet of white plastered on the face of La Grande Motte. It's a wonderful scene, and the descent through pastures prolongs the enjoyment. Halfway down the trail is joined by another, which comes from Col du Palet, and a little over two hours from the col reaches Refuge de la Glière, a small, atmospheric hut settled at the foot of the Aiguille de l'Epéna.

Back in the Ponturin valley the main route of approach to Refuge du Col du Palet is the GR5 trail which leads in about four hours from Chalet-Refuge de Rosuel. Although it's a fairly long approach, there's plenty of interest for the valley is full of charm and the surrounding mountains have lots of scenic appeal. The way passes the Chalets de la Plagne, follows a rocky crest and looks down on the Lac de la Plagne, crosses the depression of Plan de la Grassaz where an ancient lake long ago silted up, and enjoys views ahead to La Grande Motte's snow dome. Shortly after passing Lac de Grattaleu a trail breaks away left from the main GR5 and comes to Refuge du Col du Palet, set in undulating grassland with screes and grey slabs in view just ten minutes below the actual col.

The National Park boundary traces the ridge crossed by Col du Palet (2652m). To the east the ski grounds of Lac de Tignes and Val Claret make a stark contrast to the unspoiled grandeur of the Ponturin side, grandeur that is signified by the sprawling Bellecôte massif and its spiky neighbour, l'Aliet. Views east from the "spacious level of white stone" (as Martin Collins described the col) are extensive, and a short way along the descent trail includes the distant range of the Gran Paradiso. Instead of crossing Col du Palet, walkers who follow a trail heading south-west will soon come to another pass, Col de la Croix des Frêtes from which La Grande Casse is clearly seen ahead. Crossing this col the trail descends to Refuge de la Glière at the head of the Champagny valley, joining the route described above from Col de la Grassaz. Another pass to the north of Col du Palet is the 2656 metre Col de la Tourne which provides an alternative route down the eastern side of the ridge to Lac de Tignes. This route is joined about ten minutes below the hut, is much more wild on the western side and considerably less trodden than that of Palet.

Vallée du Doron de Champagny

South of the Vallée du Ponturin the Doron de Champagny cuts a major east-west valley through the Tarentaise mountains from its headwaters below the north face of La Grande Casse, to Moutiers where it swells the Isère. From Bozel, however, having already been joined by the Doron de Pralognan at Le Villard, the river is known as the Doron de Bozel. (Doron, incidentally, is the Savoie dialect word for stream, or river.) Spreading to the south of Bozel the ski grounds of Courchevel not unnaturally deflect the walker's attention elsewhere, while at Le Villard another road breaks away to the south-east towards Pralognan where there is much to concentrate the mind. We will return to this particular valley shortly. But east of the small resort of Champagny-en-Vanoise the D91 road squeezes through the Gorges de la Pontille to enter the upper Champagny valley where there are several attractive small hamlets and increasingly dramatic scenery that will repay a visit by all who are inspired by nature in its raw, untamed state. La Grande Motte looks especially fine at the head of the valley. Accommodation is limited, but there are modest bases to be had at Champagny-en-Vanoise, Champagny-le-Haut where there's another PNV *porte du parc* (Refuge du Bois) and a campsite, and at the roadhead and National Park boundary at Laisonnay d'en Haut with a gîte d'étape (Refuge du Laisonnay) from where the lovely Cascade du Py is seen above to the left. Another mountain hut exists to the south of, and about 900 metres higher than, Champagny-le-Haut. Here Refuge du Plan des Gouilles (2350m) provides climbers with a base for routes on the north flank of the Grand Bec (Refuge du Grand Bec on the west flank is accessible from Pralognan). Refuge de Plaisance occupies a glen to the north of Laisonnay d'en Haut (visited earlier by a route from Entre le Lac in the Vallée du Ponturin), and the little Refuge de la Glière nestles at the head of the valley. La Glière is owned by the Commune de Champagny and has only twenty-one beds. But there is a guardian in summer residence who serves meals, and self-catering facilities are provided as in most CAF and PNV huts. In a stone building nearby locally made cheese is usually for sale, as are drinks for passing walkers.

Hut to hut routes from the Vallée du Doron de Champagny mostly demand the crossing of cols to the north leading into the Ponturin valley, routes that were outlined in the reverse direction within the Vallée du Ponturin section above. By linking several of these huts enjoyable two- or three-day circuits could be achieved. With the Sommet de Bellecôte as the hub, for example, a hut-to-hut tour beginning at Champagny-le-Haut would lead north across Col de Frête and through the Nant Benin glen to Nancroix, then along the route of GR5 to Rosuel and Refuge d'Entre le Lac, or as far as the hut on the west side of Col du Palet. From both Entre le Lac and Col du Palet there are return routes to the Champagny valley via Col du Plan Séry, Col de la Grassaz or Col de la Croix des Frêtes. Depending which crossing is made you'll reach the bed of the valley either at Refuge de la Glière, or Laisonnay d'en Haut.

A shorter, and in many ways a better tour, could be made by simply crossing Col du Plan Séry and Col de la Grassaz, using the Refuge du Laisonnay gîte as the starting point. Two days should be sufficient for this, spending the intervening night at Refuge d'Entre le Lac. The first stage climbs north of Laisonnay d'en Haut on a good path, passing in view of the Cascade du Py, and goes to Refuge de Plaisance. The trail then swings to the right and switchbacks up to the meadows of Plan Séry before climbing again in order to cross the col at 2609 metres. The descent begins quite steeply, the trail partially eroded, but it improves lower down. About twenty minutes before gaining the hut a junction of trails is reached; the right-hand option being the one to take on the next stage to Col de la Grassaz (it also offers a way to Refuge du Col du Palet). There is a third option here where a path heads left up to the Lacs du Plan Richard in a hanging valley below the aiguille of l'Aliet. The return stage from Refuge d'Entre le Lac has already been outlined under the Vallée du Ponturin section, and has as its highlight those tremendous big mountain views from Col de la Grassaz, views that continue all the way down to La Glière. A two-day outing such as this is immensely rewarding, and would make a first-rate introduction to the delights of hut-to-hut trekking for newcomers to the Alps.

Vallée du Doron de Pralognan

Long respected as a mountaineering centre, Pralognan-la-Vanoise is one of the best-known of all the resorts in the Western Graians, although it remains quite modest in size as its growth is naturally restricted by the geography of the valley. Hemmed in by abrupt crowding mountains that define the western extent of the Vanoise massif, it makes some claim to be a minor ski resort, yet has managed to retain a traditional village atmosphere with far greater success than many of its rivals by banning all high-rise development. It has just one cableway (the Mont Bochor *téléphérique*) and a limited number of ski tows and chairlifts. Reached by bus from Moutiers Pralognan sits at the junction of three valleys and has much to offer as a base for a walking holiday. It has several modest hotels, gîtes d'étape and campsites, and access to a variety of mountain huts. Trails abound, and in the height of summer they can be very busy indeed, with accommodation at a premium in Pralognan and the surrounding huts.

The main valley flows roughly northward downstream of the resort to Le Villard and the Doron de Champagny, its upper reaches leading to wild country headed by Col de Chavière, while a steep tributary glen enters Pralognan from the east over which the Grande Casse reigns supreme. The National Park boundary crosses the summit of the Grand Bec, a mountain that effectively separates Pralognan's valley from that of Champagny, chooses a serpentine course around the east of Pralognan itself and, working southward, edges the right flank of the Chavière valley whose upper reaches it encloses by veering west and north to include Aiguille du Fruit, thereby setting a limit to the outlying Courchevel-Méribel ski playgrounds.

Of all walks splaying out from Pralognan perhaps the most popular is that which climbs steeply to Refuge du Col de la Vanoise (2517m), otherwise known as Refuge Félix Faure after the French president who visited the site in 1897. As its name suggests, the hut is situated at the col, a long trough in full glorious view of the Grande Casse and a choice selection of aiguilles and blank slab walls nearby. Considering there's a difference in altitude of some eleven hundred metres between Pralognan and the col, it is surprising the amount (and shape, size and age) of tourists who make the climb. Admitted, it's possible to drive as far as Les Fontanettes, thereby saving two hundred metres of height-gain, and there's the *téléphérique* too (use of this involves descent from the top station in order to get onto the trail), but even so there remains a lot of quite steep uphill to contend with. Red faces in early summer invariably match the brilliant alpenroses that grow beside the trail.

As a destination in its own right, the Col de la Vanoise is well worth devoting a day of one's holiday to; never mind the crowds - although, of course, it's better if you can avoid them by setting out early. The standard route from the roadhead car park at Les Fontanettes follows a dirt track/broad trail through forest, then past

Refuge les Barmettes and across the Glière torrent to enter the National Park. Now the way steepens again in many footpath braidings among low-growing shrubs and marmot burrows, mountains growing in stature all around. The shallow Lac des Vaches is traditionally crossed on stepping stones with the great slab face of Aiguille de la Vanoise soaring above to the right, and as the trail continues from the north-eastern end of the tarn, so a close and privileged view is given of climbers at work on that face. As the way curves towards the south so the Glacier de la Grande Casse is seen hanging above to the left. The way becomes increasingly stony as it switchbacks up to Lac Long, seen below to the left shortly before gaining Refuge du Col de la Vanoise, about three hours from Les Fontanettes. High above the lake soars the Grande Casse, which looks very impressive from the hut, as do the Aiguille and Pointes de l'Epéna, and Pointe de la Grande Glière to the north. The refuge, which consists of more than just one single building, is owned by the CAF, has over 150 places and a guardian in residence from mid-June to the middle of September when meals are provided. Needless to say, it's well patronised by the crowds who toil up the track during the day, but who go no farther. Those walkers in search of mountain tranquillity will do better by continuing south-eastward through the long, fairly level trough of the col where more lakes, screes, meandering streams, alpine flowers and marmots, and magnificent views, abound.

There are fine cross-country routes to tackle which continue to the Vallon de la Leisse (on GR55), or south of that to Entre Deux Eaux and the Vallon de la Rocheure, or to Plan du Lac; or even down the west flank of the Doron gorge to Refuge de l'Arpont, thereby reversing a section of the Tour des Glaciers de la Vanoise. Each of these suggestions will give a magnificent and full day's walking from Pralognan. But should a return be planned to Pralognan, rather than reverse the route of ascent there's a circuit to be made by heading south-west from the hut to Lac des Assiettes (by mid-summer this is often almost dry), then down through a wild hanging valley below the Glacier de l'Arcin. The descent is rough and more challenging than the standard route. It is also a little longer, taking almost three hours to reach Les Fontanettes.

South of Pralognan Refuge de la Vallette sits high on the right flank of the Chavière valley on a hillside shelf below the long rock wall that supports the Glaciers de la Vanoise ice sheet. A trail climbs to it from Pralognan by way of the Isertan forest, while linking trails lead to Col de la Vanoise by way of the Col du Grand Marchet (2490m) and the Fontanettes-Lac des Assiettes path. Another walkers' route heads south from the Vallette hut on a strenuous crossing of Col d'Aussois (2916m), and descends from there to Refuge du Fond d'Aussois in the Aussois glen that drains into the Maurienne. This latter route forms part of the Tour des Glaciers de la Vanoise outlined below. Incidentally, there are three further routes by which the Col and Refuge du Fond d'Aussois may be gained from the Chavière valley. The first leaves the valley road near Les Prioux and climbs to the Chalet des Nants where the Vallette trail is joined. Next is a track coming from the roadhead at Pont de la Pêche, with a path that continues above Montaimont, while the third breaks away from the GR55 trail upstream from La Motte, crosses the Chavière to the Ritort alp, and climbs in zig-zags from there to join the main Vallette-Col d'Aussois route on the right bank of the Rosoire stream.

Opposite Refuge de la Vallette, on the west side of the Chavière, rises the Petit Mont Blanc (2677m), a popular and modest peak that attracts walkers by a choice of footpaths starting from the Chavière valley, as well as via other routes of ascent beginning in a glen on the west side of the mountain made accessible from Courchevel. One of the Chavière routes begins downstream of Pont de Gerlan; one leaves the GR55 path upstream of that bridge, another from Les Prioux hamlet, and yet a fourth from a track between Pont de la Pêche and La Motte. Petit Mont Blanc (or Petit Mont Blanc de Pralognan to give its full title) is so-named for the exposed white gypsum deposits from which it is made. The summit is reached by way of a series of strange craters, and from the crown extensive views include the Vanoise glaciers seen across the valley to the east.

From the summit it's possible to link with a ridge-walk along the Crête du Mont Charvet, gained by way of the Col des Saulces (2456m) and a trail along the west flank of the Dents de la Portetta, or return to Pralognan via Col de la Grande Pierre. Alternatively descend west from Petit Mont Blanc to the little unguarded PNV hut, Refuge des Lacs Merlet in a corrie below Aiguille du Fruit, and spend the remainder of the day exploring that corrie, then make a circuit of the aiguille next day, passing Refuge du Saut where the trail divides. By heading south-east, cross Col Rouge (2731m) and descend to the GR55 at a point midway between Pont de la Pêche and Refuge de Péclet-Polset in the upper Chavière valley. From there either head upvalley to Péclet-Polset, or turn left and wander downstream to Pralognan. Those who go up to Refuge de Péclet-Polset will find it very busy by day with walkers making a visit from the roadhead at Pont de la Pêche. Above the hut a low ridge gives lovely views onto the milky-blue waters of Lac Blanc, while to the south an uncompromisingly wild patch of country encloses the valley-head in a stony amphitheatre with the dipping Col de Chavière offering an escape route to the Maurienne.

It will be seen, then, that Pralognan is not short of walking routes, and a holiday based there will serve well those who prefer their mountains tempered with comfortable sociability of an evening. The map is liberally outlined with blue-traced possibilities, while refuge symbols indicate a range of multi-day tours available for those with a taste for this kind of walking holiday. Of these, the best of all outings to be made in and around the Vanoise National Park is the ten-to-twelve-day Tour of the Vanoise described below from Modane, and the shorter version, the four-day 'official' tour of the Glaciers de la Vanoise which is publicised as starting from Pralognan. There is also a traverse of the massif to be made which begins at Landry in the Tarentaise, follows GR5 to Col du Palet, descends to Val Claret and joins GR55 across the mountains to Pralognan, and continues through the Chavière to Péclet-Polset, crosses Col de Chavière and descends to Modane in the Maurienne; a five-day crossing.

NB: At present (1997) the Péclet-Polset hut is being rebuilt after a fire. Enquire in Pralognan.

✻   ✻   ✻

TOUR DES GLACIERS DE LA VANOISE

Apart from the start and finish, this fine circuit remains above the 2000 metre contour, has two real passes to cross and numerous ridge spurs to negotiate, three nights to be spent in mountain huts and splendid views to enjoy throughout. Apart from the route over the first col (Col d'Aussois), which you may have to yourself, trails are likely to be well used during the main summer season. Snow will no doubt be lying in places until the middle of July, or even later in some years following a late spring, but while caution is naturally required, there should be no technical difficulties to face.

On the southern outskirts of Pralognan a path is taken which climbs steeply from the edge of a campsite through the Isertan forest, followed by a rough scramble to the so-called Pas de l'Âne, reached by way of an impressive open gully. The path continues up to the Roc du Tambour with the Petit Marchet rising above to the left, then swings right and eases below rock walls supporting ice cliffs edging the Glaciers de la Vanoise, and about five hours from Pralognan, arrives at the Refuge de la Vallette.

The second stage is longer and more arduous than the first, taking about seven and a half hours (plus rests) to gain Refuge du Fond d'Aussois over the Col d'Aussois, highest point of the tour. However, the day begins with a steady descent of about four hundred metres to the Chalet des Nants where an alternative trail rises from Les Prioux. From the chalet the way then makes a traverse of hill slopes below the little Glacier des Nants until a point is reached just above Montaimont. Here the trail rises into the Cirque du Génépy (Refuge du Génépy, marked on some maps, no longer exists, having been destroyed by avalanche) topped by the Dôme de l'Arpont and with the Glacier du Génépy draped below it. The way continues to climb, then eases along a belvedere trail known as the Sentier Balcon d'Ariande. Joined by the trail from the alp of Ritort, the continuing route heads south-east up the glen of the Rosoire stream before veering south for the final steep climb to Col d'Aussois, the final part of which is often over old snow on scree. The col is surprisingly broad and level, but the way down to the Aussois glen can be tiring as it descends a series of rock terraces before more comfortable slopes of grass lead eventually to the hut set beside a pleasant stream.

Next day is less strenuous, but is almost as long as the last, demanding perhaps six hours or so for the route to Refuge de l'Arpont. But there are no real passes to negotiate, the trails are good and mostly clear and, since the way is shared by both the longer Tour of the Vanoise and the GR5, there should be no navigational skills called upon.

Leaving Refuge du Fond d'Aussois continue downvalley through the lovely glen to a bridge over a stream that falls into the Plan d'Amont reservoir. At this point a crossing trail (GR5) is joined, bearing left (east) below Refuge de la Dent Parrachée, then on a track heading south-east to pass the privately-owned Refuge du Plan Sec. A short distance beyond this hut a footpath breaks away from the track near some ski tows, crosses pastureland and makes a traverse of hillside high above the Maurienne. At a junction of trails near the ruined hutments of La Turra, the way climbs the flank of Roc des Corneilles in steep switchbacks to gain a well-made path cutting round a bare cirque formed by curving ridges of the Pointe de

Bellecôte. Rounding a ridge spur projecting east of the same mountain, the trail then goes north-west and north along the GR5 into the Doron valley. As the way progresses, so views toward the head of the valley become more and more impressive; streams spill down from the Vanoise glaciers above to the left and ibex are often seen among pastures and stream-cut gullies on the approach to the hut. The Arpont hut enjoys lovely views south with the Doron gorge below to the east, while to see the full bounty of northward views it is necessary to climb a short slope behind the hut.

These views are gained next morning on stage four which leads to the Refuge du Col de la Vanoise and down to Pralognan - a demanding day's trekking. In the early part of the season snow slopes often lie just beyond Refuge de l'Arpont, and caution will be required in crossing them. However, the slope soon eases and the trail crosses gentle grassland basins below the eastern extent of the Vanoise glaciers. A little under three hours from Arpont the main GR5 trail descends steeply eastward into a glen below Entre Deux Eaux, while the route to the Col de la Vanoise is signposted off to the left, a trail that cuts along the east face of Point de la Réchasse. This eventually joins a major route (GR55) climbing from Pont de Croé-Vie. Near this junction stands a large triangular memorial stone erected in memory of two army officers who perished in the mountains. The route to Col de la Vanoise climbs left and soon enters the long windy trough that leads to Refuge du Col de la Vanoise, beyond which descends the well-marked but tiring mule-track to Pralognan.

TOUR DES GLACIERS DE LA VANOISE - SUMMARY OF CIRCUIT

Day 1: Pralognan - Pas de l'Âne - Refuge de la Vallette

Day 2: Refuge de la Vallette - Col d'Aussois - Refuge du Fond d'Aussois

Day 3: Refuge du Fond d'Aussois - Refuge de l'Arpont

Day 4: Refuge de l'Arpont - Refuge du Col de la Vanoise - Pralognan

---

✳   ✳   ✳

TOUR OF THE VANOISE

This longer route, which extends that of the Vanoise glaciers tour outlined above, makes an excellent circuit of the massif in ten to twelve days, providing a series of magnificent experiences and a first-class overview of the National Park, and is arguably the finest expedition open to walkers in the western Graian Alps. In some respects it stands comparison with the much better-known Tour du Mont Blanc, while being not so demanding as the Tour de l'Oisans in the neighbouring Dauphiné Alps. Accommodation with meals provision is available every night in mountain huts or valley hotels and gîtes d'étape. Backpacking is therefore unnecessary, and in summer walkers should be able to tackle the circuit in a two-week holiday without the burden of a heavy rucksack.

Modane makes an obvious starting point. Access is straightforward, and a short but steep approach made on the first day to Refuge de l'Orgère. It is a steep approach too, in forest for much of the way on a trail with numerous junctions, but signposts and waymarks are sufficient to ensure the correct trail is taken. On occasion momentary views are allowed through the trees down to the bed of the valley, while the upward view is almost always concealed by dense forest cover. When rare open meadows are crossed (meadows extravagant with alpine flowers in early summer), the long trench of the Maurienne is revealed off to the right, its southern walling mountains of modest appeal except towards the east where they grow in stature. Those higher peaks will be seen to good effect later on the tour. Half an hour from Orgère a track is crossed near the Pierre Brune chalet. If this is followed to the right it will lead in five minutes or so to an alternative hut, the privately-owned Refuge de l'Aiguille Doran.

From the National Park's Orgère refuge the Tour of the Vanoise crosses the mouth of the Orgère glen and follows the route of the GR5 heading north-east along an undulating trail, at first through forest, then rising over steep hillsides of grass where sheep graze high above the Maurienne, passing one or two isolated stone buildings before descending a little to the grass saddle of Col du Barbier. The col is more a shallow scoop of grass than a proper col, and in mist I was once confused as to whether I'd crossed it, until I reached a junction of trails some way beyond. When visibility is clear, however, the col is a pleasant place to rest with its gentle grass dome nearby overlooking the valley, and a clear hint ahead that the Aussois glen soon to be entered will provide good things to enjoy.

The Aussois glen is a rewarding place to wander. The trail picks its way along the western slopes some way above the Plan d'Aval man-made lake, with its thunderous roar of water floating on the breeze. The cascade seen far below is part of a hydro-electric scheme, the fall bursting from a seventeen-kilometre pipe used to divert water from streams near the head of the Doron gorge. The trail climbs over a rocky bluff, then crosses a broad, open, moorland-like stretch running with streams in the early season, and fine views across the glen to La Dent Parrachée and Pointe de Bellecôte. Beyond this moorland the way veers to the right and eventually drops steeply to a shelf bright with alpenroses, below which a bridge crosses a stream draining the upper glen. There follows a short exposed section of footpath, but this soon gives way to easier terrain and a dirt road that makes a traverse of the eastern hillside. This dirt road passes just below Refuge du Plan Sec, with a narrow trail climbing in a few moments up to it.

On the third stage the route enters the Doron valley which will later provide some of the loveliest of all Vanoise scenery. In order to gain that valley from Plan Sec, GR5 is once again adopted as the best route of access; the same trail as that used by the Tour des Glaciers de la Vanoise on the way to Refuge de l'Arpont. From Plan Sec the dirt road is followed a short way downvalley, then a narrow trail leads away from it across meadows and teetering along the steeply plunging hillside quite 1100 metres above the ribbon of l'Arc. A short gully is climbed by a tightly twisting path, then a wide and easy trail breaks away on a rising traverse followed by switchbacks to an open grass saddle near the ruins of La Turra above the unseen Monolithe de Sardières. Another twisting uphill trail leads to a comfortingly easy traverse of a coombe, beyond which one further saddle is crossed by more chalet ruins at La Loza. By straying a few paces from the trail onto a nearby hillock (2376m), an extensive panorama may be enjoyed which includes both La Grande Casse and La Grande Motte to the north of the Doron gorge, while north-east across the valley the continuing trail of the Tour of the Vanoise can just be seen, as can Termignon nestling at a junction of streams a thousand metres and more below.

After rounding a spur at La Loza the trail cuts across another large combe (snow patches early in the summer) and tops a bluff marked on the map as Montafia. Just beyond this the route curves into the Combe d'Enfer, a charming corrie wild above and vegetated below. On its north-eastern side there's a small farm advertising home-made cheese, drinks and *couchettes* - a remote lodging reminiscent of that experienced by the Victorian pioneers. Now heading north-west the trail lines the mountainside walling the Doron gorge, and on the final approach to the hut crosses numerous streams flowing from the Glaciers de la Vanoise - streams that have cut deep channels in the natural hillside shelf. Cascades pour their silver over a line of cliffs above to the left, while Refuge de l'Arpont sits perched on a narrow levelling of hillside spur projecting from the Dôme de Chasseforêt, gazing south to the far boundary of the Maurienne.

Above Arpont high mountain views increase in grandeur on one of the best of all stages of this ever-delightful tour. Continuing north along the western wall of the Doron gorge, the way hiccups over a series of bluffs and open pastures with the hint of glaciers above, and the dark face of the Pointe de la Réchasse disguising the full extent of the much bigger Grande Casse that rises behind it. Glacial torrents dash through the pastures, and through glens rough with old moraines, while other glens off to the right entice with their own mystique. La Grande Motte shows itself above shadows that tell of the Vallon de la Leisse through which the route will return in four or five days' time, then a sudden descent is made to the head of the Doron gorge and a confluence of streams - that which drains the Vallon de la Leisse itself, and the Torrent de la Rocheure coming from the east. An old dairy farm sprawling on the hillside above to the north is in use as the Refuge d'Entre Deux Eaux. Described as being "long and low, rising at one end to a second storey," the refuge seems hardly to have changed since Janet Adam Smith first stayed there in 1935. Full of character and surrounded by the calm of remote mountain country, "the way to the south lies wide open, letting the sun in at all seasons." (*Mountain Holidays*) But the Tour of the Vanoise chooses to ignore Entre Deux Eaux on this occasion, and instead rises to the south over hillsides thick with shrubs until a more open pastureland is reached which leads easily to the PNV's Refuge du Plan du Lac with its memorable outlook west to the Glaciers de la Vanoise across the depths of the unseen gorge.

Stage five leads to another PNV hut, Refuge du Vallonbrun. It's a varied day's walking of about six hours, heading south from the start and soon passing alongside the sparkling lake of Plan du Lac (spectacular reflected views looking north), then down to Bellecombe at the limit of access for private vehicles on the road from Termignon. At this point a trail cuts off to the east, crossing rolling pastures and soon leading round a huge open pastoral cirque sparsely dotted with simple farms below the Crête de Côte Chaude. The southern end of this cirque comes at the Turra de Termignon, a fine viewpoint on a spur of the Crête de la Turra (an extension of the Côte Chaude crest), which overlooks the deep valley of l'Arc. A small summer-only farmhouse nestles here under the ridge in a dramatic situation. The trail drops past it and continues to descend steeply through natural rock gardens and into dense forest. Coming to a forest track the way eases on what becomes a long eastward traverse; the track eventually giving way to a footpath that climbs to the unmanned Refuge du Cuchet, then resumes its belvedere course below the Grand Roc Noir all the way to Vallonbrun.

From Vallonbrun to Bonneval-sur-Arc is an undemanding stage in which the Tour of the Vanoise explores flower-rich meadows in the bed of the Haute-Maurienne. A short distance upvalley from Refuge du Vallonbrun, by the side of a small chapel, a path descends through pastures, creeps alongside yet more ruined buildings, and continues in a series of steep zig-zags to Le Collet, a small hamlet crowded on the Col de la Madeleine. From here to Bonneval the trail remains in the valley on the north bank of l'Arc, passes through meadows, visits Bessans and Le Villaron (both of which have accommodation), followed by a gentle trail that goes all the way to Bonneval for a night's lodging: hotels in Bonneval and nearby Tralenta, CAF chalet-refuge, and another privately-owned hut (Refuge du Criou) which stands on the mountainside to the south-east.

Bonneval is linked with Val d'Isère by a road that crosses Col de l'Iseran. The Tour of the Vanoise also uses the Iseran, but fortunately manages to avoid the road for all but a very short stretch, in so doing wanders through a charming glen (Vallon de la Lenta) and a narrow rocky gorge crossed in one place by a more or less permanent snow bridge. In order to gain the Vallon de la Lenta a sharp ascent is made of the hillside that rises immediately behind Bonneval. There follows a brief stretch along the Iseran road, then a gentle amble through the Lenta glen where a few scattered stone chalets enjoy a vision of great beauty, gazing back as they do across the Maurienne to the Albaron and Ciamarella group of mountains. A footbridge spanning the Lenta stream brings another trail in from the left - an alternative high-level route used by a variant of the GR5 from near Bessans by way of the unmanned Refuge du Molard and the Vallon amphitheatre.

Soft pastures in Vallon de la Lenta are soon exchanged for the narrow gorge, emerging at its northern end by the road bridge of Pont de la Neige. The road is ignored as a trail continues along the left-hand hillside, rising steadily to the Col de l'Iseran. Here the road is crossed and a narrow trail followed down through a northbound scoop (Vallon de l'Iseran) unhappily littered with ski machinery. However, all this is soon left behind and Val d'Isère reached by a fragrant forest trail; the best way to enter this bustling resort.

Although obviously lacking the kind of tranquillity experienced in mountain refuges adopted for overnight accommodation elsewhere on this tour, it has to be said that for such a busy resort Val d'Isère is not entirely without grace, and it certainly provides an ideal opportunity to restock with provisions for the next stage or two which return the route to the confines of the National Park across Col de la Leisse. However, before the delights of the Vallon de la Leisse may be won, a cross-country trail is taken to the ski grounds of Lac de Tignes and Val Claret. The Vallon de la Tovière, headed by an easy saddle, makes an innocent link, but all who love wild places will scurry past Tignes and Val Claret as fast as their rucksacks allow, in order to regain uncluttered landscapes. Col de la Leisse provides that renewal, although on the slopes of La Grande Motte, soaring high overhead, a string of cableways can be seen, and even in summer skiers, tiny in the distance, weave patterns on snowfields gleaming in the sunshine. Descent into Vallon de la Leisse allows spiritual refreshment through the harsh colours of nature's raw artistry. Bare rock walls, boulders patterned with green and khaki lichen, dusty screes, meandering streams and grey marsh, plus a tarn or two, black when cloud-shadows drift across, take the trail to the tent-shaped Refuge de la Leisse; three buildings, in fact, overlooking the lower western end of the glen that curves out of sight to the left. Edelweiss star the slopes around the hut, and chamois and marmot inhabit the grasslands lower down.

Stage nine of our circuit crosses Col de la Vanoise on the way to Pralognan, but walkers with sufficient days in hand may be seduced into diverting from the main tour in order to explore the delights of the Rocheure glen that runs east to west on the far side of the Vallon de la Leisse's southern wall of mountains. There are two overnight options to consider. The first is Refuge de la Femma, a PNV hut charmingly situated deep inside the Vallon de la Rocheure; the second is Refuge d'Entre Deux Eaux already described on the stage from Arpont to Plan du Lac. If the latter is chosen, the following day's walk to Pralognan will not be quite so demanding, and it also means that the Rocheure glen can be wandered without a rucksack - or at least, with an even lighter 'sack than normal. Assuming this to be the case, leave Refuge de la Leisse and walk down-valley on a good path that remains on the left bank of the stream as far as the humpbacked Pont de Croé-Vie, a stone bridge that takes the main trail to Col de la Vanoise. Ignore the bridge and continue down the left bank as far as Entre Deux Eaux, and there book a bed for the night and leave any non-essential baggage, before continuing beyond the hut to cross the Rocheure torrent a short distance below. Over the stream bear left through the glen to Refuge de la Femma, reached in a little over two hours from Entre Deux Eaux. It's a fine, undemanding walk, with gentle views upvalley, and more challenging views back to the west to be enjoyed on the return. And the hut itself is both comfortable and welcoming, providing an enjoyable interlude.

The continuing tour, crossing Col de la Vanoise, resumes its uphill course on the west side of the Pont de Croé-Vie, twisting among alpenroses, then easing a little among boulders before entering the high, bleak trough that runs between Pointe de la Réchasse and La Grande Casse. This trough can be quite a wind-funnel, but on calm days the almost level trail may be enjoyed at leisure, while severe mountain walls rising on either side add a certain air of wild grandeur. Cushion plants do their best to brighten the way, and a couple of small tarns near the col itself cast reflections of sharp aiguilles once they've lost the ice flows of spring. In three and a half hours from Refuge de la Leisse (a little less from Entre Deux Eaux) you should arrive at the Refuge du Col de la Vanoise, then decide whether to take the main trail down to Pralognan via the north side of the Aiguille de la Vanoise and Lac des Vaches, or follow a longer and less-trodden way past the Lac des Assiettes and below the Glacier and Grande Aiguille de l'Arcelin.

It would be possible for fit walkers to reach Modane in a full day's exercise from

Pralognan by way of Col de Chavière. In certain cases it may be necessary to do so, but it would be a shame to rush this final crossing for there's still plenty on the tour to absorb and enjoy. The alternatives are to either plan an easy day's walking as far as Refuge de Péclet-Polset, or continue over the Chavière but instead of going all the way down to Modane, spend a last night in Refuge de l'Orgère. Should you have a train to catch next morning, it would still be feasible to do so after breakfast at Orgère, for it'll only take a couple of hours to reach the station from there.

Leaving Pralognan the trail to Péclet-Polset goes through forest for a while on the east bank of the river, then crosses to the other side at Pont de Gerlan. A track is then followed to Les Prioux, a small hamlet with accommodation in the Chalet-Refuge le Repoju. Immediately beyond Les Prioux it becomes necessary to walk for a short distance along the valley road as far as an unsurfaced parking area near Pont de la Pêche. Back on the west bank once more the route follows a track for some way through pastures with bare mountains rising on either side, but with growing views of snowfield and glacier towards the head of the valley. The track narrows to footpath, and the way rises steadily from one natural step to the next until rolling grassland gives way to more savage terrain. And there, above the trail to the right, stands Refuge de Péclet-Polset.

South of the refuge stony mounds and scree-runnels, bony hollows and boulder tips make an uncompromising scene. But there are also poor patches of grass and a few small pools to brighten an otherwise drab landscape. Col de Chavière is reached in less than an hour and a half from the hut. A narrow saddle in a sharp crest of stone, it is without question the finest true col on the Tour of the Vanoise. Marked by a large cairn, both sides plunge steeply to scree and rock, and on the proverbial clear day views are impressive. To the north-east Mont Blanc can be seen, while to the south-west Mont Thabor and major summits of the Écrins massif swell against the horizon.

Descending scree at first, the southern side of the col soon leads to a choice of routes. One leads down the right-hand side of the Tête Noir's dividing bluff into the glen drained by the Ruisseau de St Bernard, the other traces the east flank of Tête Noir before dropping steeply to Refuge de l'Orgère. Both routes combine in forest to the south and descend directly to Modane in the Maurienne.

To summarise, the Tour of the Vanoise makes a very fine circuit; not too demanding but scenically delightful throughout. Accommodation is plentiful, trails good, waymarks sufficient without being intrusive. But as the Vanoise National Park is extremely popular during the main summer season, walkers intending to tackle this route, especially from mid-July to mid-August, are advised at least to telephone ahead to reserve places in mountain huts. The National Park authority provides a reservation facility for walkers planning to use refuges within its jurisdiction, and the guidebook (see below) gives details of this service. Note that snow often lies across some of the higher trails well into July, and caution is then advised.

```
┌─────────────────────────────────────────────────────────────────┐
│        TOUR OF THE VANOISE - SUMMARY OF CIRCUIT                  │
```

TOUR OF THE VANOISE - SUMMARY OF CIRCUIT

Day 1:   Modane - Refuge de l'Orgère

Day 2:   Refuge de l'Orgère - Col du Barbier - Refuge du Plan Sec

Day 3:   Refuge du Plan Sec - Refuge de l'Arpont

Day 4:   Refuge de l'Arpont - Refuge du Plan du Lac

Day 5:   Refuge du Plan du Lac - Turra de Termignon - Refuge du Vallonbrun

Day 6:   Refuge du Vallonbrun - Bessans - Le Villaron - Bonneval-sur-Arc

Day 7:   Bonneval - Col de l'Iseran - Val d'Isère

Day 8:   Val d'Isère - Pas de la Tovière - Col de la Leisse - Refuge de la Leisse

Day 9:   Refuge de la Leisse - Col de la Vanoise - Pralognan

   or: Refuge de la Leisse - Refuge de la Femma - Refuge d'Entre Deux Eaux

Day 9a: Refuge d'Entre Deux Eaux - Col de la Vanoise - Pralognan

Day 10:   Pralognan - Refuge de Péclet-Polset

   or: Pralognan - Col de Chavière - Refuge de l'Orgère

Day 11:   Refuge de Péclet-Polset - Col de Chavière - Modane

✳   ✳   ✳

THE EASTERN GRAIANS

To all intents and purposes the Eastern Graians mean the Gran Paradiso and its national park, a rewarding area that comprises a substantial block of crystalline mountains lying south of the Valle d'Aosta across which glorious visions of Mont Blanc, Grand Combin and assorted giants of the Pennine Alps are revealed to the fortunate wanderer.

The Gran Paradiso National Park boasts no less than fifty-seven glaciers and dozens of peaks in excess of 3000 metres, while the mountain after which it is named is, at 4061 metres, the highest entirely in Italy and, incidentally, is generally reckoned to be the easiest of all Alpine four thousanders to climb. Created in 1922 it was the country's first national park, a landmark in the protection of wildlife in general and the ibex in particular. Formerly a royal hunting ground for Vittorio Emanuel II, some 2000 hectares were ceded to the State in 1919 by one of the hunter king's successors, and since the park's inception three years later the area has expanded to include some 70,000 hectares, or more than 700 square kilometres. Within the park's boundaries roam 5000 ibex, around 8000 chamois and 10,000 marmots, so it will be a rare summer day's walking here that fails to conjure sightings of wildlife.

The range spreads eastward from the French frontier to the southern curve of

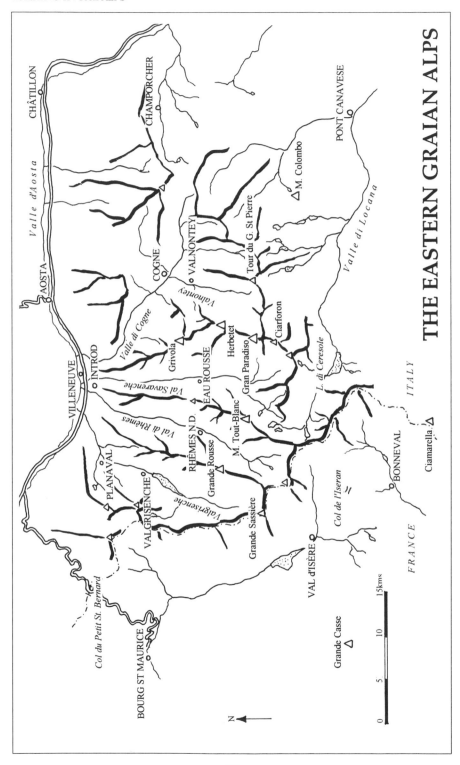

THE EASTERN GRAIAN ALPS

Valle d'Aosta where the Dora Baltea sweeps out of the mountains toward the Po, its northern limit being defined by the Valle d'Aosta itself where French has been the official language since 1561, its southern by the Valle di Susa dominated by Turin. This is a sizeable chunk of country, but so far as this chapter is concerned we will concentrate only on the central block, and the four main valleys on the northern side. Naming from west to east these are Val Grisenche, Val di Rhêmes, Val Savarenche and the Valle di Cogne with its lovely tributary glen, Valnontey. Of these, only Val Grisenche lies outside the national park's boundary. The southern valleys may be less popular, the scenery not quite so dramatic as on the northern side, but the landscape is somewhat wilder and with trails that one could enjoy in peaceful isolation from the crowds.

Naturally Valle d'Aosta holds the key to all vehicular approach from the northern side of the mountains, with public transport focused on the old Roman town of Aosta itself (once known as the 'Rome of the Alps'), although it must be said that some of the bus services to more remote areas are either greatly reduced or suspended outside the high summer months of July and August. Mid-summer is exceedingly popular in the honeypot areas, and trails and huts can be uncomfortably crowded. However, in June and September it's easy enough to find routes to wander in solitude, when the true delights of the area can be properly absorbed, although as in most regions of the high Alps snow conditions may prevent some of the loftier routes from being tackled until late June or early July.

Hotels, campsites, several mountain huts and a number of bivouac shelters on the northern side of the ridge that divides the autonomous region of Valle d'Aosta from Piedmont, provide a range of accommodation to suit most tastes. With some 450 kilometres of footpaths to choose from it will be seen that countless permutations of walks exist to suit activists of every persuasion. Trails are in the main clearly defined with waymarks and occasional signposts, including a number of old mule-tracks created for Vittorio Emanuel's hunting parties, and two multi-day routes marked on the map suggest ways of exploring the region in the best possible manner. The first of these is the Grande Traversata del Gran Paradiso (GTGP) which, after crossing dividing ridges on the northern side, then makes a high-level traverse of the southern flanks; the second is known as the Alta Via della Valle d'Aosta No 2, making an eastbound traverse from La Thuile below the Col du Petit St Bernard to Champorcher. (Alta Via No 1, the so-called 'Giants' Trail', which makes a traverse of the mountains north of Valle d'Aosta, is mentioned in the Pennine Alps chapter.)

In the following pages an outline of both long routes will be provided, following a study of walking prospects in the four north-flowing valleys, beginning first with Val Grisenche.

Val Grisenche

Flowing roughly parallel to the Franco-Italian border, this is the least-visited of the four valleys; partly because it lies outside the national park's boundary and therefore receives less publicity than the others, partly because it is farther away from Aosta than any of its neighbours and partly, I suppose, because it has the least amount of accommodation available to the visitor. Among its scattered hamlets not one amounts to anything resembling a resort, and the road that climbs into the glen is rather tortuous and narrow, managing to veil its true nature until the traveller has made his commitment to enter. However, Val Grisenche is certainly not without its charms, either in scenic values or walking possibilities, and prospective visitors attracted by unsung corners of the Alps will accept these reasons as being sufficient in themselves to go there, while those coming under their own steam from France will see it as the first valley to explore when travelling down Valle d'Aosta from Courmayeur and the Mont Blanc tunnel. With no obvious display of its appeal from the insignificant entrance at Leverogne, Val Grisenche nevertheless leads to much quiet beauty, and few who appreciate nature in the raw will be disappointed by their findings there.

In its lower reaches the valley is narrow and heavily wooded, but as you head south-westward so it widens to a few rough pastures and small, huddled hamlets, stone-built and little changed by the centuries. Planaval lies below a tributary glen through which a trail visits a ruined hamlet, with a side-path climbing to the blue-green Lago di Fondo, while the main trail continues up alongside the Château Blanc glacier before crossing a glacier pass traversed by both Alta Via 2 and the GTGP long distance routes. On the far side of the col, and some way below it, stands Rifugio Deffeyes with several tarns nearby, and another trail cutting back over Passo Alto into the Sopra glen by which a two-day circuit could be achieved.

Another major trail leading from Planaval strikes upvalley, rising on a long slant across the left-hand mountainside to Lago di San Grato which has a small stone chapel at its southern end. Several trails break away from this tarn, one of these leading to a crossing of the frontier ridge at Col du Mont, on the French side of which lies the privately-owned Refuge la Motte. Returning from this col to Val Grisenche a good path descends to a service road and the bed of the valley, passing on the way a memorial that recalls the death by avalanche during the last war, of German officers and their prisoners who were being forced to carry supplies up to the col.

Upvalley beyond Planaval there are more hamlets and clusters of simple buildings. Valgrisenche itself boasts a foodstore and a post office, and from it a walking route that heads up the true right bank of the valley before climbing to Rifugio de l'Épée. Above this hut Col de la Finestra (or Col Fenêtre) provides a high route into Val di Rhêmes. Continuing beyond Valgrisenche village you come to Bonne, set on a ledge overlooking the dammed Lago di Beauregard, the only unfortunate scar in the valley. This long ribbon of reservoir was unwanted and deeply resented by the local population when it was created in the 1960s, because it drowned the hamlet of Fornet. Resentment lingers on as, apparently, it has not yet been used to capacity.

After Bonne a service road climbs high above the lake through scarlet masses of rosebay willowherb, then descends to the main Dora di Valgrisenche below the buildings of Grand Alpe and the trail junction for Col du Mont. A farm building nearby has been adapted to serve as a simple bar/restaurant. Vehicles are not allowed beyond this point, and only footpaths and farm tracks score into the wild, upper region that entices from the south.

Here Val Grisenche rises under a glacial cirque topped by the Grande Sassière, where the Ghiacciaio di Gliairetta sweeps across the cirque's header wall which carries the international frontier in an eastward kink - *ghiacciaio*, incidentally, being the Italian word for glacier. This upper part of the valley is an untamed delight. Laced with numerous streams and waterfalls, and with the Italian Alpine Club's (CAI) Rifugio Mario Bezzi set at 2284 metres on the right bank of the Dora di Valgrisenche at Alp Vaudet, the lonely uplands may be explored at leisure. Apart from glacier crossings and summit routes that lie outside the scope of this book, more walking trails entice across both of the valley's limiting walls. On the western side Col du Lac Noir and Col du Rocher Blanc, the two separated by Point du Rocher Blanc, offer ways over the frontier to the valley of Isère below Tignes, while the east wall has a crossing point at Col le Bassac Derè leading to the upper Val di Rhêmes and Rifugio Benevolo. Another worthwhile outing from the Bezzi hut, a local there-and-back route but on a poorly defined footpath, takes you across the meadows of Piano di Vaudet and up to the tarn of Lago di San Martino north-east of the hut.

The foregoing paragraphs offered just a few suggestions of walking possibilities in the valley. There are, of course, many others, including a circular tour made by adopting existing paths, or yet more ridge crossings to west or east. By linking two or more cols demanding circuits show themselves as distinct possibilities, while activists with scrambling experience will never run short of ideas for collecting summits with outstanding panoramas.

Val di Rhêmes

Gained by road from Villeneuve, which has a useful tourist office, the next valley to the east of Val Grisenche is Val di Rhêmes, a broader, more open glen than its neighbour, whose river more or less defines the national park's western boundary. A little longer than Val Grisenche, there are clear signs that outside money is being spent on the renovation of several hamlets in a tasteful way. There's camping to be had in Rhêmes St Georges, and modest hotel accommodation in Rhêmes Notre-Dame, a small but pretty village with a useful foodstore, while set upon a grassy bluff near the head of the valley Rifugio Benevolo attracts plenty of day visitors by virtue of a short and easy (and extremely attractive) approach from the roadhead at Thumel.

Whilst there are walks to be had in the valley's lower and middle sections, the main concentration here should be focused on the Benevolo hut. Around it green pastures are buckled into hillocks and hollows backed in the south by jutting cliffs and crags, and dominated by the impressive rock tower of Granta Parei (3387m). The actual head of the valley is blocked by a low amphitheatre - a scene of ice and snow, small peaks, big rubble-strewn moraines, and level pastures pitted with marmot burrows. The French border traces the cirque crest, beyond which lies the Vanoise National Park, while to east and west projecting ridges have their own appeal.

One highly recommended day walk from the Benevolo hut makes a circuit of Truc Santa Elena, a rocky hill rising a short distance away to the south. On tackling this circuit one has an evolving variety of scenery to enjoy, from gentle pastures to rough scree bowls, from a close view of glaciers and churning moraines to big rock walls and waterfalls, boulder tips and small tarns with alpine flowers at their edges. On a beautiful September day under perfect walking conditions I had this circuit to myself, other than the marmots, that is, while around the hut dozens of visitors sat blinking in the sunlight.

Other possibilities inevitably involve the traverse of walling ridges. Although Alta Via 2 avoids the higher crossings here (it tackles cols on either side of Rhêmes Notre-Dame farther downstream), the true mountain wanderer will surely not be deterred by a rich selection of cols above the 3000 metre mark, most of which are clearly defined and in all but unseasonal weather should be easy enough to follow, whilst still being demanding enough to provide a sense of achievement at the end of the day. To the east of Rifugio Benevolo the walling ridge divides Val di Rhêmes from the upper Val Savarenche. Three high cols here offer linking routes, and since two huts lie on the far side of the ridge, on the Nivolet plateau, scattered with lakes and astride the borders of Aosta and Piedmont, more circular tours become obvious temptations.

Val Savarenche

Road access to this valley from Valle d'Aosta is the same as that for Val di Rhêmes until Introd, from which handsome village superb westward views show the Italian face of Mont Blanc shining in the morning light. Val di Rhêmes and Val Savarenche are similar in their lower reaches, both being narrow, heavily wooded V-clefts that open to green pastures. Val Savarenche is a little wilder than its neighbour, though, and with the Gran Paradiso itself forming the main attraction, shared equally with the next glen to the east, Valnontey. This dividing ridge is, however, not solely of mountain interest on account of Gran Paradiso, for the northern end proudly boasts the shapely Grivola (3969m), and there's also the Gran Serra, Herbetet and several other notable peaks that draw the eye with their graceful forms. Several hamlets are spaced along the bed of the valley, all of which have some form of accommodation. There's camping to be had just south of Creton, a wooded campsite (Camping Gran Paradiso) a little further upstream on the true right bank of the river, and another more open site at the roadhead at Pont, while no less than four huts provide accommodation on the walling mountains: Albergo Savoia and neighbouring Rifugio Citta di Chivasso set upon the Nivolet plateau at the extreme south-west end of the valley, and Rifugio Chabod and the ever busy Vittorio Emanuel rifugio on the east flank below the glaciers of the Gran Paradiso.

Not surprisingly this is one of the busiest of all valleys in the national park, but since there are no cableways or other forms of mechanical aid, the only way to see the best on offer is to leave the road and take to the footpaths, a number of which date back to the days of King Vittorio Emanuel II who kept a good part of the valley as a hunting reserve, many of whose mule-trails remain to this day.

Once again walkers' passes on both flanks of the valley provide opportunities to move from one side of the walling ridges to the next, but there are also some fine walks to be achieved at mid-height along the steep hillsides. Probably the very best is that which links the Chabod and Vittorio Emanuel huts. It leads through some rough country, with rocks and boulders and glacial slabs, and with the tongues of glaciers hanging just above, their streams dashing down in long ribbons. Ibex can often be spied from this trail, and in early summer alpine flowers add much to the walk. The Chabod hut is reached in two and a half hours from the road by a fine walk through larchwoods and a green upper corrie backed by the Herbetet-Gran Paradiso ridge, followed by a more stony landscape with a final pull up a spur that provides a magnificent viewpoint. Above the hut an entertaining path climbs to the Col Gran Neyron below the Herbetet - but has a *via ferrata* descent before linking with another trail to cross Col Lauson into the Valnontey. The route to Rifugio Vittorio Emanuel, however, breaks away from the Chabod path below the hut and makes a roughly south-bound undulating traverse, remaining about 800 metres or more above the valley.

The most popular route for climbers on the Gran Paradiso begins at the Vittorio Emanuel hut, and this *voie normale* follows more or less the route taken by the team that made the first ascent in 1860 (J.J. Cowell and W. Dundas, with the Chamonix guides, Michel Payot and Jean Tairraz). The hut itself is an incongruous building once described as "reminiscent of an aircraft hangar with its ugly aluminium roof". Janet Adam Smith called it "a gigantic aluminium dog-kennel stridently out of keeping with the setting of pasture, rock and snow." With a guardian in residence between late April and the end of September, it can sleep almost 150, while the old hut nearby can take another forty. In 1924 Dorothy Pilley and her husband, I.A. Richards, spent a night there prior to making an ascent of Gran Paradiso, but they were not happy with what they found on arrival: "The hut...was a disgrace to humanity", she wrote. "Only the most confirmed of Alpine Romanticism could overlook the polluted state of the environs. A slope of garbage tippings fell from the doorstep into a rancid litle lake...With all nature in their favour, with sun and wind and water to keep the site clean, it is sad that people should mark their presence with filth and stench." (*Climbing Days*) A decade later and Janet Adam Smith also complained of a dump of tins and rubbish, but happily the hut and its surroundings were soon improved, for in 1939 R.L.G. Irving was able to describe it as "a delectable place". Irving of course was an Alpine romantic, but he was not blind to the squalor created by men in the mountains. Yet the Vittorio Emanuel clearly charmed him. This is what he says about it in *The Alps*.

> "This hut is perfectly situated at the upper end of the pastures, above the Moncorvé Glacier. [The glacier has since shrunk considerably, and now lies some way above the hut.] Here the chuckling of hens and the tinkling of cow-bells remind one pleasantly of food which has never been inside a rucksack; across the glacier are four peaks, of which the two furthest to the right are irresistibly attractive, one, the Becca di Monciair from the loveliness of its form, the other, the Punta di Broglio because it makes one long to find out if its highest point is accessible at all."

Both these huts are busily occupied in summer, and the paths to them will invariably be heavily trodden when the weather is fine. But despite this popularity they must be recommended on account of the full glory of the mountains in view. To spend time in the Gran Paradiso National Park and to see some of the finest scenery it has to offer, one must put solitude aside for a while and absorb the delights of nature so generously displayed.

Valle di Cogne

"There is no place which more persuasively calls back the visitor who wants what the Alps themselves have to offer, rather than what has been imported into them by modern life," wrote Irving about Cogne. That was pre-war. Lately Cogne has absorbed some of what he called "modern life", yet it remains a very modest and attractive resort by comparison with many another in the Western Alps; a true mountain village, not a mongrel or hybrid.

The Valle di Cogne is a long valley at the very eastern end of the national park, curving in an exaggerated sweep to the south-east and carrying the park's boundary with it. Cogne is the only place of any size, and is located at the widest part of the valley, "in a fair open basin of meadows with the Paradis gleaming occasionally out of a chaos of cloud", and with the tributary glen of Valnontey draining from the south-west. Looking along the full length of this glen from Cogne, one sees the central block of an amphitheatre of ice-bound peaks cleft by the Col de Grand Crou, "a real depression approached by a glacier that does not let you forget its hidden depths and confronts you at the end with a wall which you prefer to be decorated in snow white rather than ice blue."

This amphitheatre, or cirque, is a wildly impressive piece of mountain architecture on a par with the Cirque de Gavarnie in the Pyrenees, the skyline in places some two thousand metres above the valley floor, and with a tremendous frozen cascade of an icefall held in suspension from the Gran Paradiso's lofty ridge. Seen from the valley floor it's an astonishing sight. But better still there is a trail that runs along the midriff of the western mountainside, from which one gains an even better perspective. That trail begins at another of the hunter king's former lodges, the Rifugio Vittorio Sella.

Named after the distinguished mountain photographer and founder of the Italian Alpine Club (his photographs display both artistic and technical perfection - especially those taken during a reconnaissance of K2 in the Karakoram in 1909), the Sella hut is easily reached in a little over two hours from Valnontey village. Just above the hut the largest herd of ibex in all the Alps may be seen during the early morning and evening, but at almost any time of day small groups or individuals may be spied grazing on the nearby hillsides.

The path which provides the fine view of the Valnontey cirque mentioned above, strikes away from the Sella refuge and heads roughly southward along a shelf of pasture containing a small tarn or two, then over boulder slopes before narrowing as a tight ledge, exposed in places, high above the valley. After digging into a knuckle indent, the way then rises to a high point about fifteen minutes above l'Herbetet (two hours from Rifugio Sella), a small stone building owned by the national park authorities. It is from this high point that the classic view is enjoyed. It is, quite simply, one of the great Alpine views; an astonishing collection of hanging glaciers, their numerous torrents falling in ribbon cascades down the walls of the cirque just to the south. A similar view, but from a slightly different perspective, may be enjoyed from Alpe Money (pronounced Monay) on the opposite side of the valley. This pasture shelf, it has been said, provides a most satisfying point from which to contemplate the whole ridge from the Grivola to Gran Paradiso, while at the same time giving a climber sufficient excuse to spend a week's holiday based there without exhausting the range of routes available.

The village of Valnontey makes a good valley base for explorations in this glen. There's a huge car park that is almost empty overnight, a foodstore, small hotels and a couple of campsites, and at the foot of the trail to Rifugio Sella, a noted alpine garden with some 1500 plant species, that is worth an hour of anyone's time.

Above the barrack-like Sella hut a one-time mule-trail heads up to Col Lauson (3296m) for a connection with Val Savarenche. Another climbs behind the hut to Col di Vermia, while a third leads to Col della Rossa (3195m) for more incredible views, this time including some of the giants of the Pennine Alps beyond the deep and sunny Valle d'Aosta.

Flowing parallel to, and east of, Valnontey is another tributary of the Valle di Cogne. With Lillaz at its entrance, Valle di Valeille is wild and uninhabited, as is the glen to the east of that, Vallone di Bardoney. The two are connected by a walker's route over Col dell'Arolla, and by another at the northern end of the dividing ridge.

✳   ✳   ✳

GRANDE TRAVERSATA DEL GRAN PARADISO

Of the two main multi-day walking routes across the Gran Paradiso National Park, the GTGP crosses higher passes and remains closer to the watershed ridge than does the Alta Via 2. It also makes a traverse of a lengthy section of the Piedmont flank east of the Nivolet plateau. Until the route crosses to the south side of the range, overnights are spent in manned rifugios or village inns, but the Piedmont flank has a few bivouac huts where, if used, walkers will need to be self-sufficient with regard to food. The walk begins, as does the Alta Via, at La Thuile, a crowded little village on the road between Courmayeur and the Col du Petit St Bernard. The first crossing, however, could cause problems for inexperienced (or unequipped) mountain walkers, in which case the route should be joined at Planaval in Val Grisenche.

Heading south from La Thuile the trail wanders through the Rutor glen before climbing to Rifugio Deffeyes in four hours. Above the hut the way edges the Ghiacciaio del Rutor and crosses the Pas de Planaval (3010m). This is a glacier crossing, and local information urges the use of rope, ice axe and crampons. But once off ice the route eases down through a hanging valley to reach the hamlet of Planaval in Val Grisenche.

It is at Planaval that the GTGP and Alta Via 2 part company. Our route strikes south-westward along the left-hand mountainside, and after dropping to the valley bed at Surier, heads upvalley to Rifugio Bezzi, and from there crosses Col le Bassac Derè, before descending through the Goletta glen to reach Rifugio Benevolo at the head of Val di Rhêmes.

Continuing the eastward trend the next pass crossing is that of Col di Nivoletta, which brings the trail down to the Savoia and Chivasso huts in that lovely lake-adorned plateau at the head of Val Savarenche, with views to the Gran Paradiso's glaciers. A minor road twists its way from the south, but the onward route ignores this and, entering Piedmont, makes a long eastward traverse linking numerous alp clusters above the Valle dell'Orco (sometimes known as Valle di Locana) which carries the southernmost limit of the national park. Along this section of the GTGP there are four bivouac huts (Giraudo, Ivrea, Revelli and Davito), and two rifugios (Pontese and Pocchiola-Menghello) - the last-named of which lies just south of the trail by a dammed lake. The trail eventually descends into the Valle di Campiglia, a tributary glen that spills into the larger Valle Soana, itself a tributary of the Orco.

GRANDE TRAVERSATA DEL GRAN PARADISO - ROUTE SUMMARY

Day 1:   La Thuile - Rifugio A. Deffeyes

Day 2:   Rifugio A. Deffeyes - Pas de Planaval - Planaval

Day 3:   Planaval - Surier - Rifugio M. Bezzi

Day 4:   Rifugio M. Bezzi - Col le Bassac Derè - Rifugio Benevolo

Day 5:   Rifugio Benevolo - Col di Nivoletta - Albergo Savoia
         (or Rif Citta di Chivasso)

Day 6:   Albergo Savoia - Col della Terra - Col della Porta -
         Rifugio Pontese

Day 7:   Rifugio Pontese - Bocchetta di Valsoera - Col le Valletta -
         Campiglia

---

*   *   *

ALTA VIA DELLA VALLE D'AOSTA NO 2

Unlike the GTGP, Alta Via 2 remains on the Valle d'Aosta flank of the mountains and links one valley after another by way of cols that are mostly situated halfway along the transverse ridges. These crossings actually reveal a better perspective than is sometimes shown from the higher cols, for one can view the larger mountains to the south at a distance, and thereby gain the full visual contrast of summit snows and deep valley greenery without the foreshortening effect occasionally experienced on GTGP crossings. It's a fine week-long route, with overnights spent in a combination of mountain huts and village hotels. Camping is also a possibility, but it should be borne in mind that within the national park wild camping is forbidden. There are campsites in several villages on the route, and it's possible to restock with food supplies once or twice along the way.

The first two stages from La Thuile to Planaval are the same as that taken by the GTGP, thereafter the two routes go their own separate ways. Alta Via 2 has two options; one follows the valley road south to Valgrisenche village, and is better suited to walkers who arrived in Planaval with plenty of time and energy left and who choose the latter village for their second overnight stay, while the alternative traces a route along the upper forest line on the east side of the valley. The two options merge a little north of the Épée hut where the route then climbs to the narrow Col de la Finestra at 2840 metres. The descent to Rhêmes Notre-Dame is a steep one of about two hours.

Leaving Val di Rhêmes the Alta Via adopts a pleasant route over wooded hillsides and open pastures to gain Col de l'Entrelor (3007m) in about three and a half hours. From this point glaciers of the Herbetet-Paradiso ridge shine across the depths of Val Savarenche, while a few blue tarns sparkle in the Nampio glen just below. An undemanding descent leads down to Eaux Rousses (Eau Rousse) on the left bank of the Savara stream, with the next col on the route being visible virtually every step of the way.

Col Lauson at 3296 metres, is the highest crossing by far on this traverse, and with five hours needed for the sixteen hundred metre climb from Eaux Rousses. At the col the landscape changes dramatically and the initial descent is safeguarded with fixed cables and chains. It then eases for the walk down to Rifugio Vittorio Sella which is in view for much of the descent. The alternative is to continue down to Valnontey, but it is better to stay at the hut in order to watch the great herds of ibex at dusk and the following dawn.

There follows a long valley stretch, descending from the Sella hut to Valnontey and Cogne, then on to Lillaz. Beyond this last village the path climbs through the Vallone di Urtier, then after crossing a brow it levels in a fertile upper alp area before climbing again to the final col, the Finestra di Champorcher (2826m). On the east side of this pass and about two hundred and fifty metres below, stands Rifugio Miserin by the lake of the same name. Champorcher, the end of the route, is a morning's walk away.

ALTA VIA DELLA VALLE D'AOSTA NO 2 - ROUTE SUMMARY

Day 1: La Thuile - Rifugio A. Deffeyes

Day 2: Rifugio A. Deffeyes - Pas de Planaval - Planaval
   (or Valgrisenche)

Day 3: Planaval (or Valgrisenche) - Col de la Finestra -
   Rhêmes Notre-Dame

Day 4: Rhêmes Notre-Dame - Col de l'Entrelor - Eaux Rousses

Day 5: Eaux Rousses - Col Lauson - Rifugio V. Sella (or Valnontey)

Day 6: Rifugio V. Sella - Cogne - Finestra di Champorcher -
   Rifugio Miserin

Day 7: Rifugio Miserin - Champorcher

✳   ✳   ✳

Finally, before leaving the Graians, mention should be made of an eight- or nine-day route for experienced mountain walkers which links Pralognan in the Vanoise National Park with Cogne at the foot of the Gran Paradiso. This route, described in reverse in Stefano Ardito's *Walking & Climbing in the Alps*, has one small glacier section to contend with on the crossing of 3109 metre Col du Carro, and uses huts on all stages bar one, when a village hotel provides overnight accommodation in

Eaux Rousses in Val Savarenche. The basic route outline is given below.

A TRAVERSE OF THE GRAIAN ALPS - ROUTE SUMMARY

Day 1: Pralognan - Col de la Vanoise - Refuge d'Entre Deux Eaux

Day 2: Refuge d'Entre Deux Eaux - Refuge du Plan du Lac - Refuge du Cuchet

Day 3: Refuge du Cuchet - Refuge du Vallonbrun - Bessans - Bonneval-sur-Arc

Day 4: Bonneval-sur-Arc - l'Écot - Refuge du Carro

Day 5: Refuge du Carro - Col du Carro - Col di Nivolet - Rifugio Citta di Chivasso

Day 6: Rifugio Citta di Chivasso - Pont - Eaux Rousses

Day 7: Eaux Rousses - Col Lauson - Rifugio V. Sella

Day 8: Rifugio V. Sella - Valnontey - Cogne

---

*   *   *

THE GRAIAN ALPS

Location:
Straddling the Franco-Italian border south of Mont Blanc. The Western Graians, which include the mountains of Beaufortain and Vanoise, are in the *département* of Savoie, while the Eastern Graians, including the Gran Paradiso, fall within Piedmont and the autonomous region of Aosta.

Principal valleys:
The Tarentaise (valley of l'Isère), with the tributaries of Ponturin, Champagny, Pralognan and Chavière, and the Maurienne (l'Arc) whose main tributaries are the Doron, Ribon and Avérole, are the main valleys of the Western Graians. In the Eastern (Italian) Graians, Valle d'Aosta, Val Grisenche, Val di Rhêmes, Val Savarenche, Valnontey, Valle di Cogne, Valle Soana, and Valle di Locana (also known as the Valle dell'Orco).

Principal peaks:
Gran Paradiso (4061m), La Grivola (3969m), La Grande Casse (3855m), Mont Pourri (3779m), Herbetet (3778m), Pointe de Charbonnel (3752m), La Grande Motte (3653m)

Centres:
Pralognan-la-Vanoise, Val d'Isère and Bonneval-sur-Arc are, perhaps, the most useful in the French Graians, while Cogne is a small resort well-placed for walks in the shadow of the highest peaks in the Gran Paradiso National Park. Rhêmes Notre Dame and Valnontey are even smaller and with limited accommodation, but with fine walking country close at hand.

Huts:
In excess of 60 huts or bivouacs cover the range, with 42 alone within the area of the Vanoise National Park, and more than 20 in the Eastern Graians. Most huts belong to the French or Italian Alpine Clubs, or to the National Park authorities.

Access:

The Western Graians are accessible by train (via Chambéry) with stations at Moutier, Landry, Bourg St-Maurice and Modane. Nearest useful airport is at Lyon.

As for the Italian side, rail access with Turin (via Chambéry and Modane), Lanzo and Cuorgne for the southern valleys, and Aosta for the northern side. Nearest international airport is Turin.

Maps:

Massif et Parc National de la Vanoise and *Massifs du Mont Blanc et Beaufortain*, published by Didier & Richard at a scale of 1:50,000, cover virtually all the Western Graians, while IGN cover the same areas in their TOP25 series of 1:25,000 scale maps. The Italian valleys are adequately covered by a series of 1:25,000 sheets published by IGC (Instituto Geografico Centrale). The Austrian publishing house, Kompass, also produces a series covering the Italian Graians at 1:50,000. Studio FMB of Bologna has published a good 1:50,000 sheet covering the Gran Paradiso National Park, complete with walking routes and rifugios prominently marked. This is entitled *Gran Paradiso*.

Guidebooks:

Walking in the Tarentaise & Beaufortain Alps by J.W. Akitt (Cicerone Press) gives a good selection of day and multi-day walks in these two regions of the Western Graians.

Walking the Alpine Parks of France & Northwest Italy by Marcia R. Lieberman (Cordee/The Mountaineers) details a number of walks, including multi-day treks, in both the Vanoise and Gran Paradiso National Parks.

Tour of the Vanoise by Kev Reynolds (Cicerone Press) describes the 10-12 day circuit outlined above, and also provides details of other multi-day tours and traverses within the vicinity of the Vanoise National Park.

Long Distance Walks in the Gran Paradiso by J.W. Akitt (Cicerone Press) is a guide to the long distance walks of the Gran Paradiso including the Via Alta (2 and 4) and the traverse of the Gran Paradiso.

Walking in Italy's Gran Paradiso by Gillian Price (Cicerone Press) is a guide to some shorter walks in the Gran Paradiso and its rugged mountains, desolate valleys and wildlife.

Walking the French Alps: GR5 by Martin Collins (Cicerone Press) is a guide to the classic long distance route from Lake Geneva to the Mediterranean, which includes a traverse of the Western Graians.

Walking the GR5: Lake Geneva to Mont-Blanc (Robertson McCarta) is a translation of the French topoguides published originally by the FFRP. The title is misleading, for the book describes the GR5 as far as Modane, and thereby includes a crossing of the Western Graians, as does the Collins guide above. Includes useful sections of IGN maps, although the route is not always accurately marked.

Other reading:

Classic Walks of the World by Walt Unsworth *(Oxford* Illustrated Press) has a chapter by Martin Collins that describes a crossing of the Vanoise region from Landry to Modane.

Classic Walks in the Alps by Kev Reynolds (Oxford Illustrated Press) includes a chapter by Andrew Harper describing a 7-8 day walk along the north flank of the Gran Paradiso from Ste Foy-Tarentaise to Champorcher. Much of this route follows Alta Via 2.

Walking & Climbing in the Alps by Stefano Ardito (Swan Hill Press 1995) contains a chapter describing an east-west traverse route between Cogne and Pralognan.

The Outdoor Traveler's Guide to The Alps by Marcia R. Lieberman (Stewart, Tabori & Chang, New York) naturally includes detail of selected valleys and centres in the

Graian Alps.

The Alps by R.L.G. Irving (Batsford, 1939) provides a romantic view of the Graians.

Mountain Holidays by Janet Adam Smith (Dent, 1946/The Ernest Press, 1997) is a charming account of pre-war holidays in Scotland and the Alps, which includes large sections devoted to the Graians. Evocative of an era long-gone, but with the surprise that some places have barely changed.

Climbing Days by Dorothy Pilley (Bell and Sons, 1935) is devoted to mountain adventures in assorted ranges, including the Graians.

Journals of Excursions in the Alps by W. Brockedon (James Duncan, 1833). Principally a painter, Brockedon traversed the Alps no less than 58 times on research, and crossed more than 40 passes. This book is an account of his travels in 1824 and 1825, which included the Graians.

Scrambles in the Eastern Graians, 1878-1897 by George Yeld (Fisher-Unwin, 1900) is a pioneer's view of the range. One-time editor of the Alpine Journal, Yeld became something of an authority on the Graians.

※   ※   ※

Col de la Seigne, on the Franco-Italian frontier, provides
a spectacular view of Mont Blanc

4: THE MONT BLANC RANGE
Including the Chablais, Faucigny & Dents du Midi

For a region so well-endowed with big mountains and glaciers, the Mont Blanc range is surprisingly compact, measuring less than forty kilometres by fifteen, and with the summit of Mont Blanc itself rising to 4807 metres as the highest point in Europe west of the Caucasus. That dome of snow and ice is attended by a large number of other peaks. Frison-Roche lists some 400 summits, which include among them Mont Maudit, Mont Blanc du Tacul, the Dent du Géant, Verte and Drus, the Grandes Jorasses and Mont Dolent, each with its own challenge to climbers and fenced in by a barrier of slender granite aiguilles that provides the massif with its own personal identity. On the northern side they bristle above Chamonix and the valley of the Arve, while the more sturdy ramparts of the Brenva face overlook the southern, Italian, side, along with the great Peuterey and Brouillard ridges.

Then there are the glaciers - literally dozens of them - that either project long tongues towards the main valleys, or hang suspended from high and remote cirques. Best-known is the Mer de Glace. Born of the Leschaux, Tacul and Géant glaciers, it's overlooked by the north face of the Grandes Jorasses and flanked by the rocky bastions of Charmoz, Grépon and Drus before snaking below the Montenvers to expire among rubble-strewn moraines. To the north-east the

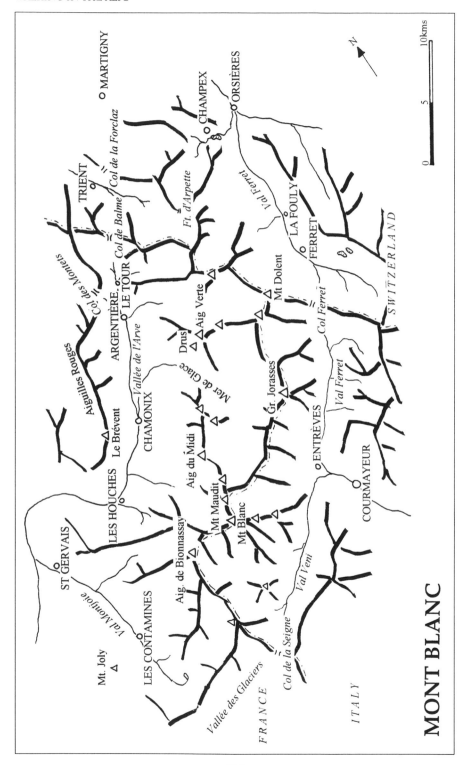

MONT BLANC

Argentière glacier is even longer, while farther down valley the Glacier des Bossons, broad at its formation almost at the summit of Mont Blanc du Tacul and tapering below the tree-line, shows the full drama of a cascading icefall to visitors who need never leave the valley in order to witness its savage grandeur. On the south side of the range the Brenva glacier snakes down towards Entrèves, while the Glacier du Miage has bulldozed a huge wall of lateral moraine across the Val Veni.

Mont Blanc's glaciers have always formed a large part of the district's appeal - especially to the non-mountaineer. In a letter dated 22 July 1816 written from Chamonix, P.B. Shelley expressed great enthusiasm for the mountains themselves ("the immensity of these aerial summits excited...a sentiment of ecstatic wonder, not unallied to madness"), but reserved true astonishment for the Bossons glacier and its icefall:

> "We saw this glacier, which comes close to the fertile plain, as we passed. Its surface was broken into a thousand unaccountable figures; conical and pyramidical crystallizations, more than fifty feet in height, rise from its surface, and precipices of ice, of dazzling splendour, overhang the woods and meadows of the vale. This glacier winds upwards from the valley, until it joins the masses of frost from which it was produced above, winding through its own ravine like a bright belt flung over the black region of the pines. There is more in all these scenes than mere magnitude of proportion: there is a majesty of outline; there is an awful grace in the very colours which invest these wonderful shapes - a charm which is peculiar to them, quite distinct even from the reality of their unutterable greatness."

Lozenge-shaped, the range follows a north-east to south-west alignment between the Col Ferret and Col du Bonhomme, and stands head and shoulders above all its near neighbours. The Franco-Italian border runs along its crest, and on the summit of Mont Dolent is also joined by that of Switzerland. Around it flow seven principal valleys that effectively define is limits. These valleys, listing anti-clockwise from Chamonix, are: the Vallée de l'Arve, Val Montjoie, Vallée des Glaciers, Val Veni, the two Vals Ferret - one Italian, the other Swiss - and the Val Trient.

❊   ❊   ❊

Vallée de l'Arve

The most important of these, in terms of size, development and tourist infrastructure, is the Vallée de l'Arve, the 'Vale of Chamouni'. When William Windham, with Richard Pococke and several companions, entered the valley in 1741 they did so with exaggerated caution, being fully armed against what they feared would be a savage peasantry, and accompanied by servants and pack horses loaded with food and camping equipment. When they arrived in Chamonix they found it a surprisingly hospitable village and the valley well established with a public market that had already been held for some 200 years under the protection of the Dukes of Savoy. While the surrounding peaks were considered by locals to be *Les Montagnes Maudites* (the accursed mountains), the valley itself was devoted largely to agriculture, with sheep and goats grazing the upper pastures. Almost twenty years later de Saussure made his first visit and was suitably impressed by the "fresh and pure air...the good cultivation of the soil...the pretty hamlets...[which] give the impression of a new world, a sort of earthly paradise...enclosed by a kindly Deity in the circle of the mountains."

Since Windham's and de Saussure's visits the valley has seen massive development. Mont Blanc has had a tunnel scored right through it to take heavy road traffic into Italy. Cableways have been strung from valley to mountain top and even across the glaciers to La Palud in Val Ferret on the south side. Rack railways wind up hillsides and the hospitable village of Chamonix has grown into a town of major significance. It has, quite simply, become the world's premier mountaineering centre.

The Vallée de l'Arve begins in a small cirque above Le Tour, where the Col de Balme (2191m) marks the border between France and Switzerland. A privately-owned stone-built refuge occupies prime position on the broad, grassy saddle of the col, and enjoys a magnificent vew over the whole valley, with Mont Blanc and the aiguilles forming the left-hand wall and the Aiguilles Rouges a rocky crest on the right. As R.L.G. Irving once said: "If that view does not thrill you you are better away from the Alps."

All the way down the valley, from Le Tour to Les Houches, glacial avenues open from the left, serving as drainage channels from the Mont Blanc heartland. First of these is the Glacier du Tour, upon whose right bank sits the Albert Premier Refuge (2702m). This very popular hut, given by the Club Alpin Belge to the CAF in 1930, is named after King Albert I of Belgium, a distinguished mountaineer who was killed in an abseiling accident in the Ardennes in 1934. The hut not only forms a base for climbers tackling peaks at this northern end of the range, but makes a worthy destination in itself for walkers anxious to gain a close view of the arctic world of high mountains without facing the tribulations of glacier travel. A path leads to it from Col de Balme, joining another from Le Tour shortly before the hut is reached.

Le Tour is far enough away from Chamonix to maintain an independent existence. Although small, it has both hotel and dortoir accommodation, and the neighbouring hillsides are immensely popular with skiers. The village receives more winter snowfall than any other in the French Alps, and part of its attraction to skiers is the number of cableways that now string the slopes above. As a result the summer walking potential is somewhat devalued by the existence of raw pistes and a clutter of tows and gondola lifts.

At Montroc, below Le Tour, the narrow-gauge railway from Martigny emerges from a tunnel under Col des Montets. That col, squeezed by the Aiguilles Rouges and Montagne des Posettes, provides road access from the Rhône valley in Switzerland and is heavily used. The col forms a boundary of the Aiguilles Rouges Nature Reserve, and there's an alpine garden on either side of the road as it descends towards the Vallée de l'Arve, where the first framed views of the massif give a foretaste of things to come.

The attractive little hamlet of Tré-le-Champ lies just off the Montets road; little more than a huddle of chalets, including a gîte, set in small, neat meadows and with a footpath that drops down to the bed of the valley at Argentière. On the other side of the road to the hamlet a path begins to climb the slopes of the Aiguilles Rouges, first among pinewoods, but then out in the open to tackle a series of metal ladders fixed against a line of cliffs. Mounting these ladders is quite safe, but exhilerating work, as there's a degree of exposure with the valley now several hundred metres below. At the top of the ladders you emerge to a natural terrace that runs along the face of the mountain, and there join another trail that has come from Col des Montets, the junction marked by a huge cairn and with fantastic views directly across the valley to the Mer de Glace. This trail is known as the Grand Balcon Sud, one of the most spectacular balcony walks in all the Alps, and one that has been adopted by both the Tour du Mont Blanc and the less well-known Tour du Pays du Mont Blanc.

To walk the Grand Balcon Sud in its entirety from Col des Montets to Les Houches, is to sample a day or two of mountain walking at its very best. The complete walk could be achieved in a single day. It would be a full and demanding day, it's true, but to a strong walker, well acclimatised to the Alps, quite feasible. But so much better to devote two days to it in order to have time to savour the panorama which takes in the full panoply of Mont Blanc's great northern wall, its upper snows, jagged aiguilles and snaking icefields seen across the depths of the intervening valley. Along that balcony trail it's possible to enjoy such a panorama hour after hour as the sun drifts across the heavens and casts a new light, with new shadows, in a procession of delight from dawn to dusk. And then at night too, perhaps graced by a full moon and a sky thick with stars to add another dimension to a scene that defies description.

Where to stay? Along the *balcon* there's the much-lauded refuge at La Flégère which is also reached by cable-car from Les Praz de Chamonix, and above that, another at Lac Blanc (2352m) that is linked to La Flégère either by a steep footpath or by a combination of the Index cableway and connecting mountain trail. Both provide unforgettable views across the valley to the Mer de Glace, with Aiguille Verte, the Drus, Grandes Jorasses, Dent du Géant, Grands Charmoz, Aiguille du Midi and Mont Blanc itself on show. With its additional height, Lac Blanc is rightly considered one of the prime viewpoints from which to study the massif, while La Flégère offers no less grandeur, though the scale and perspective may be slightly different.

Farther along the Grand Balcon Sud, below and to the west of Le Brévent, another private mountain hut perched on a steeply plunging hillside is worth considering for an overnight's accommodation. Refuge de Bellachat may lack the direct view along the highway of the Mer de Glace enjoyed at La Flégère, but this small, simple but charming building enjoys a more frontal aspect of Mont Blanc and the Bossons glacier with the toy-like buildings of Chamonix over a thousand metres below. From the communal dining room the full stature of Mont Blanc is on show, from its summit dome of ice and snow to the greenery of the valley at its feet; an altitude difference of almost 4000 metres.

Midway between Refuge de Bellachat and the summit of Le Brévent, and reached by a short footpath spur off the Grand Balcon, lies the little Lac du Brévent, a lovely tarn to sit by on a bright summer's day and contemplate the abundance of good things that nature has supplied close to hand, while above it Le Brévent itself rightly holds the crowds.

Probably no single viewpoint, attainable to all who can afford a ticket on the cable-car, will be found that better displays the full majesty of Mont Blanc than that of Le Brévent. The cable-car rises from Chamonix via Plan Praz and deposits visitors to within a few paces of the 2525 metre summit, while the walker, progressing along the Grand Balcon Sud, comes to that same viewpoint but on foot from La Flégère by way of Plan Praz and Col du Brévent. Snow often lies deep on the col and across its approaches until long after mid-summer. Otherwise there's nothing difficult about the route, although the descent from Le Brévent to the bed of the valley just below Les Houches uses an exceptionally steep path that will have tired legs straining all the way.

There's no balcony path of equivalent length along the Mont Blanc side of the valley. Paths there are, in plenty, but the intervening glaciers effectively get in the way of a continuous route from one end to the other. The Grand Balcon Nord is the best option, but this is interrupted by the projection of the Mer de Glace above Le Lavancher.

The Mer de Glace is always worth a visit despite the crowds, despite two centuries and more of it being one of *the* sites to see whilst staying in Chamonix or one of its satellite resorts, for nothing can devalue the view along that snaking river of ice to the dramatically impressive Grandes Jorasses, nor of the jutting peaks on either side. Following his visit, Windham wrote to a friend about "the tops (which) being naked and craggy rocks, shoot up immensely high; something resembling old Gothic buildings or ruins..." Early visitors were escorted there by guides using mules to convey the famous, the infamous, the unfit and the delicate. Then in 1908 the Montenvers railway was opened and mule-tours went into rapid decline. Nowadays the rack-railway does a steady business throughout the summer, while the path that climbs from Chamonix takes a pleasant route through larchwoods, crossing and recrossing the tracks on the way.

At Montenvers there's a large hotel-refuge complex with accommodation in beds and dortoirs. Formerly one of the major starting points for climbs within the heart of the range, the opening of the cableway to the Aiguille du Midi has taken much of the pressure off, although it still features as an important staging post on the way to a number of climbers' huts higher up.

For the walker it not only provides a grandstand view of an impressive array of solid-looking mountains and shapely aiguilles that rises alongside and at the head of the glacier, it also gives an opportunity to join the Grand Balcon Nord as it climbs in zig-zags to the viewpoint of Signal Forbes (2198m) where, from a northern spur of the Frêtes des Charmoz, the Aiguille Verte looks especially fine on the opposite side of the Mer de Glace.

The Grand Balcon Nord heads south-west below the Aiguilles des Grandes Charmoz, Blaitière and Plan to the small Refuge du Plan de l'Aiguille. Beyond this the path begins its steep descent to Chamonix, although the middle station of the Aiguille du Midi cableway is easily reached from the refuge in the event of bad weather demanding a speedy return to the valley.

As has already been said, Chamonix has become the world's most important mountaineering centre. Those who have known it a long time mourn its growth and not-altogether sympathetic development, but truth is, the town has never been slow to respond to the whims of visitors, and its attraction to skiers in the winter as well as to the mountaineering fraternity and coachloads of casual tourists in summer, has resulted in the bustling town we see today. Even so, we may imagine that de Saussure, who stands alongside Balmat in the square with his eyes fixed on the summit of Mont Blanc, and who above all was responsible for drawing attention to the appeal of these mountains, would not be entirely saddened by what has happened to Chamonix. It is, after all, a simple love of the mountains that is being exploited here.

Chamonix spills its way down valley. Just outside is the little Lac des Gaillands with a dark frieze of conifers making a sharp contrast to the dazzling snows of Mont Blanc seen across the waters and soaring high above; a lovely spot. Behind the lake rock slabs are invariably dotted with climbers working out their craft, and below the slabs a woodland path leads gently along the valley to the railway station at Les Houches. Thereafter the Vallée de l'Arve narrows and twists north-westward, before curving once more and losing its immediate hold on Mont Blanc and the glaciers as it broadens below St-Gervais-les-Bains.

St-Gervais, however, retains more than a passing interest in Mont Blanc, for it is from Le Fayet just below the town that the Tramway du Mont Blanc begins its ambitious ascent via Col de Voza to Nid d'Aigle overlooking the Glacier de Bionnassay. Opened in 1912, the original intention had been to push the 'tramway' to the very summit of Mont Blanc! From Nid d'Aigle a trail climbs to the Refuge de la Tête Rousse (3167m). Another leads to the glacier's moraine, then continues down to the Chalet de l'Are from where assorted paths lead either to Bionnassay and the Val Montjoie, to Les Contamines on the route of the Tour of Mont Blanc, or back to St-Gervais by way of Col de Voza. Just above Col de Voza, at Bellevue, a cableway arrives from Les Houches, thereby enabling walkers based in that lower part of the Vallée de l'Arve to gain a variety of routes without facing a long approach march.

The Bon Nant flows through St-Gervais before joining the Arve at Le Fayet. This river, less flamboyant but in some ways lovelier than the Arve, drains the second of our seven valleys, the Val Montjoie, that forms the western extremity of the Mont Blanc range.

Val Montjoie

The valleys of Montjoie and l'Arve could hardly be more different. Whilst the Arve is crowded with mountains, buildings and people, Val Montjoie gives a sense of space, of unfussed forests and open pastureland. There's development, of course, and mechanical aid strung about some of the hillsides, but this western end of the massif is comparatively untouched. And yet in Roman times it was one of the busiest of high Alpine valleys, for the Roman road linking Gaul with Valle d'Aosta ran right through it, and sections of that ancient paved route may still be seen today above the chapel of Notre Dame de la Gorge.

Despite the upper presence of the Trélatête and Bionnassay glaciers and the smaller glaciers hanging beneath the Dômes de Miage, there's far less ice draining into Val Montjoie than into the Arve. Where the valley begins, in a wild cirque above the chalets of La Balme, there is no ice or permanent snowfield of any size. Col du Bonhomme (2329m) lies among stony heights, but below it a lovely grassy basin is wound about with streams, one that spills from the Lacs Jovet under Mont Tondu, others that seep from screes and patches of last winter's snow remaining in the high corries.

This is fine walking terrain protected as a nature reserve, and those with a taste for such country could spend several worthwhile days exploring a clover-leaf of hanging valleys, intimate glens and a number of passes of varying degrees of difficulty from a base at La Balme, where there's a chalet-refuge with lovely views up to the Aiguilles de la Pennaz and the Roches Franches that wall the glen to the south-west. A little lower in the valley the Chalet Nant Borrant makes another good base on the edge of woodland.

The bright, bustling little resort of Les Contamines-Montjoie makes a more obvious centre in Val Montjoie. The village is terraced on the right bank of the river, but with camping and gîte accommodation on the opposite side at Nivorin. Here the valley is green and pastoral. Skiing is enjoyed on slopes to the south-west where Col du Joly marks a saddle between Aiguille Croche and Aiguille de Roselette, but there are other hillsides where there's been no intrusion by piste-making machines and footpaths seduce the inquisitive onto upper slopes and ridgetops with far-flung views. One such is Mont Joly (2525m) to the west of Les Contamines.

A little to the north of the village the ascent of this shaly mountain begins on the left bank of the Bon Nant near La Chapelle. There a path tacks to and fro up the hillside and tops the ridge at Mont Geroux (2288m). Below, and to the north-west, the Refuge-Pavillon du Mont Joly (2002m) provides overnight accommodation and refreshments. From Mont Geroux the way heads south to gain the summit of Mont Joly, one of the finest viewpoints west of Mont Blanc accessible to the walker, although care is required and good visibility advised.

From the summit of this little peak Mont Blanc proves its stature, a glorious mass of rock and snow and ice dominating the eastward view, a view that also presents an interesting examination of the Miage glen. Mont Blanc is seemingly flanked by the Dômes de Miage and the Aiguilles de Bionnassay, but there are other mountains to enjoy from here too, a veritable sea of peaks in every direction. Those of Beaufortain are nearby to the south, but farther away rise the Vanoise and more distant ragged crests of the Oisans, while north-east Les Diablerets guards the borders of the Vaudois and Bernese Alps beyond the Rhône valley.

On the other, eastern, side of Val Montjoie, one recommended outing visits the privately-owned Refuge de Trélatête below the glacier of the same name. While the immediate surroundings of the hut lack the pristine grandeur of some, its situation has much to commend it. From there a more serious hut approach continues along the north bank of the Trélatête glacier to Refuge des Conscrits (2730m), midway between the Dômes de Miage and Aiguille des Glaciers, while mountain walkers with considerable experience of snow and ice, who are at home on wild, unmarked mountain terrain and who are adequately equipped for the job in hand, may be tempted by a crossing suggested by the late Douglas Milner in his book, *Mont Blanc and the Aiguilles*. This involves scaling the southern ridge that overlooks the Trélatête glacier and gaining the head of the Vallée des Glaciers by either the Col

Mont Tondu (2895m) or Col des Glaciers - the former, he says, is the easier. There's another col, unmarked on the Didier and Richard map but shown on the IGN, named Col du Moyen-Age by that Alpine connoisseur R.L.G. Irving, which Irving reckoned to be the simplest and quickest pass from Trélatête to the upper Val Veni on the south side of Mont Blanc. None of these three cols is encouraged by the solid blue or red markings reserved for walking routes on either of the above-mentioned maps, so an attempt at their crossing should be reserved for walkers with well-honed mountaineering skills. Refuge Robert Blanc is situated on the southern slopes of the ridge midway between Col Mont Tondu and Col des Glaciers and this, presumably, would make a convenient halfway halt before skirting the head of Vallée des Glaciers and crossing the easy walkers' pass of Col de la Seigne into Italy.

For a less challenging, but no less interesting, extension of the walk to Refuge de Trélatête, a well-made path known as the Sentier Claudius Bernard continues north to Combe d'Armancette and its little tarn, then descends to Les Contamines-Montjoie once more. Such a walk makes a fine day's outing, but the Combe d'Armancette should be avoided early in the season, or following storm, when there's a distinct danger of stone-fall or avalanche.

Combe d'Armancette hangs above Les Contamines just to the south-east of the village. To the north-east a beautiful glen has been scooped out of the hillside by glaciers that have long since drawn back into the headland of the Dômes de Miage. The glen is soft and pastoral and bright with alpenroses early in the summer. Midway along it a collection of chalets and haybarns is set on the right bank of a torrent spawned by several minor streams that drain the small icefields dazzling from the Dômes de Miage and Aiguilles de Bionnassay. Cattle graze the pastures, their bells clattering against the constant sound of running water while marmots burrow among the rocks. North of the Chalets de Miage is Col de Tricot, crossed by a variant of the Tour du Mont Blanc. To the south-west a vegetated spur of hillside has an extension of that path climbing to the Chalets du Truc, while a dirt road snakes off to Tresse in the valley below Les Contamines.

Among the chalets and haybarns stands the Refuge de Miage, and a night or two spent there in a cradle of mountains and with the necklace of glaciers dangling high above, would give an opportunity to absorb something of the atmosphere of the world of pastoral alps, as opposed to a possibly more comfortable, but more distant, overnight in a valley divorced from the intimacy of the mountains themselves.

Apart from the trails already mentioned, there are others that could be taken from the Chalets de Miage to fill one's days. One option would be to follow a path heading north-west to Le Champel, then bear right to Bionnassay along the GR5, and from there climb through forest to the snout of the Glacier de Bionnassay. Once arrived there a well-marked footpath rises steadily over mixed terrain to Col de Tricot, from where the Chalets de Miage are seen more than five hundred metres below. The path descends directly to them, as a variant on the Tour du Mont Blanc (TMB) mentioned above.

Having now revisited the Glacier de Bionnassay where it pours its melt in a torrent which flows below Bionnassay to join the Bon Nant at Bionnay above St-

Gervais-les-Bains, this brief overview of the Val Montjoie has gone full-circle and it's time to look at the smallest of the three French valleys, reached on foot by way of Col du Bonhomme and Col de la Croix du Bonhomme; the Vallée des Glaciers.

Vallée des Glaciers

Less than ten kilometres separate the head of the valley and the hamlet of Les Chapieux where it makes a sharp southerly bend to pass through the narrows below Pointe de la Terrasse. In those ten kilometres there's no resort, no real village, no tourist infrastructure. The valley has a metalled road that comes up from Bourg-St-Maurice and goes as far as the misnamed Ville des Glaciers, a collection of alp farms on the right bank of the stream, and a rough farm track that continues beyond it. Limited accommodation is available at Selonge near the roadhead just short of Ville des Glaciers, and at a privately-owned refuge on the left bank at about 1898 metres. Apart from these, Les Chapieux represents the only concession to the need for accommodation and refreshment in the valley, so far as walkers are concerned. But at Les Chapieux there's lodging available in hotel beds and dortoirs, and an opportunity for those who stay there for a day or two to explore country to the west where tracks and footpaths link up with the GR5 where it has traversed the airy Crête des Gittes south-west of the Col de la Croix du Bonhomme.

At first glance the Vallée des Glaciers would seem to be inappropriately named, for of all the seven valleys surrounding Mont Blanc, this has the least number of glaciers. In fact apart from the remnant of the Glacier des Lanchettes there's really only one, but as that is draped from the Aiguille des Glaciers, a mountain liberally hung about with ice-sheets on every side, it becomes clear that the valley is named as much for the prominent peak at its head, as for any glacier that might drain into it.

The Aiguille des Glaciers (3816m) is one of the cornerstones of the Mont Blanc range, an elegant peak jutting from a high ridge that curves as the head of the cirque blocking the north-eastern end of the valley. The snow and ice that gathers there is all that remains throughout the summer. The rest of the valley is either brushed with a furze of grass on which sheep and cattle graze, or is bare and stony. There's little woodland cover and the shrubs that are so abundant in many other valleys, are in short supply here.

But that is not to suggest the Vallée des Glaciers is lacking in charm; far from it. It's just that its charm is one of different proportions. One wanders through the valley and over the passes that give access to it with an air of expectation, but scenes of breathtaking grandeur are not to be grasped easily. The extraordinary and beautiful are there alright, but they steal slowly upon you. By contrast with the northern and southern flanks of the massif, this south-western enclave requires the visitor to take a different attitude of mind and let the valley's magic work its spell in its own good time. It won't assault you with its wonders at first glance.

A night spent high above the valley at the newly-rebuilt Refuge de la Croix du Bonhomme, owned by the CAF, may do the trick. If not, try the Refuge des Mottets on the way to Col de la Seigne. From there the head of the valley is not far away and the drapery of ice on the Aiguille des Glaciers haunts the night with its mellow natural glow.

From Refuge de la Croix du Bonhomme there are four ways of descending to the valley. The first is on a clear and obvious trail that descends rucked green hillsides directly to Les Chapieux. The second is a devious route that takes the path of the GR5 across the Crête des Gittes, and via Col de la Sauce to Refuge du Plan de la Lai overlooking the large Lac de Roselend on the northern side of the ridge, before descending the D902 road to Les Chapieux. The third route is a variation of the second, for it breaks away from GR5 without tackling the Crête and slants south-westward to join the D902 part-way down the hillside. But perhaps the best of all is the fourth option, a route that has been hi-jacked as a variant of the TMB; the crossing of Col des Fours (2665m), about forty-five minutes above the refuge. The subsequent descent is a little difficult in places, especially when snow is still lying early in the season, and heads roughly eastwards to gain the valley at Ville des Glaciers.

Refuge des Mottets has been converted from an alp farm and has a pleasant rustic atmosphere. One-time cowsheds have been turned into clean but basic dortoirs, and the main dining room contains old farming and cheese-making implements. It lies directly on the path of the Tour du Mont Blanc, now that the path has been slightly rerouted, and will therefore be familiar to many. Above it the trail is badly eroded with deep trenches having been initially dug in the turf and deep hillside soil by countless boots, then scoured by the spring thaw and summer downpours. But as you gain height towards Col de la Seigne, so the way improves. And on arrival at the col, on the borders of France and Italy, a scene of wonder bursts upon you. There ahead soars the magnificent southern side of Mont Blanc with Val Veni, first of the Italian valleys, lying far below. Without question this is one of the great views of the Alps.

Val Veni

While the northern slopes of the Mont Blanc range have one single valley to perform the functions of a moat draining its glaciers, the Italian side has two. Val Veni and Val Ferret smile at one another across the face of the mountain, and are of similar length. The first drains north-eastward, the second south-west. Gently tilted, their waters flow towards the spur of land on which is built Entrèves, but that spur of land deflects their course and they're sent southwards to join forces above La Saxe as the Dora Baltea (or Doire Baltée), which then flows south-eastwards at right-angles to the range through Valle d'Aosta. Courmayeur acts as a counterpoint to Chamonix and is the main centre of activity. Built on the east bank of the river with the light of the warm south flooding its valley, it gazes up, not at Mont Blanc itself as does Chamonix, but at the big walls just to the east of the monarch.

Approaching from the south the full splendour of the range bursts upon the eager traveller. Dr Julius Kugy, who wrote such fine things about the Julian Alps, wrote too about this view on his way from Aosta to Courmayeur in 1887:

> "At one point about half-way up, where this beautiful valley of the Dora Baltea makes its great bend, there was a sudden stir among the company. Something had arisen before us, and it filled the background of the valley. It was neither cloud, nor rock, nor ice. It was all these in one. A fabulous structure of cloud, rock, ice and snow, a picture great

beyond the richest fantasy, a cathedral borne on giant granite columns...a dome standing brilliant in the firmament." (*Alpine Pilgrimage*)

But if that southerly approach rewards with memorable visions of beauty not only those who come on foot, but also the motorist and unathletic passenger seated in an air-conditioned coach, the scene which stretches before the walker who alone can gain the Col de la Seigne, is no less magnificent. Immediately below lies the great trough of the Vallon de la Lée Blanche which drops in a sudden step to Val Veni proper. Close at hand on the left the twin Pyramides Calcaires intrude. Immediately to their left a ridge slants up, first to the Petite Aiguille, then the Aiguille des Glaciers, and behind this the Aiguille de Trélatête. But above and beyond these, all fall subservient to the crown of Mont Blanc, more rugged and masculine from this side than when viewed from the Vallée de l'Arve; a great mass of snow and ice perched above raw bastions of rock. And through the col that divides the Pyramides Calcaires can be seen a grey triangular wedge that proves to be the Aiguille Noire de Peuterey, the finest of the upthrusting spears that stand guard round this side of the monarch. Impressive from the col, when viewed from the depths of Val Veni the Aiguille Noire is truly astonishing.

Vallon de la Lée Blanche (or Lex Blanche) is bleak by comparison with the lush green valleys on the French side of the range. Scant pastures are skeined with streams, the Pyramides Calcaires form a stark northern wall, and at its north-eastern end on a rocky bluff littered with ruins overlooking Val Veni, sits the Rifugio Elisabetta (2300m). Owned by the CAI, this hut was built as a memorial to Italian Alpine Troops, and as it is easily accessible by a relatively short walk from the roadhead near Lac de Combal, it's a very busy one, especially at weekends. Behind it the Glacier de la Lée Blanche pours from the east flank of the Aiguille des Glaciers and the south side of Aiguille de Trélatête.

Below Elisabetta the Vallon de la Lée Blanche descends in a rocky step to a lower level where the flat bed gathers numerous glacial streams into a marshy area broken by open pools that rejoices in the name of Lac de Combal. A huge wall of lateral moraine, bulldozed by the Miage glacier, blocks the eastern end of Lac de Combal, but its outflow squeezes to one side and then enters Val Veni proper.

The Val Veni pastures used to ring to the clatter of cowbells. But a military road was pushed through the valley, and after the Second World War it was opened to public access. The valley is now a justifiable tourist haunt. Buses serve it, so walkers based at Courmayeur, La Saxe or Entrèves, can ride towards the head of the valley and then spend the rest of the day in delightful exercise tracing some of the paths that provide such exquisite views of these great mountains and their glaciers.

Footpaths wander along the bed of Val Veni on both sides of the river. One climbs up to the Monzino hut (2630m) on a spur of rock between the Brouillard and Fréney glaciers immediately below Mont Blanc de Courmayeur. Another goes through forest to the grassy saddle of Col Chécroui with its famed view into the armchair aspect of Aiguille Noire de Peuterey. But perhaps the finest of all is the high belvedere trail adopted by the TMB which climbs south from Lac de Combal, then heads north-eastwards on a helter-skelter course, passing Lac Chécroui, then down to Col Chécroui where it forks. One trail descends into Val Veni, another winds down to Plan Chécroui, continues to Dolonne and across the Dora Baltea to Courmayeur, while yet a third climbs onto Mont Chétif, the 2343 metre promontory and splendid viewpoint that effectively blocks Courmayeur's view of Mont Blanc.

Italian Val Ferret

The Mont Blanc Tunnel emerges near Entrèves and spills its heavy burden of traffic down through Valle d'Aosta on a major highway where once marched the legions of Rome. East of the tunnel at La Palud is situated the valley station of the Funivie Monte Bianco, the cableway system that swings thousands of tourists each year up and over the Glacier du Géant and the once-remote world of the Vallée Blanche, to the Aiguille du Midi and down into the Vallée de l'Arve at Chamonix on the northern side of the massif. There are intermediate stops at Pavillon (Mont Fréty), Rifugio Torino and Pointe Hellbronner (3322m) on the border between Italy and France, where the close proximity of huge rock walls, cascading glaciers and gleaming snowfields allows the non-mountaineer to enjoy a privileged high mountain experience at the cost of a ticket.

La Palud and Entrèves nestle at the lower end of Val Ferret, second of the Italian valleys below the Mont Blanc range, from close by its confluence with Val Veni. A dozen kilometres or so from Entrèves the valley is blocked by a low dipping wall of mountains that stretches from the edge of the Pré de Bar glacier to the summit of the Grand Golliat. Along the crest runs the international border, and in the middle of that wall the Tête de Ferret is bounded on either side by the Petit Col Ferret and the Grand Col Ferret, both of which carry paths into the Swiss valley of the same name. Some 500 metres below the Grand Col Ferret stands the large, well-appointed Rifugio Elena which is more akin to a hotel-restaurant than a traditional mountain hut.

The Italian Val Ferret has a bed of boulder-pocked meadows and straggling pinewoods. Its northern slopes rear suddenly and with a great sense of drama in a sweep of rock and ice. Glaciers peel from the heights. Long ridge systems stutter between them, while the summits read like a climber's tick-list: Mont Dolent, Aiguilles de Triolet, Talèfre and Leschaux, the impeccable Grandes Jorasses and Dent du Géant.

The southern side of the valley, however, is very different. There are no glaciers, and hillsides rise to a natural, broad sloping terrace before rising again to less-imposing summits that lie back better to enjoy their loftier neighbours. From the Grand Col Ferret it's a powerful scene, with Col de la Seigne providing a distant counter-balance above Val Veni.

Val Ferret is popular with cross-country skiers in winter, and just as popular with Italian picnic parties in summer. A road winds up from Courmayeur and is open to motor traffic in summer only as far as the little plain of Arnuva. An irregular bus service feeds the villages of Entrèves, La Palud and Planpincieux where there's a large campsite. Better still a footpath leads from La Saxe along the east bank of the Dora Baltea to join the road at Planpincieux.

The high path above Val Veni gave magnificent views to the Brenva face of Mont Blanc and the Aiguille Noire de Peuterey. A similar high path can be taken above Val Ferret, from which the Grandes Jorasses is the crowning glory. This path enters the glen of Val Sapin behind La Saxe, then mounts the slopes of Monte de la Saxe which is the twin of Mont Chétif on the opposite bank of the Dora Baltea. At almost two thousand metres sits the Rifugio Bertone, but the path continues to climb beyond it and about two hours from Courmayeur begins a traverse of the crest where the panorama to the north is breathtakingly beautiful.

Edward Whymper and his guides went onto that crest on 23 June 1865 in order to prospect a route to the summit of the Grandes Jorasses. "Five thousand feet of glacier-covered precipices rose above us," he wrote, "and up all that height we planned a way to our satisfaction. Three thousand feet more of glacier and forest-covered slopes lay beneath...The glaciers were shrinking, and were surrounded by bastions of rounded rock, far too polished to please the rough mountaineer." (*Scrambles Amongst the Alps*) Next day, at 1.00pm, Whymper's party made the first ascent of the western summit of the Grandes Jorasses in order to obtain a view of the upper part of the Aiguille Verte, for which he also had ambitions.

Walkers enjoying the high trail above Val Ferret can make a circular tour by returning to Courmayeur on an alternative route descending through Val Sapin by way of Col Sapin (2436m), or if there's neither desire nor need to return down valley there should be plenty of time to continue towards the head of Val Ferret to overnight at La Vachey or Rifugio Elena. Rifugio Elena is of more use to walkers than climbers, for it's directly on the route of the Tour du Mont Blanc and serves as an ideal point from which to tackle the next stage into Switzerland. A little over an hour's uphill work from the refuge leads to Grand Col Ferret with the Swiss Val Ferret lost from view below.

Swiss Val Ferret

The Swiss Val Ferret traces the eastern boundary of the Mont Blanc range. Though walkers entering from Italy might at first question its charm, it's a delightful glen from the hamlet of Ferret down; a pastoral valley with rolling meadows, dark forest and several attractive hamlets and small villages whose timber chalets are bright with window boxes. At its lower end the valley joins the Val d'Entremont at the village of Orsières, by which Martigny and the Rhône valley can be reached by train.

There are several dortoirs and a number of small mountain hotels scattered along the valley, and a large campsite on the left bank of the Drance de Ferret at La Fouly. Above the campsite, in a challenging cirque, hangs the Glacier de l'A Neuve as part of a larger curtain of ice suspended from a crest linking Mont Dolent with the Tour Noir. That crest extends in company with the borders of France and Switzerland round to the Aiguilles d'Argentière and Chardonnet, but these are unseen from the valley itself and it's necessary to gain a higher vantage point to properly enjoy that impeccable mountain wall. Above the alp of Les Ars-Dessous where the Tour du Mont Blanc reaches the valley road, just such a vantage point may be gained at the Lacs de Fenêtre.

Val Ferret has a forgotten-world atmosphere. Being a cul-de-sac at the less popular end of the Pennine Alps chain, it receives fewer visitors than many of its neighbours farther to the east. To their credit its villages show little inclination to give themselves up to brash signs of modernity, and the paths that squeeze through them do so among ancient haybarns perched on staddle stones, beside chalets of ancient timber and stone, sometimes on cobbles, often through alleyways too narrow to allow access by motor vehicle. Between villages and hamlets open meadows are thick with wild flowers - until the scythe is taken to them, that is. And as you wander from one end to the other, it is the gentle beauty of the valley that attracts as much as the dramatic outliers of the Mont Blanc massif that wall it. Routes onto that wall are all severe. Paths lead to one or two huts, but these are uncompromisingly steep, although mechanical aid from Champex reduces some of the effort required to reach the SAC's Cabane d'Orny (2811m), and the higher Cabane du Trient.

Champex is a cheerful little resort set in a minor glen at the bottom end of Val Ferret, above and to the west of Orsières. The village clusters round two sides of a small lake and looks south towards the Grand Combin. Forests clothe the hillsides below, and darken the rising mountains to mid-height. There are no snowpeaks in sight, other than those of the Combin massif, but one can sense that big mountains are never far away. A chairlift rises from the ouskirts of the village to La Breya, from where a path takes off to the Cabane d'Orny. Once there a world of high mountains is again evident, with the shrinking Glacier d'Orny nearby tipping from the Plateau du Trient. It is possible, of course, to walk all the way to the hut from the village.

The chairlift begins near the mouth of a wild glen that rewards all who go wandering there. Val d'Arpette has no village, but there's a hotel with dortoir accommodation and space for camping just behind it. Thereafter a farm building or two are all that intrudes into as peaceful a glen as one could wish to find. Rocky peaks rise on either side, but the bed of the valley has sparse woodlands, rough pastures, a mass of shrubs, and a joyous stream that comes through with the unbridled vitality of youth. A path rises up the southern flank to cross Col de la Breya en route to Cabane d'Orny, but the glen's main trail works its way to the head of the valley where all is rough and stony, then climbs to the Fenêtre d'Arpette for an astonishing view onto the chaos of the Trient glacier. This path is a major, some would say *the* major, variant on the TMB; a strenuous alternative to the pretty, and much more green, standard route which goes via the Bovine alp to the last of our seven valleys, Val Trient.

Val Trient

The Trient glacier has its foundations on the broad Plateau du Trient contained between the Aiguilles Dorées, the frontier ridge topped by the Aiguille du Tour and the north-eastern gatepost of Pointe d'Orny, on the slopes of which sits the Swiss Alpine Club's Cabane du Trient (3170m). Traditionally this hut has been a very useful base from which to embark on glacier journeys to other parts of the massif, but for walkers arriving at the Fenêtre d'Arpette, the Plateau is little more than a suggestion at the roof of a long cascading glacier.

It's an exciting prospect to arrive at that pass after a steady grind up a slope of boulders, grit and stone to be confronted by the turmoil of the glacier spilling into the narrow glen ahead. The contrast with Val d'Arpette is almost total. Down in the shadows of its eponymous valley, Trient village squints up at that glacier and the sweep of the Plateau du Trient at its head which forms such a dramatic, if distant, backcloth. It's a narrow V wedge of a valley with dark forested slopes whose waters flow roughly northwards, are joined by l'Eau Noir near Finhaut, then make a right-hand bend on their journey to the Rhône below the southern flanks of the Dents du Midi. Down there the Mont Blanc Express (surely one of the slowest 'express' trains in Europe) makes its tortuous way from Martigny to Chamonix, giving passengers a teasing, seductive view into Val Trient as it winds across the glen's entrance.

The valley has barely been developed, despite the fact that it has the railway passing below it, and is traversed by the Martigny-Chamonix road between Col de la Forclaz and Col des Montets. La Forclaz (1526m) is a saddle in the hills above and to the east of Trient, to which it is linked by footpath. The Bovine trail from Champex comes out at Forclaz, while another path leads from the complex of hotel, restaurant and souvenir shops along the wooded hillside heading south beside an irrigation channel, or *bisse*, to reach the little Chalet du Glacier near the snout of the Trient glacier. This is a short but delightful walk with very little change in altitude, and the majesty of the long finger of ice is an appealing sight to lure you on.

In this short and narrow glen there's a gîte in Le Peuty, and hotel and dortoir accommodation in Trient itself. The village is small and simple. It has a shop and a Post Office, a church with a slender spire, and a huddle of stone-built dwellings. There's nothing grand or pretentious about it, no overt attempt to put it 'on the map' or to pander to the whims of the tourist trade. What you see is what you get in Trient. In that simplicity there's a breath of fresh air.

Walkers pass through on one of the closing stages of the Tour du Mont Blanc, and also make use of its facilities on the Chamonix to Zermatt Haute Route. One set of walkers heading west, the others east. And there are several trails to choose from.

The two routes out of the valley heading east have already been mentioned. These are the path via Col de la Forclaz to Champex by way of the Bovine alp, with its lovely views north over the Rhône valley, while the other crosses the Fenêtre d'Arpette and descends through Val d'Arpette to Champex.

For those heading west over the frontier ridge to the Vallée de l'Arve, one climbs directly out of Trient, goes through forest and round Pointe du Van where there's a choice of continuing either to Col des Posettes or to Vallorcine north of Col des Montets. Another option is the standard TMB trail which heads up the southern flank of the Nant Noir glen to Col de Balme, while the third alternative uses the *bisse* path from Forclaz to Chalet du Glacier, then makes its own way via Les Grands and the upper hillsides of the Nant Noir glen to join the previously mentioned path at Col de Balme. And there the length of the Vallée de l'Arve flows before you, flanked on the right by the Aiguilles Rouges, and on the left by Aiguille Verte and Drus and the bold snowy crown of Mont Blanc itself.

✳   ✳   ✳

TOUR DU MONT BLANC

Having looked at the seven valleys that surround Mont Blanc, and at some of the walking possibilities within them, we now come to the subject of a continuous tour of the range with an opportunity to stray from the standard circuit here and there to pack a fortnight's holiday with activity. Suggestions will be made for staying overnight in either high or remote parts of the mountains where possible, as well as the more usual valley bases, and pointers will be given to neighbouring glens, passes, and in some cases, easy summits, that would be worth exploring by walkers with time at their disposal. But first a word about the tour itself which forms the basis for our circuit.

The Tour du Mont Blanc (TMB) is justifiably well known and generally considered to be one of the finest walking routes of its kind in Europe. Without question the scenery enjoyed each day is of the highest quality, and if visual stimulation be the sole criterion by which to judge a walk, then the TMB would certainly qualify as one of the great routes of the world, let alone Europe. But few will walk it in solitude, and those who have previously enjoyed long treks in wilderness country may find the garrulous crowd a little off-putting, while walkers of limited experience may find comfort in a steady stream of trekkers all going the same way. Mountain walking though, as in most things, is very much a question of expectation, personal experience and taste, and the overall impression gained on this grand circuit of the Monarch of the Alps will surely be one of simple delight. The unrivalled scenery will ensure that.

The TMB links the seven valleys already described in a circuit lasting anything from a week to ten days. It was initiated, as was the ascent of Mont Blanc itself, by the enthusiasm of the Genevese Professor of Natural Philosophy, Horace Bénédict de Saussure, who made the first circumnavigation in 1767. Others, scientists like de Saussure, and general tourists too, followed his lead, mostly on the backs of mules on what would in the early days have been mostly tracks and rough country roads. But with the explosion of interest in mountain walking for its own sake, the route has been improved and refined to what it is today. There are several alternative sections, known as *variants*. Waymarking, whilst not entirely perfect in every corner, is more than adequate almost everywhere. Accommodation, including the provision of campsites, is plentiful and on all but the most extreme occasions quite capable of satisfying the needs of somewhere in the region of ten thousand people who tackle the walk annually.

The walk has international renown, and voices from the United States or Australia are as likely to be heard along the way, as are walkers speaking French, Dutch, German or Italian. Several trekking companies organise holidays tackling the route, but even for solo walkers it can prove to be an extremely sociable tour as one is forever leapfrogging others along the way, or meeting of an evening in a dortoir, hotel or on a campsite. Although it's quite possible to enjoy long stretches entirely on one's own, walking the Tour du Mont Blanc will rarely be an experience where solitude counts for much. The following suggested tour, however, includes days spent straying from the route where it may be possible to enjoy the beauty of the mountains in brief isolation. But anyone particularly keen to share the route with as few people as possible, should consider starting out midweek.

Popular opinion has the route beginning at Les Houches at the lower end of the Vallée de l'Arve. If the walker arrives by train, Les Houches has a station on the narrow-gauge railway that links with the main SNCF network at Le Fayet. The village is also served by local bus from Chamonix, or may be reached from there by a pleasant woodland path on the right bank of the Arve from Les Gaillands on the town's western outskirts. Les Houches is an unassuming, pleasant village on a slope of hillside above the west bank of the river. It has a choice of hotels and dortoirs and a large open campsite not far from the Bellevue cable-car station, beyond which the first TMB signpost will be found.

It takes a little over two hours, on a combination of road, track and woodland path, to reach the broad, busy saddle of Col de Voza (1653m) on the ridge that divides the Vallée de l'Arve from Val Montjoie. Here the Tramway du Mont Blanc is met on its way up to Nid d'Aigle. The main TMB crosses the col and descends through a series of meadows to La Villette and Tresse in Val Montjoie, then heads up the road to Les Contamines. But this should only be contemplated in the event of bad weather, for the alternative, though much longer and more demanding, remains true to the spirit of the walk and rewards with a constant variety of fine views.

First of these comes after a short climb to the old hotel-refuge of Bellevue, from where the Vallée de l'Arve is spread out below, and the view is dominated by the Dôme de Gouter with Mont Blanc to its right and a jagged line of aiguilles to the left. Across an enclosed meadow followed by woods, the way then makes a traverse of hillside before descending suddenly from a trail that would otherwise lead to the right bank of the Bionnassay glacier. That glacier will be met, but on its other bank, and the descent is necessary in order to get below the ice and across the torrent that pours from it before rising on its far side. A steel ladder aids the ascent of what would have been a tricky obstacle near the glacier's snout, but once over that the path is straightforward as it rises through undulating pastures scarlet with alpenroses and with an opportunity to study the glacier that flows nearby.

Col de Tricot (2120m) is a grassy saddle at the head of the pastures, on a long spur running down from the Aiguilles de Bionnassay. The col is marked by a low stone wall from which there's a blinkered view steeply down onto the Chalets de Miage. The path descends directly to them, and there, in the open meadows, it's tempting to throw off your rucksack and lie in the flower-starred grass to gaze at the splendours of the Dômes de Miage that block this lovely little glen.

It could be that you've had enough walking for a first day by the time you reach the Chalets de Miage. It will have taken something in the region of five or six hours, plus rests, to get here from Les Houches, and it will take another two before you reach Les Contamines. That may be perfectly feasible for walkers in training, but it could possibly be more than enough for those fresh from the lowlands and unused as yet to the Alpine scale of things. To these, as to others who wish to absorb as much of the atmosphere of the mountain world as possible, I'd suggest spending a night here in the Refuge de Miage.

The continuing route takes a twisting path up the wooded slopes of Mont Truc (*truc* means rounded summit), crosses the shoulder of this grassy spur that forms the glen's southern wall, and comes to the privately-owned Refuge du Truc. From there an hour's steady descent leads to Les Contamines-Montjoie, an important village for backpackers, as its shops offer a last opportunity to stock up with provisions before Courmayeur is reached, another two days or more away.

At this point those who chose not to stop at Refuge de Miage might consider booking in for a two-night stay, in order to make an ascent of Mont Joly - but only if visibility is favourable and there's no forecast of bad weather coming in. The ascent and descent will take a total of about seven or eight hours in a round-trip that begins down-valley at Les Hoches near La Chapelle.

Resuming the Tour du Mont Blanc out of Les Contamines-Montjoie initially involves a road walk south before breaking away on a parallel track that accompanies a clear stream as far as the baroque chapel of Notre Dame de la Gorge. The track now begins to rise among woods and is paved for a while with stone slabs. This is the old Roman road which came through the Italian Valle d'Aosta, over Col de la Seigne and Col du Bonhomme into Val Montjoie; in effect the route followed in reverse by the TMB.

The paved track becomes a dirt road that goes all the way to the alp huts of La Balme, set in a lovely pastoral glen headed by a series of rocky peaks. Walkers who have spent the previous night in Les Contamines will only have been on the go for a couple of hours or so and will continue past the Chalet de la Balme without stopping, except perhaps for refreshment. But for those who prefer hills to valleys for their overnight lodging, there is a temptation to stay here. They will have been walking for something like four and a half hours from Refuge de Miage, and the day will still be young enough to enjoy the good things in the neighbourhood of La Balme that the TMB studiously ignores in its determination to cross the next pass on the itinerary. So, book a space in the dortoir and, after a suitable period for rest and refreshment, spend the afternoon wandering up to the Lacs Jovet which lie cupped in a wild scoop of hillside overlooked by Mont Tondu and the Monts Jovet. The two tarns are almost 500 metres higher than La Balme and a couple of hours would be sufficient to get there and back again, but as there are waterfalls and mountain views to enjoy, a whole afternoon could be well spent on this diversion.

Above La Balme the TMB crosses open pastureland, then rises again towards Col du Bonhomme. A remnant snowfield is usually there to negotiate on the way to the pass, but for most of the way a clear trail slants up the shaly slopes into increasingly wild country. A small shelter tops the col from where a minor trail descends to Lac de la Gittaz and its larger neighbour, Lac de Roselend, but the Tour du Mont Blanc path curves left, rising still, before making a traverse of rough, stony mountainside brightened here and there with a rich assortment of alpine flowers.

At 2479 metres Col de la Croix du Bonhomme is just 150 metres higher than the previous col and is marked by a tall cairn. Ten minutes below to the south a large CAF refuge stands at a junction of paths, with the TMB going one way, the GR5 another. The standard TMB descends past the refuge to Les Chapieux where dortoir and hotel accommodation are on offer, but the continuation from there demands an hour's unrelieved road walking along the Vallée des Glaciers. In the event of bad weather threatening at Col de la Croix du Bonhomme, that's the way to go. Otherwise, the variant route which strikes away from the col and climbs north-east to Col des Fours, often over snow even in mid-summer, leads to a more direct descent to the upper reaches of the Vallée des Glaciers and the collection of farm buildings of Ville des Glaciers. From there it takes a little over an hour to reach the Refuge des Mottets where an overnight is recommended. This variant could be a little problematic in the initial descent from Col des Fours, but becomes easier as the path progresses.

It's possible, of course, that circumstances demand breaking the route early with a night spent at Refuge de la Croix du Bonhomme. Should time and conditions permit, a recommended outing from there leads along the GR5 trail to sample the delights of the Crêtes des Gittes south-west of the hut. This exciting ridge-path sneaks from one side of the crest to the other and enjoys airy views throughout its length. Safe but spectacular, it's worth wandering for an hour or so before returning to the hut by the same path. Or alternatively, the continuing GR5 trail could be taken down to Refuge de la Lai where the narrow D902 road is met. This is then followed eastward to Les Chapieux to rejoin the TMB.

Walkers preferring to sleep high would choose to press on for another three hours beyond the Mottets hut and continue to Rifugio Elisabetta above Val Veni, as would those who slept at Refuge de la Croix or Les Chapieux, for whom Mottets is reached too soon. The way is clear and easy, Col de la Seigne (2516m) which borders France and Italy being reached on grass practically all the way from Ville des Glaciers. It is a visually spectacular crossing, for the col introduces the TMB walker to the dramatic southern side of the range with all the splendour of rock faces, sharp-pointed aiguilles, hanging glaciers and huge domes of snow arcing against the sky. The route down to Val Veni, after crossing the remains of last winter's snow immediately below the saddle, is mostly untroubled as it later slopes down the left flank of the valley below the Pyramides Calcaires and joins scant grasslands shortly before Rifugio Elisabetta is gained.

Once again the Tour du Mont Blanc divides to offer a choice of routes through the Val Veni. This time the diversion comes at Lac de Combal where the lateral moraine from the Glacier de Miage emerges as a towering wall. The traditional route remains in the bed of the valley (where in emergencies a bus may be caught to Courmayeur), and continues through meadows below the stupendous south face of Mont Blanc, then rejoins the road as it curves round the slopes of Mont Chétif, passes the chapel of Notre Dame de la Guérison (the Italian counterpart to the chapel in Val Montjoie) before descending to Courmayeur.

That walk has its merits, but it cannot compare with the alternative high route that climbs along the southern hillside at just the right height and at just the right distance from the big crowded mountains to view them in full majesty. This breakaway trail leaves the valley road just short of a stone bridge below the Miage glacier's moraine wall. A brief diversion here is also possible, with a path that climbs the moraine to view the icy Lac de Miage, a glacial pool that attracts tourists who have driven through Val Veni for a transitory glimpse of one aspect of the high mountains.

The TMB variant heads in the opposite direction, climbs among trees and shrubs, then across an open hillside with Aiguille Noire de Peuterey soaring up and up in a needle point across the valley. Throughout the ascent and subsequent traverse of this green hillside, that majestic peak demands one's attention while

Mont Blanc de Courmayeur to its left dazzles its snows in the sunshine, and the monstrous cleft created by the Miage glacier forms a stairway to the Aiguilles de Bionnassay. Ruined buildings at l'Arp Vieille Inferior are passed by. A raging torrent is crossed by delicate moves on half-submerged rocks, and the trail continues to climb among acres of alpenrose, goes through a shallow trough with a stream flashing clear and cold, then rises again to more substantial hutments at l'Arp Vieille Superior. Now the way slants left and makes one last big effort to round a spur projecting north of Mont Favre, a superb viewpoint promontory, then drops steeply before making a long contour, sometimes on snow, then on grass, towards Col Chécroui.

Above Col Chécroui the ski industry has left its imprint. Cableways string the hillsides and bald pistes carve S-bends through the grass. There's a sadness about such places in summer. In winter, with a crisp coverlet of snow, it's possible to overlook the gross indecency that the spring melt reveals. By summer the mechanics of winter offer insult to the smiling bounty of nature.

Col Chécroui has been known and loved for a long time. J.D. Forbes, the Scots Professor of Natural Philosophy and pioneering mountaineer, visited it in 1842, but he was by no means the first to be won over by the tremendous view across the depths of Val Veni to the Fauteuil des Allemands, the great concave face of the Aiguille Noire, and the southern snows of Mont Blanc peering above it. North-east of the col rises the easy viewpoint of Mont Chétif from which the Brenva flank is seen to such good effect. Mont Chétif is the cornerstone of Valle d'Aosta, and it blocks some impressive peaks from the view of Courmayeur. But in return it has become a popular outing for walkers staying in that town, and is worth visiting too by walkers on the TMB still with sufficient energy to tackle it. But those who left Refuge des Mottets earlier in the day will no doubt be thinking in terms of descent to the valley.

If the plan is to spend a night or two in Courmayeur, it's possible either to descend via Plan Chécroui to the old village of Dolonne and then cross the Dora Baltea, or cut through forest north of the col to the large, well-appointed Rifugio Monte Bianco, and follow the road from there for much of the way down-valley. The nearest campsites are in Val Veni, so backpackers will have no need to descend to Courmayeur, unless it's to savour the atmosphere of this Italian Chamonix. Courmayeur has a number of hotels, but little in the way of low-priced accommodation. As it forms an important part of the Tour du Mont Blanc experience many will choose to stay there anyway, although Entrèves and La Palud upvalley will no doubt be a little cheaper.

Since there are two ways of continuing the TMB towards the Swiss frontier at the head of Val Ferret, walkers choosing to spend two nights in Courmayeur, Entrèves or La Palud, have an opportunity to walk them both. If the weather is clear it's advisable to tackle the high route along the crest of Monte de la Saxe for the magnificent panorama that walk affords; if clouds are down then save that route until the next day in the hope of an improvement, and walk along Val Ferret instead. The valley route is certainly not without its attraction although the drama of high mountain views so notable on the alternative trail will be lacking. The return to Courmayeur after completion of the Monte de la Saxe route can be made through Val Sapin, while buses that serve the Val Ferret would save backtracking the outward trail.

Our 'high sleeping' walkers who stayed the previous night at Rifugio Elisabetta, may still have time and energy to spare when Courmayeur comes in sight. To them a recommendation is made for an overnight to be spent at Rifugio Bertone (1991m), less than two hours above Courmayeur on the shoulder of Monte de la Saxe.

The next destination, for those who stayed in Courmayeur as well as walkers who patronised Rifugio Bertone, is the large new Rifugio Elena at the head of Val Ferret on the pastureland shelf of Pré de Bar. The original Elena hut was destroyed by avalanche, but this was replaced by a large and prestigious new building which, like its predecessor, commands a very fine view of Val Ferret and its walling mountains, and especially of the retreating Pré de Bar glacier nearby. From the tree-studded plain at Arnuva a dirt road rises easily to the hut and places the walker in a good position to tackle the crossing of Grand Col Ferret into Switzerland next day. The Petit Col Ferret (2490m), north-west of Tête de Ferret, offers an alternative possibility, but the descent on the Swiss side through Combe des Fonds, can be problematic. It's far less used than its higher neighbour.

A short climb leads to the Grand Col Ferret, little more than an hour being required in good conditions. The path to it begins a few paces from the hut and slopes easily up the hillside, making a few steep zig-zags midway to the pass. From the col itself a last look back into Italy shows a mountain world painted on a slightly larger canvas than that enjoyed at Elena. But looking ahead the Combin massif comes into view in an attempt to counter-balance Mont Dolent and other neighbouring outliers of the Mont Blanc range that crown the left-hand side of the hinted Swiss Val Ferret. That new valley system really is little more than a hint, for there are intervening hills and domes to confuse the immediate geography. However, once in the valley a short walk along a road leads to the hamlet of Ferret that immediately reveals the trim orderliness of Switzerland.

Hotel and dortoir accommodation are available here, as in several other villages in Val Ferret. With its wider choice of places to stay, and with restaurants and a useful supermarket centrally placed, La Fouly, half an hour down-valley from Ferret, provides perhaps the best base, and will certainly be of value to the backpacker on account of its spacious campsite. Our walker who prefers to sleep high has little opportunity to do so in this part of the valley, so we'll assume that La Fouly attracts the majority of TMB wanderers, despite the fact that it will have been a very short stage from the Elena refuge. Some might find it tempting to continue all the way to Champex. But that would be a mistake. Val Ferret has some good things in store for those who are prepared to divert from the main trail and not be rushed.

The advice given here, then, is to choose accommodation to suit for a couple of nights and spend the rest of the day of arrival enjoying the wild aspect of the glacial cirque that makes such an interesting background west of La Fouly. With the Glacier de l'A Neuve projecting from it a horseshoe of rocky peaks rises steeply from the valley floor. Should you arrive after a fall of fresh snow that cirque makes a tremendous sight.

Next day, instead of moving on to Champex, return upvalley in the opposite direction, but remain on the road beyond the point at which the trail from Grand Col Ferret joins it. A dirt road soon winds up to an alp farm at Plan de la Chaux, and a footpath climbs from there, quite steeply in places, to gain an exquisite high-level shelf rimmed with a tilt of rocks in which lies the Lac de Fenêtre (2456m). There are, in fact, three lakes, but the first and largest is best of all, and from its flat eastern shoreline fluffed with cotton grass, a most magnificent view is won which spreads along a great crest of peaks whose more notable features include the Grandes Jorasses, Mont Dolent, Tour Noir, a clutch of aiguilles and long glacial fingers, with the lake's sheen of water as a foreground. On a mountain circuit that rewards with so many fine panoramas, this is one of the least-known because it can only be discovered by diverting from the set route. It is certainly worth making that diversion and giving a spare day to it. The Lacs de Fenêtre also mark one of the highlights of the Tour des Combin described in the Pennine Alps chapter.

Another short and easy stage follows that from Rifugio Elena to La Fouly, for the walk to Champex demands no more than four to five hours of effort. But it's a very pleasant walk all the same that begins on the left bank of the Drance de Ferret, comes down towards Praz de Fort along a narrow wooded moraine, then crosses the mouth of the Saleina glen. Beyond Praz de Fort the path leads through lovely open meadows, but at Issert resumes on the left bank to climb among pinewoods almost all the way to Champex, where there's plenty of accommodation of all standards, including a campsite at the upper end of the village. Again, those who prefer more peaceful upper glens and hillsides for their lodging are recommended to continue beyond Champex and go up into Val d'Arpette where there's a hotel with dortoir options, and also camping space behind it.

A demanding alternative route could be taken by walkers with plenty of energy and an eagerness to see yet more of the high mountains, and with another opportunity to spend a night close to them. It's not recognised as being part of the Tour du Mont Blanc, nor even a variant of it. But enjoyment of the mountains and the exercise they offer, should be sufficient to ignore for once the 'official' way and to tackle this route. It begins at the mouth of the Saleina glen just before the TMB path swings into Praz de Fort. A narrow road pushes into the glen and after some time a path strikes away from it, climbs steeply up the scree-bound north wall for almost fifteen hundred metres and reaches Cabane d'Orny overlooking a small tarn. From the hut there's yet another option available, and that is to go even higher, along the edge of the Orny glacier to overnight in the Cabane du Trient (3170m) with the pristine grandeur of the Plateau du Trient sweeping before it. The glacier walk between huts does have some crevasses to negotiate, but in some seasons these are much easier to deal with than in others.

If our walker has chosen to overnight in Cabane d'Orny in preference to Cabane du Trient, he might be persuaded to visit the upper refuge next morning, then return to cross Col de la Breya by which Val d'Arpette may be reached. An easier descent is by chairlift to the junction of Val d'Arpette and the basin in which Champex sits, but the recommended footpath descent is not a long one, in terms of time taken, and less than a morning will be needed to reach the Relais d'Arpette. That allows the afternoon to be spent wandering through the lovely Arpette glen in a delight of lazy exploration. Such seemingly aimless meanderings often bring unexpected rewards to a mountain holiday that a strict adherence to a published itinerary may fail to do.

Resuming the Tour du Mont Blanc proper a decision has to be made about the next stage to Val Trient. Is it to be by way of the Fenêtre d'Arpette, or the Bovine alp? In truth the choice will largely depend on the weather, for only if the forecast is promising should the crossing of the Fenêtre be attempted. It's no place to be caught by storm, and there's no point in tackling it anyway if visibility is going to be limited. The Fenêtre d'Arpette offers a grand day's walking. But the crossing is quite severe, although in reasonable summer conditions it does not warrant the symbols indicating *passage dangereux* shown on some maps. Nevertheless it is the highest and probably the hardest of all passes on the TMB, and at the same time the finest. It's a true mountain pass. Not a broad grassy saddle, nor an open col, but a rocky cleft on a high ridge and with truly astonishing views to enjoy once gained.

However, it is not considered to be the main TMB route, but only a variant. By contrast the Bovine path has no pass to cross, for it skirts the northern flanks of those peaklets that form the ridge dividing not only Val d'Arpette and Val Trient, but also Val d'Arpette and the valley that sweeps down through the Gorges du Durand to join the Drance just above Martigny. While the Fenêtre is gaunt and stony, and with a glacier on its western side, the Bovine route is green throughout. It begins along a forest track, goes through an alp, climbs again among trees, then makes a lovely traverse of open hillside with views over the Rhône valley to the north, before reaching the huts at Bovine alp. Refreshments and simple dortoir accommodation are available for those who are tempted to call it a day in order to sample the unchanged and unchanging way of life of a secluded alp, but the path to Col de la Forclaz still has a little more height to gain before a shoulder of hillside is crossed and the descent made among lush vegetation to the col.

Col de la Forclaz is a road pass crowned by a hotel with little of the tranquillity experienced at the Bovine alp where cowbells alone break the peace. Here motor traffic grinds across the pass throughout the day and evening, while paths continue down to Trient in the valley just below, or alongside an irrigation channel that leads to the snout of the Trient glacier where another trail begins to climb south, then west, to Col de Balme and the Vallée de l'Arve. But that crossing belongs to tomorrow.

Trient is where the Fenêtre and Bovine routes reassemble, and from where a return to France begins. The main TMB trail heads south out of the village, then climbs through woodland along the slopes of the Nant Noir glen to reach Col de Balme. There are, however, two official variants, alternative routes that have their advocates. One has already been mentioned; the trail alongside the irrigation channel leading from Forclaz to the Chalet du Glacier, then by way of Les Grands and a high path above and to the south of the main route, which it rejoins at Col de Balme. The other variant avoids Col de Balme completely and goes round the slopes of Croix de Fer, then picks a way to Vallorcine and Col des Montets.

Since most walkers understandably choose Col de Balme as being the prime point of re-entry to France, with its well-known grandstand view of the Vallée de l'Arve and the Chamonix aiguilles, it is at Col de Balme where we will look at the options open to us for the continuing route. The official Tour du Mont Blanc suggests a safe, if uninspiring, descent directly to Le Tour. Much better is the variant which skirts the upper slopes of the Tête de Balme, then zig-zags down to Col des Posettes before going over the Aiguillette des Posettes on a splendid trail full of visual delights. This eventually drops steeply through forest to reach the road below Col des Montets near the hamlet of Tré-le-Champ with its welcoming gîte. Strong walkers could continue without staying there, but the next accommodation on the route is at La Flégère, about three hours farther along the Grand Balcon Sud, and since much of the way to it is quite demanding it would be better to tackle that section first thing in the morning when you're feeling fresh.

Yet again there is another option available for those walkers who have still not had their fill of the high mountain experience. That option is to break away from the two TMB routes at Col de Balme and follow a path heading south round the hillside to reach the Albert Premier Refuge set beside the Glacier du Tour, and next day return to Col de Balme and pick up the Posettes route already referred to. If this suggestion is followed it would be quite feasible to opt out of spending a night at Tré-le-Champ and continue to La Flégère.

In his guidebook Andrew Harper advocates a short stage from Tré-le-Champ to La Flégère in order to have time to visit Lac Blanc to enjoy its classic panorama. An alternative to this plan would be for strong walkers to go directly to Lac Blanc on a path that climbs as a spur from the Grand Balcon Sud, and then descend from there to La Flégère and continue via Plan Praz, over the summit of Le Brévent, and down to the charming little Refuge de Bellachat (2152m). This option is for strong walkers only. Others are urged to follow the guidebook's recommendation.

But both options are only valid if the weather is clear. There's no point in going up to Lac Blanc unless you can see the views that make all the effort worthwhile. If conditions are favourable this diversion will be one of the many memorable sites of the TMB. If clouds are down, make a mental note to return at the earliest opportunity.

From either La Flégère or Bellachat, the final stage eventually leads down to the station at Les Houches; the first will take much of the day because of the effort involved in climbing to the summit of Le Brévent, the second option demands no more than two or three hours along a steep downhill trail. And if there's a day or two to spare once the tour has been completed, Chamonix has plenty to offer, in addition to the many fine footpaths, short or long, that are worth exploring in the valley itself for walkers whose energy and enthusiasm remain as fresh as ever.

TOUR DU MONT BLANC - SUMMARY OF CIRCUIT

I: The Basic Tour (with optional extras)

Day 1:   Les Houches - Col de Voza - Col de Tricot - Les Contamines-Montjoie

Day 2:   Ascent of Mont Joly

Day 3:   Les Contamines - Col du Bonhomme - Col de la Croix du Bonhomme - Refuge des Mottets

Day 4:   Refuge des Mottets - Col de la Seigne - Col Chécroui - Courmayeur

Day 5:   Monte de la Saxe route & return to Courmaeur through Val Sapin, or Val Ferret route to Arnuva & return by bus

Day 6:   Courmayeur - Rifugio Elena via Monte de la Saxe or Val Ferret

Day 7:   Rifugio Elena - Grand Col Ferret - La Fouly

Day 8:   Round-trip to Lacs de Fenêtre (2456m)

Day 9:   La Fouly - Praz de Fort - Champex

Day 10: Champex - Trient via Fenêtre d'Arpette or Bovine

Day 11: Trient - Col de Balme - Col des Posettes - Tré-le-Champ

Day 12: Tré-le-Champ - Chéserys - La Flégère & visit Lac Blanc

Day 13: La Flégère - Col du Brévent - Le Brévent - Les Houches

II: The Basic Tour with Options for Sleeping High (and alternatives)

Day 1:   Les Houches - Col de Voza - Col de Tricot - Refuge de Miage (1559m)

Day 2:   Refuge de Miage - Les Contamines-Montjoie - Chalet de Balme (1706m) & visit Lacs Jovet

Day 3:   Chalet de Balme - Col du Bonhomme - Col de la Croix du Bonhomme - Col des Fours - Col de la Seigne - Rifugio Elisabetta (2300m)

Day 4:   Rifugio Elisabetta - Col Chécroui - Rifugio Bertone (1991m)

Day 5:   Rifugio Bertone - Monte de la Saxe - Rifugio Elena (2060m)

Day 6:   Rifugio Elena - Grand Col Ferret - La Fouly (1594m)

Day 7:   Round-trip to Lacs de Fenêtre (2456m)

Day 8:   La Fouly - Praz de Fort - Champex - Relais d'Arpette (1627m)
   or
Day 8a: La Fouly - Cabane d'Orny (2811m) or Cabane du Trient (3170m)

Day 9a: Cabane d'Orny (or Cab. du Trient) - Col de la Breya - Relais d'Arpette (1627m)

Day 9:   Arpette - Fenêtre d'Arpette or Bovine - Trient (1279m)

Day 10: Trient - Col de Balme - Col des Posettes - Tré-le-Champ (1400m)
   or
Day 10a: Trient - Col de Balme - Albert Premier Refuge (2702m)

Day 11a: Albert Premier Refuge - Col de Balme - Col des Posettes - La Flégère (1877m)

Day 11: Tré-le-Champ - La Flégère (1877m) & visit Lac Blanc, or to Refuge de Bellachat (2152m) via Col du Brévent

Day 12: La Flégère (or Bellachat) - Grand Balcon Sud - Les Houches (980m)

Much of the standard route provides moderately strenuous walking over well-marked paths, tracks or roads. Gradients are rarely severe but the highest crossing (Fenêtre d'Arpette) reaches 2665 metres and has its difficult passages. The TMB is subject to late-lying snow in some areas. The best time to attempt it is between mid-July and late September.

CHABLAIS, FAUCIGNY & DENTS DU MIDI

Although in no sense part of the Mont Blanc range, the neighbouring districts of Chablais, Faucigny and Dents du Midi are close enough to be included briefly within this chapter. The first two are located in Haute Savoie, the second being entirely Swiss and falling within the administrative canton of Valais. The glories of Mont Blanc not unnaturally divert the attention of most visitors away from these lower mountains and hills, but the discerning walker and lover of fine scenery will always find something worthy on which to focus for a day or two of an active mountain holiday. As a well-travelled Alpine commentator once argued: "The glaciers are small, only a few summits pass the 10,000 mark, but the valleys are full of beauty, great stretches of their green floors being studded with the two star blue gentians, verna and bavarica."

Chablais is an attractive region of flowery meadows, forests and white limestone cliffs of the Pre-Alps, rising from the southern shores of Lac Léman (the Lake of Geneva) to Morzine, while Faucigny continues to the outer edge of the Mont Blanc range. Large areas have been sacrificed to the downhill ski industry, but footpaths abound elsewhere and there is plenty of good walking to be had, from gentle half-day outings to multi-day traverse routes such as the GR5 and the Tour du Pays du Mont Blanc. Janette Norton's guidebook, *Walking in the Haute Savoie*, is a useful introduction to the region with a number of suggestions for walks of modest attainment, most of which explore landscapes of undisputed charm. Here, gentle grassy cols provide enticing views to bigger mountains, while the highest pass crossed by GR5 before entering the Mont Blanc arena is the 2257 metre Col d'Anterne which, having passed several waterfalls on the way, rewards with a breathtaking panorama. Given clear conditions one looks beyond and above the foreground crest of the Aiguilles Rouges to the great snow dome of Mont Blanc itself dominating the southern horizon. Walkers who have already tackled the TMB will sense a tinge of nostalgia as well as excitement in such a view. Others, who have yet to experience at close hand such high Alpine grandeur, will find it difficult to resist the lure.

Seen from the air as a jagged spine of peaks spattered with snow as one approaches Geneva airport, the Dents du Midi fill a small district between the eastern Chablais and the Rhône valley. Attractive limestone mountains, their highest summits are Haute Cime (3257m), Doigts (3210m) and Dent Jaune (3186m). From them views are justifiably famous. But while the walker may feel daunted by prospects of climbing such abrupt-looking peaks, there are cols and valleys easily reached whose prospects offer no scenic second-best. The view from Porte du Lac Vert (2157m) above the tarn of the same name just inside the Swiss border above the Champéry valley is, for example, nothing short of spectacular, while the Salanfe basin to the south had its praises sung long ago by Emile Javelle. Its charm remains.

A two- or three-day tour of the Dents du Midi is the best way of unravelling a fair quota of the district's charm. Overnight accommodation could be arranged by a detour to one of several outlying villages or hamlets, while Cabane de Susanfe provides lodging on the south side of the mountains. Much will depend on your plans, of course, and how gently you wish to undertake such a circuit. Tackled in an anti-clockwise direction the tour begins and ends at Vérossaz, a village reached from St Maurice in the Rhône valley, and heads south-west across the Crête du Dardeu to Signal de Soi (2054m). From there to Bonavau on the right bank of the upper Champéry valley before swinging eastward to gain the Cabane de Susanfe (2102m) in the Susanfe glen. Beyond this a climb of almost 300 metres leads to Col de Susanfe overlooking the Salanfe basin with its fjord-like lake trapped in a great well of mountains. A trail leads down to the northern shore, then rises easily to Col du Jorat where the tour now heads north to Mex and a forest trail back to Vérossaz.

❊   ❊   ❊

THE MONT BLANC RANGE

Location:
Mainly France and Italy, but the north-eastern limits lie in Switzerland. The French valleys are in the Départment de Haute-Savoie, the Italian side falls within the jurisdiction of the Valle d'Aosta region, while the Swiss valleys are in the canton of Valais. Chablais and Faucigny lie between the Mont Blanc range and the Lake of Geneva, while the Dents du Midi rise on the south bank of the Rhône valley in Switzerland.

Principal valleys:
Vallée de l'Arve, Val Montjoie, Vallée des Glaciers (in France), Vals Veni and Ferret (Italy) and Val Ferret and Val Trient (Switzerland)

Principal peaks:
Mont Blanc (4807m), Mont Maudit (4465m), Mont Blanc du Tacul (4248m), Grandes Jorasses (4208m), Aiguille Verte (4122m), Aiguille de Bionnassay (4052m). In the Dents du Midi the main peak is Haute Cime (3257m).

Centres:
Chamonix, Argentière, Les Houches, Les Contamines-Montjoie (France), Courmayeur (Italy), La Fouly and Champex (Switzerland)

Huts:
Many on all sides. Several are used on the Tour of Mont Blanc. Very few in Chablais, Faucigny and Dents du Midi districts.

Access:
a) By air to Geneva, then by train or coach to Chamonix. b) By rail to Paris and train from there to St-Gervais (Le Fayet), where narrow-gauge local train serves Les Houches and Chamonix. c) By Eurolines coach from London to Chamonix.

Maps:
Massifs du Mont Blanc - Beaufortain 1:50,000 published by Didier & Richard (Grenoble) is perhaps the best for walkers. Produced by IGN it has walking routes overprinted in blue, and mountain refuges and gîtes marked in red. Didier & Richard *Massifs du Chablais, Faucigny & Genevois* and L.S. 272 *St-Maurice* and 5003 *Mont Blanc-Grand Combin*, also at 1:50,000.

Guidebooks:
Chamonix-Mont Blanc: A Walking Guide by Martin Collins (Cicerone Press) - a pocket-sized guidebook to some of the best day-walks in and from the French valleys.
Tour of Mont Blanc by Andrew Harper (Cicerone Press) - a popular guide to this classic

126

circuit; regularly updated.

Walking in the Haute Savoie by Janette Norton (Cicerone Press) for the Chablais and Faucigny regions.

Other reading:

Mont Blanc & the Seven Valleys by Roger Frison-Roche (Kaye, 1961) - illustrated with superb monochrome photographs by Pierre Tairraz, this English translation provides an eloquent overview of the region.

Savage Snows by Walt Unsworth (Hodder & Stoughton, 1986) - a very readable history of climbing on the highest mountain in the Alps.

Mont Blanc & the Aiguilles by C. Douglas Milner (Robert Hale, 1955) - primarily intended for climbers, it contains much of interest to first-time visitors.

The Alps by R.L.G. Irving (Batsford, 1939) - contains a chapter on the Mont Blanc range that is full of interest, despite its pre-war publication date.

Scrambles Amongst the Alps by Edward Whymper (John Murray, numerous editions). Best known for the story of Whymper's obsession with the Matterhorn, 'Scrambles' also contains passages of interest to walkers visiting the Mont Blanc range.

The Mountains of Europe by Kev Reynolds (Oxford llustrated Press, 1990) has a good background chapter on this district by C. Douglas Milner.

The Outdoor Traveler's Guide to The Alps by Marcia R. Lieberman (Stewart, Tabori & Chang, New York, 1991) has a small section devoted to Chamonix and Mont Blanc.

Below Col de Louvie a magnificent view across Val de Bagnes shows
the full splendour of Grand Combin

5: THE PENNINE ALPS

Extending eastward from Col Ferret to the Simplon Pass, this tremendous range contains the greatest concentration of 4000 metre peaks in Europe west of the Caucasus. Though Mont Blanc may boast the highest summit in the Alps, such noble giants as Monte Rosa, the Matterhorn, Dom, Weisshorn, Ober Gabelhorn, Dent d'Hérens, Dent Blanche, Mont Collon and Grand Combin - to name but a few - provide the Pennines with a matchless pedigree and a long-held reputation for scenic grandeur that remains undinted by the passage of time.

Most of these summits are ranged along the Alpine watershed which here forms the frontier ridge between Switzerland and Italy; a watershed of ice and snow broken by peaks of striking individuality. Numerous glaciers swirl from these lofty peaks. Those that drain the northern, Swiss, flanks flow through a series of roughly parallel valleys to the Rhône, while Italian valleys send their streams and rivers in long complex journeys down to the Po. The range thus makes an effective divide between Central and Southern Europe.

Beyond the Simplon rise the Lepontine Alps; north of the Rhône the Bernese Alps. To the south, and separated from the Pennines by Valle d'Aosta, are the Italian Graians dominated by the Gran Paradiso, while to the south-west across the Col Ferret stand outliers of the Mont Blanc range.

The huge wall of the Pennine Alps represents the crucial front-line of pressure created when the African tectonic plate collided with that of the Eurasian block,

Above:
Pointes de Mourti and
the Moiry Glacier (Ch 5)

Left:
Lac de Louvie and
Grand Combin (Ch 5)

Top: The Dix hut and Mont Blanc de Cheilon
(*R.B. Evans.* Ch 5)

Centre: Icefields flowing from the Strahlhorn
above Saas Fee (Ch 5)

Right: The celebrated Pas de Chêvre above
Arolla (*W. Unsworth.* Ch 5)

with the projecting landmass that is now Italy acting as a buffer and forcing mountains to rise and buckle and fold nappe upon nappe into a towering, rumpled mass. But weathering over millions of years, and the sculpting tool of glaciers, has provided them with their unique shape and form; a process that continues unabated to this day.

When mountaineers first turned to the Alps for adventure the Pennines must have seemed like the Promised Land, and it is no great surprise to find that much of the drama of the so-called Golden Age was played out upon them. Whymper's tragic first ascent of the Matterhorn in 1865 may have given rise to an outburst of indignation from the Victorian Establishment, but from that date the Alps in general, and the Matterhorn in particular, grew in the public conscience. Today the Pennines have year-round appeal. Skiers flock to them in winter, climbers and mountain walkers in summer. And with so many accessible valleys linked by easy passes, the mountain walker has, in many respects, the most visually rewarding arena of all to play in. It is certainly the most extensive.

❋   ❋   ❋

The Swiss Valleys

Consider first the Swiss valleys, several of which are subdivided in their upper reaches by glens of great charm. Heading from west to east these are Val Ferret, Val d'Entremont and Val de Bagnes; the first of which also limits the eastern end of the Mont Blanc range, while the other two form calipers round the big block of the Combin massif. North-east of Val de Bagnes lies the little Val de Nendaz into whose inner reaches drains the Grand Désert glacier off Rosablanche. Then comes Val d'Hérens, subdivided by Val d'Hérémence whose upper section is known as Val des Dix. Above Les Haudères lies the Val d'Arolla with Mont Collon at its head.

Val d'Anniviers is the next main valley to the east, but the Moiry glen flows into it from the south-west, headed by a fine snub of second-echelon peaks and a chaotic icefall behind the SAC hut, while Val de Zinal, the upper stem of Val d'Anniviers proper, gives access to some of the best summits of all: Weisshorn, Zinal Rothorn, Ober Gabelhorn and Dent Blanche among them. To the north of the Weisshorn lies the charming Turtmanntal with summer-only access by road from the Rhône. A secretive valley, is the Turtmanntal, while to the east of that runs the great trench of the Mattertal, possibly the busiest mountain valley in all the Alps since Zermatt is its highest village, with the Matterhorn soaring above that. Then comes the Saastal, walled by lovely mountains on either side, and, last of all, the valley that drains the Simplon Pass.

Each of these valleys and glens will repay the walker's attention, no matter what the degree of commitment. Suggestions for their exploration will be made in the following pages, but before studying these we should first look at the opposite, southern, side of the chain, and the Italian valleys.

The Italian Valleys

For an initial introductory quotation we can do no better than to turn to R.L.G. Irving, who, at the outbreak of the last war, wrote in respect of these valleys: "All

THE PENNINE ALPS

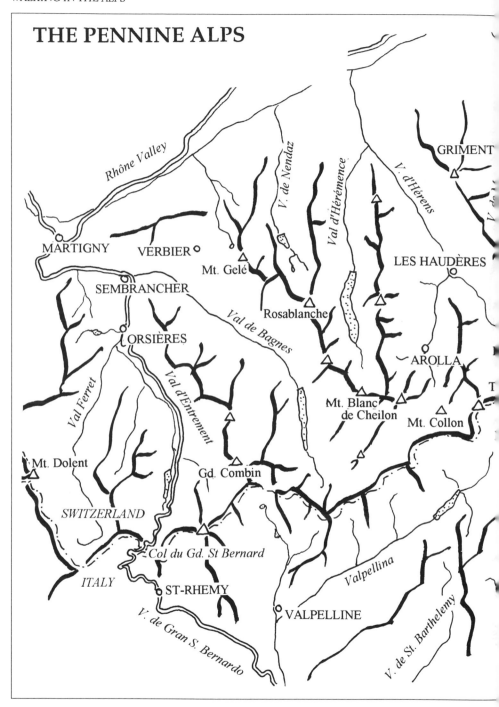

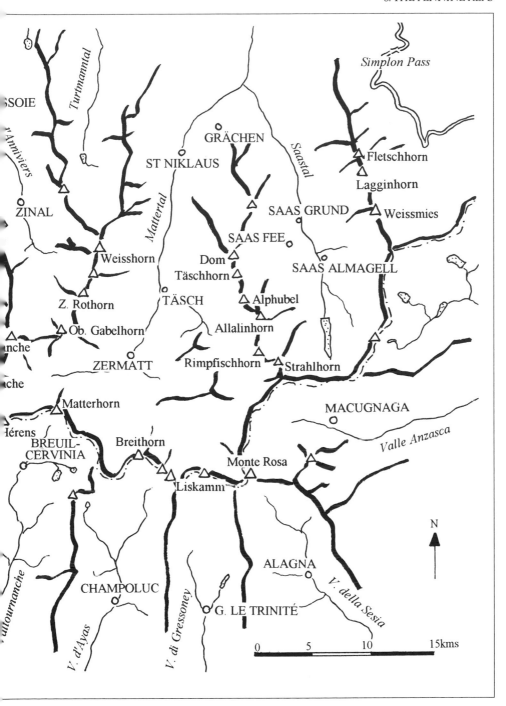

Simplon Pass

Turtmanntal

SSOIE

'Anniviers

GRÄCHEN

ST NIKLAUS

Saastal

Fletschhorn

Lagginhorn

ZINAL

Mattertal

SAAS GRUND

Weissmies

SAAS FEE

Weisshorn

Dom

SAAS ALMAGELL

Täschhorn

Z. Rothorn

TÄSCH

Alphubel

Ob. Gabelhorn

Allalinhorn

nche

ZERMATT

Rimpfischhorn

Strahlhorn

che

Matterhorn

MACUGNAGA

lérens

BREUIL-
CERVINIA

Breithorn

Valle Anzasca

Monte Rosa

Liskamm

N

ALAGNA

ultournanche

CHAMPOLUC

V. della Sesia

V. d'Ayas

V. di Gressoney

G. LE TRINITÉ

0   5   10   15kms

are beautiful, for Nature has been particularly happy in her planting of their lower parts with trees of many kinds, and in the upper parts she has done much to hide the wastes of stones that intervene between the pastures and the snows."

The Italian Val Ferret flows south-westward below the great flanks of the Grandes Jorasses to join the Dora Baltea above La Saxe, and is more properly included as one of Mont Blanc's seven valleys. But on the eastern side of the Grand Golliat, across whose summit runs the Swiss frontier, several short glens congregate at the headwaters of Valle del Gran San Bernardo which carries international traffic above the village of St-Rhemy, and down through St-Oyen and Etroubles before swinging south to Aosta. Valle de Menouve is the easternmost glen here, a quiet little valley with rough pastures topped by Mont Vélan whose long southern ridge effectively divides it from Valle d'Ollomont.

This latter valley is headed by a broad pastoral amphitheatre in which squats the tiny hamlet of By, dwarfed by the southern slopes of the Combin massif. A walker's pass, the Fenêtre de Durand, links By with the Swiss Val de Bagnes and provides trekkers with stark visual contrasts. Valle d'Ollomont, incidentally, is named after its main village, rather than its river (the Buthier), and joins the Valpelline at Valpelline village some three kilometres downstream of Ollomont, where a second Buthier river drains from the north-east.

Long and deep, the Valpelline makes an intriguing shaft through the mountains from north-east to south-west, beginning below glaciers draped on the southern flanks of the Dent d'Hérens. The rifugio at Prarayer hamlet is its highest accommodation, with walkers' passes leading across the mountain ridge which separates the valley from that of the Valtournanche, one of the best known of all these glens on the southern slopes of the Pennine Alps on account of the fact that it leads travellers to Breuil-Cervinia and the Italian face of the Matterhorn.

Between the Valpelline and Valtournanche the glen of St Barthélemy has been carved from the intervening ridge some way south of the main peaks of the Alpine watershed, its stream being one of the many tributaries of the Dora Baltea. Valtournanche extends southward away from the Matterhorn, but the general alignment of the main Pennine range breaks away to the north across the multi-summited Monte Rosa, and those valleys that flow from this bulky massif do so between a splay of ridges that projects like the fingers of an outstretched hand.

First of these is Val d'Ayas whose river, the Evançon, drains glaciers from the Breithorn, Pollux and Castor. Next comes the charming Valle di Gressoney stretching south from the Liskamm. The "exquisite verdure and beautiful scenery" of this valley was described in 1861 by William Mathews thus:

> "Lofty cliff and noble pine forest, and foaming torrent, and huge erratic
> blocks, islands in a sea of green, are here thrown together by the hand
> of nature in exhaustless variety and profusion; and the effect of all this
> natural beauty is increased by the apparent comfort of the dwellings,
> and the bright and picturesque costume of the inhabitants."

East of Valle di Gressoney lies Val Sesia, then a tributary glen, Valle Sermenza, which has two upper feeder glens, and the long trench of Valle Anzasca with Macugnaga lying beneath the vast eastern wall of Monte Rosa itself - a face more than two thousand metres high, and containing the greatest glacier wall in the Alps.

Above Macugnaga to the north the Monte Moro Pass (2832m) provides walkers with access to the Saastal in Switzerland, while the Val di Antrona also maintains access with the Saastal via the historic trading route that for centuries crossed the Antrona Pass (2838m) and where sections of medieval paving are still visible today.

*　　*　　*

Both sides of the Pennine chain having been roughly enumerated, it is now time to look at the great potential for walking holidays that exists in particular among the Swiss valleys, followed by a classic west to east traverse across projecting spurs of the range.

Vals Ferret, Entremont and Bagnes

At the western end the first two valleys, Ferret and Entremont, are united at the little town of Orsières about six kilometres south of Sembrancher. Orsières is the terminus of the St Bernard Express, a branch railway of great appeal that begins in the Rhône at Martigny, and then feeds assorted routes of the Postbus service, thus providing access to the upper glens for non-motorised walkers.

Val Ferret has been briefly dealt with in the Mont Blanc chapter, and will be revisited shortly when discussing the Tour des Combin. As for the Val d'Entremont, this is dominated by the busy thoroughfare of the Col du Grand St Bernard (2469m), a pass known to pilgrims, traders and armies of invasion since before Roman times. There are gentle walks in the bed of the valley, and more demanding trails that lead to passes - such as that of the Col du Nève de la Rousse at the head of Combe de l'A, and Col du Bastillon below Monts Telliers - that see many days of high summer drift by without a single visitor. Above Bourg-St-Pierre, and reached through the Valsorey glen, Cabane du Vélan on the northern slopes of Mont Vélan, and Cabane du Valsorey in a combe on the flanks of the Combin massif, provide worthwhile objectives in themselves, and reveal the wild nature of these upper regions. But despite these fine outings, Val d'Entremont cannot compare in riches to its opposite number on the northern side of the Grand Combin.

Val de Bagnes rises in a large open basin between the compact Combin massif and long fingers of ridge and peak that project from Mont Blanc de Cheilon, Pigne d'Arolla and the frontier, a basin into which funnel several glaciers, scree chutes and stony moraines. Overlooked by the Swiss Alpine Club's Cabane de Chanrion, rough pastures rumpled into hills and hollows contain small tarns, while above them hillsides reveal little that is harmonious - this is nature in the raw. That is not to suggest for one moment that this landscape has no appeal. On the contrary, it is a marvellous area in which to explore. It's just that its basic nature makes few concessions. Take it or leave it may be the message it imparts. And why not?

Out of this basin the upper valley has been flooded by the construction of the huge Mauvoisin dam, part of the extensive Grande Dixence hydro-electricity scheme that has so altered the character of several high glens in the Swiss Pennines. However, there is a precedent to this lake, for in the winter of 1817-18, something like one hundred and forty years before the Mauvoisin dam was built, the stream (the Drance de Bagnes) was blocked by a mass of ice which broke away from the Glacier du Giétro. A vast natural lake was created more or less where the reservoir of Lac de Mauvoisin lies today. But in June 1818 it burst its banks and swept down valley, killing thirty-four people and wreaking havoc as far as Sembrancher and Martigny where the remains of trees and houses finally came to rest.

Below the towering barrage Val de Bagnes is narrow, steep-walled and a little gloomy. But it soon opens to smiling meadows as it flows in a steady north-westerly curve flanked by the wall of the Combin on the left, and by another on the right which provides some exciting walking possibilities. Take Fionnay as a base from which to explore the area. It has a handful of hotels and dormitory accommodation, and there's a semi-wild but official campsite a short distance upvalley at Bonatchesse. The first choice of route would be that which climbs south-westward up the left-hand hillside, rounds the northern end of a gaunt rock wall, and in four hours reaches Cabane de Pannossière (2669m) set among moraines on the right bank of the Glacier de Corbassière. Destroyed by avalanche in the spring of 1988, the Pannossière hut was reopened three years later and is used as a base for climbers tackling assorted routes on the Combin group which soars in a chaos of ice and snow all around. Providing a wild yet magnificent outlook, it would be worth spending a night there, and next day varying the return to Fionnay by crossing Col des Otanes, located above the hut and below the Grand Tavé, then descending to either Mauvoisin or Bonatchesse, followed by an easy valley walk back to your base.

The right-hand mountain wall above Fionnay, topped by the unseen Rosablanche (3336m), contains the beautiful tarn of Lac de Louvie, with the privately-owned Refuge de Louvie set upon a brief level of turf just to the south of its outflow. Lac de Louvie provides a spectacular viewpoint from which to study the Grand Combin across the valley, and is surely one of the grandest sites in all the Pennines accessible to the walker. That access from Fionnay, however, is by way of an extremely steep path eased in places by a seemingly endless flight of steps. From the tarn there are possibilities of continuing exploration via the neat little corrie in which the tarn lies, but unless you choose to overnight in the refuge there and make forays from it, it would perhaps be wiser to enter this unique corner of Val de Bagnes, not from the bed of the valley itself, but from that other hut located further to the north-west, Cabane du Mont-Fort (2457m).

Perched high above the valley under the ridge of Monts de Sion, Cabane du Mont-Fort enjoys year-round popularity and a most wonderful view to the eye-catching glories of the Mont Blanc range off to the south-west. Sunset spreads long-glowing embers across those distant snows and makes a night spent at the hut a night to remember. It's used by skiers in winter and in the spring touring season, is visited by day-trippers in summer making the most of cableway access, by trekkers tackling the classic Chamonix to Zermatt Walker's Haute Route (described later in this chapter), and also by walkers on the little-known Tour des Combin. Unfortunately an unwelcome assortment of cableways has been strung around and across neighbouring crests and pinnacles in order to extend the skiing facilities for winter visitors to nearby Verbier. But these are the only negative adornments to an otherwise magnificent location.

134

TOUR DES COMBIN

This eight- or nine-day tour, as its name suggests, makes a circuit of the Combin massif. It's quite demanding at times, but since accommodation is now available at the end of each section, there will be no need for backpacking. It begins either in Martigny in the Rhône valley, or in Sembrancher. In the latter case the same route as adopted by the Chamonix to Zermatt walk would be followed as far as Cabane du Mont-Fort (ie: Sembrancher to Le Châble, then via the chapel at Les Verneys and the chalets of Clambin, on a 1600 metre climb to the hut). The alternative involves a steep haul from Martigny to Col des Planches, then passes round the upper bowl that contains Verbier before gaining the Mont-Fort refuge - a strenuous two-day approach.

From Cabane du Mont-Fort the Tour des Combin heads south-eastward along the airy trail of the Sentier des Chamois with magical views of the Grand Combin across the valley which, with its tumbling icefall, long tongue of glacier and the sparkling upper snows, creates a striking impression of a Mont Blanc look-alike. At the end of this belvedere you cross the easy pass of Col Termin and break away from the main trail on a steeply descending path which drops into a hanging valley fluffed with cotton grass and bejewelled by the romantic Lac de Louvie. As you descend to it all the untamed splendour of the Combin massif is revealed across the hinted depths of Val de Bagnes, the long grey moraine wall etched sharp against pure white snowfields, while jutting peaks and summit domes offer as fine an assortment of mountain profiles as you could wish to see. All this as a backcloth to a walk that takes you down, down and ever down beyond the tarn on a knee-wrecking descent to Fionnay deep in the valley.

However, there is an alternative to the descent to Fionnay, and that is to take another path which makes an up and down traverse of mountainside from the lake's eastern shore to the alp huts of Vasevay on the slopes of La Sale, followed by an unforgiving descent to the valley midway between Bonatchesse and Mauvoisin. If taking this option one would need to spend a night either in Refuge de Louvie or the hotel below the Mauvoisin dam.

The next stage of the circuit leads to Cabane de Chanrion, described by Walker as: "...a lovely place and a fine centre for many easy ascents affording superb views". The better of two approach routes leads along the eastern shore of Lac de Mauvoisin, then climbs to the pastures and lakes of Tsofeiret - with the Combin's dominant eastern face glaring down. Above the Tsofeiret lakes a low ridge has to be crossed, easy on its northern side, but demanding care on the descent which is very steep and exposed, but with fixed ropes to safeguard the way down grit-covered ledges. Thereafter the path threads a course over screes, glacial streams and moraines pushed aside by the Brenay glacier that is now fast-receding back to its source under Pigne d'Arolla.

Cabane de Chanrion is indeed a lovely place, and from it one gains an uninterrupted view south-south-west through a stony glen to the Italian frontier at Fenêtre de Durand (2797m), the first goal on the next day's walk. Formerly known as the Col Fenêtre de Balme this easy saddle, flanked by Mont Avril and Mont Gelé, heads the remnants of the little Fenêtre glacier upon whose flower-carpeted moraine the path climbs. Once at the pass a revealing panorama of glaciers, snowfields, moraine banks, high rocky peaks and bare screes shows the Swiss side in stark relief, while the Italian slope folds one crest into another to the Ollomont valley, and far off shapes of the Graian Alps pay homage to the Gran Paradiso, a raft of snow floating on the summer haze that hovers over Valle d'Aosta.

Descending into Italy a shaly path leads to a small green tarn, then among boulders, before reaching the open pastureland of Alpe Thoules where a number of streams gather as the Acqua Blanca, one of the major tributaries of the Buthier. A dirt road is met at a group of stone buildings. This snakes down to more huts at the Balme pastures, beyond which a narrow path breaks away on a long descent to Ollomont, while the dirt road itself continues into the vast amphitheatre of Conca di By. Tucked just below this road the tiny hamlet of By overlooks a small reservoir, with steep hillsides falling to the head of the Ollomont valley.

In the mid-1990s the Valle d'Aosta authorities built a new rifugio in the lower reaches of the Conca di By, at an altitude of about 2000 metres. The hut has forty beds and a winter room, and fills a much-needed accommodation gap for walkers exploring this enchanted region.

On the western side of this great cirque the dirt road maintains a fairly consistent contour as far as Champillon, a collection of farm buildings and a small stone chapel, where a *bisse* (a channel of water used for irrigation) flows beneath the track and along the edge of a superb level meadow adorned by a tall stone cross. Views from here show the Fenêtre de Durand to the north-east and the Grand Combin rising above the Conca di By. The *bisse* returns to the right-hand side and then cuts into pinewoods. At this point you should leave the road in favour of a narrow trail that follows the watercourse, a charming path fragrant with pine that eventually loses the *bisse* at the buildings of L'Arp de Praz where a track takes over.

Valle de Menouve is crossed on a scantily waymarked path that wrestles through a rampant cover of vegetation, then over the valley stream on a stout wooden bridge to join another dirt road leading into Bezet, a small hamlet on a nose of hillside overlooking Etroubles and a junction of valleys. From here the way is less complicated, but it will still take about two hours via the two-part village of Eternon to reach St-Rhemy on the old road leading to the Col du Grand St Bernard.

St-Rhemy has limited accommodation and no food store, but there is no real alternative if you're looking for a bed for the night, and it does at least put you in a good position from which to set out on the crossing next day of the 2698 metre Fenêtre de Ferret. This is a very fine walker's pass in the frontier ridge west of the Grand St Bernard, and the thousand metre climb to it is surprisingly moderate. At first you head up the glen behind the village on an old mule path, trade it for a short section of tarmac, then return to mule path again until, about an hour and a half from St-Rhemy, you come to the St Bernard road at a collection of dilapidated hotel buildings and a small bar selling tacky souvenirs, shown on the map as Cantina Dogana. The final climb to the pass enters a stony hanging valley which opens as undulating grassland, while the frontier ridge itself is a chaos of rocks and boulders - nature's demolition site.

From the Fenêtre eastern outliers of the Mont Blanc massif are clearly visible across minor crests to the north-west, while the Lacs de Fenêtre glimmer two hundred metres below. Now back in Switzerland several tracks lead down from the ridge and unite as one to pass between the lakes - a glorious place with a magnificent panorama in which the Grandes Jorasses, Mont Dolent and Tour Noir are prominent features.

Just beyond the third and largest of the lakes the trail forks. The main path descends to Val Ferret with an assortment of accommodation being available on the route of the Tour du Mont Blanc. One possibility for the walker tackling the Tour des Combin is to go down into that valley and follow the TMB route to Champex, and next day wander down to Sembrancher or Martigny to complete the circuit. Another option is to take the upper trail at the junction by Lac de Fenêtre, and follow it over the saddle in a ridge east of Mont Ferret, the so-called Col du Néve de la Rousse. This leads into the glen of Combe de l'A which gives into Val d'Entremont above Liddes. It's not necessary to descend into Liddes, however, for a continuing trail heads north through Vichères to Orsières (accommodation in both places), thus leaving just an easy stroll down valley to Sembrancher next day.

TOUR DES COMBIN - SUMMARY OF CIRCUIT

Day 1:   Martigny - Sembrancher - Le Châble
or: Martigny - Col des Planches - Col du Lin

Day 2:   Le Châble - Clambin - Cabane du Mont-Fort
or: Col du Lin - Les Planards - Cabane du Mont-Fort

Day 3:   Cabane du Mont-Fort - Refuge de Louvie - Fionnay

Day 4:   Fionnay - Mauvoisin - Cabane de Chanrion

Day 5:   Cabane de Chanrion - Fenêtre de Durand - Conca di By (rifugio)

Day 6:   Conca di By - Eternon - St-Rhemy

Day 7:   St-Rhemy - Fenêtre de Ferret - Col du Néve de la Rousse - Vichères
or: - Fenêtre de Ferret - Ferret (or La Fouly)

Day 8:   Vichères - Orsières - Sembrancher - Martigny
or: Ferret (or La Fouly) - Orsières - Sembrancher - Martigny

To summarise, the little-known Tour des Combin provides a good way of exploring the western end of the Pennine Alps, with landscapes of varied, but nearly always, outstanding beauty. On the Swiss side of the frontier the route for the most part uses clear footpaths, with reasonable waymarking. The Italian section of the circuit however, is less obvious and with some confusing sections. Concentration will be required in order to avoid getting lost! The two high passes by which the frontier is crossed (Fenêtre de Durand and Fenêtre de Ferret) are both straightforward in clear conditions, but the latter could be difficult in thick cloud. Both are subject to late-lying snow. The best time to attempt this route would be from July to late September.

Vals d'Hérémence and d'Hérens

The main flow of Val de Bagnes is north-westward, while the next major valley system to the east drains more or less to the north. However, between Val de Bagnes and Val d'Hérémence the little Val de Nendaz intrudes as a short, pastoral wedge headed by the ice-draped Rosablanche. This glen has been developed for skiing, with an assortment of mechanical aids linking it with the vast ski fields of Verbier. But there remain plenty of modest walks through forest and meadow in mid-valley, while above the dammed Lac de Cleuson a much more wild and stony landscape remains unblemished by the pylons of either chairlift or cable-car. The privately-owned Refuge de St Laurent, hidden above the southern end of the lake, provides overnight accommodation for those who would come wandering this way. Behind it the seemingly barren, undulating upper valley is dotted with tarns left behind by the retreating Grand Désert glacier whose moraines and rocky wastes are being invaded by lovely flowering plants. One trail here links the western fringe of the glacier with Val de Bagnes by way of Col de Louvie (2921m) and either Col Termin or the higher Col de la Chaux, while another, on the eastern side, crosses Col de Prafleuri (2965m) as a route of access to either Val d'Hérémence or its upper section, Val des Dix.

Col de Prafleuri looks into the desolate Prafleuri basin (translated inappropriately as the plain of flowers) scarred decades ago by contractors at work on the monstrous barrage of Le Chargeur which holds back the waters of Lac des Dix. Unseen from the barrage a former workman's hut has been converted into a privately-owned mountain refuge. Privately-owned it may be, but as with Refuge de St Laurent and numerous others like it, Cabane de Prafleuri is open to all and it makes an obvious overnight base for walkers tackling the Chamonix to Zermatt trek. A herd of ibex roams the surrounding basin, and small groups are often seen close to the hut where the guardian is said sometimes to leave salt out for them. On one visit the guardian had been scanning the upper slopes through binoculars, saw me and a couple friends descending, and had a weclome brew ready for us when we arrived!

The track that services the hut winds down to Val d'Hérémence where there's accommodation, and a campsite, at Pralong, an unpretentious base from which to explore that section of valley. But less than 200 metres above the hut Col des Roux (2804m) offers an easy and visually stimulating way into Val des Dix. Situated at the foot of Mont Blanc de Cheilon at the head of that valley, Cabane des Dix may be reached in about four hours or so from Prafleuri. From the Dix hut a straightforward glacier crossing leads to the ladder-aided Pas de Chèvres (2855m) which provides a popular route to or from Arolla at the head of a glen feeding Val d'Hérens. Next to the Pas de Chèvres the higher Col de Riedmatten offers an alternative crossing of the same ridge without ladder assistance. This particular pass is usually chosen by walkers tackling a magnificent trek from the dam at Le Chargeur, over the walling ridge and down to Arolla; a walk of great beauty and challenge that links the Vals d'Hérémence and d'Hérens, demanding around six hours, plus rests.

Val d'Hérémence is merely a tributary of Val d'Hérens, joining the parent valley near Vex. Evolène and Les Haudères are two of the finest of all traditional Valaisian villages and the most important centres in the main stem of Val d'Hérens with a choice of accommodation, including campsites. Above them on the eastern hillside Villa, La Sage and La Forclaz also offer beds in hotels, dortoirs and private chalets with glorious views. From them a trail climbs over Col de Torrent into the parallel Val de Moiry. Each of these is worth considering as a base for a walking holiday, though it must be said the upper three villages are somewhat limited in scope and you'd really need transport in order to make the most of the opportunities that exist throughout the valley, if staying in them for more than a few days.

Perhaps the best base of all would be Arolla, the village dominated by Mont Collon (3637m) at the head of Val d'Arolla, the tributary glen stretching south-west from Les Haudères. Arolla is noted for being one of the best of all centres for first-season Alpine climbers, but of more importance to readers of this book is the wide assortment of walking possibilities that exists there, from short and easy strolls such as that which leads to the perennially-popular Lac Bleu, to slightly more ambitious trails like the one that winds up to the alp huts of Pra Gra and continues to the Cabane des Aiguilles-Rouges, or the four and a half hour classic crossing of Pas de Chèvres and the Cheilon glacier on the way to Cabane des Dix. There are, of course, many others. More than fifty years ago it was said that: "Arolla is still small and the hills around it are big, so that even if the weather is so fine that it chases every visitor out of doors, it is easy to find solitude." That is still largely true today.

South-east of Les Haudères lies another very short tributary glen whose only village - and that a small one - is reached by Postbus from the main valley. A recommended path then leads from Ferpècle to the grassy belvedere of Bricola, a wonderful place from which to study the glaciers of Mont Miné and Ferpècle that hang like frozen waves among towering peaks, while the huge, foreshortened tooth of the Dent Blanche looms above to the east, though appearing perhaps less formidable than it really is. Dent Blanche is a cornerstone, a savage cornerstone 4357 metres high, but it is not alone in appeal and there are other peaks and corniced ice ridges also to ponder. Among them the Wandfluh, Tête Blanche and the great wall of the Dents de Bertol with the stiletto spike of the Aiguille de la Tsa jutting from it - a wall continuing northward as a support for the Pointe des Genevois and the Grande and Petite Dents de Veisivi.

Val d'Anniviers

Those who choose not to stray far from roads will never appreciate the full appeal of the Val d'Anniviers. True, the journey that leads from Sierre in the Rhône valley to Zinal at the roadhead gives a fair impression of what visual pleasures lie ahead, but it's a blinkered view, and in order to fall properly under its spell it will be necessary to discard those blinkers. That can only be achieved by walking. Baedeker did his best to open the eyes of his readers. So did J. Hubert Walker. This is what Walker said in the original *Walking in the Alps*: "..not only is the Val d'Anniviers far and away the finest valley on the Swiss side of the Pennine Alps, but also the cirque at its head is much grander even than the head of the neighbouring valley of Zermatt." Those who have been seduced by the many enticing trails of Val d'Anniviers will surely endorse that sentiment.

Something like sixteen kilometres from Sierre the valley divides as Val de Moiry and, the main branch, Val de Zinal. Take the Moiry glen first. Spread upon the true left-hand hillside a short distance inside the glen, Grimentz is a village of attractive dark timber chalets and granaries perched upon staddle stones. Geraniums and petunias blaze from practically every window and the narrow streets and alleyways are heavy with the fragrance of drying hay.

Upvalley yet another large dam has been built. A public road served by Postbus leads to it from Grimentz, with a restaurant standing at the right-hand end of the barrage where there's also a car park. Above this there's a small dortoir, regularly used by groups, and a path that climbs from it to Col de Sorebois by which access to Val de Zinal is made. But if you cross the dam to its western side a track winds up to a grassy alp from which trails explore the upper hillsides that spread out as broad pasturelands. One trail climbs to the lovely Lac des Autannes and continues to Col de Torrent (2919m) for a superb view of the western Pennines, with Mont Blanc seen far-off. The northern ridge rises from the col to the Sasseneire (3254m) where an extended view is offered from a slightly different perspective. Col de Torrent also provides a walker's route down to Val d'Hérens.

At the farm above Lac de Moiry (Montagne de Torrent) another trail cuts away heading south-east. This makes its way eventually to the Cabane de Moiry, and is useful for walkers tackling the west-to-east traverse of the range along the Walker's Haute Route, while the standard approach to the Moiry hut leads directly from the dam. From there the road continues along the eastern shore of Lac de Moiry and comes to an end near the snout of the Moiry glacier. A trail climbs alongside the glacier and traces the moraine wall to a high rocky spur where stands the Cabane de Moiry in full view of a spectacular icefall. In *The Alps in 1864* A.W. Moore described this icefall in glowing terms:

> "The lower part extends completely from one side of the glacier to the other, but higher up, under the Pigne de la Lex, is a belt of smooth ice, which we had no doubt would give access to the field of névé above the fall. Below this great cascade of séracs, the ice is as compact and level as above it is steep and dislocated. Indeed, I never saw an ice-fall confined within such plainly defined limits, or terminate so abruptly."

Cabane de Moiry is very much a mountaineer's hut, with climbs from it on the Pigne de la Lé (Moore's Pigne de la Lex), Pointes de Mourti, Pointe de Bricola and Grand Cornier, but many walkers also make a brief visit by day, thanks to the short, if steep, approach path, while a night spent there rewards with a very special atmosphere created by the looming presence of so much rock and ice. There can be few huts anywhere that are so easily accessible, yet give an impression of utter remoteness once darkness has fallen.

A new trail has recently been created which avoids the necessity of walking along the lakeside road on the descent from the hut. This trail cuts away from the original road-to-hut path and remains more or less on the two thousand five hundred metre contour and eventually joins up with another trail, leading from the barrage at the northern end of the lake to Col de Sorebois. This col gives clear witness to the great wedge of the Weisshorn (4506m), a mountain of considerable appeal soaring over Val de Zinal opposite, but which is not seen from the depths of the valley itself, since that valley is so deep and narrow that the true splendour of its walling peaks remains unguessed until you begin to climb the hillsides above. Zinal makes an obvious base for it has plenty of accommodation, including dortoirs and a simple terraced campsite at its southern end.

A walking holiday centred there gives rise to lots of possibilities. For a first day one should enjoy an easy stroll upvalley to visit the Cabane du Petit Mountet set upon a vegetated moraine on the left bank of the Zinal glacier. From there you gain a better idea of what lies ahead than could possibly be guessed from Zinal. The glacier is receding fast and is usually rubble-strewn and dirty grey in summer. But this becomes more pristine and sparkling white towards its head where Ober Gabelhorn, Mont Durand and Pointe de Zinal are hung with their own glacial armoury. Opposite stands the Weisshorn, behind rises Pigne de la Lé, and the continuing line of walling peaks includes the Bouquetins, Grand Cornier and Dent Blanche. A trail continues along the moraine crest beyond the Petit Mountet. Steep and narrow in places this path is safeguarded with fixed ropes, and there are sections of ladder to negotiate where cliffs intrude in the line of crumbling moraine. The trail ends just beyond a grassy bluff known as the Plan des Lettres (2465m), a first-rate picnic site with more fabulous views of the amphitheatre blocking the valley-head.

Cabane du Mountet stands within that cirque and enjoys what Walker reckoned to be one of the most glorious views in the Alps, while G.D. Abraham called it "an almost unsurpassed prospect of stupendous peak, and glittering glacier". The standard route from Zinal to the Mountet hut used to go via Petit Mountet and the Plan des Lettres, then crossed the glacier. But with glacial recession and the subsequent disturbed condition of the ice, this route has lost much of its appeal. Instead a different line is now taken on the eastern side of the Zinal glacier, crossing high along the flanks of Lo Besso before descending to the hut.

Another fine walk treads a narrow path high on the western hillside above Zinal and works southward to the green pastoral corrie of La Lé. From it the Weisshorn again appears magnificent. Then comes the Schalihorn with a beautiful snow ridge running round to link with Pointe Sud de Moming and Zinal Rothorn. Peaks at the head of the valley are again seen as the trail continues beyond La Lé on a steady descent to Petit Mountet.

The eastern side of the valley entices with several tremendous outings for walkers. Perhaps the best of all involves the crossing of a high grassy bluff known as Roc de la Vache (2581m), a strenuous walk of about five hours, Zinal to Zinal, plus rest stops and time to absorb the truly stunning panorama that is the main reward for tackling this route. As you descend from the high point of the Roc you come to the ruins of a stone-roofed alp hut and gain a breathtaking view of the corniced ridge of Pointe Sud de Moming with the fragmented Glacier de Moming caught mid frozen cascade. Val de Zinal lies hundreds of metres below and wherever you look majestic peaks soar heavenward.

Variations of the main walk are possible, with additional trails straying through the Combautanna corrie which leads to Cabane de Tracuit (3256m) on the ridge linking Les Diablons and Tête de Milon, or another which wanders from a collection of small tarns into the hanging valley of Ar Pitetta in the lap of the Weisshorn. Whymper came into this latter hanging valley in 1864 prior to making the first crossing of the Moming Pass from Zinal to Zermatt. Searching for somewhere in which to pass the night he found a cheese-maker's hut, "...a hovel, growing, as it were, out of the hill-side; roofed with rough slabs of slaty stone;

without a door or window; surrounded by quagmires of ordure, and dirt of every description." (*Scrambles Amongst the Alps*) The SAC now has a small refuge (Cabane d'Ar Pitetta; 2786m, 20 places) situated among moraines on the west flank of the Weisshorn from which climbers may tackle a variety of routes. The walk to it is worth considering too.

North of Zinal the somewhat eccentric Victorian Hotel Weisshorn stands on a hillside shelf more than eleven hundred metres above Vissoie, facing into the sunset and with views also across the Rhône to the Bernese Alps. After years of neglect, during which it was in danger of crumbling into romantic, but irreversible, decay, the hotel has now been refurbished. In doing so part of its former spartan appeal has been traded for more conventional standards of comfort and a healthier future, yet the views remain unchanged and as magnificent as ever.

St-Luc, a trim village above Vissoie, provides mechanical boost to walkers heading for Hotel Weisshorn from the lower reaches of Val d'Anniviers, while a spectacular belvedere trail hugs the eastern hillside to link the hotel with Zinal. A walk along this trail should be on the list of all visitors to the valley, for despite its surprising ease and lack of exposure or demand for scrambling (a price often exacted for the winning of great views) it makes one of the most delightful of panoramic outings with scenic rewards aplenty. Worth tackling in either direction, it is the southbound route that is the better option, for almost every step of the way will be an adulation of mountain scenery at its very best, the list of peaks on show reading like a Pennine Who's Who of mountains: Weisshorn, Zinal Rothorn, Ober Gabelhorn, Matterhorn (appearing over the domed snow ridge of Mont Durand), Dent d'Hérens, Dent Blanche, Grand Cornier and the rocky Bouquetins arête.

This elevated trail forms part of a four-or five-day walking circuit beginning and ending at Sierre in the Rhône valley and promoted by tourist offices within Val d'Anniviers. From Sierre the path climbs into the valley and heads south along the eastern flank to Chandolin and St-Luc, continues to Hotel Weisshorn and makes that glorious traverse upvalley to Zinal. From Zinal the circuit then takes a path round the lower, wooded, slopes of the Corne de Sorebois as far as Grimentz at the mouth of Val de Moiry. Now heading north linking trails trace a route along the western hillsides to Vercorin and, swinging above Chalais, returns to Sierre.

Vissoie and St-Luc not only provide opportunities for walks up to Hotel Weisshorn, they're also noted for the ever-popular ascent of Bella Tola (3025m) with its well-known 360 degree panorama described by Baedeker thus: "The View embraces the whole of the Bernese and Valaisian Alps; opposite, to the N., the whole gorge of the Dala is visible, up to the Gemmi. The mountains to the S., from Monte Leone to Mont Blanc, are particularly grand."

Bella Tola marks the high point on the ridge separating Val d'Anniviers from the Turtmanntal. This ridge also acts as a linguistic divide. All Swiss valleys to the west are French speaking; those to the east are German. Breaching this divide two main passes, the Forcletta (2874m) and Meidpass (2790m), are regularly crossed by mountain walkers. The first is easily gained from Zinal by way of a section of the trail to Hotel Weisshorn, the second reached through the curious hanging valley of Montagne de Nava that cuts immediately behind Hotel Weisshorn.

The Turtmanntal

This charming glen remains an unknown quantity to the vast majority of visitors to the Pennine Alps, a fact that is very much in its favour. A narrow road climbs into it from the Rhône valley and now projects some way south of Gruben, thus providing mountaineers with little more than an hour's walk from the roadhead to the Turtmann hut. Also known as Cabane Tourtemagne, it is used as a base for climbs on the Bishorn (4159m), that elegant snow peak which is, in fact, part of the Weisshorn's northerly ridge system from which the great Turtmann glacier drapes itself, effectively blocking the head of the valley.

More than a hundred years ago Leslie Stephen found himself gazing up at that scene from a pine glade near Gruben. "Above us rose the Weisshorn" he wrote, "in one of the most sublime aspects of that almost faultless mountain. The Turtmann glacier, broad and white with deep regular crevasses, formed a noble approach, like the staircase of some superb palace. Above this rose the huge mass of the mountain, firm and solid...And, higher still, its lofty crest, jagged and apparently swaying from side to side...Nowhere have I seen a more delicate combination of mountain massiveness, with soaring and delicately carved pinnacles pushed to the verge of extravagance." (*The Playground of Europe*)

Gruben boasts just one hotel, the Schwarzhorn, whose attic is given over to dormitory accommodation. Down valley a short distance, Restaurant Waldesruh also provides beds in a dormitory. There's a small food-store near Hotel Schwarzhorn, otherwise facilities for walkers passing through are practically non-existent. As far as walking routes are concerned, the main interest lies in the approach to, and crossing of, a variety of passes on either side of the valley. On the western side the two main crossings (the Forcletta and Meidpass) have already been noted. Of these the Forcletta provides the better view on the Turtmann flank, and is the more interesting route. Combined with a return via the Meidpass, a fine two-day circuit could be achieved, using Hotel Weisshorn on the Val d'Anniviers side for overnight accommodation.

Two passes on the eastern wall of the Turtmanntal entice walkers over to Zermatt's valley, the Mattertal, reached at St Niklaus. The first is the Augstbordpass (2894m), adopted by the Chamonix to Zermatt route, the other being the Jungpass (2990m), a rougher crossing than its neighbour to the north-east. From the Augstbordpass an hour's diversion will lead to the Schwarzhorn (3202m) whose summit view rivals that of the Bella Tola.

The Mattertal

Descending from the Augstbordpass the mountain walker loses some 200 metres or so of height, then turns a ridge projection to be presented with a surprise view of the Dom (4545m), Switzerland's highest mountain (as opposed to its highest *summit*, which is the 4634 metre Dufourspitze, part of the Monte Rosa massif shared with Italy) rising as a triangle of ice above the Nadelhorn, Ulrichshorn and Balfrin, and the tremendous cascading trunk of the Riedgletscher carving out a new glen for some far-off century on the opposite side of the unseen valley. The bed of that valley lies more than 1500 metres below, a deep shadowed shaft, hidden from view so that its depth remains a mystery.

The trail leads on, a paved mule-trail that hiccups along the steep hillside, gradually revealing the Mattertal in fragments until almost its full length is clearly visible, and its massive glaciated headwall above Zermatt blocks the southern horizon. Halfway along the right-hand wall the Weisshorn soars and glistens its upper ice-clad north-east face, but of the Matterhorn there is no sign.

On a steep slope of hillside between the Augstbordpass and St Niklaus, the main village slumped in the bed of the Mattertal far below, there sits a tiny alp hamlet of typical Valaisian chalets and hay barns, with a white-painted chapel perched on the very lip of the slope, and a small restaurant next to it that offers a few beds and a four-bunk dormitory for passing walkers. Jungen (1955m) occupies one of the most idyllic settings imaginable, a haven of undisturbed peace and scenic delights. By day the lofty peaks that close ranks along both sides of the Mattertal steadily rearrange their shadows so that no two hours are alike, while at night the view from Jungen is of black velvet shapes pricked with the lights of remote mountain huts on high, scattered farms and villages lower down, and, far away at the head of the valley, a snaking procession of diamonds as a silent train makes its way from Zermatt to the Gornergrat. Apart from the ancient trail linking St Niklaus with the Augstbordpass and the Jungpass, Jungen is accessible from the valley only by a do-it-yourself cable-car. A splendid walk known as the Höhenweg Vispertaler Sonnenberge passes through the hamlet.

On the opposite, eastern, side of the valley, the larger village of Grächen mimicks Jungen's airy situation. By comparison it's a teeming metropolis, yet Grächen is in reality little more than a virtually traffic-free, scattered resort of handsome chalets and flower-busy hotels set among steep pastures at the tail end of the Ried glacier. There are some grand walking trails leading from it. The classic route here being the Höhenweg Saas Fee (otherwise known as the Höhenweg Balfrin), a seven-hour epic route, nineteen kilometres long, which climbs to Hannigalp on the northern spur of the Mattertal's dividing ridge, then curves into the adjacent Saastal, maintaining a high and in some places exposed belvedere way above the valley until finally sloping down into Saas Fee. It's a marvellously engineered path which even tunnels through a cliff at one point, and with good views to the Fletschhorn, Lagginhorn and Weissmies once Hannigalp's forested spur has been turned.

Heading south through the Mattertal the valley road is busy throughout summer with a constant succession of cars and coaches filled with eager-eyed passengers making a modern-day pilgrimage of devotion to the foot of the Matterhorn. The railway keeps close company with the road for much of the way, and passes through several small villages, each of which lives in the metaphorical shadow of Zermatt.

Randa is one such, though it deserves better, for it has its own particular charm and with a few hotels, apartments and a campsite on the southern outskirts, offers more low-key facilities than its more illustrious neighbour upvalley. From it some very steep paths climb to splendid viewpoints. One route ascends the eastern hillside to the Dom hut (2940m); another fights its way up the side of the Schalikin gorge, passes a few remote hay barns and chalets, and eventually gains the Weisshorn hut (2932m) on the opposite flank. As if to emphasise the unsettled nature of the landscape here, a massive rockfall reshaped the left-hand hillside just north of Randa in April 1991, demolishing the railway, blocking the river and cutting off the upper valley for several days. Two years later a huge dust cloud from the debris still hung over part of the valley whenever a wind blew. But this was merely the latest such rockfall, for history records another monstrous landslip which completely buried a village somewhere between Randa and Täsch.

Between Randa and Zermatt Täsch is dominated by huge car parks filled to capacity for much of the time by visitors, not to Täsch itself, but to Zermatt, thanks to the latter resort's traffic-free status. Because of this Täsch has little individual charm, being seen by the vast majority of tourists as no more than a place of transit, where one exchanges car travel for that of train. It does have an assortment of hotels, however, for those who would choose to stay, and a campsite strung alongside the railway line near the ever-busy station. But none should camp there and expect seclusion.

Cutting away to the south-east of the village a glen suggests, quite rightly, that it could be worth exploring. This glen drains the western flanks of Rimpfischhorn, Allalinhorn and Alphubel. Täschalp lies in its bed some two hours from Täsch. It has an inn, an attractive little chapel, and a splay of footpaths leading from it. One climbs to the Täsch hut (2701m) in a further hour and a half, another continues upvalley, while a third option crosses the Ober Sattla below the Sattelspitz and continues roughly southward to Zermatt.

Without question Zermatt is one of the great centres of the Alps, a resort whose fame exploded with the drama of Whymper's first ascent of the Matterhorn in 1865. But while the Matterhorn is the natural lure, this stately pyramid of stone is merely one of many fabulous peaks drawn around and above Zermatt in an arc of glacial splendour. From east to west the bounding rim is topped by the Rimpfischhorn, Strahlhorn, Monte Rosa (consisting of Jägerhorn, Nordend, and Dutourspitze), Liskamm, the 'twins', Castor and Pollux, Breithorn, Klein Matterhorn, Matterhorn, Dent d'Hérens, Tête de Valpelline, Dent Blanche and Ober Gabelhorn. These are the mountains that form a backcloth to an almost limitless number of walks, and though the range of possibilities is greatly extended when glacier crossings are included, they are specifically excluded here. Those outing suggestions which follow require no specialised equipment such as ropes, crampons or ice axes, but will nonetheless present scenic rewards in abundance.

The walk to the Schönbiel hut is an obvious choice, for it is one of the finest of all outings from Zermatt. Standing on a moraine wall at the foot of Pointe de Zinal, the hut gazes across the Zmutt glacier to Dent d'Hérens and the Zmutt ridge of the Matterhorn. Ice faces form a cirque to the west, while far off to the east Monte Rosa and the Gorner glacier provide distant perspectives. There are two routes to it; one, a high trail that climbs from the middle of Zermatt to the remote Trift Hotel via the Edelweiss restaurant (from which an alternative trail cuts away to join the upper path at Höhbalmen), then swings south round the flanks of the Unter Gabelhorn, joins the Edelweiss trail and curves westward with stunning views of the Matterhorn on a high belvedere of a path. Just before reaching the little Arben glen which drains the south slopes of the Ober Gabelhorn, the trail twists down to join the main, low-level path from Zermatt. This lower option is full of variety and splendid views too.

Leaving Zermatt the trail rises gently through meadows and woodland to the hamlet of Zmutt, then heads west to pass below the Matterhorn's looming north face. Having been joined by the upper trail from Trift, the way then crosses the Arben stream (the water level often rises considerably midway through a summer's day as the snow and ice melt from the Ober Gabelhorn increases), climbs onto the crest of a moraine wall banked alongside the Zmutt glacier, and follows it all the way to the hut.

A visit to the Hörnli hut on the lower slopes of the Matterhorn is worth considering too. Not necessarily for the steep walk itself, but in order to obtain a more personal experience of one of the world's best-known mountains, and to enjoy an exceptional panorama of a glacial kingdom seen from the terrace in front of the hut. It's possible to take the easy option of cableways much of the way to a high shelf of hillside overlooking the little Schwarzsee, but that should be resisted, for the uphill walk from Zermatt is the proper way to approach such a mountain. The climb through pinewoods above the black timbers of Zum See is a fragrant one on a warm summer's morning; red squirrels in the trees, their half-chewed husks of pine-cones crushed among the needles carpeting the path, and as you emerge from the trees, so the Matterhorn reveals itself as a towering monolith with its cocked head often adorned with a dusting of cloud near the summit.

Above the crowded Schwarzsee the trail refuses to slacken a gradient that was steep enough from Zum See at the foot of the hill. In fact the whole route is quite strenuous, with only an occasional brief easing of angle. A series of ladders helps overcome sections of exposed crag, but the majority of this upper approach follows a broad winding path up a mountainside that grows increasingly barren, while views all around are simply magnificent.

Once at the hut, with the former Belvedere Hotel next door, it is the long view across the icy wastes to Monte Rosa that holds one's attention. The Matterhorn itself is seriously foreshortened, yet it reveals the truth that close-to it is nothing more than a giant pile of disintegrating rubble!

Walks to the Schönbiel and Hörnli huts are both full-day outings, but shorter walks with their own magical views abound too. One such is the route to Findeln, the much-photographed collection of dark-timbered chalets, hay barns and trim white chapel standing on a steeply sloping hillside to the south-east of Zermatt. Another extends from Findeln to visit the tiny Grüensee, from whose shoreline Zinal Rothorn and Weisshorn offer a splendid profile on the far side of the valley.

There are several teardrop tarns scattered on hills high above Zermatt that make worthy outings. Perhaps the best known is the Riffelsee on the north side of the Riffelhorn. The grass banks of this jewel are often crowded with visitors who have ridden the railway to Gornergrat, had their fill of the panorama there and then decided to walk back down to Zermatt collecting such notable viewpoints as the Riffelsee and Riffelalp on the way.

To spend days walking in the hills above Zermatt is to dispense with any dream of isolation. Unless, that is, you're prepared to study the map well, rise early and shun most of the viewpoints that form a thousand dazzling compositions on the postcard stands. Zermatt's gifts to the mountain walker, as to the mountaineer, lie not in outings of startling originality (it's been on everyone's Alpine tick-list far too long for that), but in a somewhat romantic, if tenuous, link with the past.

The Saastal

Zermatt and Saas Fee are linked by high glacier passes: the Adler, Allalin and Feejoch. Though beyond the scope of this volume, the Adler Pass is of particular interest, for it is not only the main route of access between the head of the Mattertal and that of the Saastal, but it provides one of those astonishing panoramas by which the local geography is clearly revealed. Standing at a height of 3789 metres between Rimpfischhorn and Strahlhorn, one gazes not only across the pristine arctic wastes of the combined Adler, Findeln and Gorner glaciers, not only enjoying every peak of note from Monte Rosa to the Ober Gabelhorn, but also the stark frowning upper reaches of the Mischabel wall that is the main divider between Mattertal and Saastal, and far off beyond the unseen, unguessed depths of the Rhône valley to crest upon crest of Oberland summits - the whole summed up by Alfred Wills in *Wanderings Among the High Alps* as: "a scene of such inconceivable extent and magnificence, as to beggar all description".

Such is one route from Zermatt to Saas Fee; a route though not difficult nor particularly arduous as such routes go, it is nevertheless confined to those with the necessary expertise and equipment to tackle a glacier expedition of this nature. The modest walker who follows winding trails has no such 'short cut' from one valley-head to the next, for all along that lofty dividing wall stretching from the snow domes of Monte Rosa to the Färichhorn between St Niklaus and Saas Balen, ice guards one face or the other, and one must look for more inviting ways to gain the seemingly elusive Saastal.

It is not at all elusive, of course, since the Postbus runs daily through the valley from Visp, and there are trails if you're prepared to look for them. Arguably the best linking trail is that which has already been mentioned from Grächen, the Höhenweg Saas Fee. A similar high path also traces a route along the eastern wall of the Saastal, the Gspon Höhenweg, leading from Gspon at its northern end, to Saas Grund in the valley bed below Saas Fee.

There are certain similarities between Zermatt and Saas Fee. Both are lodged among spectacular high mountains. Both deny access to motor vehicles. Both have a wonderland of walking routes leading from them. And both have a rather inflated opinion of themselves, which has resulted in what many consider to be an over-abundance of mechanical adornment that has served to devalue what is, after all, their major asset - the mountains themselves.

Lodged in a compact hanging valley above the main Saastal, Saas Fee huddles within the cradle of an astonishing mountain amphitheatre whose summits by and large are well above the four thousand metre mark. Towering above the village their glaciers shine as an eye-squinting backcloth: "...a huge curtain of ice let down from the summits of the mighty range between the Dom and Monte Rosa, cutting off half the horizon...its beauties almost unique in the Alps." That is how Leslie Stephen described it in *The Playground of Europe*. Today cable-cars dangle above those icefields and skiers swoop down the Fee glacier in summer as well as winter. The Fee glacier has suffered a gross humiliation, however, for engineers have bored through rock walls near its head to ceate the Metro-Alpin, the world's highest subway which travels from the top station of the Felskinn cableway and emerges to a revolving restaurant on the Mittelallalin. What would Leslie Stephen have to say about that, I wonder?

But there's no denying the multitude of trails that turns Saas Fee into a very fine base for a walking holiday. Trails, there are, that provide a wide range of opportunities: modest, moderate, and challenging. One of the best of the easy walks follows the Kapellenweg (Chapel Way) between Saas Fee and Saas Grund. This is an historic footpath lined with sixteen small stone shrines (the first built in 1687) and an elaborately-decorated chapel which is the scene of a pilgrimage festival every year on 8 September. For the non-motorised walker this footpath offers the most interesting way up to Saas Fee from the valley. Once there, however, more challenging routes become possible.

There's a fine, though exposed, trail that links Saas Fee with the Britannia hut (3030m) by way of the ridge-spur of Plattjen below the Mittaghorn. Despite one's natural antipathy towards the littering of mountains by cable-car, chairlift or funicular, the Felskinn cableway enables this walk to be achieved within a day starting from the Britannia Hut and ending at Saas Fee, and with a recommended extension that involves a lengthy traverse of hillsides above the village. From the upper cable-car station (2991m) a track is maintained throughout the summer across the small Chessjen glacier heading south-east through the Egginerjoch, an obvious col between the red-brown rock tower of the Egginer and the icefields of the Hinter Allalin. The track across the glacier is clearly marked and should be safe to follow, but it is important to stick closely to the precise route. It leads in about forty minutes to the Britannia hut, set at the foot of an easy ridge leading onto the summit of the Klein Allalin, whose panorama includes the Allalinhorn, Rimpfischhorn and Strahlhorn rising to the south and south-west amid a sea of snow-covered ice.

Leaving the hut a trail crosses snow at the lower end of the Chessjen glacier and joins a good path on the northern side. This cuts along the steep eastern flank of the Egginer and Mittaghorn high above the upper Saastal, and is buttressed in places by well-placed rocks. Although exposed at times, with a long drop to the valley, it always appears perfectly safe and is visually stimulating as you have before you the great peaks of Weissmies, Lagginhorn and Fletschhorn leading the eye to the distant Oberland wall. Crossing a rough boulder-field the path then curves left to cross the north-east shoulder of the Mittaghorn, and suddenly you're confronted by the stupendous face of the Mischabel peaks (Täschhorn, Dom, Lenzspitze and Nadelhorn) sharp above the turmoil of the Fee glacier. It's a view to stop you in your tracks.

The way now descends past the Plattjen gondola lift to Berghaus Plattjen and a choice of paths. Instead of taking one of those that descends directly to Saas Fee I would choose the Gemsweg (chamois path) which heads westward as an almost level trail round the hillside. In late summer, when the first frosts have sharpened the air, shrubs and larches along the way express themselves with the most amazing colours, set off by the delicate blue and silvery waves of the glacier beyond. Eventually the path slopes down to pass close below the snout of the glacier and crosses several streams issuing from it. Now the route twists among boulders, passes a small barren plain of glacial debris, climbs a moraine bank and rises along the lower slopes of the Mischabelhörner to gain the panoramic viewpoint of Hannigalp, served by gondola lift from Saas Fee. From here a forest path winds down to the village.

Whilst Saas Fee enjoys such a privileged situation below the glaciers, other villages spread among the Saastal meadows have their own appeal. Saas Balen, midway along the valley, huddles at the foot of the Fletschhorn (3993m), while Unter dem Berg and Saas Grund have both Lagginhorn (4010m) and Weissmies (4023m) as their overpowering eastern wall.

On the slopes of the Lagginhorn high above Unter dem Berg sit the two Weissmies huts at 2726 metres. From them a clear view to the south-west shows all the glory of Saas Fee's knuckle glen, its glaciers, ice cliffs and magnificent background of the Mischabel peaks. Some 300 metres below the huts is the upper station of the Kreuzboden cableway which provides access to the Hannig Panoramaweg. This trail is very steep in places, but it makes for a memorable half-day walk as it passes through the picturesque, semi-deserted hamlet of Triftalp before dropping through larchwoods to the valley.

Another recommended walk from Kreuzboden is the Höhenweg Almagelleralp, a fine belvedere that cuts along the slopes of Weissmies and Trifthorn, before cutting into the glen of the Almagellertal which joins the main Saastal near the northern edge of Saas Almagell, the valley's uppermost village. There's a mountain inn at Almagelleralp from which to explore this lovely glen. In its headwall the Zwischbergenpass (3268m) provides access to the Zwischbergental, a glen on the northern side of the frontier which flows out to the border village of Gondo on the Italian slope of the Simplon Pass.

To the south of Saas Almagell another fine glen slants away south-eastward from the main valley. Through the Furggtälli a trading route of ancient tradition crosses the Antrona Pass (2838m) into Italy. A walk of at least eight hours takes you from Almagell, across this pass and down to Antronapiana past several lakes, while at the head of the main Saastal the Monte Moro Pass is probably the most popular of all frontier crossings in this corner of the Pennine Alps. Like the Antrona, the Monte Moro Pass has been in use for centuries. The first mention of a crossing here was in a treaty of 1403, although it had been known at least since the middle of the thirteenth century. It makes a fine walk in its own right from the dam at the northern end of the Mattmark reservoir (three hours), and with the lure of another three hours of descent on the Italian side to Macugnaga in full view of the great east face (the so-called 'mirror wall') of Monte Rosa.

✳   ✳   ✳

THE WALKER'S HAUTE ROUTE

Although this chapter is primarily concerned with the Pennine Alps, it is necessary here to stray a little west of its boundary with the Mont Blanc massif in order to follow a recommended long-distance walk in its entirety, from the base of Mont Blanc to the Matterhorn; a trek known as the Walker's Haute Route.

Mention of the Haute Route today usually conjures visions among the mountaineering fraternity of the ski-touring classic that leads from one glacial col to the next between Chamonix (or Argentière) and Zermatt or Saas Fee. It is the Alpine ski tour *par excellence*, yet it originated as a mountaineer's expedition back in the days of the Victorian pioneers, among such Alpine Club stalwarts as J.F. Hardy, William Mathews, Francis Fox Tuckett, F.W. Jacomb and Stephen Winkworth who, with their guides, achieved a complete High Level Route in 1861. It was only later, after it had been hi-jacked as a ski-touring expedition, that it become known as the Haute Route.

That original mountaineer's route is still tackled today, although with the advance in glacial recession some of the high passes have become potentially dangerous on account of stonefall; where earlier crossings were eased by a covering of snow and ice, a number of cols are now bare rock or near-vertical scree. Only in the spring ski-touring season is there a virtual guarantee of good snow-cover.

But the Walker's Haute Route referred to several times in the preceding pages takes a different line between Chamonix and Zermatt. The mountaineer's route more or less hugs the crest of the range; the walker's route hiccups over the long north-projecting ridges that separate deep fragrant valleys. Crossing eleven passes, not one of which is a glacier pass, it gains and loses an accumulation of more than 11,000 metres in height, visits some of the finest villages on the Swiss side of the Pennines and provides daily views of peak and pasture that count among the loveliest in all the Alps.

Taking from ten days to a fortnight to complete, accommodation is plentiful, and as there are opportunities on most stages to restock with food to eat on the trail, backpacking with a heavy rucksack is unnecessary. Route-finding, under normal conditions, should not be problematic as the vast majority of trails are clear on the ground and the recommended maps show plenty of detail. Nowhere along the way, however, is there a sign denoting the existence of the Haute Route, so its course demands advance scrutiny of the guidebook.

The first two or three stages as far as Champex reverse sections of the Tour du Mont Blanc. Beginning in Chamonix (the TMB actually avoids the town), a series of footpaths and tracks leads upvalley largely through forest to Argentière, and on to Le Tour huddled below the Col de Balme. Above hangs the Glacier du Tour, while looking back down the Vallée de l'Arve Mont Blanc is seen as a great snow dome on the left, with the Aiguilles Rouges rising in a long wall on the right.

The first pass of the Haute Route involves an undemanding climb to Col de Balme across which runs the Franco/Swiss border. Not that there's any indication of a frontier here, except that at the privately-owned refuge food and drinks may be paid for in either French or Swiss currency. It's a scenically delightful spot dominated by views of the Aiguilles Verte and Drus, and graceful Mont Blanc itself. Looking north-east, however, the first Swiss valley appears to be rather lacking in scenes of landscape drama. But once you've descended through the Nant Noir glen, suddenly a great cascade of ice looms off to the right; the fragmented Glacier du Trient.

From the village of Trient to Champex the Haute Route walker has two options, both of which are shared with walkers on the TMB, most of whom are coming in the opposite direction. The first is to go via the high, steep and scenically spectacular Fenêtre d'Arpette (2665m), or by way of a green helter-skelter hillside on the so-called 'Bovine' route. Both have much to commend them, but the Fenêtre crossing wins hands-down by virtue of the climb to it which follows the north bank of the Trient glacier, and then provides a real surprise on arrival at the col. It should be borne in mind, however, that with nearly 1400 metres of height to gain, it's a hard day's walk - especially coming so early into a major trek. And the 1200 metre descent to Champex is no gentle stroll either. That descent begins with a very steep runnel of grit and stones, then crosses a rough boulderfield before easing into the pastures of the Arpette glen. From Trient to Champex by this route will demand at least six and a half hours of effort, plus time allowed for necessary rests - and to photograph the stunning scenery.

The Bovine route also rewards with fine views, although these are mostly pastoral by contrast with the stark high mountain scenery of the Fenêtre alternative. Though a little longer in distance, the Bovine path takes about an hour less to complete than the high crossing, while it is still fairly demanding. It leads from Trient directly up to the Col de la Forclaz, then strikes eastward, rising along a narrow trail among trees and shrubs with views down a long groove of valley to the broad cut of the Rhône. Alp Bovine is an open hillside with simple buildings at which walkers can buy refreshments from the farmer and his family who live there in summer. From the alp the way continues, rounds a curving spur and descends steeply among trees to another rough pasture (La Jure), then through forest to Plan de l'Au and on among trees once more before joining the road for the final walk down into Champex.

Once you leave Champex the way becomes less busy with walkers, for the TMB does not stray along our route now, and the gentle morning's amble down to Sembrancher at the junction of Vals d'Entremont and Bagnes presents an opportunity to witness the life of pastoral Switzerland as it has been lived untouched by tourism for many generations. Trails slant down through tiny hamlets and meadows with islands of crop (sweet corn, potato, chard) growing among them. Once at Sembrancher a short valley stroll heads into Val de Bagnes and ends in La Châble in readiness for a long climb next day to Cabane du Mont-Fort.

It is a long climb too, with more than 1600 metres of height gain over a distance of about nine kilometres. That being said, the way is full of interest for it begins with a steep footpath linking villages that seem to hang suspended from the steep hillside, then traverses round to the trim chapel and farm of Les Verneys before resuming the uphill climb through forest to the open, sunny clutch of chalets at Clambin (1701m) above, and to the south-east of, Verbier. Emerging from the dense forest cover just below Clambin one gains an impressive first view of the Combin massif filling the south-east vista. That view, that massif, will dominate the rest of the walk to the Mont-Fort hut, and the first hour or so of tomorrow's stage too.

Not only does Clambin enjoy a privileged view of the Combin massif, it also looks across an intervening ridge to the eastern outliers of the Mont Blanc range, and westward to the spiked outline of the Dents du Midi. There's a splendid restaurant here, with seats and tables outside protected from the sun with bright parasols, where it's tempting to relax with a cold drink and absorb those views in luxury. Above Clambin, when at last you can drag yourself away, there's more forest shade, but this soon gives way to open hillside above the treeline. Eventually a *bisse* is found, with an accompanying footpath that makes a gentle contour nearly all the way to the hut.

If the panorama of numerous stately mountains gives reason to rejoice at Clambin, the elevated position of Cabane du Mont-Fort only extends one's sense of privilege. Dusk is a time of particular magic, for often the Val de Bagnes far below slips into darkness beneath strips of vapour dyed by the setting sun. And out to the south-west fence-post aiguilles and distant crowns of snow catch the last of that sun and hold its reflected light until only a fading glow remains to burnish the serrated horizon.

Sharing for an hour and a half the path of the Tour des Combin, the Walker's Haute Route turns from Cabane du Mont-Fort next day and follows the trail of the Sentier des Chamois to Col Termin in a constant adulation of the splendours of the Grand Combin across the depths of Val de Bagnes. With nothing to intrude that view the full frontal glory of the mountain and its big glacier system is open for inspection, while along the trail itself there is a very good chance of spying the large herd of ibex that roams here. It's a wonderful start to a day's walking, for even the trail demands attention as it edges round exposed corners, scrambles up short, narrow buttresses with the aid of fixed ropes, and then makes a steady traverse along precipitous slopes. That being said, with due concentration there should be no cause for alarm. It is just the sort of trail that makes a long mountain journey such as this so rewarding.

There is an alternative to the Sentier des Chamois which crosses Col de la Chaux (2940m) south-east of the Mont-Fort hut, and joins the main route below Col de Louvie. When conditions are suspect along the chamois path, after snowfall, for example, or when there's ice on the trail, the guardian at Mont-Fort usually advises this alternative crossing. It's always worth asking his advice prior to setting out.

At the end of the Sentier des Chamois the trail crosses Col Termin and makes an undulating traverse north-eastward above Lac de Louvie, then rises through a stony hanging valley to Col de Louvie (2921m). A scene of gaunt austerity is revealed; a landscape of decay and destruction. Yet through this wilderness the continuing route seeks a course, crosses the lower reaches of the untroubled Grand Désert glacier and eventually scrambles up to the third and final pass of the day, Col de Prafleuri. More than 300 metres below sits the timber-built Cabane de Prafleuri.

From Prafleuri to Arolla is another splendid day's journey. It starts well, and maintains visual interest all day as you cross Col des Roux just twenty minutes above the hut and gaze on the Val des Dix and its artificial lake, with the triangular north face of Mont Blanc de Cheilon (3870m) and Pigne d'Arolla next to it joined by a long pelmet of snow blocking the valley to the south. The way leads down to the lake's western shoreline and forks at the far end. One route (the main one) goes up the eastern flank of the continuing valley above the Cheilon glacier, and crosses Col de Riedmatten at the southern end of the Monts Rouges ridge. The alternative trail follows the west bank of the Cheilon glacier to the ever-popular Cabane des Dix standing atop its rocky knoll immediately below Mont Blanc de Cheilon. From there one crosses the glacier to a pair of steep ladders leading onto the Pas de Chèvres, which is only a few paces from Col de Riedmatten.

Both cols provide amazing views eastward. Among a bevy of fine peaks on show are the Dent Blanche, Bouquetins, Dent d'Hérens, the distant unmistakable tip of the Matterhorn, and Mont Collon, the snow-gemmed mountain that so dominates views from Arolla. From either pass it will take another hour and a half, at least, to wander down to Arolla among pastures overlooked by guardian glaciers and awesome mountains, finishing the day on a fragrant trail dropping through pinewoods.

The next stage is a gentle intermission. No passes to cross, no steep ascents to tackle, no rough boulderscapes. Just an easy wander down through the Arolla glen to Les Haudères at the head of Val d'Hérens, followed by an easy uphill path that leads to either La Sage or Villa, two small neighbouring villages set above the valley gazing west from a natural hillside terrace. Both have a limited amount of accommodation; La Sage has a dortoir, while Villa has private rooms to rent and a small foodstore useful for stocking up with supplies for the next day or two.

Col de Torrent (2919m) is unseen from either Villa or La Sage, hidden as it is by folding layers of green hillside. The continuing trail slants up this hillside, enters a high pastoral basin, then makes a final series of loops onto the pass. Once there yet another fine panorama is added to a growing list of memorable views before descending past the tranquil Lac des Autannes into the Moiry glen where several options need looking at. Fit walkers should be able to continue beyond Moiry as far as Zinal in the upper reaches of Val d'Anniviers, by crossing a second pass, Col de Sorebois (2896m), above the northern end of Lac de Moiry. But this is an option worth considering only if you're running short of days, for Val de Moiry deserves better treatment than a brief scurried appreciation, and for that to be achieved at least one night should be spent there - preferably in the Cabane de Moiry. This may be gained either by a path that breaks off to the right at the farm of Montagne de Torrent (halfway between Lac des Autannes and Lac de Moiry), or by a clear trail that branches south-eastward away from the main track below the farm, slants down to the mountain end of the Moiry reservoir, then climbs to the hut along the moraine wall banked against the eastern side of the Moiry glacier.

Two other options are available, both of which will be of interest to walkers too weary to contemplate either of the alternatives outlined above. The first, and easier, suggests a night spent in the dortoir set above the north-eastern end of the Moiry dam, the second requires a further two kilometre walk downvalley to the pretty village of Grimentz. The trouble with the latter solution is that you will then have to retrace your steps to the dam next day before climbing to Col de Sorebois, or take an alternative low-level route round to Zinal, in which case you lose the 'high level' flavour of this classic walk.

Col de Sorebois is easily reached from its western side. The trail to it from the Moiry dam looks down into the deep wedge of valley beyond Grimentz, while chamois are often seen grazing the slopes just below the col. On the Zinal side, however, the upper hillside has been badly scarred by the ski industry and it is only a glorious panorama of big mountains that relieves the scene of immediate desolation. Once below the broad bulldozed pistes the descent to Zinal is unremittingly steep on a forest path that threatens to destroy knee joints and leg muscles alike, but for those who experience problems on such descents there's a possibility of riding a cable-car for this last section.

Earlier in this chapter the splendid range and variety of walking routes accessible from Zinal were briefly outlined. One of those mentioned was the balcony trail linking Zinal with Hotel Weisshorn; a four-hour visual extravaganza. It is this trail that is taken on the next stage of the Walker's Haute Route; an easy, short stage that could be lengthened by continuing over the Meidpass to the Turtmanntal. Alternatively, a useful crossing into the Turtmanntal for those running short of time, is by way of the 2874 metre Forcletta, a fine pass that produces a stimulating descent in the shadow of handsome mountains.

One of those two crossings will need to be tackled in due course in order to progress the route eastward, but Hotel Weisshorn is worth using as an overnight base - weather, time and expense permitting - for the magic of its position, the delight of the trail to reach it, and for the glories of sunset witnessed through the huge plate glass windows of its dining room.

Of the two passes linking Val d'Anniviers with the Turtmanntal, the Meidpass is lower and shorter if tackled following a night at Hotel Weisshorn, while the Forcletta is better if approached directly from Zinal (though it's easily accessible too from Hotel Weisshorn by a little back-tracking), and provides more intimate details of peaks crowding the head of the Turtmanntal.

Gruben is the only village in the Turtmanntal of use to walkers on our route, and that only a very small one. Ideally set in the bed of the valley directly between the Meidpass and the final crossing of the Chamonix to Zermatt walk, it gives immediate access to a belt of forest through which a delightful path rises to the Augstbordpass. Although the pass is more than a thousand metres above Gruben the gradient is generous and there are no horrors to face - or could it be that by the time you embark on this final crossing you feel ready to tackle anything? When forest gives way to an open shelf of pasture and a pair of alp huts, a sudden tantalising view north shows the elegant Bietschhorn rising as a conical pillar advertising the Bernese Alps. It's only a very brief view, but it forms a worthy counter-balance to all those sirens of the Pennine Alps to which the walk has been privy so far. The trail now enters the hanging valley of Grüobtälli, rising over hummocks of grass to a stony, scree-ridden upper region; a zone of silence when the wind is stilled. Above this a small pool is passed, then a final clutter of rocks and boulders before stealing up the last steep slope to gain the Augstbordpass, overlooking a landscape of wild, austere beauty.

The trail descends into that wild landscape, a stony basin giving way to the more gentle Augstbord glen with views directly ahead showing the junction of Saastal and Mattertal, that splendid deep Y of valley systems where two major glacier streams combine forces to flow north into the Rhône. Beyond that confluence the glacier-draped Fletschhorn provides a broad hint of the Saastal's beauty, while the full splendour of the Mattertal holds itself in check until you've crossed the Emdbach stream below the Inners Tälli basin, and made a steady rising traverse over a slope of boulders and rocks to a shoulder of mountain (the Steitalgrat) which, when rounded, presents the most startling vista of the whole route from Chamonix to Zermatt.

Ahead soars the majestic west face of the Mischabelhörner: Färichhorn, Balfrin,

Ulrichshorn, Dürrenhorn, Nadelhorn, Lenzspitze and Dom; a crown of snow and ice and dark rocky pyramids, with dazzling slopes of névé and icefields coming together as the long tongue of the Ried glacier, tormented with countless lines of crevasse and séracs casting shadow - mountain architecture in its most sublime and reverential form. All this seen across the unguessed depths of the Mattertal, while a few paces later another vision of beauty is revealed as the Weisshorn and Brunegghorn thrust out their ice-clad chests in an attitude of bravado. An old mule-path takes you down to the mouth of the Jungtal glen, then twists left away from the Jungtal trail, goes through a patch of woodland and emerges to the hamlet of Jungen (shown as Jungu on some maps) before steepening in a succession of zig-zags to the bed of the Mattertal at St Niklaus. All that remains is for a final day's walking upvalley to Zermatt and the Matterhorn.

CHAMONIX TO ZERMATT - THE WALKER'S HAUTE ROUTE - SUMMARY

Day 1:   Chamonix - Argentière (assuming late arrival in Chamonix)
or: Chamonix - Col de Balme - Trient

Day 2:   Argentière - Col de Balme - Trient

Day 3:   Trient - Fenêtre d'Arpette - Champex
or: Trient - Col de la Forclaz - Alp Bovine - Champex

Day 4:   Champex - Sembrancher - Le Châble

Day 5:   Le Châble - Clambin - Cabane du Mont-Fort

Day 6:   Cabane du Mont-Fort - Col Termin - Col de Louvie - Col de Prafleuri - Cabane de Prafleuri

Day 7:   Cabane de Prafleuri - Col de Riedmatten - Arolla
or: Cabane de Prafleuri - Cabane des Dix - Pas de Chèvres - Arolla

Day 8:   Arolla - Les Haudères - La Sage (or Villa)

Day 9:   La Sage (or Villa) - Col de Torrent - Cabane de Moiry
         (or Barrage de Moiry)

Day 10: Cabane de Moiry (or Barrage de Moiry) - Col de Sorebois - Zinal

Day 11: Zinal - Hotel Weisshorn
or: Zinal - Forcletta - Gruben

Day 12: Hotel Weisshorn - Meidpass - Gruben

Day 13: Gruben - Augstbordpass - Jungen (or St Niklaus)

Day 14: Jungen (or St Niklaus) - Randa - Täsch - Zermatt

An energetic but scenically spectacular route, with eleven passes to cross, some well-situated mountain huts providing accommodation, and a variety of charming villages visited along the way. Trails are good for most of the route, although several very steep descents require care. Some of the crossings are quite high, with a fair chance of snow remaining in the early summer. It is not unusual to experience the odd day of snowfall even in August. The Haute Route should not be attempted before early July.

THE EASTWARD TRAVERSE OF THE ITALIAN VALLEYS

Turning now to the southern flank of the Pennine Alps, we can look with anticipation at the potential for challenging walking tours across those projecting ridge spurs that separate the Italian valleys, and gain an insight from the Victorian pioneers whose erudition more than a hundred years on still manages to convey the spirit of the region. In his account of a tour made with his wife in 1855, the Rev. Samuel William King wrote (in *The Italian Valleys of the Pennine Alps*) of "the beautiful southern mountain ranges blending in every varying tint of ashy purple, amethyst and rosy red, exquisitely soft and transparent for such bare ridges." F.F. Tuckett described "fine mountains of picturesque forms and exquisitely wooded" (*A Pioneer in the High Alps*), while nearly a century later Hubert Walker called it "one of the most beautiful districts of the Alps [which] has hitherto been a Paradise with shut doors."

The Rev. King's tour was made a decade or so after J.D. Forbes explored both sides of the Pennines, explorations described evocatively in *Travels Through the Alps*, and which has provided inspiration for many mountain wanderers since. When Walker set out his journey across the Italian valleys in the original *Walking in the Alps*, he borrowed from both, and explained that "by passing from valley to valley from west to east, there is experienced a gradual crescendo of scenic splendour, from wildness through grandeur to sheer overwhelming magnificence."

What was good enough for Forbes, King and Walker should be good enough for us, as the following traverse is described matching in parallel form much of the Walker's Haute Route across the Swiss flanks outlined earlier. There are trails, of course, feeding along the mid-height hillsides from the western limits of the Italian Pennines, in particular the Alta Via della Valle d'Aosta No 1 (inaugurated in 1977) linking the southern side of Mont Blanc at Courmayeur with Gressoney-St-Jean on the south side of Monte Rosa, but Walker - and more recently, Chris Wright when devising his Grand Tour of Monte Rosa - began his journey on the south side of the Fenêtre de Durand which forms the walker's link between the Swiss Val de Bagnes and Italian Valle d'Ollomont. This is the traverse outlined here, in places adopting sections of the Alta Via.

As has been noted in our tour of the Combin massif, a vast pastoral cirque, the Conca di By, forms the headwall of the Ollomont valley, and any progress eastward is effectively hindered by the curving arm of this cirque created by an extensive ridge system marked on the Swiss map as the Chaine du Morion, whose crest never falls below 3000 metres in seven unbroken kilometres. There is no easy way over this wall so the walker is forced to descend steeply into the bed of the valley to Ollomont, more than fourteen hundred metres below the Fenêtre, and either continue down valley into the sultry warmth of low altitudes to Valpelline village (960m), set among vines and walnut trees at the confluence of the two Buthier mountain torrents, or climb out of the valley by way of Col de Breuson (2492m) on a mountain spur projecting from Monte Berrio. If the latter course be adopted, an early halt should be called at Voex, a little short of Ollomont, where there's hotel accommodation, for the next opportunity for a bed lies in the Valpelline at Dzovenno, almost six hours later.

The way over Col de Breuson is not difficult, although the path is obscure in places and waymarks sparse. Once at the pass, however, views are glorious, and the thousand metre descent to Close in the Valpelline, going through several small alps, is waymarked for most of the way. Close is a small hamlet with a now-defunct hotel, about two kilometres from Dzovenno where there are two hotels and a campsite.

Near the head of the Valpelline the road ends at the artificial Lago di Place Moulin, at the far end of which stand the privately-owned Rifugio Prarayer, a cluster of chalets, the remains of a small chapel and an obsolete hotel deserted on its knoll above the chalets. Prarayer was once described as being lodged in a scene of great grandeur - as indeed it is, crowded by a seemingly impenetrable cirque of lofty mountains adorned with glaciers and bristling ridges. Tuckett suggested a man should bring with him "contentment, a good appetite, and fine weather, and I venture to engage that he will not be disappointed."

A surprising number of passes breaches those circling walls. Those that lead over the frontier ridge are, of course, climbers' passes with glaciers to negotiate, while walkers' routes exist across the spiny ridge that divides the Valpelline and St Barthélemy glens. In all there are seven passes in that extensive ridge from which to choose a continuing route eastward. Those at the upper end of the Valpelline are the more demanding, but they avoid descent into St Barthélemy. Those at the lower end are necessarily longer for they add the little glen to the list of valleys to explore. The highest is Col de Valcournera (3066m), an old hunters' pass which leads from Prarayer and gives almost direct access to the Valtournanche, and which is adopted by one of the Alta Vias. Col de Vofrède also provides an almost direct route to the valley below Breuil-Cervinia and was the crossing favoured by Walker. The Rev. King started lower down in the Valpelline at Oyace. He chose Colle de Vessona (2783m) for his route over the mountains to St Barthélemy, and again it is worth quoting from his writings:

> "The view which burst upon us from the narrow ridge was more than a reward for our toil, and different from any scene we had yet witnessed. As we climbed up there was no time to look round, and now we found the mighty form of Mont Blanc, the Grande Jorasse, and others, had risen up behind us, above a long range of peaks to the westward, while the glittering heads of Mont Combin and Mont Vélan, with the glaciers of Mont Gélé, and the Crête Sèche, closed up the view to the north, giving us a perfect panorama of the well-known outlines of many familiar acquaintances, in novel and unexpected combinations."

Whichever route is taken to reach this secluded glen, a second day will be needed to reach the Valtournanche, overnight accommodation in St Barthélemy being found in one of a handful of *bivacco* (simple huts), a rifugio at Cuney or hotels in the glen's main village of Lignan. Maintaining the eastward trend involves making the passage of either Fenêtre di Tzan near the head of the glen, or of the Col Fenêtre. Both are easy and straightforward, and neither challenge a full day's activity, Col Fenêtre needing little more than a morning's walk to reach Torgnon from Lignan. From there to Breuil-Cervinia involves a valley walk heading north.

With the Matterhorn (known here as Monte Cervino) rising at its head,

Valtournanche has become the best known of all the Italian valleys ranging immediately below the frontier crest. Breuil-Cervinia, like its illustrious neighbour on the Swiss side of the Matterhorn, has seen a growth of tourist development and exploitation of the upper slopes for skiing. However, it cannot rival Zermatt in either visitor-numbers, or in the prices charged for accommodation.

Above Breuil the historic Theodule Pass (3290m) offers a scenically spectacular short-cut across to Switzerland by way of an easy glacier (in some seasons crevasses on the Swiss side demand extra care), while our onward journey in the shadow of Monte Rosa involves the crossing of Colle Superiore delle Cima Bianche from Breuil to St Jacques at the roadhead in Val d'Ayas. Walker commented that throughout this crossing "you are in the heart of the most majestic country." But he would be appalled today by the cableways and bulldozed scars of dirt roads that fuss both sides of the pass, in contrast to distant scenic delights.

Colle Superiore is not the only linking route in the eastward progress from Valtournanche of our traverse of the Italian valleys, there being several alternative options. Of these, the neighbouring Colle Inferiore delle Cima Bianche (at 2896m it is eighty-six metres lower than Colle Superiore) suffers also from dirt roads, ski pistes and cableways, while Colletto della Roisetta is about an hour or so shorter in length than the previous two. Col di Nana (2780m) similarly links Paquier in Valtournanche with St Jacques in Val d'Ayas, but has two ridges to cross and several minor peaks tempting to climb nearby. This is the option favoured by Alta Via No 1, also known as the Giants' Trail. Colle Portola, enjoyed by Forbes in 1842, is the southernmost option best begun from Antey St André. Forbes and his party started from Valtournanche village at 7.30 in the morning and made their way to the pass via the hamlet of Chamois: "We rejoiced in the beauty of the morning," he wrote, "and of the herbage spangled with drops from the early mists; and as we turned round we saw behind us the Mont Cervin rising in unclouded splendour...From thence, a gentle though pretty long ascent took us to the Col de Portola, composed of limestone, and very precipitous on the eastern side, where it immediately overlooks the village of Ayas."

Having reached Val d'Ayas via one of the northern cols either descend for accommodation to St Jacques, or make a diversion from Fiéry to Resy (2072m) where two farm buildings have been adapted for use as rifugios enjoying lovely vistas over the glen to the Grand Tournalin which forms part of the valley's western wall.

More broad and gentle than Valtournanche, Val d'Ayas is much less developed than its western neighbour, and although there are ski lifts near Champoluc, the main village, skiing here is a comparatively low-key affair. The upper valley was settled during the Middle Ages by Walsers (or Valdesi), and their descendants still speak a German dialect and inhabit timber buildings similar in architectural style to those of the Swiss Valais, as do the people of the next valley on our tour, Valle di Gressoney, otherwise known as the valley of Lys, or Lis.

Valtournanche is headed by Monte Cervino; Val d'Ayas by Breithorn, Castor and Pollux; Valle di Gressoney by a wall of snow and ice - the south face of the Liskamm (4479m). The steep Lis glacier (Ghiacciaio del Lis) curls from that snow dome, and descends to the Plateau de Lis which is reached from Gressoney-la-

Trinité by footpath. Gressoney-la-Trinité nestles among meadows and fruit trees in the upper reaches of the valley about three kilometres from the roadhead, and boasts dazzling views of the ice and snow that blocks the valley to the north.

To reach Valle di Gressoney from Val d'Ayas the walker has a remarkable number of passes to choose from. Many of these offer low, unambitious routes, albeit they enjoy tremendous high mountain scenery, while others provide a little more challenge and also grant opportunities to grab a summit or two on the way. Of these Colle di Pinter (2777m), tackled by Alta Via della Valle d'Aosta No 1 (which ends at Gressoney-St-Jean), teases with an easy scramble to the Testa Grigia (3315m) whose summit it is claimed "commands perhaps the finest view of the south side of the Monte Rosa chain." Should Colle di Pinter be selected for this crossing, the starting point would be Champoluc, rather than St Jacques or the rifugios at Resy. If, on the other hand, accommodation was had in Resy (or St Jacques), Colle di Bettaforca (2672m) provides the more obvious route. This is not recommended, however, on account of the sorry mess of ski development that disfigures much of the route. Midway between the two, Passo del Rothorn has much to commend it. Leading from St Jacques to Gressoney-la-Trinité it's a fine crossing that rewards with charming views and the chance to scramble to Monte Rothorn (3152m), first climbed by de Saussure in 1789.

Valle di Gressoney projects southward in an almost straight line with very few kinks to its alignment. But on the eastern side of its walling ridge Val Sesia writhes in long curves with numerous tributary glens feeding into it, its general flow being roughly south-east from Alagna to Varallo. Once again a generous choice of crossings punctuates the intervening mountain wall, but on close scrutiny we discover that a number of these are really the domain of mountaineers rather than general mountain walkers, leaving just two options available, Colle Valdobbia and Col d'Olen. Hubert Walker adds a third, Passo di Rissuolo (2930m) which lies south of Corno Bianco, whose summit he urges walkers to tackle for its imposing view of Monte Rosa, but C.J. Wright lists this among those adventurous crossings best left to mountaineers.

Neither Colle Valdobbia nor Col d'Olen rank among the first echelon of passes. Both offer easy, though fairly long, routes . The first, regarded by Hinchliff as "the most uninteresting I have seen" lacks the scenic quality come to be regarded as normal on this traverse of the Italian valleys, while the Col d'Olen route has degenerated under the skiers' playground of the Staffa-Orsia-Gabiet complex. Hubert Walker could not predict the skiing boom nor its affect on the landscape, but described the Col as being very beautiful. Views are indeed fine, and with several rifugios on both sides of the pass those able to ignore the cableways and ski pistes may be tempted to spend an overnight in one to experience the special evening and morning light tinting the distant snowpeaks.

The crossing of Col d'Olen is taken from Gressoney-la-Trinité; about seven hours plus rests being required in order to reach Alagna near the roadhead in the Val Sesia where accommodation may be had in a choice of hotels or a pensione. (The true name of this village is Alagna-Valsésia.) There then follows either a long, easy and comparatively 'direct' route via the Roman paved Colle del Turlo (2738m) which leads to Macugnaga in Valle Anzasca, or one of several indirect crossings that reach Macugnaga by way of the Valle Sermenza, a tributary of Val Sesia. Walkers with glacier experience, and the necessary equipment, should, however, consider the high Colle delle Loccie (3324m) which is both dramatic and magnificent - and also direct.

Of the 'indirect' routes to Macugnaga, that using Colle Piglimo is the most northerly, taking some five hours or so to gain Rima in the Sermenza glen, while the most southerly is Bochetta della Moanda, generally considered the finest approach to the Sermenza with the added advantage of a teasing diversion to Monte Tagliaferro, a noted viewpoint. The Bochetta route forks on the descent. One option cuts off to the left (north) and crosses a spur at Passo del Vallarollo, while the main trail descends into the valley at San Giuseppe. If the latter path is taken, one then wanders upvalley to Rima through beautiful scenery.

The second stage of the crossing from Val Sesia to Valle Anzasca involves the passage of either Col Piccolo Altare (2627m) or Colle delle Vallè (2625m), both of which join the Turlo path for the descent to Macugnaga, thus completing a fine traverse claimed by Tuckett to be one of the loveliest he ever undertook. Quite a claim, coming from a man who explored more of the Alps on foot than almost any of his predecessors.

Once comfortably established in Macugnaga there is much for a walker to do before leaving for home. With the magnificent east face of Monte Rosa blocking the head of the valley the natural thing to do is spend time studying it in all its glory. Walker recognised this and urged his readers to stroll up to the Belvedere from where the vast amphitheatre could be clearly seen. A chairlift now carries tourists from Pecetto to Belvedere, making it a very busy place on summer days, and from there a marked route crosses the glacier to Rifugio Zamboni-Zappa set in a meadowland idyl.

Another route for walkers to consider is the crossing of the Monte Moro Pass (Passo di Monte Moro), a classic and historic route that leads to the Saastal in Switzerland. Trekkers tackling the Grand Tour of Monte Rosa adopt that route, but even if your intentions lie elsewhere, it would still be worth ascending the trail (there is a cable-car from Staffa) as far as the former customs house converted by the CAI into the Rifugio Gaspare Oberto just below the pass, book a night's lodging there and rise early to catch the magic of sunrise from the easy Joderhorn. From there Monte Rosa looks as though it has been transported from the Himalaya, so enormous does it appear; the very embodiment of mountain grandeur.

Our traverse of the Italian valleys of the Pennine Alps now complete, one may echo the words of R.L.G. Irving: "To wander from one of these lovely Pennine valleys to another, sometimes by easy paths, sometimes by passes far above the snow-line is to have the best of both Alpine worlds, the world of grass and cows and flowers and clear streams and the world which makes a man feel he is only there by kind permission of the elements."

The sharp fin of the Finsteraarhorn and Fiescherwand in the Bernese Alps (Ch 6)

The Schreckhorn - an icy backdrop to walks on the Grindel Alp, above Grindelwald (Ch 6)

Above:
Trail to the Chelenalp hut in a tributary glen of the Göschenertal (Ch 7)

Left:
Head of the Prato valley in the Ticino Alps (*W. Unsworth*. Ch 8)

Below:
The hamlet of Äsch in the Schächental with its famed waterfall (Ch 7)

THE EASTWARD TRAVERSE OF THE ITALIAN VALLEYS - SUMMARY

Day 1:   Cabane de Chanrion - Fenêtre de Durand - Voex (if coming from Switzerland)

or: Valpelline - Prarayer (if approaching from Aosta)

Day 2:   Voex - Col de Breuson - Close - Dzovenno

or: Prarayer - Col de Valcournera - Paquier (Valtournanche)

Day 3:   Dzovenno - Close - Colle de Vessona - Lignan

Day 4:   Lignan - Fenêtre di Tzan (or Col Fenêtre) - Torgnon - Breuil-Cervinia (or Valtournanche)

Day 5:   Breuil - Colle Superiore delle Cima Bianche - St Jacques

or: Paquier (Valtournanche) - Col di Nana - St Jacques

or: Antey St André - Colle Portola - St Jacques

Day 6:   St Jacques - Passo del Rothorn - Gressoney-la-Trinité

or: Champoluc - Colle di Pinter - Gressoney-la-Trinité

Day 7:   Gressoney-la-Trinité - Col d'Olen - Alagna-Valsésia

or: Gressoney-la-Trinité - Colle Valdobbia - Alagna-Valsésia

Day 8:   Alagna - Colle del Turlo - Macugnaga

or: Alagna - Colle Piglimo (or Bochetta della Moanda) - Rima

Day 9:   Rima - Col Piccolo Altare (or Colle delle Vallè) - Macugnaga

A challenging traverse, with some high passes giving a sense of remoteness, although some crossings have been spoiled by ski pistes and cableways. Accommodation is plentiful, as are alternative crossings in the case of bad weather. The traverse stands as a fine outing in its own right, or could be used as the southern portion of a long circuit of the Pennine Alps. Following a similar course across the Italian valleys is the Alta Via della Valle d'Aosta No 1, also known as the *Alta Via dei Giganti* - the 'Giants' Trail' after the 'giant' mountains in whose shadow it wanders. The route is about 120 kilometres long, extending between Courmayeur and Gressoney-St-Jean, taking about eight days.

✳   ✳   ✳

THE PENNINE ALPS

Location:

The range forms part of the Alpine watershed, the main ridge carrying the frontier between Switzerland and Italy. The Swiss side is covered by canton Valais (Wallis in German), the Italian slopes by Piedmont and Valle d'Aosta.

Principal valleys:

Vals Ferret, Entremont and Bagnes; Vals d'Hérémence and Hérens, Val d'Anniviers, Turtmanntal, Mattertal and Saastal on the northern, Swiss, side. Italian Val Ferret, Valle del Gran San Bernardo, Vallée d'Ollomont, Valpelline, Valtournanche, Valle Anzasca and d'Antrona on the Italian side.

Principal peaks:

Monte Rosa (Dufourspitze: 4634m, Nordend: 4609m, Signalkuppe: 4554m), Dom

(4545m), Weisshorn (4505m), Matterhorn (4477m), Dent Blanche (4357m), Grand Combin (4314m), Dent d'Hérens (4171m), Ober Gabelhorn (4063m)

Centres:
Practically every valley can boast at least one reasonable base for a walking holiday. The most important are: Zermatt, Saas Fee, Zinal, Arolla in Switzerland; Breuil-Cervinia and Macugnaga in Italy.

Huts:
Something like 50 mountain huts exist within the area covered by the Pennine Alps. Most are run by the Swiss or Italian Alpine Clubs, but a few are either privately owned or maintained by local communes.

Access:
By air to Geneva or Bern for approach to the Swiss side. Milan is served by international airlines in Italy. By rail a good and fast service links Geneva with all the main Rhône valley towns from which there are Postbus (or branch line) connections with the major mountain centres. The Trans-European Express serves Bern-Brig-Domodossola-Milan via the Simplon tunnel. In Italy a main line links Turin, Chivasso and Aosta.

Maps:
Mont Blanc-Grand Combin and *Matterhorn-Mischabel* cover much of the Swiss Pennines at a scale of 1:50,000 and should satisfy most walkers' needs. Published by the official Swiss Survey (Office fédéral de topographie) their reference numbers are 5003 and 5006 respectively. The same area is covered by about 16 sheets at 1:25,000 scale.

The northern limits of the Italian valleys are also covered by the Swiss Survey, but IGC (Instituto Geografico Centrale) based in Turin, have three sheets (numbers 4, 5 and 10) at a scale of 1:50,000 which cover much of the southern Pennines, and the publishers Kompass produce sheets 85 (*Monte Bianco*), 87 (*Breuil/Cervinia-Zermatt*) and 88 (*Monte Rosa*), also at 1:50,000. Studio FMB of Bologna publish tourist maps under the general heading *Eurocart* showing rifugios and with paths numbered.

Guidebooks:
The Valais: A Walking Guide by Kev Reynolds (Cicerone Press) details 95 routes (graded 1-3) in most of the Swiss valleys covered by this chapter. Information with regard to transport, accommodation etc is also given.
Chamonix to Zermatt: The Walker's Haute Route by Kev Reynolds (Cicerone Press) describes this classic walk in 14 stages, plus alternatives, with a two-stage extension to Saas Fee.
The Grand Tour of Monte Rosa by C.J. Wright (Cicerone Press) is a two-volume guide to a route that encircles most of the Pennine Alps in an anti-clockwise direction. Vol 1 covers the walk from Martigny to Val Sesia (mostly the Italian valleys). Vol 2 describes the route from Alagna Valsesia to Martigny via the Swiss valleys.
Sentiers du Tour des Combins by Gilbert Petoud (published by the Tourist Office of Val d'Entremont and the Martigny-Orsières Railway Company). This French-language guidebook to the Tour des Combin may be found in bookshops in Martigny.

Other reading:
Walking in the Alps by J. Hubert Walker (Oliver & Boyd, 1951). Although information with regard to some areas is rather dated now, for example where certain Swiss glens have been hi-jacked for hydro purposes, what Walker wrote about the Pennine Alps is worth reading even today. He gave more space to this range than to any other in his book, which reflects its importance to the visiting walker and climber. Truly inspirational.

The Outdoor Traveler's Guide to The Alps by Marcia R. Lieberman (Stewart, Tabori & Chang, New York, 1991) provides basic detail of selected valleys and centres on both sides of the frontier.

The Mountains of Europe by Kev Reynolds (Oxford Illustrated Press, 1990) contains a chapter devoted to this district.

Classic Walks in the Alps by Kev Reynolds (Oxford Illustrated Press, 1991) describes several routes briefly mentioned in this chapter.

Walking & Climbing in the Alps by Stefano Ardito (Swan Hill Press, 1995) is a large-format glossy book, translated from the Italian. Contains a chapter describing an 8-day tour from the Simplon Pass to Zermatt via the Theodul and Monte Moro Passes.

Backpacking in Alps and Pyrenees by Showell Styles (Victor Gollancz, 1976) includes narrative of a backpacking journey from Martigny to Brig crossing several passes used by the Walker's Haute Route.

Trekking in Europe by Giancarlo Corbellini (AA Publishing, 1990) has a chapter devoted to the 'Giants' Trail' (AVVA No 1) - a traverse of the Italian valleys from Gressoney-St-Jean to Courmayeur.

Scrambles Amongst the Alps by Edward Whymper (John Murray - many editions). Of interest to all visitors to the Pennine Alps, *Scrambles* is a record of Whymper's Alpine campaigns of 1860-65, the climax being the tragic first ascent of the Matterhorn.

Men and the Matterhorn by Gaston Rebuffet (Kaye & Ward, 1973) is a well-illustrated volume dedicated to one of the world's best-loved mountains.

Several other books by Victorian pioneers mentioned in the text above provide fascinating reading for anyone interested in exploring the Pennines on foot.

The Gspaltenhorn seen above Mürren

6: THE BERNESE ALPS

Facing the Pennine Alps across the deep moat of the Rhône valley, the longest glacier in all the Alpine regions carves out an extensive highway of ice. The Grosser Aletschgletscher is formed at the Konkordiaplatz, a junction of four main glaciers that come together below the southern flanks of Jungfrau, Mönch, Fiescherhorn and Grünhorn. East of Konkordiaplatz, on the other side of the Grünhornlücke - the saddle at the head of the Grüneggfirn - a second glacier system pours south towards the Rhône from spawning grounds in an icy cirque topped by Grünhorn, Fiescherhorn and Finsteraarhorn, while from the eastern flank of the latter peak yet more glaciers drain towards the Grimsel Pass.

At the heart of the Bernese Alps, then, lies a massive core of ice.

This glacial heartland pushes tentacles in all directions, and overlays a thick carpet across the 3000 metre ridge of the Petersgrat as a last remnant of successive Ice Ages that were so influential in shaping the great mountains and valleys of the Alps. Surprisingly, perhaps, the biggest glaciers flow south, while the smallest fingers of ice are those that hang from the major north-facing peaks - the great wall of the Bernese Oberland that appears so dramatic when viewed from Interlaken, or from the autobahn south of Bern. "No earthly object that I have seen approaches in grandeur to the stupendous mountain wall whose battlements overhang the villages of Lauterbrunnen and Grindelwald." So wrote Leslie Stephen a hundred years ago in *The Playground of Europe*.

164

That Oberland wall is, however, but one small, though significant, section of the largest unbroken chain in the Western Alps, for the Bernese Alps spread south-westward from the Grimsel Pass at the head of the Haslital, to the Rhône valley's northerly curve near Martigny. The southern boundary is marked by the Rhône itself; the northern limits being drawn by the valley in which lie the lakes of Brienz and Thun, and continue as an imaginary line that extends from the Thunersee through Adelboden to Aigle.

Unlike either the Mont Blanc range or the neighbouring Pennine Alps, no international frontier divides this mountain chain, although along the main crest runs the boundary between cantons Bern and Valais. That same crest acts as a major watershed, for rivers flowing north from it feed the Aare, a tributary of the Rhine which eventually flows into the North Sea, while glaciers and streams draining the southern flanks join the Rhône on its journey to the Mediterranean. Mountains too are of varying substance, for at the eastern end of the range they are largely formed of igneous or crystalline rocks, while those west of the Gemmi Pass are mostly of chalk or Jurassic limestone.

So much for the background mountains. The valleys and projecting spurs that form foothills to the high peaks provide almost limitless opportunities for the active walker; all in a setting that has attracted travellers ever since the Alps first emerged from the dark ages of fear, replacing imagined dragons and demons that had been thought to inhabit glacier, lake and summit with a more romantic vision - where "alps upon alps arise".

✳   ✳   ✳

THE NORTHERN VALLEYS

In order to survey the range in some detail it is necessary to visit all the most important valleys and some of their neighbouring glens, and to discuss their appeal and potential, so far as our mountain walker is concerned. First then, the northern side, beginning in the east and heading west.

The Haslital

The most easterly valley is the Haslital, which flows from the austere Grimsel Pass (2165m) down to the Brienzersee at a modest 564 metres. Into the upper valley drain the Oberaar and Unteraar glaciers, and at mid-level the glens of the Urbachtal and Rosenlaui (the latter watered by the Rychenbach stream) divided by the great slabs and peaks of the Engelhörner. Meiringen is the major resort here, with nearby Innertkirchen also offering hotel and campsite facilities, while above Meiringen, on a shelf of hillside facing west, Hasliberg is a scattering of hamlets providing accommodation in apartments and hotels. There are some fine walks to be had from Hasliberg - round the flanks of the Glogghüs, to Melchsee, or into the Gental.

So far as walking holidays are concerned, the Haslital offers plenty of variety. The Alps of Central Switzerland rise immediately to the east, so additional valleys and glens become easily accessible - notably the lovely Gental which leads to the Engstlenalp below the ice-domed Titlis (3238m).

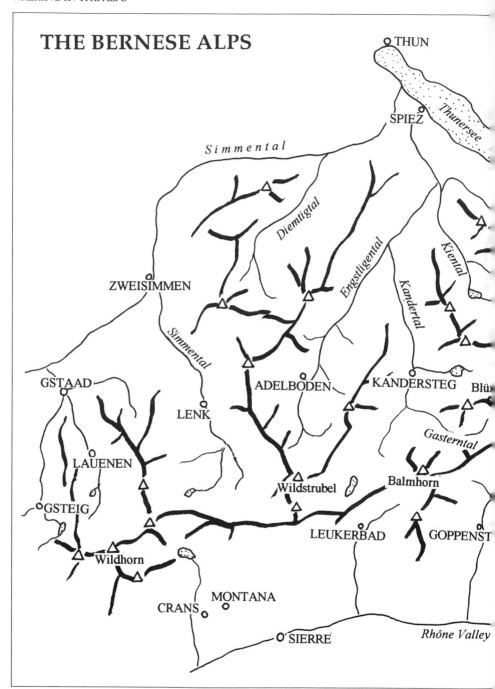

THE BERNESE ALPS

THUN

SPIEZ

Thunersee

Simmental

Diemtigal

Engstligental

Kiental

Kandertal

ZWEISIMMEN

Simmental

GSTAAD

ADELBODEN

KANDERSTEG

Blü

LENK

Gasterntal

LAUENEN

GSTEIG

Wildstrubel

Balmhorn

LEUKERBAD

GOPPENST

Wildhorn

CRANS

MONTANA

SIERRE

Rhône Valley

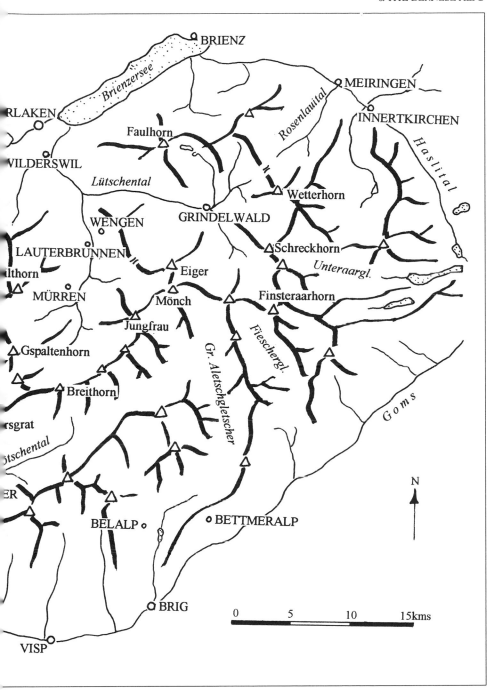

BRIENZ

MEIRINGEN

INNERTKIRCHEN

Brienzersee

Rosenlauital

Haslital

RLAKEN

Faulhorn

VILDERSWIL

Lütschental

Wetterhorn

WENGEN

GRINDELWALD

LAUTERBRUNNEN

Schreckhorn

lthorn

Eiger

Unteraargl.

MÜRREN

Mönch

Finsteraarhorn

Jungfrau

Fieschergl.

Gspaltenhorn

Gr. Aletschgletscher

Breithorn

rsgrat

G o m s

ötschental

N

ER

BELALP

BETTMERALP

BRIG

VISP

0   5   10   15kms

At the head of the Haslital the Grimsel Pass provides access to raw glens through which glacial highways entice mountaineers into the heartland of the Bernese Alps. The Oberaar and Unteraar glaciers are stark and rubble-strewn in summer, but their moraine banks, and the margins of their sullen lakes, have trails along them that enable walkers to gain an insight into a world normally reserved for mountaineers embarked upon adventures beyond the range of this book. Of the two glens the northern, Unteraargletscher's, is the larger and, with the Lauteraar hut within four and a half hours walk of the Grimsel Hospice, it offers a rewarding day out.

A clear path edges the north bank of the milky, silt-laden Grimselsee among alpenrose and juniper, and at the far end climbs onto the glacier, which here resembles something more akin to either the Himalaya, or Karakoram mountains of Pakistan, than the Swiss Alps. There is even a huge Buddhist chorten standing atop a massive boulder being carried down valley on the glacier's back! After an hour or so wandering along the glacier you leave it in favour of a narrow trail on the right which climbs over a bluff and then drops to the Lauteraar hut overlooking the convergence of the upper Lauteraar and the Finsteraar glaciers. In view are Finsteraarhorn, Schreckhorn and Oberaarhorn, with long fortress-like ridges that soar from sweeping icefields.

Further north the Urbachtal feeds into the Haslital behind Innertkirchen. In its lower reaches the glen is a green pastureland flanked by the stupendous limestone wall of the Engelhörner with a crest almost two thousand metres above the stream. At first glance one thinks of Norwegian fjords, but the deeper you go into the valley, so its character changes until, in the secretive Gaulischafberg, it is closed off by an untamed mountain cirque overhung with glaciers peeling from the Hangdengletscherhorn, Bärglistock and Ewigschneehorn. In the cradle of this amphitheatre sits the SAC's Gauli hut, reached in about six hours from Innertkirchen.

Meiringen has spread itself along the right bank of the Aare river, but on the opposite side of the valley, behind the ever-popular Reichenbach Falls, the Rosenlauital appears little more than a heavily-wooded cleft. Once you wander through that cleft, however, the glen steadily improves in appeal. Habitation is sporadic; a few chalets and farms dotted about and the occasional gasthof with simple lodgings of use to walkers and climbers choosing somewhere a little out of the way for accommodation, in preference to one of the mainstream resort villages. The valley is served by Postbus which plies a route between Meiringen and Grindelwald, the latter resort found on the opposite side of the Grosse Scheidegg, an obvious low-slung saddle in a ridge linking Wetterhorn and Schwarzhorn. Apart from the Postbus, access by motor vehicle is restricted above Schwarzwaldalp, which adds to the glen's appeal. One of the best walks here is that which explores the full length of the valley on its way to Grindelwald, a seven and a half hour stage adopted by the Alpine Pass Route.

Lütschental and Lauterbrunnental

Heading west the next major valley system belongs to the Lütschental (the valley of the Schwarze Lütschine) and the neighbouring Lauterbrunnental (with the Weisse Lütschine its river), the latter valley being a southerly stem joining the

Lütschental at Zweilütschinen. Accessible by train from Interlaken via Wilderswil, these are the two best-known valleys in the Bernese Alps, for they lead to some of Switzerland's busiest resorts overlooked by truly awe-inspiring mountain scenery. Walling the first are Wetterhorn and Eiger, with Grindelwald spread in an open basin of pastureland at their feet. Blocking the latter valley are Jungfrau, Gletscherhorn, Ebnefluh, Mittaghorn, Grosshorn, Breithorn and Tschingelhorn; a fabulous amphitheatre whose summit ridge is adorned with hanging glaciers. In addition to Grindelwald and Lauterbrunnen, Wengen and Mürren are also notable centres here with popular appeal in winter as well as summer, and along with Gimmelwald, a near-neighbour to Mürren, enjoy privileged positions high above the Lauterbrunnental. For budget-conscious walkers and climbers both valleys have plenty of camping facilities, as well as dormitory accommodation in mountain inns away from the main resorts.

Known for their great skiing potential both Lütschental and Lauterbrunnental, however, offer tremendous scope to the active mountain walker. Walks there are to please everyone, with challenging, distant goals to aim for as well as more pedestrian outings that can be eased with the aid of chairlift, cable-car or railway. The Jungfraujoch (3475m) is made accessible to all by train - if you can afford it - from Grindelwald, Lauterbrunnen, Wengen or Kleine Scheidegg. But that is of little use to our walker who prefers the winding trail and pastoral views to an expensive railway that burrows through the sunless stone heart of both Eiger and Mönch.

One of the best of all walks from Grindelwald treads a dramatic path high above the gorge created by the Unterer Grindelwald glacier between the Mättenberg and the Eiger's long north-east (Mitteleggi) ridge. This path leads to an isolated meadow in full view of a superb glacial cirque topped by the 4049 metre Fiescherhorn, and continues by way of fixed ropes up the cliff barrier of the Rots Gufer to the Schreckhorn hut, from which dazzling views of the Agassizhorn and Finsteraarhorn amply repay the time and effort required to get there.

By direct contrast to this glacial wonderland a less challenging, but no-less rewarding, walk leads to the lovely Bachsee tarns in a glen hidden to the north of Grindelwald. The best way to reach these is via the broad pastures of Bussalp (accessible by Postbus from Grindelwald), and across an easy saddle below the Faulhorn. Coming down to the tarns from this saddle a gradually expanding panorama offers Wetterhorn, Schreckhorn, Finsteraarhorn and Fiescherhorn as an incredible backdrop and, if you're lucky with the weather, these great fins will be reflected in the Bachsee itself. But it must be said, this is one of the busiest of all Alpine honeypots thanks to the Grindelwald-First gondola lift which ferries hundreds (maybe even thousands) of visitors to within easy reach on bright days in summer. Views remain magnificent, of course, despite the crowds - though they do tend to devalue the experience somewhat. There are, however, plenty of nearby alternative trails that will be less busy, which also offer scenes of splendour. I think especially of one which cuts through the wild glen to the north-east of the Bachsee, passing the wintry tarns of Hagelsee and Häxenseeli with a return to Grindelwald via the tricky Grosse Chrinne (fixed ropes on the steep descent); and of another which returns to Bussalp by way of a glorious back-country of woodland and rough pasture on a trail known as the Höhenweg 2000. Here, on the northern side of

Grindelwald's basin, the walker is spoilt for choice; and every panorama is spellbinding

A full day's walk justifiably recognised as a local classic, is that which links Schynige Platte with Grindelwald; a route nineteen kilometres long demanding from six to seven hours of effort. A rack-and-pinion railway (built 1893) climbs some 1400 metres from Wilderswil to Schynige Platte (2067m), from where you gain one of the finest of Alpine views accessible to all. From here a series of footpaths takes you first along the crest of a ridge leading towards the Laucherhorn, with the Brienzersee lying far below, then cuts roughly eastward to the Faulhorn (tremendous sunrise and sunset views from a small hotel on the summit), before descending past the Bachsee tarns to Grindelwald. It's a tremendous walk, not overly difficult under good summer conditions, although route-finding could be problematic in poor visibility. This is a walk in any case that should be saved for a fine-weather day in order to sample all the breathtaking views that have given it such a wide reputation.

Another long walk worth considering is that which crosses from Grindelwald to the Lauterbrunnental by way of either Kleine Scheidegg and the Wengernalp, or over the Männlichen ridge north of Kleine Scheidegg and thence very steeply down to Wengen and Lauterbrunnen in the valley far below. Kleine Scheidegg itself is a monstrous eyesore of railway station, hotels and overhead gantries by which the Jungfraujoch railway is powered, but with Eiger, Mönch and Jungfrau towering above, and a hint of the Lauterbrunnental's deep cleft below, the surrounding landscape is of the highest quality. In 1856 John Tyndall came here on a scientific ramble with Professor Huxley and saw: "...floods of golden light [that] were poured down the sides of the mountain. On the slopes were innumerable chalets, glistening in the sunbeams, herds browsing peacefully...while the blackness of the pine-trees, crowded into woods, or scattered in pleasant clusters over alps and valley, contrasted forcibly with the lively green of the fields."

The Grindelwald to Lauterbrunnen walk passes through Alpiglen below the Eiger's notorious nordwand, crosses Kleine Scheidegg and descends to the Wengernalp, among whose visual delights mention should be made of the avalanches that rumble from the Jungfrau most days in early summer. To quote from Leslie Stephen:

> "Surely the Wengern Alp must be precisely the loveliest place in this world. To hurry past it...is a very unsatisfactory mode of enjoyment...But it does one's moral nature good to linger there at sunset or in the early morning...It is delicious to lie upon the short crisp turf under the Lauberhorn, to listen to the distant cow-bells, and to try to catch the moment at which the last glow dies off the summit of the Jungfrau; or to watch a light summer mist driving by, and the great mountains look through its rents at intervals from an apparently impossible height above the clouds. It is pleasant to look out in the early morning from one of the narrow windows, when the Jungfrau seems gradually to mould itself out of darkness, slowly to reveal every fold of its torn glaciers, and then to light up with an ethereal fire."

The prose is typically Victorian, but the sensation that produced it transcends the decades and even the hardest of modern climbers might find himself enjoying just such a scene - even though he might find it impossible to voice his appreciation in those terms. For the wanderer passing through such is the beauty of Wengernalp (or, better still, the Biglenalp and Mettlenalp nearby) that the horrors of modern Kleine Scheidegg are quickly forgotten. But the alternative crossing from Grindelwald to the Lauterbrunnental via the Männlichen ridge is also worth tackling. From the trail up to the ridge you gain a much better perspective of the Eiger than the foreshortened Alpiglen view, and from the ridge-crest the full splendour of Lauterbrunnen's deep U-shaped valley is seen at its very best, while Mönch and Jungfrau appear utterly radiant as they dominate the scene.

The Lauterbrunnen valley is very special. Its smooth grey walls have been shaved by glaciers that withdrew long ago and now remain as little more than shadows of their former selves. Down the face of abrupt vertical cliffs shower slender cascades; above them green hillside terraces fold to high alps backed by walkers' passes that look onto Oberland giants. Wengen occupies one such terrace on the eastern flank, Mürren enjoys a corresponding position on the western hillside. Both are served by rack-and-pinion railways from Lauterbrunnen, and both enjoy a traffic-free environment.

From Mürren a good path skirts rucked pastureland in full view of the Gspaltenhorn and leads to the Sefinenfurke (2612m), a narrow col midway between the Hundshorn and Büttlassen, by which the Kiental, and eventually the Kandertal, can be reached by strong mountain walkers.

Other trails go north from Mürren to Isenfluh and the curious Soustal, or south through Gimmelwald to the Sefinental glen, or deeper south over the lofty ridge walling the Sefinental, then down to the head of the Lauterbrunnental where the rustic inn at Obersteinberg gives easy access to the charming Oberhornsee tarn and the Schmadri hut. Oberhornsee is also approached by footpath from Stechelberg, the last habitation in the bed of the valley proper whose campsite better suits walkers with a desire for peace than do the overcrowded tent cities at Lauterbrunnen. A night spent in Stechelberg enables an early start to be made to such walks as that which climbs more than 1800 metres to the Rottal hut perched high above the valley on the south-western slopes of the Jungfrau. This hut approach is very demanding and with a fixed rope section in a steep gully, but it is well worth pursuing for the incredible panorama it affords. The hut looks out at hanging glaciers and across the head of the Lauterbrunnental to a fine bevy of peaks, including Ebnefluh, Mittaghorn, Grosshorn, Breithorn, Tschingelhorn, Morgenhorn and Gspaltenhorn, while the deep well of the valley itself is little more than a hint of shadow far below.

MULTI-DAY CIRCUIT OF THE LÜTSCHENTAL AND LAUTERBRUNNENTAL

A visually spectacular circuit of about five days could be achieved here by linking several of the walks outlined above. Accommodation is available in various fine locations in addition to the well-known resort villages, so each day's stage could be shortened or lengthened to suit. The following tour will provide both excellent walking and memorable vistas.

The obvious place to begin is Wilderswil south of Interlaken, valley station for the Schynige Platte railway. Here you can either ride the railway and make the first day's stage from Schynige Platte to Grindelwald, or take the footpath from Wilderswil all the way to Schynige Platte (an ascent of 1400 metres) and spend the night there with plenty of time to enjoy the great vista of peaks blocking the southern end of the Lauterbrunnen valley. The continuing trail to Grindelwald provides a constant shuffling and reshuffling of views, and with an option of breaking the route with an overnight on the Faulhorn, whose summit was deemed worthy of a panorama in early Baedeker guides.

Leaving Grindelwald one could either cross the Kleine Scheidegg and descend through Wengernalp and Wengen to Lauterbrunnen; cross the Männlichen ridge and plunge steeply into Wengen and thence to Lauterbrunnen; or go via Kleine Scheidegg and the Wengernalp, but then break away on a sharp descent through the narrow Trümmeltal, so to reach the bed of the valley at Sandbach, and then continue south through the valley to overnight at Stechelberg or Obersteinberg - depending on fitness and/or personal preference.

Wherever you spent the previous night Mürren, or one of the little inns above it, should be your goal for the next night. Those who stayed in Lauterbrunnen might be tempted to climb directly to it by a very steep path that parallels the funicular to Grütschalp, then follow a more gentle trail along the hillside shelf to the south. However, a better way is to remain in the bed of the valley as far as Stechelberg (there's a good trail on the true left bank of the stream that avoids valley traffic), then go up to Obersteinberg to find a hillside route to Mürren. Mürren's hotels are on the expensive side, but cheaper dormitory accommodation is available at Suppenalp and in the Blumental half an hour or so above the resort. From these rustic inns the evening alpenglow on the Jungfrau makes a fitting nightcap.

The fourth stage is another short one as it traces a natural hillside terrace high above the valley heading north to Isenfluh, a small village with a limited amount of accommodation lodged above the Lauterbrunnental near its junction with the Lütschental. Anyone short of time could descend directly from there to Zweilütschinen and take the train out to Interlaken, while the fifth and final day of the circuit proper explores the neat little glen of Saxettal, reached by a 900 metre climb over a shoulder of the Bällehöchst followed by descent to Saxeten, from where an obvious downhill walk leads to Wilderswil.

MULTI-DAY CIRCUIT OF THE LÜTSCHENTAL AND LAUTERBRUNNENTAL - SUMMARY OF CIRCUIT

Day 1: Wilderswil - Schynige Platte (by funicular) - Faulhorn - Grindelwald

Day 2: Grindelwald - Kleine Scheidegg - Wengen - Lauterbrunnen
  or: Grindelwald - Männlichen - Wengen - Lauterbrunnen

Day 3: Lauterbrunnen - Stechelberg - Obersteinberg - Mürren

Day 4: Mürren - Isenfluh

Day 5: Isenfluh - Bällehöchst - Saxeten - Wilderswil

Kandertal

Running roughly parallel to the Lauterbrunnental, but with minor glens in between, is the Kandertal, subdivided at its head by the splendid Gasterntal and two hanging valleys hidden from the bed of the main valley either by crowding mountain walls or intruding hillsides. The first of these hidden glens, watered by the Schwarzbach and with the Daubensee near its head, leads to the Gemmi Pass (2322m), while the next drains north-east from the Steghorn in a series of steps before discharging into the Kandertal below the Kleine (or Chlyne) Lohner. Kandersteg is the highest village, an expanding, straggling resort that has enjoyed a long popularity with walkers, mountaineers and general tourists. Served by railway from Bern, it forms the northern terminus for car-carrying trains travelling through the Lötschberg Tunnel to Goppenstein. There are plenty of hotels and apartments for holiday rent, and a campsite situated by the chairlift which swings visitors up to the Oeschinensee, a beautiful oval lake trapped in a hollow below peaks and hanging glaciers of the Blümlisalp.

As a base for a walking holiday Kandersteg scores high. Among many excursions from it a visit to the Gasterntal is a must. This charming glen lies south-east of the village and is approached by minibus taxi from the railway station most mornings in summer. There are no villages in the Gasterntal, but two or three simple mountain inns provide accommodation in an idyllic setting. The blue tongue of the Kanderfirn glacier projects between cliffs at the head of the valley, and there's a trail climbing to it that leads from natural rock gardens in the bed of the glen, through a belt of alpenroses, and up to a stark terrain of bare rock and ice. Walkers with glacier experience and the necessary equipment may continue up the easy Kanderfirn, which forms part of the Petersgrat icefield, to the Mutthorn hut (2901m) caught amid a sea of ice north-west of the Tschingelhorn. Immediately below the hut the Tschingelfirn glacier drops to the head of the Lauterbrunnental, while due south an easy crossing of the Petersgrat gives access through a steep and narrow glen to the glorious Lötschental, the finest valley on the south side of the Bernese Alps.

A two-day crossing from the Gasterntal to the Lötschental via the Petersgrat made one mid-summer several years ago remains among my brightest memories. Shortly after first light, standing on the ice crest just above the Mutthorn hut, two of us gazed out across the head of the Lauterbrunnen valley, lost beneath the morning clouds, to the unfamiliar shape of the Jungfrau, the spear-like Eiger seen side-on, and the modest Faulhorn standing back on a minor ridge above and behind unseen Grindelwald. Beyond the Faulhorn innocent peaks and peaklets rose like islands in an archipelago from a swell of vapour in that magical hour that follows dawn.

South of the hut the lowest point of the Petersgrat ice-cap was quickly gained, with only a few narrow slices of crevasse to step across. And once again we were met by a tremendous panorama. Far off, beyond the deep gulf of the Rhône valley, the whole chain of the Pennine Alps dazzled in the morning sun. From the Dom above Saas Fee to Mont Blanc above Chamonix, a sea of peaks rose and fell among a bed of serpent-like glaciers. The Lötschental was as yet unseen, for the *grat* plunged away to nothing. But from the opposite wall the graceful pyramid of the

Bietschhorn stabbed a finger of rock and ice out of a ridge daubed with its own hanging glaciers poised above the silent, hinted valley. It took a long time before we could force ourselves away from that view and descend steeply into the head of the Uisters Tal, by which we would gain Fafleralp in the Lötschental.

An alternative crossing from the Gasterntal to Lötschental goes by way of the Lötschenpass (2690m), the oldest known glacier pass in the Bernese Alps, and is highly recommended. Although there is a small glacier to cross it is quite straightforward under normal summer conditions, and as long as walkers follow the marked route there should be neither difficulty nor danger.

The start of this walk is made almost directly from the inn at Selden where a signpost points the way to Gfällalp and the Lötschenpass. Crossing the Kander stream on a Himalaya-style suspension bridge, a trail then begins a steep uphill climb alongside the Leitibach stream to the little restaurant building of Gfällalp, and continues for a further hour and a half to gain the left bank of the Lötschen glacier, the crossing of which follows a route usually marked with poles. (In the event of recent snowfall you should not attempt the crossing as crevasses may be hidden.) Once the true right bank is gained a series of rock terraces leads directly to the pass with its small hut placed in a commanding position from which to study the Bietschhorn across the depths of the Lötschental. Just below the pass a small tarn mirrors that mountain's handsome profile, and also provides a wonderful view south to the Weisshorn and other giants of the Pennine Alps beyond the Rhône valley. A trail continues down now to Kummenalp and then more steeply to Ferden in the bed of the Lötschental.

Down valley from Selden the Gasterntal becomes rather fjord-like. Birch and pine trees grow among gravel beds where the Kander river strays in several wayward braidings, and long slender waterfalls cascade down the steep southern walls. High above soars the Balmhorn (3699m) and its neighbouring 'twin', Altels (3629m); between the two hangs the broken Balmhorn glacier, its lower ice cliffs threatening the path of approach to the Balmhorn hut.

Sheltered in a woodland glade near the mouth of the valley is the Waldhaus hotel. Behind it a path climbs into a cleft formed by the Schwarzbach torrent; the stream which drains that high hidden glen through which the Gemmi Pass is reached. This steep trail is not the only way to gain that glen, however, for at Eggeschwand at the head of the Kandertal a cableway lifts walkers effortlessly to the northern end of the glen, while another path climbs more or less beneath the cable.

The glen is a curious bit of geography and a noted flower-garden bordered on the east by Altels, Balmhorn and Rinderhorn, and on the west by outliers of the Wildstrubel massif. At its southern end the Gemmi Pass provides a surprising outlook to the chain of the Pennine Alps, with Monte Rosa, Mischabelhörner, Matterhorn, Dent Blanche, Weisshorn and many others lining up as if on parade. The Gemmi is an ancient crossing between the cantons of Bern and Valais. In the early years of the eighteenth century a remarkable staircase was created on the steep southern side, thus easing access between Leukerbad and the pass. Nowadays a cableway swings visitors in a matter of minutes from one to the other. There's a hotel at the pass, with dormitory accommodation as well as standard beds. West of the Gemmi the Lämmern hut serves climbers attempting the Wildstrubel, but also offers a night's lodging to walkers wishing to explore this somewhat secretive corner of the Bernese Alps. Elsewhere Berghotel Schwarenbach also provides accommodation in bedrooms and dormitories.

The second hidden valley above the upper Kandertal is drained by the Alpbach stream, and is accessible by two or three walkers' passes that cross the low ridge of the Üschenegrat which divides that glen from the valley of the Schwarzbach. The Üschenental is a rough pastoral trough of a glen with a few farms in its lower reaches and a little tarn (Tälliseeli, 2405m) trapped in an upper step overlooked by the Steghorn. A trail leads through the glen from just south of Kandersteg and provides opportunities for a two-day circuit when linked with a crossing of the Üschenegrat and return via the Schwarzbach glen.

Upvalley from the Tälliseeli a second path slants up the east flank of the Engstligengrat and crosses to the Engstligenalp above Adelboden, while at the lower end of the glen a more popular crossing to Adelboden is achieved by way of the 2385 metre Bunderchrinde.

Down in the valley Kandersteg is ideally situated as an overnight stop between two classic stages of the Alpine Pass Route; the crossing of the Hohtürli from Griesalp, and the Bunderchrinde route to Adelboden. Hohtürli (2778m) makes a wonderful challenge for fit mountain walkers. More than 1600 metres above Kandersteg, and reached by way of the Oeschinensee in about five and a half hours, this shaly pass offers wild and lofty views of the Blümlisalp peaks that rise immediately above it. Glaciers carve down the north-facing slopes and for much of the ascent above the Oeschinensee the trail climbs along moraine walls thrown up by these precipitous icefields. A few metres above the pass the Blümlisalp hut enjoys a lordly position with far-reaching views to the west.

Kiental

The distinctive, but distant, snow-and-ice-domed summits of the Blümlisalp are also seen to splendid effect from the meadows of the Kiental, an important but little-visited tributary valley that feeds into the Frutigtal - the name given to the lower reaches of the Kandertal - near Reichenbach.

The Kiental is a delightful, peaceful, off-the-beaten-track valley with no resort, as such, but with a few simple hotels and gasthofs in its one true village which is also known as Kiental. Beyond Kiental village the valley forks. One branch is the glen of Spiggengrund, the other known as the Gornergrund. The road through this latter glen is a toll road, but a Postbus service continues upvalley past the Tschingelsee tarn, then twists in a series of exceedingly tight hairpins to Griesalp, a small hamlet with three hotels and pensions (dormitory beds available) popular with walking parties. The best and most challenging opportunities for the walker are to be found here, with some fine wild country stretching south and south-east topped by high passes with big peaks all around.

The Kiental, as we have seen, flows into the Frutigtal at Reichenbach and is the main tributary from the eastern side of the valley. But upvalley, between Reichenbach and Kandersteg, a second important tributary glen cuts back to the south-west. This is the Engstligental, known mainly for the ski resort of Adelboden.

Engstligental

At its entrance the Engstligental is considerably more narrow and, at first, with steeper walls, than is the Frutigtal, but eventually it opens to a large grassy basin south of Adelboden where the Wildstrubel's snow crown focuses one's attention. This large basin is the Engstligenalp, a one-time glacial cirque now carpeted with lush pastureland bright with wild flowers in early summer, through which numerous streams gather before flowing as one through the narrow lip at its northern opening, then plunging in the impressive Engstligen Falls, a Swiss national monument. A path climbs up the eastern side of the falls from Unter dem Berg, while a cableway makes a less-energetic approach.

Engstligenalp is a great place in which to amble with nothing more in mind than to enjoy a unique situation below the Wildstrubel. But this almost circular highland plateau also offers two longish walks that both involve crossing the ridges that contain it. The first climbs to the Engstligengrat north of the Tierhörnli, descends into the upper Üschenental and continues over the Rote Kumme (or Rote Chumme) to gain the Gemmi Pass. The other crosses the south-west containing ridge, the Ammertengrat, and descends into the Ober Simmental by way of the wild channel of the Simmen Falls south-east of Lenk.

The last-mentioned route is a demanding one. However, there is a much easier way between Adelboden and Lenk that goes by way of the green saddle of Hahnenmoos (1956m) at the head of the Gilbach glen, while a third crossing, between the two previously outlined, takes the little Pommernpass found just to the west of the Regenboldshorn (2193m). Walkers choosing to cross here are recommended to stray from the pass to the summit of this easy little peak for an extensive panorama, while the Hahnenmoos crossing has been adopted by a six-day circuit publicised by tourist agencies of the Kandertal and Engstligental, and known locally as Tour Wildstrubel.

TOUR WILDSTRUBEL

Being a circular walk the tour could begin in any one of half a dozen places, although Kandersteg, with its ease of access by public transport, is usually the starting place with the circuit being mostly tackled in an anti-clockwise direction. The first stage, then, heads out of Kandersteg and climbs the western valley wall which is crossed at the narrow cleft of the Bunderchrinde, followed by descent to Adelboden. For a first day's walk this is quite demanding, for it's sixteen kilometres long and with a climb of more than 1200 metres starting almost directly from Kandersteg. Without rests this stage will take around seven hours of effort.

Next day is much less demanding, for there's an easy crossing to face in the Hahnenmoos Pass on the way to Lenk. Lenk sits among flat meadows in the soft and gentle Ober Simmental, and is threatened neither by looming peaks nor hanging glaciers. It's a stage of modest demands and generous views of a green and pastoral Switzerland; a direct contrast to the sometimes overpowering presence of big mountains experienced elsewhere in the Bernese Alps.

A more challenging stage follows. Heading south out of Lenk the tour now has to cross the watershed ridge west of the Wildstrubel massif. The pass chosen for this is the 2429 metre Rawil Pass gained by way of Iffigenalp, then through a wild patch of mountainside normally used as the approach route for the ascent of the Wildstrubel. A small tarn is reached just before gaining the pass - a rather desolate plateau enclosed by mountain walls that retain dirty snow patches long into summer. But as you descend, so blinkered views of the Pennine Alps begin to reveal a new and exciting landscape beyond the Rhône valley. The stage ends either in Anzère (thus adding an extra day to the circuit) or in Crans-Montana, a modern ski resort facing south from a broad hillside terrace.

From Crans-Montana the trail works a way roughly eastward high above the Rhône, and with consistently fine views to majestic peaks of the Pennine Alps. Rounding the broad spur of mountain projecting from the Trubelstock at Varneralp, the way then veers northward into the steep-walled glen in which Leukerbad is found. Alternative ways of completing the route back to Kandersteg are now possible. The most direct entails climbing the long stone staircase to the Gemmi Pass, wandering through the Schwarzbach glen and descending from its northern end into the Kandertal. This makes a tiring day's walk, but with the option of breaking it halfway at Schwarenbach. The other option is to cross the 2626 metre Restipass from which the splendid Lötschental is gained, and spend a night in Kummenalp, a small hamlet perched high above the valley, and next day climb steeply to the Lötschenpass, descend into the Gasterntal and from there wander downvalley to Kandersteg.

TOUR WILDSTRUBEL - SUMMARY OF CIRCUIT

Day 1: Kandersteg - Bunderchrinde - Adelboden
Day 2: Adelboden - Hahnenmoos - Lenk
Day 3: Lenk - Iffigenalp - Rawil Pass Crans-Montana
Day 4: Crans-Montana - Leukerbad
Day 5: Leukerbad - Gemmi Pass - Kandersteg
   or: Leukerbad - Restipass - Kummenalp
Day 6: Kummenalp - Lötschenpass - Selden - Kandersteg

Diemtigtal

The Diemtigtal lies some way north of the main crestline of the Bernese Alps, and is therefore ignored by many active visitors to the region. But those who have discovered it recognise it as a gem of a valley, unsophisticated and quite unspoilt, and with lots of possibilities for walkers who enjoy the prospect of crossing remote cols and exploring little-known glens off the beaten track.

The valley spills into that of the Ober Simmental at the little village of Oey, south-west of Spiez, and is reached by train on the Spiez-Zweisimmen line that passes its entrance. Trains are met by the Postbus that serves the valley as far south as Grimmialp, beyond which the Diemtigtal divides into two inner glens. The south-easterly of these is blocked by a green alp cirque topped by Türmlihorn, Drümännler and Männliflue; the south-western arm being overlooked by the fine craggy ridge of the Spillgerte.

There are no real tourist centres in the Diemtigtal, but accommodation will be found in most of the small hamlets that are scattered alongside the narrow road. From them a variety of trails explores the wooded hillsides, knuckle indents to the valley and, perhaps best of all, those upper inner glens that tease with remote passes. The Otterepass (2278m) in the ridge linking Wyssi Flue and Männiflue takes walkers over to the Engstligental, the Grimmi Pass (2057m) crosses a minor ridge east of the Spillgerte, and descends via the Färmeltal into the Ober Simmental, while a third option breaks away from the glen south-west of Grimmialp and tackles the 1991 metre Scheidegg (north of the Spillgerte) and reaches the Ober Simmental near Blankenburg.

These, and numerous other routes, remain to be explored by discerning walkers who are tempted more by the little-known rather than the much-heralded trails, who are not disappointed by a lack of glacier or snowfield, but who respond to the wild flowers that adorn peak and pasture, and an aura of peace that holds the mountains and glens in its summer embrace.

Simmental

Rising in the western half of the Wildstrubel massif, the Simmental is one of the major valleys of the Bernese Alps which flows in a great arcing curve through the mountains before spilling out by the Thunersee at Spiez, and by way of either Col du Pillon or the Jaun Pass forms an important route of communication between the lakes of Geneva and Thun. Most of the valley is pastorally elegant, noted for its cattle and wooden, decorated houses, while its upper reaches south of Lenk offer challenging walks in a sometimes remote setting. Lenk makes an obvious base for a walking holiday. It's an attractive little resort with a number of hotels, holiday flats and pensions, and a campsite at the head of the valley. The village is served by rail by way of Zweisimmen. Above Lenk the Ober Simmental is known as Oberried, with a secondary glen, the Poschenried, leading into the Iffigtal. Both have considerable appeal, although their nature is quite different.

First we will look at the more gentle Oberried whose waters come from the Wildstrubel glaciers and snowfields. The bed of this valley is flat and gentle, its river contained among the meadows, but in the south and west forests clothe hillsides that rise in tiers. High above the forests the Glacier de la Plaine Morte is a big sheet of ice tilted towards the north, a remarkable *firn* plateau whose scenery has been likened to that of Greenland or Spitzbergen. This is how Martin Conway described it:

> "It is so large, so simple, so secluded. It seems like a portion of some strange world. Its effect of size is increased by the insignificance of the wall that surrounds it - enough to shut out all distant views and no more... Here a man might come and, setting up his tent for a week, learn what it is to be alone. He might wander safely in any direction and, climbing the wall at any point, look out upon the world of hotels and tourists; then returning to his lonely abode, he might kindle his solitary lamp and cook for himself the cup of contemplation."
>
> (*The Alps from End to End*)

From this astonishing ice-sheet streams fan down rock slabs and screes to link forces with those that drain the higher slopes of the Wildstrubel. Suitably fortified these convergent streams come rushing through a long cleft as the lovely Simmenfälle, sending clouds of spray into the bordering woodlands to encourage a lush vegetation. Trails give access to these falls and can be linked with others that cross neighbouring cols or meander along the high hillsides to east and west. Day-long tours of the Oberried glen may be enjoyed in some seclusion, but more challenging walks will be found in neighbouring glens to the west; namely Poschenried and Iffigtal.

A narrow road climbs through Poschenried from Lenk and projects as far as Iffigenalp where there's a mountain inn. The road is two-way as far as Färiche, behind which another glen rises to the Niesenhorn-Rothorn-Fürflue ridge. Beyond the few buildings of Färiche vehicles are restricted to a timed one-way system, with access restricted to fifteen minutes every hour. Buses ply the route from Lenk to Iffigenalp in the high summer, which is useful for walkers planning a long circuit, or valley-to-valley routes.

Once at Iffigenalp trails climb south to the Rawil Pass, or south-west to the Iffigsee, Iffighore and Wildhorn hut. Walkers in training could link all three in a day's outing. It will take about two hours to reach the deep blue gem of the Iffigsee tarn, and a further hour to gain the Wildhorn hut (2301m) perched among screes in a desolate, stony valley brightened in summer by splendid alpine flowers. North of the hut a trail skirts the high screes and makes a traverse round the flanks of the Niesenhorn to reach a trough of an unnamed col at 2378 metres. It would be possible to descend from there into the Lauenental in the west, but other options remain to be considered. One alternative would be to pick up a trail heading north along the slopes of Rothorn and Fürflue, and then veer north-eastward down to Lenk. Another would be to ascend the minor Iffighore (2378m) east of the unnamed col, then wander back down the initially steep Iffigtal to Iffigenalp once more.

Lauenental

West of the Ober Simmental this green and gentle glen has none of the extravagant flair of better-known valleys further east, but is by no means without its charm. This it has in plenty. At its northern end, where the Lauibach joins the Turbach to flow into the Saane, sits fashionable Gstaad, consciously chic and apparently wishing the summer away before exploiting winter for all it's worth. But while Gstaad is a winter resort Lauenen, the only village in the valley, makes the most of the snow-free months and offers plenty of opportunities to explore neighbouring hillsides and the rough-structured slopes of the Wildhorn massif which forms such a powerful backdrop.

Seen from Lauenen the Wildhorn presents itself as a high, broad ridge of snow and ice thrusting out matching spurs, or subsidiary ridges, to embrace the head of the valley. The cirque, or amphitheatre, thus created, provides an obvious clue to the Lauenental's formation, while the Gelten glacier draped across the upper face of the mountain is the last remaining vestige of the bulldozing ice-sheet that once pushed north as far as Gstaad. Hidden within that cirque, on a shelf six hundred metres above the valley floor, is the Gelten hut (2008m), owned by the Oldenhorn

Section of the SAC. With magnificent views, and space for more than eighty in its dormitories, the hut serves not only as a useful base from which climbers tackle the Wildhorn, Arpelistock, Schafhorn etc, but is so situated as to suggest an obvious destination for a day's walk from Lauenen.

It should not take much more than about three or four hours by reasonably fit walkers setting out from the village, but there are pleasures in practically every step. Firstly a track eases along the western hillside, through pastures and passing neat chalets before coming to the green, reed-fringed tarn of Lauenensee. From the southern end of the tarn a *bergweg* begins to climb through forest to gain the open pasture of Feisseberg, a region of flower meadows protected as a nature reserve. The trail goes through the meadows towards a huge cascading waterfall (the Geltenschuss), swings to the right and climbs steep slopes in a series of switchbacks, then returns to the cascade, ducking behind a minor waterfall on the way. Alpenroses bring a flush of scarlet in early summer, and views downvalley are exquisite.

The path bears right again and teeters alongside the Geltenbach that has bored great holes and swirls in the limestone. The stream is crossed some way back of the Geltenschuss, and there's a final short climb remaining before a grassy bluff gives way to the shingle-walled hut perched above a secret inner bowl of pastureland trapped between the bluff and the Wildhorn's glaciers.

A return to Lauenen could be varied by climbing a steep, grass-covered knoll north-east of the hut, and taking a narrow path beyond it along a vegetated crest. The path is clear, though exposed in places. It passes an isolated alp hut, Usseri Gelten, makes a traverse of the west flank of the Follhore and descends steeply (in part by metal ladder) to the pastures of Chüetungel. A choice of paths is offered here; one descends very steeply (fixed cables in places), while the alternative makes a more gentle downhill slant of the northern hillside. Both lead into the valley some way short of Lauenen and leave a fairly level walk back to the village.

The Gelten hut makes an obvious destination for a day's walk from Lauenen, but so too does the Wasserngrat-Brüeschigrat - a panoramic ridge-walk high above the valley north-east of the village. The standard way of tackling this is to use the Wasserngrat cableway that rises just to the east of Gstaad to a point at 1936 metres, then wander south-eastward on an airy trail with magnificent views of Les Diablerets and Wildhorn. The path climbs to a high point of 2203 metres, then loses a little height before cutting across the face of the Lauenehore to a saddle at 1986 metres which offers an easy way down to Lauenen.

Better still, one should descend northward from the saddle, away from Lauenen, into the head of the lonely Turbach glen, then wander down valley to Gstaad - thus creating a fine day's circuit before catching the bus back to Lauenen.

Careful study of the map will reveal a range of possibilities for full-day tours based on the valley, as well as multi-day treks and circuits radiating from Lauenen. A good three-day tour, for example, links the Gelten and Wildhorn huts, descends to Lenk in the Ober Simmental, then returns to the Lauenental by way of the easy Truttlisberg Pass.

The western hillside effectively separates the Lauenental from the Saanental, the most westerly valley in this part of canton Bern. The green dividing ridge is known as the Höhe Wispile; although mostly wooded, where the trees give way to bare crests fine views abound, and there are, of course, narrow trails to exploit them. On the Lauenental side these views are somewhat limited by intruding spurs and crags, but the western slopes open to damp, boggy pastures and alp hamlets that gaze in adoration of the curious formations of the big mass of Les Diablerets that soars overhead.

Saanental

The Saane begins life as the Rüschbach on the slopes of the Col du Pillon (1546m), an important watershed in more ways than one. From the col some streams spill westward into the Rhône and thence into the Mediterranean, while the Rüschbach/ Saane flows through central Switzerland and joins the Aare, which in turn feeds the Rhine and eventually discharges into the North Sea. Col du Pillon also marks the western limit of canton Bern, and serves too as a linguistic divide. All valleys east of the col are German-speaking, while those on the western side use French as their main language.

Les Diablerets dominates the upper Saanental. This lumbering limestone massif has several summits over three thousand metres, and with glaciers hanging on its north and east-facing slopes, provides limited skiing throughout the summer, accessed by cableway from the col itself. Apart from Les Diablerets, the Saanental is predominantly green - neat pasturelands backed by forests through which modest trails lead to unsung views. One such, on the northern side of Col du Pillon, leads to the attractive little Lac Retaud, easily reached in half an hour. There's a restaurant by the tarn with beautiful views to Les Diablerets. A track continues from it, then a path breaks off to the left to climb to a drystone wall marking the cantonal boundary at an insignificant saddle (Voré; 1919m). On the north side of the wall a clear trail slopes down through a shallow groove of a valley, goes through a minor col and descends slopes bright with alpenrose, juniper, larch and rowan, and comes to a junction of paths at the farm of Seeberg. From here one may either take a trail slanting up the hillside to gain the Blattipass with its astonishing panorama of distant Oberland giants, then descend to Gsteig; or continue downhill below Seeberg to the Arnensee lake, alongside which a route takes you through the Tschärzis glen to eventually spill into the Saanental at Feutersoey.

Gsteig is an attractive little resort at the foot of the hairpins leading to Col du Pillon. It has limited hotel accommodation, but no shortage of apartments and chalets for holiday let. There's a campsite just above the village. Four kilometres downvalley, and roughly midway between Gsteig and Gstaad, Feutersoey is little more than a hamlet of chalets planted in the low valley meadows. An easy but rewarding walk links Gsteig with Lauenen by way of the Krinnen Pass, while a much longer pass crossing is that of the Col du Sanetsch to the south of Gsteig, an ancient route which leads to Sion in the Rhône valley in nine hours or more. On the south side of the col a memorable view of the Pennine Alps stretching off as far as Mont Blanc, will be one of the visual rewards.

West of Col du Pillon streams gathered on the slopes of the Diablerets massif fall as attractive cascades beside the road which runs down to the scattered village of Les Diablerets and Ormont-Dessus. South of Les Diablerets village the cirque of Creux de Champ has been scooped out of the north-west flank of the massif, birthplace of the Grande Eau whose valley twists down to that of the Rhône. An alternative, minor, road climbs painfully south-west of Les Diablerets to Col de la Croix between the Tête de Meilleret and the Culan, then eases down the glen of La Gryonne via Villars, to spill out either at Bex or Ollon on the right bank of the Rhône valley.

✳   ✳   ✳

THE SOUTHERN FLANK

Historically most of the glaciers of the Bernese Alps pushed northward from the main range, carving out those valleys already visited. But as we have seen, these northern glaciers today are little more than insignificant remnants, stubby fingers of ice by comparison with those that flow south towards the Rhône from the heartland. However, the southern flank of the Bernese Alps has, by contrast with the northern side where long spurs and ridges project far from the watershed crest, been largely cut short by the Rhône itself, and as a result there are fewer tributary valleys and glens to explore. In due time that shortage may be partly readdressed when the Grosser Aletschgletscher and Fieschergletscher have melted back far enough to leave 'new' valley systems whose glories we can at present only speculate upon. But that will be for more distant generations to discover.

The southern flank may be a little short of valleys as such, but there's plenty of grand mountain scenery to enjoy, and several charming alps and villages trapped on remote hillside shelves offer gentle day walks in spectacular surroundings.

The upper, north-eastern, extension of the Rhône valley is known as Goms. A string of modest villages lines the valley bed, and at its head three major road passes provide access to other regions of Switzerland: the Grimsel leads north to Meiringen and the lake of Brienz; the Furka descends on its far side to Andermatt and central Switzerland, while the Nufenen crosses into Val Bedretto and Ticino. Walkers coming to the Upper Rhône from the northern valleys via the Grimsel could use a track that breaks away from the southern end of the Totesee (the tarn on the actual pass), then rounds the mountainside high above the valley, and serves a scattering of alp hamlets on the slopes of the Sidelhorn before swinging down into the valley at Obergesteln.

A steady ribbon of streams drains into the Goms valley from knuckle indents on the northern mountain wall, some of which have footpaths climbing into them, and above Fiesch the long tongue of the Fieschergletscher has bulldozed through a block of mountains headed by Finsteraarhorn, Fiescherhorn and Grünhorn. The glacier is in retreat, drawing back towards the big mountains of its birth, leaving a short glen, the Fieschertal, through which the milky torrent of the Wysswasser pours down to the Rhône. Fiesch is a small resort in the mouth of the Fieschertal that gives pedestrian access to the icy heart of the range. From it a tempting trail heads north along the right bank of the glen for about five kilometres, rising along the moraine that once walled the Fieschergletscher. An alternative path goes through the ablation valley below the moraine, then curves leftward, climbing alongside the Seebach stream to reach the Märjelensee, a small glacial tarn often dotted with iceflows on the left bank of the Grosser Aletschgletscher.

This tarn is also reached by way of Kühboden (cable-car access from Fiesch) along a hillside shelf below the Eggishorn - that famed viewpoint and, at 2927 metres, the highest summit on the ridge separating the Grosser Aletschgletscher from the Rhône valley, which is itself served by cable-car to within a twenty minute walk of the summit. The Eggishorn panorama is spectacular, not only on account of the near and middle views, but by virtue of far off ranges filling every horizon. Positioned directly above the great curve of the Grosser Aletschgletscher, this tremendous icefield is, of course, the main focus of attention; a vast highway of ice with its bands and stripes of medial moraine and crevasse all contained between shapely mountains. The Aletschhorn soars across the glacier to the north-west, with its own Mittel Aletschgletscher filling the corrie between Geisshorn and Olmenhorn. At the head of the main glacier Jungfrau, Mönch and Eiger appear relatively insignificant; to the right of them the Finsteraarhorn's fin-like tip, while the dark shapes of the Wannenhorn peaks nearby form a part of the glacier's great eastern wall, here known as the Walliser Fiescherhörner.

On the southern side of the Rhône valley one instinctively looks to Monte Leone, the Fletschhorn, Monte Rosa, and the Mischabel summits above the hinted Saastal. The Matterhorn is also in view, as is the Weisshorn, and far off the snow crown of Mont Blanc catches the sun.

Clearly the Eggishorn provides one of the finest lookouts from which to study the southern flank of the Bernese Alps, but there are several other viewpoints nearby, not so elevated of course, but hardly less interesting in themselves, where footpaths entice. As a base, the growing resort of Bettmeralp, trim and modernised but without motorised traffic, takes some beating. Isolated upon a sunny terrace more than a thousand metres above the Rhône (reached by cable-car from Betten Fo), it gazes south to the Pennine Alps. But wander away from the village on a trail that leads to Hotel Bettmerhorn, then break away to the north and climb for fifty minutes to the saddle of Hohbalm, and you'll have a similar view to that from the Eggishorn.

From Hohbalm you can either follow a trail along the western slopes of the Eggishorn directly above the glacier, and so reach the Märjelensee and return via Kühboden on the Rhône side, thus making a long circuit in effect of the Eggishorn; or bear left along the broad crest among boulders and shrubs of alpenrose, juniper and bilberry, with contrasting views to enjoy all the way - Grosser Aletschgletscher and attendant peaks to the right, Pennine Alps to the left across the unfathomable depths of the Rhône valley. By taking this ridge-crest trail it is possible to gain the neighbouring resort of Riederalp or, if time is short, cut back across the ridge to the little Blausee and descend easily from there to Bettmeralp.

Below the snout of the Grosser Aletschgletscher to the west of Riederalp lies a dammed lake and the narrow gorge of the Massaschlucht, and on a hillside shelf on the far side of that Blatten provides a way up to Belalp, that magnificent vantage-point much-loved by the Victorians. Ruskin visited in 1844, and in 1877 Professor John Tyndall, scientist and mountaineer, built a chalet there to enjoy what he considered the most beautiful view in the Alps. From it he would peer across the Rhône to the Weisshorn, of which he had made the first ascent. Above Belalp a way leads to the summit of the Sparrhorn (3021m), for a view comparable to that from Eggishorn; another cuts round the eastern flank of the Sparrhorn and reaches the moraine bank of the Ober Aletschgletscher - a climber's route to the Grosser Fusshorn, Geisshorn, Aletschhorn and Schinhorn. On the western side of the Schinhorn another icy tongue spills out of the great glacial spawning grounds of the Bernese Alps heartland, and drains into the finest valley on the southern flank of the range, the Lötschental.

The Lötschental

This is one of the loveliest of all Alpine valleys, a delight "... for anyone who loves unspoiled Alpine beauty" (R.L.G. Irving); a valley whose wonders are kept hidden from both north and south by being blocked from view by the configuration of its guardian mountains. The Lötschental is hemmed in on both sides by high mountain crests running roughly north-east to south-west, while the Rhône at this point flows almost due west below its partly disguised entrance. A road climbs out of the Rhône valley at Steg, about twenty kilometres west of Brig, and is signposted to Goppenstein, southern entrance to the Lötschberg Tunnel that takes a car-carrying railway through the mountains to Kandersteg - the only access for non-walkers or climbers between the Rhône valley and the central valleys on the northern side of the Bernese Alps.

Goppenstein is a gloomy place, and although it is only a matter of minutes away from the glories of the Lötschental proper, still there is little hint of what is to come. The valley here is a dark defile, but suddenly the steep bleak walls that form a gateway are flung aside and light and colour bursts out. At its head the Langgletscher is shrinking back towards the saddle of the Lötschenlücke, across whose innocent dipping ridge lies the Grosser Aletschfirn, the gathering ground for those icefields that come together at Konkordiaplatz to form the Grosser Aletschgletscher. As with all these glaciers, the Langgletscher is steadily receding, yet it is not difficult to imagine how great its industry has been in the past. Evidence of its sculpting power is all around you in the Lötschental.

The valley is narrow, but not too narrow to breed a sense of constriction, and as it faces south-west, so it catches plenty of sunlight. Meadows, dotted with hay barns, chalets and neat villages, line the stream; above them forests of larch and pine out of which rise the big mountains. The biggest and best is the stately Bietschhorn at 3934 metres, whose force of personality dominates practically every view. Seen from the far side of the Rhône valley it appears as a great pyramid of rock streaked with snow. Seen from one of the alp hamlets on the northern flank of the Lötschental, that elegant pyramid is different, but hardly less profound, as it rises from dark shoulders of stone down whose walls hanging glaciers are delicately poised.

The Wilerhorn, near neighbour to the Bietschhorn, acts as the southern gatepost to the valley. However, as the long southern wall of the Lötschental extends towards the north-east, so that wall (the Gletscherstafel) announces character all its own, and seen from the Petersgrat opposite - or from one of the narrow glens that descend from it to the valley - it holds immense appeal.

The ubiquitous Postbus serves each of the valley's half dozen or so villages, from Goppenstein to Fafleralp and as far as a large car park at the head of the Lötschental, on a frequent basis through the summer months, and there's no shortage of accommodation of all standards except, perhaps, the very grandest - which is no bad thing since one of its charms is its lack of sophistication. On the northern slope a string of alp hamlets, between three hundred and six hundred metres above the valley, look to the Bietschhorn as if in homage. There's accommodation to be had in some of these too, and in the hut at the Lötschenpass, by which the lovely Gasterntal above Kandersteg is reached.

The best of all walks here links these alp hamlets by a trail known as the Lötschentaler Höhenweg, a superb outing that reveals a whole series of classic views, from those that look across the Rhône to Monte Rosa and the Pennine Alps, others that reveal the full glory of the Lötschental in a single glance, the inevitable spectacle of the Bietschhorn on the opposite flank, and a succession of alp hamlets through which the trail makes its meandering way. It begins by climbing steeply for an hour and a half above Ferden to Faldumalp, a charming collection of typical Valaisian timber chalets (the southern slopes of the Bernese Alps fall within canton Valais) and a picturesque shingle-walled chapel tied down against the winds with cables.

From here the trail heads roughly northward to Restialp, then on to Kummenalp, from where an alternative path climbs to the Lötschenpass and beyond to Kandersteg. From Kummenalp the way follows a gentle contour to the cluster of chalets of Hockenalp, and in a further twenty minutes reaches Lauchernalp, from which it's possible to descend quickly and painlessly to Wiler by cable-car. Weritzstafel (or Weritzalp) comes next, a hamlet of red-shuttered chalets and a small restaurant perched on the steeply-plunging hillside. Leaving Weritzstafel the path now slopes downhill a little through patches of forest to gain the few hay barns and alp hutments of Tellistafel (Tellialp) in the narrow opening of the Tellin glen. Across the stream flowing from the glen the trail continues through more patches of forest, passes the little tarn of Schwarzsee and comes to Fafleralp, which has a superb modern chapel half hidden in the woods behind Hotel Fafleralp. In another ten minutes you reach the large car park at the head of the valley where, if you're lucky, the Postbus is ready to whisk you back to your valley base at the end of a magnificent seven-hour walk.

The Bernese Alps provide almost unlimited scope for active mountain holidays at all grades of seriousness. There are desperate (and notorious) routes for top-grade mountaineers on such faces as the Eiger's north wall; snow and ice routes on peaks like the Jungfrau; rock routes on the Engelhörner; modest summits like Wildhorn and Wildstrubel; glacier tours and ski tours along its icy core; prime downhill skiing grounds at Grindelwald, Wengen and Mürren; long-distance walking routes and a super-abundance of day walks and short tours, a brief sample of which has been outlined above.

Two first-rate multi-day walking tours traverse a goodly proportion of the range. The first explores the ice-bound heartland and is only for those experienced in, and equipped for, glacier travel; the second crosses a series of non-technical passes along the northern flank.

185

BERNESE ALPS GLACIER TOUR

This tour makes an east-west crossing of those glaciers and glacier passes which lie between the Grimsel at the head of the Haslital, and the Lötschental, and is just one of several options for such travel that exist here. In good conditions the route could be achieved in about three days, but tempting peaks line the way, and adepts could extend the journey by several days through adding peaks to their passes. It goes without saying, however, that none should attempt this tour without the necessary expertise to deal with crevasse rescue.

The route begins at the Grimsel Pass where a track heads roughly westward to the milky Oberaarsee, beyond which stretches the Oberaargletscher. On the left of the glacier runs the mountain wall (the Aargrat) which flanks the upper Rhône valley; on the right the dividing ridge between the Oberaar and Unteraar glaciers. At the head of the glacier is the Oberaar Joch (3223m), a small saddle immediately below the south ridge of the Oberaarhorn. Tucked among the rocks on the western side of the pass, and a little above it, is the SAC's Oberaarjoch hut.

North-west of the hut rises the Finsteraarhorn, the highest peak in the Bernese Alps at 4274 metres, its south-east ridge apparently blocking further progress westward across the narrow Studergletscher. But in that ridge, just below the Finsteraarrothorn, is the little pass of the Gemslücke (3335m). Through this a descent is made to the Finsteraarhorn hut and the head of the Fieschergletscher. (An alternative exit from the east-west tour could be made by following this last-named glacier downstream to Fiesch in the Rhône valley.)

Continuing westward the tour then crosses the Grünhornlücke (3286m), between Grünegghorn and Fiescher Gabelhorn. Ahead now sweeps the glacier of Grüneggfirn, one of a star-like finger of glaciers that converge at Konkordiaplatz, that magnificent junction of icefields from which the Grosser Aletschgletscher curls off to the south-east. Where the Grüneggfirn spills into Konkordiaplatz the Konkordia huts will be found perched high and dry above the glacier on the slopes of the Fülbärg. The position of these huts (there are two) clearly shows the amount of glacial shrinkage in the last few decades, for they originally stood on the edge of the icefield, now some way below, where the early pioneers sought shelter in a damp cave.

Opposite the Konkordia huts the Grosser Aletschfirn is a great white sheet rising between Dreieckhorn and Aletschhorn on the left, and Gletscherhorn, Ebnefluh and Mittaghorn on the right. A three-hour plod up the length of the glacier leads to the Hollandia hut (also known as the Lötschen hut) and the final pass on the tour, the Lötschenlücke. Descent into the Lötschental is by way of the Langgletscher, which could be the most difficult of all to negotiate. But eventually snow and ice are traded for pastures and streams, pinewoods, cowbells and hay barns which so epitomize the summer alps.

BERNESE ALPS GLACIER TOUR - ROUTE SUMMARY

Day 1:   Grimsel Pass - Oberaargletscher - Oberaarjoch Hut
Day 2:   Oberaarjoch Hut - Gemslücke - Grünhornlücke - Konkordia Hut
Day 3:   Konkordia Hut - Lötschenlücke (Hollandia Hut) - Lötschental

Standard safety procedures for glacier travel must be adopted on this crossing (ie: three or more on the rope; all equipped and with an understanding of crevasse rescue techniques). In good visibility route-finding should not be problematic, but in mist severe difficulties could arise.

✳   ✳   ✳

OBERLAND PASSES

On the northern flank of the range, as we have seen, a series of transverse ridges and spurs projects from the main crest-line, effectively separating each of the valleys that lie between the Haslital in the east, and Col du Pillon towards the western end of the Bernese Alps. Non-technical passes provide access from one valley to the next, and when linked these make a challenging traverse of the range possible for strong mountain walkers. The week-long trek outlined below forms part (some would say the most spectacular part) of the classic Alpine Pass Route which crosses Switzerland from Sargans, near the Liechtenstein border, to Montreux on the Lake of Geneva.

In its entirety the APR covers some 325 kilometres, crosses sixteen passes (none of which is a glacier pass) and gains an accumulation of almost 18,000 metres in height over a period of fifteen walking days. This central section, beginning at Meiringen and ending at Gsteig on the eastern side of Col du Pillon, has eight passes to contend with, the highest being the Hohtürli (2778m) above Kandersteg, the lowest at 1659 metres being the Krinnen Pass between Lauenen and Gsteig. It's a first-class mountain tour with an equal amount of challenge and visual reward to highlight each stage.

The APR is six days old by the time the trekker reaches the Haslital, and a welcome easy stage advances the route south-westward to Grindelwald by way of the Grosse Scheidegg as an introduction to the Bernese Alps. For walkers just starting out on a week-long traverse of the range, however, the twenty-one kilometres between Meiringen and Grindelwald, and the demands of almost 1400 metres of height-gain, will be quite enough for a first day. Happily that height gain is nowhere too severe, and the route is peppered with refreshment opportunities.

It leaves Meiringen heading south, crosses the Aare river to Willigen, then begins to climb among pasture and forest into the mouth of the Rosenlauital. This narrow tributary valley has a road running through it (only permit-holders and the Postbus are allowed to drive as far as the Grosse Scheidegg), but footpaths enable walkers to avoid most of the tarmac. With the towering walls of the Engelhörner rising to the left, and pastures dotted with hay barns and dark timber chalets on the right, the walk as far as Schwarzwaldalp makes a very pleasant start to the day.

From Schwarzwaldalp to Alpiglen the way is best followed on the true right bank of the stream, now with the craggy towers of the Wetterhorn dominating the valley from the south. The obvious saddle of Grosse Scheidegg below the Wetterhorn, with its large hotel and crowds of tourists gathered there to enjoy the view, is gained in about five and a half hours, and it will only take another two hours to complete the easy descent to Grindelwald. An interesting descent it is too, for the side-on view of the Eiger, and the blue glimmer of ice exposed below the

187

Wetterhorn's south-west face, make a direct contrast to the neatly shorn meadows and gentle fold of hillside rising to the Männlichen ridge ahead. Grindelwald has no shortage of accommodation, including a youth hostel, numerous campsites and hotels of every level of sophistication. It's a busy place year-round, and seclusion is not one of its assets. Its setting is.

The next stage from Grindelwald involves crossing the green dividing ridge running north from Kleine Scheidegg to Männlichen, and descending from there to the Lauterbrunnen valley. This ridge crossing may be achieved either at Kleine Scheidegg itself, or by a trail that descends very steeply under the cableway linking Männlichen with Wengen. Both routes have their advocates. The first leads past Alpiglen, suffers the indignities of Kleine Scheidegg's railway clutter, but rejoices in the glory of the Jungfrau from Wengernalp; the second provides a better and slightly more distant prospect of the Eiger's north face, as well as a lovely backward view of the Schreckhorn from the trail to Männlichen, and a tremendous bird's-eye view of the Lauterbrunnen valley from the ridge, but is slightly devalued on the descent to Wengen by avalanche fences projecting just below the ridge. Both options unite in Wengen where the final drop to Lauterbrunnen will take another two hours. Lauterbrunnen has two huge tent cities and several hotels, with more modest accommodation to be found towards the head of the valley.

An early start is recommended for the next stage which crosses the Sefinenfurke. That pass - a bare, craggy notch in the crest linking Büttlassen and Hundshorn - is a little over 1800 metres above Lauterbrunnen, and it'll take around six hours or so to reach. Add to that another three hours for the descent to Griesalp, and it will be evident that this is a hard day's trek. But it is also a very rewarding mountain day.

Once you've climbed out of Lauterbrunnen's deep trench and emerged to pastures on the outskirts of Mürren, the full scenic splendour of the Bernese Alps is revealed like a giant, multi-dimensional backdrop. Looking back to the north-east the Wetterhorn's coronet of summits can be made out beyond the Eiger's sharp profile; then there's Mönch and Jungfrau and, to the south, nature's own wall of great architectural merit topped by Ebnefluh, Mittaghorn, Grosshorn, Breithorn and Tschingelhorn, interrupted by the equally fine Gspaltenhorn, with the Tschingelgrat balancing a pristine shelf of glacier above its walling crags. This is the very stuff of dreams, a powerful backdrop that threatens to delay further progress.

The final climb to the pass is through the glen of the Sefinental that effectively closes off much of the visual splendour of the day. But once the Sefinenfurke has been reached, so a new prospect opens out, and it's the Blümlisalp that now takes command. Looking back, both Eiger and Mönch demand a last farewell. A steep slope of grit and scree, safeguarded by fixed rope, begins the descent. This eases a little to hummocks of grass above a lonely alp farm, then drops to another farm, Burgli, at a junction of trails. The main trail continues to descend to the hamlet of Griesalp, while the left-hand path makes its way through the Gamchibach glen to find the Gspaltenhorn hut. An alternative option descends a short distance, then breaks away from the main trail to cut short tomorrow's route by rising to the alp of Oberi Bund where there's dormitory accommodation available in the farmhouse, while next door the Swiss Alpine Club maintains a berghaus. The main route goes down past the chalets of Steinberg to Griesalp, a tiny hamlet grouped round a square, where there are hotels and a small food store.

The Hohtürli crossing next day is the highest on this traverse. The pass is at an altitide of 2778 metres, making a climb of nearly fourteen hundred metres from Griesalp, followed by a knee-twisting descent of 1600 metres into Kandersteg. A hard day, but a very rewarding one. Just above the pass the Blümlisalp hut tempts with prospects of refreshment in a stunning location, and after a climb of four hours plus from Griesalp to the pass, he would be a very single-minded mountain walker indeed who would shun this minor diversion from the route for at least a half litre of tea, and plod all the way down to Kandersteg without being fortified there. When it comes, the way down leads past the snout of the Blümlisalp glacier, edges a moraine cone, drops into a green, former glacial hollow with an alp farm set among huge boulders, then overlooks the fjord-like basin of the Oeschinensee.

Descending to Kandersteg at the end of summer one year on a crossing of the Alpine Pass Route with three friends, we found ourselves caught in a procession of cows and goats departing the alp of Ober Bergli. The lead cows were queens of the herd, wearing headdresses of flowers and wreaths, with tiny trees fixed to their horns. It was a bright and attractive scene, but the novelty soon wore off as we were unable to overtake and had to shuffle our way down the trail to the Oeschinensee along a moist brown carpet.

Between Kandersteg and Adelboden the way is blocked by a ridge crossed by the stony Bunderchrinde immediately to the south of the Chlyne (or Kleine) Lohner. The route to the pass goes via the entrance to the Üschenental and a lonely cheesemaker's alp on a shelf 500 metres above it, from which a grandstand view is gained into the Gasterntal. The final drag to the pass itself crosses a long scree drape at a comforting angle. The narrow gash of the Bunderchrinde is a windy gateway; a wild and inhospitable place with two trails breaking from it on the western side. One cuts off to the right to pass below the final crags of the Chlyne Lohner on its way to the Bunderspitze; the other drops into a stone-filled corrie, then descends among rough pastures to the Bunderle glen and Adelboden; a tough crossing.

The sixth stage of our Oberland Passes trek is an easy one which ends in Lenk. The standard crossing goes by way of the Gilbach (or Geilsbach) glen, the low saddle of Hahnenmoos and Hotel Büelberg on the Ober Simmental flank, and can be achieved in about four and a half hours, while a more entertaining choice is the neighbouring Pommernpass reached by a glen cut by the Bütschibach. This latter route takes another two hours or so to complete, but is recommended on account of the greater solitude to be found throughout most of the walk, for the Hahnenmoos alternative is cluttered with a gondola lift that spills the crowds carried there from Geilsbüel on a bright summer's day. Walkers on their way to the Pommernpass, however, will not only have the trail mostly to themselves, but may enjoy an unusual view across the Engstligenalp to the snowfields of the Wildstrubel from Tronegg Grat, as well as an opportunity for a wide panorama won from the summit of the Regenboldshorn overlooking the pass, and a delightful descent leading past the Simmen Falls near the head of the Ober Simmental.

Finally, the stage leading from Lenk to Gstaad crosses two low saddles; the

Trüttlisberg (2038m) and Krinnen at a modest 1659 metres. Between the two lies Lauenen in its pastoral valley overshadowed by the glacial dome of the Wildhorn, while Gsteig looks up at Les Diablerets. Although neither pass is high nor particularly demanding, and despite the fact that there are no close views of the major peaks of the Bernese Alps on show, it is still a worthy day's trek of twenty-two kilometres through charming countryside that will keep most walkers on the move for a good eight hours.

An alternative finish to the trek could be either Gstaad or Saanen. Gstaad has rather high-class accommodation; Saanen boasts a campsite. Both are linked by railway with Montreux and Bern, which could be useful for those with an early flight home next day. (Transport from Gsteig relies first on a Postbus ride to Gstaad for a homebound railway journey.) Walkers choosing the Gstaad/Saanen option would be advised to cut away north-west from the Trüttlisberg Pass to a saddle known as Turli (not marked as such on the 1:50,000 map) at 1986 metres, and descend from there into the head of the lovely Turbach glen. This flows north then west all the way to Gstaad, and is utterly delightful.

Finally, the Alpine Pass Route proper, of which the above tour forms a part, breaks away from the main alignment of the Bernese Alps chain on leaving Gsteig, and in two long days reaches Montreux on the Lake of Geneva by way of the road pass of Col des Mosses and 1437 metre Col de Chaude below the Rochers de Naye.

OBERLAND PASSES - ROUTE SUMMARY

Day 1: Meiringen - Grosse Scheidegg - Grindelwald

Day 2: Grindelwald - Kleine Scheidegg - Wengen - Lauterbrunnen
 or: Grindelwald - Männlichen - Wengen - Lauterbrunnen

Day 3: Lauterbrunnen - Mürren - Sefinenfurke - Griesalp (or Oberi Bund)

Day 4: Griesalp (or Oberi Bund) - Hohtürli - Kandersteg

Day 5: Kandersteg - Bunderchrinde - Adelboden

Day 6: Adelboden - Hahnenmoos - Lenk
 or: Adelboden - Pommernpass - Lenk

Day 7: Lenk - Trüttlisberg Pass - Krinnen Pass - Gsteig
 or: Lenk - Trüttlisberg Pass - Turli - Turbachtal - Gstaad (or Saanen)

A tremendous route for fit mountain walkers, some of the pass crossings are quite demanding; fixed ropes safeguard awkward sections that could be potentially dangerous in icy conditions. Mostly trails are straightforward and well-marked. Accommodation is plentiful and scenery spectacular. This route is part of the longer Alpine Pass Route (fifteen stages from Sargans to Montreux). As some of the crossings are quite high there is a danger of snow cover early in the season. In a 'normal' year the traverse should not be attempted before July.

---

* * *

THE BERNESE ALPS

Location:
North of the Rhône valley the Bernese Alps stretch from the Grimsel Pass in the east, to the Rhône's northerly curve near Martigny. The southern flank is in canton Valais (Wallis in German), the northern slopes fall mostly within canton Bern, while the western extremity is in canton Vaud.

Principal valleys:
From east to west on the northern side of the watershed, these are the Haslital (with the tributary glens of Urbachtal and Rosenlauital), Lütschental, Lauterbrunnental, Kandertal (and the subsidiary glens of Kiental and Gasterntal), Engstligental, Diemtigtal, Simmental, Lauenental, and the Saanental. On the southern flank the main valley is that of the Lötschental.

Principal peaks:
Finsteraarhorn (4274m), Aletschhorn (4195m), Jungfrau (4158m), Mönch (4099m), Schreckhorn (4078m), Fiescherhorn (4049m), Eiger (3970m), Bietschhorn (3934m), Lauterbrunnen Breithorn (3782m), Wetterhorn (3704m) Blümlisalphorn (3664m), Wildhorn (3248m), Wildstrubel (3244m), Les Diablerets (3210m)

Centres:
The range boasts numerous resorts and villages from which to base a walking holiday. A selection only is given here: Meiringen, Grindelwald, Wilderswil, Wengen, Lauterbrunnen, Mürren, Kandersteg, Adelboden, Lenk, Lauenen and Gstaad on the northern side; Fiesch, Bettmeralp, Wiler, Blatten and Kippel on the south side.

Huts:
There's no shortage of SAC huts (and some privately owned) situated in remote positions throughout the Bernese Alps. Mostly erected for the use of climbers, a number make interesting destinations for mountain walkers.

Access:
By air to Geneva or Zürich, both airports being linked to the region by rail. By rail the key towns to make for are Thun, Interlaken or Kandersteg for the northern valleys. Kandersteg (for the Lötschberg rail tunnel) is also important for walkers intending to concentrate on the south side. The reliable Postbus service fills any gaps missed by the railway.

Maps:
The majority of the range is conveniently covered by two sheets at 1:50,000 scale published by the Swiss topographical survey - Landeskarte der Schweiz. *Berner Oberland* (sheet 5004) serves the eastern valleys and mountains from Haslital to Kandertal - and a small section of the upper Rhône (Goms) valley; *Gstaad-Adelboden* (sheet 5009) covers the range west of the Kandertal to Ormont-Dessous west of Les Diablerets. This sheet also includes country south of the Gemmi. For the Lötschental sheet 264, *Jungfrau*, also covers the region of Fiesch, Bettmeralp, Belalp etc.

Guidebooks:
The Bernese Alps by Kev Reynolds (Cicerone Press) describes 115 walking routes on the northern side of the watershed, while *The Valais*, by the same author and publisher, includes routes based on the Lötschental and Bettmeralp on the south side of the range. *Alpine Pass Route* by Kev Reynolds (Cicerone Press) describes this long-distance route, plus variations, in 15 day stages.

Other reading:

Rambles in the Alps by Hugh Merrick (Country Life, 1951) - a large-format book, long out of print but available on loan from public libraries on special order, much of the content eulogises the Bernese Alps as a walking area.

Backpacking in Alps and Pyrenees by Showell Styles (Victor Gollancz, 1976) contains an account of a backpacking tour of part of the Bernese Alps.

Classic Walks in Europe edited by Walt Unsworth (Oxford Illustrated Press, 1987) contains a chapter by Andrew Harper describing part of the multi-day circuit of the Lütschental and Lauterbrunnental, which Harper calls The Grindelwald Cirque.

Classic Walks in the Alps by Kev Reynolds (Oxford Illustrated Press, 1991) - a large-format book with a number of routes relevant to this chapter described and illustrated.

The Mountains of Europe by Kev Reynolds (Oxford Illustrated Press, 1990) includes a chapter devoted to the Bernese Alps.

Wanderings Among the High Alps by Alfred Wills (Blackwell, latest edition 1939), gives an interesting pioneer's-eye-view of early mountaineering in the range.

The Playground of Europe by Leslie Stephen (Blackwell, latest edition 1936) is one of the classics of early mountaineering literature, and includes several essays of interest to visitors to the Bernese Alps.

The Dammastock massif blocks the head of the Göschenertal

7: THE CENTRAL SWISS ALPS
Including the Eastern Bernese Alps, Uri Alps and Glarner Alps

Loosely defined under a general heading of the Central Swiss Alps, this chapter looks at those mountains that extend, in effect, the chain of the Bernese Alps eastward of the Haslital to the Reuss valley, the Uri Alps, and the block of the Glarner Alps between the Reuss valley and the Rhine. The boundaries of this group (or groups) are not precisely followed nor given comprehensive coverage, but selected mountains, valleys and passes will be explored in some detail. Though not so well-known as the Bernese or Pennine Alps, the scenic delights and walking potential of the area offer no poor second-best. On the contrary, it may well be said that in the comparatively little-known, as represented by some of the unsung glens and remote hamlets and pasturelands here, pleasures may be found that have additional appeal in their apparent isolation.

Of our various groups, that which rises immediately to the east of the upper Haslital and forms a near neighbour to the Alps of canton Bern, is neatly contained within a rough square of major road systems. Sometimes known as the Urner Oberland, it's also referred to as the Eastern Bernese Alps, despite a large portion being in canton Uri. The Grimsel and Furka Passes cross at the south-western corner, the Susten links the Gadmen and Meien valleys on the northern boundary,

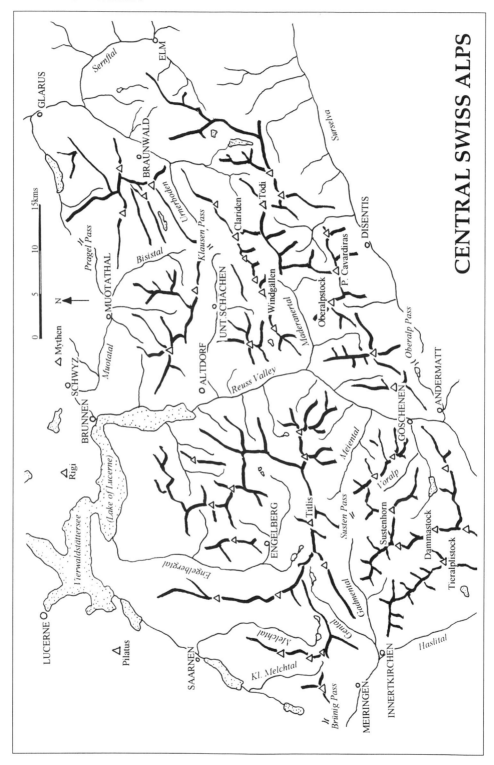

CENTRAL SWISS ALPS

while the Gotthard route along the eastern flank makes the Reuss valley one of the most important of all trans-alpine thoroughfares.

There are no 4000 metre summits in this road-encircled region, but numerous shapely peaks well in excess of 3000 metres are adorned with permanent snowfields and bright dazzling glaciers: Galenstock, Tieralplistock, Dammastock, Tierberg, Sustenhorn - their names may mean little or nothing to the majority of mountain lovers reading this book. But once seen as a backdrop to a bevy of enchanting walks, their individual characters will become woven in the tapestry of mountain days.

✳   ✳   ✳

THE EASTERN BERNESE ALPS

This relatively small and compact group contains the highest and most interesting of all the mountains of the Central Swiss Alps. The Winterberg massif - an impressive ridge system running roughly north-south, with an easterly kink between the Tierberg and Sustenhorn - effectively divides the group and forms the canton boundary. The western flank is the more heavily glaciated with the Triftgletscher flowing north from a *firn* basin on one side of the Tieralplistock, the Rhônegletscher tumbling south towards the Furka Pass from a matching *firn* basin on the other.

The western side of the group falls into the Haslital at too steep an angle for much walking comfort, although there is a trail climbing to the Gelmer hut (2412m) just north of the Grimsel Pass, and one or two others that link remote alps, effectively making a high traverse possible way above the valley. The northern valleys of Gadmental and Meiental, draining either side of the Susten, are not devoid of charm, but without question the finest of all is the Göschenertal that rises to the south-east of the Tierberg and flows out to the gloomy defile of the Reuss valley at the village of Göschenen.

The Göschenertal is one of the most beautiful and dramatic of all those valleys of the Central Swiss Alps. With the glacier-clad Dammastock apparently blocking its western end beyond the dammed Göscheneralpsee, a gaunt rocky wall extending along its southern length and a barely-hinted tributary glen (the Voralp) cutting to the north halfway through it, the valley is as grand as any mountain lover could wish as a base for an active holiday. Walkers relying on public transport to get to their mountains will find that Göschenen is easily accessible from Zürich and other major Swiss centres, for it sits at the northern end of the St Gotthard railway tunnel, and plenty of trains call at the station there. The village has a handful of hotels and a youth hostel, while the hamlet of Gwüest, situated midway between the entrance to the Voralp glen and the Göscheneralp reservoir, has simple accommodation in a *touristenlager*. Beds are also to be had in a large *gasthof* at the roadhead. From Göschenen to the roadhead at the dam the valley is served by Postbus daily between late-June and October.

Five huts strategically placed around the valley are easily accessible without treading glaciers or permanent snowfields, and although each one may be gained on day-walks with the initial aid of motorised transport from a single valley base, by linking four of them on a short tour it is possible to gain a very fair overview of the best the Göschenertal has to offer.

TOUR OF THE GÖSCHENERTAL

We will assume our walker has arrived by train at Göschenen. If she has that day flown to Zürich and taken the Gotthard rail route from there, time will probably be a bit tight to make a start on our short tour of the valley's huts, so it will be as well to a find a bed for the night and set out next morning fresh of limb and with an eagerness to get into the heart of the mountains, with the aim of wandering as far as the comfortable Voralp hut set deep in the narrow glen of the same name overlooked by the Sustenhorn (3503m).

It will only take a few minutes to walk out of Göschenen heading west into the Göschenertal on a trail that eases through patches of forest and open meadow on the south bank of the river. The valley rises gently, and the deeper you intrude, so the grandeur of its situation grows more and more impressive. One footpath breaks away just beyond Abfrutt and climbs to an alp some 500 metres higher, but our trail keeps company with the river all the way to its confluence with the Voralpreuss. A footbridge then allows access to the north bank where the road snakes its persistent way, and from which a path climbs into conifer woods guarding the Voralp glen's narrow entrance.

From the crossing of the road to the hut will take about two and a half hours of walking time, with the path remaining on the true left bank of the stream throughout. It's a wild little glen, its pastures littered with rocks and boulders. Immediately on entry the pinnacled ridge of the Salbitschijen towering above the northern wall provides rock climbing of an extreme nature - the Salbit hut from which a number of routes are tackled, stands on a shelf of hillside on the other side of the ridge and is reached by path from Abfrutt, while a bivouac hut is perched about 800 metres above the Voralp glen. An hour or so from the valley's entrance the way leads past the few alp hutments of Horefalli, then climbs again. Now you enter an upper level where the glen changes character, becomes squeezed by crags on the right and draped with glaciers on the left, the trail winding among alpenroses and tufts of alder; the flanking peaks creating a rugged boundary on either side, and at the head of the valley.

The Voralp hut is finally reached by a twist of zig-zags. Owned by the Uto Section of the Swiss Alpine Club, it replaces an earlier refuge destroyed by avalanche in 1988. With bedspace for about forty, it's well appointed and enjoys fine views to the graceful Sustenhorn which, hung about with glaciers, dominates the glen. I arrived there one stormy afternoon, soaked through after plodding in torrential rain all the way from the main valley, to find the hut deserted save for the guardian, who plied me with hot drinks until I was steaming. The Sustenhorn disappeared into cloud, its glacial apron grey and oppressive in the rain. But when the clouds finally lifted, everything shone in glory.

After using this opportunity to explore the glen further, return down valley next day to the Göschenertal, then head south-west to the dammed lake from whose north-eastern end a trail climbs steeply to the Bergsee hut (2370m), built alongside a small tarn high upon the southern flanks of the Bergseeschijen. Views from the path, as from the hut, are magnificent, with the great spread of the Winterberg massif seen in all its splendour to the west. By virtue of its proximity to the roadhead, from which it is easily reached, the hut is extremely popular during the day, but by nightfall the number of visitors dwindles to enable an atmosphere more akin to that enjoyed at more remote mountain huts to be recreated.

The map of the region published by the official Swiss survey suggests that it's necessary to retrace the upward path upon leaving, but an alternative trail (marked on the Kümmerly & Frey 1:50,000 sheet: *Urner Oberland*) skirts the southern shore of the Bergsee tarn, climbs to a high point on the Vorder Mur (a shoulder of the Bergseeschijen), then makes a high traverse above the lovely Chelenalptal, before coming to the Chelenalp hut (2350m). The Chelenalptal is the upper, north-westerly, projection of the Göschenertal, through which the standard route of approach is made to this third hut on our tour. This glen will be explored on our descent route.

The high belvedere trail linking the Bergsee and Chelenalp huts demands a little care and a head for heights, and is likely to be impassable early in the season, but once again the world of high mountains and glaciers on display makes it a trail worthy of this Alpine wonderland. The hut itself is perched in a bold, elevated position below the Rot Stock, with a cascade of glaciers peeling from the head of the valley a short distance away. It's the largest of the SAC huts in the Eastern Bernese Alps, with room for about eighty in its dormitories.

The next stage on our walking tour will lead to the Damma hut, built on an exposed spur of grass-cushioned rock at an altitude of 2438 metres below the Dammastock, due west of the Göscheneralpsee. An easy morning's walk is all that's required to reach it from the Chelenalp hut, but so delightful is the countryside through which the route leads, that a full day could justifiably be spent in getting there. The Chelenalptal is a natural flower garden, and those who readily acknowledge the broad treasures of the Alpine world, rather than concentrate solely on the grandeur of mountain architecture, will find sufficient to charm them in this valley back-of-beyond. Not only the alpine flowers, but the marmots and chamois too; and the wildlife in and around the streams that dash from the glaciers. And the glaciers and snowfields that adorn every mountain running along the western flank.

Descent from the hut to the Chelenalptal is by a steep trail that passes a granite slab on which a huge cairn has been built. Further down the rocks are stained rust-red, and the glaciers are often likewise stained with a rusty grit from the mountains. But the valley itself is a charming little glen, full of innocence, bright with alpenroses and starred with cushion plants that adorn numerous boggy patches. Midway through the glen you pass the little alp hut of Hinter Röti, camouflaged beneath a boulder pile. Lower down, near the start of the Göscheneralpsee, there's another hut; Vorder Röti. The trail divides. Ours heads south among alder scrub and alpenroses before climbing a little and crossing boulder slabs at the entrance to the Dammareuss glen. This is a small, glacial carved basin topped by the Dammastock upon whose eastern face the Dammagletscher makes a broad apron. From it a lively torrent comes dashing through the centre of the stony basin; a wild fury of spume and spray. The trail follows its true left bank, then breaks away to climb steeply over a series of rock terraces, often with no obvious trail other than a guiding line of paint flashes or small cairns, to gain the hut.

Views from the Damma hut are inevitably dominated by the Winterberg massif. But to the south-east the spiked crags of Feldschijen and Müeterlishorn also impress by their rugged topography; in fact the whole line of the southern wall provides a focus of interest, while the Göschenertal projects a deep trench through which the morning light will send its early shafts next day.

Return to Göschenen is not without its charm, and is best achieved by descent into the Dammareuss glen, crossing the torrent to its south bank by footbridge, then taking a path which makes a high traverse above the Göscheneralpsee. Cross the dam to the *Berggasthaus* at the roadhead, then follow the trail down valley, soon treading soft pastures nearly all the way to Göschenen to conclude a rewarding four or five day tour, summarised as follows:

TOUR OF THE GÖSCHENERTAL

Day 1: Göschenen - Voralp Hut

Day 2: Voralp Hut - Göscheneralpsee - Bergsee Hut

Day 3: Bergsee Hut - Chelenalp Hut - Damma Hut

Day 4: Damma Hut - Göscheneralpsee - Göschenen

None of these stages should be found too taxing for mountain walkers in good shape. The route from the Bergsee hut to the Chelenalp hut, for example, requires only a morning's effort, but the situation of the latter hut is so good that it is quite possible that you'd be tempted to spend a night there, and either have a longer fourth day by visiting the Damma hut and continuing down to Göschenen, or extending this little tour into one of five days. In such country distance covered each day is almost an irrelevance. The important yardstick is how much pleasure can be squeezed from each hour.

---

*   *   *

THE WESTERN URI ALPS

North of the Susten Pass and on display from the shores of the Lake of Lucerne (Vierwaldstättersee), another fine mountain block stands with a knuckle of ridges enclosing exquisite little glens and valleys well worth exploring. The snowy Titlis (3238m) is the main peak here, with an extensive south-westerly ridge effectively dividing the Gadmental from the Gental; while a subsidiary block immediately to the south (containing the aptly named Fünffingerstock) guards the Susten. A ridge pushing north and east of the Fünffingerstock, given additional character by the Spannort pinnacles, provides a barrier to the Meiental, while the northern side of that overlooks the Engelbergtal in which Engelberg, of course, is the main resort village.

Seen from above, the landscape here is contorted into curious sworls and anarchic ridge spurs. Numerous minor glaciers, many long vanished, are responsible for the arthritic nature of this mountainscape, having gouged out clover-like indents that are, in effect, attractive little cirques containing rough pastures bright with alpine flowers and grazed by cattle and sheep where once the ice lay deep.

The western edge of this block is accessed from Innertkirchen in the Haslital by way of a short stretch along the Susten Pass road. Less than four kilometres into the Gadmental a minor road breaks away to the north and twists into the Gental (Baedeker sniffed at this valley, calling it 'monotonous' - though it is hardly that) through which the Postbus makes its way past tiny hamlets and waterfalls streaking the southern mountain wall, as far as the roadhead at Engstlenalp, described in 1866 by John Tyndall as "one of the most charming spots in the Alps." The alp here has hardly changed at all in the century and more since Tyndall's visit; still a few timber farms and an old Victorian *Berghotel* with a commanding view to the south-west where the Wetterhorn stands supreme. Behind the hotel the Engstlensee lake draws crowds of day-trippers, while a path climbs beyond that among a clutter of chair lifts to the Joch Pass west of the Titlis, and descends from there to Engelberg.

Engstlenalp has a number of good walks emanating from it in addition to that which crosses the Joch Pass. One popular tour heads over the Gental's north-west wall to Tannensee and Melchsee; another goes down into the Gental itself or, perhaps the finest of all, a high belvedere trail that makes a full traverse of the right-hand wall of the Gental to Hasliberg and Meiringen. From Engstlenalp the route over the valley's north-west ridge to the high plateau containing the Tannensee and Melchsee, is surprisingly straightforward, but no less worth tackling for that. Having crossed a stream below a cascade the path begins a rising traverse under a line of cliffs, then slants up to a grassy crest which provides a grandstand view of the Gental leading the eye towards the Wetterhorn, Schreckhorn, Lauteraarhorn and Finsteraarhorn forming a rough sea of peaks to the south-west; while to the east the snow-and ice-crested Titlis and its near-neighbour, the Wendenstöcke, contrast the greenery of valley pastures.

The Tannensee-Melchsee plateau is a strange landscape, a nature reserve with a rich alpine flora and patches of limestone pavement. A variety of paths scores through it, and in winter it's popular with cross-country skiers. There's accommodation to be had (including a youth hostel) in Tannensee, and hotel and dormitory beds in Melchsee-Frutt, from which it's possible to take a gondola cableway down to Stockalp in the lower Melchtal - itself served by Postbus out to Saarnen. Not far away, Älggialp above the Klein Melchtal is acknowledged as the geographical centre of Switzerland.

Rather than end the walk from Engstlenalp here, our walker will either make a short tour of the plateau, then return to the ridge crest at the Balmeregghorn (following the line of a cableway) south of the Melchsee, and wander north-east along the ridge to rejoin the outward trail from Engstlensee or, if the plan is to continue roughly westward, take the right-hand trail at Balmeregghorn and traverse the Rothorn's sharp flank in order to find a path leading down to Hasliberg and Meiringen. This latter route would give a long, fine and very varied day's walking.

The recommended alternative trail to Hasliberg and Meiringen, however, hugs the upper flank of the Gental's right-hand wall all the way from Engstlenalp on a delightful natural shelf that leads hour after hour in a glory of long views, running streams, tiny alps, flowers and peace. Although it has been adopted by the classic Alpine Pass Route, it's not a busy trail. In places it's quite narrow and a little exposed, although never dangerously so, and it is only as you approach the village of Reuti that the outside world intrudes; while it traces high above the Gental there's little other than wild nature to distract.

The Gental has no resort villages and, apart from Engstlenalp, practically no facilities for holiday makers. It's a peaceful valley, unspectacular but full of simple charms. By marked contrast, on the northern side of Titlis the Engelbergtal is served by railway as far as Engelberg where there are numerous hotels, apartments, youth hostel and shops, and a campsite a short way upvalley. The Engelbergtal offers a choice of cableways by which to gain access not only to high shelves of pastureland with stunning views, but to mountain peaks too, with one series of lifts rising almost to the summit of Titlis. Even so, it's possible to ignore these, and the crowds, for there's plenty of unspoilt walking country to enjoy.

Towards its head, the Engelbergtal curves north-eastward below the Gross Spannort, and is blocked by a lovely glacial cirque (now minus its ice) topped by the Wissigstock and Blackenstock. Blackenalp, a secluded farm, lodges in this pastoral bowl, with a neat white chapel perched on a rock nearby. In the lower north-eastern ridge of the cirque the Surenen Pass provides an opportunity for fit mountain walkers to cross over to Attinghausen, Altdorf, or the shores of the Vierwaldstättersee on a long, knee-straining descent. Just below the pass, on the Blackenalp side, two or three small tarns lie sheltered among grassy hummocks with grand views of Titlis to the south-west.

Streams fan out of the cirque and join forces just below the farm at the Stauber waterfall to become the Surenenbach. This then dashes through the valley below a good trail that traces its right bank, and below Titlis the river becomes known as the Engelberger Aa. Along its bordering trail another small farm, Stäfeli, doubles as a restaurant with dormitory accommodation in full view of the Spannort pinnacles. During the day it's busy with passing trade, but as evening approaches so an atmosphere of peaceful seclusion settles over the valley, disturbed only by the tinkle of goatbells. Such simple lodging places have an appeal for those of us who love the wild nature of mountains, that far outstrips the grandest and most comfortable of resort hotels.

Nearly 600 metres higher than the Stäfeli farm with its *matratzenlager*, the Spannort hut can be detected on the north-west flank of the Gross Spannort opposite. A steeply climbing trail leads to it, and continues to the north ridge of the Gross Spannort for some astonishing views.

The standard route down to Engelberg entails following the river all the way through the bed of the valley, but a better walk takes a high trail along the north wall of the Engelbergtal. First wander upvalley towards Blackenalp, but before reaching the Stauber waterfall cut back to the left on an alternative path that leads along a beautiful hillside shelf with Titlis looming directly ahead. The trail by-passes one or two huddles of alp hutments, rounds a spur of the Wissberg near the upper Fürenalp cable-car terminus, then traces a route north-westward over rough pastures and through patches of forest, until reaching the Barenbach glen where descent is made to Engelberg.

Heading the Barenbach glen to the east of Engelberg, the Wissigstock and Engelberg-Rotstock send out ridge-arms of embrace. The north side of these face the Uri-Rotstock guarding the modest Grosstal that drains out, via the little village of Isenthal, to the Urnersee finger of the Lake of Lucerne. Strong mountain walkers setting out from Engelberg could cross the mountains to the lake by one of two routes, apart from the superb Surenen Pass crossing already mentioned. The first is to follow a trail up to the Rugghubel hut, cross the north-west ridge of the Engelberger Rotstock to a little glacial drape on the north slope, then descend to the Grosstal. A longer, but slightly less demanding way of reaching the same destination, is to head roughly north from Engelberg round the slopes of the Walenstöcke to Oberrickenbach, then south-eastward through the Bannalp glen, and over the 2250 metre Bannalper Schonegg, to join the previously mentioned trail which gives into the Grosstal and down to the Mediterranean-like Urnersee, in so doing exchanging one world for another. An entertaining circuit of three or four days could be made by combining one of these routes with a crossing of the Surenen Pass, and is outlined as follows:

URI-ROTSTOCK CIRCUIT

Day 1: Engelberg - Rugghubel Hut

Day 2: Rugghubel Hut - Rot Grätli - Isenthal (Hotel Urirotstock)

Day 3: Isenthal - Seedorf (via the Swiss Path) - Attinghausen - Brüsti (gasthof)

Day 4: Brüsti - Surenen Pass - Engelberg

The Swiss Path mentioned on day three makes a thirty-five-kilometre horseshoe loop round the Urnersee from the Rütli Meadow to Brunnen, and was created in 1991 as a celebration of the seven hundredth anniversary of the Swiss Confederation. The Walk makes a pleasant two-day amble amid fine scenery, although it is seldom far from roads and could not compare with the majority of suggestions in this book for either scale or sense of grandeur. The section adopted on our circuit makes a useful link in the journey from Isleten at the mouth of the Grosstal, to Seetal at the southern end of the lake, while that part of the circuit between Attinghausen and Engelberg which crosses the Surenen Pass, is one of the stages on the Alpine Pass Route.

---

*   *   *

THE EASTERN URI ALPS & GLARNER ALPS

Rising from the eastern shore of the Urnersee a chain of limestone mountains reaches out to the Linth valley which projects north from the Tödi - the so-called 'king of little mountains'. The southern extent of this chain is determined by the Schächental and the valley of Urnerboden, the two joined by the 1948 metre Klausenpass, while the northern edge breaks up among the green hills of canton Schwyz. Cutting through the heart of these mountains a secretive little valley (the Bisistal) rises almost due north of the Klausenpass, and drains north-north-west to a forested curve opening as the Muotatal. This in turn flows roughly westward to the Urnersee near Brunnen.

Walkers who enjoy their mountains away from crowds, who delight in raw scenery with jutting peaklets whose names inspire barely an eyebrow raised in recognition, who seldom tire of pastures soft under foot, of silver cascades and sidling streams, of lonely alp farms clattering with cowbells; who are happy to explore bare ribs of limestone pavement and visit remote passes that gaze on more unknown valleys and maze-like ridges far away, will find plenty to their liking here.

Where to stay? Well, if you've transport and are content with day trips into the mountains, you could mix it with the seaside-like atmosphere of Brunnen (hotels, pensions and two campsites). For a halfway solution there's the village of Muotathal with a few hotels and a youth hostel. But for those who prefer to be among the mountains, there's *matratzenlager* accommodation to be found in the Hürital glen cutting south of Hinterthal, gasthofs at Dürenboden and Schwarzenbach in the Bisistal, and a couple of SAC mountain huts: the Lidernen above the Riemenstaldner valley, and the Glattalp near the head of the Bisistal overlooking Glattalp and the Glattalpsee high above the right bank of the valley. The first has a guardian in residence for most of the summer, the latter usually at weekends.

Several worthwhile days could be spent exploring these mountains and glens, making use of the modest accommodation available. What follows is a suggested tour in which the best of the region can be enjoyed, in the best possible manner - that is, by having a temporary base here and there in order to discover local gems, before moving on across the mountains to the next valley base.

Assuming our walker has no transport of his own, the easiest way of getting into the Muotatal is by bus from Schwyz. Leave the bus at Hinterthal, the next village upvalley from Muotathal, and wander south into the Hürital. A footpath short-cuts the narrow road which services the valley, at first across meadows, then through forest, mostly alongside the Hüribach stream nearly all the way to the little hamlet of Liplisbüel where a base should be made for the next two nights. South of Liplisbüel the valley is distinctly pastoral, but is headed by grey limestone peaks whose southern barrier is breached by a couple of walkers' passes leading into the Schächental. The western wall is almost dolomitic in appearance. There are neither glaciers nor permanent snowfields, but sharp bastions of rock soar out of screes that fan down to rough grasslands rich in wild flowers.

The first aim of our walker, then, will be to see these peaks at close hand and to tread the pastures. For that a full day will be required; a day of about six hours or so of exercise, plus lots of time to stand and stare and to absorb the graceful beauty of the region. Initially the route follows the valley road a short distance until it crosses to the east side of the stream. A vague path then continues along the west bank, and in about fifteen minutes comes to a trail junction where you take the right-hand option to climb alongside a woodland and eventually join a farm track. This leads to the alp building of Seenalp. The way now heads up a steep cone of hillside blazing scarlet with alpenroses in the early summer, and eases on a rucked pastureland below the Dolomite-like Chaiserstock-Chronenstock wall. Just off the trail to the south lies an attractive tarn (Seenalper Seeli) cupped in a grassy basin and with plenty of wild flowers forming cushions over exposed rocks.

Above the tarn the path heads among sections of limestone pavement; it then crosses more pastureland, dodges to and fro over little streams. Gaining height still a small hut is seen ahead perched below what appears to be a grassy saddle, but the trail swings left below the hut to pass through a region of limestone pits and grass bowls, goes through a cleft and descends to a junction of paths. Continue ahead, and soon veer right towards a large cross, above which you gain the pass of Chinzig Chulm (2073m).

While the northern side of the pass, and much of the crest itself, is grass, the southern side offers a complete contrast, with grey cliffs and limestone gullies plunging, and stern peaklets rising. There's a small shrine and a signpost, from which an enticing array of rock peaks, blue-hinted valleys and sloping pastures fills each horizon. The trail which crosses the pass descends into the Schächental, whose bed lies 1300 metres below. On this occasion, though, the suggestion is to ignore that option and return to the wooden cross and take a trail leading down to the Chinzertal, a minor glen which is one of the headwaters of the main Hürital. About ten minutes below Chinzig Chulm a second trail heads off to the right and is one of the ways by which to reach the neighbouring valley of Bisistal. Our descent via the Chinzertal passes through an untidy little alp partially submerged amongst a jungle of dock tight against the southern crags of the Chinzerberg, then provides an exciting prospect of jagged peaks that form the dividing wall between the upper Hürital and the Bisistal. The Chinzertal feeds into the Wangi glen, dotted with alp hutments, and this in turn opens as the Hürital for a relaxed final plod back to Liplisbüel.

Having made a brief exploration of the upper western reaches of the Hürital, and gazed at the splendours of the upper eastern portion, it is now time to move on into the next valley to the east, the Bisistal. Apart from returning down valley to the Muotatal and then joining the Bisistal at its northern end, there are two ways of crossing the dividing ridge wall. The higher option was noted just below the pass of Chinzig Chulm where a trail cut off across the head of the Wangi glen to Rindermatt alp, then eased up north-eastwards to the rock-girt pastures of Galtenäbnet before dropping into the Bisistal at Schwarzenbach. That makes a great day's crossing, but on this occasion the alternative option is advised.

A short distance upvalley from Liplisbüel a path crosses to the left-hand side of the stream and rises through a series of natural terraces, or bands of rock, below the crags of Wasserbergfirst. At the high point of 2049 metres a small tarn (Träsmerenseeli) is skirted on its northern side before sloping easily north-eastward towards the Bisistal. Overlooking the glen at 1471 metres the trail forks. Take the right-hand option to the alp of Waldhüttli, then down through forest on a serpentine track that leads directly to the hamlet of Schwarzenbach for a couple of nights in the gasthof there.

The Bisistal is the longest of the Muotatal's tributaries and, like the Hürital, is distinctly pastoral with a number of summer-only farms dotted about the valley and its hillside shelves. At its head it is enclosed by a knot of limestone peaks, the highest of which is the Höch Windgällen at a modest 2763 metres. Modest though the height of some of these peaks may be, there are some rugged and attractive forms on display which far outclass mere altitude reading. The Höch Windgällen (not to be confused with the better-known Windgällen mountains above the Maderanertal) forms a cornerstone from which the boundary ridge undulates roughly east-south-east above the Klausenpass, breached in no less than three places by foot passes linking the Bisistal with either the Schächental or the valley of Urnerboden.

The method of exploration adopted in the Hürital glen will be used here in an effort to discover some of the delights of the Bisistal. Two nights will be spent in Schwarzenbach, followed by a night in the Glattalp hut, before crossing out of the region. Carrying only a light pack for the day head upvalley from Schwarzenbach following the tarmac road on the west bank of the Muota stream for a little over a kilometre, until a rock on the right-hand side of the road bears a painted sign for Waldialp. Waymarks lead a tenuous path over grass slopes to reach the hutments of Vorderstein Hütten and on to a farm track heading south to pass along the left-hand side of a tarn (a meadow here boasts a tremendous array of orchids in early summer) with lovely views to mountains blocking the head of the valley. Continue heading south to Unter Stafel, a small alp hut at 1496 metres in the steep grassland of Ruosalp, where a narrow path rises behind it to cross a high rolling pasture. Most of the time there is no actual path to be seen, but waymarks give general guidance in poor visibility.

From pasture to a bare stony region, then across more grassland with the spiky craglets of Rau Stöckli rising above to the left. Suddenly it's a wild corner of mountains you've come to. In good bright conditions the landscape is disturbed yet somehow untroubled; but with mists writhing it can appear almost haunted or even threatening. Now the trail (as far as we may call it a trail) veers south-south-west and steepens, to be led by tall marker poles as far as the pass of Ruosalper Chulm (2178m), an obvious saddle set in a craggy ridge gazing south across the depths of the Schächental to mountains that wall the lovely Brunnital glen. Immediately below the pass lies a small tarn, and the descent route to the Schächental goes right past it.

Our aim, however, is not to descend into that valley just yet, but instead return to the welcome pastures of the Bisistal. In order to avoid backtracking take the upper of two paths branching left along the ridge crest. This soon skirts along the right-hand side of the ridge to traverse the southern slopes of Point 2318m whose crags tower above you. When I tackled this route alone one summer I found the slopes had been swept clear of any form of trail by rockfall, and picked my way with heartstopping care as mists rose from the valley to obscure all onward views. With no obvious route either forward or back, for a while it seemed safer to settle myself on a rock and wait for clearer vision, without which I found it impossible to decide exactly where the return pass could be. After what seemed an eternity the mist eventually cleared sufficiently to enable me to take a quick compass bearing in order to locate the way over the Balmer Grätli (2218m) and onto safer ground.

As a precaution I would add a warning note here that if this linking trail on the south side of the ridge has not been remade, it would be safer to backtrack down the upward trail as far as Unter Stafel where the continuing descent route to Schwarzenbach may be rejoined.

Once at the stony Balmer Grätli you'll see a waymarked path dropping steeply to the south to the Klausenpass, but for a return to the Bisistal go across to the northern side and through a nearby band of rocks where a line of waymarks leads down into a stony valley flanked by cliffs. Below this rough pastures open to the hummocks of Ruosalp where the upward trail is rejoined at Unter Stafel. Continue down a track to a large cattle byre, then bear right, soon crossing a stream beyond which you descend a little, then bear right again and eventually come to the alp of Milchbüelen. On the way to this alp a superb view left shows the powerful waterfall of the Ruosalper Bach (sometimes known as the Waldibach Falls) reckoned to be one of the finest in Central Switzerland.

A charming inner pastureland is crossed behind the buildings of Milchbüelen – soft meadows with a clear stream flowing through, on the way to Feldmoos, a high shelf of hillside where a farm track is joined. This track leads further along the hillside before snaking its way down to Schwarzenbach for a second night. After this the next stage in our plan is to look at the eastern side of the valley for which the Glattalp hut provides an obvious base. Bearing in mind the fact that this hut normally has a guardian only at weekends, it may be necessary to carry food for consumption while you're there.

During the previous day's exploration, trails were walked on both sides of the valley. We now have two options to consider. The first is to follow a marked footpath heading up the eastern hillside immediately above Schwarzenbach to the fine viewpoint at the hutments of Geitenberg, then cross the south-west flank of Mandlieggen into the Charetalp, and go up and over a ridge shoulder of Firstli to Glattalp. That makes an admirable approach, quite remote in places, but with good views throughout, while the second option provides, perhaps, greater contrasts and is outlined as follows.

Remain in the bed of the valley wandering south alongside the narrow road (there's little if any traffic) over pastures with the Muota stream foaming below to the left. The road ends a little way south of a small lake near the Sahli-Glattalp cable-car station. Just beyond this cross the Muota by bridge and follow a farm track winding uphill, with the Waldibach waterfall clearly seen across the valley. When the track forks bear left, and soon after take a waymarked trail up a series of timber-reinforced steps to a sloping pastureland - the southern end of the Milchbüelen alp, backed in the east by a curving wall of cliffs. The path skirts the pastureland, then begins to climb the right-hand headwall. The main path makes a long rising traverse, while an alternative route climbs more steeply (a little exposed in places) by way of the naturally terraced rock, and rejoins the main trail once more before edging a stream that sidles along another section of limestone pavement, then comes to a small tarn. Above this the trail forks. Take the left-hand path across further examples of limestone pavement to reach the hut.

The Glattalp hut is owned by the Mythen Section of the Swiss Alpine Club. It can sleep sixty, and cooking facilities are available when the guardian is not in residence. From it there are several possibilities for exploration, so two or three nights could be justifiably spent there, using the days to scramble onto modest summits with outstanding panoramas (notably the Ortstock at the head of the Glattalp), to visit distant passes, to make a circuit of the Chilberg-Höch Turm-Flatstock complex, or more gently to seek out the flora of this limestone wonderland.

The local *Wanderkarte*, at a scale of 1:25,000, shows some of these possibilities, and none who are inspired by such maps, and by such country as that which is overlooked by the hut, will find time devoted to the area in any way unrewarding.

Having given a suitable number of days to the region's exploration, a decision will need to be made regarding the next move. It may be that you have to return home, or feel the desire to relax by the shores of the Lake of Lucerne. In which case wander back down to Schwarzenbach and catch the bus out of the mountains to Schwyz. But if you plan to move on into neighbouring regions within the Central Swiss Alps, two further options are available. One of these leads to the crossing of the Furggele saddle (2395m) at the head of Glattalp, followed by a steep descent to Braunwald, a traffic-free resort on a natural shelf above the Linth valley. This crossing is only for experienced mountain walkers though, and should only be attempted in good settled conditions and when equipped with an ice axe (at the bare minimum), for a series of small glaciers and snowfields are found on the eastern side of the pass, and even in the middle of summer there can be large cornices on the pass itself. (A slightly easier crossing to Braunwald goes by way of the Charetalp and Eggismatt north of Furggele, but joins the Furggele route a little lower down.)

The alternative to these is a crossing of the Firner Loch, a narrow pass in the ridge that separates the Bisistal from the Klausenpass region south of the Glattalp hut. This crossing is also quite demanding, not so much by the amount of height gained between the hut and the pass (which is, after all, a little less than four hundred metres), but on account of the somewhat confusing terrain, while the descent to Urnerboden is very steep, but blessed with a charming outlook over the Urnerboden valley dominated at its southern end by the snowy Clariden.

A TOUR OF THE HÜRITAL & BISISTAL - ROUTE SUMMARY

Day 1:   Muotathal - Hinterthal - Liplisbüel

Day 2:   Liplisbüel - Seenalp - Chinzig Chulm - Liplisbüel

Day 3:   Liplisbüel - Oberen Träsmeren - Schwarzenbach

Day 4:   Schwarzenbach - Ruosalper Chulm - Balmer Grätli - Schwarzenbach

Day 5:   Schwarzenbach - Sahli - Glattalp Hut

Day 6:   Glattalp Hut - Furggele - Ortstock - Glattalp Hut

Day 7:   Glattalp Hut - Firner Loch - Urnerboden

✳   ✳   ✳

Klausenpass Region

With the Klausenpass forming a road link between the valleys of Schächental and Urnerboden, options for exploring the great block of mountains south of the Muotatal-Hürital-Bisistal region are eased with prospects of public transport, in the shape of the ubiquitous Postbus running from one end to the other. But the walker, be he so-minded, will be content to make his journeys almost entirely on foot. There is no shortage of trails, and no shortage either of fine scenic country through which to wander.

The valley of Urnerboden, for example; a remarkable U-shaped pastoral glen whose sculpting glaciers have withdrawn to the upper corries of Clariden (3267m), is a rich grazing area for dairy herds brought from lower valleys when winter's snow has retreated. There's only one village, and that little more than a hamlet which shares the same name as the valley itself. Small though it may be, it has a post office, general store and a few modest hotels, some offering low-priced *matratzenlager* accommodation, and is worth considering as a base for a night or two.

Along the northern limits of the valley runs a steep grey mountain wall broken at mid-height by a clearly defined terrace upon which lie a small handful of alps occupied in summer. With alps come footpaths of access, and although not all are linked by virtue of difficult topography, there remains the potential for several interesting walks. The nearest accessible to Urnerboden village are the alps of Zingel and Firnen, the first reached by way of a steep grassy gully bearing clusters of lilies, the latter visited by walkers crossing over from the Bisistal via the Firner Loch. Both enjoy lovely views of the valley itself, as well as the dazzling Clariden apparently lording it over all. Down valley from Urnerboden village a trail climbs towards that same mid-height terrace, then breaks away on a long traverse to reach sophisticated Braunwald overlooking the Linth valley and up to the Tödi.

On the south side of the valley a trail breaks away from the Klausenpass road near the Chlus (or Klus) headwall, noted for its waterfalls, and then rises north-eastwards along the mountainside to the Fisetengrat (the south-west ridge of the little Chamerstock), crosses at the Fisetenpass, and then continues round the flanks of the Rotstock to the Clariden hut, or descends instead into the Linth valley.

There are, of course, other opportunities for walks and explorations in and around the Urnerboden valley, and a classic trail over the Klausenpass adopted by the Alpine Pass Route. This strikes upvalley from Urnerboden village and avoids most of the road by climbing steeply to the north when the road begins its snaking course towards the pass. The trail crosses the road at Vorfrutt and continues across a high, semi-moorland-like region as far as the Klausenpass itself.

Once at the pass the deep Schächental stretches off towards the west; a steeply falling valley that drains down to the Reuss at Altdorf, just short of the southern end of the Urnersee. Apart from the road itself, there are two walkers' routes to the Reuss valley; one on the north flank of the valley, the other begins along the southern side. First we'll look at the northern route.

This uses a combination of farm tracks, narrow lanes and footpaths linking alp hamlets high above the valley on a fairly constant contour. As you progress further towards the west, so the Schächental falls deeper and deeper beneath, so one has an impression of height gain without undue effort. The way leads beneath the Schächentaler Windgällen, and all those continuing limestone mountains that form a chain to create an impressive boundary to the Bisistal and Hürital, and as there are several foot passes making a breach through that chain, it would be possible, if desired, to divert from the traverse path and return to that magical country on the far side. Accommodation otherwise is available in Biel and

Eggbergen, from which one looks south at the better-known Windgällen peaks.

The southern route from the Klausenpass is no less interesting and has some magnificent diversions available. A short distance from the pass a footpath starts to descend through a marshy area, draws close to the road then breaks away again to visit the farm buildings of Unter Balm before descending below a line of crags in a series of zig-zags. Towards the foot of the zig-zags an insignificant-looking path cuts off to the right and soon leads through meadows on the approach to Äsch. This hamlet is famed for its magnificent waterfall, the Stauben Falls, that thunders in a great burst of spray just behind the chalets. Unterschächen is reached from here by way of an easy track, and provides overnight lodging for those intending to explore the neighbourhood - there's plenty worth seeing. Although this small village sits astride the Klausenpass road, and is therefore disturbed by traffic by day, that stream of traffic tails off by evening and a semblance of peace can be gained.

Directly south of Unterschächen one of the loveliest glens in all the Central Swiss Alps entices with a dramatic cirque headwall formed by the north faces of the Windgällen and Ruchen peaks, and with cascade tassles streaking the steep flanks to right and left. The little Brunnital is a gem, and by spending a night or two in Unterschächen the walker has a chance to sample some of its delights. The obvious route of access entails a straightforward hike south from Unterschächen, at first along a road, then by way of a track/footpath that strikes through forest and over pastureland to reach the hamlet of Brunnialp. This makes a delightful short walk that could be extended by climbing the western hillside, then heading north along an easy contour to Sittlisalp and a string of alp farms enjoying favoured views.

But perhaps an even better ploy would be to make a devious approach by way of Äsch, that glorious hamlet backed by a big waterfall east of Unterschächen, visited on the way down from the Klausenpass. From Äsch continue heading east, soon climbing rucked hillsides with waterfalls to right and left until, about thirty minutes from the hamlet, you come to a small boulder used as a signpost at a junction of trails. The left-hand option continues to climb to the Klausenpass, the right-hand choice is marked Oberalp. The latter trail is ours; it leads in zig-zags among trees to gain a bowl of meadowland with clear streams draining through. Veering right the way climbs on to a high, rough meadow pitted with rocks and with a minor cascade ahead which serves a brief apprenticeship for the greater Stauben Falls that tip out of sight below.

Again there's a trail junction. We head west to Nideralp, a small, rather untidy alp from which a track leads on to another, Wannelen. This high route displays well the northern side of the Schächental and, looking back, the ice-clad Clariden-Schärhorn complex, but as it is our intention to visit the Brunnital it is necessary to continue beyond this last alp, still heading west. The way now enters forest and turns a spur of mountain guarding the entrance to the Brunnital glen, then slopes down to Trogenalp, a scattered collection of huts and dwellings used in summer only, perched on a tilted hillside shelf and with the great headwall of the glen seen as a dramatic backdrop. The trail continues towards that headwall, comes to Nider Lammerbach, crosses a stream and descends through woods to Brunnialp, with its pretty huddle of chalets, cattle byres and small white-walled chapel. From there an easy downhill walk leads through forest back to Unterschächen to conclude a very varied day's walking of six or seven hours.

As has already been noted, the cirque blocking the Brunnital is topped by the cliffs and summits of the Windgällen massif, whose southern crags soar over the Maderanertal, a valley that is central to this final block of mountains in our sample survey of the Glarner Alps. The road route to it from Unterschächen winds down to the Reuss valley near Altdorf, heads south to Amsteg, then climbs eastward into the Maderanertal proper. The adventurous mountain walker, however, will dismiss the road and take to the hills, for which a challenging route exists via the pass of Stich-Fülen (2329m), a gap in the south ridge of Hoch Fülen above the corrie of Griesstal. The crossing is not for the faint-hearted, for there's a height difference of more than thirteen hundred metres between Unterschächen and the pass, and a fairly complex route following that skirts the western flanks of the Windgällen before descent can be made into the Maderanertal. It's a long outing, but once you've entered the southern side of the Windgällen massif, you'll know the rewards are worth having.

❊   ❊   ❊

Maderanertal

Rising in the Hüfifirn glacier that sweeps like an elephant's trunk from an icy basin high on the slopes of Schärhorn, Chammliberg and Clariden, the Maderanertal eases roughly westward into the Reuss valley at Amsteg. Its northern slopes are dominated by the Windgällen peaks, its southern flank by the Oberalpstock (3328m), and by the 3256 metre Gross Düssi which guards the snout of the Hüfifirn and upon whose northern spur sits the SAC's Hüfi hut. The valley's north wall is unbroken, while the southern side is drained by several minor glens and one major tributary valley, the Etzli.

The Maderanertal is a valley of pristine beauty, largely neglected but without question worthy of the attention of walkers seeking escape from some of the better-known regions of Alpine Switzerland. It has a bare minimum of mechanical lifts, no resort development, and only one true village (Bristen) graces the valley. There are, however, a few places with accommodation - including *gasthof* and *matratzenlager* in Bristen, *gasthof* in Golzern, *matratzenlager* at Lägni, and an SAC hotel in a romantic woodland setting at Balmenegg near the head of the valley. In addition there are no less than four mountain refuges accessible to walkers: the Windgällen, Hüfi, Cavardiras and Etzli huts. Should our walker have only limited time to explore the Maderanertal, the first priority should be to visit the Windgällen hut. This allows an unrivalled opportunity by which to assess the region's appeal, and forms part of a day-long circuit that counts among the finest of the valley's outings.

We'll assume a first night has been spent in Bristen. Setting out after breakfast head upvalley until a footpath is found which climbs steeply up the northern hillside to Golzern, a hamlet set upon a terrace 600 metres or so above the bed of the valley. It has no road link with the valley, but a five-minute cable-car ride provides access for those less inclined to walk. To the east of Golzern glimmers the

Golzerensee tarn, marshy at one end, backed by a wooded bluff at the other. Between Golzern and the tarn is a huddle of buildings known as Seewen, from which the Windgällen hut trail strikes off through flower meadows, climbs in woodland, then more steeply over alpenrose-clad slopes with a magnificent panorama growing more extensive as you gain height. In a little under two hours from Golzern a huge cairn is met at a junction of trails. From it a glorious view is afforded over the valley and to the Gross Düssi in the east. The Windgällen hut is reached in only fifteen minutes from here, by way of a path which climbs alongside a stream whose cascade spray can be welcome on a shadeless summer's day. The hut, owned by the Academic Alpine Club of Zürich, is perched at the foot of the Windgällen cliffs, but overlooking a gentle grassy basin, landscape contrasts are both immediate and dramatic.

Though it may well be physically possible to push on from here, it would be a shame to do so without making the most of an opportunity to spend a night in this elevated spot with only the occasional clatter of stones falling through a nearby gully to disturb the darkness. But next day fresh landscapes beckon, and the second stage of this short tour of discovery will lead eastward, after having first descended to the large cairn at the trail junction a short way below. Instead of taking the path that leads back to Golzern bear left and wander across high pastures dotted with small pools, passing just below Alp Stafel and sloping gently to the viewpoint of Tritt before descending in long zig-zags towards the head of the Maderanertal where several waterfalls spray from both sides of the valley.

Once you've reached the valley bed two immediate options arise. One is to bear left and follow a trail which climbs almost 900 metres to the Hüfi hut (2334m; 70 beds, guardian July-September); the other is to head down valley to Balmenegg and Balmenschächen where another alternative becomes evident. This time a secondary trail breaks away to the south-east, then rises eastward to gain the Brunnital glen (a different Brunnital to that already explored from Unterschächen) through which approach is made to the Cavardiras hut, just across the canton boundary in Graubunden.

We continue down through the Maderanertal though (charming with its mixture of woodland and pasture) for a further five kilometres, before turning south into the Etzli glen. Now this little glen is a narrow shaft of forest lower down, rough pasture at mid level, and barren rock and snow higher up. At its head is a pass that leads over to the Vorderrhein, but in its western wall a corrie (the Hinter Etzli) provides a crossing via the 2506 metre Pörtilücke into the neighbouring Fellital. The Swiss Alpine Club's Etzli hut, situated at 2052 metres in the opening of the Hinter Etzli, makes an obvious overnight base here, and is reached after a full day's walking from the Windgällen hut.

Next day a moderate climb leads through the corrie to the Pörtilücke and down the western, stony side to gain the Fellital proper at a small alp. A short distance to the right stands the stone-built Tresch hut, backed by pines and with a burst of a torrent in front. The Fellital does not drain into the Maderanertal, but feeds instead the Reuss valley at Gurtnellen. A trail leads down to that village in about two and a half hours from the Tresch hut, while another climbs through the glen to cross the easy Fellilücke at its head, followed by a short downhill stretch to the

Oberalp road pass. From the Oberalp a succession of farm tracks and footpaths leads down to Andermatt in the Reuss valley where the big glacier peaks of the Eastern Bernese Alps form a handsome block to the west.

*   *   *

THE CENTRAL SWISS ALPS

Location:
East of the Bernese Alps, and roughly defined in an arc spreading south, east and west from the Vierwaldstättersee (Lake of Lucerne), with the Rhine valley bounding its outer limits.

Principal valleys:
The Göschenertal in the Eastern Bernese Alps, Gental and Engelbergtal in the Western Uri Alps. East of the Vierwaldstättersee the Muotatal, Hürital and Bisistal. Flanking the Klausenpass the Schächental (with the Brunnital glen) and Urnerboden, while south of the former runs the lovely Maderanertal with the Etzli glen as its tributary, and the Fellital west of that flowing into the Reuss valley.

Principal peaks:
Dammastock (3630m), Tödi (3614m), Schneestock (3608m), Rhonestock (3596m), Galenstock (3583m), Sustenhorn (3503m), Oberalpstock (3328m), Clariden (3267m), Gross Düssi (3256m), Titlis (3238m), Gross Windgällen (3188m)

Centres:
Engelberg is the main resort of the region, all other bases being smaller villages with varying facilities. Göschenen serves the Göschenertal, Engstlenalp the Gental. Muotathal can be useful for walkers exploring the Muotatal, Bisistal and Hürital with their own transport. Unterschächen is best for the upper Schächental and Brunnital, while Urnerboden has accommodation in the valley of the same name. Bristen or Amsteg have limited facilities for walkers concentrating on the Maderanertal.

Huts:
The region is blessed with plenty of huts, most of which are easily accessible to walkers - as mentioned in the main body of text above. The majority of these are owned by various sections of the Swiss Alpine Club.

Access:
By air to Zürich. Good rail services exist through the Reuss valley, or via Lucerne for Engelberg. The Postbus remains the final, reliable link with those valleys not served by rail. Road access to most valleys will involve a pass climb.

Maps:
The 1:50,000 series published by Landeskarte der Schweiz should be adequate for most walkers' needs. For the Göschenertal and Gental regions use sheet 255, *Sustenpass*. Kümmerly & Frey have a *wanderkarte* useful for the Göschenertal based on the LS map, but with suggested routes outlined in red; this is entitled *Urner Oberland*. The Engelbergtal, and country west of the Urnersee, is covered by sheet 245, *Stans*. Sheet 246, *Klausenpass* is good value since it covers the Muotatal, Hürital, Bisistal, Schächental, Brunnital and Urnerboden, as well as the upper reaches of the Maderanertal. The rest of the Maderanertal is found on *Disentis*, sheet 256.

Guidebooks:

Central Switzerland by Kev Reynolds (Cicerone Press) describes all the areas covered by this chapter, plus others, and outlines 90 walking routes. Since the Alpine Pass Route crosses the northern valleys see also *Alpine Pass Route* by Kev Reynolds (Cicerone Press).

Footloose in the Swiss Alps by William Reifsnyder (Sierra Club, San Francisco) includes details of a long walk which passes through the region from Engstlenalp to the Muotatal. Kümmerly & Frey of Bern publish several German-language guidebooks to the region.

Other reading:

Surprisingly, very little has been published in English of interest to walkers with regard to this region. One recent exception is Marcia Lieberman's *Outdoor Traveler's Guide to The Alps* (Stewart, Tabori & Chang, New York, 1991) which includes a brief overview of the Glarner (or Glarus) Alps.

High plateau of Nei Pini near Alpe di Chiera in the Lepontine Alps of Switzerland

8: THE LEPONTINE ALPS
Including the Alps of Ticino & the Adula Alps

O f these sun-washed, comparatively little-known mountains, Walker summed up their appeal in a couple of sentences which, nearly fifty years on, still ring with the clarity of truth. He wrote:

"The scenery is throughout of the highest order, the valleys...are among the least visited in Switzerland, the weather according to climatic statistics may be relied upon more certainly than in any other part of Switzerland, and there is little of the commercialism which so often seems to accompany the development of a popular centre. Atmospheric effects and the richness of the vegetation provide colour; which each day's journeyings, from villages round about 2,000 feet above sea-level to ridges ranging from 8,000 to 10,000 feet, will be ample tax on the energies of most people."

In a district famed for its sunshine and for the obvious appeal of such tendril lakes as Maggiore, Lugano and Como, it comes as a surprise to discover that so few wanderers find themselves enticed into the higher valleys that drain to them, or onto the secretive plateaux ringed about by granite mountains at the heart of the range where tarns lie idle beneath the sun, where streams dash in spray and where a scattering of well-sited huts provide a welcome, for those who stray to them, in

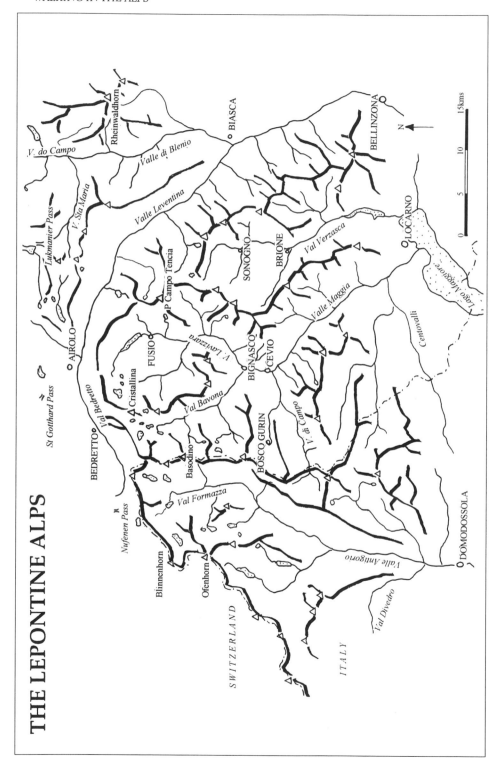

THE LEPONTINE ALPS

the most peaceful of surroundings. True, there are no stunning peaks with household names, no major glacier systems nor extensive fields of snow to dazzle from afar. The Lepontines clearly lack routes of notoriety that would otherwise bring them to the fore in mountaineering journals. Nor do they have widely-known, classic walking tours such as the TMB, Alpine Pass Route or Walker's Haute Route - although Walker himself claimed (perhaps with slight exaggeration excused by his understandable enthusiasm for the range) that "there is no single district of the whole Alpine chain better suited to a continuous walking-tour from valley to valley, from glen to glen, and there is scarcely a mountain in it whose summit cannot be reached by a rough uphill walk." There are no great resorts in their valleys nor on their hillsides, nor do they have winter playgrounds of renown for the skiing fraternity. Yet what they do have is simple grandeur in no small measure, and those who love mountains for what they are, and not what history or fashion has attached to them, who care more for solitude and untamed nature than for crowded familiarity, for the obscure rather than the famous, will find in the mountains and glens of the Lepontine Alps a veritable feast of adventure and beauty. "For the lover of pure mountain beauty," said Walker, "...this is the district."

Walker was not alone in his enthusiasm for the Lepontines. Although comparatively few books have been written in English that devote more than a very brief passage to the region, D.W. Freshfield, one of the most respected and widely travelled of all the Victorian mountain explorers, wrote in rapturous terms (in *Italian Alps*) of the appeal of Valle Maggia and its tributary glens, Val Lavizzara and Val Bavona especially, while Walter Larden, a contemporary of Freshfield's, also sang its praises in his *Recollections of an Old Mountaineer.*

On the down-side it must be said that in comparison with many other Alpine districts accommodation is strictly limited in a number of valleys during the prime summer season, and may be found wanting in some of the finest walking areas. There are hotels and mountain inns, of course, and moderately-priced pensions in the main valleys, most of which are small, family-run businesses with just a few beds, but in those villages lodged in the most delectable of glens where it would be perfect to base oneself for a few days, there is often nowhere to stay. Happily mountain huts (here known as *capanna* or *rifugio*) will be found tucked among the more secluded recesses for those of us who prefer to live as near to the heart of wild country as possible, but there are gaps in the chain, which tend to concentrate the mind when planning long expeditions. As for camping, official campsites are not so numerous as in other regions of Switzerland, and of those that do exist here, most are sited outside the main areas of interest and are extremely busy during the summer months, occupied by holiday-makers who seldom stray far from their bungalow-style tents or caravans. Off-site camping is officially discouraged, although there are numerous idyllic corners of remote glens and high plateaux where a small tent could perhaps be discreetly pitched for an overnight stay during a multi-day tour - provided, of course, that those who do so take every precaution to protect the environment.

The range lies south of the main Alpine watershed, and therein lies some of its appeal, for the landscape has such rich colouring, what with the crystalline rocks, deep-blue of the tarns and dark blocks of forest, while mountain and glen alike are bathed in the soft pure light of Lombardy. Spring comes earlier here than over the watershed, and summers are consequently longer and more penetrating. The ridge of the watershed, which separates rivers that drain to the Po from those that flow north to the Rhône and the Rhine, marks then the northern limit of the range. The western boundary is formed by the Simplon, and the eastern extent marked by the Lukmanier (or Lucomagno) Pass, but the adjacent Adula Alps that continue from the Lukmanier to the Splügen Pass, are generally considered to be an eastern extension of the Lepontines, and as such will be included here.

Largely confined to the pear-shaped Swiss canton of Ticino, the range also incorporates neighbouring ridges and valleys across the border in Italy. But whether Italian or Swiss, the language, culture, architecture, climate, the very flavour of the landscape, is that of mountain Italy. Warmth, sunshine and an almost liquid purity of light are among its characteristics. Another, which the first-time visitor will be quick to perceive, is the quality of the scenery which is in complete contrast to that of districts immediately to the north, east and west. It is a quality that will be judged by subtle measures - by detail, rather than by scale.

For example, the elevation of its mountain peaks is considerably more modest than that of the proud collection of four thousand metre summits of which the neighbouring Pennines can boast - the highest here being Monte Leone which straddles the watershed immediately above the Simplon at 3553 metres - while of the district's few glaciers, only those of the Blinnenhorn (near the Nufenen Pass), and Rheinwaldhorn group in the Adula Alps offer much to write home about, and those of the latter group only because they are considered the birthplace of the great Rhine river. But valleys of the Lepontine Alps plunge steeply southward; narrow valleys and glens with few level pastures, where the remnants of one-time alp hamlets are crumbling back to their origins; valleys with gaunt grey peaks thrusting from chestnut woods, seemingly unattainable, girdled as they are with dense vegetation - rampant shrubs, pine forest, walnut groves and spinneys of silver birch. Through those mostly uninhabited glens narrow ancient trails and mule paths, sometimes paved with flagstones, weave their devious course. Some traverse unmarked cols, others edge their way through shadowed ravines, crossing here and there on romantic arched bridges. A few vanish in a bewilderment of scree and lichen-dashed boulders.

In the major valleys of Ticino, villages add their own dimension of colour. Many of these seem not to belong to this century, but have an air of simplicity and grace reminiscent of the Middle Ages, a timeless quality sung by the shrieking swifts that race of a summer evening where shadows lengthen. Distinctive as to architectural style and mode of decoration, Ticino villages consist in the main of grey stone houses with stone slabs on their roofs and brilliant flower boxes at their windows. Some are flamboyant in appearance, where external plasterwork has been painted with murals, religious motifs or family crests - outdoor art galleries in which stone and plaster replace canvas. Between the houses cobbled alleyways lead to churches graced with tall, slender campaniles, or to terraced garden plots, while vineyards and orchards create stairways up the hillside.

These villages inhabit landscapes that make direct appeal to the soul of an artist, and to the wanderer who prefers his mountains still a little rough and raw around the edges, not shorn with the trim perfection of more populous districts where cowbells clatter hour by hour. Landscapes, these are, to wander day after day, from one glen to another, the whole district summarised so deftly by Walker that his words are worth repeating here:

"Dividing the deeply cut valleys are mountain ranges, thrust out like spokes from the enclosing rim and trending from north to south on the whole and but little lower than it in height. These are dissected and dissected again by the many branches into which each main stream subdivides near its head - and by the innumerable lateral glens cutting back into the flanks of each dividing range. Hence it will be seen that by crossing from side glen to side glen over the projecting spurs in the flanks of an individual valley, and by crossing from valley to valley over the ridges between, there is an immense variety of routes available to the discriminating walker."

In order now to look at the range in detail, and to discuss opportunities for walking tours there, it is best to enumerate those valleys travelling from west to east, irrespective of their political allegiance. The first of these, through part of which traffic bound for the Simplon grinds its way, is that of the Toce, whose upper extent is known as Val Formazza, middle section Valle Antigorio, and lower part below Domodossola, the Valle d'Ossola which empties its river into Lago Maggiore, largest and deepest of all the Alpine lakes. Valle Antigorio has a feeder glen in the Valle Devero, while the larger Val Divedro is that which carries the Simplon road out of the main Ossola valley. Trails link the head of these glens, skirting below gaunt crags and leading to such pastureland gems as Alpe Veglia, described by Irving as "one of the loveliest green basins in the Alps." Other routes cross easy passes from the head of Val Formazza, leading past the Cascata del Toce (the Tosa Falls), to the Nufenen via the Gries Pass, and by way of Passo San Giacomo into the head of Val Bedretto. Some of the high lakes have been dammed for hydro purposes, their serpentine contractors' roads intruding into country that was still virgin in Walker's day. Other remote corries, however, retain a quality of wilderness and challenge the visitor with their rich choice of trails.

The next major valley system is that of the Swiss Valle Maggia whose river is deposited into Lago Maggiore at Locarno. This is perhaps the most important of all Lepontine valleys, so far as the walker is concerned, for its upper tributaries of Vals Lavizzara, Bavona and di Prato, each with its own sub-dividing glens, lead into wonderland, and from each one walkers' passes connect with neighbouring valleys to east and west. These upper glens were much-loved by Hubert Walker: "All the way up," he wrote of Val Bavona, "the scenery has character, and is grand and striking in the extreme."

To the east of Valle Maggia, and running parallel to it, Val Verzasca is also sub-divided by a number of glens, most of which are wild and uninhabited and which, by virtue of their narrowness, give to their walling mountains an impression of greater height than the map would otherwise indicate. In such leaf-strewn glens as Vals d'Agro, Pincascia or Carecchio above the village of Lavertezzo, it is possible to wander semi-abandoned trails in welcome solitude, and experience a degree of isolation virtually unknown in other Alpine regions. Further upstream at Brione Val

Verzasca bifurcates, with Val d'Osura flowing in from the north-west. The main stem continues to Sonogno and forks again. Here the upper reaches of the Verzasca valley become known as Val Vegorness, while the shorter Val Redorta cuts back to the west. Again, walkers' passes link neighbouring valleys and thereby extend possibilities for an assortment of outstanding tours.

At its lower, southern end the Verzasca feeds into the man-made reservoir of Lago di Vogorno. Below the dam its stream flows through a gorge and out to the eastern end of Lago Maggiore. A low-lying plain, the so-called Piano di Magadino, then eases back from the top end of the lake to Giubiasco and Bellinzona, while north of the latter town stretches the longest of all the Lepontine valleys. Valle Leventina, known as the Riviera in its lower third below Biasca, cuts right through the heart of canton Ticino, which takes its name from the river, and makes a natural highway that was adopted as a major transalpine route via the St Gotthard Pass in the thirteenth century.

At first glance the deep cleft of Valle Leventina has little to commend it to the lover of mountain scenery - there's far too much intrusive engineering for that, what with a busy international railway, power lines, a motorway on stilts and the old valley road too. But this valley does have its own special appeal for those prepared to seek it out, and there are some exquisite, unspoilt villages and old stone hamlets lodged upon the hillsides where there's welcome tranquillity to be found, and two or three charming glens well worth exploring, such as the little Val Canaria behind Airolo, Val Piora to the east of that, and Val Piumogna south of Faido which curves into a cradle of mountains topped by Piz Campo Tencia and Pizzo Campolungo. On the north-west side of the latter peak an easy pass invites walkers to cross from Valle Leventina to the upper Val Lavizzara.

Valle Leventina makes a long bow curve, a clockwise arc starting at 12 o'clock (Airolo) and reaching Bellinzona at five, at which point the arc is flattened by the Piano di Magadino mentioned above. Above Airolo the westerly extension of the curve is known as Val Bedretto. This is topped by the Nufenen, a road pass linking Ticino with the Rhône valley, constructed only after the Second World War. Whereas Leventina rumbles with the sound of road and rail traffic, Val Bedretto is sparsely populated and surprisingly peaceful, and walkers intent on finding some wild country to explore need look no further than the southern wall of mountains which rises to the Cristallina massif, or to the Gries Pass, an old 'wine pass' on its western edge with lovely views to the Bernese Alps. This leads from Val Corno, the first tributary glen feeding into Val Bedretto, down into the head of Val Formazza.

Returning to Valle Leventina, another important tributary comes down to join it at Biasca. This is Valle di Blenio, shaped like a crooked letter Y and known locally as the *valle del sole* - the valley of the sun. The upper western arm of the Y is Valle Santa Maria which carries the Lukmanier road over this ancient pass (crossed as early as AD700) and down to Disentis in the valley of the Vorder Rhine. As was noted earlier, the Lukmanier Pass is the boundary, not only between cantons Ticino and Graubunden, but also between the main Lepontines and the Adula Alps.

The eastern arm of the Y is Val Camadra, a secluded inner glen partially divorced from the main stem by a narrow ravine above the village of Olivone. At its head trails entice through little-travelled country to valleys north, east and, by way of further cols, to the south, while high pastoral country to the west has its own appeal with routes crossing to Valle Santa Maria. Topping the eastern wall of Valle di Blenio is the 3402 metre Rheinwaldhorn, first climbed in 1789 by Father Placidus à Spescha from the Benedictine monastery in Disentis, a mountain whose modest glacial armoury catches the eye of walkers from passes off to the west, and whose summit is the highest of the Adula Alps. Apart from the glen of Val Malvaglia which flows into the lower Valle di Blenio, the main valleys draining south out of the Adula Alps are, from west to east, Val Calanca, Valle Mesolcina which carries traffic over the San Bernardino, and finally Valle San Giacomo with the Splügen Pass at its head. While the first two drain their waters into Lago Maggiore by way of Bellinzona, streams from San Giacomo swell the Mera on its way out of the Bregaglia before emptying into Lago di Como.

So much for the Lepontine valleys en masse, it is now time to study the potential of selected valleys and glens so far as the walker is concerned, then look at options for making a multi-day tour of a large part of the district.

✳   ✳   ✳

Valle Maggia

The first and most obvious centre of attention must be Valle Maggia and its many subsidiary glens, for a vast array of outings splays from it. Within its boundaries sufficient expeditions may be attempted to last any discerning mountain walker a full and active fortnight's holiday, and still leave enough plans unfulfilled to demand a return visit.

Unless the visitor enters on foot across one of the northern passes among the Cristallina mountains, say from Val Bedretto, and then descends through those delightful upper glens, the normal route of approach will be from the south, from the lakeside towns of Locarno and Ascona. Locarno is served by rail via Bellinzona, and buses work through the valley from there to Bignasco and the upper glens, thereby providing the non-motorised visitor with reliable access.

Although the Maggia region includes all the upper glens which begin under peaks of the Cristallina massif and covers an area of 568 square kilometres, the first point to note about the main stem of Valle Maggia itself is that it does not appear to be Alpine in any real sense. It's a broad, flat-bottomed trench with a barely-perceptible fall in the twenty-eight kilometres that lie between Bignasco, where the tributaries of Val Bavona and Val Lavizzara join the main valley stem, and Locarno on the north shore of Lago Maggiore. Its mountains are largely forested and only in a few cases do they rise above 2300 metres. In this flat trench of a valley the river is little more than a lazy blue stream in summer sifting through a wide bed of stones. On its banks holiday-makers spread themselves as though on a Mediterranean beach, ignorant of, or uninterested in, the scenic delights to be found by delving into higher country upvalley. There are campsites at Gordevio and Avegno, and small hotels at Gordevio, Maggia, Cevio and Bignasco. But other than Bignasco these villages are situated a little too far from the main country of interest to walkers, unless our visitor be motorised. The valley in these lower levels then, is of primary value in reaching wilder, less-tamed landscapes, and those neat tributary glens that flow from the west down to Cevio.

At Cevio a side road climbs a sinuous route among houses built on terraces they share with vines above the Rovana torrent. Beyond these the way leads through chestnut woods, passes through Linescio, Collinasco, and then Cerentino where the road forks. The way ahead goes deeper into Valle di Campo, while the right-hand option rises through more woods into the smaller glen of Valle di Bosco - both of which are served by Postbus from Cevio.

Valle di Campo opens as a green, pastoral swathe closed at its western end by a north-south ridge topped by Piz del Forno, on the far side of which runs Valle Antigorio. Along this ridge one might expect to find the Swiss-Italian border which hereabouts makes its sharp kink to enclose the 'pear' of Ticino. Not so. In fact the border slopes down from the north wall of the valley via a spur projecting from Piz Quadro, several peaks short of del Forno, cuts directly across the pastures and up the southern wall to the arête of Tramalitt, which is itself separated from Piz del Forno by Valle di Campo's cirque headwall. One or two small alp huts are dotted about the Italian slopes at the head of the Campo glen, while a small handful of villages and hamlets inhabits the Swiss side of the frontier, most important of which is Campo itself where there is limited accommodation. In Ticino it is unusual for a village to be spaced across a hillside in the way that Campo is, for by far the majority huddle in tight clusters of houses as if to offer mutual protection against a hostile environment, or to conserve valuable farmland. But Campo is different, for it sprawls in the sunshine on the south-facing hillside high above the river. From it trails climb over the ridge which divides the glen from Valle di Bosco. Other trails visit lonely alps, or fight a way up to a high point from which to make a traverse of hillside before descending steeply to other villages. One particularly enjoyable outing leads to the alp of Corte Nuovo, then crosses the hillside among alpenrose, juniper and clumps of bilberry to Alpe di Quadrella, from where one option climbs again over the Quadrella Pass (2137m) to Grossalp at the head of the Bosco glen, while another descends to Fontanella, Cimalmotto and thence back to Campo.

The walker deciding to settle for a few days in Valle di Campo will find virtually empty footpaths to explore. There are few waymarks, and in some cases the trails are not always evident on the ground. But the scenery is quite lovely, if undramatic, and there will be rewards enough for those who have eyes to see and, perhaps most of all, an inquisitive nature that is not deterred by trails that disappear. Whilst sufficient single-day outings will be found to justify a short holiday based in the glen, perhaps Valle di Campo has more to offer those whose delight it is to move on day after day, conjuring a round of unsung mountains. A study of the map reveals a number of possibilities, which include crossing Passo della Fria (2499m) and the Forcoletta (2359m) in the valley headwall, and descent from there into Valle Antigorio; or via those same passes into Valle dell'Isorno which gives into Valle d'Ossola; or across Passo della Cavegna in the southern wall of the Campo glen which leads into the Vergletto valley - a two-day circuit could be made here which would return you to Campo by way of an alternative pass - or, indeed, by one of two possible crossings of the north wall above Campo into the neighbouring Bosco glen.

As for Valle di Bosco itself, this is a much shorter, more intimate glen whose sole village, Bosco-Gurin, is the highest in all Ticino at 1503 metres; a curiosity in that its inhabitants speak a form of Swizzer-Deutsch, rather than Italian, and its architecture reflects the origins of the Valaisians who first settled there in the thirteenth century. There is limited accommodation in the village, while a mountain hut owned by the UTOE (*Unione Ticinese Operai Excursionisti*) is reached in a little over an hour's walk from the roadhead. Capanna Grossalp is located on the partially-deserted alp of the same name, a collection of rough stone huts overrun by goats. Above Grossalp the U-shaped pass of Guriner Furka (2323m) in the headwall south of Piz Stella makes an obvious destination for a walk, while if linked with another pass (Hendar Furggu) on the north side of the same mountain and below the impressive Wandfluhhorn, a fine day's circuit could be achieved. Alternatively, if one were eager to make a long tour, and the traverse of Valle di Bosco were but one section of it, the crossing of the Guriner Furka, otherwise known as Passo di Bosco, would lead to a trail descending into Valle Antigorio. From there an assortment of routes upstream would suggest ways of regaining Valle Maggia by one of its higher tributary glens.

Returning now to Valle Maggia proper we move upstream from Cevio towards Bignasco, gateway to the promised land of Vals Bavona, Lavizzara and their tributary glens. As far as Cevio the valley was not especially remarkable, but as Freshfield noted, beyond it "the landscape takes a more romantic character. The valley-walls close in and bend, and huge knobs of ruddy-grey rock thrust themselves forward." Bignasco has been planted at the junction of two of the loveliest of Ticino glens, where the Bavona stream flowing from the north-west joins that of the Maggia, emerging from the narrows of Val Lavizzara. Served by bus from Locarno, and with two one-star hotels, three restaurants, a bakery, post office and bank, there can be few finer places in the district to choose as a base for a walking holiday. "As we draw near the first scattered houses of Bignasco, the mountains suddenly break open, and reveal a vision of the most exquisite and harmonious beauty, one of the masterpieces of nature which defy the efforts of the subtlest word-painters," said Freshfield again. Gazing up Val Bavona from a nearby hillside, through a framework of chestnut woods and huge boulders, mountains fill the horizon. "In the distance the snows of the Basodino seen through the sunny haze gleam, like a golden halo, on the far-off head of the mountain."

Val Bavona

Not unnaturally it is to Val Bavona that we are drawn first, for it is in this valley, which Freshfield described with such exuberance, that "the strength of granite is clothed in the grace of southern foliage, in a rich mantle of chestnuts and beeches, fringed with maize and vines, and embroidered about the skirts with delicate traceries of ferns and cyclamen." He should have mentioned the walnuts too, the sumptuous waterfalls, secluded glens, hidden tarns, deserted alp hamlets (though these were probably inhabited in Freshfield's day), and streams of astonishing clarity that wash through gravel beds sparkling with crystals. The tiny villages too, settled for centuries in their brief woodland glades, represent at their best prime examples of Ticinese vernacular architecture; sturdy stone walls bathed in the delicate light of the south, their chapels adorned with frescoes, while sunken windows look out on nature's artistry. The Bavona road snakes through the glen beneath vast slab walls of granite as far as San Carlo, a hamlet that looks up to the Basodino, and down onto the forests of the lower valley. It's a little over ten kilometres from Bignasco to San Carlo, and throughout that distance the valley is full of character, the juxtaposition of soaring cliff and luxuriant woods providing scenery that is "grand and striking in the extreme." Linking footpaths that cross and recross the valley stream give the walker an opportunity to absorb that scenery at leisure all the way to San Carlo and beyond.

Foroglio is one of the best villages set among stands of chestnut, linden and beech trees, and is especially noteworthy for the powerful cascade that bursts from the lip of a hidden glen two hundred metres above. Standing back from the road from which it is protected by the Bavona stream, it's a crammed huddle of stone dwellings with narrow pathways inching between them. One of these pathways climbs above the village and arrives at the top of the Froda di Foroglio cascade to discover the V-shaped Val Calnegia stretching ahead, brightened with spinneys of silver birch. Inside this glen the few buildings of Puntid are set in a rough meadowland, and a picturesque hump-backed bridge crosses the Calnegia stream where a footpath entices upvalley.

One full day of a holiday based on Bignasco should be spent exploring Val Calnegia. Within that glen there's a semi-deserted hamlet (Gerra), and a fully deserted one (Calnegia) near its head, whose handful of stone houses, stables and granaries are being strangled by a rampant vegetation. Val Calnegia must once have been a productive glen, but that productivity has ceased and wild nature is taking over, leaving the walker, at least, with delicious raspberries to feed on in summer. A thousand metres above the uppermost deserted hamlet the tarns of Laghi della Crosa lie in a high corrie formed by the linking ridges of Piz Solögna, Piz Forera and Madone di Formazzöö, and though it's a stiff climb to reach them, there is a trail, and the distant outlook won from the corrie entrance provides a splendid overview of the main Val Bavona cutting across one's field of vision.

At the Bavona roadhead San Carlo has a large car park for customers using the Robiei cableway, an out-of-place construction that is a legacy of the Robiei dam and hydro-electricity project that has partially scarred some of the high corries of the Cristallina massif. The existence of the cable-car has, of course, opened up parts of this former wild landscape to tourists. But there remains much empty country to wander in solitude for those who seek it.

To the west of San Carlo, for example, the little glen of Val d'Antabia has a pair of tarns caught in stony hollows more than a thousand metres above the Bavona stream. These tarns, the Laghetti d'Antabia, lie in a mountain cradle a little south of the impressive slab walls of Basodino (3272m). A trail climbs to them, through the alp hamlet of Corte Grande above which the Tamier Pass (2772m) is one of the crossings recommended by Walker in order to reach the Tosa Falls in Val Formazza, the Italian valley which runs roughly parallel to Val Bavona on the far side of the mountains. In pastures a little below the tarns stands Rifugio Piano delle Creste. Owned by the SAV (*Società Alpinistica Valmaggese*), a member group of the Federazione Alpinistica Ticinese, this is one of three mountain huts accessible from San Carlo, the others being Capannas Cristallina and Basodino.

The Basodino and Cristallina huts are separated from each other by some wonderful wild mountain country overlooked by Basodino and its glacier, and the mountain which lends its name to the area, Cristallina (2912m) itself. That the hydro engineers have been busy taming some of the high corries, building their dams and creating additional lakes, is a sad and undeniable fact. In truth, some of these man-made lakes don't look entirely out of place now, except when their concrete walls are on show. But the presence of a contractor's road is truly a cause for regret. Happily there are plenty of opportunities to explore mountainscapes within the Cristallina massif where that road and those dams are not in view.

The Robiei cableway swings above the upper Val Bavona and passes close to the Basodino hut. Apart from the incongruity of this cableway's close presence, the hut has a fine situation, set as it is on a hillside perch overlooking the glen that plunges away in screes and steep grass slopes from its door. But it also has a grandstand view of the handsome, glacier-draped mountain after which it is named - one of the most prominent and attractive of Lepontine peaks brooding off to the south-west.

Rather than take the cableway from San Carlo, it is preferable to walk up to Capanna Basodino on a track that takes you initially through forest, then by footpath to the alp hamlet of Campo, beyond which the way enters a rocky defile and at last climbs through the short upper glen at the head of which the hut can be seen. Owned by the SAC, it can sleep seventy and has a guardian in residence from mid-June to mid-September. It is, of course, used as a base for climbs on the Basodino and numerous other peaks, as well as serving walkers who plan to explore the stony, tarn-littered region that spreads from it.

The other hut in the vicinity is Capanna Cristallina. This is much larger than the Basodino, reflecting its popularity, and is also owned by the Swiss Alpine Club. Standing near the head of a rather bleak glen on the northern slopes of Cristallina itself, it's reached by one of two cross-country routes from Capanna Basodino. The first of these is by way of Lago Sfundau and the easy Passo di Cristallina (2568m), passing below the Cristallina's west flank, while the alternative route is not quite so straightforward, and for a large part is only guided by a tenuous line of cairns. In poor visibility this route demands some care, but in good conditions the wilderness quality of the area is an endearing feature. It makes a circuitous arc via Lago Nero, the Bochetta del Lago Nero (2563m), Passo del Sasso Nero (2420m) and Passo del Naret (2438m) - a rough and sometimes lonely route, it is however, a most rewarding one. By combining these two contrasting ways a longish full-day circular walk could be achieved which would provide an excellent series of unkempt mountain views and serve as a first-rate introduction to the massif.

There are mountains to climb here, many of which should be within the capabilities of those with a degree of scrambling experience, but who otherwise would not consider themselves Alpine mountaineers. Cristallina is one such, from whose summit the full extent of upper Ticino is revealed. Basodino is another, though on this there is a glacier to negotiate, and standard precautions should therefore be taken.

In good weather any mountain walker with common sense and map-reading skills could spend days wandering from lake to lake, corrie to corrie and across ridge after ridge in an orgy of exploration, spending the nights in either of the huts or in Albergo Robiei at the upper terminus of the cableway from San Carlo. But there will come a time when one must move on, and here again the walker is spoilt for choice. If he has commitments to fulfill down in Val Bavona or the lower Valle Maggia, the most obvious way will be to descend directly to San Carlo and continue down valley from there. But the choice may be to head north, in which case a clear mule-path goes down through Val Torta from the Cristallina hut to Val Bedretto. Another trail climbs from that hut to cross the 2562 metre Folcra Pass just to the west, then descends through the Cassinello glen to Bedretto, while yet another goes west by way of Lago Sfundau and Passo Grandinagia (2698m) to San Giacomo, from where it is easy to head south across the Giacomo Pass to Rifugio Val Toggia at the head of Val Formazza. Next day would be a short descent to the Tosa Falls (considered by Baedeker to be "the grandest in the Alps, especially when the river is high") and from there either continue down valley, or find one of several alternative routes back to Val Bavona.

Yet another option for leaving the Cristallina mountains would be to cut across country from either the Basodino or Cristallina huts to Sasso Nero, and from there descend to Valle di Peccia, another lovely glen that spills out into Val Lavizzara midway between Bignasco and Fusio.

Val Lavizzara

Back in Bignasco, having spent time getting to know Val Bavona, there comes an opportunity to study the second of our main tributaries of Valle Maggia, Val Lavizzara and its side glens. Lavizzara, like Val Bavona, has true Alpine stature, for although there are no great glaciers, nor much in the way of permanent snow, its mountains rise in towering walls of rock to cast morning and evening shadows over the valley, while the side glens, with their tumultuous cascades and fast-running streams, provide enchantment for all who are drawn into their embrace.

Upstream of Bignasco there are six small villages whose architectural style and grouping are so characteristic of Ticino. Brontallo and Menzonio reside upon terraces above the river and are connected to the highway by snaking access roads. Broglio nestles in the valley bed beside a slender strip of pasture. Then comes Prato, a handsome village with direct access to the glen which takes its name, at the head of which stands Piz Campo Tencia (3072m). Beyond Prato is Peccia, and this too has a tributary glen cutting back from it with more fine walking country to explore. And finally there's Fusio, a popular and attractive place with pastel-coloured houses built steeply above the river. Fusio is served by Postbus. The village has accommodation, restaurants and a foodstore useful for walkers and climbers taking to the hills, while above it to the north-east there's a direct way over the mountains to Rodi-Fiesso in Valle Leventina. Beyond Fusio the valley curves north-westward to the edge of the Cristallina massif, and is known as Val Sambuco.

Assuming our walker, based on Bignasco, has not exhausted all his holiday entitlement within the environs of Val Bavona, there will be much to do in Val Lavizzara. First there are the immediate glens to explore. Of these the steep little Val Chignolasc scoops the mountainside to the south-east, and is accessible directly from the village. Freshfield wandered a trail through this glen after finding one that linked it with Giumaglio down in Valle Maggia. This he reckoned to be "...probably the most beautiful path to Bignasco." Next is Val Serenello with a few isolated alp hutments in it, and then comes Val Cocco, the third glen on the eastern side of the valley, with Passo del Cocco at its head providing a way over the ridge system emanating from Monte Zucchero, and down to Val d'Osura which in turn feeds into Val Verzasca. Walker recommended this crossing (though he called Val d'Osura the Val d'Osola) as part of a short tour returning to Val Lavizzara by way of the Forcarella di Redorta and Val di Pertüs to Prato.

Between Broglio and Prato two further glens drain the eastern wall of mountains. The first of these is Val Tomè which leads to the west face of Monte Zucchero. Under that face in a stony, steep-sided basin brightened with alpenrose and a few stands of larch, lies the little Lago di Tomè at 1692 metres - almost a thousand metres higher than Broglio, although it's only four kilometres by footpath from that village. This tarn makes an interesting destination for a walk, and the map shows a trail climbing beyond it to cross a shoulder of mountain into the neighbouring Val di Pertüs, although I have no personal experience of this route. If this trail is still usable - and not all those shown on Lepontine maps exist in reality - a fine day's circuit could be achieved with a return to Broglio through the lower Val di Prato.

Val di Prato itself is one of the jewels of the Maggia region, a glen of immense charm whose beauties are evident as soon as you begin to penetrate its rather secretive heart. Travellers journeying along the Lavizzara by road have little more than a brief glimpse of this glen, and a glimpse is not enough. One must leave the valley and wander into it, to be seduced by its warm fragrance and the promise of chestnut woods, its misted mountains, stone-built huts, its sun kissed hamlets. And its waterfalls. In less than an hour from Prato you come to the little hamlet of Monte di San Carlo, which is shown as Monte di Predee on the LS map. San Carlo is set at a junction of glens with cascades tipping over rock slabs above and below. To the south is Val di Pertüs, to the north-east the continuing Val di Prato.

It is easy to appreciate Hubert Walker's enthusiasm for Monte di San Carlo, which he called "one of the loveliest alps I know". It can hardly have changed in the fifty-odd years since he was there and when I visited, I found it just as he described it: "The alp occupies an angle between two tremendous waterfalls, and from its green lawns whichever way you look you see glittering cascades backed by forests of chestnut and ringed by graceful peaks." If you delve deeper into Val di Prato the way follows the true left bank of the stream amid beautiful mountain scenery, then climbs a veritable staircase of stone in a tight little gorge from which another waterfall thunders, to emerge by the most enchanting of rock-girt pools. The walls of the glen open out a little to allow sunlight to pour onto yet more waterfalls and deep green pools, with tufts of alpenrose, bilberry and juniper, and a few stands of trees artistically placed, it would seem, as if by the hand of a landscape gardener. After exploring the upper reaches of this magical glen, out of which soars Piz Campo Tencia, a return to Prato should be made by cutting back along the eastern hillside by way of a broad grassland shelf occupied by a small goatherder's hut with more fine views across the valley, then descend by another stepped path to the main trail which is rejoined below the gorge.

The southern glen, at whose mouth sits Monte di San Carlo, is the choice of those who plan to visit Val Verzasca. Val di Pertüs is another lovely forested glen whose walls rise abruptly and curve at the southern end to create a tight little cirque topped by Monte Zucchero (or rather its subsidiary peak, Triangolino) and Corona di Redorta. The Forcarella, or Passo, di Redorta (2181m) provides a way over this cirque headwall with a descent through Val Redorta, yet another charming glen, to Sonogno (seven hours or so from Prato). With Sonogno as a base there will then be plenty to enjoy in both Val Vegorness and Verzasca. But more of those valleys later.

Continuing a short distance upstream through Val Lavizzara from Prato, we come to Peccia where again the valley forks. The left branch here is Valle di Peccia, the central of three valleys that drain the south and eastern flanks of the Cristallina massif. Within this glen there are a few small villages and hamlets - Cortignelli, another San Carlo and Piano di Peccia among them - and high quality marble is extracted from a quarry reached by a dirt track that extends the paved road beyond Piano di Peccia. High on the western hillside half-forgotten alps are crumbling into decline, and the trails that once linked them are in danger of becoming overgrown and lost. It is still possible, though, to enjoy a day's walking along that hillside visiting Alpe Srodan and Corte di Fondo, during which the landscape value of productive alps will become evident, and lessons learned of how nature's grip on vegetated hillsides is not always benevolent unless kept in check.

In Alpe Masnaro above Alpe Srodan, at an altitude of about two thousand metres, stands the unmanned Rifugio di Braga, owned by the Peccia Friends of Nature. With self-catering facilities the hut can sleep twenty, but should you plan to spend a night there, arrangements for collecting the key should be made in Piano before setting out. From the head of Valle di Peccia a trail climbs to Passo del Sasso Nero in the Cristallina mountains, from which point a choice of cross-country routes leads to Capanna Basodino, Capanna Cristallina or, via Lago di Naret, down Val Sambuco to Fusio at the head of Val Lavizzara.

Fusio offers itself as a base for walkers to challenge that of Bignasco - although, of course, it does not have ready access to Val Bavona. But what it does have is Val Sambuco and the outer rim of the Cristallina massif nearby, the possibility of crossing Sentiero dei Vanisc into Valle di Peccia to the west, and some high routes to tackle on the eastern mountain wall. Of these, one of the best climbs through larch forest and past a few chalets to reach the alp of Corte Mognola, an open pasture with cascades spraying from a hillside shelf behind it. Arriving here one lovely cloudless summer's day we found goats basking on the rooftops, ignoring the lush sweet pasture all around. The continuing trail climbs to the left of the waterfall and emerges half an hour later beside Lago di Mognola at 2003 metres, a splendid tarn to bathe in. This tarn is locked in an almost complete bowl formed by ridges and arêtes of outlying peaks thrust from the crown of Piz Campo Tencia, and its outlet stream is the source of the waterfall seen earlier cascading onto the alp below.

From the north shore of the tarn another trail climbs to a grassy saddle that affords superb views, then continues on an undulating traverse, more or less following the 2050 metre contour, to cross a shallow cirque with the solitary alp hut of Cana at its entrance. Beyond this you round a spur descending from Cima di

Sassalto to be confronted by a huge panorama in which the glacier-clad Basodino draws one's attention, looking impressive as it does in the distance, with a great cluster of peaks representing the Cristallina massif to the fore, and the man-made lake of Sambuco apparently filling the valley some six hundred metres below. From this airy position the trail suddenly descends to the alp of Corte Vacarisc, and later passes through more larch forests on the way back to Fusio.

A little further north along the same hillside is the route to Passo Campolungo (2318m), a route that continues on the far side with descent to Lago Tremorgio and the bed of Valle Leventina. This is a classic crossing amid very fine mountain scenery, the pass itself spoilt only by a pylon carrying high-voltage power lines. From the pass magnificent views include the mountains of eastern Ticino and the Adula Alps, while not far from Alpe Campolungo, 250 metres below, overnight accommodation is possible in the SAC's Capanna Leit. Not that it's necessary to break the crossing here (six hours should be sufficient to get from Fusio to Rodi-Fiesso), but by so doing an opportunity then arises to explore other possibilities on that side of the mountain. Such possibilities will be discussed when we come to study Valle Leventina.

Val Sambuco above Fusio leads, as we have seen, to the eastern rim of the Cristallina massif, green and pastoral below, gaunt and stony above. Lakes on this eastern rim have been harnessed for electricity, and a road winds painfully through the valley and up to the lakes of Scuro and Naret caught in the granitelands that promise so much. A trail cuts away from the road about a kilometre or so north-west of Lago Sambuco and climbs through the upper glen known as Campo la Torba, to reach the barrage at Lago del Naret in about three and a half hours from Fusio. From this lake Capanna Cristallina is only an hour and a half away via Passo del Naret, while Capanna Basodino is about four hours from the lake shore by way of Passo del Sasso Nero and Bochetta del Lago Nero. From these huts, as we have already seen, there are numerous possibilities for exploratory tours to be made in and around this core of bare stone mountains.

Val Verzasca

This valley flows in parallel fashion to the east of Valle Maggia, though it begins further south than either Maggia's tributary of Val Lavizzara, or Valle Leventina its eastern neighbour. Through it winds one of the loveliest of Ticino's streams. Dazzlingly pure, it either glides in deep boulder-girt pools, or dashes through narrow defiles with a boisterous flash of spray. Its bed has been moulded and scoured into patterned whorls, and here and there bleached ribs and grooves reveal strips of grey, black or blue like the grain of well-seasoned timber. Verzasca has few hotels, no official campsites, and access to just four unmanned huts. But for the walker there's a wonderland to explore.

About ten kilometres from the valley's southern entrance, the village of Lavertezzo is a honeypot for day-visitors on account of the beautiful medieval stone bridge that spans the river there. It has two small hotels with a total of just thirty beds: Osteria Vittoria and Ristorante-Garni Posse. The valley road is invariably crowded with parked cars and coaches in summer when the river bank takes on an atmosphere not unlike that of a Mediterranean beach. But cutting behind the village on the eastern side, three small glens offer tranquillity to those prepared to walk. The streams that drain these three glens, Vals Carecchio, Pincascia and d'Agro, unite a short distance from Lavertezzo among woodland narrows, and it is through these broad-leaved woods that an old mule trail provides access to these semi-deserted back-of-beyonds. A narrow road also projects a short way through the narrows, but for the needs of the walker the mule trail makes a preferable alternative. At the hamlet of Cugnera the way forks, with one option descending to the stream. This then cuts into the easternmost glen (Val Carecchio) which is blocked by a lovely cirque not properly appreciated until you're within its curving arms. The main trail curves northward and passes a number of stone buildings, most of which are deserted and falling apart. Remaining high above the stream you come to Forno, a one-time alp hamlet at the junction of Val Pincascia (branching north-east) and Val d'Agro which veers north-west. Across a hump-backed bridge below Forno the trail forks again. The right-hand option leads to Alpe Fumegna at the head of the Pincascia glen, the alternative plunges into dense hazel thickets and climbs steeply through a defile into Val d'Agro. In this glen there's a cluster of deserted alp hutments (Arai) to visit, as well as the partially restored hamlet of Agro, and the higher alps of Corte Nuovo, Mazer and Cremenze lodged high on the western hillside, or those of Alpe Lignase and Pianca to the north-east of Agro. There is enough in this glen alone to keep any mountain wanderer happy for a day or two.

Upvalley at Brione the Val Verzasca bifurcates. Branching north-west here Val d'Osura is one of the major tributary glens from which the valley gains its true character. Rising in the Sambuco cirque under the south face of Monte Zucchero we have already seen that it provides access to Bignasco by way of Passo del Cocco, but even without climbing high and crossing ridges it is still worth wandering into. At the turn of the century Baedeker sniffily referred to the path through the glen as "uninteresting". It is not. Neither is the glen it explores. Gently pastoral in its lower reaches, it becomes more rugged in the enclosing cirque where at about 1420 metres the little Capanna Alpe d'Osola provides sleeping quarters for about a dozen. (There are no facilities for cooking, so users must take their own stove, food and utensils.) A narrow surfaced lane travels into the glen for just over three kilometres from Brione to serve the hamlet of Bolastro, beyond which a track continues a little further past the old buildings of Daghei. Thereafter footpaths explore the head of the valley as well as one or two higher alps.

The simple hut at Alpe d'Osura (or Osola) conjures an atmosphere reminiscent of that enjoyed by the Victorian pioneers, and it's interesting to consider those who came here a hundred years ago. The glen will have changed very little since then. From the hut a route climbs to Alpe Sambuco, and continues steeply from there to the pass of Bochetta di Mugaia (2518m) on the south ridge of Monte Zucchero. From the pass a short and easy scramble up the ridge leads to the summit where views are extensive and well worth the effort. But on the east side of the ridge the way descends into Val Redorta, at whose entrance sits one of Verzasca's most handsome villages, Sonogno. This classic route from Brione to Sonogno via the Bochetta will take about nine and a half hours, or about seven if starting from Capanna Alpe d'Osola.

Travelling through Val Verzasca from Brione to Sonogno a footpath takes the east side of the river while the road follows the west bank most of the way. The road passes through Gerra, but then crosses to the east bank just before reaching Frasco. Cutting into the mountains to the east of Frasco the little Val d'Efra is topped by jagged peaks and long ridges that form a deep and wild mountain bowl containing Lago d'Efra. This is a mysterious glen that repays a day's exploration, while above the tarn two possible ridge crossings lead to Val Gagnone, a minor feeder glen that drains via Val d'Ambra into the Leventina near Biasca.

Sonogno has unquestionable appeal. Reached by the ubiquitous Postbus it stands at the northern extent of Val Verzasca where Val Redorta breaks away westward, and the upper valley, known as Val Vegorness, veers a little north-east before later making a westward curve. Attractive buildings line the few streets where cottage industries have been encouraged to arrest migration away from the mountains. Accommodation is limited, and there's brisk competition for a bed in summer. But there are foodstores within the village and two unmanned huts accessible from it (Capannas Alpe Barone and Cognora - the latter also known as Capanna Mezzodi). Both have simple self-catering facilities, and prospective users should enquire first in Sonogno for the key.

Val Redorta is less than five kilometres in extent. Its southern wall is that which runs from Monte Zucchero across Rasiva (2684m) to Cima di Cazzai and Poncione della Marcia, whose south-east spur descends to Brione, while the north boundary wall spreads east from Corona di Redorta (2804m) and remains above 2500 metres as far as Cima di Cagnoi, effectively separating the Redorta glen from that of Vegorness. A paved road goes through the glen as far as Fraced, passing a number of stone barns squatting in trim valley meadows on the way, then a trail climbs a short distance to cross two footbridges before splitting. Both options lead to the Forcarella, or Passo, di Redorta, the right-hand trail being the more direct, the left-hand option first visiting the little semi-deserted hamlet of Püscen Negro. The Redorta Pass is that which leads walkers down through Val di Pertüs to Prato in Val Lavizzara, and is, from all accounts, a magnificent route, if somewhat rough under foot. It was impassable from rockfall when I hoped to cross, but a friend completed it a year later when the rocks had stabilised, and he rated it highly, as did Walker.

By using the Redorta Pass here, and Passo del Cocco at the head of the Cocco glen near Bignasco, an entertaining circuit could be achieved, as suggested by Walker. This is outlined as follows: from Sonogno walk through Val Redorta and over Forcarella di Redorta, and descend through Val di Pertüs and the lower Prato glen to Val Lavizzara. There spend a night in Prato-Sornico and next day wander down valley towards Bignasco. Before reaching Bignasco, however, turn into Val Cocco and cross the pass at its head, then descend to Val d'Osura. Either spend a night in Capanna Alpe d'Osola and next day walk to Sonogno via the Bochetta di Mugaia, or descend through Val d'Osura to Brione and find a bed there (Ristorante Ai Piee has just six beds), before taking a short valley walk to Sonogno, thus completing the round in three days.

Val Vegorness, stretching beyond Sonogno, is quite twice as long as Val Redorta and rewards with some lovely Alpine views. The Verzasca stream that flows through it is wild in places, a gentle meandering brook in others. At one point it forms a series of cascades above which an inner basin is lush with alpenroses while rugged mountains soar overhead. Capanna Alpe Barone sits up here at 2172 metres on the southern flank of Piz Barone, with a tarn another 600 metres above that, and above the tarn Passo Barone is a walker's route over the mountain wall to Chironico in Valle Leventina. West of the hut another pass, Bochetta della Campala, suggests an alternative way to regain Val di Prato and Val Lavizzara.

An enterprising walker, then, will appreciate that within the Maggia-Verzasca complex of valleys and glens, an almost unlimited bounty of walks are available. Day walks and multi-day mountain tours provide vast scope for an active holiday spent in a most enchanting yet surprisingly 'undiscovered' country. These valleys may be the pick of the bunch, however in turning from them we have not finished with the Lepontines, for there are yet more valleys to discuss, including Bedretto and di Blenio. But first we will study that underrated and much-abused channel of access, Valle Leventina.

Valle Leventina

Whether you approach this important transalpine artery from north or south, first impressions are bound to be unfavourable. Major highways, an international rail link, silver marching pylons - all these are unwelcome visual intrusions, and the first-time visitor would be excused for scurrying through in search of less-troubled landscapes. But surprising though it may seem, there are glories to behold, peaceful glens to explore where tarns of brilliant hue lie restful in the lap of the mountains, stony saddles to cross, soft pastures starred with flowers, and a handful of rifugios on which to base active days 'away from it all'.

From the little Efra glen in Val Verzasca it was noted that a cross-country route exists between that valley and the Leventina by way of Val d'Ambra, one of the lower glens draining the west flank of the Leventina near its junction with that of Valle di Blenio. Val d'Ambra is, however, but one of a series of short glens, each joined by linking trails that either cross the ridges that divide them, or cut across their entrances while alternative paths project through their centres. These glens are, from Val d'Ambra heading north: Val Marcri, Val Nedro, Val Cramosino, Val d'Usedi and the larger Val Chironico that curves delightfully beneath rugged walls that plunge at right-angles from ridges extending south and east from Piz Campo Tencia.

The village of Chironico nestles at the entrance to this glen, and is settled on a hillside shelf above the Leventina with which it is joined by a twisting access road. The road extends beyond the village and pushes further into the glen, but thereafter footpaths accept the challenge of steep hillsides to visit a number of small alp hamlets, a tarn (Laghetto) at 1763 metres, and a choice of routes over the southern mountain wall into Val Vegorness. The higher of these crossings is by way of Passo Barone (2582m), the other being Passo di Piatto (2108m) directly above the Laghetto tarn.

The high east ridge extending from Piz Campo Tencia remains above 2700 metres as far as Piz Forno (2907m), from which arthritic spurs project down to Valle Leventina, effectively curving that valley, and at the same time creating another important glen, that of Val Piumogna. This glen twists like an upturned comma, its upper reaches cupped within a cirque created by a ridge system running from Pizzo Campolungo across Campo Tencia to Piz Forno, its lower forested narrows facing north and with the village of Dalpe at its entrance. In common with Chironico Dalpe is also divorced from the main Leventina by occupying a hillside shelf nearly 500 metres above the Ticino river, and hidden from it by a convenient wooded bluff. This hillside shelf is spacious enough to host two other villages in addition to Dalpe. These are Prato Leventina and Cornone, and the Postbus offers a convenient link with all three from Rodi-Fiesso.

Val Piumogna, and country to the north, provides plenty of good walking opportunites on an assortment of trails, and with three huts offering overnight accommodation (two of which have permanent summer guardians), those who prefer a hint of remoteness to more sophisticated and upmarket hotels, are well-catered for here. Of these the first is Capanna Campo Tencia, a Swiss Alpine Club hut of modern design set at mid-height on the face of the cirque enclosing the Piumogna glen at 2140 metres. Reached by a three-hour walk from Dalpe there's a guardian usually in occupation between May and the end of September. An interesting route links the Campo Tencia hut with Capanna Leit in a little over two hours by crossing Passo Morghirola (2420m), which is found on a spur of the east ridge of Pizzo Campolungo. Capanna Leit (2260m) is ideally situated in a stony landscape below the pinnacle of Pizzo del Prévat, and with easy access to the Campolungo Pass, by which Fusio at the head of Val Lavizzara is reached in three hours. The hut is owned by the SAT (*Socièta Alpinistica Ticinese*) and can sleep more than sixty in its dormitories. It's open from June to October, has no permanent resident guardian, and may be gained in a lovely walk of three to four hours from Dalpe via Alpe Cadonighino and Passo Venett, the latter a saddle of grass and stone in a ridge of glistening white rock, from which a splendid view shows the glaciated Rheinwaldhorn off to the east. Below Capanna Leit lies the delightful grassland basin of Alpe Campolungo, and below that Lago Tremorgio, on whose north-east shore stands Capanna Tremorgio. This is owned by the Ticinese electrical company which operates a pumped hydro scheme from the lake, and also controls a cable-car that rises from Rodi-Fiesso. Capanna Tremorgio has a resident guardian from July to September, and offers a full meals service.

To the north of Tremorgio, on the opposite side of Valle Leventina, Val Piora is one of the finest of Leventina's glens. Completely hidden from the main valley, this elevated glen of lake and pastureland fills the high-country between Valle Leventina and Valle Santa Maria, one of the tributaries of Valle di Blenio. Access from the south is by way of either a tortuous road which climbs out of the valley from Piotta, or by funicular, also starting from Piotta. The upper terminus of this funicular is beside the road just short of the dammed Lago Ritom where there's a convenient restaurant. With such ease of access it comes as no surprise to find parts of Val Piora are extremely popular during the high summer. This popularity, however, is usually confined to the period mid-morning to late-afternoon. By the time twilight settles over the pastures most visitors have drifted back to the valley, leaving the glen to those who spend their summers in the alps there, and walkers booked for the night at Capanna Cadagno.

Apart from the road and funicular access, walkers keen to make their own way from the Leventina will find linking trails from Airolo that cross the entrance to Val Canaria and eventually gain Lago Ritom at its south-western end - or a longer approach which goes all the way through Val Canaria to the Bochetta, or Passo, di Cadlimo (with Capanna Cadlimo nearby), then south past Lago Scuro and Lago di Tom into Val Piora proper.

The Piora glen is a gentle tilt of grassland with a mean altitude of nearly two thousand metres. Lago Ritom lies at 1850 metres, while the upper pastures are around the 2200 metre contour. Marking its upper eastern limits stands Piz dell'Uomo (2663m), on either side of which easy walkers' passes lead to the Valle Santa Maria. These are Passo dell'Uomo which takes a trail through Val Termine to the Lukmanier Pass, Passo Colombe between Piz dell'Uomo and Pizzo Colombe, and to the south of the latter peak, Passo Sole. From these last two, major peaks of the Adula Alps show themselves in snowy splendour, while the walks they encourage down into Valle Santa Maria are very pleasant indeed. Linked with the Lukmanier Pass and Passo dell'Uomo a fine day's circuit can be achieved.

The north wall of Val Piora hides another glen, that of Cadlimo, whose character is quite different to that of Piora's. A trail cuts all the way through this glen, and when combined with that through Val Termine at the eastern end, and one cutting south from Capanna Cadlimo at its western extent, yet another grand, though fairly short, walking tour is possible. Both the Cadagno and Cadlimo huts are wardened throughout the summer. The first is owned by the Lugano Section of the SAT and can accommodate sixty or so, while Capanna Cadlimo belongs to the Uto Section (Zürich) of the Swiss Alpine Club. Not quite as spacious as its neighbour, it can sleep about fifty, and is useful for several walking tours in the immediate tarn-littered countryside, and for the ascent of such peaks as Piz Rondadura, Piz Curnera and Piz Ravetsch whose linking ridges form part of the Alpine watershed that runs along the north side of the Cadlimo glen, before dipping to the lake on the Lukmanier Pass.

Before discussing walking possibilities in and around Valle Santa Maria which descends southward from the Lukmanier into Valle di Blenio, we will briefly visit the upper extension of Valle Leventina where, beyond Airolo, it is known as Val Bedretto.

Val Bedretto

From Airolo Val Bedretto arcs to the south-west. North of this the watershed ridge makes an impressive wall, while to the south outliers of the Cristallina massif drain numerous streams into the Ticino river. At its head the Nufenen Pass carries a road which squirms its way from the Valais, while the older and busier St Gotthard Pass and tunnel filters traffic from Central Switzerland out to the Leventina at Airolo. One would be forgiven for thinking that caught between the two Val Bedretto would be unbearable with the constant laboured sound of the internal combustion engine. Happily the reality is not quite like that. Off the main valley road tiny villages slumber quietly, paths edge their pastures. Other trails sneak through forests that clothe the ankles of the mountains, while still more wander from alp to alp on mid-height flanks on both sides of the valley.

The main interest for walkers here, though, lies in Val Corno, the subsidiary glen that hangs at the south-western limit of the valley, and from whose head the ancient Gries Pass provides access to Valle di Morasco and several other glens in the upper Val Formazza. There's also Passo San Giacomo to the east of the Gries Pass and reached by footpath from All Acqua, which similarly leads into Val Formazza and the Tosa Falls. Both of these passes, by the way, carry the Italian frontier before it swings south to Basodino and all along the ridge which divides Val Formazza in Italy from the Cristallina massif in Swiss Ticino. And the third point of interest from Val Bedretto lies in its usefulness as a means of getting into the Cristallina mountains through Val Torta, a neat little glen cutting south of Ossasco.

Valle di Blenio

The final selection of valleys to come under scrutiny here begins with the *valle del sole* which, as we have seen, runs roughly north to south along the borders of the Lepontine and Adula Alps immediately to the east of Valle Leventina. In its lower reaches Biasca is the main town and prime point of access, since it has rail connections on the Airolo-Bellinzona line, and from which buses serve the rest of the valley. Just to the north of Biasca the village of Loderio is the start of a long high route for walkers known as the Sentiero Alto di Blenio, a series of footpaths that leads eventually to Lago Ritom at the western end of Val Piora.

A few kilometres north of Loderio Val Malvaglia cuts away to the right behind the village after which it is named. This tributary glen curves north-east then north towards the Rheinwaldhorn. Along the north and west slopes many alp hamlets and collections of old haybarns catch the sunshine. Paths and trackways go from one to another, while yet another route leads to the very foot of the Rheinwaldhorn where the buildings of Alpe di Quarnei provide an excuse and a destination for an interesting day's outing.

Streams draining the west face of the Rheinwaldhorn flow down into a small, well-contained glen to the east of Dangio and Torre, neighbouring villages situated three quarters of the way up Valle di Blenio. Val Soi not only drains the Rheinwaldhorn, but also serves as a useful access ramp to Val di Carassino, a north-sloping trench caught between the main ridge of the Adula Alps and a smaller block of mountains extending from Cima di Pinadee. At the southern end of Val di Carassino the Swiss Alpine Club has provided a fifty-bedded hut, Capanna Adula (2012m), while the larger Rifugio Adula (2393m) stands about an hour's walk above it on the slopes of the Rheinwaldhorn, and is owned by the UTOE. At the northern end of Val di Carassino its stream twists sharply to the south-west and spills down to the Blenio just above the village of Olivone. A circuit of Cima di Pinadee, starting and ending at Olivone, is possible by following a trail that climbs into the glen at its northern end and wandering all the way through it to Capanna Adula, then descending steeply to Val Soi. Instead of taking the trail out of Val Soi to Torre, follow an alternative path heading roughly northward at mid-height along the west flank of the Pinadee block. This leads directly to Olivone.

At Olivone the valley forks. Off to the left the road twists in long loops up the hillside to gain Valle Santa Maria and the Lukmanier Pass, while straight ahead a tight little defile hides from view the delights of Val Camadra. A road tunnels through the western slopes of this defile, while a mule trail squeezes between rock walls and the river to join the road where it emerges from the tunnel just short of Campo Blenio. This little village spills onto pastures at a junction of streams. Served by bus it has two modest hotels, dormitory accommodation for groups, and some fine walking country on its doorstep.

The glen continues ahead through Ghirone, beyond which rough pastures lead towards the watershed mountains. At the head of the glen is the unmanned Capanna Scaletta which could serve as a useful base for walkers exploring this seemingly remote corner of the Alps. Above the hut to the east Passo della Greina (2357m) provides a way into some very empty country overlooked by peaks whose names mean little to any but the most dedicated of alpinists in search of unsung places in which to practise their sport. Various cols too suggest a rich assortment of tours for the inquisitive walker; tours that lead to the Vorder Rhine, or deeper into the Adula Alps, or south across Crap la Crusch from Plaun la Greina on a walk that passes below Piz Terri to the dammed Lago di Luzzone and finally back to Campo Blenio.

West of Campo a splendid high pastureland invites walkers on a crossing that slopes down to the Lukmanier Pass at the head of Valle Santa Maria. This Val di Campo is broad and featureless in places, and in thick mist can be quite eery. But in fine weather views are lovely, and the high point of Passo di Gana Negra (2401m) offers a wide panorama over a landscape that at once inspires dreams for more lengthy walking tours. This may not be bold dramatic country as will be found in the Western Alps, but it is certainly not short of charm. It is, indeed, a walker's landscape, and on the eastern slopes a little over two hours from Campo Blenio, Capanna Boverina (built by the Bellinzona Section of the UTOE) may be useful as a temporary base. From the hut an easy trail heading north leads to Lago Retico (2372m), an attractive little tarn from which the crossing of Pass Cristallina involves a climb of little more than twenty metres. On the north side of this pass Piz Cristallina (not to be confused with the Cristallina mountains south of Val Bedretto) is one in a group of peaks that overlooks Disentis in the valley of the Vorder Rhine. Trails from the pass eventually lead down to Disentis via Val Cristallina which disgorges into Val Medel below the Lukmanier.

Most walkers drawn to Val di Campo will, no doubt, cross from one side to the other via the Gana Negra Pass. If starting from Campo Blenio in Val Camadra one's destination will invariably be the final valley in this selected survey of the Lepontine Alps, namely Valle Santa Maria. Unlike so many other valleys and glens in the Lepontines, Santa Maria is broad and pastoral, an open scoop of hill country where cattle graze, where open meadows dotted with pine trees give the air of a neat tended parkland. There is no tourist infrastructure, no shops, ski tows or cableways, and in Acquacalda there's just one hotel, with modest camping facilities behind it, although there's hotel accommodation also at the Lukmanier Pass.

Gentle valley walks abound, as do options for crossing ridges to north and south. Favoured trails head west of Acquacalda via Passo Sole or Passo Colombe in order to gain the tarn-bright pastureland of Val Piora. Another breaks away from the Passo Sole route and heading south climbs to Passo Predelp (2452m), on whose southern side the way descends steeply to Predelp and a string of lovely villages perched high above Valle Leventina. Yet another trail accessible from Acquacalda goes south-east over high grassland to cross Passo Bareta on a shoulder of mountain that effectively divides Valle Santa Maria from Valle di Blenio, and thereafter goes from alp to alp heading south, our walker squinting into the sunshine, being reminded full well why it is called the valley of the sun.

✳   ✳   ✳

A TOUR OF TICINO

Hubert Walker's recommendations for a circuit of the Lepontines, and what he called the Alps of Ticino, ignored the splendours of Valle di Blenio and Val Piora, and concentrated heavily on the western valleys. By contrast the tour outlined below provides a broader view of the district and is based upon a circuit I devised a few summers ago on behalf of friends who had already tackled several of the well-known Alpine classics, but who came to regard this particular tour as one of their all-time favourites. It has several short and easy stages allowing plenty of time to explore neighbourhood glens, to laze beside a tarn or two, to scramble upon a nearby peak, or simply to amble through green pastures without constant reference to one's watch. Some Alpine trips should be treated to a leisurely approach. This is one such.

The tour begins in Valle di Blenio for it is easy of approach by public transport, having a railway station at its junction with Valle Leventina, and bus service north from there. Take the bus from Biasca to Torre or Dangio and start by walking up into Val Soi on the path which climbs to Capanna Adula at the southern end of Val Carassino. With about 1200 metres of height to gain from the road, this will be quite enough for a first day, so one would spend a night there in the shadow of the Rheinwaldhorn, at once enjoying a high Alpine atmosphere.

The second day leads north-west through Val Carassino on a gentle descent to the small dammed lake at its northern end, then swings left on a downhill trail leading to Olivone, from where you resume northwards on the mule-track which squeezes through the entrance defile hiding Val Camadra. On reaching Campo Blenio bear left to work up the western hillside to the alp hamlet of Ronco di Gualdo, from where a path goes directly to Capanna Boverina. Views east from the hut, and from the trail leading to it, show the fine granite peaks of the Adula Alps, and the barrage at the end of Lago di Luzzone blocking a cirque topped by Piz Terri (3149m) across the Camadra glen, while to the south-east the upper reaches of the Rheinwaldhorn gleam with snow and ice.

From the Boverina hut the next stage now heads roughly westward to Capanna Cadagno and Val Piora. There are two ways of achieving this, both of which begin by wandering over the broad open pastures to Passo di Gana Negra, on the western side of which the trail forks. The right-hand option goes to the Lukmanier Pass, whence one would walk through Val Termine, cross the easy Passo dell'Uomo and descend to the Cadagno hut. The left-hand choice drops to the Lukmanier road a short distance upstream of Acquacalda, then crosses the valley on a steady ascent of some five hundred and sixty metres to gain Passo Colombe in the walling ridge between Piz dell'Uomo and Pizzo Colombe. From this pass an enjoyable downhill

235

stretch leads into Val Piora where Capanna Cadagno sits in pastureland not far from the south-eastern end of the lovely Lago Cadagno.

Since Val Piora and its neighbourhood has such delightful walking potential it is worth spending at least two nights at the Cadagno refuge. A rewarding day's exercise could be won by going initially from Lago Cadagno to Lago di Tom, not by the trail marked on the LS map, but by another (waymarked to Alpe di Tom) which crosses a shoulder of hillside between the two lakes, then veers north high above the eastern shore of Lago di Tom. At the far end of this tarn cut left into a grassy bowl to find a crossing path. Bear right then, climbing north again to Lago Scuro and Capanna Cadlimo. Here another trail breaks away south-eastward to descend the Cadlimo glen. When it forks just beyond the alp buildings of Stabbio Nuovo, cross the stream and follow a path cutting round the hillside spur at the eastern end of the glen, and continue through Val Termine, over Passo dell'Uomo and back to Capanna Cadagno. This is a pleasant circuit, not too demanding, but visual rewards are in abundant supply.

The fifth stage of our tour is a short one. It retraces part of yesterday's route to the Cadlimo hut, then crosses Bochetta di Cadlimo to Pian Bornengo at the head of Val Cañaria. A trail then follows the stream all the way down through this glen to Airolo, a small resort at the foot of the St Gotthard Pass, with several hotels in the one, two and three-star categories.

Stage six takes us into the northern corries of the Cristallina massif on a day of contrasts. Airolo, of course, looks onto major transalpine road and rail routes, and the day begins with a crossing of the Leventina with its busy highway complex, but finishes in the stony silence of Val Torta beneath the north face of Cristallina itself. In between these two extremes there's an interesting belvedere path known as the Strada degli alpi Bedretto to follow, which runs along the hillside high above Val Bedretto and visits a series of alps as well as providing good views of the watershed ridge forming the north wall of the valley opposite.

South-west of Airolo the Sasso della Boggia cableway provides a quick and painless alternative to the 600 metre climb to Alpe di Pesciüm where the strada degli alpi trail is joined. The uphill trail to Pesciüm will add a little over an hour and a half to the walk, but since the route is not overlong anyway, this should be quite acceptable. Those who choose to ride the cableway, however, are warned that it's an unmanned service, and to alight at Pesciüm (the midway point) involves stepping out onto a pylon with a landing stage, and descending an iron stairway. From Pesciüm the walk heads roughly westward among alpenrose and bilberry, crossing two minor glens and passing huddled alp hutments before coming to Piano di Pescia at the mouth of Val Torta. From here a track goes to Alpe Cristallina where a footpath then heads upvalley on the west bank of the stream initially drawn by Pizzo del Naret, but as the glen curves into its upper cirque, so Cristallina looms overhead. Capanna Cristallina is found below Passo di Cristallina, following a walk of about five or six hours from Airolo.

The next stage makes a north-south crossing of the Cristallina massif to the Basodino hut. There are two ways of achieving this. The first is the standard direct route by way of Passo di Cristallina; a very fine walk but a short one of less than three hours, and since the longer alternative is recommended here, it would be worth taking a stroll over this pass after arrival at Capanna Cristallina, and descending to the eastern shore of Lago Sfundau in its scree-walled well, then continue to the little rocky saddle at the southern end of the tarn from where some lovely views are won across folding ridges to Basodino. But the route to Capanna Basodino recommended here is that which makes a devious curve round the eastern side of the main Cristallina mass by way of Passo del Naret. Over this a minor trail is then taken round to Lago del Naret, up and over a saddle a little west of Passo del Sasso Nero, then guided by cairns across a rugged landscape of boulder tips and wild depressions before gaining a col overlooking Lago Nero. Turning this above its northern shore (fixed cables in exposed places) a trail now leads to a more welcoming and better-trod corner of the mountains, with Capanna Basodino on its perch above a tight little glen.

As has already been suggested, the Cristallina massif has plenty of opportunities for day-long walking tours and scrambles, but in order to fulfill our circuit of the Ticinese mountains within a two-week holiday it is necessary to move on after just one night at the Basodino hut. Stage eight then involves an easy downhill walk through the woods and little pasturelands of Val Bavona to Bignasco. If you make an early start it would be well worth making a diversion at Foroglio to climb a short way into the mouth of Val Calnegia merely to sample the character of this little glen.

Leaving Bignasco we follow in Walker's footsteps by wandering through Val Cocco and crossing Passo del Cocco at its head, and from there descending as far as Capanna Alpe d'Osola where you spend a night in this remote and simple lodging. From here next day cross Bochetta di Mugaia in the south ridge of Monte Zucchero, and then descend sixteen hundred metres by way of Alpe di Mugaia, Cortign and Val Redorta to reach Sonogno at a junction of valleys.

Day eleven of our tour involves the crossing of Passo di Redorta, that classic 2181 metre link between Val Verzasca and Val Lavizzara. Starting from Sonogno one retraces part of yesterday's route along the Redorta glen before climbing through its upper reaches beneath the south face of Corona di Redorta. On the west side of the pass the trail is rough for a while, but it's a magical place where the walls of Val di Pertüs are steep and, in the words of Walker, "sweep down grandly to the depths of the gorge below." When eventually you come to the little alp of Monte di San Carlo where the Pertüs enters Val di Prato, continue downstream to the main trench of Val Lavizzara where overnight lodging may be found in Prato-Sornico at the end of a full but very rewarding day's trek.

Linking trails enable you to avoid much of the road between Prato and Fusio where the next night will be spent, and as this is a short journey that will confine you to the bed of the valley and be somewhat restricting so far as mountain views are concerned, the suggestion is offered here to make a diversion to Mogno, two kilometres or so short of Fusio. From Mogno a forest trail climbs steeply to Lago di Mognola, from whose northern shore a continuing path leads on an airy hillside traverse before descending once more to the valley at Fusio itself.

The final day's walk is designed to get you back to Valle Leventina in readiness for the homebound journey. The obvious way to achieve this is via Passo Campolungo, a pass more than a thousand metres above Fusio to the north-east, whose crossing involves a descent on the eastern side of some 1300 metres to Rodi-

Fiesso. It's a popular route, albeit a tiring one, on mostly good paths, and with consistently fine views on both ascent and descent. There are various alternative ways down to Valle Leventina. The first option comes at a trail junction at Alpe Campolungo where the right-hand branch leads to Dalpe (with a way from there to either Faido or Chiggiogna). Another alternative is offered at Lago Tremorgio from whose north shore a route leads by way of Pian Mott to Ambri or Piotta, while the main descent to Valle Leventina is that which twists steeply through forest from the lake to Rodi-Fiesso. Finally, should you find yourself short of time, or excessively weary on arrival at Lago Tremorgio, there's temptation to ride the cable-car down to the valley. But at the tail end of a fortnight's walking tour that option, surely, is for emergencies only!

A TOUR OF TICINO - ROUTE SUMMARY

Day 1: Torre (or Dangio) - Val Soi - Capanna Adula

Day 2: Capanna Adula - Campo Blenio - Capanna Boverina

Day 3: Capanna Boverina - Passo di Gana Negra - Lukmanier Pass - Val Termine - Capanna Cadagno

or: Capanna Boverina - Passo di Gana Negra - Passo Colombe - Capanna Cadagno

Day 4: Capanna Cadagno - Capanna Cadlimo - Val Cadlimo - Capanna Cadagno

Day 5: Capanna Cadagno - Bochetta di Cadlimo - Airolo

Day 6: Airolo - Pesciüm - Capanna Cristallina

Day 7: Capanna Cristallina - Passo del Naret - Bochetta del Lago Nero - Capanna Basodino

Day 8: Capanna Basodino - Foroglio - Bignasco

Day 9: Bignasco - Passo del Cocco - Capanna Alpe d'Osola

Day 10: Capanna Alpe d'Osola - Bochetta di Mugaia - Sonogno

Day 11: Sonogno - Passo di Redorta - Prato-Sornico

Day 12: Prato-Sornico - Lago di Mognola - Fusio

Day 13: Fusio - Passo Campolungo - Lago Tremorgio - Rodi-Fiesso

---

※   ※   ※

THE LEPONTINE ALPS

Location:

Immediately to the east of the Pennine Alps. The Lepontines proper stretch from the Simplon to the Lukmanier Passes, but the adjacent Adula Alps extend as far as the Splügen Pass and are generally considered to be part of this range. Most of the Lepontines lie within the Swiss canton of Ticino.

Principal valleys:

Val Formazza and Valle Antigorio in the west. Then Valle Maggia and Val Verzasca with their many tributary glens. Valle Leventina and its upper feeder, Val Bedretto. Valle di Blenio whose tributaries of Valle Santa Maria and Val Camadra are also important. Those that drain the Adula Alps are Val Calanca, Valle Mesolcina and Valle San Giacomo.

Principal peaks:
Monte Leone (3553m), Rheinwaldhorn (3402m), Basodino (3272m), Piz Medel (3211m), Piz Terri (3149m), Piz Campo Tencia (3072m), Cristallina (2912m)

Centres:
There are no real centres as one knows them in the Western Alps, but the following villages are located on the edge of good walking country, and have limited accommodation: Cevio, Bignasco, Lavertezzo, Sonogno, Fusio, Airolo, Biasca, Campo Blenio

Huts:
A number of huts (known here as capanna or rifugio) will be found in assorted districts. A few belong to the Swiss or Italian Alpine Clubs, but the majority are provided by local Ticinese organisations. Many are unmanned. Consult the guidebook for details.

Access:
The Zürich-Milan route provides access by rail, with the towns of Airolo, Bellinzona or Locarno being the best places to aim for. Also by train the Trans-European Express serves Bern-Brig-Domodossola-Milan via the Simplon tunnel. Nearest international airports are Zürich and Milan. Road passes are the Simplon, Nufenen, St Gotthard, Lukmanier, San Bernardino and Splügen.

Maps:
The 1:50,000 series published by the Swiss survey (Landeskarte der Schweiz or Carta nazionale della Svizzera) provide the best coverage for walkers. Principal sheets are, from west to east: 265 *Nufenenpass*, 275 *Valle Antigorio*, 256 *Disentis*, 266 *Valle Leventina*, 276 *Val Verzasca*, 267 *San Bernadino*

Guidebooks:
Walking in Ticino by Kev Reynolds (Cicerone Press) details 75 routes in the Swiss Lepontines. All the main valleys are covered, and the book also contains accommodation and public transport information.
The Swiss publisher, Kümmerly & Frey of Bern, produces a series of walking guides to Switzerland. Coverage for the Lepontines will be found in two volumes, *Locarno* and *Tre Valli*. Both are published in Italian and German editions (no English language translation).
Walking Switzerland the Swiss Way by Marcia Lieberman (Cordee/The Mountaineers) includes a small section on Ticino, with the Strada Alta Leventina described, plus two walks in Val Verzasca.

Other reading:
Walking in the Alps by J. Hubert Walker (Oliver & Boyd). Walker's enthusiasm for the Lepontines is contagious, and his chapter on these mountains remains one of the best things in his book.
Italian Alps by D.W. Freshfield (Longmans, 1875 - latest edition published by Blackwell, 1937). This is one of Freshfield's earliest books, in which his travels among the Lepontine Alps (among others) are well described.
Recollections of an Old Mountaineer by Walter Larden (Arnold, 1910) includes some of the Lepontines in this climbing autobiography.
The Outdoor Traveler's Guide to The Alps by Marcia R. Lieberman (Stewart, Tabori & Chang, New York, 1991) contains basic detail of selected valleys.

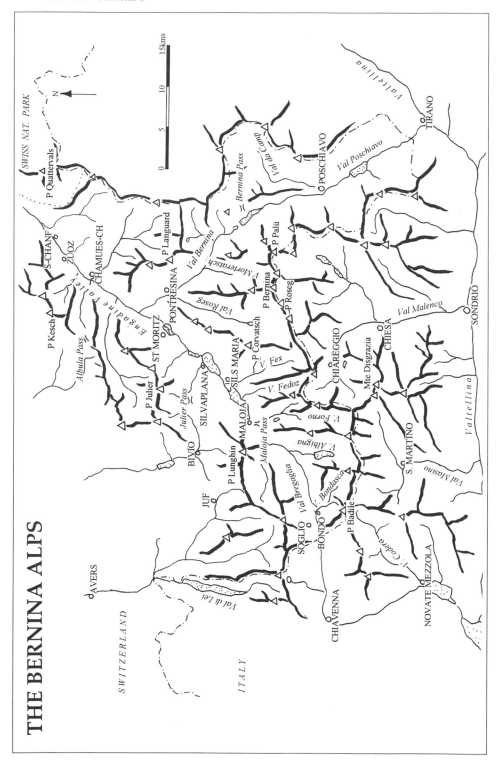

THE BERNINA ALPS

Monte della Disgrazia

9: THE BERNINA ALPS
Including the Alps of Bregaglia, the Engadine Valley and the Swiss National Park

The Bernina Alps, of which the granite spires of Bregaglia form an important adjunct, contain the most easterly four thousand metre summit of the whole Alpine chain and display a refreshing variety of mountain and valley scenery. The district is more extensive than is generally assumed, stretching from Lago di Como in the south-west to the Reschen Pass (Passo di Rèsia) in the north east. That great but sometimes maligned valley of the Engadine traces its northern edge, while the low-lying Valtellina roughly marks its southern boundary.

Though the district covers a large area, the block of the Bernina massif itself is a comparatively small one; a compact group of snow mountains caught in a triangle of valleys - Upper Engadine, Val Bernina and Val Malenco; the first two Swiss, the third flowing down into the Italian Valtellina whose vine and fruit-clad course extends from the Stelvio Pass to Lago di Como. Piz Bernina (4049m) holds court from the centre of this block, while neatly gathered around it rise other peaks whose outlines may fall a little short of the magical four thousand metre contour, but which are no less graceful for all that: Piz Roseg, Piz Scerscen, Piz Morteratsch, Piz Zupò, Bellavista and the elegant, triple-buttressed Piz Palü.

Across the green scoop of Val Malenco stands Monte della Disgrazia in a massive upthrust of ice-daubed rock, like a long-lost outlier of the Mont Blanc massif, and from whose outstretched north-west ridge extend the Bregaglia mountains - a crest of "jagged peaks interspersed with craggy precipices, with hanging glaciers and with towering pinnacles" (E.S. Kennedy). The classic snow arêtes and glaciers of the Bernina group attract mountaineers by their similarity to the Western Alps, while the Bregaglia mountains draw climbers with their promise of near-vertical sport on sun-warmed granite without the queues associated, for example, with the famed aiguilles of Chamonix with which they are sometimes compared.

In his survey of the region Walker not unnaturally confined his attention to the immediate and obvious pleasures of the Bernina and Bregaglia massifs, for within those two neighbouring groups, joined by the easy Muretto Pass, will be found the major mountain appeal of the Bernina Alps. But grand though they undoubtedly are, in this chapter we will range further afield, and in so doing unravel the full landscape diversity of the district which owes its wider attraction for the walker to its extensive valleys and numerous tributary glens, to the little corries and vegetated spurs crossed by ancient trails, to its highly decorated villages, and to the siting of Switzerland's only national park.

But first to the main mountain groups, among whose surrounding glens we will wander in full gaze of some very fine Alpine scenery.

✳   ✳   ✳

THE BREGAGLIA ALPS

These mountains form a dividing line between Switzerland and Italy like that of a graph traced by a barometer in unsettled weather, and run roughly eastward from Piz dei Vanni to the Passo del Muretto. The great slab walls of Piz Badile and Cengalo, appropriately dubbed 'the grey twins' by Freshfield, the delicate Sciora spires, the little glacial napkins that dangle above such glens as Val Bondasca, Albigna and the raw moraine wilderness of Val Forno, all these provide a romantic backdrop to expeditions that will both challenge and reward the walking connoisseur. "He must be very dull of soul indeed," wrote Walker, "who could not see without a catch of his breath the sudden upward surge of the Bondasca peaks of Badile and Cengalo, as he turns into that glen, or the cascading sheer descent of turret on turret of rock, falling from the perfect peak of Bacone, as seen from the Albigna glen. They are wonderful mountains, and no less wonderful on the south, or Italian side of the range, than the Swiss."

On the Italian side the mountain walls plunge just as steeply into deep glens with charm all their own: the enchanting Val Codera, "a long narrow gash, closely set about by steep granite cliffs" that squirms down to Lago di Mezzola, the Vals dei Bagni and di Mello which form the crossbar to the T of Val Masino, banked to the east by the soaring Monte della Disgrazia, and the long north-south trench of Val Malenco that effectively separates the Bregaglia from the snow and ice-crusted Bernina massif. While Val Codera and Val Malenco drain directly out to lower country, the great walls that surround the glens of dei Bagni and di Mello form an almost complete circle as if to protect them from outside influence. That circle is broken only where the two glens come together at San Martino, their combined waters then rushing south through the narrow gap of Val Masino. It's a dramatic, mountain-girt sanctuary, full of wild and rugged grandeur.

While the upper and best part of Val Bregaglia on the north side of the district between the Maloja Pass and Castasegna lies in Switzerland, the valley bears the full flavour of Italy. Though they may display the neat orderliness of Switzerland, villages with their cobbled alleys bear Italian names, their buildings are graced by Italian architecture and voices heard in both street and meadow speak the language of Italy too, while the soft warmth of Lombardy embraces chestnut-wooded hillsides through the long days of summer.

Val Bregaglia is usually approached from the Upper Engadine by a descent of the Maloja Pass. There is no railway, but the Postbus runs a frequent service from St Moritz. Vicosoprano is probably the best village centre for valley-based walkers, having hotels, pensions and a campsite, but Promontogno also has limited accommodation and a youth hostel, while Soglio, perched on a sunny hillside terrace some three hundred metres above the river, boasts one of the finest situations of any village in the Alps, gazing as it does across the valley to Val Bondasca - a veritable Alpine wonderland. "Lofty Alps, like lofty characters, require for their due appreciation some elevation in the spectator." Writing thus in *The Playground of Europe*, Leslie Stephen could well have had Soglio in mind.

As we have seen, the Postbus serves Val Bregaglia via the Maloja Pass. It's a fine route, described by Lord Schuster as follows: "the road winds down through forest into a gorge that ever narrows, hung round with the blue mystery of the South, and lost at last in the shadow of mountains that stand round about the Lombard Plain." A fine route indeed, but it is not the way of the walker, so let us examine the alternatives available to him.

Supposing our walker has the necessary days available to make his approach in the time-honoured way, he (or she) will begin outside the immediate district in order to experience the full drama of the valley and its attendant mountains from a distant perspective. This is the true way of the mountain wanderer. Speed has little place in our scheme of things, for the pilgrim knows that scenery (as in matters spiritual) is best appreciated after it has been earned through effort and endurance. Assuming we agree with this premise, there are five main routes of approach open to us; three of which combine at the Septimer Pass (2310m) north-west of Maloja, the remaining two crossing the high ridge above Soglio to reward with scenes of startling beauty. First the Septimer Pass options.

Starting from the Engadine valley a rather devious approach is necessary; devious because the obvious way would be to descend southward by paved way over the Maloja Pass, while we head west to a watershed behind the lump of Piz Lunghin. By taking a trail from Maloja (or from Sils Baselgia) a little tarn is reached in a desolate bowl of scree and boulder below the Lunghin Pass. This tarn is the birthplace of the great river Inn, the pass above it marking a major Alpine watershed. To the north of the Lunghin Pass an innocent stream is an early tributary of the Rhine which of course empties into the North Sea. To the west a meagre brook becomes the Maira (or Mera), which flows out to the Adriatic, while the Inn, draining Lägh dal Lunghin, scores its way through the Eastern Alps, swells the

Danube and eventually enters the Black Sea.

From the pass an easy scramble of half an hour leads to the summit of Piz Lunghin (2780m) for an impressive view onto the beautiful Engadine lakes, into the depths of Val Bregaglia and across to the cluster of peaks that lines that valley's eastern end. The pass itself overlooks a basin of poor grassland that slopes northward to Bivio below the Julier road pass, from where the second of our options begins. Bivio is on the Chur to St Moritz Postbus route, an unassuming village from which a small handful of cross-country walking routes could be devised. From it a clear and easy trail follows the Rhine's tributary stream through the Tgavretga glen all the way up to the Septimer Pass, while a short descending traverse from the Lunghin Pass leads to the same place.

For centuries the Septimer (in Romansch, Pass da Sett) was used as an important crossing by traders with their mules passing from the warm south to the Central Alps and beyond into northern Europe. The Roman legions are said to have used it too, but today it is the haunt of chamois, marmot and the occasional walker, and is the meeting place of our third route into Val Bregaglia. This comes initially from Juf, Switzerland's highest permanently-inhabited settlement (some say the highest in Europe) in the Averstal, and first entails crossing the 2672 metre pass of Forcellina before dropping to the Septimer.

Our three route options having combined, the continuing walk now leads southward in company with the lively Maira stream, soon descending in tight zig-zags to the junction with Val Maroz, a glen flowing from the west. Here the Maira curves left and drops to the neat white village of Casaccia nestling at the foot of the Maloja Pass. Unless you are fit and have made an early start, it will be necessary to go down to Casaccia for overnight accommodation, for the continuing route will require about five hours or more to gain Soglio by way of Val Maroz.

The way through Val Maroz is along a broad track at first, but this soon narrows to a footpath coloured here and there with paint flashes, and leads to the isolated alp of Maroz Dent, consisting of a simple dwelling house, cattle byre and a pentagonal walled sheepfold. From here two further options present themselves. The shorter route crosses the stream and climbs steep grass slopes to a minor saddle giving access to Val da Cam and a belvedere trail to Soglio. The alternative also crosses the stream, but then continues upvalley to the Val da la Duäna, from which a 2694 metre pass breaks through the Bregaglia's north wall above Soglio itself. Since this latter crossing is used by one of our other options, we will concentrate on the Val da Cam route here.

The entrance to Val da Cam is guarded by a row of tall cairns, beyond which the way eases through gentle pastures, rises to a second level and winds among several hillocks that obscure the rocky gateway of Pass da Cam (2433m). Suddenly the Bregaglia falls at your feet, to where Borgonovo squats astride the road some 1300 metres below. Beyond, on the far side of the valley, granite peaks burst out of the forests; a strident ridge system from which grey spurs and arêtes thrust forward, separating the glens of Albigna and Bondasca. It's a view to stop you in your tracks, but for the next three hours there will be many more such views to make this a very staccato journey indeed as the trail picks its way mostly above the two thousand metre contour among rampant shrubbery, across plunging pastures, over streams, and leading from one collection of alp chalets to the next. Coming to Plan Vest Val Bondasca cuts directly ahead on the far side of the Bregaglia. The great grey blade of Piz Badile shines to one side of the Trubinasca glen. On the other the sharp teeth of the Scioras are intermixed with fillings of snow and little daubs of ice, while below these savage but immaculate peaks, chestnut woods add a more homely dimension. From the stone hutments of Plan Vest to Alp Tombal demands a descent through extraordinarily steep pinewoods with brief snatched views between the trees. Tombal, though smaller, is no less magical than Plan Vest, while Soglio itself shares the same wonderful view and is in itself utterly charming.

So much for the approach from the Septimer Pass. Now we will look at the two alternatives mentioned above which come from the north. These centre on the Averstal, that remote and somewhat secluded valley that lies beyond the Bregaglia's north wall of mountains. A road, some twenty-four kilometres long, feeds into the Averstal from the Hinter Rhine near Andeer, and rises to Juf where there's youth hostel accommodation. From Juf, as we have already seen, there is a way over the mountains at the head of the valley to the Septimer Pass. There's another which crosses the Stallerberg (2579m) to Bivio. But we are, after all, interested here in ways to gain Soglio and the Val Bregaglia and these lead, not from Juf itself, but from either the Bergalgatal below Juf where a way leads over the Bergalga Pass into Val da la Duäna, or from Crot, a small hamlet some nine kilometres downstream where the Val Madris cuts back to the south, with the Italian frontier scored along its west-walling ridge.

Walker scorned the Bergalga route as having little to commend it, preferring instead the Madris alternative. It's a longish walk through the Madris glen, almost ten kilometres before it bifurcates at the alp of Munt da la Sovrana. Here the main valley curves to the south-east, while one of its headstreams flows from the south-west down through Val da Lägh. Ignoring this we continue alongside the Madris stream and shortly come to a second bifurcation. To the south entices Val da la Prasignola, while the main stream of the valley, now called Val da Roda, continues to the south-east with a trail rising with it to gain a high point at 2727 metres below the Bergalga Pass, followed by descent to the head of Val da la Duäna. From there a sharp turn to the right leads to the Duäna Pass (2694m) where the glory of Val Bregaglia is suddenly revealed, "especially", says Baedeker, "of the Val Bondasca with the shovel-shaped Piz Badile." The route down to Soglio soon joins the belvedere trail from Pass da Cam already described.

That route is very fine and much better than Walker intimated, but it is to Val da la Prasignola that we are drawn by his outright enthusiasm, and by the almost breathless delight of Freshfield who preceded him. At the head of this glen will be found the Pass da la Prasignola (2724m), from which Bregaglia is revealed. This is how Freshfield described it: "Opposite, and separated from our stand-point...only by the deep but narrow trench of Val Bregaglia, a great mountain-mass glowed in the afternoon sunshine. Its base was wrapped in chestnut woods, its middle girt with a belt of pines, above spread a mantle of the eternal snow. The sky-line was formed by a coronet of domes and massive pinnacles carved out of grey rocks, whose jagged yet stubborn forms revealed the presence of granite. Full in front the curving glacier of Val Bondasca filled the space beneath the smooth cliff-faces."

(*Italian Alps.*) More than a century later that glacier has shrunk considerably, but otherwise the scene remains unchanged. It is a memorable feast of mountain beauty and a worthy introduction to this magical region, and from the pass a trail sweeps down in steep twists, across high pasture and through fragrant forest, to reach enchanted Soglio.

Having gained Soglio by one of the above-mentioned routes there may well be a reluctance to move on. After all one can hardly expect much more in the way of easily-attained visual splendour than will be seen from the village itself, with its cobbled alleys, its communal covered washplace, and its surrounding meadows. But there are short walks to be enjoyed here too that offer slightly different perspectives and are worth exploring, so a day or two at comparative leisure can be put to good use. In the mid 60s, working in the Engadine, I would often travel down to Soglio when I had a few hours to spare, and scurry up and down the spider-leg trails that lead from it. Never did I find one that failed to reward with a scene of startling grandeur.

But any true mountain walker with a love of wild places will, however, eventually, inevitably, be drawn to Val Bondasca. Ignore the temptation to ride the special short wheel-based Postbus down to Promontogno, and take instead the descending footpath through lovely chestnut woods below the churchyard wall, pass through Promontogno and take the side road to Bondo - a romantic place in which to spend a late-summer's evening when yellowing leaves are beginning to drop from the trees onto the *boccia* court, the rumble of the Bondasca torrent scoring through its stony bed nearby.

None with a sense of mountaineering history could enter the Bondasca glen without sparing a moment's thought for Christian Klucker, the greatest guide the Engadine has known who, in the last two decades of the nineteenth century especially, made dozens of climbs on these towering mountains. There will also be a thought for Riccardo Cassin who, in July 1937 with his companions Esposito and Ratti, spent three days on the huge north-east face of Piz Badile (3308m) making its first ascent; a route long regarded as one of the most daring in the Alps. During the ascent, which was hindered by storms, they came upon two young climbers from Como, Valsecchi and Molseni, both of whom suffered terribly in the blizzard which accompanied their arrival on the summit. The two Como men died of exhaustion before they could be brought down to the valley. The route was not repeated for a further twelve years.

Val Bondasca rises steeply from summer-warm pastures to a bold savagery of granite spires and modest glacial writhings, and as you are drawn into its embrace, so you step from an almost sub-tropical vegetation with ferns as high as a man's shoulders, to a world of lichened rocks, tiny cushion plants and soaring slabs. From one world to another, from one season to another, from one climate to another. In its narrow, lower reaches deciduous woods give the lie to this Alpine wonderland. But above, the glen spreads wide its welcome with one of the most enchanting cirques imaginable. Bounded by the great walls of Badile and Cengalo on one side, and the craggy Cacciabella ridge on the other, the stark outline of the chiselled Sciora peaks blocks the head of the valley: Sciora di Fuori, Punta Pioda, Ago di Sciora, Sciora Dadent - a most exotic backdrop that adds something very special to the walker's day.

If you have only one day to spare for an exploration of this glen, the best course of action here for the fit and experienced mountain walker is to make an anti-clockwise circuit, beginning with a visit to the Sasc Furä hut (Capanna Sasc Furä; 1904m), continuing to the Sciora hut across Colle Vial on a spur extending from Badile's north ridge, then completing the circuit by way of the direct valley path to Promontogno or Bondo. There's not an uninteresting step anywhere. In his book Walker advised going directly up to the Sciora hut from Bondo. That is indeed a very fine walk, and those with sufficient days in hand may well choose to do that *in addition* to the circuit outlined below. But fine though that walk is, it is not in the same league as this tough yet immensely rewarding circuit, which is a true classic (I repeat) for the fit and experienced walker.

Capanna Sasc Furä stands among rock slabs, shrubs and pine trees high above the valley in the Trubinasca cirque. Above it tower Piz Trubinasca and Piz Badile, while the hut itself faces out across Val Bregaglia towards Soglio and the valley's north wall. In order to reach the hut from the depths of Bondasca involves a very steep ascent through dense vegetation; trees and shrubs, huge ferns and wild raspberry canes like thorny tentacles threatening the path. In one place steps have been cut in a living tree trunk to facilitate the ascent. Beyond this the trail eases a little, crosses a stream, and makes a rising traverse through woodland that soon begins to thin out. Shrubbery takes the place of woodland, peaks soar overhead, their walls appear to lean forward and shrink with foreshortening. After rain the great slabs gleam and glisten; in dry conditions the granite gives off a warm glow; in brooding cloud they loom threateningly.

The route from Sasc Furä to the Sciora hut could be difficult and even dangerous in poor visibility, and walkers are advised to study weather prospects before setting out for Colle Vial. That being said, no experienced mountain trekker is likely to find this route too demanding under normal clear summer conditions, and will delight in its wilderness quality. Behind the hut paint flashes guide the continuing way up smooth slabs. There's no real path above these, just a few cairns and more paint marks that lead in less than an hour to Colle Vial, a little nick of a pass confused among great granite boulders, with the north-east face of Piz Badile rising directly above. On the eastern side a fine view is afforded of the Sciora peaks, and the red speck of the Sciora hut dwarfed at their feet. The descent demands caution, for the way leads via a series of grit-covered ledges to a boulder field, then across the moraine rubble deposited by the Cengalo glacier. The route continues over glacial slabs running with streams, followed by more chaotic boulder-tips, more moraine, yet more streams and a short stretch of glacier ice until you come at last to Capanna di Sciora gazing west over the valley, the depths of Val Bondasca falling below, the Scioras rising like sharp fenceposts above. Descent to Promontogno can be tiring at the tail-end of such a day, for there's a lot of height to lose, and for a good part of the way the trail is rough underfoot. But what a day this will have been! A round trip of about sixteen kilometres, and with a height-gain and loss of more than 1400 metres. And magic all the way.

The next glen to the east is that of Albigna which flows almost due north, while Val Bondasca is set at a tilt and drains north-westward, the two divided naturally by the Cacciabella-Sciora Dadent ridge system. From the bed of Val Bregaglia the full impact of Val Albigna is lost, shielded as it is by a great white wall of a dam that effectively blocks the upper glen. In his own inimitable style, Baedeker approved of this glen, saying it was "repaying". Of course, when Baedeker wrote his guides, the dam was not even thought of. In those days one of the highlights of the approach was the Cascata dell' Albigna - "a fine fall in a wild ravine, near the foot of the Albigna Glacier." Nowadays most visitors to Albigna take the cable-car used by maintenance staff working at the dam, thus avoiding a stiff walk of about three hours. Of course, much depends on your forward plans whether you choose to walk, but if you can afford that three hour approach, and when the sweat starts running can ignore the teasing fifteen minute alternative ride in the sky, you'll find enough of interest along the woodland trail from Pranzaira or, indeed, from Vicosoprano where another path sets out for the same destination. It was a descent of this trail about which Walker wrote: "...that rough path down to Vicosoprano through a glen of almost legendary wildness and beauty ought to be trodden by the feet of all mountain pilgrims."

From the eastern side of the dam a path leads from the shoreline of Lago da l'Albigna, up and over rough boulder slopes and in a little over half an hour comes to the Capanna da l'Albigna (2336m). The hut commands a savage panorama. With this upper glen now divorced from the lower reaches of forest and scant pasture by the presence of the dam, the contrasts which lend to such places their colour, scale and considerable appeal are missing. Instead Val Albigna is a somewhat monochrome landscape - especially when clouds deny access to the sun. Then the lake is moody with black water into which dark grey slabs plunge steeply. And yet, clear those clouds for a moment and the stark ridges come alive, backed as they are then with sheets of blue. And snowfields and the dying glacier grow suddenly more appealing.

For the non-climbing walker the Abigna glen has two immediately obvious options. One is to cross the Cacciabella Pass (an old chamois-hunter's pass) in the western ridge leading to Val Bondasca, the other involves crossing the Casnil Pass in the walling ridge to the east and descending from there to Capanna del Forno in Val Forno. Since we have just visited Val Bondasca, at this point we will look at the route over to Val Forno. It's not an unduly difficult one by the Casnil Pass (2975m). There are, in fact, two passes, but it is the northerly one just below Piz Casnil that is recommended. It will take about two and a half hours for the climb from the hut to the pass, while descent to the Forno hut takes another hour or more by a steep zig-zag route down to the Forno glacier, which it reaches at a point almost opposite the hut.

The original Forno hut (the first to be built in the Bregaglia Alps) was paid for by Theodor Curtius, built under the supervision of Christian Klucker in 1889, was passed to the SAC in 1920 and rebuilt in 1924. Incidentally, during the years that Klucker acted as non-resident guardian there, he was vehemently against the use of playing cards. "As former hut guardian," he wrote in his *Adventures of an Alpine Guide*, "I had allowed no playing-cards there, and if any were found, threw them into the fire at once. Only weak creatures resort to 'Jass' in the high Alps, when they have such ample opportunity for devoting themselves to it down in the valley."

A night spent at the Capanna del Forno will allow an opportunity to study this rather gaunt but not altogether austere region of glacier and rock, and also, for those so inclined, to cross the 2775 metre Sella del Forno for a direct route down to Chiareggio in the Italian Val Malenco. This crossing has a snowfield to negotiate on the Forno side, which should not prove unduly problematic, while immediately to the north of this rises Monte del Forno (3214m), whose modest ascent is extremely rewarding for the views which are, of course, more extensive than those from the saddle. In an article published in the long-defunct *Mountain Craft* (the journal of The Mountaineering Association), Hubert Walker recommended this easy ascent. "From its top," he wrote, "you look down on to the Maloja Pass on the Swiss side, eastwards you look along the whole length of the Bernina range, with the giants of Piz Roseg and Piz Bernina looking especially grand, while to the south the eye is first taken with a view of Disgrazia, the Mountain of Ill Omen, and beyond it all the golden land and wild tangle of valleys of Alpine Italy."

Upvalley of the hut the fine glaciated summit of Cima di Rosso shows its avalanche-prone north face, while behind it the partially hidden Monte Sissone forms the glen's south-east bastion. Cima di Castello acts as the valley's south-west guardian and the three Torrone peaks create the southern headwall along which runs the Italian border. The south side of this headwall plummets steeply into Valle di Mello, while from Monte Sissone a ridge projects south-eastward to Monte Disgrazia. Down through the valley sweeps the Forno glacier which is often represented as a model Alpine-type icefield. Flowing north from an almost perfect névé basin cupped by the Sissone-Torrone-Castello cirque, the glacier shafts its way through the rock-girt valley before spilling among desolate moraines some way north of the hut. From the hut the marked route to Maloja follows the glacier, soon picking a way along the old moraine dump that is being turned into one of nature's remarkable rock gardens, then curves left into a region of rough meadowlands, with trees and shrubs and more flowers. Another world is entered. Gone is the land of ice and snow and granite pinnacles; ahead lie pastures, lakes and haybarns. The Engadine.

THE BREGAGLIA CIRCUIT

By combining several of the routes roughly outlined above, a circuit of the Swiss Bregaglia could be achieved that would provide an excellent introduction to the district, and bring focus to a few days of a walking holiday. The circuit described here makes a counter-clockwise loop with Maloja forming the initial base. Although standing at the head of the Upper Engadine, Maloja belongs politically to Val Bregaglia. It has several hotels, a youth hostel and campsite, and is accessible by Postbus from the railhead of the Rhaetian Railway at St Moritz.

The first stage of our circuit makes a tilted U-shaped course round the block of Piz Lunghin by way of the Lunghin and Septimer Passes, ending after about five hours or so at Casaccia at the foot of the Maloja Pass. Casaccia, incidentally, marks the start of the *Sentiero panoramico*, a more gentle traverse of the Bregaglia's northern hillsides than that adopted by our route, but which also provides fine (if lower) views and similarly leads to Soglio.

From Casaccia one must retrace part of yesterday's route upstream, then cut left into Val Maroz as far as Maroz Dent, before climbing southward to the hanging valley of Val da Cam. Passing through the rocky gateway of Pass da Cam the way descends a little towards the isolated farmstead of Plan Lo, then makes a long traverse of steep mountainside high above Val Bregaglia, with magnificent views south to the jagged frontier ridge and those glens that plunge from it. In places the trail is confused among boulders and shrubs, but then continues from alp to alp as far as Plan Vest. From here the way drops steeply to Soglio where it is recommended to spend the night. It would be possible to continue down to Promontogno or Bondo for accommodation, but such is the charm of Soglio's elevated position that if at all possible one should make the most of it by spending at least one night there.

For the third stage of our circuit we have a choice of destination; being either Capanna Sasc Furä, or Capanna Sciora. In truth Sasc Furä may seem a little close, requiring perhaps five energetic hours in all for the walk from Soglio, while it will take quite eight hours to gain the Sciora hut by way of Sasc Furä and the Colle Vial. On weighing up all the considerations, perhaps Sasc Furä is the favoured option, leaving a longish day for the next stage.

When leaving Soglio use the valley-bound path which leaves the village near the church and drops through lush chestnut woods to Promontogno. Taking a quiet road opposite Pension Sciora walk towards Bondo, then break away through the lower reaches of Val Bondasca on a broad track (a dirt road used by climbers) that eventually narrows to a footpath. The trail leading to Sasc Furä now crosses the Bondasca torrent by footbridge and begins a steep ascent to the Trubinasca glen. It's a demanding approach, but vegetation provides plenty of shade on a hot summer's day, and at last you emerge from woodland to a flood of light to find Capanna Sasc Furä gazing at mountains across the Bregaglia, while overhead soar Piz Badile, Cima Santa Anna, Punta Trubinasca, Piz Trubinasca and Piz dei Vanni. Between these two last-named lies the saddle of Passo della Trubinasca (2701m) by which Val Codera may be gained.

Our continuing route leads not over that pass, however, but initially by way of Colle Vial to the Sciora hut, giving as it does a close though foreshortened view of the great slab face of Piz Badile. Since it takes rather less than four hours to gain Capanna Sciora from Sasc Furä, it would be worth considering an extension of the walk eastwards across the Cacciabella ridge into Val Albigna. There are two passes, one on either side of the rock tower of Piz Eravédar (2934m). The southern Cacciabella Pass is preferred, and the route is indicated from the Sciora hut by large letters having been painted on a nearby rock. Waymarks and occasional cairns lead the way, but walkers are advised to avoid this route altogether if inclement weather is expected. On the eastern side of the pass the route edges north to cross below the alternative Cacciabella Pass, then over a wild region of rocks, snow and glacier-smooth slabs, before grass slopes take you down to the man-made Albigna lake. Capanna da l'Albigna sits above the eastern shore, and is reached in about eight hours from Sasc Furä.

Stage five involves a climb of about six hundred and forty metres above the hut in order to cross the Casnil Pass, followed by descent to the Forno glacier, on the opposite side of which stands the Forno hut among granite slabs on a green terrace overlooking the glacier. This is a four-hour crossing, and although it should be possible to walk down to Maloja the same day, that would leave no time to study the delights of Val Forno proper. The suggestion here, then, is to book in at the hut, and spend the rest of the day either contemplating the wild scenery from it, or scrambling up to the Sella del Forno behind it to gain a different perspective, including views into Italy. The following day involves an easy stroll down valley to Maloja, with a chance to loiter by the side of the ever-popular pine-fringed Lägh da Cavloc (Cavalocciosee) tarn on the way.

THE BREGAGLIA CIRCUIT - ROUTE SUMMARY

Day 1:   Maloja - Lunghin Pass - Septimer Pass - Casaccia

Day 2:   Casaccia - Val Maroz - Val da Cam - Pass da Cam - Soglio

Day 3:   Soglio - Promontogno - Capanna Sasc Furä

Day 4:   Capanna Sasc Furä - Colle Vial - Capanna Sciora - Cacciabella Pass - Capanna da l'Albigna

Day 5:   Capanna da l'Albigna - Casnil Pass - Capanna del Forno

Day 6:   Capanna del Forno - Maloja

＊   ＊   ＊

The Italian Bregaglia

The general topography of the southern valleys was briefly described earlier in this chapter, but without any detail or suggestion of what the walker may hope to achieve there. In truth there is much that the enterprising walker can do, but the very best will be reserved for those who are fit and experienced in wild mountain travel. Some of the trails, and much of the terrain, are such that newcomers to the Alpine scale of things could so easily become overwhelmed.

How to reach these southern valleys? Well, it depends upon your mode of transport and direction of approach. The motorist coming from Switzerland may choose to drive from the Engadine over the Bernina Pass, thereby having a glimpse of the main snowpeaks of the Bernina Alps on the way, then down through the delightful Val Poschiavo to Tirano in Valtellina. If the plan is to first visit Val Malenco, then one drives west to Sondrio which sits at the southern outlet of that glen. If however, Val Masino and its tributary glens are your priority, continue beyond Sondrio to Masino village. The same destination may also be reached by way of the Maloja Pass, which gives an opportunity to enjoy the Swiss Bregaglia first. This road continues through Chiavenna, now heading south towards Lago di Como. Before reaching that lake, however, the smaller Lago di Mezzola is met, at the northern end of which access (on foot only) is gained into Val Codera. Continuing down towards Lago di Como an alternative road cuts east along the Valtellina, and soon reaches Masino.

By public transport the Rhaetian Railway travels from Chur to Tirano by way of the Bernina Pass and Val Poschiavo - a wonderful journey that is one of the most romantic in the Alps. From Tirano an Italian train can then be taken west to Sondrio (for Val Malenco) or Ardenno (for Val Masino). Alternatively, take a train from Milan.

These approaches have plenty to commend them, but better by far is it to come on foot by way of some lonely pass, from which one swings down into sun-warmed Italy with the hazy blue of an insect-seething glen teasing you into its embrace. There are several such passes to consider, and we'll study these in order, travelling from west to east. The first then, is Passo della Trubinasca (2701m) above the Sasc Furä hut in Val Bondasca. This gives direct access into the head of Val Codera, and via Passo Porcellizzo (2862m) to the Gianetti hut perched high in the Porcellizzo glen on the south side of Piz Badile. Porcellizzo is a tributary of Valle dei Bagni, which is also reached by three alternative crossings from Val Codera, namely those of Passo del Barbacan (2620m), Passo dell'Oro (2574m) and the easier Passo Ligoncio (2557m). On the Bagni side of these last two will be found Rifugio Omio, with a splendid outlook along Valle dei Bagni and its crowding mountains.

The next crossing point for our walker coming from Switzerland into Italy must be Passo di Bondo (3169m) at the head of the Bondasca glacier. Since this glacier is steep and heavily crevassed, the Bondo Pass will only be tempting to those of the mountain fraternity who are equipped for such terrain and experienced in glacier travel, although in a normal summer a path of sorts will have been trodden in the snow on the Swiss side. Be that as it may, all necessary precautions must be taken. Perhaps, as Walker hinted, you might find some well-disposed party of climbers at the Sciora hut who would be willing to shepherd you in safety to the frontier ridge. "The pass is much frequented and is used by smugglers," said Walker in 1951. "On the Italian side you drop down over rocks and snow-slopes and keep going westward and make for the north-east corner of Valle Porcellizzo, where you strike the path coming from the Badile hut [Rifugio Gianetti] and follow that path down to Masino."

There's only one possible crossing point between Val Albigna and Valle di Mello, and this is Passo di Zocca (2749m) which leads directly to the Allievi hut. Walker called it "a very fine route and quite easy." The West Col guidebook says it is the easiest way across the frontier ridge between these two glens, but I have no personal experience of it. Beyond this our next possibility is the Sella del Forno which, as we have already seen, takes the trekker from Val Forno to the head of Val Malenco, while the nearby Muretto Pass (Passo del Muretto; 2562m) similarly leads to Val Malenco from Val Muretto, an offshoot of Val Forno. Of all these passes the Muretto is the easiest. An old trading route that has been in use since at least the fourteenth century, it will take about eight hours or so to walk via this pass from Maloja to Chiesa, enjoying on the way a wonderful view of Monte Disgrazia.

Having successfully gained these southern valleys we must now look at their prospects for walkers, and move back to the western end of the district where we begin with the delightful Val Codera, described by Klucker as "the wild, romantic rock-valley." Wild and rocky though it may be, it is also beautifully forested lower down, and with a number of steep tributary glens draining into it. As we have seen, Val Codera rises on the south side of the Trubinasca cirque and flows roughly south-westward in a sinuous course down to Lago di Mezzola. There is no road into this glen, but a steep path climbs from Novate Mezzola, passes through the hamlets of Codera and Bresciadega and continues to Rifugio Luigi Brasca, situated at the wooded entrance to the tributary glen of Spassato and reached in three and a half to four hours from the lakeside village. From this hut several possibilities arise, each of which entails the crossing of a pass. Continuing to the head of the glen is the trail to the Trubinasca, while another breaks away from that to traverse the frontier ridge at Bocchetta della Tegliola (2490m) from where a descent leads to Castasegna or to Bondo. Another track rises alongside the Spassato stream with imposing cascades in view and, passing the Valli bivouac hut, continues to Passo Ligoncio (2557m) overlooking Valle dei Bagni. North-east of this pass Pizzi dell'Oro throws out three ridges, on the far side of which is Passo dell'Oro, also gained from the Luigi Brasca hut. It would be possible, then, to make a circuit of Pizzi dell'Oro by descending from the Ligoncio Pass to Rifugio Omio, then return to Val Codera by way of the Oro Pass.

The main trail through the glen, however, is the classic Sentiero Roma, a truly challenging walk that begins in Novate Mezzola, rises through Val Codera and makes a long traverse of the Italian flanks of the Bregaglia mountains where waymarking is not always clear, and in places the route is safeguarded with cables and all the metalwork of a full-blown *via ferrata*. Leaving Rifugio Luigi Brasca the trail climbs eastward to cross Passo del Barbacan, situated just below Cima del Barbacan (2588m), then makes a cautious traverse of steep slopes above the Porcellizza glen to reach the Gianetti hut.

Valle Porcellizza is a deep cauldron scooped out of the mountains by a long-departed glacier. At its head a great horseshoe ridge is topped by Piz Badile, Piz Cengalo, the twin points of Pizzi Gemelli (insignificant when seen from the south) and Cima della Bondasca. The southern extension of this ridge is that which divides the Porcellizza and Ferro glens, and which Douglas Freshfield described as "a long comb, whose teeth had been tortured by time and weather into all sorts of quaint shapes; one rock bent over like a crooked finger, in another place a window was pierced through the crest." The Porcellizza glen sweeps down into Valle dei Bagni, at whose head will be found the Bagni del Masino "under its horse-shoe of granite precipices." A road twists up to the spa buildings from San Martino, and is accessible by bus in high summer. San Martino (923m) is the main centre for visitors to both Valle dei Bagni and Valle di Mello, being strategically placed between the two, both of which now have modest campsites. A useful bus service links these upper glens with the railway station at Ardenno in Valtellina. San Martino offers a selection of hotels and shops.

In recent years the road into Valle di Mello has been extended a little, thus making it more accessible to tourists. However, not even the road can properly destroy the true splendour of this glen, with its soaring granite slabs, its sparkling river with occasional deep clear pools, the boulder-strewn grass and the trifling glaciers of Monte Disgrazia balanced high above. Rock climbing really took off here in the late 'seventies, and with its numerous firm, sun-warmed slabs has become something of a Mecca. Because of the steepness of its walls practically all walks out of the bed of the glen demand considerable effort and a certain amount of caution. Those that scale the south-facing wall (and there are several) can be uncomfortably warm in the middle of summer, and each one links with the high traverse path of the Sentiero Roma.

This waymarked trail was last seen arriving at Rifugio Gianetti, from where it continues round the head of the Porcellizza cauldron remaining above the two thousand metre contour as it crosses a series of moraines, snow patches and a succession of ridge spurs heading east. The first of these ridges is crossed at Passo Camerozzo (2765m), followed by a two hundred metre descent to the south-east where the traverse then continues on the upper slopes of Valle del Ferro. The Molteni/Valsecchi bivouac hut is passed, then Passo Qualido and Passo d'Averta crossed in quick succession. The way now veers north-east below the Zocca-Castello frontier ridge and comes to Rifugio Allievi at the head of the Zocca corrie, about six hours or so after setting out from the Gianetti hut.

Leaving Rifugio Allievi the Sentiero Roma continues eastward to the great headwall of Valle di Mello that carries the high ridge linking the Bregaglia frontier crest to the graceful block of Monte Disgrazia. There are some tricky sections on this stage, and passing round the glen's headwall there's a possibility of stonefall too. In that headwall Passo di Mello (2992m) offers a traditional way over to Val Malenco. First crossed in 1865 by a large party which included Freshfield, Tuckett and H.E. Buxton, a heavily crevassed glacier has to be negotiated on the far side. This route long ago lost favour and as a consequence it is rarely used today. The Sentiero Roma route is not tempted by this either, and remains west of Disgrazia crossing the south-west ridge extending from Monte Pioda at the Bocchetta Roma (2850m). This ridge forms the dividing wall between Valle di Mello and the glen of Preda Rossa which flows into Valle di Sasso Bisolo. Two hundred metres below the Bocchetta, and just above the lateral moraine of the Preda Rossa glacier, will be found Rifugio Cesare Ponti in which the final night of the Roma traverse is to be spent, the following day needing only a downhill walk through green valleys to gain Val Masino.

SENTIERO ROMA - ROUTE SUMMARY

Day 1:   Novate Mezzola - Codera - Rifugio Luigi Brasca

Day 2:   Rifugio Luigi Brasca - Passo del Barbacan - Rifugio Gianetti

Day 3:   Rifugio Gianetti - Passo Camerozzo - Passo Qualido - Passo d'Averta - Rifugio Allievi

Day 4:   Rifugio Allievi - Passo Val Torrone - Bocchetta Roma - Rifugio Ponti

Day 5:   Rifugio Ponti - Cataeggio

Having outlined the ultimate walking experience on the south side of the Bregaglia Alps, it is now time to work our way round Monte Disgrazia (3678m) in order to look at Val Malenco, to put ourselves in a position from which later to explore the Bernina massif, and also to view this grand Mountain of Ill Omen from a variety of angles for it is, quite simply, one of the most picturesque in the Italian Alps.

Colonel E.L. Strutt, one-time president of the Alpine Club and censorious editor of its journal, was something of an expert on the Bregaglia, for which he edited the original English guidebook published in the Conway and Coolidge series in 1910. Of Monte Disgrazia he wrote: "The name, as well as the euphamistic appellation of Pizzo Bello, seem to point to some disastrous mountain slip in days gone by...which the Austrian map surveyors translated into polite Italian as Monte della Disgrazia." Such a disaster, he surmised, must have occurred on the Val Masino side, for "...in the Malenco valley the peak bears the special name of Pizzo Bello, because of its splendid appearance from that direction."

In order to gain the Malenco side and to see this splendid appearance for ourselves, we are faced with prospects of a long and strenuous, but by no means uninteresting, cross-country walk. This begins in Valle di Sasso Bisolo through which we made our descent from the Ponti hut to Cataeggio at the conclusion of the Sentiero Roma. This time, instead of descending that glen, we must walk back up it. Four kilometres from Cataeggio the road to Preda Rossa has been cut by a massive rockfall, returning the glen to some of its former primitive sparkle. This is what Claud Schuster had to say about it in 1911, in that most enjoyable of his books, *Peaks and Pleasant Pastures*:

> "I remember no more beautiful hut walk. There is no haymaking in the Upper Alps here, and the beasts were still higher up among the stones, so that, late in August as it was, the meadows were still dressed in green and gold. I spare you descriptions of the lonely loveliness both of the woods and the green open space which ought to be lake and is not, just before the last great step of the valley. The Disgrazia alone would make the walk memorable, and, lying by the hut, turning sometimes to the glowing rocks of the Corno Bruciato, and sometimes to the deep blue and gleaming silver of the Lombard Alps, I passed afternoon and evening, in a lull of every faculty but that of vision."

At the rock-strewn Preda Rosso basin the Sasso Bisolo glen is sub-divided by a spur jutting south-west from Corni Bruciati (3114m). The left branch is that which leads to the Ponti hut and the Preda Rossa glacier, while the right-hand glen rises to another short ridge, this time pushed south-south-east from Corni Bruciati. A trail eases into this glen, passes along the north bank of a small tarn, then climbs to Passo di Scermendone (2595m) from which, according to Walker, a great view is obtained. Descent is then made to the head of Valle di Postalesio, followed by a short climb to the neighbouring Passo Caldenno (2517m), a saddle in the south-east ridge of Corni Bruciati, almost due south of Monte Disgrazia's crown, and which provides access to Val Torregio. A long descent follows, first down to the Torreggio stream, then across this heading roughly north-east over hillsides rippling across the lower flanks of Monte Disgrazia to the hamlet of Lago set in a hollow of the hills. A trail continues from there down to Chiesa, the main village of Val Malenco.

Chiesa is situated on the true right bank of the Mallero river under the east flank of Monte della Disgrazia, and to the south of the Bernina massif. As a resort it has some interesting excursions in the neighbourhood, one of the best of which (Lago Palü and the neighbouring Monte Motta) is now adorned with a cableway. During one of his lengthy wanderings through the Alps that energetic Victorian, Francis

Fox Tuckett, topped the modest Passo Campolungo (2167m) between the lake and Monte Motta and entered in his diary: "Such a view burst upon us as amply rewarded us for all our toil. Right in front, but separated from us by the width of the Val Malenco, rose the noble form of the Disgrazia." It is a view that many others can now appreciate without the necessary commitment of walking, thanks to that cableway.

Just below the village both the valley and its road forks. The east branch winds up to a pair of dammed lakes below Sasso Moro, while the main, northern extent of Val Malenco leads to Chiareggio, a charming little village with limited accommodation from which Passo del Muretto is easily gained. Before Chiareggio, however, a trail climbs north into the little Forasco glen, to Alpe Fora and Rifugio Longoni (2450m). On the way to it once again views south are dominated by the ice-bound north face of Monte Disgrazia.

The standard route to the Muretto Pass is via Chiareggio, but walkers who have been tempted to spend a night in the Longoni hut, can save themselves descending all the way to that village by dropping to Alpe Fora, then taking a belvedere trail round to Alpe dell'Oro, and climbing to the pass from there. At Passo del Muretto spare a thought for those who formerly crossed with mules heavily laden, either with stone roofing slabs (*piode*), or with casks of wine. Once over the pass you will have returned to Switzerland and a long descent then follows, usually over old snow to begin with, then down through the stony Muretto glen to the lower reaches of Val Forno which spills out by Maloja, thus closing once again the round of the Bregaglia Alps.

✳   ✳   ✳

THE BERNINA MASSIF

It is now time to concentrate our attention on that block of snow and ice mountains at the heart of the district, to explore the valleys that surround it and to look at ways over intervening ridges in order to create a walking circuit that will complement those multi-day routes described above for the Bregaglia. The scenery here will be very different to that enjoyed west of the Muretto Pass. It is no more beautiful nor less lovely, but very different.

At the centre of this block stands Piz Bernina, the borders of Switzerland and Italy passing over its summit and continuing along a crest of ice and snow to both east and west. South of this crest a series of glacial basins ends in a terrace of cliffs down which waterfalls spray as they drain those icefields into Val Malenco. But on the northern side cascading glaciers, much riven with crevasses, pour down towards Val Bernina through the parallel glens of Roseg and Morteratsch, the two separated by a long dividing ridge projecting north from Piz Bernina itself. "No part of the frontier Alps offers a more striking illustration of the contrast between the snowy beauties of the northern slopes and the great bare walls that extend along the south side of the watershed," commented R.L.G. Irving.

East of Piz Bernina the watershed crest is carried over wave upon wave of corniced splendour to Piz Palü and Piz Cambrena. From Cambrena a rather more

Above:
Piz Bernina and Piz Morterasch from Diavolezza (Ch 9)

Left:
Soglio and the Bregaglia peaks (Ch 9)

The Crozzon di Brenta (Ch 10)

Valle di Mello (Ch 10)

bare and rocky ridge slopes down to the Bernina Pass which effectively divides the austere Val Bernina from the luxuriant vitality of the deep Val Poschiavo, a narrow finger of Switzerland projecting into Italy. So different are these two valleys in altitude, climate, scenery, architecture and cultural allegiance, that to travel from one to the other is to experience some of the diversity which makes the Bernina Alps so special.

West of Piz Bernina the frontier ridge stutters its way over the headwall of Val Roseg, curving south-west across the top of Val Fex and Val Fedoz, then slanting north-west to the Muretto Pass and the Bregaglia mountains. Val Fex and Val Fedoz are intimate little glens that run parallel to one another and drain gently down to the Upper Engadine, and it is in the Engadine that we will begin our survey.

Between Maloja at the head of the valley and the confluence with Val Bernina below St Moritz, the Engadine boasts four large lakes and a mean altitude of around 1800 metres. There are no major snow mountains in view from the bed of the valley, although the ski playground of Piz Corvatsch wears a snow crown most of the summer. It's a valley with numerous walking possibilities ranging from easy lakeside strolls to mid-mountain belvederes, and from energetic pass crossings to the ascent of several non-technical peaks that make fine viewpoints from which to study the whole district. Accommodation is mostly on the expensive side, although there are youth hostels in Maloja, St Moritz and Pontresina (in nearby Val Bernina), and a number of campsites too. The public transport system is first-rate, with a branch of the Rhaetian Railway terminating in St Moritz. One line goes along Val Bernina and spirals down to Val Poschiavo, while another travels through the valley to the Lower Engadine resort of Scuol. The Postbus, of course, travels just about everywhere served by road, and is both frequent and punctual. The Engadine, then, has plenty going for it. If there is a down-side, that will be in the over-abundance of ski machinery lacing the hillsides (mostly above St Moritz) and the reputation (not entirely undeserved) which St Moritz has gained in its appeal to the ultra-rich, royal and famous. Mountain writers from Leslie Stephen to R.L.G. Irving and Hubert Walker poured scorn on the wealthy crowds who gather there. But these should not worry our visitor who has his eyes to the hills. The Upper Engadine no less than Val Bregaglia has scenic grandeur aplenty, and it is our intention here to reveal the best on offer.

Since we came to the Engadine from the Bregaglia Alps at Maloja we may assume this is where we will make our base for a few days. Not only does the village stand at the head of the Upper Engadine, but it also commands the depths of Val Bregaglia into which the road pass wriggles its tortuous way to the south-west. It will be seen, then, that Maloja has the best of both worlds. Should the weather be bad in the Engadine, there's a chance that better conditions will prevail down in the Bregaglia, and vice-versa.

South of Maloja there is the perennial enticement of Val Forno and the Muretto Pass leading into Val Malenco, but we have already wandered there. On the north side we've also made a partial loop of Piz Lunghin on our long Bregaglia circuit, but there's also a gentle but rewarding day which could be spent visiting the little alps of Blaunca and Grevasalvas, both of which lie in a grassy trough divorced from sight and sound of the valley road, and with lovely views across the Engadine to its southern wall of mountains. A trail continues from Grevasalvas along the north flank of the valley to St Moritz, and is waymarked as the *Via Engiadina*. If such a walk were tackled at the start of a holiday some of the Engadine's appeal would immediately become apparent.

On the south side of the valley a short distance above Maloja, Piz da la Margna (3159m) oversees much of both the Engadine and Bregaglia and, from a position just north of the frontier ridge, surveys an extensive region of peak, valley and hinted glen, with Monte della Disgrazia seen to good effect to the south, and Piz Bernina and its snowy satellites demanding attention from the east. The ascent is neither technically difficult nor unduly arduous when tackled from Val Fedoz, but early in the season an ice axe will be required. Allow about four hours from Maloja, with another two or so for the descent.

Val Fedoz cuts back into the mountains behind the charming little hamlet of Isola huddled on the bank of the Silsersee (Lej da Segl in Romansch). Fedoz is a rough, raw little glen with stony pastures, cliffs and a small glacier hanging at its head, which makes a contrast to the neat meadows and sunny aspect of its 'twin' Val Fex. Val Fex is a welcoming little glen that all who are based for a few days in the Upper Engadine should make it their business to visit. Sils Maria is the place to aim for first, and this is reached in a little over an hour and a half from Maloja by a level lakeside path. Immediately behind the village a trail enters a small gorge and gains height along a covered walkway that emerges to pastures in the mouth of Val Fex among the farms and haybarns of Platta. An easy, undemanding, but extremely pleasant walk now takes you towards the head of the valley between lush pastures in which the guide, Christian Klucker, spent his early childhood. The Bernina region is, of course, Klucker country, as is the Bregaglia. But Val Fex was his home, and it is in the trim little churchyard at Fex Crasta that he is buried.

Midway along the glen the hamlet of Curtins marks a break-off point for walkers planning to take a high route to Marmorè, from where a fine belvedere trail skirts along the mid-height hillside below Piz Corvatsch to Surlej and St Moritz. Just beyond Curtins the track reaches a hotel, and beyond that the way continues to Plaun Vadret, the 'plain of the glaciers' where marmots scamper and wild flowers bloom in the spring. This is where the young Klucker enjoyed what he called "The free life in God's lovely world of Nature, amongst the beautiful flowering pastures of the Fextal..."

At the southern end of Val Fex the shrinking Vadret da Fex (*vadret* is Romansch for glacier) forms a ramp leading to the Fuorcla dal Chapütsch (Chapütsch Pass; 2929m), while another, higher, pass is that of the Tremoggia (3014m). Both these passes are old hunters' ways over the mountains to Chiareggio in Val Malenco. The glacier is crevassed and, below the Chapütsch Pass, the bergschrund is sometimes a little tricky, but to adepts with the necessary safety equipment neither route should present undue difficulties, and once again Monte della Disgrazia looks most impressive from the ridge.

Moving down valley a little, beyond the Silsersee to Silvaplanasee (Lej da Silvaplauna) with Silvaplana at its northern end and a large, well-equipped campsite on the very lakeside, we approach the main ski slopes of the Engadine. Here the valley's north wall is strung about with cableways, while on the south side a cable-car rises in two stages from Surlej to Piz Corvatsch for some of the most exciting downhill skiing in the whole valley. From the upper slopes of Corvatsch one gazes east across the sudden depths of Val Roseg to the soaring walls of Piz Bernina and Piz Roseg, caked as they are with encrustations of hanging glacier. Beyond these stand Monte della Disgrazia and the Bregaglia mountains, but to the north Piz Kesch and the Albula Alps also demand their share of attention. It is a glorious view that I once experienced in the light of a full moon from my tent pitched at over three thousand metres one crisp February night. Much of that night was spent viewing in solitude a flotilla of soft blue shadows easing across the face of those mountains as the moon drifted through the heavens, watched stars that appeared to settle on peaks far away and the outline of distant ridges rimmed with silver lunar beams. But the sunrise that I awaited did not happen next morning, for a blizzard came from nowhere in the early hours and made for an epic descent.

That view, or one very similar to it, of Bernina, Roseg and assorted neighbours across the depths of Val Roseg, may be enjoyed from a slightly lower elevation at the Fuorcla Surlej (2755m), an easy saddle in the ridge between Piz Corvatsch and the domed mass of Il Rosatsch. The crossing of Fuorcla Surlej is one of the recommended walks of the Upper Engadine, and one that will be adopted later on our circuit of the Bernina massif. The middle station of the Surlej-Corvatsch cableway provides a short-cut for walkers, but the full route from the valley, beginning either at Surlej or St Moritz, is worth the extra effort involved. Indeed, one of my favourite excursions here leads from Sils Maria by way of Val Fex, the spur of Marmorè, and a fine belvedere trail along the hillside heading north-east to Lej da la Fuorcla and the pass above it. At the pass there's a small pool which catches clear reflections on a still summer's day, and a restaurant close by with dormitory accommodation that provides an opportunity to capture moonlight and sunrise views without resorting to the spartan protection of a snowbound tent. On the east side of Fuorcla Surlej descent is made into Val Roseg with wonderful views each step of the way, followed by a gentle valley stroll to Pontresina.

Before going round to Pontresina and into Val Roseg mention should be made of possible ascent of one of the Rosatsch summits in the dividing wall between Val Roseg and the Upper Engadine above St Moritz. Any fit mountain walker should be able to romp up this sprawling mass without difficulty, by a footpath which begins behind the French church in St Moritz-Bad and is signposted, among other destinations, to Hahnensee, a hillside tarn and restaurant at 2153 metres with lovely views onto the Engadine lakes. Do not follow the Hahnensee path, however, but climb through the forest on a zig-zag trail which has several options. Points to make for are Piz da l'Ova Cotschna, Piz Mezdi, or Piz Rosatsch itself which, at 3134 metres, is the highest summit of the little massif. The Ova Cotschna peaklet is the easiest to gain, and from it the scenic delights of the Upper Engadine are well displayed. Better still are the higher viewpoints of Mezdi and Rosatsch, for other mountains and glens then inhabit your field of vision. Up there one can wander about almost anywhere.

Engadine forests are haunted by red and roe deer, and cautious early morning walks in summer will invariably reward with close sightings. The little Lej da Staz tarn and nearby forests to the east of St Moritz are especially favoured, while chamois can be seen on the more open slopes of Rosatsch.

A pleasant walk leads from St Moritz to Pontresina by way of Lej da Staz and suggests an easy route into Val Bernina. Like St Moritz Pontresina is also a fashionable resort that attracts the wealthy and famous, which tends to inflate prices somewhat, but as mentioned earlier, there is a youth hostel near the railway station where accommodation prices are more affordable. With its back to mountains Pontresina gazes south into Val Roseg. With this alone it would be worth coming here, but the resort has other points of recommendation too. Among them the open suntrap terrace of Muottas Muragl, and the well-known Piz Languard whose extensive summit view was deemed worthy of a pull-out panoramic illustration in Baedeker.

Muottas Muragl may be reached by funicular from Punt Muragl on the Pontresina to Samedan road. This is a popular belvedere in a privileged position at 2453 metres, with an unbroken view directly along the lake region of the Upper Engadine, a view that includes the topmost slabs of Piz Badile and Cengalo about thirty-five kilometres away to the south-west. Two or three scenic walks could be made from here. One favourite crosses a low ridge above Alp Muragl to the little tarn of Lej Muragl, above which Fuorcla Muragl leads into the Val Prüna glen for a longish cross-country walk through Val Chamuera, eventually rejoining the Engadine near La Punt. Another route cuts back from Lej Muragl and climbs over the ridge at a higher point to find the Chamanna Segantini set in a most idyllic position with an exquisite panorama spread out for inspection. It was here in September 1899 that the painter, Giovanni Segantini, spent the last days of his life. He is buried in Maloja, but a museum devoted to his life's work will be found in St Moritz. From the Segantini hut a steep descent leads to Pontresina, while an alternative path eases round to Alp Languard, and makes the final descent from there.

Piz Languard (3262m) must be one of the easiest 3000 metre peaks to ascend in all the Alps. The top may be gained with hands thrust deep in your pockets, for a clear footpath leads all the way from Pontresina to the summit. In summer the small, privately-owned Georgy hut is often full night after night, while during the day a steady stream of walkers calls there for refreshment on the way to or from the top.

So popular has Piz Languard been for generations, that its summit view is sometimes decried in hackneyed terms. That thousands of mountain lovers have laboured their way to the hut, situated just eighty-six metres below the stony crown, and from there made the pilgrimage to the summit in order to be uplifted by the cavalcade of sunset or sunrise spilling over a scene of great beauty, should be a cause for rejoicing. It matters not one jot to the quality of the scenery whether just two or ten thousand feet have stood on that summit over the years, for the view remains magnificent. Across Val Bernina to the south the crystal heart of the range is on show, "spread in white-washed perfection" is how Hamish Brown once described it in a magazine article. It is, of course, an immense panorama dominated by the graceful symmetry of Piz Palü, by the creamy sea of peaks and peaklets that lead to the jutting Piz Bernina (Biancograt to the fore) and the long moraine-striped trunk of the Morteratsch glacier pushing toward the valley at your feet. The snowless mass of Il Rosatsch makes a stark contrast to the white-washed perfection of the Bernina group, yet far-off, far, far-off the eager eye of the Alpine connoisseur may pick out the gleaming snows of the Mischabel peaks above the Saastal, and Monte Rosa too just to the left of them. Then in other directions Italian and Austrian summits jostle for attention and challenge one's skills of identification.

The stony crown of Piz Languard is yet another place where I've pitched my tent and spent the night in solitude. Sunset was on that autumnal occasion full of expected magic, the topmost snows of Piz Palü, Bellavista and Bernina held the last pink stain long after valleys had drawn darkness to them and the gold of late-September larches had dimmed to black velvet. Night was followed by the dazzle of sunrise; a memorable privilege. Instead of descending the normal route I chose the north-west ridge and soon heard the wooden sound of ibex horns clashing in battle. Slipping in shadow down the rocks until I was below these stocky creatures, I then worked my way slowly towards them, and within a few minutes found myself surrounded by a dozen or more ibex, the huge sickle-shaped horns now locked in a wrestling bout to determine which male would dominate the year's rut. At last I was only a couple of paces from them, the musty smell heavy in my nostrils, the sound of their sneezing and grunting disturbed the morning's peace, and dim bulging eyes met mine. Suddenly the sun flashed across the ridge and shone in the lens of my camera. The mountainside was cleared in a matter of seconds.

Pontresina's main attraction is its close proximity to the Bernina group. Climbing and touring courses run by the local mountain guides have gained a reputation throughout Switzerland, but one has no need to resort to glacier and ice slope, rock face or corniced ridge to enjoy the splendour of the Bernina Alps. One glance along Val Roseg will underline that fact. The valley extends in a south-south-westerly direction opposite Pontresina, and cuts into the western core of the mountains. Leading from forest to rough pasture, and from rough pasture to morainic desolation and the tumultuous frozen cascade of glacier upon glacier, soaring mountain peak and a gentle crescent of snow peaks blocking its head, the valley is one of the most beautiful in the whole district. A dirt road delves into it from the approach to Pontresina station, and goes as far as Hotel-Restaurant Roseg on the edge of the stony plain; a distance of about six kilometres. Fortunately this dirt road is not open to general traffic, only hotel delivery vehicles may use it, and the horse-drawn carriages that ferry those hotel guests who choose not to walk, and in winter horse-drawn sleighs, their bells jingling in the crisp air.

Behind the hotel rises a trail that climbs to Fuorcla Surlej and continues from there down to the Engadine. Another delves further upvalley to Alp Ota, from which a better view is obtained across the glen to where the Tschierva glacier tumbles in a huge complex of serac and crevasse between Piz Morteratsch and Piz Bernina, with Piz Scerscen and Piz Roseg rising from that wall of ice. Continue deeper into the glen and you'll reach the Coaz hut, an attractive sixteen-sided building perched on the Plattas rock overlooking the Roseg glacier. A night spent there will be a night to remember should the sky be busy with stars or a full moon casting its glow on the chaos of ice outside.

A party with modest ability and the necessary equipment to afford themselves protection, might do well to consider an interesting training excursion from the

Coaz hut up to the snow dome of Il Chapütschin (3386m), the so-called 'monk's cowl' which is reached in less than two hours. From there it is feasible to descend by way of the Fuorcla da Chapütschin into Val Fex, and then wander down to the Engadine at Sils Maria.

On the east side of Val Roseg, on the moraine bank of the Tschierva glacier commanding an excellent panorama of high peaks and tumbling icefalls, stands the Tschierva hut. Larger than the Coaz, it's a very popular refuge on account of the array of fine climbs accessible from it. One of the most modest, in terms of difficulty rather than visual rewards, is that of Piz Morteratsch (3751m), highest summit on the ridge north of Bernina which divides the Roseg and Morteratsch valleys. The summit is reached in less than four hours by way of the Fuorcla dal Boval, a glacier pass used by climbers moving between the Tschierva and Boval huts. From the summit yet more wonderful mountain views are on display, and there "...one gets an unusually fine and instructive picture of the mountain world of the Upper Engadine," wrote Klucker in his autobiography.

Running parallel to Val Roseg on the east side of the Morteratsch-Chalchagn ridge is Val Morteratsch, a glen dominated by the fast-shrinking Morteratsch glacier which flows from a headwall *firn* basin formed by the converging ridges of Piz Bernina, Crast' Agüzza, Piz Argient, Piz Zupò and the lovely virginal crest of Bellavista. "The snows of Bernina look almost Andean in their creamy depth, and flow down in glaciers which are extravagantly broken." (Hamish Brown) Not so very long ago the Morteratsch glacier reached almost to the bed of Val Bernina which cuts across its northern end. But a series of marker poles placed a few years ago along the moraines shows quite clearly just how serious is the recession of Alpine icefields, and the shrinking of this particular glacier is one of the most obvious and alarming in all Switzerland. On its left bank stands the Boval hut, the path to it being exceedingly popular with day visitors as well as climbers basing themselves there prior to making a wide range of ascents. Despite the summer crowds it would be worth following the trail to the hut in order to enjoy the spectacular arc of snow mountains that rises ahead, and to sit outside with a cold drink and with binoculars trained upvalley watch ropes of mountaineers working their way across the glistening snows.

Across the glacier to the east, beyond the lump of Munt Pers, a cable-car lifts visitors to Berghaus Diavolezza, a beautifully-situated restaurant that also has dormitory accommodation for climbers and walkers. In winter the restaurant is constantly busy with skiers, in summer with tourists squinting into the glare of sun on glacier. And those who spend a night there may enjoy a superb sunrise from the comfort of the dining room whose huge plate glass windows look onto a truly magical scene, described in an early Baedeker as "...a view of surpassing grandeur, especially in the rosy tints of dawn, of the near Bernina group."

One need not pander to the ease of mechanical uplift to reach Diavolezza, for in summer there's usually a well-trodden pathway across the glacier leading from the Boval hut by way of the rognon of Isla Persa, though normal safety precautions should be taken as there are crevasses to avoid. Diavolezza provides a stunning close view of Piz Palü which rises as a buttressed wall just to the south, as well as to the Piz Bernina-Piz Morteratsch complex to the south-west. The ascent of Piz

Palü is not unduly difficult from here for those with glacier experience and equipment, but the summit ridge affords one of the finest panoramas hereabouts; a contrast of snow wave and rock face, of glacial wonderland and a multitude of green distant pastures. And once again Monte della Disgrazia looms across Val Malenco.

Below Diavolezza Val Bernina appears rather drab and forlorn as you work your way towards the Bernina Pass (2304m), another major watershed whose draining rivers eventually feed into the Black Sea on the one hand, and the Mediterranean on the other. Along here the railway keeps close company with the line of the road, the two only going their separate ways at the pass itself where Lago Bianco invariably carries drifts of ice into early summer. It's a bleak, often windswept spot, and having ploughed my way to it one Easter in deep drifts of snow, I stood at the southern end of the lake in arctic chill gazing down to the springtime glories of Val Poschiavo some thirteen hundred metres below. Down there I could make out haloes of blossom in the trees, saw the Mediterranean blue of the lake at Le Prese and green, lush meadows which I knew would be starred with flowers. Yet I stood thigh-deep in snow and shivered in the wind while a more benevolent season taunted from below. R.L.G. Irving wrote about an experience he once had at the Bernina Hospice nearby which, he noted "must be difficult of access in some winters, judging by the depths of snow recorded on the wall, which reach well up among the first floor windows." He went on: "...there was unmistakable evidence to more senses than one that the hospice sheltered animals as well as men. The first night my party stayed there, thunder, lightning, wind and snow gave us a boisterous welcome. Several windows were blown in and though the heads of the beds in which my sons were sleeping were at the greatest possible distance from where the window had been, the snow blew straight upon their faces."

Of the two non-walking ways down to Val Poschiavo, that of the railway is infinately more enjoyable and scenically rewarding than the route taken by the road, although the road, it must be said, provides access to the lovely glen of Val da Camp that rises to a collection of tarns below Passo di Val Viola. That pass leads over the frontier ridge on the eastern side of Val Poschiavo and, by way of Val Viola, eventually reaches Bormio at the foot of the Stelvio Pass, on the edge of the Ortler Alps. Val da Camp is a delightful place from which to study at a distance the east flank of Piz Palü. Another superb viewpoint nearby is Lago del Teo, reached by a path from the mouth of Val da Camp, while the walker's trail from the Bernina Pass down to Val Poschiavo leads via Alp Grüm immediately below the Palü glacier. Continuing down into Val Poschiavo one way descends through the Cavagliasco gorge, while an alternative trail skirts the hillside to Alp Varuna before dropping to the valley.

As its name suggests Val Poschiavo, like Val Bregaglia, is Italian in all but political allegiance. Tall, slender campaniles signal from afar the village churches, and the sweet meadows, heated by the bright sun of the south, seethe with insects. Only the distant snows of Piz Palü remind you of the Alpine world left behind. Gentle valley walks and hillside trails that pass through mid-height pastures offer modest excursions that charm the senses. Below Lago di Poschiavo the valley floods out to Italy and the Valtellina which, crossing at right-angles, effectively closes the southern line of the Bernina Alps. Across that valley rise the Bergamesque Alps.

THE BERNINA CIRCUIT

A complete circuit of the Bernina massif will provide an outstanding series of mountain and valley views; a tour full of contrasts and heavy with reward. There is no 'official' route, and with a rich assortment of trails to choose from the circuit described below could be varied at will. In *Trekking in Europe* Giancarlo Corbellini suggests an eight-day tour he calls the Bernina Trail. Inevitably our route traces some of his circuit, but we divert from it in several notable places.

The first section has two distinct options. The first begins in Maloja and follows the Via Engiadina through the alp of Grevasalvas and continues along the north flank of the Upper Engadine to Silvaplana, before crossing the valley and climbing to Fuorcla Surlej where the night is spent in a *matratzenlager*. The second is a high route option which remains on the south side of the valley from Maloja, and goes via Sils Maria into Val Fex as far as Curtins, and there joins the high trail that works its way along the Engadine flank of Piz Corvatsch, then round to Fuorcla Surlej by way of Lej da la Fuorcla. The first option has the advantage of views across the lakes of Sils and Silvaplana, but is somewhat devalued by the sound of valley traffic once you've left Grevasalvas, while the high level route gives an opportunity to enjoy the delights of Val Fex and provides more elevated views on the belvedere trail between Marmorè and the point where you turn the north spur of Piz Murtel round to Lej da la Fuorcla. As for the choice of an overnight resting place, this could hardly be bettered, as far as situation is concerned, for the view is an uninterrupted one across Val Roseg to the glacier-draped slopes of Bernina, Scerscen and Piz Roseg.

That is the view for much of the descent next morning to the bed of Val Roseg. The trail is easy, and the scenic quality of the highest order. Just below the pass the trail forks, with the main route slanting left to hit the valley at Hotel-Restaurant Roseg, the right-hand path going via Alp Ota to the Coaz hut on the left bank of the Roseg glacier. I'm tempted to suggest taking the Coaz option, for it will increase your awareness of the glacier world and reward with a whole series of perspectives, not least being study of the Sella peaklets at the head of the valley. Below the hut you turn down valley and, after passing Hotel-Restaurant Roseg, exchange glacial moraine for larch woods and rough pastures on the way to Pontresina. Yet another option, for experienced trekkers who have passed their apprenticeship in Alpine scrambling, is to go to the Tschierva hut and next day cross the high ridge above it at the Boval Pass, descending then to the Boval hut. But this is not for our average mountain walker. He will go down to Val Bernina and bear right. If he has a tent he will camp in the valley near the mouth of Val Morteratsch, otherwise continue into that valley and aim to spend the night at the Boval hut.

The route of our third stage much depends on one's experience of glacier crossing, and of the Morteratsch glacier's condition. If it is good and dry (that is, free of snow-covering so that crevasses can be easily seen), and you're confident of tackling it, the way heads upvalley a short distance from the hut, then crosses the ice directly to the Isla Persa rognon, and from there strikes across the Pers glacier to Berghaus Diavolezza. Often in summer local guides lead parties across the ice between the Boval hut and Diavolezza. Enquire at the hut for up-to-date information. If, however, the ice is not in condition, or you're unhappy with the prospect of glacier crossing, return down valley to Morteratsch station, bear right and take another trail leading up to Diavolezza. Whichever route is taken to get there, continue from the Berghaus down to the south-east into the scoop of the Arlas glen and beyond a small tarn on a trail that brings you to the lakes at the Bernina Pass. Wander along the right-hand shore of Lago Bianco and either continue down to Alp Grüm where there are three hotels, or make a diversion to the right just below the lake, on the south-east slopes of Sassal Mason, to gain an alp with a restaurant at 2355 metres, which has a glorious outlook to the Palü glacier. From the restaurant the trail descends directly to Alp Grüm.

Below Alp Grüm our circular tour of Bernina involves crossing the ridge which carries the Italian frontier along the western wall of Val Poschiavo, in order to begin passage across the southern slopes of the massif. There are three walkers' passes to choose from, namely Canfinale, d'Ur and di Canciano. Passo Canfinale (2628m) is the most convenient. It is not at all difficult and may be reached from Alp Grüm by way of a trail that crosses the stream tumbling through the little Val Varuna, and soon after joins a road heading up the hillside from the northern outskirts of Poschiavo. Leave this at a left-hand hairpin to climb through the wooded Ursé glen to Alpe Canfinale, and from there gain the pass about four hours after setting out. The pass is more than sixteen hundred metres above Poschiavo town, and it is fortunate that we were able to join the route to it without the need to descend all the way to the valley from Alp Grüm. From the Canfinale Pass one gazes west across a very different landscape. To the north-west the upper slopes of Piz Zupò and Piz Argient at the left-hand end of the Bellavista ridge, are plastered with glaciers; Vedret di Fellaria and Altipiano di Fellaria. Below the western of these ice-sheets lies Alpe Gembrè, with the artificial Lago di Alpe Gera below that. Descend through meadows to the abandoned hutments, cross various streams that drain the glaciers (late in the day the water level in some of these can be high and cause difficulties), and climb by way of a winding path to Rifugio Bignami, which is owned by the Italian Alpine Club and is situated near Alpe di Fellaria.

Stage five is a short one of about three hours, but a good part of it ranges over a glacier in order to gain Rifugio Marinelli, which is set upon a rocky outcrop above the right bank of the Caspoggio glacier, at a midway point along the southern side of the Bernina massif. Walker made this his base for some fine glacier tours, which could be followed by those with the necessary time and experience. But our main aim here is to complete our loop of the mountains and will therefore remain true to that ideal. The shortest way between the Bignami and Marinelli huts crosses Bocchetta di Caspoggio (2983m), the final approach being on glacier ice. The Bocchetta is an opening between Cima di Fellaria and Cima di Caspoggio, and from it the way descends easily, veering to the right across the gently-sloping Caspoggio glacier, which should not create problems although caution must be taken. Once you mount the lateral moraine, join a good trail which rises up the rocks in zig-zags to find Rifugio Marinelli, busiest of all the huts on the Italian side of the massif. It has some two hundred beds, is owned by the Italian Alpine Club, and with a guardian in summer residence who provides meals.

The penultimate stage crosses a rough patch of mountainscape in order to locate Rifugio Longoni. Good visibility is essential as some of the route is poorly marked in places. The way descends to the left-hand lateral moraine discarded by the retreating Upper Scerscen glacier, crosses a couple of racing torrents and drops into the glen scoured out by the two Scerscen glaciers, both of which are now suspended high above. On the western side of this glen one climbs to Forcella d'Entova (2831m) in a rocky spur jutting from the cliffs that form a retaining wall for the lower of the two glaciers. Across the pass the way then descends to a road that winds down to San Guiseppe in Val Malenco, a hamlet midway between Chiesa and Chiareggio. Some way down this road a signpost directs a trail off to the right to Rifugio Longoni above Alpe Fora, with its glorious view south to Monte Disgrazia.

Departing the Longoni hut, go down to Alpe Fora, then take the trail cutting off to the right which makes a long contour of hillside below Piz Fora, passes above Chiareggio and comes to Alpe dell'Oro in the glen below the Muretto Pass. The way now crosses the pass back into Switzerland and descends to Maloja, thus completing the circuit in seven very fine days of mountain walking.

BERNINA CIRCUIT - ROUTE SUMMARY

Day 1:	Maloja - Via Engiadina - Silvaplana - Fuorcla Surlej
or:	Maloja - Curtins (Val Fex) - Fuorcla Surlej
Day 2:	Fuorcla Surlej - Val Roseg - Pontresina - Boval Hut
or:	Fuorcla Surlej - Val Roseg - Tschierva Hut
Day 3:	Boval Hut - Diavolezza - Alp Grüm
or:	Tschierva Hut - Boval Pass - Boval Hut
Day 4:	Alp Grüm - Passo Canfinale - Alpe Gembrè - Rifugio Bignami
Day 5:	Rifugio Bignami - Bocchetta di Caspoggio - Rifugio Marinelli
Day 6:	Rifugio Marinelli - Forcella d'Entova - Rifugio Longoni
Day 7:	Rifugio Longoni - Alpe dell'Oro - Passo del Muretto - Maloja

---

✳   ✳   ✳

THE ENGADINE VALLEY

This tremendous valley is a major feature of south-east Switzerland. It not only directs the River Inn from its source above Maloja to the gorge at Martina where it enters Austria, but is one of the country's prime tourist areas that contains the only national park within Swiss territory, and is a stronghold of Romansch, Switzerland's official fourth language which is spoken by just one per cent of the population. Most named features within the valley - mountains, passes, villages etc - have two spellings; one being Romansch, the other usually German. At times the valley is cut off from the rest of Switzerland, for the only direct road routes into the rest of the country cross passes that are sometimes blocked by snow. These are the Julier (2284m), Albula (2312m) and the Flüela (2383m). At its south-western end the Maloja Pass, as we have already seen, drops into Val Bregaglia and thence to Italy. The Bernina Pass leads into the deep Val Poschiavo which in itself drains directly into the Italian Valtellina, while the Ofen Pass (Pass dal Fuorn; 2149m) crosses into Val Müstair and out to the Stelvio-Reschen Pass road.

The valley is ninety-four kilometres long between Maloja and Martina, and with numerous tributary glens draining to it, it will be seen that there is plenty of scope here for the adventurous walker. Having looked at the major high mountain features of the Bernina Alps, this section concentrates on the walking potential of the rest of the valley from its confluence with Val Bernina, including of course that of the national park.

Heading down valley from Samedan where the road from Val Bernina joins the main Engadine through-route we come to Bever. On the opposite, right flank of the valley just before Bever the narrow, steep, and little-visited Val Champagna has been sliced in the mountainside below Piz Vadret. It's a lonely little glen worth giving a day to its exploration. A trail strikes through it as far as the solitary hut at Alp Champagna, and above that becomes a little unclear in places. However, it's not difficult to work out a route towards the head of the valley where you can either cross to the south to Lej Muragl and from there take a trail round to Muottas Muragl - or via the Segantini hut to Pontresina - or cross Fuorcla Muragl (2891m) and descend through Val Prüna to Val Chamuera which drains out to the Engadine near La Punt, the next village down valley from Bever.

While the Engadine itself is busy with roads, railway and a long string of resorts, just to the east there's a delightful complex of little glens and valleys linked by easy walkers' passes that one could wander for days on end without seeing more than an occasional cowherd or chamois hunter. Val Chamuera is really the key to any exploration there; a valley with woods and meadows, narrow gorges, and rocky crests leading to bigger peaks innocently dusted with snow or adorned with tiny glacial remnants. Cutting back behind the strung-out village of Chamues-ch a route leads for six kilometres to the alp of Acla Veglia where the valley splits three ways. The southern glen is that of Val Prüna, to the south-east the main Val Chamuera continues towards the Italian border, while to the east is the little Val Lavirun. Each of these glens has at least one route through. Let's look at these in turn.

Val Prüna, as we have already discovered, is linked to Val Champagna and Val Muragl by the Fuorcla Muragl. But there's another route too, which continues to the head of the glen, passing below Piz Languard and climbing towards Piz Albris. On the north side of that peak one can either cross Fuorcla Pischa and take a trail round the flanks of Crasta Languard, or bear left round the slopes of Piz Albris (watch for ibex here) and drop into Val da Fain which comes down to Val Bernina below the Diavolezza cableway.

The upper reaches of the main Val Chamuera are tempting with two possible routes. The first follows the valley stream to its very source, then crosses the ridge at Fuorcla Chamuera (2790m) just west of the Italian border, and then descends to Val da Fain. Should you wish to return to the Engadine, simply bear right and wander down valley to Val Bernina and catch the train from Bernina Suot back to

Bever via Samedan. But should you be flexible enough to try a new area, turn left in Val da Fain and cross an easy saddle at its head leading directly into the Italian Valle di Livigno. Once down there you could, perhaps, hitch a lift north to its far end, and then return to Switzerland in the national park area below the Ofen Pass.

The second option in Val Chamuera breaks away from the main route outlined above, and slants up the hillside heading roughly eastward to gain Fuorcla Federia (2901m) which carries the Italian border. Just below this on the eastern side there's a small tarn. The trail drops past this and descends into Valle di Federia which eventually enters Valle di Livigno at the southern end of Lago di Livigno. But before it does so, other trails cut off to return to Switzerland - and the Engadine - by an assortment of walkers' routes.

The third glen cutting away from Acla Veglia also has a trail leading to Valle di Federia, but the main interest here will be the crossing of Fuorcla Chaschauna (2804m) followed by a long downhill stroll through a curving glen that finally enters the Engadine below S-chanf.

Those were just a few ideas based on one valley, but they should be sufficient to illustrate what rich pickings are available, for on both sides of the Engadine tributary glens provide ample opportunities to reward a lifetime's exploration. On the left bank the Albula Alps are drained by neat little glens and moated by larger valleys, one of my own favourites being Val Susauna whose entrance is found between S-chanf and Cinuos-chel. At first glance this modest glen is just another wooded backland with no special appeal. But it is in such unremarkable beginnings that surprises are found. Val Susauna will provide a few surprises for those with senses alert. I will provide no more specific detail, except to point out that at its head you swing left into Val Funtauna and, climbing on, reach the Kesch hut (Chamanna digl Kesch) below the north face of Piz Kesch (3418m). An entertaining loop of this mountain could be achieved by wandering westward down into Val Tuors which leads to charming Bergün, from where a train could be taken back to the Engadine at Bever. Alternatively, a cross-country route could be made from Val Susauna to Davos by way of the Scaletta Pass (2606m) and the Dischmatal.

On the right bank of the Engadine opposite the entrance to Val Susauna, Val Trupchun marks the southern limit of the Swiss National Park. The park was the first in Europe, being established in 1914, and today it covers an area of 169 square kilometres. There are several valleys within its boundaries, most of which are densely forested, but with natural open meadows where marmot, chamois and red and roe deer are frequently seen. Ibex are common on the higher mountainsides, but access to human visitors is restricted to set paths. There is no wholesale freedom to roam here, but the sensitive, observant wanderer will appreciate that in this small corner of the Alps, Nature is left to her own devices. For once Man has to accept a secondary role. Accommodation is limited to Blockhaus Cluozza, a rustic inn secluded among larches in Val Cluozza south-south-east of Zernez, and Hotel Il Fuorn on the Ofen Pass road, the only road within the park. Camping is forbidden throughout the national park, yet both the blockhaus and Hotel Il Fuorn have dormitory facilities, thereby keeping the cost of accommodation down. Several dolomitic peaks rise from the northern valleys as part of a small chain known locally as the Engadiner Dolomites, while the boundary extends as far north as the edge of Scuol in the Lower Engadine, its north-eastern outline scoring alongside the rushing Clemgia stream which flows through Val S-charl - a gem of a valley for those who like their walking to be among attractive but little-known mountains.

One way of seeing as much of the national park as possible within a few days, is to make a three-day traverse, beginning at S-chanf and ending at S-charl. In between, the route will take you through Val Trupchun (the Varüsch hut is set in meadows near the park entrance in this glen), over Fuorcla Val Sassa (2857m) and down to Blockhaus Cluozza. Next day wander through forest and up to the broad, grassy, Murtèr saddle at 2545 metres, on the eastern side of which you descend through flowery meadows and forest again into Val dal Spöl. A rather devious, but extremely pleasant route leads from here to Il Fuorn for the second night's lodging. For the final day's trek there are two passes to cross. The first is Fuorcla da Val dal Botsch (2678m) with lovely views of glacial cirques and dolomitic spires, the second being Il Foss (2317m) from which the graceful Piz Plavna Dadaint is seen nearby, craggy fingers of rock punctuating its south ridge. Descent from Il Foss is via the beautiful Val Mingèr, a glen of innocent charm with crystal streams, flower-rich meadows, sparse woods of Arolla pine, and a curious sandstone outcrop whose rocks have been fashioned by wind, frost and rain into shapes recalling the face of a witch and a raven's head. Val Mingèr flows out of the national park and into Val S-charl, a short distance downstream from S-charl hamlet.

S-charl is reached by Postbus from Scuol, a summer-only service for the glen is blocked by snow throughout winter. The hamlet closes up in autumn and reopens only when snow conditions allow. There's limited accommodation here, but it is most certainly worth a visit. Peaceful, secluded, and surrounded by delightful mountain scenes, it would make a romantic base for a few days of a walking holiday. Val Sesvenna curves off to the north-east and is dominated by the square-topped Piz Sesvenna whose thrusting ridges carry the Italian border and help close the glen in an attractive cirque. Fuorcla Sesvenna (2819m) in the north ridge provides a walking route across the border and, via Valle Slingia, down to the Adige at Burgusio. An alternative long route could be achieved by crossing Fuorcla Sesvenna and descending to Alpe di Slingia at the head of the Slingia glen, then bearing left to cross Pass da Slingia back into Switzerland, followed by a lengthy descent through Val d'Uina to the Engadine at Sur En, downstream of Scuol.

Other opportunities for the walker based in S-charl include crossing the 2296 metre Cruschetta on the frontier ridge south-east of the hamlet, and dropping through Val d'Avigna into Val Müstair, or of continuing through the upper Val S-charl into the moorland-like Tamangur glen as far as Alp Astras, from where one route leads over the mountains to Val Müstair, and another crosses a minor pass with a trail descending directly to the Ofen Pass.

Val S-charl is not unique in the Lower Engadine, so far as walking opportunities are concerned. One glance at the map of the region will reveal many more glens on both banks of the River Inn, and hillside shelves dotted with picturesque villages and hamlets that, strung together, make a very rewarding day's outing. Making a high wall to the Lower Engadine between the Flüela road pass and the end of the valley, rise mountains of the Silvretta Alps, a range shared with Austria: Piz Linard,

Piz Buin, Dreilanderspitz and many, many more. More backcloths to dreams.

This chapter could have continued with close scrutiny of many more glens where memorable days have been spent wandering from alp to alp, over modest cols and onto ridge crests with vistas of enchantment. I recall early summers emerging with an extraordinary display of alpine flowers from reluctant winter drifts; winters crisp and pure when I'd walk at night through forests whose trees held great baskets of snow and the only sound was the soft squeak of boots on calf-deep powder. But perhaps best of all were golden autumn days when every Engadine larch had been touched by Midas artistry, and hillside shrubs shone orange, yellow or silver; early morning walks then spooked by ptarmigan, afternoons stalking ibex, and hour upon glorious hour romanced by scenes of genial splendour.

✳   ✳   ✳

THE BERNINA ALPS

Location:
South-east Switzerland and neighbouring valleys of Italy; to the east of the Lepontine Alps. The district extends roughly from the lake of Como to the Stelvio and Reschen Passes.

Principal valleys:
Val Bregaglia, Engadine, Val Bernina, Val Malenco and Val Masino. Many tributary glens of great appeal, including Val Bondasca, Val Albigna, Val Codera, Valles dei Bagni and di Mello, Val Fex and Val Roseg.

Principal peaks:
Piz Bernina (4049m), Piz Zupò (3996m), Piz Scerscen (3971m), Piz Roseg (3937m), Piz Palü (3905m), Monte della Disgrazia (3678m), Piz Cengalo (3370m), Piz Badile (3308m)

Centres:
The district has a large number of suitable bases. In the Swiss Bregaglia these include Promontogno, Vicosoprano and Soglio. San Martino and Chiesa on the Italian flank. Maloja, St Moritz and Pontresina for the Upper Engadine/Bernina. Zernez, Scuol and S-charl for the Lower Engadine.

Huts:
There are many huts, particularly in the Bernina and Bregaglia massifs, mostly belonging to the Swiss and Italian Alpine Clubs, but one or two are privately owned. Elsewhere a scattering of huts, some unmanned. In the Swiss National Park Blockhaus Cluozza has dormitory accommodation.

Access:
Both sides of the Bernina Alps (except the Swiss Bregaglia) are accessible by train. Most useful is the Rhaetian Railway from Chur to St Moritz, Pontresina, Poschiavo and Tirano (meeting the Italian railway through the Valtellina), with a branch line through the Lower Engadine to Scuol. There is also a Postbus route from Chur to St Moritz. Nearest international airports, Zürich and Milan. A small airstrip is located at Samedan in the Upper Engadine.

Maps:
The whole district is given first-rate comprehensive coverage by the Swiss survey

(Landeskarte der Schweiz) in assorted scales. The 1:50,000 series is adequate for most walking excursions. The very western end (Val Codera) will be found on sheet 277 *Roveredo*. Bregaglia north and south, and the main block of Bernina, are covered by 268 *Julierpass* and 278 *Disgrazia*. The Prasignola approach to Soglio is on 267 *San Bernardino*. The rest of the region will be found on sheets 258 *Bergün*, 249 *Tarasp*, 259 *Ofenpass*, 269 *Berninapass*, and 279 *Brusio*.

Guidebooks:
Walks in the Engadine, Switzerland by Kev Reynolds (Cicerone Press) describes 107 routes in all areas covered by the present chapter, except the Italian Bregaglia.
Trekking in Europe by Giancarlo Corbellini (AA Publishing) contains outline of an eight-day circuit of the Bernina under the heading Bernina Trail.

Other reading:
Walking in the Alps by J. Hubert Walker (Oliver & Boyd, 1951) remains fresh and inspirational, so far as the Bregaglia and Bernina are concerned. Naturally some of his information is out of date, but his text is worth reading for the landscape he draws.
The Alps by R.L.G. Irving (Batsford, 1939) has some good paragraphs on these mountains, but is limited in scope.
Italian Alps by D.W. Freshfield (Longmans, 1875/Blackwell, 1937) includes his journeys among the Bernina and Bregaglia Alps.
A Pioneer in the High Alps by F.F. Tuckett (Arnold, 1920) The Alpine diaries and letters of this mountain wanderer include passages of interest to visitors to the Bernina Alps.
Peaks & Pleasant Pastures by Claud Schuster (Clarendon Press, 1911) is a minor classic by one-time President of the Alpine Club. In this book he writes lovingly of the Bregaglia.
Adventures of an Alpine Guide by Christian Klucker (Murray, 1932). The memoirs of the finest guide produced by the Engadine; contains numerous references to the Bregaglia and Bernina mountains.
Starlight & Storm by Gaston Rébuffat (Dent, 1956/Kaye & Ward, 1968) The well-known Chamonix guide and author describes his ascent of the north-east face of Piz Badile; good description of Val Bondasca.
The Mountains of Europe by Kev Reynolds (Oxford Illustrated Press, 1990) includes a chapter on the high mountains of the Bernina Alps.
Classic Walks in Europe by Walt Unsworth (Oxford Illustrated Press, 1987) contains a description of the Bregaglia Circuit.
Classic Walks in the Alps by Kev Reynolds (Oxford Illustrated Press, 1991) describes a traverse of the Swiss National Park.
Walking & Climbing in the Alps by Stefano Ardito (Swan Hill Press, 1995) has a section that describes the Sentiero Roma with an extension to Poschiavo.

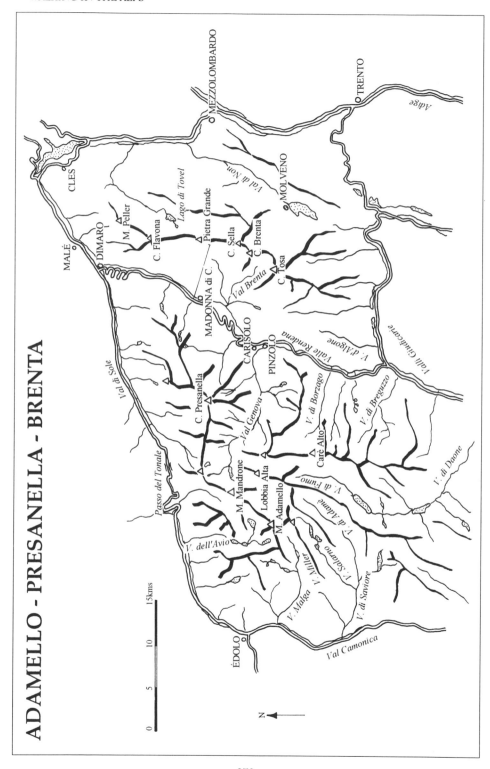

ADAMELLO - PRESANELLA - BRENTA

Near Refugio Brentei

10: ADAMELLO-PRESANELLA-BRENTA
Including the Adamello-Presanella Group,
and the Brenta Dolomites

R ising south-east of the Bernina Alps, and separated from them by the lesser heights of the Bergamesque Alps, the Adamello-Presanella Group teases the traveller on its outer rim with an impressive series of deeply cut glens draining a high, central mass of ice-crowned summits, while the compact Brenta district challenges with ranks of fairy-tale spires and turrets like the soldiers of some medieval legend turned to stone.

The two districts are almost totally different from one another in structure, appearance, character, and appeal, not to mention the very nature of walking among them. Yet despite such stark contrasts they are brought together in this chapter by their close proximity (close enough, in fact, to be united within the Adamello-Brenta Nature Park), for walkers using a base in the popular Rendena valley that runs between them could theoretically explore the glens of one in the morning, and move to the other in the afternoon.

According to Coolidge these are just two disparate mountain groups that form part of what he called the Lombard Alps, a definition that originated with John Ball, and which also included the Bergamesque Alps. However, that definition is rarely used today, and so far as this chapter is concerned, we will concentrate on the two

273

main districts whose boundaries are neatly defined by parallel south-flowing valleys; on the west Val Camonica (the valley of the Oglio), and on the east the Adige. To the north Val di Sole, linked with the Camonica across the Tonale Pass, divides the Adamello-Presanella Group from the Ortler Alps, while the southern limit is drawn by Valli Giudicarie which angles roughly across country from Trento to Bréscia.

While the western group, the Adamello-Presanella, is composed mostly of crystalline rocks, the Brenta to the east is sedimentary. The coarsely-grained tonalite (named from the Tonale Pass) of the former group has given the district its massive Alpine appearance, with steep and craggy flanks falling from a broad rounded upland draped with snowfields and glaciers. The Brenta's dolomitic material, on the other hand, has weathered into a series of parallel blocks of masonry, bold, precipitous, and chipped away at their edges into fantastic shapes; at the same time being seamed with vertical fissures that reveal quite astonishing shades and colours unknown among the glistening granite peaks of the adjacent Adamello.

The Adamello was described by Douglas Freshfield as "an enormous white cloth unevenly laid upon a table, and its shining skirts hanging over here and there between the dark massive supports." (*Italian Alps*) As for the Brenta, F.F. Tuckett wrote of "...the tall pinnacles and mighty cliffs of the Dolomite rocks [that] towered grandly aloft." He described "spires of white and brown and bronze coloured stone...[and] we were obliged to confess that in sublimity and fantastic grandeur they beat anything we had ever seen." (*A Pioneer in the High Alps*)

Yet another difference between the two districts lies in the result of their attraction to visitors. The Brenta is often crowded, especially in mid-summer when dusty dry trails stream with walkers and huts are almost bursting at the seams. The Adamello is wilder, less busy, with valleys and glens largely unspoilt. Yet in both areas the walker will find among the glens and rocky slopes a veritable wonderland of adventure, all set in landscapes as rich and rewarding in the sense of scenic grandeur, as may be found in almost any other part of the Alpine chain.

✳   ✳   ✳

ADAMELLO-PRESANELLA

The central core of mountains that forms the most impressive part of this district contains a number of peaks in excess of three thousand metres. Cima Presanella is the highest of the group at 3558 metres. This dominates the northern half of the range and overlooks the superb Val Genova that almost divides the district in two. Just four metres lower than the Presanella is Monte Adamello, while Carè Alto follows at 3453 metres. As for icefields, the Adamello glacier, or Vedretta del Mandrone, which lies within a catchment area bordered by Adamello, Monte Mandrone and Lobbia Alta (3196m), is claimed to be Italy's largest with an area of more than eighteen square kilometres.

"The central mass of the Adamello...is a huge block, large enough to supply materials for half-a-dozen fine mountains. But it is in fact only one. For a length and breadth of many miles the ground never falls below 9,500 feet.

The vast central snowfield feeds glaciers pouring to every point of the compass. The highest peaks...are merely slight elevations of the rim of this uplifted plain. Seen from within they are mere hummocks; from without they are very noble mountains falling in great precipices towards the wild glacier-closed glens which run up to their feet." (D.W. Freshfield)

It was Walker who pointed out that one of the group's characteristics is its series of extensive ridge-spurs pushing outwards from the central core or hub, the ridge-spurs becoming longer on the south-western side, thus creating a number of deep valleys that give a greater impression of height to the peaks from which they flow, than mere altitude measurement might otherwise suggest. Fortunately for the walker these ridges are crossed by a succession of passes of a uniform height, whereby one valley after another may be linked in a tour to delight "the man whose joy it is to move in comparative solitude up wild and unspoilt glens and to pass from glen to glen over the heights dividing them."

Taking the head of Val Genova as the pivot, the glens that drain the massif and provide access to it, begin with the short Val di Borzago flowing a little south of east from Carè Alto via the upper glen of Val Conca, and draining out to Valle Rendena at Pelugo. This is an attractive wild glen in its upper reaches where an impressive glacier draped cirque is popular with climbing courses based at Rifugio Carè Alto, set on the east ridge of the mountain after which it is named. The sharp horn of Carè Alto is noted for its far-reaching views, which stretch to great distances both east and west. Wandering down valley one descends among forests with occasional views east to the soaring Brenta Dolomites.

Flowing parallel to the Borzago glen a little to the south, Valle di San Valentino opens to the Rendena at Villa Rendena, having at its head a 2765 metre pass on the Cresta di San Valentino leading into the south-flowing Val di Fumo. Continuing clockwise, the next glen starts from a cirque crowned by Cima di Breguzzo, Cima Bissina and Cima d'Arnó. There Val di Breguzzo flows south-eastward to Bondo on the River Arno, and is fed by a tributary, Val d'Arno, both of which glens have crossing points in their upper ridges that also give access to Val di Fumo.

From a glance at the map it will be seen that Val di Fumo, being centrally placed in our wheel of spoke-like glens, acts as a major access route into the heart of the district. Born of the Vedretta di Fumo under Monte Fumo, the upper part of the glen is trapped between soaring ridges and glaciers with two or three bivouac huts lodged among them. Draining southward the valley, originally formed by rivers, then moulded by glacial action, becomes gently pastoral. Rifugio Val di Fumo lies upstream of the dammed Lago di Malga Bissina, below which the river pours in a series of cascades to Lago di Malga Boazzo where the valley becomes known as Val di Daone. This now flows for some twenty kilometres (road all the way) to Daone and Valli Giudicarie.

Whereas the east wall of the upper Val di Fumo is bothered by a row of hanging valleys bearing icy cravats and topped by the broad Lares glacier, the west wall is virtually bare of ice. Just south of Carè Alto lies Passo delle Vacche (2854m), highest of the four main crossing points on this side of the valley, while the opposite, west, flank has a corresponding number of passes that lead into a trio of glens. Each of these is a tributary of Val di Saviore which drains out to Val

Camonica, whose road provides a scenic link between Milan and Bolzano via the Tonale Pass. That road, then, provides the main point of access to these glens which, naming clockwise from Val di Fumo, are as follows: Val Ghilarda, with the fjord-like Lago d'Arno towards its head; the solitary Valle di Adamè, and Valle Salarno. This last-named glen is a magnificent cleft shut in by a series of great buttresses supporting the ridges that contain it. Lakes dazzle the lower glen, while Rifugio Prudenzini stands on a streamside meadow near its head at 2245 metres, and provides accommodation for a hundred in its dormitories.

Those glens drain the south-western edge of the Adamello heartland. On the west flank Val Miller, and the adjacent tarn-jewelled, deep corrie of the Baitone glen, are feeders of Val Malga, whereupon an arthritic confusion of ridges effectively directs the next two glens on north-bound courses. These are: Val Paghera (or d'Aviolo) flowing from a cirque with its own small glacier under Corno Baitone (3331m) down to Vezza d'Oglio, and Valle dell'Avio boasting a whole series of lakes, and with Monte Adamello as its crowning glory. Sadly the 'adornment' of this latter glen with pylons and overhead cables, not to mention the damming of its lakes as part of a major hydro-electric scheme, has somewhat devalued its former glory. Valle dell'Avio spills out to Val Camonica at Temu, while a short distance along the road towards Passo del Tonale a hairpin bend shows the lovely Narcanello glen digging back into the massif to the south-east. This glen makes a dog-leg curve at its midway point, then rises south-westward to the Pisgana glacier flowing from Monte Mandrone.

A little west of the Tonale Pass a cable-car ferries skiers up to the crevasse-free Presena glacier, at the foot of which sits Capanna Presena, a 76-bedded hut used by summer skiers as well as by walkers intending to traverse the district into Val Genova via the 2973 metre Passo del Maroccaro.

Val Genova, as we have already noted, almost divides the Adamello-Presanella Group into two unequal parts. The north wall of the valley is part of an extensive ridge system linking the Adamello-Mandrone peak and glacier complex with Cima Presanella. Below the northern-most part of this ridge, a spur pushes forward, with a bit of a kink above the Monticello tarn, and slopes down to the Tonale Pass, east of which the next few glens flow into Val di Sole. First of these is Val Presanella with the Presanella glacier at its head. Rifugio Francesco Denza stands on the west flank of this glen with a good view of the glacier and its cascading streams, while the valley entrance is at the hamlet of Velòn below the one-time strategically-placed Forte Tonale.

Val Piana, accessed from Ossana (which also provides an approach to the lovely Val di Péio cutting into the Ortler Alps to the north) forks in its upper reaches with the Bon and Caldara glens pushing towards the ridge wall linking Cima Scarpaco, Cima di Bon, Monte Caldura and Cima Baselga. Above the Venezia tarn in Val di Bron a 2617 metre pass takes walkers over that ridge and down into a landscape of tarns and bare rocks near the head of Valle di Nambrone, thereby making a north-south traverse possible of this northern part of the district. (Valle di Nambrone empties into the Rendena valley above Carisolo.)

Valle di Nambrone is noted for its tarns, as is Val Nambino to the north. This latter valley has cable-car access from Madonna di Campiglio and is very popular with tourists whose vision of the Brenta Dolomites across the depths of Valle di Campiglio is one of stunning beauty. Above the tree- and meadow-rimmed Lago Nambino a number of tarns have been distributed in clusters among rough-grained peaklets. Footpaths, aided by painted waymarks, link these tarns and also offer a choice of ridge crossings for walkers seduced by prospects of distant valleys. One of these crossings is via Passo di Val Gelata, on the north side of which a trail leads down to Pellizzano in Val di Sole. Another goes south over Passo Ritorto to Lago Ritorto and a cableway back to Madonna, while a third is by way of Passo di Nambron into the head of Valle di Nambron, the last in our ring of glens and valleys before returning to Val Genova.

Val Genova

This well-known valley, flowing roughly eastward from Monte Mandrone, has excited the attention of countless visitors since its early 'discovery' by the Victorian pioneers who wrote with unrestrained delight of its forests, pastures and waterfalls and, not least, of the fine Alpine scenery of its headwall. It's a classic, glaciated U-shaped valley, its lateral glens cut off by the main ice sheet that flowed downstream at a considerable depth some ten thousand years ago. These tributary glens now hang at their original level, thus providing a steep drop for the streams that drain them. Best known and most impressive of these waterfalls is the lovely Cascata di Nardis, about five kilometres from Carisolo, the village that guards the valley's entrance. A controversial road has been scored through the valley for a distance of about seventeen kilometres, and a shuttle bus service carries visitors along it in the high summer season as far as Malga Bédole, just below the Bédole hut. Despite this, it's a fine valley for wandering in, and there's a whole series of inns dotted alongside the road offering either refreshment or accommodation or both; the privately-owned Rifugio Bédole being the last of these.

Behind the hut a path climbs steeply through forest, with snatched views to Cima Presanella and its glacier off to the right, then curves left over steep rocky slopes to gain Rifugio Mandrone (otherwise known as Rifugio Città di Trento) in a little over two hours. Shortly before reaching the hut one passes a stone building that houses the Julius Peyer glacialogical study centre; this is worth a visit for the displays alone which provide evidence of the extent of glacial retreat throughout the valley. Nearby is a small alpine garden, and beyond this a line of gravestones forms a stark reminder of the madness of warfare that took place here in 1916.

The Mandrone hut (2480m) is a large, solid-looking building owned by the SAT. It stands in an almost perfect mountain setting, with whale-backed glacial slabs dotted with countless tarns and small ponds, and the snout of the Mandrone glacier clearly seen tipping from its high *firn* basin across the head of the valley, the Lobbia glacier to the left of that. Lobbia Alta is but one of several peaks forming the wall that divides these two glaciers, while Lobbia Bassa (2966m), though two hundred metres lower than the former, impresses with its graceful symmetry and by the manner with which it soars out of the valley as a tapering pyramid of grey granite. To the right of that Monte Mandrone guards the western gateway of the Vedretta del Mandone. From the hut a route leads onto this last-named glacier for access to a variety of summits that contain it; among them being the Adamello which by reputation enjoys one of the most extensive and varied panoramas in all the Alps. It was by this route that Tuckett made his ascent before crossing Passo dell'Adamello (the first time this had been achieved) and descending through Val Miller to Val Camonica - one of numerous classic traverses made by this wide-ranging Alpine pioneer. Other trails from the Mandrone hut meander among the tarns just beyond; another goes up to Lago Scuro and a brace of passes above it - one which leads into the head of Valle Narcanello, the other (the Maroccaro) already mentioned as being useful for crossing to or from the Tonale Pass, while yet another trail makes a rather demanding high-level traverse of Val Genova's left flank to the Cercen glen, from which one could either descend directly to the valley bed, or go up to the Passo Cercen (3022m), then via the Sella di Freshfield whereby Cima Presanella may be climbed. (Freshfield's party made the first ascent of Presanella in September 1864.)

On the south side of Cima Presanella the long tongue of the Nardis glacier pokes down into Val di Nardis, at the outflow of which the Cascata di Nardis sprays its magic into Val Genova. A trail goes up the eastern side of the waterfall to the Roberto bivouac hut, and beyond this it forks. The right-hand option here crosses Passo dei Quatro Cantoni to Rifugio Segantini in one of the feeder glens draining into Valle di Nambrone. By following these trails a loop trip could be made back to Carisolo.

The right-hand, or south wall, of Val Genova also has its fair share of attractions for walkers. These range from forest trails leading to tarns in Val Seniciaga, a crossing to Caderzone in Valle Rendena via the Acqua Fredda Pass, a route to the Carè Alto hut via Passo di Altar at the head of the Seniciaga glen, and a trail through Val Lares to a tarn at the snout of the Lares glacier.

✳   ✳   ✳

AN ADAMELLO CIRCUIT

In keeping with the method already established in previous chapters, of giving an outline of the district's valleys and feeder glens, then working out a multi-day route for walkers linking one valley after another, we now come to the stage when we can look at the possibility of making a complete circuit of the Adamello Group. Walker managed a partial circuit, and in her guidebook to the Central Italian Alps, Gillian Price makes a similar tour. Most of their suggestions will be incorporated in the following loop, which is probably best suited to activists with some experience of trekking in the Alps behind them. It begins for convenience at Carisolo, about twelve kilometres south of Madonna di Campiglio, the main resort situated between the Adamello-Presanella and Brenta Groups. Madonna is served by bus from either Trento or Malé, both of which may be reached by train, while local buses pass through Carisolo from Madonna.

The initial stage then, heads west through Val Genova to the Mandrone hut. It's a long valley walk, but as was mentioned above, in the peak summer season a shuttle bus service plies the route between Carisolo and Malga Bédole, thereby offering an alternative short walk from the Bédole hut/inn up the steep trail to Rifugio Mandrone. (Only the first two runs of the day begin at Carisolo; thereafter the bus begins its shuttle at Ponte Verde.) But given fine weather the full valley walk, through forest alternating with open smiling meadows, and with huge soaring crags on either side glistening with cascades, with birds singing and deer in the woods, cowbells and the shrill call of marmots disturbing the peace - all these things will make a rewarding prelude to a succession of pass crossings that will follow in the days ahead.

The first of these crossings is taken next morning, but there's a choice of two passes to consider, the trail from the hut dividing at Lago Scuro. The right-hand option climbs to Passo del Maroccaro (2973m), the left-hand choice leads to Passo di Lago Scuro (2870m). The first of these presents a glorious introductory view north to the Ortler Alps, then follows descent of the straightforward Presena glacier and a continuing route leading down to the Tonale road pass where there's hotel accommodation. Passo Lago di Scuro, on the other hand, is mostly ice-free but with a reputation for being 'fatiguing' on the descent into Valle Narcanello. In common with its neighbour, this pass also offers striking views of Adamello, Presanella and the Ortler mountains, while the glen below is a delight to wander through. There is, however, a high trail along the left flank of the Narcanello glen which leads to Rifugio Petitpierre, thus avoiding the necessity of descending all the way to Val Camonica. It is this option that is to be preferred above the Maroccaro crossing, if for no other reason than it keeps the walker within the mountain ring by shunning outlying valleys and their traffic.

Day three leads, then, from the Petitpierre hut to Rifugio Garibaldi nestling by Lago di Veneròcolo, and with a view directly across the lake to the north face of Monte Adamello. There's a choice of ways to achieve this stage. The first involves descent along a service road beneath a chairlift, followed by a forest trail heading south-west into Valle dell'Avio. Once this glen has been reached the way heads south, goes up to the dammed lakes of Avio and Benedetto and, from the southern end of the last of these, with superb high mountain views despite electricity pylons and overhead cables, a mule-trail veers left and climbs to the Veneròcolo dam. The Garibaldi hut stands on the north shore at 2550 metres.

The alternative crossing from Petitpierre to Garibaldi involves rather more effort along a trail that requires a little care. Backtracking a short distance from the hut veer right at Baita di Pastore, then head through a short glen past a tarn and go up to the Bocchetta dei Buoi (2671m), a pass in the ridge south of Punta dei Buoi. This gives access to Valle di Salimmo, the trail descending to Malga Caldea on the service road in Valle dell'Avio below the dammed lakes. Take this road up to the third lake (Lago Benedetto), then follow the mule-trail from the southern end, veering east to Rifugio Garibaldi.

There follows a fairly demanding stage to Rifugio Gnutti in Val Miller. It could, however, be broken by an overnight spent at the Tonolini hut after about five hours, although if this were done, it could make for wet going on the next stage where the route crosses a permanent snowfield.

From the south side of the dam wall at the end of Lago di Veneròcolo a trail marked Alta Via Adamello crosses an old moraine and curves below Monte Adamello's north face. Bocchetta del Pantano (2650m) then provides access to the head of Valle dell'Avio and its highest dammed lake, Lago Pantano, almost three hundred metres below the *bocchetta*. Descending to this lake, cross the dam wall and make the long climb south-west, often over snow patches but with tremendous views to lighten the effort, to gain Passo di Premassone (2847m), one of the highest crossings on this circuit. This is reached with the aid of fixed cables, while descent on the far side is straightforward, tucking round the Premassone tarn and going down to Lago Rotondo and Rifugio Tonolini. Should it be decided to remain here for the night, the experienced scrambler may be tempted by the opportunity to climb Corno Baitone (3331m) which rises almost due north of the hut. This can be achieved in three or four hours from Rifugio Tonolini, while the nearer Cima di Plem (east of the hut) requires about three hours of scrambling. Neither are said to be difficult, and Corno Baitone especially rewards with a very fine panorama.

Moving on from the Tonolini hut go down to Lago Baitone and the dam at its southern end, and from there find a trail heading south-east round the lower slopes of Corno del Lago where Passo del Gatto (2103m) is protected by more fixed cables. The narrow trail continues (still as Alta Via Adamello) and is exposed in places, but nowhere is it difficult. Entering Val Miller the way leads directly to Lago Miller and Rifugio Gnutti, with Corno Miller dominating the head of the glen to the north-east. There is an alternative route into Val Miller which avoids descent from the Premassone pass to the Tonolini hut. This is an option recommended by Walker, and it involves the crossing of Passo di Cristallo (2885m) below Cima di Plem.

The south enclosing wall of Val Miller consists of a series of summits projecting from a ridge that extends south-west then roughly westward from Corno Miller. On the far side of this ridge lies Valle Salarno, a beautiful wild glen from which the ascent of Adamello may be achieved in about five hours. Our intention here is not to climb mountains, though, but rather to work our way round their flanks and to view them in all their finery, from green glen to snow-proud crown. And having crossed the north side of Adamello at the start of our circuit, then progressed along its west flank, it is now time to head east over the south-projecting ridges. The stage leading from Rifugio Gnutti to the Prudenzini hut marks the beginning of this east-bound section, with Passo del Miller being the key to the crossing. It will only take a little over two hours to gain the pass, but in a high cirque on the Val Miller side there's a snowfield to cross which ought to be tackled fairly early in the day, otherwise the snow becomes soft and mushy and makes for unpleasant walking. On the south side of the col grass is soon traded for boulder-hopping. An extensive ridge, marked on the map as the Coster di destra, separates the upper hillside from the main valley bed, so this has to be crossed in order to work a way down to the Italian Alpine Club's Rifugio Paolo Prudenzini. "From this point," said Walker, "the huge tonalite buttresses supporting the rim of the great central plateau are dramatic and imposing in their sweep. The scenery is wild in the extreme."

Stage six continues the eastward trend, although it involves a long push south in the next valley to be visited, Valle di Adamè. This is the way chosen by the Alta Via (or Sentiero) Adamello, the crossing of Passo di Póia at 2810 metres. The climb to the pass involves plenty of snow and occasional ice, but otherwise is straightforward, while the descent into the Adamè glen provides a variety of terrain, from rock walls to boulder fields, and steep grass slopes brightened with shrubs to flowery meadows. Upvalley the small Adamè glacier protrudes to the left of Corno di Adamè, and on the east side of the glen a splendid jagged crest tops the containing wall. The map shows a route over that wall at Porta di Buciaga, a col tucked below Cima Buciaga Nord at almost exactly the same height as the col just crossed on the west side of the glen, but ignoring this option, we follow the Alta Via trail downstream for an hour to reach Rifugio Lissone in order to tackle a lower pass next day.

That pass, the Passo di Forcel Rosso, lies south-east of the Lissone hut and, at 2598 metres, involves ascent (steep in places) of a little under 600 metres, or less than two hours of effort. The pass is littered with First World War fortifications and, not for the first time on this tour, it is hard to move on without giving thought to those unfortunate men who found themselves defending these remote mountain ridges in the days when this particular pass lay on the frontier between Austria and Italy. It now carries the border between Trentino and Lombardy, and marks the point where the boundary of the Parco Naturale Adamello breaks away from the ridge it has followed all the way from Lobbia Alta.

Two paths descend from the pass into Val di Fumo. That which drops to the right goes to Lago di Malga Bissina, while ours, the left-hand option, slants gently north-eastward; a scenic walk into a pastoral valley, and with Carè Alto forming a majestic triangle on the far side. Overnight lodging here is in Rifugio Val di Fumo, owned by the SAT (Società Alpinisti Tridentina).

By taking this route from Rifugio Lissone, our tour of the Adamello has deserted the 'official' Alta Via. That route wandered south to Rifugio Brescia and continued away from the high mountains, still among fine scenery, it is true, though with some fairly difficult sections. Walker too, in his survey of the district, wandered down valley from Valle Salarno and the Prudenzini hut as far as Saviore, then returned to higher country via Rifugio Brescia and Passo di Campo, followed by a long walk up Val di Fumo, thus rejoining the general trend of our circuit. Here, Walker listed the options available for crossing out of Val di Fumo, and suggested Passo di San Valentino as being the easiest, pointing out that this pass had long been used by local herdsmen taking their cattle into the east-flowing valleys on the far side. Gillian Price recommends the higher Passo delle Vacche (2854m) which lies to the north of the San Valentino crossing. Of this crossing, Walker said: "The fourth and highest pass is undoubtedly the most enterprising and interesting...It lies close under the great spur descending to the south-west from the Carè Alto itself, and having crossed it, it would then be an easy matter to gain the Bocca di Conca, and so the Carè Alto hut." He also went on to summarise this route by saying, "For the walker the Passo di S. Valentino is the way to choose, but the man who likes a bit of hard work and a good scramble will cross the wall by the Passo delle Vacche." And so will we.

Perhaps Walker overplayed his estimation of Passo delle Vacche. Or maybe things have changed a little in the fifty-odd years since he tackled it. Certainly today there is adequate waymarking, and with the pass visible for much of the way, in good conditions no walker who has got this far on the tour should be overly concerned by this crossing, although the following stretch as far as the Bocchetta di Conca (2678m) could be a little problematic in misty weather - especially when crossing a snowfield to the south of Carè Alto. Otherwise the trail is easy enough, and the *bocchetta* should be gained within three and a half hours of leaving the Fumo hut. Once at the pass our circuitous tour has completed its eastward trend and begins to move north along the east flank of the massif.

Rifugio Carè Alto is gained in another hour from the pass, and next day the circuit is closed by a longish, though fairly easy, stretch that involves crossing Passo di Altar (2388m), north-east of the hut and reached by way of the Conca di Niscli cirque below the Lares glacier. The pass makes a splendid vantage point from which to study Carè Alto back across the cirque, now seen with the Niscli glacier curving from it, while the Brenta Dolomites are visible in the opposite direction. As you descend into Val Seniciaga, Cima Presanella is glimpsed across the hinted depths of Val Genova, and for those with plenty of energy (and time) to spare, the summit of Monte Palone (2378m) offers a broader view and may be reached by a vague trail leading from Malga Seneciaga alta. Continuing down, the Seneciaga glen finally spills out to Val Genova at Ponte del Casöl, while the best way to reach Carisolo is via the Sentiero delle Cascate whose best-known feature is the lovely Nardis waterfall.

AN ADAMELLO CIRCUIT - ROUTE SUMMARY

Day 1: Carisolo - Val Genova - Rifugio Bédole - Rifugio Mandrone

Day 2: Rifugio Mandrone - Passo di Lago Scuro - Rifugio Petitpierre
or: Rifugio Mandrone - Passo del Maroccaro - Passo del Tonale

Day 3: Rifugio Petitpierre - Valbione - Lago Benedetto - Rifugio Garibaldi
or: Rifugio Petitpierre - Bocchetta dei Buoi - Rifugio Garibaldi

Day 4: Rifugio Garibaldi - Passo di Premassone - Rifugio Tonolini - Passo del Gatto - Rifugio Gnutti
or: Rifugio Garibaldi - Passo di Premassone - Passo di Cristallo - Rifugio Gnutti

Day 5: Rifugio Gnutti - Passo del Miller - Rifugio Prudenzini

Day 6: Rifugio Prudenzini - Passo di Póia - Rifugio Lissone

Day 7: Rifugio Lissone - Passo di Forcel Rosso - Rifugio Val di Fumo

Day 8: Rifugio Val di Fumo - Passo delle Vacche - Bocchetta di Conca - Rifugio Carè Alto

Day 9: Rifugio Carè Alto - Passo di Altar - Val Genova - Carisolo

---

✻   ✻   ✻

THE BRENTA DOLOMITES

Moving eastward across Valle Rendena from the Adamello-Presanella Group may involve little more than a short morning's stroll, but the impact created by a totally different landscape is as great as if one had journeyed from one mountain range to another. The former district was classically Alpine; the Brenta is theatrically spectacular, its grey, cream, brown or orange spires and towers changing tone and texture (it seems) with each succeeding hour. In the Brenta there are practically no scree slopes and the cliffs are abrupt and severe; a few small glaciers still remain, though nothing as extensive as those of the neighbouring group's, while the change from forested valley to soaring pinnacle is about as dramatic as imagination can allow.

This is how Walker described the visual impact upon leaving Valle Rendena for the Val Brenta:

> "The scenery immediately becomes the scenery of a different world. We are confronted with a changed landscape. Crags, turrets, bastions of rich colouring and fantastic size rear their heads boldly into the sky; flaming walls of masonry rise along the sky-line; and a mountain world is revealed of surpassing grandeur."

In an earlier age, Freshfield wandered the same glen towards the Crozzon di Brenta:

> "Full opposite to us rose a colossal rock, one of the most prodigious monuments of Nature's forces. Its lower portion rose in diminishing stories like the Tower of Babel of old Bible pictures. Above it was a perfect precipice, an upright block, the top of which was 4,000 to 4,500 feet above our heads. Behind this gigantic keep a vast mountain fortress stretched out its long lines of turrets and bastions. But as we approached its base the great tower rose alone and unsupported, and the boldness of its outline became almost incredible." (*Italian Alps*)

If this smacks of hyperbole to the modern Alpinist used to tracts of unemotional understatement, I would merely say, "Go and see for yourself."

The Brenta district is neatly contained by two parallel valleys, the Rendena on the west, and Val di Non (an offshoot of the Adige) on the east. In the less-trodden areas some of Alpine Europe's last remaining brown bears are said still to survive, and farmers in Val di Non are able to claim compensation for any damage caused to their fruit trees by these protected animals. Chamois and roe deer range more widely and may well be sighted by observant walkers following the rich variety of trails for which the Brenta is noted.

The district is not a large one, for the dolomitic spine stretches north to south for a distance of little more than thirty kilometres, and spans barely a dozen kilometres at its broadest. South of Cima Tosa this spine is divided like a tuning fork into two separate ribs, with Val d'Ambiez flowing between them down to Valli Giudicarie. The northern section has a small, secondary rib branching from it which runs parallel to the main range, and this encloses a glen breaking out at Lago di Tovel, one of the Brenta's classic landmarks noted for its intense red colouring under certain conditions, caused by a rare algae threatened today by pollution.

In the west the main base is undoubtedly Madonna di Campiglio, a bustling resort on a Chamonix-like scale, with hotels and boutiques and cableways that service an enthusiastic winter ski clientele as well as the masses of summer visitors who gather there. Molveno on the opposite side of the range is nowhere near so large or grand, but is picturesquely located on the north shore of a lake, and with chairlifts to carry visitors up to a fine viewpoint from which to gaze on the Brenta towers. These two resorts are easily linked by walking routes that score through the very heart of the range via three main passes (Passo del Grostè, Bocca del Tuckett and Bocca di Brenta), while numerous scenic trails give access from the outer valleys to a plentiful supply of inn-like huts perched in the midst of fairytale mountains.

Perhaps the most popular of all huts are those in the central area immediately south of the Grostè Pass. They are, quite frankly, extremely busy in the peak summer season when, according to the guidebook, they're "taken by storm by tourists". Trails leading from one to another are dotted with walkers, and if you are unable to take your holiday other than in August, or find yourself on such a trail on a sunny weekend outside the main season, you will simply have to accept the gregarious nature of walking in the Brenta, or look elsewhere for more solitary exercise.

Assuming Madonna di Campiglio is used as the springboard from which to explore the region, several huts become readily accessible; notably the Graffer, Vallesinella, Casinei, Tuckett (and adjacent Sella), Brentei, Alimonta, Pedrotti (and the nearby Tosa) and the Dodici Apostoli. The first of these, Rifugio Giorgio Graffer (2261m), stands below Passo del Grostè, with the pale grey walls of the Pietra Grande looming overhead and a view south to Cima Tosa. The hut is usually approached by the Grostè cableway which rises from the northern end of Madonna and virtually sails over the hut itself. A good path, which joins another from the upper gondola lift terminus, leads to Rifugio Tuckett in less than two hours, while a second trail crosses the range via Passo del Grostè and Passo della Gaiarda and reaches Rifugio Malga Spora on the eastern side in under three hours.

The Vallesinella hut is a large inn, standing on the edge of mixed woods at the end of a dirt road, whose huge car park is used by walkers and climbers going deeper into the mountains. Most visitors arrive either in their own vehicle or by taxi (the hut runs a mini-bus service from Madonna), although the woodland walk to it can be rather pleasant if you go early enough to avoid the traffic. The privately-owned Rifugio Casinei is gained by a multi-braided woodland path in less than an hour from the Vallesinella hut. Casinei stands on a slope of meadowland at a junction of trails. One leads on to Rifugio Tuckett, a second heads south to gain the beautiful Val Brenta, while a third path climbs south-eastward to join a linking trail coming from the Tuckett hut, then skirts the north-east wall of Val Brenta in a delightfully scenic traverse that ends at Rifugio Brentei.

The Tuckett and Sella huts stand together in a tremendous location, the first just below the second, and with the deep portal of the Bocca del Tuckett clearly seen to the south-east between the crags of Cima Sella and Cima Brenta. These huts are used as a base for climbers as well as walkers, for there's much to keep the rock man happy for many a long day right on the doorstep. From these huts easy walkers' trails, *via ferrata* routes and rock climbs aplenty are all accessible. No wonder they're among the busiest of all Brenta rifugios.

One of the linking trails from here heads west into a chaos of glaring white boulders, crosses the Sella del Freddolin, goes through tuffets of dwarf pine and alpenrose where it joins the alternative route from Rifugio Casinei mentioned above, then veers south-eastward along the flank of Val Brenta with the most astonishing views of the towering Crozzon di Brenta directly ahead, and reaches Rifugio Alberto o Maria ai Brentei in about an hour and a half - a beautiful, short and undemanding walk. The Brentei hut is situated in the midst of some truly impressive rock scenery; everywhere you look extraordinary towers and buttresses jostle for attention; some wear bruise-like patches, some are stained light orange or pink, while most are of a creamy white tone tinged with blue shadow. A stony glen cuts back behind the hut to the Bocca di Brenta (Bocca may be translated as 'mouth'), the most important and accessible walker's pass between Madonna and Molveno, and visited by John Ball in July 1864.

Tucked into a short side glen east of the Brentei hut, the privately-owned Rifugio Alimonta (2580m) stands among limestone pavement below the west shoulder of Cima Molveno, and is reached in less than an hour from the Brentei. It's very useful for walkers tackling the classic *via ferrata* route of the Brenta district, the Sentiero delle Bocchette, which passes nearby.

Just below the Bocca di Brenta, and settled on more limestone pavement in an open situation on the Molveno flank of the mountains, two further huts are accessible from the Brentei rifugio in one and a half hours. Rifugio Pedrotti, and the older Rifugio Tosa are both owned by the SAT, although the former was built by the German Alpine Club (DAV) in 1912, and was subsequently transferred to SAT ownership as a result of a legal dispute. Molveno lies some four hours' walk away via the Valle delle Seghe.

The last of those Brenta huts listed as being accessible from Madonna di Campiglio, is the Dodici Apostoli (Twelve Apostles) hut, built in 1908 at the head of Val di Nardis and with a direct view across Valle Rendena to the Adamello-Presanella Group. The usual way of approach is from Pinzolo, some way down valley from Madonna, where ascent of Dos del Sabion (2101m) is first made by cableway and chairlift, followed by a three-hour walk. As to the approach from Madonna itself, it is better to drive through Val d'Agola to Lago d'Agola, from where a trail heads south then south-east into Val di Nardis, and gains the hut in a little under three hours. (The full walk from Madonna is not recommended.) Best of all is the route from Rifugio Brentei, a tremendous four-hour walk that initially drops into Val Brenta Alta and tucks against the base of the Crozzon tower. Climbing into Val dei Camosci the crevasse-free Camosci glacier is negotiated and the Bocca dei Camosci traversed before descending to the Dodici Apostoli hut; a truly memorable walk with impressive views throughout.

So much for the huts clustered around the central Brenta and a hint at linking routes between them. No walker with an ounce of imagination (and sufficient time at his disposal) could possibly grow tired of the options available for day walks and multi-day hut routes in this part of the district alone. But as was pointed out earlier, these huts and trails will almost certainly be very busy, especially in August, while the further north you travel, so the trails grow less crowded. Less crowded maybe, but at the same time the landscape is not quite as dramatic as in the heart of the chain, though it is certainly no less lovely. The northernmost hut along the main Brenta spine, for example, is located on a green hill dotted with dwarf pine at the foot of Monte Peller. This, the new Rifugio Peller (2022m), is reached through dense evergreen forest in about four hours from Malé. From there paths head south-west via Cima Cesta and Cima Nana to the Constanzi bivouac hut, then on sections of *via ferrata* the Sentiero Costanzi continues south to link with Sentiero Gustavo Vidi (more *via ferrata*), and in turn leads to Passo del Grostè. Yet more standard mountain trails hug the lower flanks of the dolomitic towers, penetrate valley forests and high open pastures and always, it seems, with vistas of vertical enchantment on which to focus the eye. The Sentiero delle Palete is a likely trail to consider for anyone planning to walk the northern half of the Brenta spine, for this links the Peller hut with the Grostè Pass (on the east flank throughout) in six hours or so.

Of all the Brenta walks one in particular immediately offers itself; a suggestion endorsed by no less an authority than R.L.G. Irving. "If possible," he wrote, "any active visitor should go from Pinzolo or Campiglio to Molveno by the Bocca di Brenta. The views are grand, the surroundings on both sides are lovely, and the gateway of the pass with its colossal walls of limestone on either hand is wonderful, while the lake of Molveno is just the place where a man should end a journey." (*The Alps*) This same route was summarised by Baedeker with less words, but with equal emphasis: "A fatiguing but grand route", and Walker himself devoted two pages of text to the same journey.

`*   *   *

A TOUR OF THE CENTRAL BRENTA

Bocca di Brenta is not the only point of crossing, as we have already seen, so it may be worth making a short, four-day tour, setting out from Madonna (or Pinzolo) on the first stage as far as the Pedrotti hut, then descending to Molveno on day two. Day three would be spent in regaining height to cross Passo del Grostè, then dropping to the Graffer hut, while the final stage consists of a return to Madonna via the Tuckett and Vallesinella rifugios.

In order to gain the Bocca di Brenta on day one, several possibilities present themselves. Three of these begin at the Vallesinella hut, a fourth starts by riding the cableway to Passo del Grostè, while a fifth heads directly for Val Brenta and then follows path 323, the so-called Scala di Brenta. The Passo del Grostè route descends to the Tuckett hut and there joins one of the Vallesinella paths round to the Brentei hut. The other two Vallesinella options are combined as far as Rifugio Casinei where they divide. One then climbs south-eastward (Sentiero Bogani) and is joined by the Tuckett route, while the alternative takes a much less-trodden way along the Sentiero Violi, a wilder and lower trail than that of the Bogani option. The last of our possibilities follows Val Brenta throughout. Each one has its own special appeal.

This is how Walker described the way from Val Brenta:

> "Full in front you have those amazing and fantastic pinnacles that have excited so much admiration. The beautifully wooded valley falls in three terraces; the lowest portion, the first two terraces, ends at the level lawn of Malga Brenta Bassa, and here is the place whence the view of the Tosa cluster of peaks is seen in all its wonder. Rising in an almost vertical

286

precipice to a height of 4,500 feet above the alp tower the immense cliffs of the Crozzon di Brenta...while nearby soar the sharp pinnacles of the Fulmini di Brenta. This terrace is closed by a steep rock wall, which is surmounted by a track that swings away and back again, to cross the Passo dell'Orso and reach the Malga Brenta Alta, the highest terrace, an alp where the upper limit of trees is reached and crossed by many waters. Here the mountains are closer, and on the left are the Torre di Brenta, the massive Campanile di Brenta, and the elegant Guglia di Brenta; while to the right are the Crozzon di Brenta and Cima Tosa."

At this point the Sentiero Violi, one hundred metres or so above the alp, has emerged from woodland too, and the walker there finds himself on a ledge of a path with that same astonishing view before him, while those who choose the upper, Sentiero Bogani, trail another three hundred metres above that, have the valley's great depth below to add a different perspective on the way round to the Brentei hut, where all the routes converge. Back to Walker again for the final approach to the Bocca di Brenta:

"Heading straight for the hills, the path crosses the terrace and ascends a snow-slope through an ever steepening and narrowing gash in the looming wall above. The walls gradually close in until at the summit of the pass, the Bocca di Brenta...they form the soaring uprights of a narrow portico. A little beyond the pass and then some slight distance to the south of it, a terraced track leads in some 20 minutes to the Tosa hut, an inn, standing on a broad, rocky platform on the edges of a deeply hollowed cauldron called the Pozza Tramontana."

From either Rifugio Pedrotti or Tosa our continuing route avoids descent of the Tramontana cauldron, and instead cuts north-eastward where it soon forks. The left-hand trail here, the Sentiero Osvaldo Orsi, works a way northward to Bocca del Tuckett, thereby offering an alternative return to Madonna. Of this particular trail, Walter Pause once described it in awesome terms as: "One of the most daring stanchioned climbing paths in the Alps, negotiable by non-climbers provided they do not suffer from vertigo. The exposed nature of the path demands a steady head and familiarity with mountains." (*Salute the Mountains*) However, since the development of more severe *vie ferratae*, German climbers have come to dismiss this as the "Lower Cycle Track". Our route, which continues to Molveno, descends through natural rock gardens to some ruins at the base of the Massodi peaks, then more steeply towards the Selvata hut and the deep, "strangely beautiful" Valle delle Seghe. This gorge-like glen is luxuriant with conifer woods, and as you progress through it so glimpses of Lago di Molveno lead you down. In truth it's not necessary to descend all the way to Molveno, for one could break away at Rifugio Selvata on an alternative trail that leads shortly to the Croz dell'Altissimo hut, then over Passo del Clamer to the Malga Spora rifugio where the Molveno-Passo del Grostè route is joined. If this alternative were to be adopted, the circuit could be reduced to a three-day loop.

On leaving Molveno it might be worth riding the cableway to the Pradel viewpoint, thus saving a seven hundred metre climb, then following a trail round the flank of Pizzo Gallino and crossing Passo Dagnola, by which the Malga Spora dairy farm rifugio is gained. From here a two hundred metre climb leads easily to Passo di Gaiarda (2242m). Between this and the Grostè Pass the way goes through the upper pastureland of Campo di Flavona, across a grass saddle at 2242 metres between the two Turrion rock peaks, and then into a curious karst landscape that forms such a feature of the east side of Passo del Grostè. The gondola lift at the pass provides a tempting opportunity to cut out a fourth day's walk by riding down to Madonna, should time be at a premium. But it is surely preferable to overnight at Rifugio Graffer, and next day walk to the Tuckett hut and descend to Madonna from there via the Sella di Freddolin, Rifugio Casinei and the Vallesinella, thus completing a very satisfactory circuit.

A TOUR OF THE CENTRAL BRENTA - ROUTE SUMMARY

Day 1: Madonna di Campiglio - Passo del Grostè - Rif. Tuckett - Rif. Brentei - Bocca di Brenta - Rif. Pedrotti

or: Madonna di Campiglio - Rif. Vallesinella - Rif. Tuckett - Rif. Brentei - Bocca di Brenta - Rif. Pedrotti

or: Madonna di Campiglio - Rif. Vallesinella - Rif. Casinei - Sent. Bogani (or Sent. Violi) - Rif. Brentei - Bocca di Brenta - Rif. Pedrotti

or: Madonna di Campiglio - Malga Brenta Bassa - Malga Brenta Alta - Rif. Brentei - Bocca di Brenta - Rif. Pedrotti

Day 2: Rif. Pedrotti - Rif. Selvata - Molveno

Day 3: Molveno - Pradel - Passo Dagnola - Rif. Malga Spora - Passo di Gaiardo - Passo del Grostè - Rif. Graffer

Day 4: Rif. Graffer - Rif. Tuckett - Sella di Freddolin - Rif. Casinei - Rif. Vallesinella - Madonna di Campiglio

---

✳　✳　✳

VIE FERRATAE

The above tour, plus the hut approach routes that preceded it, provide a few examples of the region's walking potential. But it is the amazing number and variety of *via ferrata* routes that sets the Brenta aside as a playground *par excellence* for walkers and scramblers with a good head for heights. In the Brenta the Italian passion for airy protected 'trails' has reached its ultimate expression.

For the uninitiated, these protected trails strike a middle course between ordinary mountain walking and rock climbing. Being translated as an 'iron path' a *via ferrata* is, in most cases, a route so safeguarded with fixed cables, ladders, rungs and occasional bridges, that a walker unaffected by exposure is able to experience regions that would otherwise be the sole preserve of the rock gymnast. The considered official recommendation is that all who attempt such aided routes ought to be capable of climbing up to Grade III, but the reality is that every summer thousands of non-climbers eagerly set out upon the vertical environment of the Dolomites, teased and lured by the fame of such *vie ferratae*, and are generously rewarded by the experience. As prerequisites, fitness and an ability to move safely in almost every kind of mountain terrain, plus the ability to act swiftly in the event

Lac Nero and Palon de la Mare (Ch 11)

Val Tuoi and Piz Buin in the southern Silvretta Alps (Ch 12)

The Taschachferner from the Fuldaer Höhenweg, Ötztal Alps (Ch 13)

Old moraines now green with vegetation carry scenic trails among the Stubai mountains (Ch 14)

of sudden bad weather (metal cables and ladders are notorious lightning conductors!) should be part of the activist's background before setting out. A history of dizziness or vertigo will preclude anyone from completing one of these trails, for in the Brenta they exploit natural airy ledges created by geological bedding planes; they rise up perpendicular, and in some places even overhanging, walls and gullies, and provide safe passage in places of breathtaking exposure. "The common factor [is] exposure," wrote Walt Unsworth in a magazine article some years ago, "tremendous, awe-inspiring, sweeping exposure." Curiously, Walker makes no mention of such routes, even though some sections were created nearly twenty years before he published his book and the oldest *vie ferratae* protected routes (not those of the Brenta) date from the late nineteenth century.

Protected routes extend across much of the region's dolomitic spine from north to south and, when linked with 'standard' mountain trails, enable one to make multi-day traverses of the complete Brenta from either Malé or Cles in the north, to San Lorenzo in the south. These *vie ferratae* cover a variety of terrain, and range from short stretches of ladder aid to the full works; some are popular as family outings, others would be best left to fit and experienced activists. This is not the place to discuss safety precautions, equipment or techniques useful on such routes, for these will be found in the recommended guidebook: *Via Ferrate, Scrambles in the Dolomites*, but the following quotation so perfectly sums up the *via ferrata* experience, that one will soon know whether such routes will appeal or appal. If the former, I would say, buy the guidebook and go for it. If the latter, move swiftly to the next chapter.

In the following quotation, the author describes a section of the Sentiero SOSAT, a protected route linking the Tuckett and Alimonta huts:

"We stopped smiling when we came to the gully. We couldn't believe our eyes. We had popped out of a limestone crevasse like a couple of jack-rabbits and found ourselves on the brink of an enormous chasm. Across the chasm we could see an iron ladder bolted to the opposite wall and leading up to what was obviously a path. I say obviously because there was nowhere else it could go, but it was the sort of path our Victorian forefathers with their usual modesty, would have described as tenuous. Moreover, the ladder leading up to it was a good hundred feet of vertical ironmongery.

"The suddenness of the view was so startling that for some time it banished the thought that first of all we had to descend our side of the canyon to get to the ladder. The route turned out to be a complex maze of grooves, cables and ladders threading a way down the wall until eventually it led to an enormous chockstone wedged in the inner recesses of the gully. From this chockstone, the great ladder soared upwards...We climbed it conscious of the thousand feet of space below, our sacks dragging us outwards, our palms unduly moist on the iron rungs." (Walt Unsworth)

The first of the Brenta's *via ferrata* routes was begun in the 1930s where a high-level 'trail' was equipped with pegs, ladders and cables between the Bocca di Brenta and Bocca dei Armi. Others soon followed, and in time individual protected routes were linked to create the exciting Sentiero (or Via) delle Bocchette - the 'way of the little passes' - which, with its variations, travels between Passo del Grostè and the Dodici Apostoli hut in a sort-of figure of eight tour through the heart of the district. It is, without question, the most acclaimed of all protected routes that each summer draws mountaineers and mountain walkers of all degrees of competence to the Brenta Dolomites. The Bocchette has virtually become the district's trademark.

In order to tour the region using the main Sentiero delle Bocchette and all its variants without hurrying, about five or six days will be needed. Half a dozen huts lie on or near the route, most of which have non-*via ferrata* trails leading from them which would allow escape in the event of bad weather settling in. These huts, and the linking protected path sections, are noted below:

Rifugio Tuckett	- *Sentiero Alfredo e Rudolfo Benini* (4hrs from Passo del Grostè)
Rifugio Brentei	- *Sentiero SOSAT* (3hrs from/to Rif. Tuckett)
Rifugio Alimonta	- *Sentiero delle Bocchette Alte* (5hrs from Rif. Tuckett)
Rifugio Pedrotti	- *Sentiero delle Bocchette Centrale* (3hrs from Rif. Alimonta)
Rifugio Agostini	- *Sentiero Brentari* (4hrs from Rif. Pedrotti)
Rifugio Dodici Apostoli	- *Sentiero dell'Ideale* (4¹/₂hrs from Rif. Pedrotti)
	Sentiero Castiglioni (2-2¹/₂hrs from Rif. Agostini)

The Sentiero delle Bocchette embodies all the qualities of the *vie ferrata* system, but even with its many variations it does not exhaust all the possibilities along the Brenta spine. Others may be followed north of Passo del Grostè, but there are few south of the Rifugio Dodici Apostoli. The Cicerone guidebook, a translation by Cecil Davies of the German original, gives detailed descriptions of a selection of the best routes, not only in the Brenta, but in the main Dolomite region east of the Adige.

⁂   ⁂   ⁂

ADAMELLO-PRESANELLA-BRENTA

Location:
In Italy, the outline of the range is defined by Val Camonica on the west, the Adige on the east, Val di Sole to the north and Valli Giudicarie to the south. The Adamello-Presanella block is divided from the Brenta by Valle Rendena. The main Dolomite mountains are east of the Adige, Ortler Alps north of Val di Sole, and the Bergamesque Alps lie between the western Adamello and the Bernina Alps.

Principal valleys:
In the Adamello-Presanella district these are: Val Genova, Val di Fumo, Valle dell'Avio, Val Nambino and Valle di Nambrone. As for the Brenta, Vallesinella, Val Brenta and Val di Tovel are, perhaps, of most interest.

Principal peaks:
Cima Presanella (3558m), Monte Adamello (3554m), Carè Alto (3453m), Monte Mandrone (3294m). In the Brenta Dolomites the most important are: Cima Tosa (3173m), Cima Brenta (3151m), Crozzon di Brenta (3135m), Cima Sella (2913m).

Centres:
Madonna di Campiglio serves the Presanella and Brenta districts. Pinzolo is also useful

for the Brenta and Adamello-Presanella, although much time will be spent travelling into the latter range to be really convenient. Molveno on the east side of the Brenta serves as a good, if small, base.

Huts:
There's no real shortage of inn-like huts in any of the districts. It should be noted that those which serve the Brenta often close on or around 20 September. Most huts belong to either the CAI or SAT, but a few privately-owned rifugios also exist.

Access:
Madonna di Campiglio is served by bus routes coming from Malé or Trento, both of which have rail access. The northern side of the Presanella district is approached by train as far as Malé from Trento.

Maps:
Tabacco sheet no.10 covers most of the Adamello-Presanella at 1:50,000. The same coverage is to be found on Kompass sheet 070, *Parco Naturale Adamello-Brenta* also at 1:40,000. This Kompass map is a good buy in that the reverse of the sheet contains the Brenta district. Alternatively try sheet 73, *Gruppo di Brenta* at 1:50,000.

Guidebooks:
Walking in the Central Italian Alps by Gillian Price (Cicerone Press) includes some good suggestions for the Adamello-Presanella district.
Walking in the Dolomites by Gillian Price (Cicerone Press) contains a small section (2 walks only) in the Brenta.
Via Ferrata: Scrambles in the Dolomites by Höfler/Werner and translated by Cecil Davies (Cicerone Press) includes the Sentiero delle Bocchette.
Huts and Hikes in the Dolomites by Ruth Rudner (Sierra Club, San Francisco), although published more than 20 years ago, the Brenta Dolomites are represented with a useful section.

Other reading:
Walking in the Alps by J. Hubert Walker (Oliver & Boyd). Once again Walker excels in his chapter on the Adamello-Presanella, with some delightful descriptions too of the Brenta.
Classic Walks of the World by Walt Unsworth (Oxford Illustrated Press). In this book the Sentiero (or Via) delle Bocchette is enticingly described in words and pictures.
Salute the Mountains by Walter Pause (Harrap, 1962). This translation from the German original, is a description of the author's 100 favourite walks in the Alps. Includes the Brenta.
A Pioneer in the High Alps by F.F. Tuckett (Arnold, 1920). Interesting reading on almost every page.
Italian Alps by D.W. Freshfield (Longmans, 1875 - latest edition published by Blackwell, 1937). More richly-worded observations by this Victorian pioneer.

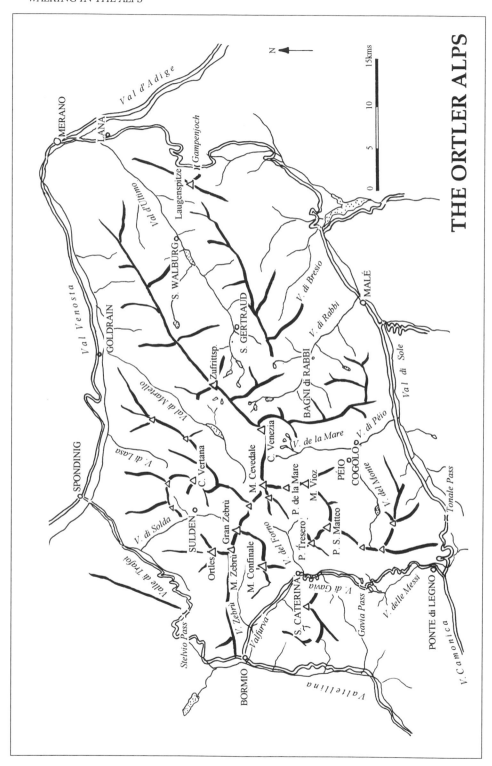

THE ORTLER ALPS

N

15kms

10

5

0

Val d'Adige

MERANO

LANA

Val d'Ultimo

Laugenspitze

Il Gampenjoch

S. WALBURG

Val Venosta

GOLDRAIN

S. GERTRAUD

Zufrittsp.

V. di Bresio

V. di Rabbi

MALÉ

Val di Sole

Val d'Martello

BAGNI di RABBI

SPONDINIG

V. di Lasa

C. Venezia

V. de la Mare

V. di Péio

C. Vertana

M. Cevedale

PÉIO

COGOLO

V. del Monte

Tonale Pass

SULDEN

Gran Zebrù

P. de la Mare

M. Vioz

V. di Solda

Ortles

M. Zebrù

M. Confinale

V. del Forno

P. Tresero

P. S. Matteo

Stelvio Pass

Valle di Tryòi

V. Zebrù

Valfurva

S. CATERINA

V. di Gavia

V. delle Messi

PONTE di LEGNO

Gavia Pass

V. Camonica

BORMIO

Valtellina

292

Cevedale from Rif. Larcher

11: THE ORTLER ALPS

T he imposing Ortler Group, situated between the sources of the Adige and the Adda, and notable for their boldness of form, great height, and magnificent glacier-scenery, present a most interesting field to the tourist," wrote Karl Baedeker more than a hundred years ago.

Until the spoils of the First World War altered political boundaries, the Ortler (3905m) and Königspitze (3851m) were the two highest mountains in Austria. During the war fierce fighting took place in the surrounding valleys, and even the summits were occupied - by Austrians on the Ortler, Italians on Monte Cevedale. But after peace was declared South Tirol was ceded to Italy and with it, the whole of this lovely ice-crusted range, "in shape like some monstrous bird with wings widespread, and heading northward," is how Walker described it. Now most of the peaks, glaciers, valleys and villages, not to mention the numerous huts, bear dual identities, and the Ortler becomes the Ortles, Königspitze the Gran Zebrù.

The Ortler Group is really a geographical extension of the Engadine, acting as a buffer between the Bernina and Brenner Passes. The long Valtellina separates it from the Engadine-Bernina range, and carries the western boundary across the Stelvio Pass into Val di Trafoi which flows down to Spondinig in Val Venosta (or Vinschgau). This forms the northern boundary of the range, beyond which rise the snowy Ötztal mountains, while the southern limit is drawn by Val di Sole and continues across the Tonale Pass along Val Camonica, in so doing outlining part of the boundary of the neighbouring Adamello-Presanella Group to the south.

The central core of mountains is crowned by Monte Cevedale (3769m) whose four main ridges, supporting a variety of glaciers and high snowfields, lead to numerous summits and clusters of summits in a crooked swastika formation overlooking an array of very attractive valleys. These valleys and their feeder glens flow out as major tributaries to river valleys that ring the massif, and provide access for walkers to the very hub of the range.

Taking these valleys in a clockwise circuit we begin with Val di Martello, one of the longest in the district, which flows north-east between two projecting ridges bearing peaks well in excess of three thousand metres. It begins in a high glacial cirque and empties into Val Venosta between Silandro and Latsch, its few hamlets lodged in the middle and lower reaches, leaving the upper valley virtually undeveloped. Writing in his diary of a journey over these mountains, the indefatigable Tuckett came down into Val di Martello (then known as the Martell Thal, or Martelltal - as it often is today) after climbing the Hinter Rotspitze, or Cima Rossa di Saént: "The chalets were unfortunately all uninhabited," he wrote, "and we therefore had to go a long way down the Martell Thal before we could find sleeping quarters, but the valley is so lovely that I scarcely regretted the necessity, though it involved a long grind back again the next morning."

Val d'Ultimo is next. This flows roughly parallel to Val di Martello and joins the Adige just below Merano with several minor glens creating a herring-bone effect. This is a very long and pastoral valley with the reservoir of Lago di Zoccolo (Zoggler Stausee) trapped roughly midway between Lana at its entrance and St Gertraud at the roadhead. While the Ultimo drains north-east, thanks to the general alignment of the range at this point the next valley worth mentioning is the unspoilt Valle di Rabbi which drains south-eastward into the Val di Sole. Much shorter than Val d'Ultimo, Valle di Rabbi is a sinuous glen with some good cross-country routes escaping over its walling ridges. About eleven kilometres from Malé, where the glen opens into Val di Sole, the old Bagni di Rabbi spa was, a hundred years ago when such places were fashionable, the most important in Tirol, the waters of which being strongly impregnated with iron. It is now a growing resort in its own right.

Heading west along Val di Sole the next valley on our clockwise circuit is Valle di Péio whose name changes to Val de la Mare above Cogolo. A great glacial scoop on the east flank of Cevedale forms the head of this delightful and gentle glen. One or two high lakes have been dammed for hydro purposes, but apart from these the valley remains virtually unscarred, its soft green pastures and patches of forest in the lower levels forming a welcome contrast to the glacial slabs and snowfields of the upper region. An important feeder glen here is Valle del Monte which drains eastward into the main Péio-Mare valley at Cogolo.

The upper Valle del Monte is cradled by ridges that splay out from Corno di Tre Signori, on the west side of which two valleys run at right angles to the del Monte glen, joined by Passo di Gavia, a minor road pass linking Ponte di Legno below the Tonale Pass with Bormio below the Stelvio. The glen flowing south from Passo di Gavia is Valle delle Messi, while that which drains to the north is Valle di Gavia.

Valle di Gavia is but one of two early tributaries of Valfurva; the other being

Valle del Forno, while some way downstream Valfurva is joined by Val Zebrù. These three feeder glens, together with the main Valfurva, represent the major access routes on the west side of the range. The winter resort of Santa Caterina Valfurva sits at the confluence of the Gavia and Forno glens at the foot of Monte Confinale to the north, Monte Sobretta on the south side and Pizzo Tresero to the east. In his classic collection of Alpine essays that appeared under the title, *The Playground of Europe*, Leslie Stephen wrote in glowing terms about this lovely spot:

> "Imagine an Alpine meadow, a mile or two in diameter, level as a cricket field, covered with velvet turf of a mountain pasturage...On two sides purple forests of pine rise steeply from the meadow floor and meet a little way below the inn to form the steep gorge through which the glacier torrent foams downwards to join the Adda at Bormio. In front the glen is closed by a steeper mountain, whose lower slopes are too rough and broken to admit of continuous forest. Above them rise bare and precipitous rocks, and from the platform thus formed there soars into the air one of the most graceful of snow-peaks, called the Tresero. It resembles strongly the still nobler pyramid of the Weisshorn, as seen from the Riffel at Zermatt...[but] the Weisshorn only reveals its full beauties to those who have climbed to a considerable height above the ordinary limits of habitation, whereas the Tresero condescends to exhibit itself even to the least adventurous of tourists."

Elsewhere in the same essay Stephen refers again to this mountain which, at 3594 metres, is by no means one of the highest in the range, but nevertheless imposes its character over the western part of the district. He referred to "the towering cone of the Tresero, with torn glaciers streaming from its sides, and glowing with the indescribable colours of sunset on eternal snow."

More than 200 metres higher than the Tresero, the Gran Zebrù, or Königspitze, overlooks the Zebrù glen to the south, while on the opposite side the main west-east ridge system pushes a major spur almost due north, topped by the Ortles (Ortler) itself. This ridge-spur effectively divides two valleys: that of Trafoi which carries the Stelvio road, and Valle di Solda (Suldental), one of the most popular in the range, which lies in the position of eleven o'clock on our circuit of the Ortler Alps.

Thanks to well-maintained road systems that effectively encircle the range, all of these inner valleys and glens are made easily accessible in summer, and since it is almost entirely absorbed within the boundaries of the Stelvio National Park (Parco Nazionale dello Stelvio), the region's popularity with a wider public whose numbers swell those of the general mountaineer and mountain wanderer, is assured. Dating from 1935, this is the largest national park in Italy; an area of 1340 square kilometres of mountains, valleys, lakes and forests - forest covers a fifth of the park's territory up to an altitude of just over two thousand metres, while one tenth is covered in ice. In the west it shares a common boundary with the Swiss National Park of the Lower Engadine, while the park's headquarters and Visitors' Centre are located in Bormio on the south side of the Stelvio Pass.

As a playground for the mountain wanderer the Ortler has plenty to commend it, not least a choice of comparatively easy routes over ice and snow for walker-mountaineers who are properly equipped. In 1918 Claude Wilson wrote with great enthusiasm for the wealth of expeditions along the ridges: "[The range] is, *par excellence*, the land of the ridge wanderer. One can walk or climb over summit after summit along every one of the sky-lines of the district...in the Ortler *all* the ridges 'go'. And yet the mountain forms are grand, and the outlines often singularly bold." (*Alpine Journal vol.32*) Add to this reputation a network of some 1500 kilometres of trails below the snowline within the national park alone, most of which will be followed on single-day outings chanced from a valley base or, maybe, from a more remote lodging in a mountain hut. But as has been hinted at more than once in the previous chapters, those whose delight it is to travel on day after day, from hut to hut or from village to village over intervening ridges, will be well rewarded here. There is no surer way of discovering an 'unknown' country than this. Our guru Hubert Walker underlined that, and his enthusiasm for this particular range is eloquently expressed in the closing words of his chapter, thereby articulating an Alpine philosophy echoed within the pages of this present book:

> "The true lover of mountain country will have been privileged to enjoy days of freedom and fresh air in country as truly beautiful as any he can find. He will have been little troubled with the noise of crowds; he will have been able to commune with himself and his kindred spirits in the presence of unsullied, unexploited and undespoiled masterpieces of Nature."

In order to emulate Walker, then, we will visit some of the most rewarding of these valleys, hint at trails to follow, enjoy landscapes of 'unsullied Nature' and then look at ways of connecting some of these in a multi-day round of exploration. First the northern valleys, for received wisdom has these as being the most beautiful, looking up as they do to crests of ice and snow that represent the range's essential characteristic.

✳   ✳   ✳

Valle di Solda (Suldental)

In full view of a great cradle of snowpeaks, including Ortles and Gran Zebrù (the latter reckoned by Irving to be the most beautiful in the Tirolese Alps), Valle di Solda is gained by way of Valle di Trafoi via a road cutting into it from Gomagoi. A bus route serves this valley during summer only, climbing in about fifteen kilometres to Solda di dentro, or Sulden, a small resort with a couple of chairlifts nearby and a cable-car that rises to Rifugio Citta di Milano. This hut overlooks the Sulden glacier and its huge moraines, and commands a noted view of the Cima di Solda directly above, while following the ridge north-westward the eager eye sweeps along a line containing Gran Zebrù, Monte Zebrù and the rocky precipices of the Ortles. It was from this hut that Kurt Diemberger set out to make the first *direttissima* on the Gran Zebrù's great Königswand, the story of which is included in his eminently readable *Summits & Secrets*.

North-east of the Milano rifugio the Madritsch hut stands below the ice-free Madritschjoch (2817m) which provides a useful link with the neighbouring Val di Martello. Walkers choosing to cross this are recommended to divert onto the Hintere Schöntaufspitze where the reward is a fine panorama that includes mountains of the Adamello-Presanella and Brenta Groups in the south-east, and Engadine summits to the north-west, while near at hand Gran Zebrù and Ortles are the most prominent features on which to concentrate one's attention.

The Milano hut is built upon the ruins of the original Schaubach hut, erected in 1878 when the Suldenferner flowed way below it down to the valley. (In 1818 and again in 1856 this glacier pushed its way down valley, but then began its retreat leaving great moraine tips as a reminder of its former threat to Sulden.) Several other huts are situated along the left-hand mountainside, while two more are found on the opposite flank, thus providing plenty of accommodation for walkers planning to sleep in more secluded lodgings than will be found in the valley itself. The Zaytal hut (Rifugio Serristori), set high in the glen of the same name, offers particularly fine views of the majestic face of Ortles, and is reached by a direct path from St Gertraud, while directly above and to the west of this hut the Hinter Schöneck (3128m) provides an outstanding vantage point. This summit is similarly reached by path from St Gertraud via Stieralm and the Vorder Schöneck.

The Ortles is also seen to dramatic effect from Rifugio Coston (the Hintergrat hut), placed on the shore of a small tarn to the north-west of the Milano hut. The walker's route to it comes up from Sulden, while a shorter approach is possible from the middle station of the cable-car that serves Rifugio Citta di Milano. Following a trail that continues north and north-west along the mountainside a two-day traverse takes you via Rifugio K2, Tabaretta hut and Payer hut (Rifugio G. Payer), before descending to Trafoi.

Another longish trail useful to walkers planning to leave Valle di Solda other than by road, is that which cuts along the right flank of the valley, mostly through forest heading north, then skirts round to the right in a lengthy traverse above Val Venosc before coming to the Lasa glen (Laaser Tal - Laas being noted for the marble quarried there). Study of the map reveals an opportunity to link this trail with others in order to create a multi-day circuit of the Ortler Alps by keeping mainly to the outer ring, from which the walker would snatch mostly distant views of the high peaks, whilst at the same time enjoying the green luxury of foothill vegetation and the delights of neighbouring massifs to north or south.

Val di Martello (Martelltal)

"The head of this valley," said Walker, "is magnificently crowned with the great snowfields of the centre of the system, it is much more remote than any other part of the district, being on no through route and not so obviously accessible as the other villages and hamlets."

The way in by road is from Goldrain (Coldrano - bus service to the Enzian hut in summer). As you progress deeper into the valley, passing several hotels, inns or guesthouses on the way, so the scenery grows in drama. On reaching the artificial lake of the Zufritt See (Lago Gioveretto), at whose southern end there are more mountain inns, the massive shape of Cevedale, its twin peaks and glacial splendour, its extensive ridges and neighbouring summits, closes the way ahead. It's a tremendous view. Several footpaths take off from the lake, making for various destinations on both sides of the valley, while an even greater assortment of trails spreads out from the roadhead two kilometres beyond the lake.

Val Madriccio, the Madritsch glen, lies just to the west of the roadhead, with the popular walkers' pass of the Madritschjoch at its head. This has already been mentioned as a crossing point between Valle di Solda and Val di Martello, as has the easily-attained summit of the Hintere Schöntaufspitze immediately north of the col. Further down valley other peaks in that dividing ridge are also accessible to the walker; accessible summits that enjoy far-reaching views.

Easy passes, tempting to the lover of fine views and good exercise, lead to neighbouring glens, while the novice Alpine mountaineer will find much to excite the imagination when based for a few days at the foot of Monte Cevedale. The Enzian hut (Rifugio Genziana) is located at the roadhead, the ever-popular Zufall hut (Rifugio N. Corsi) is a little further to the south-west, situated in a magnificent cirque topped by Cima Venezia, Monte Cevedale, Cima di Solda and Cima Madriccio (Madritschspitze). Above the Zufall hut, at 2610 metres on the slopes of the Cima Venezia and edging the Zufallferner, or Cevedale glacier, the Marteller hut (Rifugio Martello) makes a useful base for climbers tackling the Cevedale, and for the crossing of assorted easy glacier passes leading to the southern valleys. There are several of these to choose from, were we equipped to tackle them, and it would surely be an understandable temptation to stray to the Cevedale's summit while it's close at hand, for this great but uncomplicated mountain claims a panorama of rare expanse and beauty, while its central position in the range enables the whole district to be studied in some detail. "A view which extends from Monte Rosa to the Alps of Tirol and the Dolomites, which includes Adamello, Presanella and the Brenta Alps, and takes in all the valleys and ranges of Ortler itself, such a view is a thing to treasure."

Val d'Ultimo (Ultental)

A useful number of crossing points enable walkers to move into this valley over the ridge divider from Val di Martello. In her guide to the Central Italian Alps, Gillian Price recommends the grassy 2882 metre Soyscharte which has a trail beginning roughly midway along the Martello glen and comes down to St Gertraud at the roadhead in Val d'Ultimo. The pass itself provides an opportunity, according to Walker, to add another summit or two to one's tally of uncomplicated Ortler peaks by following the ridge south-westward, over the Soyjoch to the Zufrittspitze (or Gioveretto; 3439m). Without such a diversion the basic traverse of the Soyscharte is a seven-hour crossing, while there's another, also ice-free, route via the Flimjoch (2892m) to the north-east, which similarly leads to St Gertraud, the two connected by trails on either side of the ridge, while south-west of the Zufrittspitze others are partially hindered by glacial cravats draped in high upper corries.

Without tackling high ridges, however, the normal way to approach the valley is from Lana in the Val d'Adige below Merano. A bus service all year round feeds into Val d'Ultimo as far as St Gertraud, at which point the valley forks. The north-west glen leads to two dammed lakes, both of which have inns or huts located by them. The upper of these lakes is the Grünsee, and above this rises the Zufrittspitze. On the ridge cutting south from this peak the Zufrittjoch is one of those glacier passes (on the west side only) that links with Val di Martello. From the dam-end of the Grünsee a trail cuts south across the slopes of Cima Sternai to the Langsee.

Here a route filters south-west and, passing a string of small tarns, climbs to a 2825 metre pass leading to the upper Valle di Rabbi, while yet another crosses the south-eastern ridge to Passo di Rabbi, an easy but less interesting pass at the head of Valle di Montechiesa, the upper feeder glen for Val d'Ultimo.

If you should be attracted to a crossing into Valle di Rabbi the best way would be via the 2825 metre pass mentioned above. This is the Schwarzer Joch, or Giogo Nero Pass. From it a scramble is recommended to the Collecchio, a minor peak to the south-east, from where a view is obtained of the Adamello-Presanello Group off to the south, as well as the southern flank of the Ortler Alps spread before you in a fluster of ridge, peak and valley.

These routes merely represent a small selection at the head of the Ultimo. But trails in plenty exist throughout the valley, crossing pastures, cutting through the rich forests, onto upper alps and ridges and minor summits. St Walburg, a village with guesthouse accommodation located down valley beyond Lago di Zoccolo, gives access to some fine walking possibilities on the walling mountainside to the north-west, and for energetic walkers the possibility of gaining fine viewpoints on sub-three thousand metre peaks - to be attempted in good conditions only. There are also groups of tarns lodged in lofty saddles, and yet more ways over cols that lead into either Val di Martello or the main Val Venosta.

Down valley further still a side road goes up to the baths of Mitterbad in the Marauner feeder glen, from where the ascent of the Laugenspitze (Monte Luco, 2434m) is made by walkers drawn there by its local fame as a viewpoint, and also by the opportunity to descend on the far side to Senale below the Gampenjoch on the road between Merano and Fondo, a charming back-country that is, nevertheless, outside the boundaries of the real Ortler Alps. But what lovely gentle country it is - certainly worth a visit by anyone with plenty of time in hand and an eye for unheralded scenic gems.

Valle di Rabbi

This is an unspoilt valley with something of an out-of-the-way feel to it. Public buses travel from orange-roofed Malé (the 'capital' of Val di Sole which has access by rail from Trento) as far as the Bagni di Rabbi spa where there's a small National Park Visitors' Centre. There's no shortage of accommodation, including a campsite and a couple of mountain huts. There are feeder glens to explore, and high tarns and waterfalls accessible to the walker. There are opportunities for crossing into neighbouring valleys, minor summits to visit and much fine scenery to enjoy.

Travelling into the valley from Val di Sole one reaches the village of San Bernardo about seven kilometres from Malé. Here the Valorz stream pours into the main Rabbies torrent, having drained a beautiful quiet glen which digs into the mountains to the south-west. This glen is topped by a cirque formed by the combined ridges of the Mezzana, Valletta and Tremenesca peaks, and cupped within that cirque there's a cluster of tarns worth visiting. The walk up is both interesting and picturesque, including a section where the path has been tunnelled through the rock. Larchwoods adorn the lower hillsides. Higher there's alder scrub and swathes of alpenrose, then scattered boulders and rubble and a delightful wave formation where the rock appears to have been moulded when hot, but in fact owes its curious shaping to the work of a one-time glacier. There are seven lakes of varying size, linked by clear streams, and above the highest of them all, the broad col of Passo Valletta (2695m) affords spectacular views not only of the lakes, but of the distant tip of the Grossglockner visible in the north-east, and the impressive Brenta Dolomites to the south-east. A wider view may be obtained from the crown of the easy Cima Valletta (2857m), reached by way of a short scramble from the col, while an optional descent leads southward down to Mezzana in Val di Sole.

North of Piazzola, Val Lago Corvo is headed by Passo di Rabbi, the main cross-country route by which the valley is gained from Val d'Ultimo. Just below the pass, on the Rabbi side, is the handsome, stone-built Rifugio Lago Corvo (or Haselgruber hut) facing south and with views that focus one's attention on the pale shapes of the Brenta spires and turrets beyond the nearer Adamello-Presanella Group. Heading west from this hut a trail leads shortly to the tarn after which it is named, then continues to the summit of Collecchio before tracing the ridge down to the Giogo Nero Pass, that fine crossing point already mentioned above when discussing possibilities from Val d'Ultimo.

Our walker based for a day or two at the Lago Corvo hut would find his time well spent by crossing this pass and descending to Lago Lungo (Langsee) and continuing down to the Weissbrunsee (Lago Fontana Bianca), from where he may either complete a circuit via St Gertraud and up Valle di Montechiesa to Passo di Rabbi, or heading south-west to the Höchster hut (Rifugio U. Canziani), from where a direct route leads back to Lago Lungo.

The next tributary glen is that of Val Cércena where a few alp farms adorn the pastures. This glen flows into the main valley from the south-west and joins the Rabbi beyond the spa buildings and growing resort of Bagni di Rabbi. According to Walker this glen is all grand country. Grand country indeed, especially for the walker, for once again there are feasible pass crossings to draw one on; Passo Basetta in the southern ridge wall, Passo Cércena at 2622 metres at the head of the glen to the west, and Passo di Cadinel in the ridge south of the Cércena pass. This latter pass commands a very fine view of the southern peaks of the Ortler Alps, and carries the national park boundary out of Valle di Péio and down through the Cércena glen. An attractive route follows that boundary on the west side of the pass all the way to Cogolo.

Flowing parallel to the Cércena glen in the north is Val Maleda, a shorter glen than the former and with another crossing between the Péio and Rabbi valleys, less frequented than the Cércena and recommended by Hubert Walker. This is Col Verdignana, unmarked as such on the Kompass map but said by Walker to involve no more than rough scrambling.

The main Valle di Rabbi continues roughly westward beyond Piazzola before curving northward then kinking north-west into the amphitheatre known as Valle Laghetti di Sternai. It is up here that the second of the Rabbi huts is located. Owned by the SAT (Società Alpinisti Tridentina), Rifugio Silvio Dorigoni was opened in 1903 but has recently been renovated and enlarged to sleep eighty. Reached in about three hours from Piazzola, it makes a comfortable base from which to explore this backwater, with accessible tarns lodged above it and a choice of trails teasing away on traverse routes heading south, or up to rocky cols that reward with big panoramas. One of these is Passo di Saént (2984m) on the ridge linking Cima Rossa di Saént and Cima di Saént. This is one of the traditional ways of gaining Val di Martello, but whether or not your plans are to head over the glaciers on the north side of the ridge, this pass ought to be on the 'must visit' list of any walker worth his salt planning to explore this corrie. West of the hut is another. Bocchetta di Saént sud overlooks the Cima Vanezia and Careser glacier, a smooth and almost level icefield hanging above the dammed Lago Càreser near the head of Val de la Mare, the northern extension of the pastoral Péio valley.

Valle di Péio

"The ever-lovely Péio" (Tuckett) is the longest of the south-draining valleys of the Ortler Alps, and a real gem it is too, with emerald green pastures banked by dark forest and with crisp snowpeaks at its head scraping the sky. Almost as soon as you enter from Val di Sole there is a gleam of welcome from the north-bound heights. A bus service visits Cogolo, the main village where the valley forks, and continues to Péio-Fonti (or Terme, a spa) in Valle del Monte, the western tributary glen. Above the spa buildings a road twists up the hillside to Péio (or Péjo), a handsome village of Celtic origin at 1579 metres facing the sun from a shelf on the lower slopes of the pyramid-shaped Monte Vioz. Just below the spa there's a well-appointed campsite approached through trees off the Cogolo road, while there's plenty of hotel accommodation in both Cogolo and Péio-Fonti. Cogolo also has some useful shops, a bank and a tourist office dispensing literature about the Stelvio National Park.

Almost a thousand metres above Péio, Cima di Vioz (2504m) was said by Baedeker to "afford a good survey of the grand environs." This is now accessible by cable-car and chairlift (Rifugio Doss dei Cembri nearby), while a trail continues above it for another eleven hundred metres along a sharp ridge, with fixed cable in places and some snow, to gain the summit of Monte Vioz, a renowned viewpoint at 3645 metres. The panorama from this lofty spot is truly spectacular and well worth the effort required to gain it. In fact it's one of the finest of all high points accessible to the walker, for Monte Vioz is virtually an outlying peak of the Ortler range, set upon the periphery of the main mountain block from where it holds the rest of the group at arm's length, so to speak, and thereby gains a proper perspective of its higher neighbours - including those of the gleaming Adamello-Presanella Group to the south across the depths of Val di Sole. The broad sweep of the Forni glacier (second largest in the Eastern Alps) lies just below on the western side, with Punta San Matteo on its opposite bank, Palòn de la Mare to the north-west and Monte Cevedale beyond that. Gazing onto the glacier from the summit of Palòn de la Mare, Tuckett said that "the snow and ice scenery is as magnificent as anything that is to be met with in the choicest portions of Switzerland."

Just twenty minutes below the summit on the Péio flank, Rifugio Mantova al Vioz stands on an elevated perch on the southern shoulder of the mountain; a fabulous location for a hut with an amazing, far-reaching panorama - a great place from which to rise early in order to capture sunrise from the summit. This is another SAT hut, although it was originally built by the German Alpine Club and used as a garrison for Austrian troops during the First World War.

Walkers with the necessary Alpine experience, and equipped to tackle glaciers and snowfields, may well be tempted by the classic traverse of thirteen summits of the Ortler Alps that are seen from Monte Vioz's crown. This traverse, known locally as the *Traversata delle 13 cime*, is perhaps the grandest mountaineering tour available in the district. All the summits included in the tour are over 3500 metres high, and the route is seventeen kilometres long, leading over fairly modest glaciers and snowfields. Two to three days are usually taken for this tour, with overnights in the Mantovi al Vioz and Larcher huts, and the Meneghello bivouac. Monte Vioz is crossed roughly halfway along the traverse, the route beginning usually at the Larcher, or Cevedale hut at the head of Val de la Mare, and descending from the final summit (Pizzo Tresero) into either Valle di Gavia or Valle del Monte.

For our walker who prefers to stay away from glaciers, and is not tempted by prospects of summit-bagging, Valle del Monte may be explored by paths that radiate from Péio (mid-height trails) and Péio-Fonti (valley-bed walks). There's also a path known as the Sentiero dei Tedeschi which begins at the top station of the chairlift above Péio, and skirts the north flank of the del Monte glen before returning to Péio-Fonti, on which the distant splendour of the Brenta Dolomites serves as a highlight. Yet another option is a long one-, or easy two-, day walk out to the Tonale Pass. Leaving Péio-Fonti this route goes upvalley to Lago di Pian Palù, then cuts up into the Montozzo glen, crosses Forcellina di Montozzo with its First World War trenches, and descends to Rifugio A. Bozzi. From there an undemanding three-hour walk with the magnificent Adamello-Presanella Group ahead, leads to the road west of Passo di Tonale. Gillian Price's guide to *Walking in the Central Italian Alps* describes this, and several other walks in the district, and is highly recommended.

As for the main Val de la Mare that extends Valle di Péio beyond Cogolo, this holds enough opportunities for wild-country walks to satisfy an activist for several days. A road continues through the valley between pastureland and patches of forest, and twists its way to a car park at the Malga Mare power station, thereby putting the upper glen of Val Venézia within easy reach of day-trippers. However, the non-motorised walker has a good alternative to consider, with two paths that cut along the western hillside from Péio; one from the village itself, the other a higher option that begins at the top of the cableway from Péio-Fonti. The two join forces shortly before reaching Malga Mare, then follow a standard route upvalley to Rifugio Larcher, otherwise known as the Cevedale hut which preceded it on the same site.

Rifugio Guido Larcher may not have an extensive panorama to match that of the Mantova hut, but it occupies a stony corrie of glacier-ringed mountains, gazing directly across to the tumbling, heavily-crevassed Vedretta de la Mare and above it a broad crest of snow and ice. It's a popular place for mountaineers tackling climbs on the Cevedale, Zufallspitze or Cima Venezia, and for the start of the long traverse of thirteen peaks referred to above. But the modest walker is also catered for in the rather wild surroundings, and the col of La Forcola (3032m) makes a worthwhile destination for a half-day outing from the hut. From this point, you stand not only on the edge of an ice sea with a breathtaking panorama to absorb, but the col marks the border between the administrative districts of Südtirol and Trentino; one German speaking, the other intrinsically Italian.

Another first-rate outing to tackle from the Larcher hut visits four lakes and may be used as a novel way of descent to Malga Mare. It begins just one minute away from the hut with a path that rises gently eastward to a ridge-crest overlooking Lago Marmotta. Instead of descending the east side of the ridge on a trail signposted to Lago Lungo, it's worth cutting left along the crest, then sloping down to the Marmotta lake and from there making a clockwise circuit. There is no path as such at the northern end, but the way is uncomplicated and you gain a splendid view across the water to the distant snows of the Adamello-Presanella, while from the eastern shore you look back to Palòn de la Mare and Cevedale and the glacial scarf that hangs between them.

Next lake on this tour is Lago Lungo, but there's an alternative trail that remains above it and follows a contour of about 2630 metres, with consistently fine views as a major distraction, before reaching the jade-green Lago Nero from whose north shore the scenic highlight of the walk is gained. Sitting alone in that rocky bowl one day, with Palòn de la Mare looking magnificent beyond the rippling waters of the tarn, I had to strain all senses in order to capture any sound beyond the settled buzz of distance. It was a glorious early autumn day, with the crisp tinge of frost in the air, and mountains perfectly etched against the blue. A perfect day for collecting tarns and soaking the delights of these southern Ortler glens.

Just beyond Lago Nero is the larger Lago del Càreser, blocked at its south-western end by a huge dam - the only scar in a landscape of great beauty. Then the way plunges down to Malga Mare, at first over rocky terrain, then on grass slopes, and last and best of all among fragrant pine trees. Other trails cut along the left-hand hillside, teased by distant mountains, the soft blue Italian light settled in the valley below; occasional sightings of chamois, the shrill call of a marmot, finches in the pinewoods and cowbells clattering from some far-off pasture. Such are the shades of days spent wandering in the Alps.

Valfurva

As was seen earlier at the start of this chapter in our outline of the Ortler valleys, Valfurva drains westward to Bormio and the Adda below the Stelvio Pass, and is fed by three tributaries: Valle di Gavia, Valle del Forno and Val Zebrù. Bormio, then, holds the key to an exploration of these valleys, but one should first take the opportunity to stock up with assorted goodies for days on the mountains, and to call in at the National Park Visitors' Centre for up-to-date information. Walkers without their own transport have a year-round bus service to Santa Caterina Valfurva where there's accommodation to be had, as well as camping nearby, while assorted rifugios provide lodging in more remote glens and corners of these mountains.

Before disappearing into these feeder glens and visiting the huts, the ascent of one particular peak should be on the programme of all walkers wishing to form a general view of the neighbourhood from a base at Santa Caterina. And here I refer to Monte Confinale (3370m), the mountain which rises almost due north of the village, for it offers the finest vantage point available nearby. The ascent demands but four or five hours by a path that climbs above the village, then skirts to the right along the lower slopes of the mountain in order to gain Val della Manzina, through which the ascent proper is made, passing on the way the little Lago di Manzina. Of the summit view, Baedecker was brief and to the point: "Admirable survey of the Ortler chain from the summit," he wrote. "W. the Bernina and Piz Linard, S.W. the Monte della Disgrazia, S. the Presanella." Leslie Stephen was in more voluble mood in *The Playground of Europe*, and it's worth quoting him at length here, for although his style is distinctly Victorian, his general outline of the neighbouring peaks can scarcely be faulted.

> "It stands approximately at the centre of a gigantic horseshoe of snowclad mountains, from which it is divided by a deep trench, except at the point where a low isthmus connects it with one of the loftiest summits (the Königspitz), and divides the waters of the two streams at its base...[On the left] a long wall of tremendous black cliffs...sinks into the wild valley of the Zebru, inhabited only in the summer months by a few herdsmen. Above this wall, at some distance, towers the massive block of the Ortler Spitze, cleaving the air with its sharp final crest. About the centre of the crescent, in front of the spectator, the ridge culminates in the noble Königspitz, falling on this side in a sheer cliff towards the valley. The mighty precipices of this segment of the crescent, through which one or two huge glaciers have hewn deep trenches towards the valley, are well contrasted with the graceful undulations of the long snow-slopes and streaming glaciers which clothe the ridges to the right. The ever-beautiful Tresero marks an interruption to the wall, where a lateral valley [Valle di Gavia] comes in from the south, but it is continued in the long swell of the Sovretta. This half of the semicircle is divided from the Confinale by the green valley of the Frodolfo, into which the eye plunges for some thousand feet...There are nobler mountains, steeper cliffs, and vaster glaciers elsewhere, but it would be hard to find any point from which the sternness and sweetness of the High Alps are more skilfully contrasted and combined."

Of the two feeder glens that have their confluence above Santa Caterina, that which flows from the south is Valle di Gavia, with Passo di Gavia at its head. This is an old pass said to have been used as far back as 1200 by Venetian merchants. A road was built across it during the First World War, connecting with Valle delle Messi which descends to the west side of the Tonale Pass, but the road is only open to traffic in summer, while there's a trail running parallel to it that is useful for walkers either coming into or out of Valfurva. On the approach to the pass there are two huts; Rifugio A. Berni (CAI owned) and the privately-owned Rifugio Bonetta, both of which are situated at the roadside. Some way up the glen from Santa Caterina a secondary glen breaks off to the south-west, with another walkers' route that crosses Passo dell'Alpe into Valle di Rezzallo and thence down to the Valtellina at Le Prese. Also accessible from Valle di Gavia is an ascent route to Pizzo Tresero, Leslie Stephen's "most graceful of snow-peaks." This is not, however, in the realm of most walkers following routes in this book, although a crossing of

Passo di Sforzellina (3006m) into the upper Valle del Monte, and thence to Péio, could be. This route begins, as does the Tresero path, at the Berni hut, and, according to Walker, there are no difficulties and the pass is gained in two hours. Peaks on either side of the pass, Pizzo di Sforzellina (3100m) to the north, and Corno di Tre Signori (3360m) to the south, could be ascended over broken rock without problem. Both summits, he assured his readers, give views worth seeing.

Leaving Valle di Gavia now it is time to look at the other two glens that make Valfurva such a rewarding place from which to explore the western Ortler Alps; Valle del Forno and Val Zebrù.

Let's backtrack for a moment, heading downstream from Santa Caterina. On coming to San Antonio, about four kilometres from Bormio, the main Valfurva is joined from the north-east by Val Zebrù, a rugged and imposing glen noted for its wildlife (marmots, chamois, ibex and roe deer) and great dolomitic cliffs. The north wall is spectacular; a massive shaft of rock leading at its eastern end to the glacier-hung Monte Zebrù and Gran Zebrù (Königspitze), while the southern wall is taken up with the bulk of Monte Confinale and its attendant peaks, hanging glaciers and small cirques. The head of the glen is closed by a ridge running from Monte Confinale to the Gran Zebrù, and this is crossed by the walkers' pass of Passo di Zebrù (3001m), on which there's a small timber-built bivouac shelter. From this point a wild view is gained back down through the glen; a view that includes Gran Zebrù and Cima della Miniera, Monte Zebrù, Thurwieserspitze and Kristallspitze (Punta di Cristallo) along the right flank, and of Cime dei Forni near at hand on the left. A trail descending the east side of the pass leads into Val di Cedec which flows at right-angles to Val Zebrù and becomes the Valle del Forno below the buildings of Baite dei Forni.

So much for the glen's simple outline, what of the walker's prospects? In truth, apart from a long but exceedingly rewarding traverse from one end to the other and over the Zebrù Pass, they're somewhat limited by the severity of the landscape, although there's a way onto Monte Forcellino, a western peaklet thrust out by a spur from Monte Confinale, and a circuit of the same peaklet made possible by using the Passo di Forcellino on its southern shoulder. And there's Rifugio Alpini to visit.

Rifugio V° Alpini (V° meaning *quinto* - Italian for 'fifth') dates from 1884 when it was erected by the Italian Alpine Club and then known as Capanna Milano. It stands in a magnificent position on a rocky outcrop at 2877 metres on the edge of the Zebrù glacier below the south face of Monte Zebrù, and is reached by a variety of trails that converge above the Pastore alp. Above the hut a famed vantage point offers a splendid panorama of peaks and glaciers that crowd the valley. But this is primarily a mountaineer's hut, for there's a rich assortment of summits accessible from it, and a choice of glacier routes leading on the far side of the walling ridge down to either the Trafoi or Sulden valleys.

Back in Santa Caterina the last of our tributary glens awaits discovery, and as an introduction to Val del Forno again we turn to the words of Leslie Stephen in which he described, "the beautiful gorge which gradually rises from the level of Santa Catarina [sic], to the foot of the Forno glacier, the path through which shows as charming a variety of valley scenery as is to be found in any similar walk in

Switzerland."

By taking this walk as far as Rifugio Branca set below the Forni glacier, this "charming variety of valley scenery" can be enjoyed at a morning's leisure. Wandering through the Forno glen, fragrant with pinewoods and the Frodolfo stream below bringing the melt from several icefields, two rifugios (Stella Alpina and Rifugio Forni) are passed before the way forks at a parking area near the buildings of Baite dei Forni. Rifugio Ghiacciaio dei Forni, to give its full name, was formerly known as the Forno Inn or Albergo Buzzi. Walker was an eager patron, while seventy years before his book appeared it was the Baite dei Forni that provided rustic accommodation. In the 1880s this was described as being "grandly situated opposite to the huge Forno Glacier, which descends to the valley in an imposing ice-fall, and surrounded by the finely-shaped Piz Tresero, Punta di S. Matteo, Mte. Saline, etc." (*Karl Baedeker*) The glacier has withdrawn considerably since then, of course. To the left stretches Val di Cedec, while the right-hand track leads up to the Branca hut with glacier views increasing in extent as you progress towards it.

The Branca hut is situated near a small tarn lying at the foot of the Rosole glen. Owned by the CAI it was built in 1932 and can sleep one hundred. Walker called it a fine inn, and a good base from which to tackle Punta San Matteo at the head of the glacier. The glacier is split 300 metres above the hut by the rocky island of Isola Persa which looks onto the glacier's icefall, and the map shows a route leading to this from the parking area referred to above.

The northern stem of Val del Forno, Val di Cedec, is headed by Gran Zebrù, Kreilspitze and Suldenspitze. South-east of the latter peak Monte Cevedale rises across the broad swathe of the Cedec glacier, then the eastern walling ridge is carried by Monte Pasquale, whose south-west arête is the divider between Val di Cedec and the Rosole glen. The west wall of the Cedec glen consists of the sweeping flank of the Confinale massif. A track (no private vehicles) scores through the glen above Baite dei Forni, and continues to a point midway between Rifugio Pizzini-Fràttola and Rifugio Casati. A path cuts into it from the Branca hut and joins this track forty minutes before reaching the Pizzini rifugio at 2700 metres near the head of the valley. Three hundred metres above this hut to the west is Passo di Zebrù, while more than 500 metres above it to the north-east Rifugio Casati, and its annexe, Rifugio Guasti, are found virtually on the 3260 metre Passo del Cevedale. As might be imagined, a wonderful vista of icefields and snowpeaks, dominated here by the double-peaked Monte Cevedale, rewards all who arrive under cloud-free conditions.

✳   ✳   ✳

A TOUR OF THE ORTLER ALPS

So much for our review of the main Ortler valleys and glens. Having gained some impression of the layout of the district, and of its potential for valley-based walks, it is now time to work out a continuous tour that will link these various valleys with the aid of huts and, where possible, modest village hotels. The first consideration must be method of approach. Assuming public transport is used, access is possible by train to the Austrian town of Landeck, and bus from there to Spondinig or Merano for those glens draining into Val Venosta. An alternative route for the northern (and eastern) valleys is by train (say Innsbruck-Brenner-Bolzano, then to Merano), or for the western side of the range via Switzerland (Zürich-Chur-St Moritz-Bernina-Tirano), followed by bus to Bormio below the Stelvio Pass. Tirano is also reached by train from Milan, while Val di Sole has rail access (via Malé) from Trento, thereby putting the southern valleys within reach too. Since the tour sketched out below is a circuitous one and, following Walker's lead, goes in a counter-clockwise direction, it should be possible to join the route at almost any given point. But for convenience sake we begin here at Bormio in company with Walker, with the warm invitation of Valfurva and its scenic glens close at hand.

To begin the first stage, it is recommended to take the Santa Caterina bus as far as San Antonio, and there leave Valfurva to wander up through the adjacent Zebrù glen, climbing at its head to Passo di Zebrù, a rise of a little over 1600 metres from the point at which you left the bus. For a first day this is quite a haul, but it will have been one of the best possible introductions to the district, as the pass itself provides eloquent witness to glories yet to come. Descend on the east side to the head of the Cedec glen, there to spend a night in Rifugio Pizzini.

The next stage is basically a very short one, but it will give an opportunity to take in the delights of the Cedec glen and the big Forni glacier, while a diversion at the very start of the day adds a vision of other icefields streaming from Monte Cevedale. Given settled weather and prospects of good views, it would be as well to leave your main baggage behind at the Pizzini hut and walk unencumbered up the track and subsequent path rising above it, to gain Rifugio Casati, there to enjoy a grand ice-bound panorama at the very heart of the range, before returning to the Pizzini hut. Having collected your rucksack amble down through the glen a short way until you come to the trail cutting off left ahead leading to the Branca hut at the foot of the Forni glacier.

Stage three follows Walker's advice on a high route into Valle di Gavia. But while it's clearly marked on the map, it has to be admitted I have not personally taken this trail which, after descending from Rifugio Branca to the Forno glen, breaks away at Campec and rises along the north-west flank of Pizzo Tresero to the summit of Dosso Tresero (2354m). From there Walker directs his readers up a ridge to P. di Segnale (3133m) with the ruins of a one-time hut just below it. "Here, on the edge of the Tresero glacier," says Walker, "with the Tresero itself less than a mile away on its further side, the situation has airiness and a sense of the upland world to commend it." The path continues with a descent to Rifugio Berni on the roadside in Valle di Gavia.

From Rifugio Berni the onward route traces the southern edge of our circuit with the crossing of Passo di Sforzellina, descent from which takes us into Valle del Monte. Instead of restricting oneself to the bed of the glen, it is preferable to take the left-hand trail that goes along the hillside to Pèio, where the fourth night of the trek will be spent in a hotel. Should there be sufficient allowance made for it, the next day would be well spent by climbing Monte Vioz above Pèio and having a night in the Mantova hut just below the summit. Whilst not adding any productive distance to the circuit, the sheer pleasure gained by such an experience, not to mention yet another magnificent high point from which to study the layout of these southern valleys, completely validates such a diversion.

Moving on, the mid-height trail pushing north from Pèio to the Malga Mare hydro station gives easy access to Val Venezia, the stony upper glen at whose head stands the Larcher hut. If there's time and energy left when you arrive there, the climb to the col of La Forcola is worth considering.

Leaving the Larcher (or Cevedale) hut, our route parts company with that devised by Walker. In his book, Walker suggested descending the same way as the upward route to Malga Mare, continuing from there down valley to Malga Pontevecchio, then up and over Col Verdignana. From this col above the Maleda glen that drains into the upper Valle di Rabbi, he then headed for Rifugio Dorigoni. We, however, will choose a more varied route.

Departing the Larcher hut take the easy path heading south-east over the low ridge above it, and then follow a good trail passing above Lago Lungo to Lago Nero and the Càreser reservoir. From the south-eastern end of the reservoir dam descend towards Malga Mare on a steepish path, until another breaks off to the left. This should then be taken along the eastern flank of Val de la Mare, through the alp of Malga Verdignana and continuing roughly southward until coming to a crossing trail just above Malga Levi. This trail climbs up and over Passo Cércena, and down through the Cércena glen to Bagni di Rabbi or Piazzola where accommodation for the night should be found without too much difficulty.

Valle di Rabbi marks the end of the southern section of our circuit, as the continuing tour moves northward to the head of Val d'Ultimo. To advance this route a direct path heads up the Lago Corvo glen above Piazzola, to reach the Haselgruber hut (Rifugio Lago Corvo) just below Passo di Rabbi. Walkers who want a short day should cross this pass and follow a continuing trail over the Kirchbergalm to Lago Lungo (not to be confused with the Lago Lungo of the previous stage), and from there continue to the Höchster hut (Rifugio U. Canziani) set beside the Grünsee in a feeder glen above Val d'Ultimo. However, a better though longer crossing is recommended. This involves a traverse west from Lago Corvo, followed by the ascent of Collecchio, then descending a little over a hundred metres to the Giogo Nero Pass. From this col bear right and slope down to the north-east among a collection of tarns. On reaching the Langsee, or Lago Lungo, head to the left on the path which leads directly to the Höchster hut. Alternatively, should you prefer a night in a village atmosphere, do not turn left at Lago Lungo, but instead continue down through the glen to St Gertraud where there's limited accommodation and a shop for supplies.

The next ridge to cross is that which divides Val d'Ultimo from Val di Martello, and the pass chosen for this is the Soyscharte, almost due north of, and some three hundred metres or so above, the Höchster hut. However, there is no direct route from the hut to the pass, although the map suggests it would be feasible to adopt the ascent route to the Zufrittspitze, then follow the ridge north-eastward, in order to gain the Soyscharte by an interesting high level route. But once again I have no personal experience of this, and can only recommend the standard trail which meets another coming up from St Gertraud at the picturesque alp of Pilsbergalm. Once over the pass and having descended into the glorious Val di Martello, wander upstream to the Zufritt See and Rifugio Gioveretto, there to spend the evening in adoration of the fabulous amphitheatre which blocks the glen a short distance away.

From Val di Martello the circuit now heads west, crossing the Madritschjoch above Valle di Solda, but instead of dropping into that valley after reaching the Milano hut, it is better to remain above it. First, however, it's necessary to descend to the middle station of the cableway, then cut off on the trail that leads to Rifugio Coston (Hintergrat hut) and the K2 hut below the Ortles.

The final day's walk of the tour visits the Tabaretta hut, then turns the ridge-spur projecting north from the Ortles, first by way of the Barenjoch, and then the Tabarettajoch (2883m), above which Rifugio G. Payer is perched in a dramatic location. From here it's descent nearly all the way to Trafoi on the north-east side of the Stelvio Pass.

A TOUR OF THE ORTLER ALPS - ROUTE SUMMARY

Day 1: Bormio - San Antonio (bus) - Passo di Zebrù - Rifugio Pizzini

Day 2: Rifugio Pizzini - Rifugio Casati (optional) - Rifugio C. Branca

Day 3: Rifugio C. Branca - Dosso Tresero - P. di Segnale - Rifugio Berni

Day 4: Rifugio Berni - Passo di Sforzellina - Péio

Day 5: Péio - Monte Vioz - Rifugio Mantova al Vioz (optional)

Day 6: Rifugio Mantova (or Péio) - Malga Mare - Rifugio G. Larcher

Day 7: Rifugio Larcher - Passo Cércena - Bagni di Rabbi (or Piazzola)

Day 8: Bagni di Rabbi (or Piazzola) - Haselgruber Hut - Collecchio - Giogo Nero Pass - Höchster Hut (or St Gertraud)

  or: Bagni di Rabbi (or Piazzola) - Passo di Rabbi - Lago Lungo - Höchster Hut

Day 9: Höchster Hut (or St Gertraud) - Soyscharte - Rifugio Gioveretto

Day 10: Rifugio Gioveretto - Madritschjoch - Rifugio Citta di Milano - Rifugio Coston - Rifugio K2

Day 11: Rifugio K2 - Tabaretta Hut - Barenjoch - Tabarettajoch - Trafoi

---

✳ ✳ ✳

THE ORTLER ALPS

Location:

Entirely in Italy, between the Adige and Adda, the range straddles two administrative regions, Alto-Adige and Lombardy. Much of the district is contained within the boundaries of the Stelvio National Park.

Principal valleys:

Valle di Solda, Val di Martello and Val d'Ultimo on the north and eastern flanks; Valfurva, with the Zebrù, Forno and Gavia glens on the west, Valle di Péio/Val de la Mare and Valle di Rabbi draining to the south.

Principal peaks:
Ortles (Ortler; 3905m), Gran Zebrù (Königspitze; 3851m), Monte Cevedale (3769m), Monte Zebrù (3740m), Palòn de la Mare (3708m)

Centres:
Sulden, Santa Caterina in Valfurva, Cogolo, Bagni di Rabbi/Piazzola.

Huts:
The region is well stocked with huts and bivouacs, mostly owned by the CAI, but with a number of rifugio/mountain inns in private ownership.

Access:
Coming by public transport from the U.K. a choice of routes are possible: by air to Innsbruck, then train to Landeck, and bus via Nauders to Merano; or from Innsbruck by train via the Brenner Pass to Bolzano and change for Merano. The same route to Bolzano, then change for Trento where a local train goes to Malé in Val di Sole. By air to Zürick and train to Chur, St Moritz and over the Bernina Pass to Tirano, from where a bus may be taken north to Bormio. By air to Milan, train to Tirano and bus to Bormio. Local buses serve most of the inner valleys.

Maps:
All but a very small corner of the region is covered by Kompass sheet 72, *Ortler/ Ortles Cevedale* at 1:50,000. Sheet number 53 includes the lower reaches of Val d'Ultimo not covered by sheet 72. Tabacco map number 08 at 1:25,000 is useful for several valleys, giving finer detail than the Kompass sheets.

Guidebook:
Walking in the Central Italian Alps by Gillian Price (Cicerone Press) serves as an excellent companion to the area.

Other reading:
Walking in the Alps by J. Hubert Walker (Oliver & Boyd) continues to inspire, despite being out of date in several respects.
The Alpine Journal (Alpine Club) - early volumes contain entertaining articles of specific interest to visitors to the Ortler Alps. In particular volume 1 (1864) with F.F. Tuckett's article: 'Contributions to the Topography of the Orteler and Lombard Alps' and Claude Wilson's 'The Ortler in 1911' published in volume 32 (1918).
A Pioneer in the High Alps by F.F. Tuckett (Arnold, 1920), taken from the diaries and letters of this energetic traveller and mountaineer in the years 1856-1874.
The Playground of Europe by Leslie Stephen (Longmans, 1894). His chapter entitled 'The Baths of Santa Caterina' contains some very fine descriptions of the mountains around Valfurva. But be prepared to wade through pages of heavy Victorian discourse first.
Wild Italy by Tim Jepson (Aurum Press) has a good chapter on the Stelvio National Park.
Summits and Secrets by Kurt Diemberger (Allen & Unwin, 1971; paperback version by Hodder, 1983). This well-written collection of autobiographical pieces includes an account of the first ascent of the Königswand *direttissima* on the Gran Zebrù. Most definitely *not* a walker's route! But it makes fascinating reading for anyone having visited the region.

Piz Buin above the Wiesbadener hut

12: THE SILVRETTA ALPS
Including the Rätikon and Verwall Groups

By contrast with the Western Alps where the various mountain groups generally cover a large area comprising numerous valley systems, Austria appears from the map to host a surprising number of Alpine chains; far more than a country of this size would normally warrant. In truth many of these are simply neighbouring massifs that border a single district, and which have been conveniently named after a local valley by those who live in their shadow. Thus we have the Ötztal Alps, Stubai Alps and Zillertal Alps, for example, that are easily located by reference to their 'home' valley. In our survey of the Eastern Alps of Austria though, a number of other groups will be gathered together under one chapter heading, such as the Northern Limestone Alps, while just a few of the more important regions will be subjected to closer individual scrutiny; among them each of those mentioned above. So it is that we begin with a trio of neighbouring groups whose total area is considerably less in extent than many of those chains previously described, but whose close proximity provides the walker with an opportunity to drift from one to another as the whim decrees, and whose scenic quality is invariably inspiring.

With Germany to the north, Switzerland to the south and west, the tiny principality of Liechtenstein neatly contained in a block of one hundred and fifty-

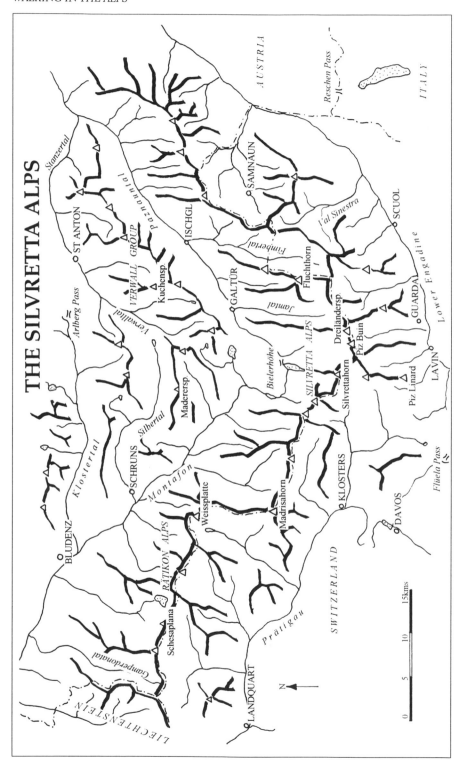

THE SILVRETTA ALPS

seven square kilometres to the south-west, and with Tirol to the east, Vorarlberg is Austria's westernmost and second smallest of its nine provinces. Cutting right through the centre, and effectively dividing it into north and south, the Klostertal carries the Feldkirch-Bludenz-Landeck highway - the main link with the rest of the country across (or beneath) the Arlberg Pass which straddles the provincial border with Tirol. To the north of this divide the Lechtaler Alps form part of the Northern Limestone Alps, but to the south the Rätikon and Silvretta Alps follow the Austro-Swiss border, while the Verwall (or Ferwall) group is contained within an inverted triangle of valleys: those of Montafon and the Paznauntal forming the down-strokes of the V, and the linking valleys on either side of the Arlberg Pass closing that V with a bar to the north, thereby completing the triangle. Of these mountains the Rätikon Alps are composed of limestone, while the Silvretta marks the western end of a long crystalline band that stretches across much of southern Austria, a mountainous band comprising the so-called *Hochgebirge*.

Although the three districts are conveniently brought together here under a common heading, it will be easier to outline their walking potential if we look at them separately. For this we begin with the Verwall group whose identity is rather different to that of its neighbours to the south.

* * *

THE VERWALL GROUP

Despite the fact that a handful of peaks exceeds 3000 metres, the Verwall group gives the impression of being somewhat lower than either the Rätikon, which has no 3000 metre summits, or Silvretta, which has many. Cecil Davies once described them (in *The Mountains of Europe*) as "...solemn mountains of darkly coloured rock, with steep flanks and corries filled with stony rubble." By contrast with their close neighbours in the Silvretta, these mountains are devoid of all but their last glacial remnants, and reveal little permanent snow. They are nonetheless bold but welcoming peaks, their abrupt walls interspersed with green hills and hollows and glens bright with tarns - in addition to those more solemn features of rock and rubble noted by Davies. They have an abundance of climbing routes; summits too that may be reached by little more than a vigorous uphill walk, others that demand an exciting scramble, while there's a refreshing supply of walking trails that criss-cross from one side to the next. Deep little glens bite into their flanks, effectively sub-dividing the range into even smaller groups and, without reference to provincial boundaries, intrude into both Vorarlberg and Tirol.

As we have seen, the northern limit of the Verwall group is drawn by the Klostertal and Stanzer Tal, the two valleys linked by the 1793 metre Arlberg Pass (crossed as long ago as AD945), on the eastern side of which lies the ever-popular winter sports resort of St Anton. Access from the north, then, is either by the major highway of the Arlbergstrasse, or by the Feldkirch-Landeck-Innsbruck railway line which tunnels beneath the pass. From St Anton a narrow road slips into the Verwalltal, one of the central glens in the northern part of the district; another runs parallel to this into the Moostal, thus providing two easy access points, and with accommodation available in both in *Alpenverein* huts. Of these, the Konstanzer hut sits at a junction of glens deep in the Verwalltal; the Darmstädter hut has a glorious location at the head of the Moostal and below the Kuchenspitze, at 3170 metres, the highest of the Verwall mountains. A high route links these two huts (with a small glacier to negotiate) across the 2739 metres Kuchenjöchl. Immediately to the north of this col the small summit of the Scheibler is worth aiming for, since it rewards with arguably the finest mountain panorama of the district.

Other access routes for walkers coming from the north are via Klosterle and Stuben, both of which are located on the Klostertal side of the Arlberg Pass. From Klosterle the Stubener Weg crosses the mountain wall west of the Kaltenberg and then divides; one path drops into the Gaflunatal, the other branches east along the Pfluntal glen to the Konstanzer hut. The route from Stuben, our second entry point, also aims for the Konstanzer hut passing first the Kaltenberg hut. This is a trail of high regard, and a little more demanding than the previous route. It passes below the Kaltenberg glacier, skirts a tarn and crosses the 2573 metre Gstansjöchl before swooping down to the Pfluntal just short of its junction with the Verwalltal.

From the south a public road served by bus climbs out of the Paznauntal a short distance upstream of Galtür, and goes as far as the dammed Kops lake in beautiful rolling green countryside that surrounds the Zeinisjoch. This pass, and also that of the broad, tarn-bright saddle of the Winterjöchl to the north, forms a watershed between tributaries of the Rhine and the Danube; one whose outlet is the North Sea, the other which flows to the Black Sea. The Zeinisjoch is of particular geographical significance since the Zeinisbach which rises just above the pass, divides in two near the actual *joch*, with one branch spilling south-westward to the Montafon valley (and thence to the Rhine), whereas the south-east stream flows down to the Paznauntal and via the Trisanna and Inn eventually to the Danube. Footpaths follow both these infant streams. Others traipse across pool-speckled pastures to the south, enjoy views of inverted mountain peaks and, from the upper ridges, gaze off to the Silvretta where an impressive line of glaciated summits creates a bold horizon. Routes also descend to the Bielerhöhe, the road pass that links Montafon and Paznauntal at the Silvretta Stausee, but the Zeinisjoch is also a good springboard from which to explore northward beyond the Verbella Alpe and into the very heart of Verwall across the Winterjöchl, on which sits the Neue Heilbronner hut with the twin Schiedsee tarns nearby which cast reflections of the impressive Patteriol (3056m) and its rugged consorts.

In the far west the Silbertal makes a long inroad towards the heart of the Verwall from Schruns, the major resort of Montafon where Ernest Hemingway spent the winters of 1924-25 and 1925-26 writing, skiing and gambling. Named from the mining of silver which was carried on there prior to the sixteenth century, the nearby village of Silbertal may be reached by bus from Schruns. Upstream the valley is joined by a tributary from the north, but further still at the Untere Gafluner Alp it splits either side of a dividing spur with one glen becoming the Gaflunatal, the other continuing as the upper Silbertal. Again, walking routes abound. One option would be to make a circuit of that dividing spur along the Emil-Roth-Weg. Another possibility is to cross the Silberttaler Winterjöchl (with a direct view of the jagged Patteriol opposite) into the Schönverwalltal glen and either wander downstream to the Konstanzer hut, or upvalley to the Neue Heilbronner. A third option is to follow through the Gaflunatal, then break away northwards on a trail that climbs over the walling ridge via the modest little Reutlinger hut, and then continues down to the Klostertal.

The Verwall's eastern edge is flanked by the Paznauntal, a lovely gentle valley that makes a moat for both the Verwall and Silvretta mountains. On the Verwall side a cable lift alleviates some of the uphill struggle of gaining high trails. Yet high routes score across and along these green hills, with more huts inviting an overnight stay and making possible a rich assortment of routes. From Kappl, on the left bank of the Trisanna, a trail loops its way up the hillside overlooking the village, goes into the little Blanka glen, then crosses the Kappler Joch (2672m) and descends 200 metres or so to the Austrian Alpine Club's Edmund-Graf hut. Originally built in 1885 this enjoys a wonderful situation in morning shadow of the Hoher Riffler. That mountain rises to the north-east, the 3168 metre summit marked by a cross, and the steep little Pettneuer glacier hanging in a corrie between the Kleiner and Hoher Riffler. Ascent from the hut is highly recommended. There is nothing unduly difficult in the route to the south summit, although a short stretch of grade II climbing is required to gain the main peak. The panorama revealed from the crown is quite magnificent, while an alternative walking route from the hut goes down through the Malfontal along a jeep track to Pettneu in the Stanzer Tal; another follows the Riffler Weg (which becomes the Kieler Weg on the south side of the Schmalzgruben Scharte) to the Niederelbe hut. Another route worth considering from the Paznauntal begins in Ischgl, rises through the Madleintal to a little tarn under the dolomitic Seeköpfe, then crosses the 2786 metre Doppelsee Scharte to gain the Darmstädter hut in about five hours. This could be used as the first stage in a two-day north-bound crossing of the Verwall, the second stage consisting of an easy stroll down through the Moostal to St Anton.

Having given a very rough outline of the district, it is now time to offer suggestions for a multi-day tour or two to add to those already made. A glance at the map immediately produces a litany of ideas, the first of which makes a long traverse of the south side from Schruns in the Montafon valley to Valzur, midway between Ischgl and Galtür in the Paznauntal. Basically this is a two-day traverse, plus time to reach the Wormser hut where a marked route begins. The hut is easily reached by cableway from Schruns to Kapellalpe, followed by a fifteen minute stroll. Unsurprisingly this makes a very popular day out for visitors to Montafon, and it may be that you prefer an alternative approach. In which case take the footpath from Silbertal that climbs southward to the Schwarzsee tarn cupped below the Hochjoch, then via the Kreuzjoch to reach the hut. This involves a height gain of more than thirteen hundred metres, and all the early part of the walk is through forest. From the sixty-bedded Wormser hut the Wormser Höhenweg traces a meandering line as far as the Heilbronner hut on the Winterjöchl. This twenty-kilometre trail makes a demanding eight- or nine-hour day, but with a whole series of fine viewpoints to enjoy. The next section of the traverse is comparatively gentle. By taking another marked trail heading roughly south-east the Friedrikshafener hut is reached in about three and a half hours, followed by a plunge downhill to Valzur.

Instead of making a traverse of the district, however, you may prefer a circuit, finishing back in Schruns. Just such a tour is feasible by diverting from the traverse at the Neue Heilbronner hut. Here you simply wander down valley a short distance, then veer west over the Silbertaler Winterjöchl and walk all the way through the lush green Silbertal - there's a choice of accommodation on offer long before you reach Schruns. But let's suppose you are more interested in going to St Anton, and have the inclination to explore something of the Verwall heartland on the way. For this a minimum of four days should be allowed; but much better to ease the route into five stages, including a first one up to the Wormser hut via Silbertal, and the second day spent walking along the classic Wormser Höhenweg. Once again Heilbronner is the point at which the next phase of the route is determined; in this instance we make our subsequent destination the Konstanzer hut. There are two ways to achieve this, but the first (two hours directly down the Schönverwalltal) is not really worth taking unless the weather is such that a recommended high route alternative is out of the question. This high route goes by way of the Wannensee tarn and the 2683 metre Wannenjöchl, a col in the splendid ridge south of the Patteriol, then down into the Fasultal which leads to the Konstanzer hut. Although this should take no more than about four hours in good conditions, there's much to see and to enjoy, and it's a good preparation for the next stage which leads across the Kuchenjöchl to the Darmstädter hut. Although it may well be possible to continue down to St Anton after this crossing, the Darmstädter hut is not one to scurry away from in undue haste. Spend a night there and appreciate the charm of its location, then amble down through the Moostal on the fifth day.

In his guidebook to Austria's mountains, Cecil Davies outlines another hut to hut route which makes a loop of the eastern Verwall from St Anton to Pettneu. In this he suggests as the first stage a three-hour walk through the Verwalltal to the Konstanzer hut, and the second a crossing of the Kuchenjöchl to the Darmstädter hut including, for those inclined, the ascent of the Scheibler. For the third day Davies chooses the Hoppe-Seyler Weg to the Niederelbe hut for its witness to some grand rock scenery, and with a summit or two to collect from the hut. Day four follows the Kieler Weg and Riffler Weg as far as the Edmund-Graf hut, then wanders down the Malfontal on the final stage to Pettneu in the Stanzer Tal.

This brief outline of routes does little more than scratch the surface of possibilities; suffice to say that the Verwall group will repay the attention of any mountain walker, especially if he or she intends then to move on to one of its more southerly neighbours. Which is precisely what we will do here.

✳   ✳   ✳

THE RÄTIKON ALPS

Tracing a line that follows a rough south-easterly direction along the borders of Liechtenstein, Austria and Switzerland these mountains present a series of ragged skylines; rocky profiles of peaks wearing aprons of scree, eased here and there with green ridge and comforting spur. None quite reaches 3000 metres, the highest being the popular snow peak of Schesaplana at 2965 metres, so these are not big mountains by standards set in the Western Alps. However, neither bulk nor extremes of altitude are essential to the enjoyment of mountain scenery, and the walker here will appreciate a rugged form of beauty and sufficient huts and valley bases from which to explore the best on offer.

On the Swiss flank the valley of Prättigau (alias Val Pratens - the 'valley of meadows'), which flows between Klosters and Landquart, marks the southern extent of the region, and has a number of tributary glens draining to it from the Rätikon ridge crest. Exploiting these glens a series of cross-border trails provides access for walkers to the Montafon valley on the Austrian side; among them crossings of the Kleine Furka just west of the Schesaplana, Schweizertor and Drusentor on either side of the Drusenfluh, Grubenpass and Plasseggenjoch for Schruns, Sarotlapass and St Antönierjoch leading to Gargellen, and the Schlappinerjoch which also links Schlappin above Klosters with Gargellen, and which marks the eastern limit of the Rätikon Alps. A high trail traverses the head of these glens eastward from above Maienfeld and is known as the Rätikon Höhenweg Sud; a parallel route on the Austrian side of the border is called the Rätikon Höhenweg Nord.

The Rhaetian railway from Chur rattles its way between Landquart and Klosters, and continues on to Davos, providing a reliable service throughout Prättigau for non-motorised visitors. From the main valley at Pardisla, west of Grüsch, a minor road goes up to Seewis from which ascents are often made of the Schesaplana, while the next glen to the east has a road as far as Schuders. The Schweizertor trail strikes upvalley from this village, and several Rätikon peaks are accessible from it. Küblis guards the entrance to the St Antöniental. This glen, drained by the Schanielabach whose source is a tarn under the impressive limestone crags of the Sulzfluh (2818m), provides opportunities for several good walking excursions, among them two border crossings and a circuit via the Swiss Alpine Club's Garschina hut which may be reached in two and a half hours from St Antönien. Striking north-east from Klosters Dorf, the Schlappintal is much shorter than its neighbours to the west although above Schlappin it curves sharply to the right and flows parallel with the frontier crest.

There are only two Swiss Club huts on the southern slopes of the Rätikon (the Garschina and Enderlin - this last-named being located at the western end of the chain above Maienfeld), while the Austrian side boasts almost a dozen huts of the German and Austrian *Alpenverein*, including the latest Douglass hut which replaces the first mountain hut ever built (in 1872) by the German Alpine Club (DAV) whose Vorarlberg section had only been formed three years before.

The Austrian side of the Rätikon Alps is largely dominated by the important valley of Montafon which, as we have already discovered, forms one of the outlines of the Verwall group and rises south-eastward from Bludenz to the Bielerhöhe, the lake-trapped saddle traversed by the sinuous Silvretta Hochalpenstrasse. However, before reaching the Bielerhöhe the border between the Rätikon and Silvretta Alps is reached at the straggling village of St Gallenkirch, the dividing line running through the Gargellental to the south.

It is from the Montafon valley that we will concentrate most of our attention on the northern flanks of the Rätikon Alps, beginning at Bludenz, south of which the River Ill flows into the main Klostertal. In fact the old town stands at the intersection of no less than five valleys, two of which give access to the Rätikon mountains. The first of these is the Brandner Tal, a neat glen digging into the mountains south-west of Bludenz. Twelve kilometres into the glen lies the winter sports resort of Brand, and from there the road (bus from Bludenz station) continues to a vast car park at the base of the Lünersee cableway. The Lünersee is a high lake dammed to service an important hydro-electric scheme. When the dam was built the rising waters drowned the second of the Douglass huts (the first had been destroyed by avalanche in the winter of 1876-77), but a third building to carry the name of this British mountaineer and industrialist, now stands by the lake at the cableway terminus at an altitude of 1976 metres, with glorious mountain and valley views. To the west of the Douglass hut and only a short walk away, stands the Totalp hut between the lake and the Schesaplana, while two more huts are accessible from Brand on the route leading to the elegant cone of the Schesaplana.

This peak is a natural lure for walkers based for a day or two in or above the Brandner Tal. The ascent is quite straightforward, but whilst there is no glacier to contend with, the approach from the south involves crossing snowfields and for inexperienced Alpine walkers it could be a serious undertaking. For all its modest height and comparatively innocent appeal (by Alpine standards, that is), the Schesaplana still deserves to be taken seriously and the German guidebook makes a point of warning ill-equipped and inexperienced tourists against attempting it. From Brand the route, via the Oberzalim and Mannheimer huts, is quite strenuous ("rather fatiguing" is how it was described a hundred years ago) and takes from five to six hours to achieve. But from the Douglass hut three hours should be sufficient in good summer conditions. Being the highest of the Rätikon peaks the summit panorama is vast. Here is how Baedeker described it in 1888:

> "The magnificent view embraces the whole of Swabia as far as Ulm on the N., the Vorarlberg and Algäu Alps to the N.E., the Oetzthal, Stubai, and Zillerthal Alps to the E., and to the S. and W. the Swiss Alps from the Silvretta and Bernina to the Gotthard and the Bernese Alps, the Prättigau, the valley of the Rhine, the Appenzell Mts., and the Lake of Constance; immediately below us on the N. are the extensive Brandner Glacier and the Brandner-Thal."

West of Schesaplana the Kleine Furka crosses the frontier ridge between Seewis on the Swiss side of the range and the lovely Gamperdonatal which drains north alongside the Liechtenstein border and spills into the River Ill between Bludenz and Feldkirch. There are two routes on the Austrian side that link up with the Kleine Furka crossing; one that comes from Brand in the Brandner Tal, the other from Nenzinger Himmel in the Gamperdonatal. By combining these an enjoyable loop could be created, using the Oberzalim hut for accommodation should the plan be to extend it into a two-day tour.

East of Schesaplana the frontier ridge stutters above the Lünersee over assorted minor summits, then drops beyond the Kirchlispitzen among imposing crags to the Schweizertor (2137m), the 'Swiss Gate'. On the north side of this the Rellstal flows down to the lower Montafon valley. The Rellstal is the next glen to the east of the Brandner Tal, and the dividing ridge is topped by the pyramid-shaped Zimba, locally known as the Matterhorn of Austria. At the mouth of the valley sits Vandans, an old settlement of Rhaeto-Roman origins whose houses, hotels and bridges are almost swamped in summer beneath an extravagence of flowers. From it an unsurfaced private road projects deeply into the Rellstal, and a trail climbs out of the glen to gain the Lünersee and the Douglass hut. Another continues from the roadhead up and over the Schweizertor, then down into the Swiss glen that leads to Schuders and, eventually, to Schiers. A third trail option cuts below the northern flanks of the Drusenfluh (2828m), crosses the Öfa Pass and descends steeply to the DAV's Lindauer hut set appealingly beneath the three towers of the Drei Türme; a romantic location with a well-kept alpine garden. An alternative route to this hut crosses the Schweizertor, where the scenery is transformed with savage abruptness, then makes a traverse of the Swiss slopes of the Drusenfluh before returning through the Drusentor. Walkers planning to spend a night or two at the Lindauer hut, having come up from the valley, might contemplate a circuit of the massive Drusenfluh or, should they be experienced scramblers, could be tempted to give part of a day to the ascent of one or more of the Drei Türme towers - but note that the smallest of these should be left to the rock climbing fraternity. There's also a brace of north-bound walking routes from the hut, both of which eventually lead to Latschau, Tschagguns and the Montafon valley.

Tschagguns and Schruns virtually face each other across the River Ill, but whereas Schruns occupies the mouth of the Silbertal with the Verwall mountains beyond, Tschagguns provides immediate access to two glens draining the Rätikon Alps; the Gauertal and Gampadelstal. Latschau huddles by a small lake at the entrance to the Gauertal, and is connected to Vandans by chairlift, while a funicular climbs the hillside behind Latschau up to the Golm where high trails strike out along the green ridge and down into neighbouring glens. At the head of the Gauertal the Sulzfluh and Drei Türme stand guard either side of the Drusentor; at the foot of the latter mountain sits the Lindauer hut, at the foot of the former is the Tilisuna, overlooking the little Tilisunasee in a bowl of pastureland. The two are linked by an energetic half-day trek along one of the loveliest sections of the Rätikon Höhenweg Nord which takes in the Bilken Grat; but one of the most popular ways of reaching the Tilisuna hut from the Montafon valley is by way of the chairlift from Tschagguns to Grabs, followed by a steady climb south to Alp Alpila, then to the little pool of the Tobelsee and skirting the 2460 metre Schwarzhorn before coming to the hut in about two and a half hours. A longer route leads through the Gampadelstal to the Tilisuna Alpe, then heads west from there. Once at the hut the ascent of the Sulzfluh is seen almost as an obligation; there are no difficulties, but the route is interesting and the summit panorama quite magnificent.

Having maintained a rough easterly trend across the head of several valleys, the frontier ridge now makes a severe southerly turn above the Tilisuna hut and rises over the Weissplatte (2630m), the mountain which blocks the Gampadelstal. Almost at the head of this glen the Plasseggenjoch entices a trail across the border where it forks; one option leads down to Partnum and St Antönien, another edges west to the Garschina hut, while a third choice renounces the pleasures of descent on the Swiss side and merely skirts the upper slopes (fixed rope safeguards), returns to the Austrian side at the Sarotlapass (2389m) and then heads directly downhill to Gargellen.

The Gargellental is the uppermost glen on the Austrian flank of the Rätikon Alps, the longest tributary of the Montafon, and the dividing line between the Rätikon and Silvretta districts; one mountain face a light grey limestone, the other showing dark igneous rock. The valley is narrow and wooded in its lower reaches, and above the resort of Gargellen, with its chairlift to the Schafberg, the glen forks. Striking south-eastward the Vergaldatal pokes into the edge of the Silvretta, while the main valley continues southward before curving as the Wintertal under the frontier ridge among broad meadows and alpenroses. South of Gargellen, and before the glen makes its curve, the Madrisa hut sits on the left bank of the stream at 1660 metres. It's only a small hut, mostly unguarded, but the key is available from an address in Gargellen for those who plan to use it as a base.

There's plenty of good walking here, both in the valley itself, and across a variety of frontier cols. These passes are listed in a counter-clockwise direction round the head of the valley, beginning south-west of Gargellen at the 2379 metre St Antönierjoch which gives access to the St Antöniental. Next is the Gafierjoch which is linked on the Swiss side with the Madrisajoch (2612m); then comes the Schlappinerjoch at the very head of the valley. This is an old crossing, formerly one of the 'wine routes' which these days makes an obvious choice for those planning to visit Schlappin or Klosters. Recollecting the wine trade, the multi-day route of the Via Valtellina uses the Schlappinerjoch on its way from Bregenz. Beyond the col it then marches across the south-eastern corner of Switzerland and into the Italian Valtellina.

On the approach to Gargellen from the Montafon valley, the village appears to be dominated by the 2770 metre peak of Madrisa. Behind this, just south of the frontier ridge, rises the larger Madrisahorn (2826m). A three-day circuit of this 'home mountain' of the Gargellental could be made by crossing the Schlappinerjoch from either the village or the Madrisa hut, and descending the Schlappintal to Klosters where a night is spent. The next day wander down through Prättigau to Kublis, then ascend the St Antöniental to spend the second night in St Antönien itself. The final day involves crossing back into Austria via the St Antönierjoch with a return to Gargellen.

A rewarding one-day circular walk at the head of the Gargellental involves going south from Gargellen towards the Schlappinerjoch, then swinging left into the Wintertal, and steadily rising past a few scattered farm buildings to the Valzifenzer-Joch (2485m) on a ridge spur that separates the Wintertal from the Vergaldatal. Descending the east flank of this spur the route (not always clear on the ground) eventually hits a major trail in the valley bed, then follows this glen downstream all the way back to Gargellen.

Finally, at the head of the Vergaldatal a route crosses the Vergaldnerjoch and drops beyond the limits of Rätikon to the Tübinger hut, first of the DAV's Silvretta mountain bases. Having thus reached the eastern limit of the Rätikon Alps in a brief overview of the various glens that flow from it, it is time to look at a multi-day west to east traverse along part of the Rätikon Höhenweg Nord which flanks the Montafon valley.

RÄTIKON HÖHENWEG NORD

The complete *höhenweg* is a multi-day extravaganza that begins on the outskirts of Feldkirch, follows the Liechtenstein border southward, then crosses that border and cuts through the south-eastern corner of the principality before returning to Austrian soil and heading roughly eastward along the mid-height flank of the mountains. In the two English-language guidebooks that include this route, both suggest a much shorter version, with a start being made at the Lünersee above the Brandner Tal. This is perfectly understandable, since the Douglass hut on the shoreline has easy access by public transport, which is useful for those who have spent a day or so travelling from home to get there. The approach route therefore is by bus from the railway station at Bludenz to the valley station of the Lünersee cable-car which, in a few painless minutes, swings you up to the Douglass hut. On arrival there an hour and a half's stroll round the lake will go some way towards salving your conscience and easing muscles of travel-ache. A better alternative, of course, should you have the necessary time and inclination, is to ignore the option of transport and walk all the way to the hut from Brand, or even to the Totalp hut nearby.

The three-day route to Gargellen consists of short (half-day) stages with optional extras. But none should decry prospects of a four hour walk from one hut to the next, for with fine scenery to absorb, those four hours could so easily stretch to six or more. The first real day's trekking along the high route, then, is a four-and-a-half-hour stage from the Douglass hut to the Lindauer hut. Being well-marked and of easy access it is a popular trail that edges the lake and wanders over grassy hillsides to the Verajöchl (2330m), enjoying on the way good views of the north face of the Kirchlispitzen, the Schesaplana behind you to the west, and the big, bold Drusenfluh ahead to the east. A two hundred metre descent then leads to the gash of the Schweizertor, with its abandoned customs house, where a decision needs to be addressed with regard to the onward route.

The standard Rätikon Höhenweg remains on the Austrian flank, rises to the third pass of the day (the Öfa Pass), then makes a longish descent of the Sporentobel below the towering Drusenfluh before arriving at the Lindauer hut. However, an alternative trail cuts round the Swiss flank of the Drusenfluh, makes a loss then gain of about two hundred metres in height (with a desolate stony bowl in between), and returns to the northern side at the Drusentor whence the Lindauer hut may be reached via slopes of scree and old moraines. The standard route is very fine; the Swiss alternative provides a different outlook and will add a further two hours to the route.

Stage two is even shorter than the previous day, requiring probably no more than three hours in all for the direct Lindauer to the Tilisuna hut route, despite the fact that the trail is an aggravated one, being steep in places and with many windings. But this could be seen as a distinct advantage, for the extra time won from the afternoon may be used in climbing the Sulzfluh which forms a powerful backdrop to the Tilisuna. The day begins among pinewoods, then up the vegetated rim of the scenic Bilken Grat where the trail exchanges pale limestone of the Sulzfluh for the surprise of dark igneous-metamorphic rock, and then on gaining the Schwarze Scharte (2336m), one discovers green-black serpentine. From the

'Black Col' the Verwall group is seen clearly beyond the Montafon valley, while just below lies the Tilisunasee - the hut itself cannot be seen from here, although it will only take about twenty minutes of descent to reach it.

While the Lindauer hut was snug on the edge of pinewoods at the base of the Drei Türme, the setting of the large Tilisuna hut is more open and spacious, the Sulzfluh rising in sprawling terraces of limestone pavement behind, green pastureland ahead. Conditions being favourable, having booked in and taken refreshment at the hut, it would be worth setting out for an ascent of the Sulzfluh. There is nothing technically difficult about the normal route; there are guiding cairns, glorious views, and the large summit cross as a constant lure. And from that crown a fine panorama that includes the plunging south flank that disappears into blue misted valleys.

The third and final stage of this high route tacks south-eastward to the frontier crest at the Grubenpass. Instead of crossing into Switzerland, however, the trail remains well to the left of the border and, heading south now, makes a traverse of the east flank of the Weissplatte before gaining the crest once more at the Plasseggenjoch which marks the head of the Gampadelstal. At this point the Höhenweg Nord passes through to the Swiss side and follows a good belvedere of a trail aiming south-east to the attractive Sarotlapass (another heads south then west to Hotel Sulzfluh). Through the pass, guarded by towering walls, the hillside falls away into the deep and wooded Gargellental. The trail twists its way down to Röbialpe, and from there to the welcome of Gargellen.

RÄTIKON HÖHENWEG NORD - ROUTE SUMMARY

Day 1:   Douglass Hut - Schweizertor - Lindauer Hut

Day 2:   Lindauer Hut - Schwarze Scharte - Tilisuna Hut (ascent of Sulzfluh optional)

Day 3:   Tilisuna Hut - Plasseggenjoch - Sarotlapass - Gargellen

The route is waymarked and there should be no orientation problems. Under normal summer conditions there is nothing difficult about the route; snow patches may be lying in the early part of the season, but there are neither glaciers nor permanent snowfields to contend with. It is a very short hut to hut route, and walkers with time at their disposal are urged to consider linking it with a crossing of the neighbouring Silvretta range. Details of this continuing route will be found at the end of the following sub-chapter which deals with the Silvretta Alps.

---

*   *   *

THE SILVRETTA ALPS

Of the three districts included in this chapter the Silvretta Alps are the most scenically dramatic and appealing, thanks to the heavy glaciation that plasters many north-facing slopes. This glacier cover extends to a small degree on the southern, Swiss, side of the range, yet Piz Linard, the highest of its mountains which stands well within Swiss territory and overlooks the Lower Engadine, has no permanent ice at all.

The boundaries of the Silvretta group follow obvious river valleys. Those on the Austrian flank are the Ill (Montafon) and Trisanna (Paznaun) on either side of the Bielerhöhe running along the northern edge, with the Gargellental on the west and Fimbertal on the east. The Swiss boundaries are formed by the Schlappinabach above Klosters on the west, then south from there to Davos, and through the Flüelatal, over the Flüela Pass and down to the River Inn at Susch in the Lower Engadine. This is the southernmost point of the district, from where the unmarked boundary follows the Inn downstream to its junction with Val Sinestra. Follow Val Sinestra north and up the Val Chöglias to the Austrian border to outline the eastern limit.

It will be noted then, that the bulk of these mountains lies south of the border, despite the fact that the Silvretta is generally spoken of as an Austrian range. As mentioned above, the Austrian side is daubed with glacial ice and broad snowfields that not only add a lustre, but provide a dimension of grandeur that is sometimes absent on the southern flank. The north side is also, perhaps, easier of access, and better equipped with huts in the higher regions. Some of the Swiss glens are tightly cleft and forested lower down; their Austrian counterparts are more open. On the Engadine side villages will be as memorable as some of the mountains. On the Tirolean slope the contrast of green meadow and bold ice-clad peak is often the very thing that calls a walker to the Alps year in and year out; yet valleys, glens and mountain walls as seen from the south have an undeniable attraction too.

The Swiss Valleys

Let's look first at the southern side and assess its qualities and its rewards for walkers, beginning with those valleys immediately accessible from Klosters. As was pointed out earlier, Klosters is served by trains of the Rhaetian Railway out of Chur. With its sheltered position, lovely views to the Silvretta glacier, lots of accommodation and facilities for the active as well as the non-active visitor, and with plenty of good prospects as a base for a walking holiday, its main appeal where we are concerned is in the surrounding glens. Of these the northern valley of the Schlappintal has already been visited in our survey of the Rätikon district, with a crossing of the Schlappinerjoch at its head. However, east of the little hamlet of Schlappin (immediately below the *joch*) the upper reaches of the glen project eastward, following the line of the frontier crest. The mountains that wall this upper glen maintain a fairly constant altitude of around 2800 metres, but just short of the north-east corner the Garnerajoch offers a way over the frontier at a modest 2490 metres. On the Austrian side, just three hundred metres below, sits the Tübinger hut at the head of the Garneratal. If one were to spend a night there it would be possible to create a splendid circuit by crossing the Plattenjoch next day and descend via the little Seetal glen below the Gross Litzner, followed by a long valley route back to Klosters. It is a long walk too, about twelve kilometres from Alp Sardasca. The route to the Plattenjoch involves a glacier crossing, but there should be no crevasses to confuse the way and the col is gained in about two hours from the hut. Note that there is also a small unguarded hut on the Seetal side of the ridge at an altitude of 2050 metres, found near a small tarn.

The long valley by which Klosters is reached from the Seetal glen makes a profound cut in the mountains east of the resort. Most of the walking appeal is centred on this valley for it forks upstream of Monbiel (private cars allowed as far as this village), thereby doubling one's options. The north-east branch leads to the Sardasca alp where it sub-divides beneath a great curving wall of mountains. A minibus service from Klosters-Platz railway station may be taken as far as this point. Due north of Alp Sardasca the Plattenjoch trail climbs into the Seetal glen, with the Seetal hut perched some four hundred metres higher than Sardasca; eastward a trail noses up to the Unter Silvretta Alp and continues climbing to the frontier ridge; another branches off to gain the SAC's Silvretta Haus at 2341 metres (reached in about four and a half hours from Klosters). This three-storey hut stands just twenty minutes below the Silvretta glacier, the ice of which is crowned by the Silvrettahorn, Silvretta Egghorn and Signalhorn. Ibex and plenty of marmots are likely to be seen in the vicinity. A recommended route for experienced mountain walkers links the Silvretta Haus with the Bielerhöhe (or either the Saarbrucker or Wiesbadener huts) on the northern side of the frontier across the 2688 metre Rote Furka, which is gained by a short stretch on the Silvretta glacier.

The south-forking branch of the main valley which flows down to Klosters, offers a number of walking opportunities. This glen, the Vereinatal, has a roadway (bus from Klosters) forcing into it from Alp Novai which projects as far as the Berghaus Vereina at 1943 metres, a traditional inn with dormitory places as well as standard hotel rooms. Here the glen opens to the Vernela glen just north of east, the Süsertal sneaking south of east, and the Jörital which continues southward. Each one is worth exploring. The first is blocked by the Verstanklahorn but has the walker's pass of Fuorcla Zadrell crossing behind Piz Linard into Val Lavinuoz; the second has a trail leading up and over the Vereinpass by which Val Sagliains and eventually the Lower Engadine may be reached; and also gives access to the Flesspass which leads via the little curving Val Fless to Val Susasca midway between the Flüela Pass and Susch. As for the Jörital, this has a trail which explores a wilderness of tarns, dying glaciers under the Flüela Weisshorn, and the secluded Jöriflesspass which also leads a trail into Val Fless.

While Davos forms a cornerstone of the Silvretta district it is a little too far removed from the main walking action provided by these mountains, other than for the motorised visitor who is prepared to spend part of the day driving to and from various access points. Nonetheless, this major resort of canton Graubünden, noted mainly for its skiing, does have plenty of good walking nearby, albeit mostly among those valleys and glens that dig into the Albula Alps to the south.

Remaining with the Silvretta Alps we now turn to those glens that drain into the north side of the Lower Engadine. The south side of this important valley has already been visited in the earlier chapter dealing with the Bernina Alps. But in order to study the Swiss slopes of the Silvretta district proper we will concentrate on that section of the valley between Susch at the foot of the Flüela road pass, and the small village of Ramosch with the glen of Val Sinestra enticing behind it. Accommodation will be found in most, if not all, villages along the bed of the valley. Scuol has the best choice, including a campsite, while other villages, especially those along a terrace above the river, offer more peaceful lodgings and some extraordinarily attractive *sgraffito*-patterned buildings. Every village in the Lower Engadine displays a sturdy vernacular architecture that has more than a hint of Italian influence in it. Thick, solid-looking walls with tiny inset windows peeking behind wrought-iron grilles; elegant arched doorways that open to an enclosed inner courtyard from which various rooms emerge; the outer walls often adorned with a frieze of well-crafted symbols, patterns or pictures, and with geraniums dazzling against the clean white or soft pink plasterwork.

Above Susch to the north soars the conical Piz Linard (3411m), highest of all the Silvretta mountains. The village is set rather too close beneath it to be able to form a proper opinion of this peak, for it appears foreshortened from this angle and one really needs to stand back a little further to the south in order to assess its qualities. Zernez is better placed for this, and when travelling down valley suddenly the mountain provokes an involuntary lift of the head, for it rears up in a graceful sweep of dark rock to a fine point created by four equal ridges that taper pencil-like with Val Sagliains to the left and Val Lavinuoz carving along its right-hand flank. Yet despite the graceful line drawn, it is hard to believe that Piz Linard is quite as high as the map suggests, for it has no glaciers, no permanent snowfield, no extensive ridge systems. And should you feel impelled to attempt a route on it, you will discover that its rock is brittle and forbidding - as my wife discovered to her cost many years ago when we were climbing without helmets. But even if you are uninterested in climbing, or are not equipped for it on this occasion, a visit to the hut on its southern midriff would be well worthwhile, followed perhaps by a walk up into the little corrie of Val Glims which creates a central scoop in the face of the mountain, then bear left to gain the south-west ridge at Fuorcla da Glims (2802m) for a truly fine view across a maze of ridges and shadowed glens. The Linard hut (Chamanna dal Linard; 2327m) is an old-fashioned, traditional hut with modest facilities, mostly unguarded other than at weekends, and without any meals provision. It evokes a wonderful atmosphere, especially if there's practically no-one there, and forms a complete contrast to some of the large, semi-luxurious inn-like huts on the Austrian side of the border. It may be reached by an obvious trail in about two and a half hours from Lavin, while the walk up to Fuorcla da Glims will take another hour and a half from there.

While Piz Linard stands well to the south of the frontier, that frontier snakes its way along an ice-encrusted series of ridges that links the most popular of the district's mountains. Probably the best known of all is Piz Buin (3312m) which looks so impressive from the north, especially with the tumbling Vermunt glacier sweeping down towards the Wiesbadener hut. When seen from the south, however, the mountain takes on an entirely different personality. Not less attractive, but certainly very different, like a towering cocked hat dashed with a sparing amount of ice and snow. The glen which drains from it is Val Tuoi; a real charmer with enchanting Guarda at its entrance.

Originally built in 1913, but modernised in the late 1980s when it was enlarged to accommodate ninety people, Chamanna Tuoi stands in the upper basin of Val Tuoi below the Vermunt Pass at an altitude of 2250 metres. An easy walk of about two and a half hours along a track takes you to it from Guarda, with pleasures all the way. The hut itself is perfectly placed for ascents of Piz Buin, Dreiländerspitz

(3197m) and Jamspitz (3178m), as well as the crossing of two glacier passes: the Vermunt and Silvretta - the first of which leads to the Wiesbadener hut in the Ochsental, the second to the Silvretta Haus below the Silvretta glacier. Without rising to any temptation to climb any of these peaks or cross these passes, a there-and-back stroll to the Tuoi hut would have value in itself, for the delights of Val Tuoi are such that time spent there will always be time well-spent. However, a full-day's circuit could be accomplished by tackling the ice-free pass known as Furcletta (2735m) in the east walling ridge of the valley, followed by descent of Val Tasna on the other side down to Ardez, completing the round along the lane that links that village with Guarda. There's some pretty rough ground on either side of the pass (one and a half hours from Chamanna Tuoi), and the Tasna side could be a little problematic when late-spring snow is still lying; but other than this the route is fairly straightforward and immensely rewarding. Allow eight hours or so for the full circuit.

The wild Val Tasna which empties into the Inn between Ardez and Ftan has options worth considering by those walkers for whom border crossings have particular appeal. Though wooded in its lower reaches, above the forests there are fine meadows lush with flowers in early summer. Just beyond Alp Vermala about three hours from Ardez, the glen forks; the left branch is Val d'Urezzas by which the Furcletta and Val Tuoi are reached, while the continuing main valley is here known as Val Urschai. This latter glen curves north-eastward and becomes increasingly stony. A trail continues through it, crosses to the north bank and climbs over moraine and scree round a spur of Piz Futschöl to gain Pass Futschöl at 2768 metres. Across this runs the Swiss-Austrian border from which a grandstand view is to be had of the Fluchthorn beyond the upper basin of the Jamtal, and with the Augstenberg rising over your left shoulder. The Jamtal hut lies 600 metres below the pass and is reached by an obvious path.

Another pass option accessed from Val Tasna is the icy Fuorcla da Tasna (2835m) east of Pass Futschöl. This leads to the Fimbertal and the Heidelberger hut. However, the route to it from Val Tasna is both long and arduous, and the pass is more frequently crossed in reverse, from north to south.

The final glen on the Swiss side of the Silvretta is the long and winding Val Sinestra, with Ramosch at its south-eastern gatepost, the tiny village of Vnà set on a terrace 400 metres up the hillside behind it, and Sent facing south across the Engadine just to the west of the glen's wooded entrance. That entrance is a deep shaft which becomes something of a gorge, dark, narrow and forested, and with a road leading along the west bank as far as the large Victorian spa hotel, Kurhaus Val Sinestra. North of this a trail eases along the east bank and joins a track some forty minutes or so from the Kurhaus. At Alp Zuort the valley forks. Off to the left rises Val Laver in which there are several small alp buildings, and at its head Fuorcla da Champatsch (2730m) between Piz Nair and Piz Champatsch offers a walking route over the mountains and steeply down to Scuol (about eight and a half hours from Sent) with fine views across the Engadine to the dolomitic peaks of the south side, while Fuorcla Davo Dieu (2807m) suggests a poorly marked route over the north rim of the glen to the Heidelberger hut. The continuing valley above Alp Zuort is Val Chöglias which also forks twice more; the first time by the hamlet of

Griosch, and the second at Alp Chöglias. By swinging left at Alp Chöglias the 2608 metre saddle of Cuolmen d'Fenga takes a path down to the Heidelberger hut which, though it belongs to the DAV and sits on the northern side of the watershed, is still within Swiss territory. The Austrian border crosses the Fimbertal a little below the hut. This crossing will require about six hours of effort from Sent.

Having studied the various Swiss valleys of the Silvretta Alps it would seem appropriate before transferring to the northern side, to map out a multi-day route that traverses this southern flank. Such a tour would reward with an assortment of views, would give an opportunity to see both the wild side and the settled nature of these mountains, to enjoy the solitude of the inner glens and the architectural splendours of some of the best of Lower Engadine villages.

TOUR OF THE SOUTHERN SILVRETTA

Klosters is the obvious place to begin our journey. Not only is it easily accessible by public transport, but should you choose to link this tour to a multi-day trek along the Austrian flank, it would be perfectly feasible to come down to this resort from one of the frontier ridge crossings above it. Our first day, then, will be spent walking to the Silvretta Haus in order to enjoy close views of the Silvretta glacier. The full day's walk could be drastically shortened by taking the minibus to Alp Sardasca, which would leave a two-hour approach, but much will depend on your state of fitness, weather conditions and so on.

Next day descend to Alp Sardasca and continue downstream as far as the junction with the Vereinatal where you bear left and walk through the gorge as far as Berghaus Vereina. With time in hand, spend the rest of the day exploring either the nearby Jörital or Süsertal, and on the third day follow a trail behind the Berghaus aiming north-east through Val Vernela to cross Fuorcla Zadrell at its head. It is interesting to note that a century or more ago this crossing was frequently made by the pastor of Lavin, Fr Zadrell (after whom it is named), who would walk from his own parish to that of Klosters in order to conduct services on the same day. Shades of Pastor Johann Imseng of Saas Fee. Once over the *fuorcla* descend into Val Lavinuoz and continue down to Lavin where you either spend a night, or arm yourself with provisions and go up to the Linard hut for a more remote and atmospheric lodging.

Day four leads to Chamanna Tuoi in the shadow of Piz Buin. Initially follow a track along a low hillside terrace towards Guarda. It eases into the mouth of Val Tuoi and makes a visit to that village non-essential. However, such is the beauty of this Engadine gem that a half-hour spent wandering Guarda's cobbled streets will add, rather than subtract from the day's pleasures. Only when you've satisfied curiosity should you then take the path that climbs through meadows above the village, and soon joins the main track nosing into the Tuoi glen. Follow this upvalley to the Tuoi hut and book a bed for the night.

On day five the tour continues with a crossing of the east-walling ridge at the saddle of Furcletta, which leads into Val Tasna. Once down into the bed of this valley one has a choice of either bearing left and taking the trail over Pass Futschöl to the Jamtal hut on the north side, or of turning right and wandering downstream towards the Engadine, skirting hillsides to Ftan, then down to Scuol for the next night's lodging. Should you choose the latter suggestion I would urge you to ignore 'upper' Scuol where modern buildings have no particular appeal, and wander down towards the river where 'old' Scuol is far more attractive.

A final day could be spent in one of three different ways. Assuming the plan is to end the holiday in the Lower Engadine, a full day's walking could be enjoyed by taking a bus to Sent, then wandering through Val Sinestra to Alp Zuort and heading left into Val Laver for a short, steep ascent to Fuorcla da Champatsch, which gives a long descent back to Scuol - with an option of a cable-car ride down from Motta Naluns if your knees have had it by then. The second choice is less demanding, and entails taking the morning bus again to Sent, and walking through Val Sinestra to Alp Zuort, then back by way of Vnà and Ramosch, while the third alternative involves crossing Cuolmen d'Fenga to spend a night in the Heidelberger hut on the north side of the ridge, and from there amble down valley and over the border into Austrian territory, thence to Ischgl in the Paznauntal.

TOUR OF THE SOUTHERN SILVRETTA - ROUTE SUMMARY

Day 1: Klosters - Alp Sardasca - Silvretta Haus

Day 2: Silvretta Haus - Alp Novai - Berghaus Vereina

Day 3: Berghaus Vereina - Fuorcla Zadrell - Lavin (or Linard Hut)

Day 4: Lavin (or Linard Hut) - Guarda - Tuoi Hut

Day 5: Tuoi Hut - Furcletta -Ftan - Scuol (or Furcletta - Pass Futschöl - Jamtal Hut)

Day 6: Scuol - Alp Zuort - Fuorcla da Champatsch - Scuol
or: Scuol - Alp Zuort - Vnà - Ramosch - Scuol
or: Scuol - Alp Zuort - Cuolmen d'Fenga - Heidelberger Hut

✳   ✳   ✳

The Austrian Valleys

On the northern side of the frontier ridge the Silvretta Alps are confined to a series of glens draining into either the Montafon valley or the Paznauntal. The district's western limit is marked by the Gargellental which, as we have already discovered, is the divider between the Rätikon and Silvretta Alps, while the easternmost glen is the Fimbertal which empties into the Paznauntal at Ischgl. The link between the Paznauntal and the Montafon valley is the Bielerhöhe, the summit of the impressive Silvretta Hochalpenstrasse toll road between Galtür and Partenen. It is this road which provides the main point of access for all but high foot pass approaches to the Austrian flanks. A public bus service through the Montafon valley is usefully linked with the main railway station at Bludenz, while coming from the east buses run through the Paznauntal from Landeck station. A choice of villages provides bases in both valleys with a good range of comfortable lodgings, while Club huts of the Austrian or German *Alpenverein* will be found in practically every inner glen.

Our review of the Austrian glens begins in the Gargellental and works eastward. Under the sub-chapter dealing with the Rätikon Alps it was noted that this glen cuts into the mountains south of St Gallenkirch and forks above Gargellen. All the western slopes of the valley belong to the Rätikon, those of the eastern flank to the Silvretta Alps, while above Gargellen the south-east branch, known as the Vergaldatal, is the first of the true Silvretta glens in that it is not shared with the neighbouring range. (The southern glen at the fork is the Wintertal, in which the Madrisa hut is set.) The north-east walling ridge above the Vergaldatal holds an interesting walk along its crest, an opportunity to climb the modest Zwischenspitz (2685m), and a crossing into the little Vermeltal. But of major interest is the crossing of the Vergaldnerjoch to the head of the Garneratal where the Tübinger hut is conveniently placed for both climbers and hut touring walkers.

The Garneratal is approached from Gaschurn by a road-cum-track that projects deep into the valley. An alternative high-level trail along the west-walling ridge gives greater interest, better and more extensive views and is eased at the start by optional use of the two-sectionVersettla chairlift. From the top of the upper lift a clear trail, waymarked and popular in its early stages, follows the ridge crest which soon maintains a rough south-westerly direction to the Matschuner Jöchli. Splendid long vistas are companions for much of the way; there is a series of summits to cross (none difficult) and plenty of interest throughout. From the Matschuner Jöchli the ridge kinks south-eastward; the trail crosses the Kuchenberg and the high point of Vorderberg (2553m) before descending to the Vergaldnerjoch where it joins the route from the Vergaldatal, dropping to the Mittelbergjoch and finally to the Tübinger hut. A very fine walk of about six hours. The hut has accommodation for more than a hundred people, and is owned by the German Alpine Club (Section Tübingen). There are several routes linking it with other Silvretta huts on both sides of the frontier, including a trail that crosses the Hochmaderer Joch in the ridge dividing the Garneratal from the little Kromertal, and which descends to the Madlener Haus, or by a valley trail to the Saarbrücker hut. On its own this makes a useful connecting route, but even without fulfilling the route in its entirety, it would still be worth going up to the *joch* (2505m), and then scrambling the 300 metres to the summit of the nearby Hochmaderer; a fine viewpoint demanding only a half-day's exercise. Better and more dramatic views are obtained, however, by climbing south-east of the hut to gain the frontier ridge at the Plattenjoch with options of descending on the south side to the Seetal hut, Alp Sardasca and Klosters, or eastward to the Saarbrücker hut by a route adopted on our traverse of the Austrian Silvretta outlined below.

Flowing roughly parallel to the Garneratal is the Vermunt valley, the lower part of which carries the Silvretta Hochalpenstrasse up to the Bielerhöhe. South of the dammed Vermunt Stausee an upper glen is known as the Kromertal, with a trail climbing through to gain the Saarbrücker hut (highest in the district) with its view of the Litzner glacier and with the Gross Seehorn and magnificent Gross Litzner standing proud above it. (The rocky pyramid of the Kleiner Litzner is gained in half an hour from the hut on a route equipped with cables and ladders.) There are two routes of approach from the Silvretta road; one by a track cutting upvalley from the dammed lake, the other being a more pleasant trail working round the hillside from the busy Madlener Haus at the Bielerhöhe.

With road access right to its door the DAV-owned Madlener Haus is often crowded, and is lacking in any mountain atmosphere such as that which often gives the inn-like Austrian huts the edge over commercial hotels. In fact the nearby Berggasthof Piz Buin offers a better outlook with views across the large expanse of the Silvretta Stausee (in the shadow of whose massive concrete dam the Madlener Haus crouches), and not overly expensive rooms. In view of this I'd suggest spending a night or two there should you arrive at the Madlener Haus to find it packed with motorists.

Another option is to wander a clear trail alongside the lake and at its southern end veer left into the Ochsental glen, near the head of which is found the two hundred bedded Wiesbadener hut at the foot of Piz Buin. Its situation is truly Alpine, even if the waitress service in the dining room suggests a more sophisticated environment than one of glacier-hung peaks and a wilderness of moraine, such as revealed by the view out of the window. Walkers with some Alpine experience and the necessary equipment to deal with crevassed glaciers could happily spend several days here romping from peak to peak or touring the high snows weaving among summits and cross-border cols. None of the peaks are especially difficult; most have non-technical routes, and the glaciers are seldom complicated. But they all deserve to be taken seriously.

A walkers' circuit that takes in the Wiesbadener hut, stony Hohes Rad and the Bieltal provides a very fine and rewarding day out from the Bielerhöhe, with good close views of Silvrettahorn, Piz Buin and Dreiländerspitz and their dazzling glaciers, as well as a lovely panorama from the 2934 metre summit of the Hohes Rad, or the lower Radsattel that has plenty of charm too. That is but one option from the Bielerhöhe. Another is an exploration of the Klostertal, the glen which cuts back to the south-west from the mountain end of the Silvretta lake. The Klostertaler glacier hangs at the southern end of the glen, but on the western side of this a trail climbs to the Kloster Pass on the frontier ridge. This is an old crossing between the Bielerhöhe and Klosters which descends on the Swiss side to Alp Sardasca and thence down the long valley to Klosters itself - a full day's walk of about eight hours.

The Bielerhöhe marks the boundary between the provinces of Vorarlberg and Tirol, as well as the districts of the Verwall to the north and Silvretta Alps to the south. On the eastern side of the pass the pastoral valley of the Kleinvermunt is really an extension of the upper Paznauntal. Coming down from the pass one wanders a vague path along the right bank of the Vermuntbach with barely a snow crown in view, pastures rattling with cowbells, tiny pools here and there showing a palette of green reflections. Then the valley bows to the right and the long trench of the Paznauntal proper sweeps ahead; a typically Tirolean valley of neat meadows, rolling pastures and trim villages lit with balconies of flowers. The first of these villages is Galtür, cramped astride the main road and with a minor paved road cutting south into the Jamtal.

The Jamtal is a long valley, deep and narrow and headed by a crowding wall of glacier peaks. On either side extensive ridge spurs push northward from the main watershed crest, and both these high spurs also hold glacial cravats draped around summits at altitudes in the region of three thousand metres. The narrow paved road from Galtür penetrates as far as the Jamtal hut, ten kilometres into the glen, although hut users may drive only as far as the Schiebenalm, roughly halfway through. There is also a footpath which parallels the road for much of the way on the right bank of the Jambach that offers a much more pleasant means of approach to the hut. The original Jamtal hut was built in 1882, when it was described as being "well fitted up by the German Alpine Club." It has since been rebuilt, considerably enlarged and refurbished, and can now accommodate more than two hundred walkers and climbers. Baedeker wrote of its situation as "picturesque...above the junction of the Futschölbach and the Jambach, commanding a magnificent view of the majestic Fluchthorn to the E., and the Augstenberg and the great Jamthal Glacier to the S." The 'great Jamtal glacier' has withdrawn considerably in the century or more since those words were written, although it remains one of the largest of Silvretta icefields. But the view from the hut remains very impressive. For an even better view and a wider perspective, the 2987 metre Westlichen Gamshorn above to the north-east is highly recommended. The Fluchthorn, second-highest peak of the Silvretta Alps, rises to the east, its southern ridge carrying with it the frontier that curves round a neat corrie at whose entrance the Jamtal hut nestles. In the crest of the south wall of that corrie Pass Futschöl invites a route over to Val Urschai, Val Tasna and the Lower Engadine. East of that the Kronenjoch (2974m) offers a four-hour crossing to the Heidelberger hut, while the Zahnjoch between Fluchthorn and Zahnspitze is a more traditional way between these two huts, although in recent years its popularity has been overtaken by the easier but longer Kronenjoch route which has no crevasses to contend with.

The main valley to the east of the Jamtal is the Fimbertal, shared unequally between Switzerland and the Austrian Tirol, despite being geographically on the northern, or Austrian, slope of the mountains. In extent it is even longer than the Jamtal, but the dividing spur splits north of the Fluchthorn, the two parallel ridge systems effectively cradling the smaller Laraintal (the Kompass map gives the spelling as Lareintal). This is one of those rare Silvretta glens that boasts no mountain hut, but the Äussere Larainalpe a little south of the entrance has restaurant facilities and is served by a minor road from Tschafein, midway between Galtür and Mathon. The Laraintal is a lovely peaceful glen, flush with alpenroses in summer and with the snow-patched Larainferner presenting a white face at the southern end. The Fluchthorn's north summit marks the south-east crown of this glacier and the point where the two ridge spurs combine. A trail explores the valley as far as the lower reaches of the glacier, but another breaks away by a locked customs hut at 2133 metres and climbs the eastern hillside to gain the Ritzenjoch (alias Fuorcla Larain). This col is marked by a frontier sign, and descent on the far side takes you into Swiss territory, with the large white Heidelberger hut set on the right bank of the river in what is known here as Val Fenga, but lower down becomes the Austrian Fimbertal.

A jeep track from Ischgl is the usual route of approach to this hut, a popular place for an overnight stay on account of its ease of access (transport to the door can be arranged), pleasant setting and friendly atmosphere. The first Heidelberger hut was built in 1889, but the present building, with room for about one hundred and fifty, is a result of extensions made in the late 1970s. It stands some fourteen kilometres or so from Ischgl, but those who choose to walk have a gentle, welcoming valley to wander through above Gampenalpe. The lower reaches are wooded, their slopes strung about with various lift systems that form part of the so-called 'Silvretta-Ski-Arena'. But beyond Gampenalpe the scene takes on a more natural and grander appeal. Here an alternative route breaks off to the south-east and climbs to the Zeblasjoch (also known as the Samnauner Joch; 2545m) on the frontier ridge. This is an old crossing point which links the Paznauntal with the Swiss Samnauntal, and from the pass a splendid view is to be had of the Ötztal Alps in one direction, and the towering Fluchthorn in the other. A second route joins the Gampenalpe trail at the *joch* having come from the Heidelberger hut by way of Fuorcla da Val Gronda on a subsidiary spur.

With pastures cut by numerous streams spread across the valley floor, and with an attractive rim of mountains on show to the south, the hut enjoys a restful setting - a good place to wind down at the end of an energetic holiday perhaps. But there is more to the valley than a simple environment for peaceful relaxation, for our walker who is lured by high cols and remote back-country glens will find rich pickings here. A glance at the map shows at least nine passes (two of which admittedly are glacier passes) that seduce in an arc around and above the Heidelberger hut, and the mountain activist with imagination, ambition and the energy to match, could conjure an assortment of tours that dodge back and forth across the ridges; cross-border loops or into neighbouring glens that also spill into the Paznauntal. In short, the valley offers much; its hut enables that potential to be fulfilled.

THE SILVRETTA TRAVERSE

Matching the Tour of the Southern Silvretta outlined above, this multi-day hut to hut route explores the Austrian side of the mountains and could be usefully tacked on to the three-day Rätikon Höhenweg Nord, also described elsewhere in this chapter, to give an eight-day trek, or linked with the southern tour (which would need to be reversed) thereby creating a trek of eleven or twelve days - a complete circuit of the Silvretta Alps. But even without these extensions the traverse on its own is well worth tackling for its landscape value, sense of challenge and pleasures to be gained on staying at some of the huts along the way. The straightforward six-day traverse would effectively begin by walking upvalley from St Gallenkirch through the Gargellental, and there to either spend a first night in a Gargellen hotel or guesthouse, or at the Madrisa hut. But note that a bus service runs from St Gallenkirch to Gargellen, while the Madrisa hut stands about forty-five minutes' walk to the south of that resort.

The trek proper starts in earnest next day with a crossing of the Vergaldnerjoch which leads to the Tübinger hut. It's not a long route, four to five hours only should suffice, but with a height gain of some eleven hundred metres from Gargellen to the pass, that will probably seem quite enough for the early part of a walking tour. If the previous night were spent at the Madrisa hut you'd need to descend to Gargellen first in order to return the key. But if others are staying there with responsibility for the key, an alternative route could be taken. This would entail heading upstream through the Wintertal, then crossing the Valzifenzer-Joch and descending to the head of the Vergaldatal, before tackling the steep uphill trail that leads to the Vergaldnerjoch. That would certainly add something to the day and provide extra challenge, were any needed. Once over the Vergaldnerjoch a second ridge (in effect this is more a spur) is crossed at the Mittelbergjoch from where the Tübinger hut can be seen below.

A full day is required for the next stage but with two possible routes to take, the choice of which will depend largely on weather conditions. The preferred route climbs very steeply to the south-east above the Tübinger hut, crosses a small, crevasse-free glacier and reaches the Plattenjoch (2728m) in about two hours. Excellent views of the Gross and Kleine Seehorn are won from this frontier pass, although fine views are ten a penny on this route. From the Plattenjoch the way continues towards the east to gain the 2745 metre Schweizerlücke, then the descent begins over two further small glaciers and boulder slopes, and on to the Saarbrücker hut in time for lunch. The next section of the day's walk takes an easy trail to the Madlener Haus at the Bielerhöhe, followed by a two-hour stroll that goes south alongside the Silvretta Stausee and south-east through the Ochsental as far as the Wiesbadener hut in full view of Piz Buin.

The alternative, poor weather, route between the Tübinger and Wiesbadener huts avoids the lofty Plattenjoch-Schweizerlücke crossing, and instead goes by way of the lower Hochmaderer Joch to the Madlener Haus, and there joins the final stage of the outlined route.

Stage four is quite short (four to five hours) but strenuous in places. Study of the map clearly shows that the most direct way from the Wiesbadener to the Jamtal hut involves a lot of glacier work, and since the assumption is made here that our trekkers are neither equipped with ice axes or ropes that would offer a form of safeguard against crevasses, we must look for an alternative crossing. Happily there is one such that avoids an over-long valley slog, and that is via the Getschnerscharte, a 2839 metre col above the Madlenerferner, a little glacier that has all but disappeared now. From the Wiesbadener hut a clear and popular trail climbs northward and goes over the steep Radsattel - an hour's detour left at this saddle gives an opportunity to collect the summit of the Hohes Rad - and down to the Bieltal glen. A faint waymarked trail leaves the main path, crosses the Bielbach, makes a rising traverse northward, then swings right for the climb to the Getschnerscharte via snow slopes, scree and boulders. On the east side of the ridge descent to the Jamtal is uncomplicated but tiring on the legs since the mountainside is a steep one down to the Jambach. The hut is located on the opposite side of the stream, with the Fluchthorn rising behind it to the east.

The penultimate stage of our traverse is destined to finish at the Heidelberger hut. It would be feasible to continue down through the Fimbertal to Ischgl, but it would be a shame to do so for the hut's situation is such that one ought to give time to enjoy it. And a night spent there also provides an opportunity to tackle alternate ways out.

But first the route from the Jamtal hut. Jonathan Hurdle's guidebook which includes this route (*Walking Austria's Alps Hut to Hut*) suggests using the Zahnjoch by which to gain Val Fenga, but in the more recently published West Col guide to the *Silvretta Alps* Jeff Williams warns of crevasses on the eastern side and suggests the Kronenjoch as a safer alternative. The latest Kompass map also marks the Zahnjoch route as being the 'old way', while the Kronenjoch trail is the 'new way'.

By this latter route the Heidelberger hut should be reached in about four hours, exclusive of rests.

For a last day's walking on this traverse, rather than take the obvious valley route down to Ischgl, I would advocate crossing the Ritzenjoch into the parallel Laraintal and then ambling slowly down through this quiet glen to either Galtür or Mathon. Or, should your plan be to make a full circuit of the Silvretta region, the outward route from the Heidelberger hut would lead across the Cuolmen d'Fenga and down the long Val Sinestra to the Lower Engadine, there to join the Tour of the Southern Silvretta. Whichever option is taken, a good day's walking is almost guaranteed.

THE SILVRETTA TRAVERSE - ROUTE SUMMARY

Day 1: St Gallenkirch - Gargellen (or Madrisa Hut)

Day 2: Gargellen (or Madrisa Hut) - Vergaldnerjoch - Tübinger Hut

Day 3: Tübinger Hut - Plattenjoch (or Hochmaderer Joch) - Madlener Haus - Wiesbadener Hut

Day 4: Wiesbadener Hut - Radsattel - Getschnerscharte - Jamtal Hut

Day 5: Jamtal Hut - Kronenjoch - Heidelberger Hut

Day 6: Heidelberger Hut - Ritzenjoch - Galtür (or Mathon)
or: Heidelberger Hut - Cuolmen d'Fenga - Val Sinestra - Sent

---

* * *

THE SILVRETTA ALPS

Location:

On the Swiss-Austrian border, the neighbouring Rätikon Alps also share a border with Liechtenstein, while the Verwall group lies just to the north within Austria's far western province of Vorarlberg, and part of Tirol. The Swiss side of the Rätikon and Silvretta lies within canton Graubünden.

Principal valleys:

In the Verwall group these are the Verwalltal, Moostal, Silbertal and Paznauntal. The Rätikon glens on the Austrian side are: Gamperdonatal and Brandner Tal near Bludenz, while the Rellstal, Gauertal, Gampadelstal and Gargellental all flow into the Montafon valley. On the Swiss side the main glens are St Antöniental and Schlappintal that drain to the Prättigau valley. The principal Silvretta valleys in Switzerland are the Vereinatal, Lower Engadine, Val Tuoi, Val Tasna, Val Sinestra. In Austria these are the Paznauntal, Garneratal, Jamtal and Fimbertal/Val Fenga.

Principal peaks:

Piz Linard (3410m), Fluchthorn (3399m), Piz Buin (3312m), Silvrettahorn (3244m), Dreiländerspitz (3197m), Kuchenspitze (3184m), Schesaplana (2965m), Drusenfluh (2628m)

Centres:
Bludenz, Schruns, St Gallenkirch for the northern Rätikon and western Verwall; Galtür and Ischgl for the eastern Verwall and northern Silvretta; Landquart and Klosters for the southern Rätikon; Klosters and Scuol for the Swiss Silvretta.

Huts:
Many huts on both sides of the border. The majority belong to the German, Austrian or Swiss Alpine Clubs; a few are privately owned.

Access:
By train to Bludez for the northern Rätikon and western Verwall, or to Landquart or Klosters for the Swiss side of the Rätikon. Rail to Landeck or St Anton for the eastern Verwall or Austrian side of the Silvretta; rail from Chur to Scuol for the southern Silvretta. Nearest international airports, Zürich and Innsbruck.

Maps:
For the Verwall group and northern side of the Silvretta, the Kompass Wanderkarte sheet 41, *Silvretta Verwallgruppe* at 1:50,000 is perfectly adequate. The Swiss side of the Silvretta is contained on 1:100,000 LS sheet 39 *Flüelapass*, while the Rätikon Alps are represented on Kompass Wanderkarte sheets 21, *Feldkirch, Vaduz* and 32, *Bludenz, Schruns, Klostertal*, both at 1:50,000. Freytag Berndt produce a single sheet at 1:100,000 scale which covers all three areas - sheet number 37, *Rätikon, Silvretta & Verwallgruppe*

Guidebooks:
Mountain Walking in Austria by Cecil Davies (Cicerone Press).
Walking Austria's Alps, Hut to Hut by Jonathan Hurdle (Cordee/The Mountaineers) gives details of a seven-day tour of the Rätikon and Silvretta Alps.
Walks in the Engadine, Switzerland by Kev Reynolds (Cicerone Press) includes routes on the Swiss side of the Silvretta range.
Silvretta Alps by Jeff Williams (West Col) is mostly for mountaineers, but with useful information on huts and hut approaches on both sides of the border.

Other reading:
The Mountains of Europe by Kev Reynolds (Oxford Illustrated Press, 1990). A chapter by Cecil Davies on the Austrian Alps includes these three districts.
Classic Walks in the Alps by Kev Reynolds (Oxford Illustrated Press, 1991) includes a three-day section of the Rätikon Höhenweg Nord described by Cecil Davies.
Over Tyrolese Hills by F.S. Smythe (Hodder & Stoughton, 1936) tells of a long traverse of the Austrian Alps from Schruns to Mittersill in Pinzgau in the summer of 1935, during which Smythe climbed a number of peaks in the Silvretta, Ötztal, Stubai, Zillertal and Venediger groups.

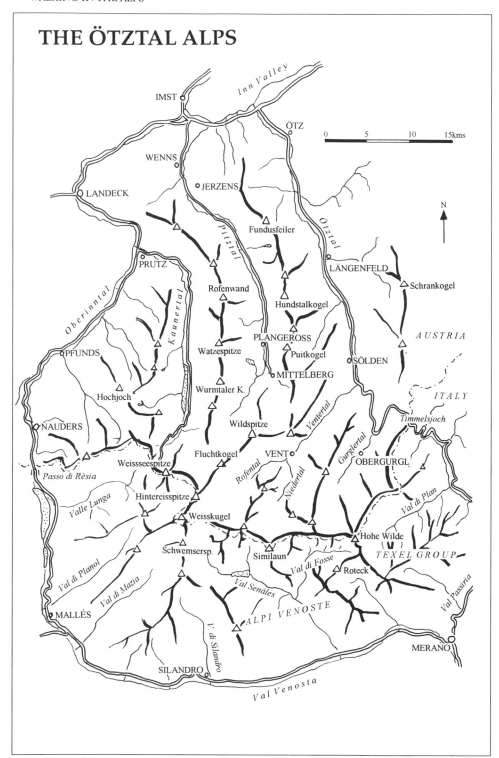

THE ÖTZTAL ALPS

Inn Valley

IMST

ÖTZ

0   5   10   15kms

WENNS

LANDECK

JERZENS

N

Pitztal

Fundusfeiler

Ötztal

PRUTZ

LÄNGENFELD

Rofenwand

Schrankogel

Oberinntal

Kaunertal

Hundstalkogel

AUSTRIA

PFUNDS

Watzespitze

PLANGEROSS

Puitkogel

SÖLDEN

Hochjoch

Wurmtaler K.

MITTELBERG

ITALY

NAUDERS

Wildspitze

Ventertal

Timmelsjoch

Fluchtkogel

VENT

Gurglertal

OBERGURGL

Weissseespitze

Rofental

Niedertal

Passo di Rèsia

Valle Lunga

Hintereisspitze

Val di Plan

Weisskugel

Hohe Wilde

Schwemsersp.

Similaun

TEXEL GROUP

Val di Planol

Val di Fosse

Roteck

Val Senáles

Val di Mazia

V. di Silandro

ALPI VENOSTE

Val Passiria

MALLÉS

MERANO

SILANDRO

Val Venosta

Taschachferner from the Riffelsee trail

13: THE ÖTZTAL ALPS

Though Austria has its loftiest mountain further east in the Hohe Tauern, the Ötztal group in the western Tirol has produced the country's most extensive series of snowfields and glaciers amid an impressive range of Alpine scenery. It is one of the major districts of the Eastern Alps, an ideal range for the newcomer to snow mountains with numerous uncomplicated routes on comparatively high peaks, and with a plentiful supply of huts from which to tackle them. Glacier expeditions are popular, as are hut to hut tours, while our walker, eager to avoid all but the most innocent of icefields, will find almost unlimited opportunities to make expeditions of assorted lengths below the snowline, all with a glorious mountain backdrop.

The district is neatly outlined by river valleys traversed by major through-roads. The northern boundary is scored by the River Inn and the Landeck-Innsbruck highway. The Inn also marks the western limit from Landeck down to the Swiss border, with the Silvretta Alps on the far side, and is then continued southward over the Reschen Pass (Passo di Rèsia) which links the valleys of the Inn and the upper Adige on the Austro-Italian border. The Adige then flows in an anti-clockwise curve to the east, thus lining the southern extent of the Ötztal Alps with a major road leading through orchard country of Val Venosta (or Vinschgau) to Merano, which also edges the Ortler Alps to the south and has the Texel group rising northward. Merano acts as the south-east cornerstone of the district with Val Passiria (formerly the Passiertal) effectively outlining the lower eastern limit as far north as the 2509 metre Timmelsjoch, on the Austrian side of which flows the Ötztaler Ache, draining the valley whose name has been adopted for the whole area. All the mountains and glens on the east flank of the Ötztal, however, belong to the neighbouring Stubai Alps.

A glance at the map shows that although the district has little respect for international frontiers, by far the greater part falls within the Austrian province of Tirol, while that of the Italian flank belongs to the Alto-Adige, or South Tirol, the mountains here known as the Alpi Venoste. The dividing frontier ridge runs roughly west to east and carries the main Alpine watershed with it, yet the highest summit and the biggest glaciers do not stride this ridge, instead they are gathered near the midway point of the chain where a spur breaks away north-east from the frontier crest at the Weisskugel and culminates on the Wildspitze (3772m), undisputed monarch of the region.

So much for the general outline. Within those boundaries two major valleys flowing parallel to one another on the northern side of the watershed give access to the heart of the range, while the Italian slopes are cut by lesser glens flowing out like the spokes of a wheel to the Adige rim. These southern glens are listed from west to east. The first is Valle Lunga which curves under the Hintereisspitze and Weisskugel, and flows out to Lago di Resia. Then comes Val di Planol which drains the Falbonairspitze and joins the Adige at Málles, and then Val di Mazia whose river is the Saldurbach and whose southern end is guarded by the thirteenth century Castel Coira (Schloss Churburg). The fourth glen flows roughly north to south, with Silandro at its entrance. At the head of Val di Silandro a walkers' pass crosses into Val Senáles (formerly known as the Schnalsertal), the largest of these southern valleys. A road projects almost to the head of this latter valley, passing the dammed Lago di Vernago (Stausee Vernagt) on the way, and from the roadhead cableway access is given to the glacier of the Hochjochferner to exploit its potential for skiing at almost three thousand metres. To the east of the Hochjochferner, between the Hauslabjoch and Niederjoch, the remains of a Stone Age traveller (nicknamed Ötzi, the Ice Man) were discovered in September 1991 preserved in the ice where he had lain trapped for some 5000 years and more.

Val Senáles has an important tributary glen in the Val di Fosse, whose upper reaches curve eastward parallel to the frontier crest and lie within the Texel Nature Park. Continuing counter-clockwise from the lower Val Senáles several minor glens drain the Texel group and the outer flanks of the Alpi Venoste, and have a scattering of huts on their slopes, but the last major valley of the Italian Ötztal Alps is Val di Plan (Pfelderer Tal) which flows north-eastward into Val Passiria.

So much for the Italian flanks. The two major valleys cutting into the heart of the range on the Austrian side are the Kaunertal and the Pitztal, while a shorter glen, the Ventertal, forks away from the upper Ötztal proper between Sölden and Obergurgl and is sub-divided just above Vent into the Rofental and Niedertal. Beyond the Ventertal's opening the Ötztal veers south as the Gurglertal with the icesheet of the Gurglerferner at its head. Glaciers adorn the head of all these valleys and glens, but those that block the southern end of the Kaunertal and Pitztal flow from the highest part of the district; a lofty mountain barrier liberally plastered with ice and snow, with an extensive ridge wall separating the two which maintains a mean altitude above 3000 metres for the greater part of its length, while the mountain wall dividing the Pitztal from the Ötztal is only marginally lower.

It might be imagined, then, that with such an abundance of glacier and snowfield, and with such consistently high mountain ridges, the general hillwalker here might be severely limited in scope, restricted, perhaps to the green forested valleys. The truth, however, is far different. In the Ötztal Alps a wealth of cross-country routes awaits exploration. From hut to hut, valley to valley, glen to glen, with rugged cols to cross, high alms to visit and an array of glorious high mountain views to gaze upon. I say 'high mountain views' because to all intents and purposes these are high mountains. Not high in the sense that the major ranges of the Western Alps are high, for there are no four thousand metre summits this side of the Bernina Alps. But in their regal and snowy domination these Ötztal peaks give every impression of seriousness, of mountains that deserve to be noticed. And it's only when seen through the eyes of the experienced alpinist that the modest nature of their challenge becomes apparent. The walker, though, does not seek the challenge of arduous or exacting ice slopes or rock walls. Instead he looks for ways that give safe passage over sometimes wild, sometimes gentle and pastoral, landscapes, but with one predominant aim; that is, to gaze on as much scenic beauty as is possible. In such an aim the adventurous walker in the Ötztal Alps may be daily blessed.

* * *

The Kaunertal

Walkers without transport planning to begin their exploration of the district from this valley, will approach by bus from Landeck station which is on the main line from Innsbruck. Buses journey south-east from the town alongside the Inn as far as Prutz where the Kaunertal empties into the Oberinntal. From there another bus links this lower part of the valley with its upper reaches above a large dammed reservoir, the Stausee Gepatsch, leading up to which the way passes in summer through a veritable forest of blue lupins. The road actually winds high into the mountains that block the valley where summer skiing is possible on the glaciated headwall. By comparison with some districts the valley has limited accommodation. Way down valley a few modest hotels and gasthofs are located in a string of villages, or there's the rustic inn of the Gepatsch Haus, owned by the Frankfurt section of the German Alpine Club (DAV), that is attractively set on a bluff among pine trees at the southern end of the lake. Gazing upvalley from this inn one looks directly at the Gepatschferner, the largest glacier in the Tirol, and the second in extent in all Austria.

The Kaunertal is at first an unremarkable green trench, pastoral here, forested there, but gaining in drama the deeper you go through it. At almost every stage there are walking routes up onto the right-hand mountain wall, and routes too that wander onto and over the western flank. Upvalley from Feichten, the highest village, one such trail climbs over the western ridge to gain the Anton-Renk hut which sits high above Ried in the neighbouring Oberinntal. Another, from Feichten itself, goes up the eastern hillside to the Verpeil hut in the little Verpeiltal glen. A continuing route climbs above the hut and crosses the 2830 metre Verpeil Joch, then descends steeply into the Pitztal. A more popular crossing of this ridge, however, cuts south from the hut before swinging south-east on a long climb to the Madatsch Joch (3010m), a col on the north ridge of the 3533 metre Watzespitze, highest of the Kaunergrat's peaks. On the east side of the ridge the trail descends to the Kaunergrat hut and eventually as far as the hamlet of Plangeross. Two further crossings of the Kaunergrat are possible from the bank of the Gepatsch reservoir. The first and northernmost of these is by way of the 3083 metre Rostiz Joch, the other is marked as the Offenbacher Höhenweg, with a small section of glacier to negotiate on the Pitztal side of the Wurmtaler Joch. Both these routes descend to the Riffelsee above Mittelberg at the head of the Pitztal.

But perhaps the finest eastbound crossing is that of the Ölgrubenjoch from the Gepatsch Haus to the Taschach Haus, a fairly strenuous route that provides stunning views of Austria's second highest mountain, the Wildspitze. However, before we look in detail at this route, and discuss the prospect of making a three-day traverse of the district, we should see what else is possible from the Gepatsch Haus itself.

Taking our lead from Hubert Walker, one outing that ought to be considered is a visit to the Rauhekopf hut perched among glaciers about three hours to the south-east of the Gepatsch Haus. There is a narrow portion of glacier to cross here, and the usual precautions should be taken. After refreshing yourself at the hut Walker then recommends making the ascent of the Grosser Rauher Kopf (2990m) which rises behind it. This, he says, provides a splendid view over the Gepatsch glacier to the frontier snow ridge that extends from the Weissseespitze to the Weisskugel.

As mentioned above the finest eastbound crossing of the dividing ridge between the Kaunertal and Pitztal is that of the Ölgrubenjoch at 3095 metres. With an altitude gain of more than 1100 metres from the Gepatsch Haus, and an optional ascent of another 200 metres from the col to a neighbouring summit, followed by descent over snow-covered ice, boulders and moraine as far as the Taschach Haus, it will be seen that it's not the sort of crossing you'd choose to make on the first day of a walking holiday. It is, nonetheless, a magnificent route, and one which gave my wife and me one of the most rewarding days of a memorable Alpine summer recently, despite being undertaken in heat-wave conditions.

The lower hillside is clad with vegetation; at mid-height the trail borders a long boulder-field, a tongue of stone daubed with yellow and lime-green lichens. There are patches of snow and a small glacier plastered on the face of the Hinterer Ölgrubenspitze nearby, and below it a dirty green tarn unmarked on the map. The final pull to the pass is by way of a steep ramp of scree and grit, and one emerges there to be greeted by one of the great panoramas of the Austrian Alps. Ahead to the south-east the graceful shape of the Wildspitze conducts the view, its attendant peaks and flowing glaciers shining like great white mirrors, while snowfields and glaciers adorn numerous other mountains stretching far into the blue haze of distance.

The Ölgrubenjoch may be just a broad saddle of bare rock, but it truly is a splendid place from which to study the central block of the Ötztal Alps, the Wildspitze being just one of a great assembly of peaks and deep hinted valleys. And for those with sufficient energy the Hinterer Ölgrubenspitze (3296m) which borders the pass to the south is worth a visit for the extended view its summit affords. Both Walker and Baedeker gave it their recommendation; there is no difficulty and the top should be reached in less than an hour from the saddle.

We sat on the pass in the sunshine and let the minutes conjure hours; studied the mountains through binoculars and counted thirty climbers on the Wildspitze alone, then peered into a wild corrie below to where the Taschach Haus could be identified on its grassy shelf beside the Taschachferner icefall. The descent to it leads along the top edge of a cliff, then down glacial slabs and grit-covered ledges to a snowfield. From snowfield to boulder-field, and from boulder-field to moraine bank extravagent with alpine flowers; then over streams furious with afternoon melt, and up a short rise to the Taschach Haus itself.

This DAV hut is situated on a spur projecting north of the Pitztaler Urkund, and with a remarkable close view of the splintered séracs and crevassed welts of the Taschachferner's icefall which cascades through a rocky cleft nearby. Thanks to its privileged position the Taschach Haus (2434m) is crowded in summer with climbers and aspirant climbers taking part in ice-climbing and general mountaineering courses based there. A few paces away stands the original Taschach hut which dates from 1874; a very simple affair by comparison with facilities on offer at the main building. Below to the north stretches the Taschachtal, one of the tributary glens of the important Pitztal, a valley with primary appeal to walkers. But before we turn to a study of that valley, it is worth noting that a much recommended three-day traverse of the central Ötztal Alps continues from the Taschach Haus to the Braunschweiger hut, then over the Pitztaler Jöchl for descent to Sölden in the main Ötztal. Individual stages of this route will be described in a little more detail below.

The Pitztal

> "A visit to the Pitzthal, a valley running parallel to the Oetzthal on the
> W., is recommended not only to mountaineers, who will find many
> attractions here, but also to less ambitious travellers who desire to
> obtain a glimpse at the Oetzthal glacier-region."

So said Karl Baedeker in the 1888 edition of his guide to the Eastern Alps. What he wrote then is still true today, for the scenic attractions have not diminished with the years. They may have changed, in terms of glacial extent, but retreating icefields have not lessened their impact on the region. Indeed, in their wake nature's artistry has been allowed full expression, and new tarns glisten in hollows left behind, and moraine deposits now flourish with alpine plants bright in summer glory. Baedeker's Pitztal had been threatened not by global warming, but by glaciers that were still advancing. In the early nineteenth century such was the fear of inundation by ice, that services of intercession were held on the edge of the Mittelbergferner. Those prayers were answered, the advance was checked and the glaciers are now in reluctant retreat. But the splendour remains; indeed, many would echo the view that the Pitztal rewards with some of the finest Alpine scenery in Austria.

Longer than the Kaunertal, its neighbour to the west, the Pitztal scores deeply into the mountains south of Imst between the Kaunergrat and Geigenkamm, a distance of almost forty kilometres from the mouth of the valley to Mittelberg, the highest village. The northern, lower, section is a broad smiling valley populated with many villages; the principal ones being Arzl, known as the *Torl zum Pitztal* (Gateway to the Pitztal), Wenns, on a fertile terrace above the left bank of the river, and the old village of Jerzens above the river on the right bank. Beyond Wenns the Pillarbach tributary flows in from the south-west (road to Prutz and Landeck), and at the head of this the 1558 metre Pillarhöhe is a notable viewpoint.

Midway along the valley St Leonhard-im-Pitztal is the main village. From it a walkers' route climbs over the western walling ridge at the Wallfahrtsjöchl (2770m) and descends through the Gallrutt glen to the Kaunertal. Continuing south through the Pitztal the scenic grandeur increases, the road passing through the hamlets of Stillebach, Neurur and Trenkwald. From Trenkwald a respectable path climbs up the western hillside to a small tarn reached through the Lorbachtal glen; a more demanding trail crosses the Verpeil Joch, while a third climbs 1100 metres up the east flank in order to cross the Breitlehnjöchl (2630m), followed by descent to Huben (in six hours) in the Ötztal.

Plangeross is popular with walkers, and justifiably so, for it has some fine expeditions virtually on its doorstep. That some of these involve long, steep ascents should be seen to its credit rather than be slipped into the debit side of the hamlet's account. Of these, one crosses the Madatsch Joch under the Watzespitze by way of the glen that cuts west of the hamlet. The col is almost 1400 metres above Plangeross, but the Austrian Alpine Club's Kaunergrat hut is conveniently placed at 2817 metres on the Pitztal side, and thus gives an opportunity to turn the crossing into a two-day journey. In his guidebook (*Mountain Walking in Austria*) Cecil Davies speaks highly of the Grade III ascent of the Watzespitze east ridge from this hut, although I have no personal experience of it. Halfway through the Plangeross glen an enticing route (some possible stonefall danger) marked as the Cottbuser Höhenweg breaks away to the south to make a traverse round the flanks of the 2635 metre Steinkogel and its twin, the Brandkogel, to the Riffelsee tarn.

On the eastern hillside above Plangeross the Neue Chemnitzer hut at 2323 metres enjoys an inspiring view across the valley to the Watzespitze and Verpeil Spitze and their modest glaciers that catch the morning light. Just above the hut a junction of paths extends one's opportunities for further exploration. These opportunities may be summarised as follows. The first choice for many would be to make the ascent of the Hohe Geige (3395m), highest summit of the Geigenkamm. Despite the fact that this mountain boasts three glaciers, the normal route of ascent ignores each of these, and will not be found too difficult by most hillwalkers with a bit of Alpine experience. Snow will often be encountered though, and in such cases caution is advised. The summit, reached in a little over three hours from the hut, provides an excellent panorama, as one might expect. The second option from the Neue Chemnitzer hut breaks away from the Hohe Geige route, makes a long traverse of the hillside heading north, and either crosses the Breitlehnjöchl to the Ötztal, or descends through the Hundsbach Alm to Trenkwald, down valley from Plangeross. Next to consider will be the right-hand trail at the path junction above the hut. This leads directly to the 2959 metre Weissmaurach Joch, yet another of those high crossings of the Geigenkamm (the ridge that divides the Pitztal from the Ötztal); this time descending first through the Pollestal. Finally the map indicates a scrambling route leading south from the Weissmaurach Joch. This, the so-called Mainzer Höhenweg, keeps on the east side of the ridge until ascending the Wassertalkogel (3247m), upon whose crown there's a small, orange-coloured bivouac hut, then continues south along the crest to the Polleskogel (3035m), from which descent is made either to the Braunschweiger hut via the Pitztaler Jöchl (a brief dip in a shattered ridge), or eastward to the roadhead serving the Rettenbachferner ski playground. This high route is a demanding one, and for experienced mountain walkers only. It is waymarked throughout its length, but in places the rocks are alarmingly loose and there's quite a bit of exposure. But the visual rewards are memorable; especially when tackled from north to south.

South of Plangeross the valley road leads to the hamlet of Mittelberg, located at a junction of glens. To the south-east a short and wild-looking glen carries the infant Pitze river from the Mittelbergferner via a series of cliffs; to the south-west the Taschachtal leads to the Taschachferner, unseen from here. Mountain huts are set high in both glens, while a third, the Riffelsee hut stands as its name suggests, by the little Riffelsee tarn on a green shelf above and to the west of Mittelberg. When Walker was here Mittelberg consisted of little more than an inn. Baedeker spoke of it as being the last farm in the valley. Now it can be crowded in summer and in winter too, thanks to the construction of the Pitztaler Gletscherbahn ('Pitzexpress'), an underground funicular that leads to the edge of the Mittelbergferner, a huge glacial snow bowl grossly exploited by the ski industry. From the upper station a cable-car continues to the Hinterer Brunnenkogel (3440m), a peak to the north of the Wildspitze, while the funicular station itself has a restaurant at 2841 metres which provides spectacular views that include the Dolomites.

Earlier in this chapter we came over the Ölgrubenjoch from the Kaunertal and descended to the Taschach Haus. Now we can approach the same hut, but from Mittelberg. There are two routes to choose from; one leads directly through the valley, at first along a dirt road, then on a broad track edging slopes coloured with alpenroses, and finally up a steepening trail that leads directly to it. The other rises along the western hillside via the Riffelsee. Of the two the second is far the nicer and should be adopted if the plan is not to return to the Pitztal. If, however, you decide on a there-and-back walk from Mittelberg it would be better to approach the hut by the low route, and return by way of the the left-bank trail, shown on the map as the Fuldaer Höhenweg, pausing for refreshment, perhaps, at the Riffelsee hut before descending the final slope to the roadhead.

Walkers based for a day or two at the Taschach Haus have a privileged opportunity to capture many fine views of the glacier world of the high mountains. Among the options available you are urged to wander upvalley at least as far as a small ice-locked tarn on the edge of the Sexegertenferner, if not to the Ölgrubenjoch above it - although the summit of the Hinterer Ölgrubenspitze will repay the extra effort involved. The moraine spoils on the north side of the glacier display a wonderfully rich variety of alpine plants, and will surely underline once and for all the abundant diversity of habitats provided by the mountain kingdom. Though these moraines may appear from a distance to be the epitomy of moribund decay, upon closer inspection colour, movement and life in vivid exuberance bursts from the debris churned out of the base mountain block by the bulldozing ice. It's a wonderland set amid a scene of arctic splendour.

Returning to Mittelberg along the Fuldaer Höhenweg allows the perspective of distance. Instead of rubbing your nose against the mountains, so to speak, the division of the valley in that view makes a profound difference. One stands back as in an art gallery, in order to balance scale, depth and height, to better gauge the varying levels of light, to appreciate an umbrella sky as part of the overall scene. To bear witness to the mountains as a whole. From the Fuldaer balcony (a balcony with fixed cable safeguards in places) grass and foreground flowers play a part. So do streams and tiny pools trapped in hillside hollows, and marmots and butterflies and the seething of insects when overnight dew has dried - all this with a backdrop of ice-draped peaks. I have before me as I write a photograph taken along that trail on a July morning a couple of years ago. A clutter of grey, lichen-spattered rocks pokes through a yellow-starred bluff softened with grass, beyond which the hillside disappears to the hint of the Taschachtal. Across that unseen glen the white-blue-grey trunk of the Taschachferner pushes through a funnelled hillside, its snout smooth on top but cleft at the edges into claw-like toes. Further back a chaos of séracs, tumultuous and forbidding from this distance, announces the icefall on which apprentice climbers learn their craft (unseen from here). Above that deep folds and runnels reveal a multitude of crevasses. On either side of the glacier grey screes have been shunted aside; that on the right tapers to a wave-like wall, grey on the glacier bank, dusted lime green on the other. The left-hand slope is part-concealed in morning shade. At the back of the glacier a wall (the Taschachwand) rears steeply; a wall of blue-black rock speckled with piebald patches of white and topped with a liberal coating of snow and ice painted here and there with the soft blue shadows of clouds. One or two cloud wisps trip across the horizon; others sail in innocence through warm summer skies.

Back in Mittelberg our next excursion must be to the Braunschweiger hut on a route that will be adopted as stage two of our crossing of the central Ötztal Alps. This hut too gives a close view of the glacier world, but it's an even more intimate view that is provided here than that from the Taschach Haus. There one had the contrast of green grass and white, blue or grey ice; the comforting subtleties of vegetation from which to safely gaze on glacial mysteries. Not so at the Braunschweiger, for up here you're very much a part of that ice world, living in a man-made oasis on a bony island washed up on an arctic tide.

At an altitude of 2759 metres, the Braunschweiger hut is almost a thousand metres higher than Mittelberg, and some of the ascent to it is quite gruelling. But it's a fine route all the same, with no chance of boredom setting in. Halfway along the upper glen of the Pitze river the Gletscherstübele restaurant is the final remnant of tourist gaiety with bright-coloured parasols over outdoor tables. Beyond that the glen is blocked by a cliff-like barrier from which a fearsome waterfall explodes with a halo of spray. The trail picks a way up and over this barrier and enters a rocky trough with a fine view of the lower, steep slope of the Mittelbergferner. Now the trail steepens considerably; first a rocky section, then along an uphill ramp with alpenroses and yellow anemones adding colour to the scene. Natural stairways of stone lead on, now with more open views onto the glacier's icefall as the trail weaves to and fro. Then at last the hut is spied from a bend where a bench seat has been placed in order to encourage passers by to collapse there and enjoy at leisure the glacial landscape laid out for inspection.

The Braunschweiger hut belongs to the DAV, by whom it was built in 1892. It's a large building with sleeping places for more than a hundred in its dormitories and bedrooms, and with a dining room that gazes out across an arc of glaciers that curves around the rocky knoll on which it is perched. It's a popular base for climbs on the Wildspitze, for the Mittelbergferner serves as a straightforward approach route and has few crevasses to worry about. For a big mountain the Wildspitze offers surprisingly easy ways to its crown. Our purpose in coming here, however, is not to climb mountains but to cross them by non-technical means, although that is not to suggest we are disinterested in summits or ways to them, for we may often be tempted. It's just that summits are not our primary aim.

By virtue of its location the hut is limited in expeditions for non-glacier trekkers. Walkers with the necessary scrambling experience, and a good head for heights, will find interest in following a section of the Mainzer Höhenweg (already mentioned) which teeters along a ridge leading to the Wassertalkogel. This could be taken as a one day there-and-back route from Braunschweiger; or it could be continued beyond the Wassertalkogel high point to the Weissmaurach Joch and from there either bear left to the Neue Chemnitzer hut, or right for a descent through the Pollestal to Huben in the Ötztal (a long day's walk). Another route through the Pollestal may be accessed from the Braunschweiger hut via the Pitztaler Jöchl and a point just beyond the Polleskogel. But our recommendation will be to leave Braunschweiger for the Ötztal with descent through the Rettenbachtal. This too crosses the rocky 2995 metre Pitztaler Jöchl (look for ibex on the ridge above the hut leading to the col), and descends a short stretch of snowfield before coming to a parking area used by skiers on the Rettenbachferner whose tows and cableways will have been in view since before gaining the col. The rest of the descent to Sölden wanders through a mixed glen below the road that services those ski grounds, alongside a stream on soft turf with flowers bright among the wayside rocks. Then down steeply through forest (glades flush with orchids in July) to the beaming Ötztal, thus completing the three-day crossing of the district.

ACROSS THE CENTRAL ÖTZTAL ALPS - ROUTE SUMMARY

Day 1: Gepatsch Haus - Ölgrubenjoch - Taschach Haus

Day 2: Taschach Haus - Mittelberg - Braunschweiger Hut

Day 3: Braunschweiger Hut - Pitztaler Jöchl - Sölden

The Ötztal

Forming an unmarked divide between the Ötztal Alps and the Stubai Alps, the well-populated Ötztal is the longest and busiest of the district's valleys, and with the upper tributary glens of the Ventertal and Gurglertal, not to mention the various glens that drain the eastern side of the valley, it provides a wealth of walking opportunities. Those eastern glens will be included in the following chapter which deals with the Stubai Alps, but there is quite sufficient scope for the eager walker here on the left flank to hold one's attention throughout many a fine Alpine day.

So far as basic detail is concerned, sufficient to say that access by public transport is both frequent and reliable. At its confluence with the Inn, trains plying the Innsbruck-Landeck line stop at a small village that has grown up round the railway station known simply as Ötztal Bahnhof. Buses connect with stopping trains and ferry passengers to Sölden and beyond. Accommodation is plentiful throughout the valley with varying degrees of luxury, and as elsewhere in these mountains there are some fine *Alpenverein* huts in outstanding settings. Of the many villages the main ones for our purposes are Umhausen, Längenfeld, Sölden and Obergurgl.

In its lower reaches the Ötztal is a broad, green and fertile valley. Halfway up it contracts into a series of gorges which alternate with open sunny stretches of meadowland; and in its upper reaches the feeder glens curve towards big mountains of snow and ice. A few of the higher slopes have been snagged by the ski industry which has brought financial stability to the area, but not all such development is beneficial, and one may regret some aspects of this exploitation of a fragile environment.

Making our way upvalley from Ötztal Bahnhof we pass a road breaking away to the east (a cross-country route which goes by way of the Kühtaisattel to the Sellraintal), and come to Ötz (also spelt Oetz) on the right bank of the river. This has a few interesting walks on both flanks of the valley, including a short stroll to the Piburger See set on a wooded terrace to the south-west, the Tumpental which cuts under the Hoher Karkopf, and a scrambling route onto the Hoher Karkopf (2686m) itself.

Umhausen is the next resort of note. Though not as large as Ötz, it's the oldest village in the valley and with the nearby Stuiben Falls (said to be the largest in Tirol) as one of its prime attractions. Behind it the Horlachtal digs into the western Stubai Alps, but across the valley a trail enters the Leierstal glen and climbs to the Erlanger hut, a small DAV lodging built on the shores of the Wettersee under the eastern crags of the Wildgrat. From this hut an interesting ridge route traces a considerable portion of the Geigenkamm heading south towards the snowy high peaks of the range. This is a multi-day epic that links several huts, finishes along the Mainzer Höhenweg and leads eventually to the Braunschweiger hut.

Längenfeld lies to the south of Umhausen at the mouth of the Sulztal, and is noted as the birthplace (in 1831) of Pastor Franz Senn, the man who was largely responsible for opening the area for tourism in an effort to arrest the poverty he saw when working in Vent, his first parish, from 1860-1872. As a base for a walking holiday much of Längenfeld's attraction will be focused on the Sulztal, although since our aim here is to concentrate on the west flank of the valley it should be noted that the Hauertal glen opposite gives access to that long ridge route mentioned in the previous paragraph. Part of that route could be adopted for a one-day circuit. But even without joining that longer trail, this glen is well worth exploring for the charming tarn of Hauersee which lies cradled beneath the craggy peaks of the Geigenkamm. A small hut beside this tarn (2331m; 8 spaces) is unmanned and locked. The key for it needs to be collected from either the Frischmann hut, Neue Chemnitzer hut, or from an address in Umhausen.

A short distance upvalley from Längenfeld, Huben nestles on the left bank of the Ötztaler Ache at the mouth of the Breitlehntal, at the head of which the Breitlehnjöchl gives access to Trenkwald in the Pitztal. But also accessible from Huben is the wildly attractive Pollestal, with a gorge defending its entrance opposite the hamlet of Winkel. Avoiding this gorge a woodland trail enters the glen on the north side of the Pollesbach and follows the river first on one bank, then on the other, to its source under the 3035 metre Polleskogel, some ten kilometres from its confluence with the Ötztaler Ache. The glen is an uninhabited delight and with some tough routes out. One climbs the western slopes to the Weissmaurach Joch (reached from the opposite side by a trail from the Neue Chemnitzer hut, and is adopted by the Mainzer Höhenweg); another climbs at its head to the Polleskogel on a challenging route to the Braunschweiger hut. Both routes are demanding.

Sölden is the main resort of the Ötztal, attracting crowds of visitors in summer and winter alike. Above the village on the western hillside the ski-slopes of Hochsölden are reached by both road and cableway. In fact the left bank hillsides are well-endowed with tows and cables, while the road through the Rettenbachtal leads to summer skiing on the Rettenbach and Tiefenbach glaciers, the latter being connected with the former by way of a road tunnel which, it is claimed, is the highest in Europe. Sölden lies at a junction of valleys. To the east the Windachtal noses into the Stubai Alps, but to the south the main Ötztal is squeezed by the gorge of Kühtraienschluct, then rises steadily to Zwieselstein where the Ventertal breaks away to the south-west.

The Ventertal & Gurglertal

The Ventertal runs deep into the mountains and forms a south-eastern moat to the long and important ridge spur of the Weisskamm that breaks away from the frontier crest and contains the lovely Wildspitze. Having already seen this, the highest mountain of the Ötztal Alps, from the west and north, the narrow Ventertal provides opportunities to explore its southern aspect. Vent, a simple village with modest ski facilities, lies at the foot of the mountain where the valley divides; the south-western arm is the Rofental, the southern being the glen of Niedertal. With the reputation for being the highest permanently-inhabited settlement in Austria, the hamlet of Rofenhöfe is located a short distance beyond Vent in the Rofental, and with a number of huts within easy reach.

Above the Rofental the Breslauer and Vernagt huts can both accommodate in excess of a hundred people in their dormitories and separate bedrooms, and are linked by a trail that hugs the mid-height slopes of the Weisskamm. The Breslauer hut is used as a base for climbs on the Wildspitze, the Vernagt is set at a junction of moraines below a high glacial basin. Further round the flank of the mountain, on a rock spur in a sea of glaciers, the Brandenburger Haus (3272m) makes a tempting destination, but walkers should note that any approach necessarily involves a glacier crossing and safety precautions ought therefore be taken. At the head of the glen, approached by a trail that is protected in places by cable where it teeters along the edge of a deep gorge, the Hochjoch Hospitz also provides accommodation for walkers and climbers, and provides a grand outlook with Weisskugel, Langtauferer Spitze, and the frontier crest sweeping round to the Hinter Hintereis Spitze gleaming above a fine glacial drapery. The present building is situated a little lower than the 1869 original which was destroyed by avalanche and whose remains are to be seen further upvalley, and from it a straightforward trail climbs south then south-west alongside the Hochjochferner to gain the Austro-Italian border at the 2861 metre Hochjoch. On the south side of the frontier the privately-owned Rifugio Bellavista (Schöne Aussicht hut) overlooks the upper Val Senáles. To the north of this the summit of Am Hintern Eis (3270m) is worth visiting for the first class view it affords of the Weisskugel a short distance away to the west. The route has some waymarks and a few cairns, and requires about an hour and a half of effort from the hut.

On the other side of the ridge which separates the Rofental from the Niedertal the DAV has yet another hut, the Martin-Busch Haus, with a link route traversing that ridge from the Hochjoch Hospitz. On the west side there's a glacier to contend with, while the route actually crosses over the 3360 metre Seikogel which enjoys a splendid vista of big, ice-hung mountains. If approached by the normal route from Vent, the stone-built Martin-Busch Haus (or Neue Samoar hut) is reached along the left bank of the Niedertaler Ache by a straightforward track in less than three hours. The hut is in a delightful setting below glaciers on three sides. Four hundred metres above it to the west the little Brizzisee tarn offers dazzling reflected views of the frontier peaks. The Niederjochferner curls down from the frontier ridge south-west of the hut, with the Niederjoch at its head and the Similaun hut (3019m) beside it being ideally situated for an ascent of the 3606 metre Similaun to the east. Views from the pass are of the Ortler Alps to the south-west across the distant suggested trench of Val Venosta. Over this pass each year come thousands of sheep returning to the South Tirolean valleys, their shepherds having continued an ancient tradition that gives them grazing rights over the Vent pastures.

An enterprising walker with a modicum of Alpine experience and an eager partner, both of whom have the necessary equipment to safely tackle crevassed glaciers, could make a very fine tour combining each of these huts, beginning and ending at Vent. And even those who shy away from icefields could still create a first-rate expedition, missing out only the Brandenburger hut. The following route outline provides one option, while an extra day would be needed to include the Brandenburger hut.

HUT TO HUT IN THE VENTERTAL - SUMMARY

Day 1:   Vent - Breslauer Hut - Vernagt Hut

Day 2:   Vernagt Hut - Hochjoch Hospitz - Rifugio Bellavista

Day 3:   Rifugio Bellavista - (Am Hintern Eis) - Hochjoch - Seikogel - Martin-Busch Haus

Day 4:   Martin-Busch Haus - Similaun Hut - Martin-Busch Haus - Vent

---

Flowing roughly parallel to the Ventertal the Gurglertal is shorter than its neighbour, but skiing development above Obergurgl has made this one of the most important glens in the Ötztal, so far as tourism is concerned. Skiers flock here in winter when snow in the lower resorts is a bit thin on the ground, but in summer the valley provides abundant walking opportunities and, not surprisingly, Walker made it his first choice as a temporary base. Obergurgl rests in the midst of imposing scenery with the frontier crest enclosing the valley on two sides, and the dividing wall blocking the Ventertal running along its west flank. Glaciers defend the Gurglertal to the south, while other ice-sheets shrink back towards the high ridge crests on either side. Again, as we discovered in the neighbouring Ventertal, several well-situated huts conjure prospects for hut to hut tours.

Of these the nearest to Obergurgl is the Schönweis, a privately-owned ski hut at 2266 metres in a glorious location in the mouth of the Rotmoostal glen. Next is the Langtalereck hut (also known as the Neue Karlsruher) on the right-hand hillside overlooking the Gurglerferner's icefall, with a material lift connecting with the Hochwildehaus (2883m) over a shoulder of the Schwarzen Spitze. The Hochwildehaus is built on the edge of the Schwärzenkamm rock rib coming down from the Hochwilde, and with the impressive Gurglerferner flowing below. It's a magnificent situation on the glacier's lateral moraine, while the route to it is safeguarded in places by fixed cables. On the west side of the valley, almost directly opposite the Langtalereck hut, the Ramolhaus (3006m) stands on a rocky shoulder above the snout of the Gurglerferner, about half an hour's walk from the Ramol Joch. This hut commands a privileged view across the Gurglerferner and up to an impressive sweep of mountains.

So much for prospects of accommodation upvalley from Obergurgl, what then are the main attractions here for walkers? First we should consider perhaps those several little glens that elbow their way into the right-hand wall of the valley. There are no less than five of these (six if we include the head of the valley where the great Gurglerferner bullies its way) with trails of one sort or another that tease with opportunities to gain a closer inspection of the glacial draperies, the snowfields and ancient architecture of the peaks that line them. Listing from north to south these glens enumerate as follows: the Königstal (between Obergurgl and Hochgurgl) with a possible crossing into Italy by way of the 2810 metre Königs Joch; the Ferwalltal with one trail prospecting straight through the glen to the glacier at its head, while another veers away from this and climbs to a col just below the Königs Kogel, with a second opportunity to descend into Italy south of the Timmelsjoch road pass. From the col, incidentally, it is but a short scramble to the Königs Kogel, where one gains a broad vista. The next glen is that of the Gaisbergtal with the steep and narrow Gaisbergferner nosing down the valley from the Liebener Spitze and its neighbour, the Seewer Spitze. A footpath edges up to this glacier, and a rough trail then breaks away south to climb the rib that separates this from the next glen. Once on the crest of the rib a better path goes to Hohe Mut (2659m), reached by chairlift from Obergurgl. Hohe Mut is one of the resort's finest and most accessible viewpoints from which all the world and his wife can admire a spectacular landscape without straining leg muscles on the way. From it you can either descend directly to Obergurgl, or cross into the next glen to the south, the Rotmoostal.

Flowing parallel to the Gaisbergtal the Rotmoostal is a broader, deeper, U-shaped valley grazed by horses in summer, and with the Heufler Kogel towering over the glacier that is responsible for scouring it out. At the mouth of this glen the Schönweis hut sits at a junction of trails, one of which climbs to the lovely belvedere of Hangerer (3021m) which, marked by a large cross, enjoys a much more extensive panorama even than that claimed by the Hohe Mut.

The fifth of our glens is the Langental, with the Langtalereck hut at its entrance. During the nineteenth century this glen was effectively blocked by the Gurgler-ferner which flowed beyond its entrance, thus damming the stream discharged from the Langentalerferner. When the spring melt came a substantial lake built up in the glen, and sometimes burst its banks to cause devastation down valley. No such threat remains today, of course, thanks to glacial retreat, and it's possible to wander into the Langental and up the north bank towards the Seelenferner. On the far side of the Schwärzenkamm rib which forms the glen's left wall a trail winds round to the Hochwildehaus on the moraine bank of the Gurglerferner.

On the left-hand wall of the Gurglertal a long trail makes an almost complete traverse of the valley from Zwieselstein to the Ramolhaus; about eighteen kilometres. Along this trail a handful of small tarns adds a sparkle to the landscape, and there are possibilities of reaching modest summits from it in order to extend one's field of vision even more than that obtained from the mid-height trail. One of those shown on the map as having a marked route to it, is the Nederkogel (3163m) at the northern end of the dividing ridge, while Walker recommends the Schalfkogel (3540m), a high snowy dome towards the southern end of the same ridge. This he points out as being beautifully set in the heart of the snowy region at the head of both the Gurglertal and Ventertal. Although the ascent involves crossing snowfields, Walker says it is only a walk and a most delightful expedition at that.

But of all expeditions available for the non-mountaineer here, a hut to hut tour enjoys the best of all worlds. A very fine two-day outing could be achieved within the Gurglertal, walking on the first day from Obergurgl to the Hochwildehaus, calling on the way at the Schönweis and Langtalereck huts, and the next day returning to Obergurgl along the western hillside after crossing the usually dry glacier of the lower Gurglerferner, climbing to the Ramolhaus and then following the Ötztaler Jungschützenweg north-eastwards. Variations on this theme are possible. A longer option is to combine huts in the Gurglertal and the neighbouring Ventertal in one single expedition. The location of each of the huts has already been discussed, with mention of the various routes available from them, and the following outline provides a summary of one such recommended expedition.

GURGLERTAL-VENTERTAL HUT TOUR - ROUTE SUMMARY

Day 1: Obergurgl - Schönweis Hut - Langtalereck Hut - Hochwildehaus

Day 2: Hochwildehaus - Ramolhaus - Ramol Joch - Martin-Busch Haus

Day 3: Martin-Busch Haus - Niederjoch/Similaun Hut - Martin-Busch Haus

Day 4: Martin-Busch Haus - Seikogel - Rifugio Bellavista

Day 5: Rifugio Bellavista - Am Hintern Eis - Hochjoch - Hochjoch Hospitz

Day 6: Hochjoch Hospitz - Vernagt Hut - Breslauer Hut - Vent

The Italian Valleys of Alpi Venoste

South of the border mountains, huts, valleys and villages suffer a confusion of names, thanks to the political redefining of international frontiers that is an almost inevitable result of warfare between nations. South Tirol, now Italian, was formerly part of the Austrian Habsburg empire, and the German language continues to be spoken by many who live there, despite the fact that those who do so carry Italian passports. This dual linguistic confusion is recorded on maps and in guidebooks. But no matter what they are called at any one time, the mountains retain an elegant aloofness, the valleys attract with their sun-shafts of a morning irrespective of political allegiance and the huts continue to look out at scenes of visual grandeur whether payment for the privilege of being there is made in Austrian schillings or Italian lire.

In the far west of the region, tucked in a quiet corner of Italy near that knot of mountains that gathers the frontiers of Austria and Switzerland, the Valle Lunga (or Langtauferstal) digs into the Ötztal Alps from the shores of Lago di Resia, and curves under the ice-dazzling peaks of the border itself. The lower part of the valley, which extends nearly a dozen kilometres from the lake shore to Melago the last village, was considered by Walker to be rather monotonous and dreary, although Baedeker used the adjective of 'smiling' when he referred to it. Whatever your view, the upper section with the Weisskugel at its head will certainly inspire. From the roadhead at Melago a track continues upvalley through meadows before narrowing to a trail, then climbs in less than two hours to Rifugio Pio XI (2544m) set upon a moraine crest near the Langtauferer glacier. Nowadays owned by the CAI, this refuge was originally built by the German Alpine Club in 1893, by whom it was named the Weisskugel hut. To add to the confusion, it is also sometimes referred to as Rifugio Pala Bianca, the Italian name for the Weisskugel.

All the high country spilling out from the watershed ridge down to Val Venosta is wild and appealing and worth exploring. In his book Walker outlined a way of moving on from the head of Valle Lunga over two ridge spurs extending from the frontier crest by way of Val di Planol (Planeiltal) to the upper reaches of Val di Mazia (Matscher Tal). With the Oberettes hut as the destination this would make an interesting stage in a hut to hut tour along the southern flanks of the Ötztal Alps.

Walker's suggestion, then, was to take a steep trail south from below Rifugio Pio XI in order to cross what he called the Planol col, then descend a short way into Val di Planol (with an option of staying overnight at the Hinterberger hut), before taking a track up the eastern wall of the glen where a crossing could be made at the Schnalser Schartl. It's very much an up-and-down route, for descent must be made from this pass into Val di Mazia, followed by another climb up the opposite hillside to the Oberettes hut perched at 2670 metres near the cliffs of the Weisskugel. This would be a long but rewarding day's trek through unfussed country.

On a site not far from the Oberettes hut, the original Karlsbader hut was built at the foot of the Oberettes glacier in 1882 by the Prague section of the DAV, and six years later it was described as being 'well fitted up'. After the First World War ownership transferred to the Italian Alpine Club when it was renamed Rifugio Diaz. As if the change of name from Karlsbader hut to Rifugio Diaz were not bad enough, it has also been known at various times in its history as the Höller hut and Rifugio

Mazia. The present (Oberettes) hut belongs to the South Tirol Alpine Club (Alpenverein Südtirol - AVS), and is used by climbers bound for the southern flanks of the Weisskugel.

Below the Oberettes hut Val di Mazia offers pleasant walking amid attractive scenery. In its lower reaches, not far from the ruins of the old Matsch castle, a romantic footpath edges alongside one of the district's irrigation channels, known here as a *waale* (the accompanying path is a *waalweg*) - in French-speaking districts of the Alps such an ingenious watercourse would be called a *bisse*. Midway through the valley one wanders pasture and woodland, farmhouses speckle the meadows and hillsides; there's limited accommodation to be had at the hamlet of Glieshof, and at the ruined building of Innere Matscher Alm a fine view is won towards the valley headwall. Above this more woodland, slopes of alpenrose, the ice-bright Ramudler Ferner and the little tarns of Sadlerseen lodged in a side glen.

To continue the eastward trend round the southern flank of the Ötztal Alps, the next crossing to contemplate from the Oberettes hut is that of the 3097 metre Bildstöckljoch by which the ski resort of Kurzras (or Corteraso) in Val Senáles is reached. The route is waymarked, and the four hundred metres of ascent to the pass should not be unduly taxing. There's some snow to contend with on the final approach and a descent of more than a thousand metres to face before hitting the roadhead at Kurzras, which is served by bus from Merano.

Arriving at Kurzras we now have an alternative to consider. From the Bildstöckljoch looking north-east Rifugio Bellavista (Schöne Aussicht hut) could be seen by the Hochjochferner. From Kurzras a popular and easy trail leads to it in a little over two hours, and it is tempting to take that option. Much depends, of course, upon your onward plans. Walker himself chose to return to Austrian soil at the Hochjoch, with a descent then into the Rofental glen which feeds into the Ventertal. And so could we, although our main aim here is to continue across the head of these Italian valleys, remaining as near as possible to the frontier wall. But it would be a shame to ignore what is potentially an interesting and scenically attractive two-day cross-border circuit, so we will set aside for a few moments our ambitious eastward journey and be teased into a diversion.

From Kurzras we need to follow the trail which is used by generations of shepherds from Val Senáles (Schnalsertal) who take their flocks each June over the mountains to graze pastures in the Ventertal. By this route the aptly-named Rifugio Bellavista is reached much too early for an overnight stay, so one would continue alongside the glacier over the Hochjoch, with retrospective views across Val Senáles to the 3435 metre Punta Saldura (or Salurnspitze), and ahead to the glacial crown of the Stubai Alps. The route now wanders downhill beside the sizeable Hochjochferner until a timber-creaking suspension bridge leads across a glacial torrent for a short climb to the Hochjoch Hospitz (four hours from Kurzras). It'll take another two hours to reach Vent, where overnight accommodation will probably be sought, unless you've energy enough to turn right into the Niedertal at its junction with the Rofental, and then head up the track to the Martin-Busch Haus. This latter option would mean a walking day of about seven hours.

It will take another seven hours to return to Val Senáles by the Niederjoch, if starting from Vent, or six and a half if you spent the night at the Martin-Busch Haus.

A clear trail takes you all the way to the pass, over pasture, moraine and a final patch of snow-covered glacier, well trodden in summer, to refreshment at the Similaun hut. Then it's downhill all the way to Vernagt, set by Lago di Vernago, from where a bus may be caught back to Kurzras, or out to Merano.

TWO-DAY CROSS-BORDER TOUR - ROUTE SUMMARY

Day 1: Kurzras - Hochjoch/Rifugio Bellavista - Vent (or Martin-Busch Haus)

Day 2: Vent (or Martin-Busch Haus) - Niederjoch/Similaun Hut - Vernagt

Note: this tour is fully described in Gillian Price's excellent guidebook, *Walking in the Central Italian Alps.*

To resume our journey across the head of the Italian valleys, we need to make our way to Val di Fosse (Pfossental), that major tributary glen that joins Val Senáles below Karthaus. One way of achieving this would be to take the valley bus from Kurzras, but that would defeat the object of the exercise. A better way is to take a cross-country trail round a ridge spur projecting south from Grawand. This trail, a little exposed in places, goes by way of Finailhof and the farm of Tisenhof (accommodation in both), then down valley past Vernagt to Karthaus. Heading north now through the deep Val di Fosse, there's a road as far as the hamlet of Vorderkaser (Casera di fuori - nine kilometres), but for much of the way there's an alternative footpath. There's guesthouse accommodation in Vorderkaser which may appeal to some in readiness for a fairly long stretch next day. Otherwise continue upvalley to the farm at Rableid Alm.

This final stage in our multi-day traverse ends in Val di Plan (Pfelderer Tal), and although it's nowhere difficult, it will be a longish day if started from Vorderkaser. The altitude of this hamlet is 1693 metres; the Eisjöchl, our crossing point in the ridge pushed south by the Hochwilde, is almost exactly twelve hundred metres higher. Upvalley the Meraner Höhenweg (a 100 kilometre circuit of the Texel Nature Park) crosses the park's boundary and rises to Rableid Alm (2004m) and Eishof (accommodation at both farms, the latter once considered the highest in the Tirol) now heading east with the Texelspitze-Roteck basin walling the valley to the south. Above the treeline the way climbs steadily over pastures, then up towards the pass with the sweeping walls of the Hohe and Kleine Weisse making an impressive show off to the right. The Eisjöchl (2895m), or Eisjöchl-am-Bild, rewards with a magnificent panorama - better still a short scramble up the slope towards the Hochwilde presents an even broader view which includes the handsome Tribulaun (in the Stubai Alps), and beyond that the Zillertal Alps, Grossvenediger, Grossglockner, and also the Dolomites. Just below the pass sits the Stettiner hut, otherwise known as the Eisjöchl hut or Rifugio Petrarca. Walker recommends spending a night here, and from it climbing the Hochwilde which, he says, involves no snow or ice from this side, just a rough scramble of two or three hours.

Below the Stettiner hut the way descends some twelve hundred metres to Pfelders at the roadhead in Val di Plan, by way of Lazinser Alm and the secluded hamlet of Lazins (accommodation). From Pfelders buses run down to Merano, but experienced walkers with more time at their disposal, and a desire (or need) to finish their holiday on the northern side of the border, could take an alternative trail from Lazins which climbs towards Rifugio Plan (alias the Zwickauer hut; 2980m), then break away on an airy route that remains high on a north-easterly traverse above Val di Plan as far as the 2844 metre Rauhejoch (Passo di Mont Scabro). This col is in the ridge extending from the Seewer Spitze, on the northern side of which the trail continues into the Seewer glen with two options for returning to Austria. The first is via the Aperer Ferwall Joch (2903m), the second being the lower Königs Joch. Both lead to the Gurglertal below Obergurgl.

An outline of this multi-day crossing of Alpi Venoste is given below, while those walkers interested in spending more time exploring these southern mountains and glens, are advised to consult the Cicerone guide, *Walking in the Central Italian Alps*, which details a variety of routes, especially in the Texel Nature Park.

ACROSS THE ALPI VENOSTE - ROUTE SUMMARY

Day 1:   Valle Lunga - Melago - Rifugio Pio XI

Day 2:   Rifugio Pio XI - Val di Planol - Schnalser Schartl - Oberettes Hut

Day 3:   Oberettes Hut - Bildstöckljoch - Kurzras

Day 4:   Kurzras - Vernagt - Karthaus - Vorderkaser (or Rableid Alm)

Day 5:   Vorderkaser (or Rableid Alm) - Eisjöchl/Stettiner Hut - Pfelders (or Lazins)

Day 6:   Lazins - Rauhejoch - Aperer Ferwall Joch (or Königs Joch) - Obergurgl

Notes: a) Day six is only appropriate if returning to Austria, otherwise one would make a way out of Val di Plan to Val Passiria. b) For a longer tour the two-day border crossing from Kurzras outlined above could be included, thus creating a very fine eight-day expedition.

---

*   *   *

THE ÖTZTAL ALPS

Location:

East and south of the Inn valley, with the Ötztal forming the eastern boundary on the Austrian side of the border. On the Italian flank the mountains are known as the Alpi Venoste, with Val Venosta forming the western and southern boundaries, and Val Passiria on the eastern side.

Principal valleys:

In Austria these are the Kaunertal, Pitztal and Ötztal, with major tributaries of Ventertal and Gurglertal. On the south side of the frontier, Valle Lunga, Val di Mazia, Val di Silandro, Val Senáles and Val di Plan.

Principal peaks:

Wildspitze (3772m), Weisskugel (3739m) Hintere Schwärze (3628m), Similaun (3606m), Weissseespitze (3526m), Hochwilde (3482m).

Centres:
Sölden, Längenfeld, Obergurgl, Plangeross, Mittelberg in Austria; in Italy these include Merano, Kurzras, Schluderns and Mals.

Huts:
The district is well-equipped with huts and mountain inns. Some are privately owned, but the majority belong to the various Alpine Clubs - German, Austrian and Italian.

Access:
Public transport on the Austrian side focuses on the Inn valley, with the Innsbruck-Landeck railway being met by buses that serve the various valleys. South of the frontier Merano may be reached by coach from Landeck; a railway serves Val Venosta as far west as Mals, and buses feed into several higher valleys. Merano may also be reached by rail from Innsbruck via the Brenner Pass-Bolzano line. Change trains in Bolzano. Nearest international airport: Innsbruck.

Maps:
Kompass Wanderkarte sheet 43, *Ötztaler Alpen* (1:50,000) covers all the Austrian mountains and valleys of the district, bar the very western limits along the Oberinntal. Sheet number 52 is useful for the Italian side, although the Tabacco maps are often preferred for their clarity. Various 1:25,000 sheets are needed for this area.

Guidebooks:
Walking Austria's Alps, Hut to Hut by Jonathan Hurdle (Cordee/The Mountaineers) suggests two hutting tours.
Mountain Walking in Austria by Cecil Davies (Cicerone Press) describes a dozen routes, including a few summits.
Walking in the Central Italian Alps by Gillian Price (Cicerone Press) is a useful guide to the south side of the border with several good routes described.

Other reading:
Walking in the Alps by J. Hubert Walker (Oliver & Boyd, 1951). In this Walker is both eloquent and ethusiastic, and of course, full of good ideas.
The Outdoor Traveler's Guide to The Alps by Marcia R. Lieberman (Stewart, Tabori & Chang, New York ,1991). The section on the Ötztal Alps provides basic detail of the better-known areas.

THE STUBAI ALPS

Inn Valley

KARWENDELGEBIRGE

INNSBRUCK

Nedertal

KUHTAI

Sellraintal

SELLRAIN

○ ÖTZ

GRIES

Foltschertal

Horlachtal

Zw. Rosskogel

Sch. Seespitze

Stubaital

FULPMES

Luisenstal

Sillptal

NEUSTIFT

STEINACH

LÄNGENFELD

Oberbergtal

Unterbergtal

Pinnistal

Gschnitztal

Schrankogel

Sulztal

Habicht

OBERTAL

Obernbergtal

Ruderhofsp.

Tribulaun

Ötztal

W. Freiger

Feuerstein

Brenner Pass

SÖLDEN ○

Windachtal

Zuckerhütl

Val di Fleres

ÖTZTAL ALPS

Val Ridanna

VIPITENO

Timmelsjoch

RIDANNA

Val di Racines

Val di Passria

V. di Racines

N

AUSTRIA

ITALY

0   5   10   15kms

The Bremer hut used by trekkers on the classic Stubai High Route

14: THE STUBAI ALPS

East of the Ötztal and its several tributary glens, the Ötztal Alps merge comfortably with the Stubai Alps, perhaps the best-known, and certainly one of the most easily accessible, of all the mountain groups in Austria. This accessibility (Innsbruck is only an hour away), coupled with magnificent scenery, a rich choice of snow and ice climbs, and numerous comfortable huts, have combined to make this one of the leading districts of the Eastern Alps for both mountaineers and walkers alike. It is an immediately attractive area whose typically Alpine peaks are composed mainly of granite, schist or gneiss, although several at the eastern end, notably the rugged Kalkkogel, are formed of limestone and bear a striking resemblance to the Dolomites. The lush valleys are dotted with picturesque villages whose chalets, farms and hotels are gay with flower-hung balconies, the lower hillsides are mostly wooded, the upper slopes a patchwork of grass and rock while dome-shaped, glacier-clad mountains form an impressive wall to the south. In the Stubai Alps we have the quintessential Tirolean landscape which, with a network of entertaining trails, makes a first-rate destination for mountain wanderers. "All things considered," said Walker, "this is pre-eminently a walker's country and as such it is as fine as any." To that I would only add, "and better than some."

The boundaries of the group are drawn by river valleys: the Ötztaler Ache in the west, the broad valley of the Inn to the north, and in the east by the Sill, whose valley is known as the Wipptal and through which the Brenner Pass (1375m) is easily gained. The Brenner is Austria's main arterial route through the high mountains into Italy, while at the head of the Ötztaler Ache the toll road over the Timmelsjoch (2509m) provides a more elevated alternative crossing, although this is snowbound in winter. Though they are generally considered to be Austrian mountains, the Stubai Alps do not end at the crest carrying the Italian border, for south of the frontier they continue with more icy summits drained by Val Passiria (formerly the Passiertal), Val Ridanna (Ridnauntal), Val di Fleres (Pflerschtal) and the Eisack flowing through the busy Valle d'Isarco which carries traffic from the Brenner Pass down to Bolzano and the Dolomites.

Although the frontier watershed crest runs vaguely west to east, the various draining glens do not conform as one would expect to a straightforward south-north or north-south flow. True, the Ötztal itself, and the opposite boundary valley of the Wipptal, do follow one's expectation, as do their Italian counterparts. But they are the exception rather than the rule. Austrian valleys of the Stubai, in the main, descend north-eastward from a high point in the south-west where a swell of lofty peaks twists against the grain, while Italian glens rise in the north-west and flow south-eastward to Valle d'Isarco. Of the northern, Austrian valleys, most of these are subdivided by tributary glens that provide additional access to the high mountains and their projecting ridge systems, thus creating a seemingly complex geographical arrangement, but which in reality plays into the hands and dreams of our ambitious walker.

In this chapter concentration will primarily be on these Austrian valleys where some of the finest walking opportunities are to be found, so it is necessary first to enumerate these valleys and their tributary glens, travelling from north to south and then west to east, in order to explore some of their potential.

*   *   *

The Ötztal & Its Tributary Glens

As we have seen, the valley of the Ötztaler Ache not only lends its name to an important group of mountains, it also forms a seam between the Ötztal Alps and the Stubai Alps. All the mountains and glens west of the valley belong to the former; all those on the east are included in the Stubai Alps. Having already studied the western side of the valley in the previous chapter, we now look at the outer fringe of the Stubai, beginning with those glens that drain westward into the main Ötztal valley. The northernmost of these is the Nedertal (or Kühtai valley), the glen of the Stockacher Bach which links with the larger east-flowing Sellraintal over the 2017 metre Kühtaisattel. A minor road crosses this pass, thus making possible a west-east traverse by motorists of the lower part of the range running parallel with the Inn valley. Just below Kühtai, the highest resort which, with its cableways and ski lifts is almost lifeless in summer, sits the luxurious, hotel-like Dortmunder hut. This is directly accessible by road, and from it several tarns lodged in the mountains to the south-east make an obvious goal, while the ascent of the Rietzer Griesskogel (2884m) to the north is another option available to energetic walkers based there.

The next glen to the south is that of the Horlachtal which enters the Ötztal downstream of Umhausen. Beginning under the ice and snow of the Zwiselbachferner, the upper reaches of this glen are known as the Zwiselbachtal, flowing roughly north and north-north-west before curving sharply leftwards as the Horlachtal proper, and then collecting the waters of two tributaries from the south; the Larstigtal and Grastal, the first with a trail climbing to its glacial headwall, the second with a fine walk up to the Grastalsee at 2533 metres. A minibus journeys through the Horlachtal as far as Niederthai, but a gravel road continues upstream to the DAV's Guben-Schweinfurter hut, which provides a useful base for a variety of expeditions. One recommended outing heads up the Zwiselbachtal to the Zwiselbach Joch (2870m) to gain a very fine view of the snow-covered Breiter Griesskogel. On the south side of the col a trail descends directly to the Winnebachsee hut. Another crosses the Finstertaler Scharte via the Gubener Weg, and then descends to the Finstertaler lake, with a trail continuing from there down to Kühtai and the Dortmunder hut, while a third suggestion is to take a path over the Gleirschjöchl (2751m) to the Neue Pforzheimer hut and thence to the Sellraintal.

Halfway through the valley, about fifteen kilometres south of Ötz, Längenfeld is the major village of the middle Ötztal, a popular health resort conveniently situated at the mouth of the Sulztal. Five kilometres into this glen, and served by minibus, lies the small village of Gries at an altitude of 1573 metres. Here the Sulztal forks. The main glen continues to the south-east, while to the north rises the Winnebachtal. Remaining with the Sulztal a trail follows the Fischbach stream, first on one bank, then on the other, until it reaches the Amberger hut lodged in the valley at the foot of the Schrankogel, at 3497 metres the second highest summit of the Stubai Alps. Whilst the ascent of the Schrankogel is naturally the main focus of attention here, trails also lead to a choice of glaciers, all in a wild setting.

A climb of some two hours from Gries through the northern glen of the Winnebachtal brings you to the Winnebachsee hut (2372m), set beside the tarn after which it was named and with excellent waterfall views. This is the starting point for several interesting climbs, and with trails crossing various ridge systems into neighbouring valleys the hut is also used by walkers embarked on some fine cross-country tours, including a route that leads to the Franz Senn hut at the head of the Oberbergtal stem of the Stubaital. This route is a minor classic of the region, a two-day expedition that crosses a brace of respectable passes, the Winnebachjoch through a wilderness of boulders, and the demanding Grosses Horntaler Joch at 2812 metres. The second night of this trek is spent in the Westfalenhaus, a DAV hut in a secluded tributary glen that feeds into the Lüsensertal.

The final Stubai glen that eases into the Ötztal is that of the Windachtal, a gorge-like glen that cuts into the mountains east of Sölden and drains the highest mountains of the frontier crest. With the Hochstubai (3174m), Hildesheimer (2900m) and Siegerland huts (2710m) accessible from it, most of the interest in this valley is directed to climbers, for whom big peaks and glacier passes provide local challenge. However, a walk up to the Hildesheimer hut is worth the effort for the privileged view it claims of the Pfaffen glacier and Zuckerhütl seen rising above the ice to the east. By taking a high level path from Hildesheimer to the Siegerland hut, and descent from there back to Sölden, a fine outing can be achieved in magnificent big mountain country.

The Sellraintal & Feeder Glens

Access to the ten kilometres long Sellraintal is either from Kematen in the Inn valley, or from the Ötztal across the Kühtaisattel. Sellrain is the main resort, from which a number of attractive walks begin, but the valley as a whole attracts winter visitors as well as walkers in summer, and provides a variety of ways into the main Stubai Alps from the north. Several glens drain those higher mountains and thus secure access to the heartland of the district. Listing from west to east, these are as follows: first is the little Kraspestal cutting south-west from Haggen. At its head rises the Zwiselbacher Rosskogel with a small glacial cravat round its upper north face. Below the glacier lies a tiny tarn, and a path goes up to it from Haggen; another breaks away from this trail and crosses the left-hand ridge by the modest Pockkogel, then descends to Kühtai.

Running parallel to the Kraspestal is the Gleirschtal. This is twice as long as its neighbour, a twisting glen that opens into the Sellraintal at St Sigmund. A little over halfway through the valley a trail leads to the Neue Pforzheimer hut (Adolf-Witzmann-Haus) from where several routes disperse. One climbs westward over the Gleirschjöchl to the Zwiselbachtal which, as we have already seen, flows into the Horlachtal and this, in turn, discharges into the Ötztal valley below Umhausen. Taking this route all the way is, says Baedeker, "fatiguing". Another option heads east from the hut, crosses the Satteljoch below the Lampsenspitze and drops to Praxmar in the Lüsensertal, from where a rich choice of trails gives possibilities of multi-day treks.

The Lüsensertal (alias Lisensertal) is one of the finest for walking opportunities of all the glens feeding into the Sellraintal. Served by road from Gries-im-Sellrain (bus to Praxmar) this valley flows almost due north from its birth in a corrie topped by the Lüsener Fernerkogel, whose glacier system is the largest hereabouts. Just below this peak the main stem of the valley is joined by a subsidiary glen flowing from the south-west, in which the isolated Westfalenhaus is located at a junction of trails. Heading down valley the Melach stream is fed by numerous other streams that drain the walling mountains to east and west. A variety of trails tackle these mountain walls, and exploit any possible weakness in their defences. So it is that our walker based for a few days in this glen will find sufficient challenge to exercise his passion for tough days in a rewarding landscape by crossing high cols into neighbouring glens, or scrambling to snow-free summits with fine views in prospect. Of these pass crossings the Grosses Horntaler Joch provides a classic route over the headwall to the Franz Senn hut in the Oberbergtal; the Höchgraffjoch in the ridge north-east of the Lüsener Villerspitze takes a route over to the Fotschertal to the east, while another crossing to the same glen can be made from Praxmar and which includes the summit of the 2832 metre Roter Kogel and a collection of little tarns on the east flank. Heading west from Praxmar it's possible to cross the Satteljoch (2735m) to the Neue Pforzheimer hut in the Gleirschtal, thus reversing a route suggested above, then descend from there to St Sigmund and take a high trail back along the west flank of the Lüsensertal to Praxmar, thereby creating an entertaining circuit.

East of the Lüsensertal the Fotschertal opens out at Sellrain. This glen projects south of the Sellraintal between ridge systems whose map outlines are etched with walking routes, and where accommodation is possible at either Bergheim Fotsch, or the DAV-owned Potsdamer hut above the Seealm. The glen's headwall is crowned by the Hohe Villerspitze (3087m), a mountain whose southern slopes pour into the upper reaches of the Oberbergtal. The only way over this headwall is via the 2599 metre Wildkopfscharte, but other crossings are possible into the parallel glens, and ridge walks are also a feature here. For a splendid day's round try gaining the Wildkopfscharte from the Potsdamer hut and descend on the southern side to Seduckalm. Once there follow the Franz Senn Weg heading north-east to the Sendersjöchl where you branch left along the east flank of the upper Senderstal, before crossing back to the Fotschertal over the Kreuzjöchl.

Topped by the soaring rock peaks of the Kalkkogel, the Senderstal offers a choice of walking routes, from valley-based trails in forest and pasture, to more dramatic tours that scuff the dust of tumbling screes and edge graceful limestone crags that appear for all the world as though they've been transported from the Brenta. Access to the glen is from Grinzens, with a road going to the Kemater Alm where the valley forks. The south-west branch leads to a craggy but modest headwall whose crest runs between the Schwarzhorn and Gamskogel, while the south-east stem eases below the Kalkkogel, and is occupied by the Adolf-Pichler hut. Owned by the Academic Alpine Club of Innsbruck, this has twenty five beds and fifty dormitory places, and may be gained by a three-hour walk from Grinzens. A number of options become available to walkers based here, and a glance at the map will reveal the richness of the area. Ignore for a moment the ski-lifts that adorn slopes to the east, and concentrate on the savage splendour of the Kalkkogel, for it is this powerful upthrusting group that will dominate your plans. There are circuits to be made and, for the adventurous, *klettersteig* teasings on the Riepenwand, Grosser Ochsenwand and the Marchreisenspitze. And when you've finally exhausted all possibilities from this hut, a comparatively short walk to the south, over the Seejöchl and along a scree-slope trail below the south-west face of the Schlicker Seespitze, leads to the Starkenburger hut from whose terrace all the Stubaital is set out before you. Another landscape of dreams.

The Stubaital

Of all these valleys on the northern side of the frontier crest the largest and most important is the Stubaital itself. Rising within an arc of glacier summits all above three thousand metres, including the Zuckerhütl at 3507 metres the highest of the group, the valley maintains a straight north-east alignment and enters the Wipptal close to the impressive Europa Bridge just above Innsbruck. At Neder an enchanting glen, the Pinnistal, cuts deeply into the southern wall of mountains, at the head of which rises the Habicht. Further upstream at Milders, a little south-west of Neustift, the Stubaital forks. The main stem here is known as the Unterbergtal, while the other, shorter glen is the Oberbergtal which branches off to the north-west, then curves to the south-west towards a white crest of mountains. From the head of the road in the Oberbergtal an easy trail rises to the busy Franz Senn hut, named after the 'glacier-priest' who did much to promote the Stubai as a mountaineering district.

As for the Unterbergtal, this has several short feeder glens draining into it from the southern mountain wall, and but one (the Falbesonertal) from the north. At Mutterbergalm in the upper reaches of the valley, known here as the Mutterbergtal, a lift system ferries walkers, climbers and skiers up through the Fernautal to the Dresdner hut and the extensive snowfields above it. Downstream a little the valley is fed by the Sulzaubach, with the Sulzenau hut settled in a glen backed by the Zuckerhütl, while a short distance from Ranalt the Mutterbergtal is joined by the Langental, a little glen with a trail climbing through it to the Nürnberger hut.

While the head of the Stubaital is crowned with snow and ice, and small glaciers carve down towards green pastures, the long walling ridges that project from the main summits to direct the valley's flow, are mostly snow-free for much of the summer and are thereby inviting to walkers. In those walling ridges will be found a number of passes accessible to all with power in their legs and hard-working lungs, that not only extend the scope for multi-day tours leading from one valley to the next, but add considerably to the district's attraction. That attraction is, of course, mostly conducted by the exquisite scenery. From the bed of the valley an artistic blend of forest, pasture, rock, snow and ice is matched by the neat orderliness of its villages, the trim sentry-like stooks of drying hay, the old barns and heavy-timbered farms, the waterfalls, clear-running streams, flower meadows - and a hint, no more than that, of more majestic scenes to be discovered beyond a low screening spur. There are cableways, it is true, that swing visitors up to noted viewpoints and provide a glimpse of those majestic scenes without resorting to a long uphill walk, but the finest views and the greatest rewards await those who are prepared to follow the winding trail. Walkers with glacier experience and who are adept at modest snow and ice work, were they suitably equipped, would also find among the Stubai Alps a range of possibilities for adding summits to their tour. Such outings will be mentioned in passing as we make our way hut to hut round the classic Stubaier Höhenweg (Stubai High Route), without doubt one of the finest of all such routes in Austria, from which a veritable wonderland of mountain scenery is revealed.

But first to such practical matters as means of approach, valley bases and logistics. A little local train from Innsbruck serves the Stubaital as far as Fulpmes, the largest village with a resident population of about 3000, but buses also run from Innsbruck station to Neustift and beyond. Several small communities, from the valley's entrance at Schönberg upward, offer a range of accommodation and incentives to stay there. Neustift is probably the best; certainly as far as situation is concerned, while facilities on offer for the less-committed members of a walker's family are of a fairly wide appeal, including reliable public transport throughout the valley and out as far as Innsbruck. Should the enterprising walker need to consider the needs of other, valley-bound, members of the family whilst tackling a multi-day tour such as the Stubai High Route, Neustift will surely serve as an almost perfect base for them.

THE STUBAI HIGH ROUTE

In simple outline the Stubaital is a trident-shaped valley, the main stem having as a neighbour to the south the Gschnitztal which flows parallel to it. Positioned at a convenient distance from one to another in a rough horseshoe pattern around the valley and at the head of the Gschnitztal, eight huts (more like mountain inns) provide staging posts for walkers along the high route. The route itself makes an ideal introduction to Alpine walking, for it is well-marked, avoids all but the very briefest of glacier crossings, and many of the stages are of such a length that plenty of time should be left over to allow a leisurely enjoyment of individual features in the landscape. It has to be said, though, that many sections are deemed potentially dangerous, enough so to warrant safeguarding by fixed cables, and in one or two places unseasonal ice could pose serious difficulties. That having been said, the Stubai High Route should be well within the cababilities of the majority of fit and active hillwalkers who are unaffected by vertigo. Being a circular tour it could be tackled either clockwise or anti-clockwise. On this occasion the route is described as my wife and I walked it, that is to say, clockwise beginning at Neder, the next village downstream of Neustift.

Neder nestles below the mouth of the Pinnistal through which the first stage leads to the Innsbrucker hut on the far side of the Pinnisjoch. In the summer months a minibus ferries visitors through the glen from Neder as far as Pinnisalm, but the Pinnistal is such a charming valley that no walker worth his salt will consider using motorised transport to scurry through it. However, I would advise in favour of setting out at a reasonable hour in the morning, and not do as we did, which was to start walking after two o'clock on a stifling July afternoon, having just arrived by air from England. It's about ten kilometres from Neder to the hut, with a height gain of almost fourteen hundred metres, and for much of the way there will be no shade. The moral is clear: should the weather be hot and cloud-free, set out early and drink plenty of liquids along the way.

The Pinnistal is a delightful glen, forested part way, shorn meadows and pastureland in its middle reaches, and great scree fans out of which soaring walls of honey-coloured limestone hem it in on the eastern flank. These walls buttress the Serleskamm along whose crest runs the Jubilaumssteig, a fine scrambling route with distant views of the Dolomites. On the west flank of the valley an easy trail leads to a balcony viewpoint, but the Stubai High Route ignores both of these diversions and aims directly for the saddle of the Pinnisjoch (2370m) at the southern end, midway between the Kalkwand and Habicht. Just below it, on the south side of the pass and overlooking the depths of the Gschnitztal from which a trail drops to the village of Gschnitz, the large Innsbrucker hut enjoys a wonderful view across the valley to the towering Tribulaun peaks.

The approach to the Innsbrucker hut (a comfortable lodging in a spectacular setting) will take care of a good five hours or so from Neder; Williams says four in his guidebook, Walker says seven from Neustift. Once there it is quite likely that you'll want to do no more than sit on the balcony with a cool drink and gaze at the scenery until the guardian has the evening meal ready. However, assuming you've energy and time to spare it would be worth returning to the Pinnisjoch and from there scramble along the craggy, broken Kalkwand ridge to the Ilmspitze (2692m) - but not as far as the Kirchdachspitze (2840m), as encouraged by Walker. Note though, it is a scramble, and not simply a walk. Although not really difficult or dangerous, due care will be required. The Ilmspitze klettersteig on the east side of the ridge is an extremely exposed *via ferrata* of about 300 metres, and although it has become very popular, it is definitely not for beginners and should only be attempted by parties properly equipped with helmets, harnesses, tape slings and karabiners.

If you are interested in adding summits to your tour, it will be as well to book a second night at Innsbrucker in order to enjoy the ascent of the nearby Habicht, whose crown is some nine hundred metres above the hut. At 3277 metres it's the highest in this corner of the Stubai, and its north face looks most impressive from the terrace outside the Starkenburger hut at the end of the tour. The ordinary route climbs by way of the east ridge; there is a small glacier and some snow to cross, and in several places fixed ropes aid troublesome pitches. But for experienced scramblers there's little cause for concern, while the summit, gained in about three hours, repays with a broad panorama.

The second stage of our high route goes as far as the rustic Bremer hut, a longer and more arduous stage than that which led to Innsbrucker, and which will take from six to seven hours without rests. Unlike most stages on this circuit, where there's usually just one ridge to cross, the trail to the Bremer hut is something of a helter-skelter, a corrugated route that climbs and descends a series of ridge spurs. The first of these is crossed immediately above the Innsbrucker hut on a spur of the Alfeirkamm; the second a very narrow crest to the west of the little Pramarnspitze, although between these two a few fixed rope descents guide the way into and across a stream-cut corrie that makes a brief relaxing interlude. More ridge spurs are tackled, and more fixed ropes aid steep or potentially troublesome sections. In early summer snow is almost certain to be lying, and on exposed slopes this should be tackled with circumspection. Having crossed the final grass-covered spur to the east of the Ausserer Wetterspitze, the way descends to the rumpled pastures of Simmingalm before scrambling up boulder slopes and over patches of snow that lead directly to the Bremer hut, set just above a small tarn.

This small, shingle-walled hut is the simplest of all those on the tour, but in many ways it is the nicest. Owned by the Bremen section of the DAV it has twenty beds and forty-six dormitory places, with a guardian in residence from the end of June until the end of September. When we were there a group of Welshmen arrived; one of whom learnt that evening that he'd just become a grandfather. The guardian opened a bottle of Schnapps in his honour, and a celebratory drink enlivened the atmosphere somewhat as a storm rattled the shingles outside.

At the head of the little hanging valley behind the hut the frontier ridge is carried by a crest running between the Ostlicher Feuerstein and the Schneespitze over the Pflerscher Hochjoch. Draped down the mountain flank from this crest is the Simmingferner glacier, while the glen is walled along its western edge by a ridge pushed north of the Pflerscher Hochjoch. The third stage of our high route has to cross this ridge at the 2764 metre Simmingjöchl. This is not so much a pass, or col, as an easing of the crest south-west of the hut, from which it is gained in about an hour. The route to it is an entertaining one that involves an unrelenting scramble up steepish crags safeguarded in places by fixed cable. On the crest is a tiny hut apparently used by border guards. Views include the handsome snow-plastered Wilder Freiger, while the Nürnberger hut, the day's destination, is clearly visible across a deep valley (the Langental) to the west.

From the Simmingjöchl it is feasible to climb the Ostlicher Feuerstein (3267m) in about two and a half hours, or alternatively make a shorter ascent of the Aperer Feuerstein (2965m) in little more than one hour. Both ascents involve snow slopes and glacier work; the first has some crevasse danger and possible bergschrund difficulty, the second is apparently less demanding. Both offer outstanding views of course.

To continue hut to hut along the Stubai High Route, the way descends the west side of the Simmingjöchl into a stony corrie; a tip of screes, larger rocks and snow patches beneath the crags of the Innere Wetterspitze. In the bed of this corrie soft turf takes over; streams running clear of their grim birthplace unite to wash over smooth slabs into an enclosed bowl with ox-bows and one or two small pools that provide reflections, with Wilder Freiger looking grand to the south-west. With nothing particularly demanding about the rest of the route it's tempting to laze here and simply enjoy the peace of this wild yet extremely pleasant spot. Later the waymarked route goes down a series of glacial slabs that spill over convex slopes - beware if ice glazes these rocks. Then down cliffs fixed with cables to a glacial torrent crossed by plank footbridge and fringed with alpine flowers, before beginning the climb up the west flank of the valley to gain the large, four-storey Nürnberger hut. The hillside on which this hut stands betrays its glacial origins. With long whale-back slabs sloping valleywards, and various levels of former glacier-scrape on display on the opposite flank, this is textbook geography writ large upon the landscape.

It should take no more than three hours to reach Nürnberger from the Bremer hut, but we took a full six - which is less a comment on our fitness than acknowledged celebration of the scenery through which the route travels. A similar doubling of hours taken on the next stage also says much about the magnificent countryside enjoyed on this route.

South of the Nürnberger hut wave upon wave of snowpeaks grace the horizon. Wilder Freiger (3418m) is the highest nearby. This is often climbed directly from the hut, a four-hour ascent that is one of the most popular in the Stubai Alps. High route activists with time to spare and the necessary equipment for dealing with glacier crossings, should consider spending a second night at the hut and making the climb from there. As an alternative, if you have neither the equipment nor experience to tackle the Wilder Freiger, the Seescharte (2762m), just south of the Urfallspitze, provides a magnificent viewpoint from which to study the glacier world beyond.

The ascent of Wilder Freiger itself is usually included as one of a number of summits collected on an expedition starting from the Nürnberger. Hubert Walker did just this, ending his day at the Hildesheimer hut to the west of the Zuckerhütl, and in his book he summerized the experience thus: "It is very pretty country all the way, and I cannot recall any day which gave me more pleasure...The particular charm of this otherwise unsensational and undramatic country to me lay in the shape of the mountains and the trend of the ridges, the ever-lovely snowfields and the treasuries of the snow, and the light glinting on the sea of mountains stretching away to the far horizon." In such phrases does Walker conjure the simple pleasures to be gained among the Alps.

Moving on from the Nürnberger hut the way continues westward along the southern base of our circuit, working parallel to the frontier crest but avoiding glaciers that stream from it. Rising steeply above the hut a craggy ridge has been thrust forward from that frontier crest, and it is this that effectively divides the Langental from the little glen of the Sulzaubach, both of which flow into the upper reaches of the Unterbergtal. The dividing ridge is steep and broken, and narrow along its rim, and its crossing involves the descent of some exposed crags that could cause problems for anyone with a history of vertigo. From the hut a large wooden cross is easily seen on the skyline marking a saddle in the ridge; this is the crossing point of Niederl (2627m), midway between the Urfallspitze and Maierspitze. The route to it is part path, part scramble, with fixed wire ropes on the steepest sections. The ridge is gained in about an hour.

A little to the north of the Niederl a second crossing point offers an interesting alternative, as well as an opportunity to make the ascent of the easy Maierspitze (2781m). The route to this breaks away from the Niederl path a short distance from the hut and also involves some scrambling with fixed rope aid. From the col (2553m) a thirty minute diversion northward leads to the crown of the Maierspitze, which is also marked by a large cross. From the Maierspitze, as from the Niederl, views are quite magnificent in both directions; yesterday's route from the Simmingjöchl is clearly seen, while the way ahead, littered as it is with gleaming tarns, and with a backdrop of snow mountains and tumbling glaciers, is an enticement to move on.

The west side of the ridge, if taken from the Niederl, calls for a cautious descent from one grit-covered ledge to the next, safeguarded yet again by fixed wire ropes, down the broken crags to a zig-zag trail that weaves among nurseries of alpine flowers, then over scree and boulder slopes to the shores of a little tarn reflecting the most exquisite of mountain scenes. Gazing across this tarn one looks directly at the Wilder Freiger glacier suspended from the mountain's north face. From this angle one notices the ice folds, the blue sliced crevasses revealed here and there, the rock ribs and ice-shaved slabs that border it, and then up and up to a pure white crest sharp in outline against the sky. Then move the head slowly so the eye builds piece by piece a landscape that consists of one snow-bound summit after another, one peeling icefield after another, one strip of newly-vegetated moraine after another... It is one of the loveliest of many lovely panoramic views to be enjoyed along the Stubai High Route.

As with yesterday's stage, three hours should be quite sufficient to walk from the Nürnberger to the Sulzenau hut, but as yesterday, the connoisseur will take twice as long. For there are other tarns along the way, others to stray to that multiply visions of glory. There are moraine walls scarlet edged with alpenroses to trip along; streams to cross, wild meadows to laze upon, ablation troughs to explore, marmots to watch, views to absorb. Given favourable conditions this three hour stroll could easily turn into an all-day epic.

The Sulzenau hut is accessible from the Unterbergtal by a comparatively short walk, and it comes as a rude shock to be able to see (if you are foolish enough to look) a few cars parked some way down valley below the hut. But to the south-west the highest of all Stubai peaks, the Zuckerhütl (3507m), sends down the glacier of

Sulzenauferner into a wildly attractive glen, and it is through part of this glen that stage five makes a way to the Dresdner hut. Blocking the way to the Fernautal, the glen in which the Dresdner hut is situated, the dark lump of the Grosser Trögler (2902m) is a high point in a long ridge system extending from the Aperer Pfaff right down to the Unterbergtal. The standard way across this ridge is over the Peiljoch (marked on some maps as Beiljoch; 2672m), a stony col marked by numerous cairns below, and to the south-west of, the Grosser Trögler. But an alternative crossing can be made by going right over the summit of this snow-free mountain, a route that will add just one hour to the Peiljoch's three-hour stage. The climb is nowhere technically difficult, although there are one or two short exposed moves, and summit views are said to be magnificent. When we tackled the high route we woke at Sulzenau to find rain falling from a heavy-clouded sky. By the time we were ready to set out for the day the rain had ceased, but clouds remained obstinately low. There were no views to be had anywhere, but I calculated that we had a chance of winning some by climbing above the clouds over the Grosser Trögler, rather than follow the Peiljoch trail. Armed thus with optimism we took the high option, scrambling blind over shelves of rock and along the south-east flank just below the ridge crest until we came onto the summit proper, with yet another large wooden cross guyed against the winds. Up there one sensed space and a broad panorama. But visual proof was sorely missing, and it was only after we descended to the Dresdner hut that we met four others who had gone by way of the lower Peiljoch and been rewarded with surprise views onto the icefall of the Sulzenauferner!

The Peiljoch route shares that of the Grosser Trögler's for a short way upvalley from Sulzenau, and joins it again on the final approach to the Dresdner hut. On both sides of the ridge alpine flowers speckle the otherwise drab moraine and scree with bright extravagence; the lower moraines of the Sulzenauferner are especially fine with natural rock gardens everywhere. Regrettably the site of the Dresdner hut has been vandalised by a conglomeration of cableways. Until now we have enjoyed some of the most delightful mountain scenery available to the non-climbing wanderer anywhere in the Alps. Yet the final approach to the Dresdner hut is sufficient to fill you with despair. Mechanical hoists, a clatter of machinery, an endless stream of red bubble gondolas swinging overhead, bulldozed scars on the landscape - all the accoutrements deemed necessary to service the downhill ski industry, for above the hut the linking glaciers and snowfields of the Stubaier Wildspitze and Schaufelspitze are strung about with tows and cables. The mountains have been tamed and defiled. Perhaps under a thick winter coat of white such 'adornments' may present a more benign face. But in summer, when the mountain wanderer comes calling, the camouflage of snow is missing and there's no way to disguise such gross disfigurement.

The Dresdner hut, however, provides a warm welcome, and with a longer day in store for the morrow there is more to consider than the ugliness of the immediate environment outside. On this sixth stage the highest pass of the tour, followed by the only stretch of glacier on the route, will be crossed on the way to the Neue Regensburger hut set on the eastern lip of a marshy glen about a thousand metres above the Unterbergtal. But before setting out for that hut, perhaps it would be a good idea to examine the geography of this part of the Stubaital.

As we have seen, the upper reaches of the Unterbergtal are fed by tributary glens. On the southern side these are the Langental, with the Nürnberger hut near its head, the Sulzaubach glen that gives access to the Sulzenau hut, and the Fernautal leading to the Dresdner hut. North of the Dresdner hut the Egesengrat makes a 300 metre high wall dividing the Fernautal from the open basin which gives birth to the Unterbergtal proper. This basin, and the initial valley section flowing from it, is known as the Mutterbergtal. Now the north wall of the Mutterbergtal maintains an altitude well in excess of three thousand metres for the greater part of its length, and the eastern third of this wall protects the Falbesonertal, the glen occupied by the Neue Regensburger hut. It is this glen that forms the only tributary on the north bank of the Ruetz until the Unterbergtal is joined by the Oberbergtal at Milders.

In order for the Stubai High Route to progress beyond the Dresdner hut it becomes necessary to break away from the east-west trend it has followed since leaving the Bremer hut, for any further advance westward becomes effectively blocked by one glacier or another. So, the way now curves north then north-east across a low saddle on a shoulder of the Egesengrat, and picks a route along the north wall of the Mutterbergtal which it crosses at the 2881 metre Grawagrubennieder, the high pass from which the way drops steeply into the glen leading directly to the Neue Regensburger. It is a fine route, and one that will take care of seven or eight hours. It is, apparently, a scenically rewarding one too, with very fine views of a bevy of glaciers, and of the Wilder Freiger, Zuckerhütl, Aperer Pfaff, Grosser Trögler and Maierspitze. I say apparently, because this was another of those stages on which we were blinkered by cloud and denied all views, save for a momentary glimpse of an unguessed summit briefly marooned above the shifting vapour. But none of that mattered, for the route itself was entertaining enough. The descent from the Grawagrubenneider, a wind-blown col on the east ridge of the Ruderhofspitze, demands great care should there be other walkers below, for the way twists down a steep gully of very loose and broken rock. From the foot of this you then cross the lower reaches of the Hochmoos glacier and wander down an easy path to the hut, one of the most comfortable and welcoming on our tour.

One of the comforting things about the Stubai High Route is the number of easy escape routes that exist in case of accident, lack of time, or in the event of the weather turning so bad as to make a continuation inadvisable. All huts bar one have straightforward descent trails that lead into one branch or another of the main Stubaital; the exception being the Bremer hut from which descent leads straight into the Gschnitztal. Escape from the high route at Neue Regensburger is by trail that drops virtually from the front door down to a bus stop at Falbeson in the Unterbergtal. Our route, however, shuns that option and follows a short belvedere trail heading north-east high above the valley, then breaks away at a signed junction to make an easy climb northward in order to gain the wild Schrimmennieder, a rocky 2714 metre col, the final fifty metre scramble to it being aided by fixed wire rope. This is the only ridge crossing on the short stage to the Franz Senn hut, and the descent from the col makes an easy slanting traverse across the head of a stony basin before dropping below crags guarding its lower levels. Down there yet more alpine flowers brighten the wilderness of stone; soldanellas gather in open patches, and there are primulas and big yellow alpine asters and cushions of pink androsace. Then grassland at the foot of the corrie, luxuriant with streams and alpenroses and a few pine trees.

Franz Senn is reached in only four hours, leaving sufficient time to explore the surroundings of this exceedingly popular hut. One of the easiest and most rewarding of outings is the walk up to the little Rinnensee, a much-loved tarn sheltered among boulders on a hillside terrace upvalley of the hut from which it may be reached in about an hour and a half. Reflected views in this tarn include several peaks and glaciers walling the valley to the south, and on summer days many wanderers go no further than its shore and there spend the day wallowing in its beauty. Others with more ambition and energy will be tempted by the ridge above the tarn. In this ridge, a little west of the three thousand metre summit of the Rinnenspitze, the Rinnennieder is a 2899 metre col which overlooks the Lüsener Ferner (Lisenser Ferner), as well as extending the view south. This is one of Walker's recommended outings.

Another easy walk leads through the glen behind the hut, rising in stages to the Alreiner Ferner with views to a crowding cirque of mountains. Yet another recommended trail leads south in a short ascent of the Sommerwand, marked on some maps as Point 2676 metres. For adepts with time and equipment, a day snatched from the high route at this stage provides an opportunity to make the five-hour ascent of the Lüsener (or Lisenser) Fernerkogel (3298m), an easy mountain that offers one of the most striking panoramas in the Eastern Alps, and listed by Walker as one of his favourites. This peak is gained by way of the Rinnennieder, then across the crevassed Lüsener Ferner, finishing with a scramble up the south ridge.

Opportunities for extending one's tour seem almost limitless, for there's another col accessible from the Franz Senn hut that leads over the walling ridge into the Lüsensertal, a north-flowing glen that drains into the larger Sellraintal with numerous tempting diversions to be made there. At this point, however, we should complete the Stubai High Route, for we have so far made a horseshoe loop that needs to be closed, and to effectively manage that we need to head roughly eastward from Franz Senn to either Neustift or Fulpmes by way of the Starkenburger hut. The easiest way to reach either of these villages, of course, would be to wander directly down valley from the hut and stroll along the bed of the Oberbergtal. But that would defeat the object of our high route exercise. This is splendidly addressed by the so-called Franz Senn Weg, a balcony trail that makes a long traverse of the valley's left-hand hillside, keeping always well above the 2000 metre contour. It's the longest of all stages on the High Route, in terms of distance, but practically every step of the way is a delight of fine scenery. Not as dramatic as some previous stages, perhaps, but beautiful nonetheless.

This penultimate stage then begins along a well-marked trail cut along the north flank of the valley, at first on an even contour, then climbing over small rocky promontories, edging narrow ravines and over steep pasture on the approach to Seduckalm. Beyond the farmhouse the trail slants uphill to gain the Sendersjöchl (2477m) with a glimpse of the shallow but broad Senderstal on the north side, a green scoop thrust between innocent ridges. The Franz Senn Weg now hugs the right-hand side of the ridge crest, moves onto the crest itself, then through a gentian-starred trough on the left-hand side before dropping into a rough basin with the stark walls of the limestone Kalkkogel forming a dramatic backdrop. These savage, Dolomite look-alikes rearing out of long fans of grey scree make an astonishing contrast to the snowpeaks at the southern end of the valley, and provide yet another highlight of the tour. Across the screes which buttress organ-pipe towers of Schlicker Seespitze and Hoher Burgstall a trail can be seen as a neat scar. This is the route we must take from the broad saddle of the Seejöchl (2518m). The reality of this path is much kinder than the initial view suggested, and at the southern end of the screes the way crosses a vegetated spur, then descends in a series of twists to the suntrap of the Starkenburger hut.

Set on a ridge spur below the Hoher Burgstall this hut enjoys a very fine panorama. From the terrace both the Oberbergtal and Unterbergtal project away in die-straight lines to snow mountains and their tongue-like glaciers. Across the Stubaital to the south a clear view shows the north face of Habicht, wearing its modest glacial scarf. Just to the left of that the Tribulaun peaks also show above a mid-distance ridge, while the shadowed Pinnistal merely hints of good things. Neustift spills across the valley more than sixteen hundred metres below, hidden from view by a dense girdle of forest. It will take about an hour and a half of knee-wrenching descent to reach it, and at the end of a full day's walking from Franz Senn that would seem like purgatory. Better to spend a night at the Starkenburger hut with the following options to consider for the next day. Either descend directly to Neustift on the steep trail that drops below the hut and passes through delicious pinewoods and small open pastures; or take a continuing trail along the hillside heading north-east and make a more gradual descent to Fulpmes, or spend the first part of the day on an ascent of the Hoher Burgstall (2611m) before heading for the valley. There is nothing difficult about this ascent, in fact a path goes all the way to the summit, but it makes a splendid viewpoint from which to study so much of the Stubai Alps and the high route you've just completed, and would make a worthy finale to a memorable tour.

STUBAI HIGH ROUTE - SUMMARY

Suggestions for optional ascents are given which would add several days to the standard itinerary. Climbs requiring additional equipment or experience beyond that of the standard hillwalker are noted with the bracketed letter (c).

Day 1: Neder - Pinnisjoch - Innsbrucker Hut

Day 2: Innsbrucker Hut - Bremer Hut
   or: Innsbrucker Hut - Habicht - Innsbrucker Hut

Day 3: Bremer Hut - Simmingjöchl - Nürnberger Hut
   or: Bremer Hut - Simmingjöchl - Aperer Feuerstein (c) - Ostlicher Feuerstein (c) - Nürnberger Hut

Day 4: Nürnberger Hut - Niederl (or Maierspitze) - Sulzenau Hut
   or: Nürnberger Hut - Wilder Freiger (c) (or Seescharte) - Nürnberger Hut

Day 5: Sulzenau Hut - Peiljoch (or Grosser Trögler) - Dresdner Hut

Day 6:	Dresdner Hut - Grawagrubennieder - Neue Regensburger Hut
Day 7:	Neue Regensburger Hut - Schrimmennieder - Franz Senn Hut
Day 8:	Franz Senn Hut - Franz Senn Weg - Starkenburger Hut
or:	Franz Senn Hut - Rinnennieder - Lüsener Fernerkogel (c) - Franz Senn Hut
Day 9:	Starkenburger Hut - Hoher Burgstall (optional) - Neustift

As several of these stages are very short (three to four hours only), some could be doubled-up; for example it would be feasible to combine days three and four, making a single stage from the Bremer hut to Sulzenau, or stages four and five from Nürnberger to the Dresdner hut. It would also be possible to finish the tour by walking all the way from Franz Senn to Neustift via the Starkenburger hut, without spending a night there. However, as has been pointed out in the route description, the countryside is so fine as to warrant a leisurely journey through it. If you have time to divert from the waymarked route in order to enjoy an extra tarn, meadow or glacier, I would urge you to do so. Few hours thus spent will be regretted by the true lover of the hills.

✳ ✳ ✳

The Gschnitztal & Obernbergtal

The final two valleys to be included in this overview of the northern side of the Stubai Alps are the Gschnitztal, which flows roughly parallel to the Stubaital on the south-east side of its walling ridge, and the little Obernbergtal tucked under the frontier crest to the south of the Gschnitztal. "For wildly beautiful and comparatively lonely country this remote corner of the Group has few stretches to equal it and very few to beat it," was Walker's view.

Rising under an amphitheatre of peaks surrounding the Simmingalm, the Gschnitztal is about twenty kilometres long and discharges into the Wipptal at Steinach-am-Brenner, the latter resort conveniently served by rail from Innsbruck. There's a good supply of accommodation throughout the valley. Most hotels, of course, are concentrated on Trins and Gschnitz, the two resorts reached by bus from Innsbruck (the bus continues beyond Gschnitz to Feuerstein), while four huts are accessible from one or both of these: the Padasterjochhaus (2232m) on the slopes of the Wasenwand, three hours above Trins; Innsbrucker hut (2369m) on the Pinnisjoch, three hours from Gschnitz and included on the Stubai High Route; Bremer hut (2411m) also visited on the high route, but reached here in a little over four hours from Gschnitz; and the Tribulaun hut (2064m), two and a half hours to the south of Gschnitz in the Sandestal. This latter hut replaces an earlier refuge which was destroyed by avalanche in the winter of 1974-75, and should not to be confused, by the way, with the small Italian Tribulaun hut (Rifugio Calciati al Tribulaun; 2373m) which is found on the south side of the Sandesjöchl by the Sandessee tarn.

The Obernbergtal is a broad basin of a glen with two lakes near its head. Accommodation may be had in Obernberg-am-Brenner (hotels and youth hostel), and the valley is served by bus. Of the many walks available here, opportunities abound for easy pass crossings, not only across the dividing ridge into the Gschnitztal, but into the Italian Val di Fleres which runs behind the splendid Tribulaun, described by Walker as being one of the finest of all Tirolean mountains.

Combining these two valleys, and including Val di Fleres in the occasional tour, a fine selection of walking routes could be achieved. For a start, consider exploring the head of the Gschnitztal, say from an initial base at Obernberg. From that village either make a direct crossing of the Gstreinjöchl (2540m) to reach the Tribulaun hut, or adopt a longer and more complicated route from the Obernbergsee to the Obernberger Tribulaun (2780m), then via the frontier crest over the Schwarze Wand to the Schneetalscharte, a col on the Austro-Italian border from which descent is made to the Tribulaun hut. Next day head west to the Bremer hut, first by following the Dolomieu-Weg, then the Jubilaumssteig. The third stage reverses day two of the Stubai High Route by travelling from the Bremer to the Innsbrucker hut, and on the final day drops into the Gschnitztal and, if need be, returns to Obernberg via the 2398 metre Muttenjoch.

That is but one multi-day option. Other tours could be created by crossing from the Tribulaun hut to Val di Fleres, then straying west to spend a night at the Magdeburger hut (also known as the Schneespitz hut or Rifugio Cremona alla Stua) set on the edge of the fast-shrinking Stubenferner glacier, and returning down valley next day to cross back to the Austrian side by one of several possible cols. Instead of visiting the Magdeburger hut there's the Pflerscher Höhenweg to consider. This high trail makes a traverse of the southern flank of the Tribulaun peaks from the Italian Tribulaun hut eastward to the Portjoch which gives access to the Obernbergtal. This is an exciting route with sections of *klettersteig* to overcome otherwise difficult rock features, and when used in conjunction with trails on the northern side, makes possible yet another circular tour.

There are also a few ascents that hillwalkers could achieve here too. Of these Walker recommended the Pflerscher Pinggl (2767m) from the Sandesjöchl, Gschnitzer Tribulaun (2946m) from the Schneetalscharte, and the Schwarze Wand and Obernberger Tribulaun already 'collected' on the suggested tour mentioned as starting from Obernberg village.

✳   ✳   ✳

The Italian Valleys

With the Timmelsjoch at its head connecting with the Austrian Ötztal, Val di Passiria (Passeiertal) is the westernmost valley on the southern flank of the Stubai Alps. In the summer months a bus service links San Leonardo (St Leonhard - birthplace in 1767 of Tirolean patriot Andreas Hofer) with Sölden. From a sharp left-hand hairpin on the Timmelsjoch road at Schönauer Alm, a marked track breaks away northward on the left bank of the Timmelsbach, and along this a walk of about two hours will lead to the Schneeberg hut at 2355 metres. Formerly used as a miners' canteen for workers at the nearby zinc, lead and silver mine, it was taken over by the CAI in 1962 when mining work ceased. From here a cross-country route leads to Masseria/Maiern in Val Ridanna (Ridnauntal), and another to the Becherhaus, at 3191 metres the highest of all Stubai huts, perched on rocks below the Wilder Freiger at the head of the latter valley.

Val Ridanna cuts into the heart of the Italian Stubai with a road, served by bus from Vipiteno, projecting just beyond Masseria. In the lower reaches of this valley a tributary glen breaks away westward; this is Val di Racines, otherwise known as the Ratschingstal. Both Ridanna (Ridnaun) and Masseria have a modest amount of accommodation, while the Grohmann, Teplitzer and Becher huts are all within reach of the roadhead. The first of these is also known as Rifugio Vedretta Piana, or Übeltalferner hut; a tiny stone building at 2254 metres used as an overflow for the Teplitzer hut and reached in about two and a half hours from Masseria. In common with the multiplicity of names now taken as standard for huts, mountains, villages and valleys in South Tirol, the CAI's Teplitzer hut is also known as Rifugio Vedretta Pendente, or the Feuerstein hut. It was built in 1889, but following a lightning strike in 1986 it was refurbished and now caters for a total of eighty-five people in bedrooms and dormitories. It stands on a rocky plateau at 2586 metres above and to the north of the Grohmann hut, from which it is gained by a good path in about forty-five minutes. The route to the Becherhaus continues from here for a further three to four hours, and involves a short glacier crossing. Its location is spectacular, and for adepts with the necessary equipment, provides opportunities for cross-border forays to the Nürnberger or Sulzenau huts, and for the ascent of Wilder Freiger.

The most easterly of the Italian valleys is Val di Fleres, formerly the Pflerschtal, which begins by flowing roughly eastward from the Feuerstein peaks, then takes a more south-easterly trend before joining Valle d'Isarco midway between the Brenner Pass and Vipiteno (Sterzing). The south wall is the divide on the far side of which Val Ridanna runs its parallel course, the northern side carries the Austrian frontier, with Gschnitztal and Obernbergtal beyond that. It's a fine valley served by bus from Colle Isarco (Gossensass) to the last village, Innerpflersch (otherwise known as Fleres, or St Anton in Pflersch), which crouches at the foot of the massive Pflerscher Tribulaun. Accommodation is available here with a few hotels, and in addition the Tribulaun and Magdeburger huts are both accessible along clear trails in about two and a half hours each. The first of these (Rifugio Calciati al Tribulaun) is small, modest, and set beside the Sandessee tarn with the Sandesjöchl above it, while the Magdeburger hut stands a little further west near the head of the valley at 2423 metres commanding, said Baedeker, a magnificent view. Above both these huts looms the frontier crest, here a soaring mass of rock, there a dash of ice and snowfield.

A high trail links these huts; although waymarked at times the route could be a little difficult to find - especially early in the season when the spring thaw has effectively rearranged rocks in a stony amphitheatre between the Magdeburger hut and the Weisswand. The way passes round the flanks of this mountain to gain a col before climbing the Hoher Zahn (2924m) on the frontier ridge. Views are splendid almost throughout this route; it's rather exposed in places, but nothing to deter most Alpine walkers, and the Tribulaun hut should be reached in less than four hours.

If you choose Innerpflersch as a valley base a fine, energetic, very full day's expedition could be won by going first to the Magdeburger hut, then following that high trail to the Tribulaun hut and descending from there to the valley again. Other suggested outings to be tackled include a crossing of the Sandesjöchl to the Austrian Tribulaun hut; the ascent of various frontier summits, and the airy Pflerscher Höhenweg that makes a traverse along the mid-height slopes of the north wall of the valley, as already mentioned as part of a multi-day excursion from the Gschnitztal and Obernbergtal. But armed with the necessary maps, and ambition to match one's dreams, any enterprising walker will find sufficient ways to fill every waking hour among these delightful mountains and valleys of the Stubai Alps.

❋   ❋   ❋

THE STUBAI ALPS

Location:
On both sides of the Austro-Italian border running eastward from the Ötztal Alps to the Brenner Pass; in the Austrian Province of Tirol, Italian Alto-Adige or South Tirol.

Principal valleys:
On the Austrian side these are the Sellraintal and its feeder glens, in particular the Lüsensertal and Senderstal; the Stubaital, with the Oberbergtal, Unterbergtal and Pinnistal; and the Gschnitztal. South of the frontier Val Ridanna and Val di Fleres.

Principal peaks:
Zuckerhütl (3507m), Schrankogel (3497m), Wilder Pfaff (3456m), Wilder Freiger (3418m)

Centres:
The best are, perhaps, Neustift and Fulpmes in the Stubaital and Gschnitz in the Gschnitztal. Längenfeld and Sölden in the Ötztal serve the western glens. Innerpflersch in Val di Fleres, and Masseria in Val Ridanna on the Italian side.

Huts:
Numerous huts on both sides of the frontier; mostly owned by the Austrian, German or Italian Alpine Clubs.

Access:
The nearest international airport is Innsbruck, from which town rail access is given to the north and east sides of the range, and across the Italian border too. Frequent buses serve the main valleys on both sides of the border.

Maps:
Kompass Wanderkarte, sheet 83 *Stubaier Alpen: Serleskamm* at a scale of 1:50,000 is sufficient for most walkers' needs in the Austrian Stubai. The Austrian Alpine Club produce two useful sheets (Alpenvereinskarte) with more detail at 1:25,000 scale. These are sheet 31/1 *Stubai Alpen: Hoch Stubai* and sheet 31/2 *Stubai Alpen: Sellrain*. Freytag Berndt Wanderkarte cover the Italian valleys with two sheets at 1:50,000: numbers S4 *Sterzing-Brixen* and S8 *Passeier-Timmelsjoch*.

Guidebooks:
Hut to Hut in the Stubai Alps by Allan Hartley (Cicerone Press) describes the Stubai High Route, which Hartley calls the Stubai Rucksack Route, and a six-day glacier

tour which takes in a number of summits.

Stubai Alps and South Tirol by Jeff Williams (West Col) gives hut details and approach routes, plus climbing routes on both sides of the border. Of more use to the mountaineer than the mountain walker.

Walking Austria's Alps, Hut to Hut by Jonathan Hurdle (Cordee/The Mountaineers) includes a multi-day hut-to-hut route in the Stubai, starting at Gries in the Sulztal and ending with a descent to Neustift from the Nürnberger hut.

Mountain Walking in Austria by Cecil Davies (Cicerone Press) details eight walking routes, including two multi-day tours.

Hut Hopping in the Austrian Alps by William E. Reifsnyder (Sierra Club, San Francisco, 1973) outlines the Stubai High Route in reverse order to that described above, from Franz Senn to the Nürnberger hut and down to Ranalt.

Other reading:

Walking in the Alps by J. Hubert Walker (Oliver & Boyd, 1951) contains a chapter on the Stubai Alps, with some fine ideas.

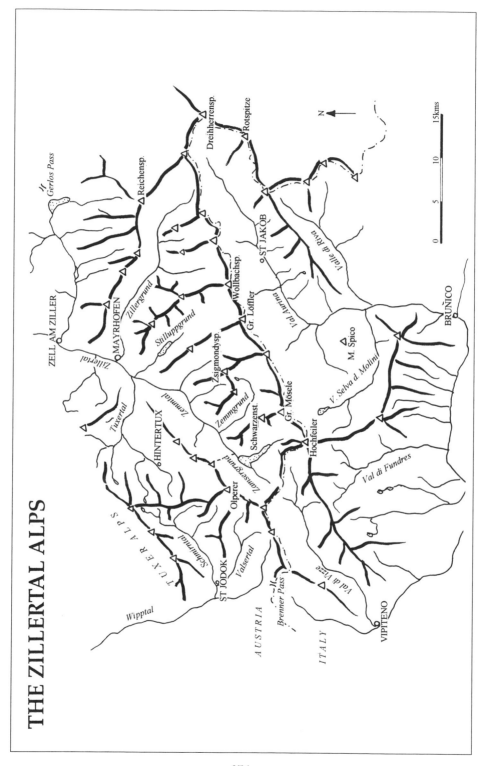

THE ZILLERTAL ALPS

Hay meadows high above the Zillertal

15: THE ZILLERTAL ALPS

S preading east from the Brenner Pass the Zillertal Alps are considered by many to be the shapeliest and most rugged of all mountain groups of the Austrian Tirol. Primarily frontier mountains, they continue the chain of the Ötztal and Stubai Alps along the Austro-Italian border as far as the Dreiherrenspitze, beyond which rises the Venediger group of Hohe Tauern. Roughly half the district falls within Italian territory, the south-east portion draining into Val Aurina (Ahrntal), while the western half of the Italian flank flows via Val di Vizze (Pfitschertal) into the Isarco, or by way of south-trending glens into Val Pusteria (Pustertal) above Bressanone. But it is from the Austrian side that the Zillertal Alps are better known, and it is from the main valley which drains the northern slopes that the district takes its name.

The watershed crest contains a whole series of snow and ice-capped summits in excess of 3000 metres (the highest being the Hochfeiler; 3510m), while a second major ridge, the so-called Tuxer Kamm, pushes north-east from the Hohe Wand (3289m) along the edge of the Zamsergrund and Zemmtal, and offers the glaciers of its north flank to the ski industry. A large portion of the north-facing frontier ridge is glaciated, as are several subsidiary spurs pushing from it. However, other spurs that are now clear of permanent snow and ice have routes across them that link one glen after another and thereby create numerous opportunities for the enterprising walker. Most of the valleys form deep trenches, with level pastures in their bed and forests lining the hillsides, their upper reaches being known as *grund,* their glaciers called *kees.*

Approached from the Inn valley north-east of Innsbruck the important Zillertal projects deep into the mountains to the south, effectively dividing the Tuxer Alps on the west from the Kitzbüheler Alps to the east. In its lower reaches the valley presents an open expanse of meadowland, but it's a densely populated one, whose village resorts attract crowds of visitors in winter and summer alike. Once a mining village, Zell am Ziller is now the foremost resort of the lower Zillertal. It sits at the junction of the Gerlostal which forms the southern limit of the Kitzbüheler Alps, and provides facilities for winter skiing on the slopes of the Kreuzjoch and the Gerlossteinwand. The road through the long Gerlostal is a scenic one, rising to the Gerlos Pass that marks the north-east limit of the Zillertal Alps before descending to Krimml in the upper Pinzgau. There is a small ski resort just to the west of the pass, and good views south to the Reichenspitze rising from the Wildgerlos Kees icefield. On the south side of the Gerlostal successive glens drain the mountain ridge which walls the upper Zillertal, known here as the Zillergrund.

The main valley road continues south of Zell along the right bank of the river and comes to Mayrhofen, situated very much at the hub of the district with valleys fanning from it. Working clockwise these are the Zillergrund to the east, the Stilluppgrund, then the Zemmtal, and finally the Tuxertal roughly west of Mayrhofen which has been heavily developed for skiing and which, as its name suggests, borders the Tuxer Alps. Tourism has transformed Mayrhofen from a slumbering village into a major resort with plentiful accommodation and a wide range of facilities. Hillsides accessible from it are adorned with cableways and, to a greater or lesser degree, most of the adjacent valleys have been tamed in one way or another - either by flooding for hydro purposes, made accessible to motor traffic by the construction of roads, or exploited for skiing. And yet the vast majority of mountains of the Zillertal Alps remain undefiled and from viewpoints on practically every walk reveal a backdrop of tremendous appeal.

As elsewhere in the Eastern Alps the bulk of mountain exploration was carried out in the nineteenth century by Austrian or German climbers, but such Victorian notables as Tuckett, the Pendlebury brothers and the ubiquitous D.W. Freshfield made visits in the 1860s and '70s, while Yorkshireman Russell Starr made his mark by climbing the 3381 metre connoisseur's peak of the Fussstein in 1880. Today the range provides a wealth of glacier expeditions and classic mixed snow and ice routes, but little in the way of rock climbing other than on the Fussstein and the spiky Zsigmondyspitze (formerly known as the Feldkopf; 3087m) climbed in 1879 by the Zsigmondy brothers.

But this book is concerned with *walking* expeditions, rather than climbing, although there are plenty of summits accessible to walkers without technical expertise. For our purposes the Zillertal Alps are alive with prospects on both sides of the international divide where there are nearly thirty Club huts of the Austrian and German Alpenverein or the Italian Alpine Club (CAI), and others that belong to the Austrian Touring Club (ÖTK), South Tirol Mountain Association (AVS) and some that are privately owned. It will be seen, then, that hut to hut touring is a very viable proposition here; not only along well-established routes, but with many opportunities to create tours of varying length and severity to suit the individual. A few suggestions will be made below, but first we should study the district in a little more detail in order to better appreciate the lie of the land.

✲   ✲   ✲

Schmirntal, Valsertal and Venntal

The western outline of the Zillertal Alps is drawn by the Wipptal on the Austrian side of the border and Valle d'Isarco on the Italian, the two being joined by the Brenner Pass. Feeding into the Wipptal at Stafflach, just seven kilometres short of the Italian frontier, the combined waters of the Schmirnbach and Valser Bach provide a choice of access glens to the district's outer limits. At St Jodok the Schmirntal forks. The main valley veers north-eastward, while the Valsertal cuts off to the south-east with a metalled road going as far as the Touristenrast gasthof. The Schmirntal digs into mountains that border both the Tuxer and Zillertal Alps and, by way of other tributary glens, offers walking routes over the boundary ridges. The Tuxer Joch (2310m) is an obvious crossing into the head of the Tuxertal, but on emerging at the saddle one is confronted by a heavy concentration of cableways with summer skiing practised on glaciers to the south. There is an ÖTK hut here, the Tuxerjochhaus, which is reached by chairlift from Hintertux, and a number of trails that either go along the ridge to the Frauenwand, north into the Tuxer Alps proper, or down into the Tuxertal itself where other possibilities present themselves.

A higher, better and less-fussed crossing than that of the Tuxer Joch would be won from the head of the Valsertal where the 2959 metre Alpeiner Scharte below the Fussstein provides views of the snowy Zillertal chain and a descent to the Zamsergrund, as well as options to the Pfitscherjoch on the Austro-Italian border to the south, or to the Olperer hut above the valley east of the pass. On occasion steep frozen snow slopes create problems on both sides of the pass. In such conditions caution is advised. If unsure, before attempting such a crossing it would be worth enquiring of current conditions at the Geraer hut which is situated some six hundred metres below the pass in a dramatic location at the foot of the soaring west flank of the Fussstein.

At this stage it is worth mentioning the Weitwanderweg, a national walking route across the mountains of Austria, which comes this way. On maps and some waymarks the series of trails which have been adopted for this long-distance route are numbered 502. So far as the Zillertal Alps are concerned the Weitwanderweg crosses from west to east just below the frontier ridge, coming from St Jodok to the Geraer hut, then over the Alpeiner Scharte to the Olperer hut. There it joins the Berliner Höhenweg as far as the Berliner hut, and continues via the Greizer and Kasseler huts along the route of the Zillertal Hut Tour described later in this chapter. But whilst the hut tour outlined below breaks away to the north from the Kasseler hut and finishes at Mayrhofen, the Weitwanderweg becomes more challenging as it continues eastward over glacier passes to the Venediger group.

A second access glen on the Austrian side of the border is the Venntal, which emerges close to the Brenner Pass. A road, then track, scores into it, with a footpath continuing up among pastures and trees to the Landshuter Europa hut set on a ridge overlooking the Italian Val di Vizze. Reached in about four hours from the Brennersee (three hours from Platz in Val di Vizze), the hut dates from 1889, but has been rebuilt and enlarged and now has room for about a hundred in dormitories and bedrooms. Built on the very frontier it is jointly owned by the DAV and Italian Alpine Club. Above it the 2999 metre Kraxentrager may be reached in about an hour by an uncomplicated scramble, and the summit rewards with views to the Dolomites. Snaking eastward from the hut the Landshuter Höhenweg makes an interesting traverse high above Val di Vizze and in two and a half hours leads to the privately-owned Pfitscherjoch Haus (alias Rifugio Passo Vizze; 2277m), with a tiny tarn nearby, and the actual *joch* a little lower to the north-east by which the head of the Zamsergrund may be reached.

The Zemmtal and Zamsergrund

The Zamsergrund trends roughly north-east to Breitlahner, then continues as the Zemmtal to Ginzling where the Zammbach and Floitenbach streams converge. The valley then makes a more northerly sweep to Mayrhofen and the Zillertal. Several tributary glens feed into it from the glacial frontier crest, while the Tuxer Kamm marks the valley's left-hand wall. Assuming our approach is by road from Mayrhofen (the main route of approach), these tributaries are as follows: the Floitengrund with an access road from Ginzling; the Gunggltal (a short glen draining a cirque formed by the Grosse Ingent-Ochsner-Zsigmondyspitze ridge system); the Zemmgrund glen which leads to the Berliner hut; and lastly the Schlegeisgrund glen with a large dammed lake at its entrance and glaciers hanging between the Hochfeiler and Grosse Möseler (3478m) at its head. A public bus service travels from Mayrhofen as far as the dam at the north end of the fjord-like Schlegeisspeicher reservoir, but there are car parks beyond this. The road above Breitlahner, however, carries an expensive toll for private vehicles. From Mayrhofen up accommodation is to be had in Ginzling and Breitlahner, while each of the feeder glens has either gasthofs, inns or mountain huts that could usefully be employed for either a single overnight's lodging, or as the base for a longer stay in order to explore that particular valley's potential to the full.

On the western edge of the Schlegeisspeicher the privately-owned Dominikus hut is accessible by road, but just beyond it a path climbs steeply through the Riepenbach gorge to gain the DAV's Olperer hut in an hour and a half. Being perched at 2389 metres views are spectacular, overlooking the Schlegeisspeicher to the Hochfeiler, the crusted ridge leading round to the Grosse Möseler and the blue-etched Schlegeiskees plastered across the face of the mountains that enclose the glen opposite. From the Olperer hut trails link with neighbouring huts: the Friesenberg is reached in two hours by the classic Berliner Höhenweg; the Geraer hut in four hours across the Alpeiner Scharte, and the Pfitscherjoch Haus by a choice of routes. At the upper end of the Schlegeisgrund, and reached by a trail along the south-west bank of the reservoir followed by a final steep approach over grass slopes, the Furtschagl Haus gazes directly up to converging glaciers, with the Grosse Möseler rising above to the east. The Berliner Höhenweg trail climbs above the hut and crosses the ridge pushing north-west from the Grosse Möseler - the ridge which separates this from the next glen to the north-east, the Zemmgrund.

With Breitlahner at its entrance the Zemmgrund entices towards a glacial basin of considerable charm. A private jeep road scores into the glen along the true right bank of the stream and leads in an hour and a half's walk to the Grawand Haus which offers accommodation, as does the Alpenrose-Wirtshaus half an hour further on into the valley. From this latter establishment the scenery takes on a more dramatic and imposing character with glaciers looming from an impressive natural amphitheatre ahead, and in another thirty minutes you come to the Berliner hut (2040m), the largest in the Zillertal Alps with accommodation for upwards of one hundred and eighty people. Dating from 1879 this so-called 'hut' hardly compares with many of those simple refuges of the Western Alps, for it has an impressively large entrance foyer and the dining room, complete with chandeliers, is more like a baronial hall than the communal eating-place of climbers and walkers. There's plenty to do from a base here. Trails climb rock spurs that divide glaciers hanging from the frontier crest; another goes up to the 3133 metre Schönbichler Horn (reached by a brief diversion from the Berliner Höhenweg) for a very fine mountain vista; and another strikes north-east from the hut and visits the popular Schwarzensee tarn in a wild location from which yet more tremendous views are won. It's possible to continue above the tarn to cross a shoulder of the Zsigmondyspitze at the Melkerscharte (2880m) and descend from there into the Gunggltal. Note, however, that the initial descent section from the col can sometimes be awkward with a troublesome bergschrund to negotiate.

Less-frequented than either of its neighbours, the Gunggltal is an unspoilt glen hemmed in by rocky walls and crowned at the southern end by the Ochsner and Zsigmondyspitze. There are no Alpenverein huts here, but the privately-owned Max hut is shown by the map to be located a short way inside the glen. Any route other than a there and back walk will involve a high ridge crossing at the Melkerscharte.

The last of the Zemmtal's tributary glens is also its longest. The Floitengrund projects south-east from Ginzling, an almost die-straight glen leading to the base of the symmetrical Grosse Löffler (3376m). At its foot stands the Greizer hut with a backcloth of glaciers, reached in about four hours from Ginzling by a route described by Cecil Davies as "probably the most romantic valley walk in the area." Initially the way leads along a private road as far as Sulzenalm - a road served by minibus from Mayrhofen. Beyond this the walk grows in interest and visual delight. This is how Davies describes it in his guidebook:

"It is a narrow valley, green and partially wooded at first. Higher it has more scattered boulders. Higher still you feel the weight of the steep mountain slopes impending on each side; the path is forced near the stream and the glacier and permanent snow at the valley head can be seen. When the hut comes into view it is higher and rather to the left. The path becomes steeper, the valley stonier and as we climb to the left, the stream is below us on our right. Now, over stony slopes the path climbs the valley side in zig-zags until the hut is reached, perched on a sort of spur, looking out on the ice-fall of the Floiten Glacier, and also away down the valley."

(*Mountain Walking in Austria*)

In common with other huts built at the head of these parallel glens, marked footpaths lead from it across neighbouring ridges to link with other huts. In this instance the western trail eventually leads to the Berliner hut, while the continuing route over the east-walling ridge goes to either the Grüne Wand Haus or the Kasseler hut, both of which are situated in the Stilluppgrund, a lengthy valley which leads directly down to Mayrhofen.

The Stilluppgrund

Protected at its northern end by the wooded gorge of the Stilluppklamm, a toll road winds into the valley and alongside a reservoir to the Wasserfall gasthof. There is a bus service from Mayrhofen to this point, and a minibus continues from there as far as the Grüne Wand Haus, followed by a track and footpath leading finally to the Kasseler hut (2177m). Perched on the steep hillside below the Hinter Stangen Spitze, and with an outlook that includes a string of small glaciers hanging from frontier peaks, this DAV-owned hut has been enlarged considerably since it was erected in 1927, and can now accommodate more than a hundred in bedrooms and dormitories. Reached in about two hours from the roadhead, a longer route of approach, which avoids the road entirely, follows a high path for something like fifteen kilometres along the hillside from the Edel hut. This is more attractive to walkers than the road alternative, but will take eight or nine hours to achieve - with good mountain views to draw you on. The Edel hut sits below the striking Ahornspitze with a bird's-eye view onto Mayrhofen, from which it may be reached by way of the Ahornbahn cableway followed by a walk of about an hour. If one were to go up to the hut by the cableway, it should be perfectly feasible to make an ascent of the Ahornspitze (2976m) the same day (there is a marked route all the way to the summit, with a little easy scrambling), and set out for the Kasseler hut along the Aschaffenburger Höhensteig the following morning.

The east ridge wall of the valley wears several glaciers on its eastern side, so limiting any further advance in that direction for our mountain walker. But a marked route strikes round the valley's headwall below other glaciers heading west, and crosses the Lapen Scharte (2707m) in the opposite ridge with a descent to the Greizer hut in the neighbouring Floitengrund.

ZILLERTAL HUT TOUR

This initial review takes care of the western glens on the Austrian flank of the district, but before we move on to look at the eastern half, it is worth giving a brief description of a quite splendid hut to hut tour that reveals some of the finest and most dramatic scenery available to view by the mountain walker in all the Zillertal Alps. Study of the map will show the existence of a major system of trails at mid-height along the Zemmtal-Zamsergrund slope of the Tuxer Kamm which, linked as one, becomes the Berliner Höhenweg. This stretches almost the complete length of the valley, then drops to the northern end of the Schlegeisspeicher where it is joined by the ultra-long Zentralalpenweg (the Weitwanderweg, path 502), and then crosses below the Grosse Möseler to the Berliner hut in the Zemmgrund. By following this route from one hut to another, then extending it to the Stilluppgrund, a magnificent touring holiday of about eight days could be achieved.

Mayrhofen makes an obvious start and finishing point, from where the first half-day stage will entail wandering upvalley to Finkenberg before taking a steeply-climbing forest trail up a spur of the Gamsberg which effectively separates the lower Tuxertal and Zemmtal valleys. On this spur, about three hours from Finkenberg, the little Gams hut provides a convenient first night's lodging. Nine hundred metres above it the triple-summited Grinbergspitzen makes a tempting half-day's outing; two and a half hours should be sufficient to gain the first summit, the popular Vordere, by a marked route, while an additional thirty minutes of scrambling will lead to the middle summit at 2867 metres. The connecting ridge which leads to the higher, Hintere Grinbergspitze (2884m), involves sections of grade III/IV rock climbing over a series of pinnacles.

Following the Berliner Höhenweg next day the route makes a long undulating traverse of the Tuxer Kamm heading south-west, with a vista of high mountains developing in both extent and grandeur as the trail progresses. Depending on ambition, fitness and weather conditions, the choice of accommodation at the end of this stage will be either the Friesenberg Haus (seven hours) or the Olperer hut in a further two hours. The first is situated on the slopes of the Hoher Riffler at 2498 metres, the second overlooks the Schlegeisspeicher from a site below the Olperer. In view of the comparative shortness of tomorrrow's route it would be as well to opt for the former.

Whichever hut was chosen for the second night's lodging, the Furtschagl Haus will be the destination for day three. For this one must descend almost 600 metres from the Olperer hut to the shores of the Schlegeis reservoir, then follow the south-west bank into the glen headed by the glacial wall running between the Hochfeiler and Grosse Möseler. It's a scenic approach along a broad track, easy underfoot and clear all the way to the final uphill path (waterfalls in view) over grass slopes leading to the hut, which sits on a broad terrace above the Furtschaglbach about four hours' walk from the Olperer hut.

The highest point on the tour is tackled on the crossing of the lofty dividing ridge beyond which lies the Zemmgrund, the next glen to the north-east. This is achieved by way of the Schönbichler Scharte at 3081 metres, an oft-crossed col on the narrow north ridge of the Grosse Möseler, and with a clear trail leading to it in about two and a half hours. From the rocky col a short scramble leads to the summit of the nearby Schönbichler Horn which rewards with very fine views. According to the West Col Zillertal guide, this is (not surprisingly) the most frequented of all the district's three thousand metre tops and was once described by Eric Roberts who did the research for that guide, as having the banality of a seaside outing. Be that as it may, few walkers would want to forego that diversion, which is safeguarded with fixed ropes in places and will not add much in the way of time or effort to their day, although the gains in respect of visual appreciation will be many. Descent to the Berliner hut, which is seen from the summit, requires some caution but should not be too troublesome under normal summer conditions.

The fifth stage leads to the Greizer hut via the Schwarzensee and Mörchen Scharte. There are two such cols bearing this name between the Zsigmondyspitze and the Kleine Mörchner, but path number 502 uses the north option at 2872 metres. By this route the Greizer hut at the head of the Floitengrund is reached in five to six hours. The way is not unduly difficult but there are some steep sections, and with a fair amount of height gain and loss.

Next day cross the Lapen Scharte, nearly 500 metres above the Greizer hut. On the east side of the ridge where the path forks, take the right-hand option to skirt below the Lapen, Löffler and Stillupp glaciers on a traverse of the valley-head which leads directly to the Kasseler hut in about four hours, hut to hut. The penultimate stage involves a full day's walk north (boulder-hopping and scrambling in places with fixed rope aid) along the right-hand wall of the Stilluppgrund following the Aschaffenburger Höhensteig to the Edel hut, with Mayrhofen seen in the valley below. The author of a chapter in *Walking Austria's Alps Hut to Hut* dealing with part of this Zillertal traverse warns that the high route stage between the Kasseler and Edel huts should not be attempted if the ground is wet, suggesting that in such conditions the steep grass slopes could be extremely dangerous. In which case the straightforward valley route should be adopted. Since the descent to Mayrhofen from the Edel hut requires little more than a steep two-hour descent (or a ride on the Ahornbahn cableway), a visit to the summit of the Ahornspitze is recommended first, thus ending the tour on a high note, in more ways than one.

ZILLERTAL HUT TOUR - ROUTE SUMMARY

Day 1: Mayrhofen - Finkenberg - Gams Hut

Day 2: Gams Hut - Berliner Höhenweg - Friesenberg Haus (or Olperer Hut)

Day 3: Friesenberg Haus (or Olperer Hut) - Schlegeisspeicher - Furtschagl Haus

Day 4: Furtschagl Haus - Schönbichler Scharte (Schönbichler Horn) - Berliner Hut

Day 5: Berliner Hut - Nördlicher Mörchen Scharte - Greizer Hut

Day 6: Greizer Hut - Lapen Scharte - Kasseler Hut

Day 7: Kasseler Hut - Aschaffenburger Höhensteig - Edel Hut

Day 8: Edel Hut - Ahornspitze - Mayrhofen

* * *

Zillergrund

The Zillergrund makes deep inroads into the mountains to the south-east of Mayrhofen. This is the last of the district's valleys, the ridge that runs over the Dreiecker and Reichenspitze forming the provincial boundary between Tirol and Salzburg, east of which rise the Venediger mountains. The granite blades, pyramids and domes of the Reichenspitze group, rising from attractive little glaciers, lend to the area comparisons with the Bregaglia. But Zillergrund attractions are not monopolised by these mountains alone. The walker in search of long trails with fine views and enough challenge to provide physical and spiritual satisfaction will not face disappointment here.

Above:
The Kalser Tal gives access both to the south side of the Grossglockner and the Granatspitze (Ch 16)

Centre left:
On the Austro-Italian border above the Gailtal the limestone of the Carnic Alps offers good scrambling and ridge walking (Ch 16)

Bottom left:
The Reichenspitze in the Zillertal Alps (Ch 15)

Above:
In the Wilder Kaiser
(Ch 17)

Centre left:
The pastures of Elmau Alm
above Werfen in the
Tennengebirge
(Ch 17)

Bottom left:
The Wengerwinkel glen in
the south-west
Tennengebirge (Ch 17)

A road goes through the valley as far as yet another reservoir, the Speicher Zillergründl. Only permit-holders are allowed to drive beyond Brandberg, just five kilometres from Mayrhofen, although a minibus service ferries passengers as far as Bärenbad a little short of the reservoir, where there's a gasthof. There are several inns scattered along the valley, but only one Alpenverein hut (the Plauener) despite its length and the fact that there are two important tributary glens feeding into it from the south-flanking wall. These tributaries are the Sondergrund and the rather desolate Hundskehlgrund; the first cuts south of In der Au, the second digs into the mountains to the south of Bärenbad. Both offer routes over the frontier mountains into the Italian Val Aurina (Ahrntal), as does the Zillergründl above the reservoir.

The Sondergrund has a private jeep track pushing as far as the Schönhütten at 1771 metres. Beyond this one trail branches off to the west and rises to a spur of the Hintere Stangenspitze where a glacier pass suggests a way over the ridge to the Kasseler hut, while another climbs to the glen's headwall in order to cross the frontier crest at the Hörndljoch (2553m), then plunges on the Italian side to St Jakob in Val Aurina. Baedeker called this full day's route "fatiguing".

In the parallel glen to the east a waymarked route works through the valley on the right bank of the Hundskehlbach almost the whole way to the Hundskehljoch (2561m), where views are won of the Dreiherrenspitze and Rötspitze walling Val Aurina to the east. From the col one route descends to St Peter in the valley bed; one (the Lausitzer Weg - also known as Via Vetta d'Italia) cuts along the ridge eastward, then traverses round the Italian flank of the Rauchkofel, Winkelkopf and Schientalkopf to the CAI-owned Neugersdorfer hut (alias Rifugio Vetta d'Italia; 2562m), while yet a third trail begins a short way from the col and makes a devious descent to the valley via the Waldnersee tarn. A pleasant two-day tour could be achieved here, starting and ending at the Bärenbad gasthof. On the first day (a long one with eighteen kilometres to cover, so start early) go through the Hundskehlgrund and up to the frontier ridge, then strike off along the Lausitzer Weg to the Neugersdorfer hut and spend the night there with tremendous views across the head of Val Aurina to the Dreiherrenspitze. Above the hut cross the 2633 metre Krimmler Tauern, then take the higher of two paths, make a traverse north-westward and cross back into Austria at the Zillerplattenscharte, a col in the ridge walling the upper Zillergrund. Below this bear right on the Hannemannweg which leads to the Plauener hut and, eventually, the Bärenbad gasthof.

The Plauener hut dates from 1898 and is located on a ledge below the Kuchelmoos glacier with the Reichenspitze above that, and a glacier pass (Gamsscharte; 2976m) on the north ridge of the Schwarzkopf forming a link with the Richter hut on the far side. From the Plauener hut the Hannemannweg makes a steady rising traverse towards the head of the glen where the Heiliggeistjöchl (Feldjöchl or Forcla di Campo; 2657m) provides a rough route to Kasern in Val Aurina. On the Italian side of this pass the descent crosses the Lausitzer Weg traverse path mentioned above, and thereby offers a tempting, shorter alternative to the two-day tour outlined in the preceding paragraph.

✳   ✳   ✳

385

The Italian Valleys

Very briefly the two valleys with which we will be concerned on the south side of the Austro-Italian border are Val di Vizze (Pfitschertal) and Val Aurina (Ahrntal). Both drain roughly south-westward, but are separated by a block of snow mountains crowned by the Hochfeiler. Other glens flow from this block, the most important of which is Val Selva dei Molini (Mühlwalder Tal) which curves counter-clockwise from the Neves reservoir and joins the lower Val Aurina at Mühlen (Molini di Tures) where the latter valley becomes the Val di Tures. Above the Neves reservoir the Edelraute and Nevesjoch huts are both conveniently placed on a lengthy trail that gives a high route along much of this southern side of the chain, the Pfunderer Höhenweg.

Val di Vizze

Val di Vizze slices through the mountains below the west face of the Hochfeiler. At its outflow at Vipiteno (Sterzing) below the Brenner Pass a road breaks away from the busy Innsbruck-Brenner-Bolzano highway and pushes through the valley as far as St Jakob (not to be confused with St Jakob in Val Aurina). A bus service reaches this point from Vipiteno, whilst an unmade road continues up to the Pfitscherjoch (Passo di Vizze) on the Austrian border, where the privately-owned Pfitscherjoch Haus offers hut-standard accommodation and access to a high trail known as the Landshuter Höhenweg, as already mentioned earlier in this chapter. Several villages within the valley provide hotel, gasthof and campsite accommodation as well as some provisioning, and towards its head a number of trails climb the walling hillsides to exploit viewpoints or to cross into parallel glens. At Saletto (Wieden) the valley forks. Here the Grossbergtal breaks away to the right and is dominated by the Wilde Kreuzspitze whose ascent was once said to be "fatiguing but highly remunerative". At the head of this glen the Pfundersjoch is a walker's route over the mountains to Fundres (Pfunders) in Val di Fundres - one of the south-draining glens that feeds into Val Pusteria. Here an enterprising walker could join the Pfunderer Höhenweg and make a multi-day hut route roughly heading eastward to St Johann in Val Aurina.

Above St Jakob Val di Vizze forks once more. Beyond this point the main valley is known as the Oberbergtal, the right-hand glen being the Unterbergtal, a glacial scoop whose bulldozing ice tools are receding back to the Hochfeiler. A trail goes through the Unterbergtal and climbs to the Hochfeiler hut (2710m) built above the ruins of the former Wiener hut on a rib dividing two glacier systems. From here the ascent of the highest Zillertal mountain by its west-south-west ridge is an uncomplicated three-hour scramble in good conditions - the easiest route on the Hochfeiler which is, elsewhere, heavily glaciated. At the head of the neighbouring Oberbergtal the Hochferner bivouac hut offers simple lodging at 2429 metres below the north-west face of the Hochfernerspitze; an impressive situation.

Among the lofty viewpoints on the south side of the valley that may be reached without having to resort to technical climbing, the Grabspitze (3059m), Felbespitze (2849m) and Rotes Beil (2949m) are highlighted on the map, while the Landshuter Europa hut on the frontier crest above Platz is linked by trails that go to such accessible summits as the Wildseespitze and Kraxentrager, and two other paths that descend to the Austrian Valsertal.

Val Aurina

Considerably longer than Val di Vizze, this valley offers a range of walking opportunities from gentle valley strolls to tough cross-border routes, and high trails that link one valley with another and suggest interesting multi-day expeditions. There are several tributary glens, the most profound being those that divide the upper reaches of the valley where ridges carrying the Austrian border make a right-angle over the 3499 metre Dreiherrenspitze and effectively contain the headwaters within a cirque bearing a handful of small glaciers.

Buses go as far as Kasern. Accommodation may be found throughout the valley, and there's an official campsite at Trinkstein midway between Kasern and the Birnlücken hut. This hut (CAI owned) lies just two hundred metres below the Birnlücke (2667m), a col that gives access to the top of the Krimmler Achental on the edge of the Venediger group. From this hut the Lausitzer Weg (Via Vetta d'Italia) makes an interesting traverse round to the Neugersdorfer hut under the Krimmler Tauern, the crossing point for the Windbachtal, Richter hut and the route west and north to the Plauener hut already mentioned.

Below Trinkstein the Windtal drains the Rosshut-Ahrnerkopf-Untere Rötspitze ridge that carries the border south of the Dreiherrenspitze. A trail climbs through this glen on the way to the Lenkjöch hut (Rifugio Giogo Lungo; 2590m) which sits on a ridge dividing the Windtal from Röttal. An alternative approach path comes through this latter glen from Kasern, and when linked with the former enables a day's circular walk to be achieved. A cross-border trail climbs from the Lenkjöch hut, goes over the Vordere Umbaltörl (2926m) and, via the Kleine Philipp-Reuter and Clara huts, descends to Prägraten in the Virgental on the south side of the Venediger mountains.

Walking routes abound and a glance at the map is sufficient to reveal the range and extent throughout the valley. Some of these have already been outlined in this chapter where non-glacial passes could be crossed from one side of the main Zillertal watershed crest to the other, and it is unnecessary to repeat them here. Let the map provide inspiration. The mountains and valleys themselves will do the rest.

✳   ✳   ✳

THE ZILLERTAL ALPS

Location:
East of the Stubai Alps, from which they are separated by the Brenner Pass, the Zillertal Alps are frontier mountains whose eastern limit is bounded by the Tirolean border which runs roughly northward round a series of ridges from the Dreiherrenspitze to the Gerlos Pass. South of the Dreiherrenspitze the Austro-Italian frontier forms the boundary. To the north lie the Tuxer and Kitzbüheler Alps.

Principal valleys:
The Zamsergrund, Zemmtal, Floitengrund, Stilluppgrund and Zillergrund on the Austrian side of the border. Val di Vizze and Val Aurina on the Italian flank.

Principal peaks:
Hochfeiler (3510m), Dreiherrenspitze (3499m), Grosse Möseler (3478m), Olperer (3476m), Grosse Löffler (3376m)

387

Centres:

Mayrhofen is the main base in the Austrian Zillertal for its easy access to the best valleys and glens. On the Italian side perhaps St Jakob in the upper Val di Vizze is the most useful for the south-western glens, and St Johann, St Jakob or Kasern in the Val Aurina.

Huts:

The Austrian side is well endowed with huts, mostly those of the DAV. The Italian side has a few belonging to the CAI, and some that are privately-owned.

Access:

By rail or road on either side of the Brenner Pass for the western fringe. Otherwise by rail or road from Innsbruck along the Inn valley to Jenbach, then south through the Zillertal to Mayrhofen. Nearest international airport, Innsbruck.

Maps:

A number of publishers produce maps of this region. For our purposes the Kompass Wanderkarte 1:50,000 series, sheet 37 *Zillertal Alpen* should be adequate. Freytag Berndt cover much the same area on sheet 152 *Mayrhofen-Zillertaler Alpen* also at 1:50,000.

Guidebooks:

Mountain Walking in Austria by Cecil Davies (Cicerone Press) has a small section devoted to these mountains.

Walking Austria's Alps Hut to Hut by Jonathan Hurdle (Cordee/The Mountaineers) outlines a multi-day hut route from the Brenner Pass to Mayrhofen following much of the route described above as the Zillertal Hut Tour.

Zillertal Alps by Eric Roberts & Robin Collomb (West Col) is a mountaineer's guide, but with useful hut and access information, although some is a little out of date now.

Other reading:

The Mountains of Europe by Kev Reynolds (Oxford Illustrated Press, 1990) contains a chapter by Cecil Davies which briefly includes this district.

Over Tyrolese Hills by Frank Smythe (Hodder & Stoughton, 1936) describes a journey over these mountains undertaken in 1935.

Europa Panoramaweg, between Matrei and Kals

16: THE EASTERN AUSTRIAN ALPS
Including the Alps of the Hohe & Niedere Tauern,
the Gailtal & Carnic Alps

When Martin Conway made his epic west to east traverse of the Alps in 1894, as recorded in *The Alps from End to End,* he concluded his journey at the foot of the Grossglockner. But that is not to say the Alps end there. Indeed, the Alpine chain continues eastward, diminishing in height it is true though seldom lacking a particular kind of magic, almost as far as Vienna, with other spurs straying south of the Austrian ranges across the brow of Italy and well into Slovenia. Those southern spurs are treated within these pages to chapters of their own, as are the Northern Limestone Alps extending beyond Salzburg through the Dachstein and Totes Gebirge on the northern side of the Enns river valley, while here we will gather those mountains that spread roughly eastward from the Zillertal Alps, as well as the limestone ranges that run close to, and in some cases carry, the Italian and Slovenian borders along Austria's southern fringe.

This collection of districts is, admittedly, a remarkably disparate one, but in that diversity of form lies some of the glory that is the very essence of the Alps. To those of us who are happy to stray from region to region where a whim decrees, the Eastern Austrian Alps provide a rich feast of adventure with a kaleidoscopic range of landscapes to enjoy. That kaleidoscope changes from bold snow and ice-capped

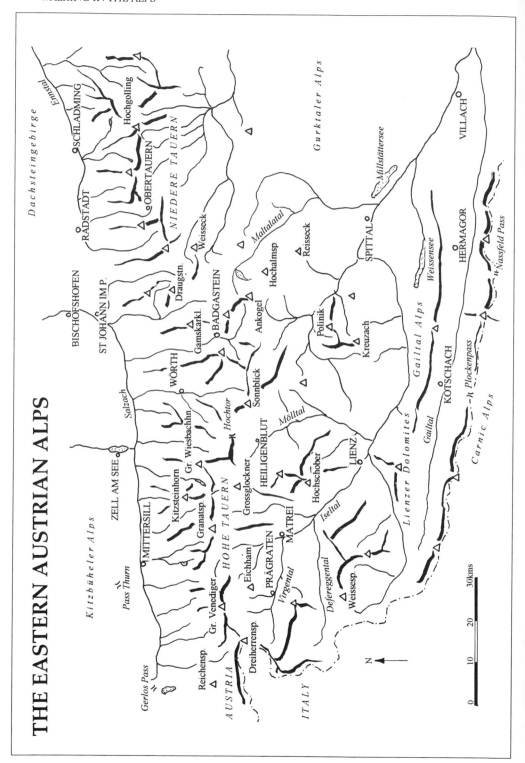

THE EASTERN AUSTRIAN ALPS

mountains of the Venediger and Glockner groups in the Hohe Tauern, to the pitted limestone crags of the Gailtal Alps, Carnic Alps and the Karawanken, and the bare, rocky Niedere Tauern with their wooded valleys and numerous lakes.

Travel from one district to the next is reasonably straightforward by public transport, given time and deep enough pockets, for the Austrian railway network tours the dividing valleys, and where there is a terminus - or a valley without a line - buses invariably fill the gaps. The popular lakeside resort of Zell am See on the north-west edge of the region provides a springboard from which to set out on an exploration. From it trains scurry westward on a branch line through the upper Pinzgau valley to Krimml at the foot of the Venediger group, on the way passing through Mittersill. Mittersill sits at a junction of valleys, and has a bus service heading south through the Felbertauern tunnel to Matrei-in-Osttirol and Lienz on the Drau. To the south of this chief town of East Tirol rise the rugged Lienzer Dolomites, while trains follow the Drau downstream to Villach in the province of Carinthia, which gives access to both the Carnic Alps and the Karawanken. The Drau forms a geological divide; to the north the high Alps of the Venediger and Glockner are composed mostly of gneiss or schist, while south of the river limestone dominates.

Zell am See lies close to Bruck at the foot of the Grossglockner-Hochalpenstrasse, the multi-hairpinned toll road that crosses the Hohe Tauern from north to south and leads to Heiligenblut, traditional starting place for climbs on Austria's highest mountain, the Grossglockner (3798m). The road is a great feat of engineering and one of the finest in the Alps for panoramic views, but it has become an environmental eyesore with the construction of numerous car parks and tourist facilities, and during the high summer season traffic is almost nose-to-tail along it day after day. It is very much a modern horror-story that threatens the peace of the hills and destroys any remote sense of tranquillity. At the head of the Mölltal Heiligenblut is also reached by public transport from Lienz, while Zell am See offers yet another point of access to the eastern Hohe Tauern and the mountains and valleys of the Niedere Tauern by way of the Zell-Salzburg railway line which has a secondary branch cutting from it at Schwarzach. This goes south and south-east via Badgastein and the Tauern Tunnel to Spittal and Villach, while one further railway line breaks away from the Zell-Salzburg route at Bischofshofen and runs east to the Enns valley along the northern edge of the Niedere Tauern. Between these two railway routes the Hafner group contains the most easterly snow peak of the Alps.

❋   ❋   ❋

THE HOHE TAUERN

This sub-chapter will concentrate on the Venediger and Glockner groups, and the smaller Granatspitze district wedged between the two. Along its northern edge the river Salzach flows eastward through the Pinzgau valley, the Kitzbüheler Alps forming that valley's north wall from the Gerlos Pass to Zell am See. Along this green wall the Pinzgauer Spaziergang makes a splendid day's traverse (twenty-four kilometres from Zell to the simple Bürgl hut above Mittersill) with consistently fine views south across the Pinzgau to the long white crest of the Glockner-Venediger chain. A series of glens sends down one glacial torrent after another from that chain to the Salzach, while the south-facing slopes fan to the two main valleys, those of the Tauerntal and Mölltal. The Virgental effectively slices west to east between the Venediger and the Lasörling group, while the Kalser Tal provides an obvious way into the south side of the Glockner; the ridge between these two important massifs being topped by the Grosse Muntanitz, 'king' of the Granatspitze group which forms a three thousand metre linchpin. A greater part of this region is contained within the boundaries of the Hohe Tauern National Park that was established in various stages subsequent to the signing of an agreement in 1971 between the provincial authorities of Carinthia, Salzburg and Tirol. But the reality of this national park was only achieved after the damming of several lakes and the construction of cableways for ski playgrounds had threatened to overrun some of the finest high mountains of the Austrian Alps.

The Venediger Group

The most westerly of the Hohe Tauern's mountains are those of the Venediger group which extends from the Zillertal Alps along a crest running from the Dreiherrenspitze over the lovely snow-bound summit of the Grossvenediger to the windy pass of the Felber Tauern. "A crown of ice, some 30 kilometres in circumference, extends further tentacle-like glaciers on all sides and is topped by a mountain of 3674 metres with its attendant peaks and rock islands," wrote Cecil Davies in *The Mountains of Europe*.

A dozen huts of the Austro-German Alpenverein, and a further fifteen or so privately owned huts and mountain inns provide lodging in some exquisite locations, thereby enabling a goodly assortment of expeditions to be tackled. Given the amount of ice that is draped on both sides of these mountains, however, a fair number of routes demand the use of ice-axe and rope for protection on crevassed glaciers, although plenty of rewarding walks may still be found that remain well below the permanent snowline. Day walks lead out of the valleys to the huts themselves on both sides of the district for some memorable views - especially on the south side of the Virgental where from the slopes of the Lasörling group the Venediger look magnificent. And there's a north-south crossing of the main chain to be made which takes advantage of an ice-free pass in the ridge high above the Felbertauern tunnel; lots of small lakes and fine views to the Venediger in one direction, the Glockner in the other, and deep valleys on either side. But to gather the best the group has to offer, the multi-day Venediger Höhenweg is a recommended classic that takes a lot of beating.

THE VENEDIGER HÖHENWEG

Making a great arc round the southern flank of the mountains above the Virgental, and skirting the majority of Venediger glaciers, this week-long hut to hut tour remains above the two thousand metre contour and crosses the head of several tributary glens, including the Maurertal, Dorfertal and Timmeltal before descending into the Gschlosstal at the end of the walk. Matrei-in-Osttirol is the resort to aim for when travelling into the area. This attractive little town sits in the deep valley of the Tauerntal at its junction with the Virgental. This latter glen drains in from the west;

a lovely pastoral valley dotted with small villages and with the Dreiherrenspitze at its head. The main village bases are Virgen and Prägraten, but a bus service from Matrei travels the seventeen kilometres to Hinterbichl and continues a short distance west of there to the large parking area of Ströden (also spelt as Streden).

Three huts are accessible from the roadhead: the Neue Reichenberger to the south, the Clara (three hours to the west) and the Essener-Rostocker hut which lies to the north and is also reached in about three hours. In the past the *höhenweg* began on the slopes of the Lasörling group at the Neue Reichenberger and made a curve round the head of the valley to the Clara hut, then on to the Essener-Rostocker. But this fell out of favour when the linking path was considered too dangerous, so the first night of the tour is now spent at the Essener-Rostocker hut, thus shortening the route by two days. However, it is possible that the original route will be reinstated, so make enquiries locally if you plan to attempt it.

From Ströden a track heads up the Maurertal through light woodland to Stoanalm, and continues as far as the hut's *materialbahn* (supply lift). A footpath now climbs above a waterfall over grass slopes, then twists among rock outcrops to reach the two tall three-storey huts set side-by-side among old moraines at 2208 metres. Above the huts other trails lead to glacier views and two small glacial tarns, and time can be well-spent exploring the neighbourhood. Of these huts, the original stone-built Rostocker was built in 1912, the adjoining rather bland and utilitarian Essener hut was constructed in 1964. The combined accommodation is now capable of sleeping about a hundred and thirty people, yet may still be crowded in the height of the season.

It should be possible for fit walkers to take the second stage of the tour as far as the privately-owned Eissee hut, but this is not country to scurry through and it would be better to make an unhurried walk instead to the Johannis hut by way of the scenic 2790 metre Türmljoch. This is a morning's walk, with the option of continuing to the Defregger Haus in the midst, it seems, of glaciers and snowfields. Unfortunately the Johannis hut can be reached by taxi and as a consequence it has many day visitors, so peace may not be very evident until the afternoon crowd has gone. It is the oldest hut in the district, dating from 1857, while the Defregger Haus is the highest at 2962 metres. This also has a long history, being built originally in 1887 by the Austrian Touring Club (ÖTK) "on a rocky crest between the Mullwitz and Rainer Glaciers" above which rises the summit of the Grossvenediger.

Day three leads to the Eissee hut in about four hours, but allow another hour or so from the Defregger Haus if you spent the night there and will be returning first to the Johannis hut; there is a glacier route alternative. The trail climbs steeply with views growing in splendour as you gain the Zopetscharte (2958m), a rocky col below the Zopetspitze, and with a vista sparkling with glacier and snowpeak. Fixed cables aid the descent in places, and it is important to be wary of dislodging stones onto parties below - the rock is very friable here. Over boulder slopes, then across the Timmelbach stream, over a bluff then round to the Eissee hut. If you've sufficient energy left after having booked a bed for the night, it might be worth wandering upvalley to visit the Eissee tarn at the head of the valley.

The next stage is slightly longer and leads to the Bonn-Matreier hut (2750m) located under the Sailkopf to the south-east of the Eissee hut. Once again the route, whilst narrow in places, is adequately marked, and despite a short, sharp uphill climb and a steep descent through a stony gully that provide the day with their moments of entertainment, there are no undue difficulties to face, although the very steep grass slopes can be dangerous when wet. Once at the hut, set theatrically, as Cecil Davies described it "on a fine spur, as on a stage, with neighbouring rock spurs as wings and a backdrop of picturesquely jagged peaks," you may be tempted to climb the easy Sailkopf (3209m) for the magnificent panorama its summit affords. The Grossglockner shines its icy spire off to the north-east, and it is easy to understand how Austria's highest has gained a reputation for being one of the most elegant of all Alpine peaks.

On stage five the *höhenweg* heads east at first across the 2884 metre Galtenscharte, a crossing marked *nur für Geubte*, which means 'only for the experienced'. Difficulties arise on the descent from the scharte on slopes of steep, loose shale which is made dangerous when wet or if covered with late-spring snow. Before setting out on this stage it is advisable to consult the guardian at Bonn-Matreier as to current conditions. Once over the scharte the way swings north to gain the smaller Badener hut (2608m), which is more easily reached by a trail up the glen of the Frossnitzbach, a glen that drains not into the Virgental, but directly into the main Tauerntal below Gruben.

The Badener hut stands just below the Frossnitzkees glacier south-east of the Grossvenediger, and the trail to the privately-owned Venediger Haus in the hamlet of Innergschlöss provides one of the best views of this great ice-bound mountain so far achieved. It's not a long stage by any means, and it would be perfectly feasible to continue to Matreier Tauernhaus and catch the bus from there down to Matrei in order to conclude the tour the same day. But unless the demands of time or weather dictate thus, it would be far preferable to spend a full day wandering the trail to the Venediger Haus and linger wherever the mood suggests in order to squeeze the maximum enjoyment from this handsome massif. It's a day of tremendous vistas of glacier and icefall, of tarns and low-lying meadows that contrast with lofty snows and wave-like peaks. A day full of mountain beauty and a worthy one on which to end the Venediger Höhenweg.

If, however, you still have time for more, it would be worth heading west upvalley to where the Alte and Neue Prager huts (one at 2489m, the other at 2796m) provide opportunities for an ascent of the Grossvenediger itself, albeit with ice-axe and rope, and some fine glacier excursions for those experienced in travel over crevassed icefields. Even without claiming summits (and most are reached without major difficulty) there are other huts to be visited by various glacier routes, including the Defregger Haus south of the Venediger and already mentioned along the *höhenweg*, and the Kürsinger hut on the north side of the crest, a hut normally reached via the Obersulzbachtal which drains into the Salzach downstream of Krimml.

VENEDIGER HÖHENWEG - ROUTE SUMMARY

Day 1: Ströden - Stoanalm - Essener-Rostocker Hut

Day 2: Essener-Rostocker Hut - Türmljoch - Johannis Hut (or Defregger Haus)

Day 3: Johannis Hut (or Defregger Haus) - Zopetscharte - Eissee Hut

Day 4: Eissee Hut - Bonn-Matreier Hut (Sailkopf - optional)

Day 5: Bonn-Matreier Hut - Galtenscharte - Badener Hut

Day 6: Badener Hut - Venediger Haus/Innergschlöss

Day 7: Venediger Haus - Matreier Tauernhaus - Matrei (by bus)

✳   ✳   ✳

The Granatspitze Group

This group acts as a hinge linking the Venediger and Glockner ranges east of the Felbertauern tunnel. Basically the mountains congregate on or near a north-south ridge system which rises above Mittersill and descends below Matrei-in-Osttirol, forming an effective divide between the valleys of the Felbertal and Stubachtal on the north side of the main crest, and the Tauerntal and Dorfer/Kalser Tals on the south side. There is much less ice covering these peaks than those of the neighbouring districts, and but few short, steep tributary glens. A handful of tarns cluster in high corries, and just five Alpenverein huts are strung along the mountain flanks to facilitate walking or climbing expeditions. Of these the St Pöltner and Grünsee huts are linked by the St Pöltener Ostweg which, with other trails, makes an exploration of three tarns under the Hochgasser-Riegelkogel ridge a highly recommended outing. The first of these huts occupies the rather bleak pass of Felber Tauern and is gained from the north, from the roadhead in the Felbertal reached from Mittersill; the second hut is approached via Matreier Tauernhaus on the south side of the crest.

The St Pöltener Ostweg continues eastward (as its name suggests) from the Grünsee hut and makes a link with the simple, twelve-bedded Karl-Fürst hut, while the St Pöltener Westweg goes from the St Pöltner hut round the mid height flank of the Gschlösstal to the Neue Prager hut and, eventually, joins the Venediger Höhenweg.

On the eastern side of the Granatspitze ridge system the large and busy Rudolfs hut sits on the shores of the Weissee, the surrounding landscape somewhat tamed by cables - one of which comes up directly from the Sulzbachtal to the hut itself, another being a chairlift rising towards the main ridge. The route of the St Pöltener Ostweg comes down to the Weissee from the Karl-Fürst hut, having edged the glacier hanging between the Sonnblick and Granatspitze - the latter mountain lending its name to the whole group, despite the fact that several others are higher than its 3086 metre summit. The Rudolfs hut (2315m) was taken over in 1979 as the Austrian Alpine Club's mountain training centre (*Alpinzentrum*), as a result of which it is heavily booked and organized to the extent that the more relaxed atmosphere enjoyed at many other huts may be missing.

Above the hut to the south a crossing of the ridge at the Kalser Tauern east of the Granatspitze leads to several possible routes. One of these descends to the head of the Dorfer Tal, while another remains high and forges a way along the slopes of the Grosse Muntanitz (3232m; highest of the Granatspitze group) to the Sudetendeutsche hut. While this is the last of the five Alpenverein huts here, mention should also be made of the privately-owned Kals-Matreier Törlhaus built in a saddle midway between Kals-am-Grossglockner in the Kalser Tal, and Matrei in the Tauerntal - "the prettiest pass I ever saw" according to Tuckett in 1866. This hut is extremely busy by day since it is so readily accessible by chairlift from both Kals and Matrei, and an easy, almost-level walk publicised locally as the Europa Panoramaweg leads past the door. On a fine summer's day hundreds of tourists wander this broad but scenically spectacular trail which winds between the two chairlift stations and gives, so the publicity has it, views of no less than sixty-three 3000 metre peaks. On the occasion that I walked it every summit wore a beret of cloud!

Perhaps the best walk here, however, is that of the Sudetendeutscher Höhenweg which heads north from the Kals-Matreier Törlhaus along the ridge with the Grossglockner seen across the valley to the east, and the Venediger group to the west. This ridge-walk edges a series of rocky summits over 2500 metres, is safeguarded with fixed rope in places and leads eventually to the hut after which it is named. From here the ascent of the Kleiner Muntanitz is recommended; the Grosse Muntanitz too, but for walkers only with a high standard of scrambling experience.

The Glockner Group

Containing Austria's highest, and one of its most distinctive, mountains, the Glockner group packs a relatively small area with high peaks and a mass of ice and snow. On the eastern side of the Grossglockner itself the Pasterzenkees is the longest glacier in the Eastern Alps. Spawned in a cirque of mountains formed by the ridges of Eiskögele, Johannisberg and the Hohe Riffel, each one of which is more than 3300 metres high, this great ice-sheet forces its way down valley below the walls of the Grossglockner towards the head of the Mölltal. The Möll and its upper tributary of the Leitertal forms part of the group's boundary. That boundary continues on the south side of the Grossglockner over the Peischlachtörl and down to Kals, a small resort that rivals Heiligenblut as starting point for climbs on the highest peaks. The boundary now pushes north up the Dorfer Tal to its head where the Kalser Tauern acts as a bridge between the Granatspitze and Glockner groups. On the northern side of that high ridge the Glockner's outline continues down the Stubachtal to the Salzach at Uttendorf. The Salzach, or Pinzgau valley, forms the northern limit of the group stretching eastward past Zell am See to Taxenbach. From there it heads south through the Raurisertal to Wörth, then south-west along the Seidlwinkeltal. The 2626 metre Hochtor on the high watershed crest carries not only the arbitrary boundary of the Glockner group, but also the provincial border (Salzburg to the north, Carinthia to the south) and the outline of the national park. The Grossglockner-Hochalpenstrasse tunnels beneath the Hochtor and traces the eastern boundary of the group as it spirals down to the Mölltal at Heiligenblut.

So much for the extent of the Glockner group in bald terms. But that unadorned nomenclature says nothing of the delights to be found there; the beautiful green valleys with their flowering pastures, neat haybarns and gleaming white villages whose church spires match in elegance the graceful spire of the Grossglockner - "no true mountaineer can behold that beautiful peak without longing to attain its summit" (John Ball). The mountains have a freshness about them, a pristine glacial flourish on every side that creates a misleading impression of inaccessibility. In truth there's much that can be achieved here by mountaineers of fairly modest ability - although there are, of course, routes of some severity too, including the north faces of the Grossglockner and Eiskögele first climbed by Willo Welzenbach in 1926. The skier has also been catered for with a concentration of cableways on the handsome Kitzsteinhorn overlooking Kaprun and the large dammed lakes that lie between that mountain and the Grosse Wiesbachhorn.

But once again it is the walker for whom this book is written, and it is the walker of pastoral alps, lonely passes and sun-bright valleys who will find plenty to his taste here, although it must be admitted that solitude is likely to be in short supply during the best weeks of high summer. Where to stay? Much depends on your mode of transport and ambition, but most valleys have their small resort villages that will provide a clean bed and a menu full of temptation. If you want to nibble at the outer edges of the district try Zell am See if you have transport and plan to concentrate on the northern glens. Avoid anywhere along the Hochalpenstrasse unless traffic doesn't bother you. Kals-am-Grossglockner and neighbouring Grossdorf provide a variety of walking options and scenic locations on the south side, while a score or more huts (private and Alpenverein-owned) provide closer contact with the mountain heartland.

Each of the northern glens has its walking routes edging up towards the watershed crest, and others that stray from one glen to the next across the intervening ridge spurs, thus creating opportunities for long day circuits and multi-day traverses that journey from hut to hut without actually treading ice. The southern valleys are no less welcoming to the walker, for they too have their valley trails and cross-ridge footpaths and no shortage of mountain huts. In some ways the southern side is preferable to the north, for here the big-mountain views are more profound, and the valleys less developed than their northern counterparts. But the north flank has a wider choice of routes.

A multi-day hut-hopping tour which crosses the range from north to south makes for an exhilerating holiday, and displays some remarkable mountain scenery. It begins south of Zell am See, where the Kaprun hydro scheme has provided access to what was formerly wild and remote country. From a high, lake-trapped region the way heads south-west to the Rudolfs hut and crosses the main crest at the Kalser Tauern, then wanders south through the Dorfer Tal before climbing to the Stüdl hut beneath the Grossglockner. From there the tour continues roughly southward into the neighbouring Schober group (still within the Hohe Tauern National Park) before descending eastwards through the Wangenitztal to Mörtschach in the Mölltal. Such a route provides a very fine overview of the major summits of the Hohe Tauern. It illustrates too the threat brought to the high mountain environment by the powerful hydro lobby, and the contrasting, appetizing peace of more remote, undeveloped glens and ridges. The tour is briefly described below, while a route almost identical to this one is treated to more detail in the guidebook, *Walking Austria's Alps Hut to Hut*.

A TOUR OF THE GLOCKNER & SCHOBER GROUPS

Kaprun, south of Zell, would seem a logical place from which to begin such a tour since it is easy of access, and as the first hut may be reached by public transport it would be possible (assuming the timetable works in your favour) to get to the hut on your first day out from home. A summer bus service travels through the Kaprunertal, then grinds its way up the road built to aid construction of two hydro-dams at the Speicher (or Stausee) Wasserfallboden and Speicher Mooserboden; the first at 1672 metres, the second at 2020 metres. A night would then be spent in the Dr Adolf-Schärf-Haus, a hut belonging to the Touristenverein Naturfreunde built at the northern end of the upper lake, with some awe-inspiring scenery to gaze on. An alternative hut, this one owned by the DAV, stands another eight hundred metres above the lake on the flanks of the Untere Fochezkopf in a very lofty, impressive position. The Heinrich-Schwaiger Haus offers spectacular views, but if one were to be teased into staying there, it would be necessary to descend almost to the lake shore next day in order to join the onward route to the Rudolfs hut.

The way to the Rudolfs hut traces the eastern shore of the Mooserboden reservoir, and from its southern end climbs to the 2639 metre Kapruner Törl, a narrow col in the ridge linking the Kleine Eiser and Hohe Riffl. The descent on the western side is steep to begin with, and later winds through a chaos of boulders before gaining the hut, behind which the Hintere Schafbichl provides an extensive panorama. As has already been mentioned, the Rudolfs hut is often crowded with Austrian Alpine Club members taking part in various mountaineering courses run there.

In fair conditions the next, short stage is uncomplicated and offers a complete contrast with regard to landscape values. It begins with a 200 metre climb to the Kalser Tauern on the watershed ridge, from which views are rather limited. Once there a steep and stony descent follows with the long Granatspitze ridge stretching ahead to the right (west), the Glockner ice crest to the left, and the Dorfer Tal cutting a deep furrow between the two. Not far below the col the trail forks. Bear left to the Dorfer See and continue down to the Kalser Tauernhaus, set among larches and pines near the head of the charming Dorfer Tal due west of the Grossglockner; a panoramic view exploits this aspect of the mountain and its glaciers. As the walk will have taken only a morning to achieve, one may be tempted to continue down valley in search of other accommodation, but to do so would only shorten the stage leading on the morrow to the Stüdl hut which, although it demands a longish climb from the hamlet of Taurer, is not so demanding as to make it imperative to reduce its impact.

Next day continue down valley and through the narrow gorge of the Dabaklamm where a trail has been blasted from the rock wall, and which opens just above Taurer. The way then breaks off to the east and rises through the Teischnitztal to gain the Stüdl hut (2801m) on the Fanatscharte, a gap in the south ridge of the Grossglockner; the hut being named after Johann Stüdl of Prague, one of the founding fathers of the Alpenverein who built it in 1868. This hut is on the popular ascent route of the Grossglockner. From it climbers continue over the Kodnitz glacier to the highest hut in the Eastern Alps, the Erzherzog-Johann (3454m) on the Adlersruhe, which gives a short final climb to the summit.

This south side of the Glockner is well set with huts, and our walker has a rich choice to make for on the fifth day. For a very short walk (less than three hours), the Glorer hut is reached by way of the Johann-Stüdl Weg. A longer, more devious route to that same hut leads over the Pfortscharte and visits first the Salm hut (four hours), then heads south to the Glorer hut in a further three hours. Or one could go direct to the Glorer hut and continue from there over the Peischlachtörl and Kesselkees Sattel in order to reach the Elberfelder hut in about eight hours. Much will depend on your onward plans, or weather conditions. A short escape route down from the mountains in inclement weather is possible from one of several points, but given good conditions it would be better to aim at some stage to spend a night at the Elberfelder hut, the first on our tour that is set in the Schober group. After this cross a section of the Gössnitz glacier which should be free of crevasses, to gain the 2732 metre Gössnitzscharte. A few minutes west of this col an emergency bivouac shelter has been provided with room for about eight to sleep in. Once over the scharte follow the Elberfelder Weg down to the Lienzer hut, an Austrian Alpine Club hut dating from 1892 and standing among pastures flush with alpenroses.

This is set at a junction of trails. The Lienzer Höhenweg heads south, as does the Karl-Ech-Weg through the Debanttal to Lienz. The Franz-Keil-Weg winds off to the west and goes by way of the Hochschober hut to St Johann im Walde in the Iseltal, midway between Matrei and Lienz. Another crosses the mountains north-east of the hut and descends through the Gradontal to the Mölltal, while yet a fourth (our route) breaks away eastward, crosses the easy Untere Seescharte and then drops to the Wangenitzsee hut, a modern-looking building on the north shore of a mountain lake. Above the hut to the north rises the easy 3283 metre Petzeck whose summit, according to Baedeker, commands a magnificent view. It may be reached in about two and a half hours by a scramble on a marked way.

The final stage leads down to the Mölltal, but there are two options to consider. The first and most obvious is to descend eastward through the Wangenitztal, but a more sporting route (the Alpinsteig marked on the Kompass Wanderkarte) suggests a bit more excitement with some protected sections of high trail to add spice. This eventually descends to join the alternative trail above Mörtschach.

A TOUR OF THE GLOCKNER & SCHOBER GROUPS - ROUTE SUMMARY

Day 1:   Kaprun - Dr Adolf-Schärf-Haus (Berghaus Mooserboden) (by bus)

Day 2:   Dr Adolf-Schärf-Haus - Kapruner Törl - Rudolfs Hut

Day 3:   Rudolfs Hut - Kalser Tauern - Kalser Tauernhaus

Day 4:   Kalser Tauernhaus - Dabaklamm - Taurer - Stüdl Hut

Day 5:   Stüdl Hut - Medlscharte - Glorer Hut

or:	Stüdl Hut - Pfortscharte - Salm Hut - Glorer Hut
Day 6:	Glorer Hut - Peischlachtörl - Kesselkees Sattel - Elberfelder Hut
Day 7:	Elberfelder Hut - Gössnitzscharte - Lienzer Hut
Day 8:	Lienzer Hut - Untere Seescharte - Wangenitzsee Hut - (Petzeck - optional)
or:	Lienzer Hut - Lienzer Höhenweg/Karl-Ech-Weg - Lienz
or:	Lienzer Hut - Hochschober Hut - St Johann im Walde
Day 9:	Wangenitzsee Hut - Wangenitztal - Mörtschach

It has to be said that several of the stages outlined above are very short and could be combined in order for strong walkers to reduce the overall length of the tour to about a week. However, as has been proclaimed elsewhere in this book, the mountain connoisseur will always find plenty of ways to fill his day, and it is invariably more rewarding to take longer over a multi-day route than to hurry - unless the weather dictates otherwise, that is.

Using part of this north-south tour as the stimulus for exploration of the Glockner group, the map shows possibilities for creating a full circular tour by straying further east into the Goldberg group on the far side of the Hochalpenstrasse. Though I have neither made such a tour personally, nor spoken to anyone who has, I've seen enough of the district to believe that dreams of a circuit could be turned into reality. Others with imagination may wish to work out such a route for themselves.

＊　　＊　　＊

THE NIEDERE TAUERN

The great band of mountains carried through south-central Austria by the Hohe Tauern continues eastward as the Niedere Tauern, a largely-unspoiled region that stretches for about 120 kilometres, and varies in breadth of between thirty and fifty kilometres from north to south. But while the Hohe Tauern displays a bounty of snow and ice and many of its peaks rise well above 3000 metres, the Niedere Tauern range has no glaciers, its mountains are mostly bare and craggy and the highest of its summits, the Hochgolling, climbed as long ago as 1791, is just 2863 metres high.

Be that as it may, as we have discovered elsewhere the modest altitude attained by some peaks is not necessarily to their disadvantage, for landscape appeal relies on more than a simple spot height, and the Niedere Tauern has charm of its own in no small measure - as that great Victorian pioneeer John Ball was quick to point out:

"The scenery of the interior valleys of this part of the range [the Hochgolling district] is of a very wild and somewhat savage character. They divide into numerous short branches, mere recesses in the mountains, in each of which a small tarn is usually found, while peaks of dark and menacing aspect rise above them with extreme steepness. The general effect more resembles that of the valleys of the Northern Carpathians than any scenery familiar to the traveller in Switzerland or Tyrol."

Four separate districts, or groups, make up the Niedere Tauern, in keeping with the Austrian custom of naming a mountain area after a nearby town, valley or river. Naming from west to east these are the Radstädter Tauern, which extends from the Murtörl to the Tauern Pass; the Schladminger Tauern which has the highest peaks and a number of very attractive lakes; then the remote Wölzer Tauern whose mountains are mostly grass-covered; and lastly the Rottenmanner Tauern outlined by a triangle of major valleys whose eastern limit is marked by St Michael, about ten kilometres from Leoben.

The Enns river valley separates the Radstädter and Schladminger districts from the bristling white crags of the Dachstein, and the road and railway that exploit that valley provide easy access to the northern edge. Few roads successfully traverse the range from north to south, although the Salzburg-Klagenfurt autobahn crosses through the central Radstädter district with a six kilometre tunnel boring through the mountains at its highest point, and just to the east of this the old main road from Radstädt also crosses via the Tauern Pass (with its unlovely ski resort of Obertauern) to the Murtal, the valley which outlines the southern extent of the whole Niedere Tauern range. A number of parallel valleys and lesser glens penetrate the southern flanks of the mountains directly from the Murtal; fewer do so on the northern side from the Enns valley.

As for mountain huts, the Alpenverein's very useful 'green book' lists eleven huts and inns for the Radstädter, eighteen for the Schladminger, and a total of just ten for the combined Wölzer and Rottenmanner Tauern groups. On the Tauern Pass on the edge of both the Radstädter and Schladminger districts, the large DAV-Haus Obertauern provides ready access to both regions. Convenient though it may be (it can be reached by bus or private vehicle) the surroundings leave much to be desired, although the trails that disappear into the neighbouring mountains soon lose the eyesore of ski pistes and cableways. By general consensus the best walking and the finest mountain landscapes are to be found in the Schladminger district where a choice of trails traverse the range from north to south, although naturally enough there is good walking to be experienced in all regions, and there's a high-level route (the Tauernhöhenweg) which traverses the main range from west to east.

The Schladminger Tauern has a very special flavour; qualities exist here that have been driven from the mainstream Alpine areas further west, where development in one form or another has destroyed any real concept of wilderness. Apart from the outer edges much of the central arc retains that sense of tranquillity hinted at by John Ball long ago when he was preparing his famous series of guidebooks. Among his "peaks of dark and menacing aspect" the district contains more than two hundred and thirty summits in excess of 2000 metres, in an area of some 500 square kilometres of wild and largely undeveloped country. Forests clothe the valleys and lower hillsides. Above tree-level the upper slopes are often grass-covered with rocky crags bursting through. There are more than three hundred tarns and lakes, many of them in the spectacular basin of the Klafferkessel, and countless waterfalls that add a romance to the glens and hillsides. It is just this country that we will explore on a short hut to hut tour beginning at Obertauern.

Hut to Hut in the Schladminger Tauern

Heading roughly eastward the route goes up to the Austrian Alpine Club's Seekarhaus, and then makes for the Klammlscharte, a pass which offers an opportunity for a diversion to the easy Sonntagkarhöhe (2245m), before continuing over a further series of cols, including Ahkarscharte, Znachsattel and Preuneggsattel on the way to the Ignaz-Mattis hut. Built in 1910 overlooking the Untere Giglach See it has twice been enlarged until it can now accommodate something like eighty people. Commenting on the first extension Philip Tallantire wrote (in *Felix Austria Vol III - Niederen & Hohen Tauern*) "Anyone who...survived a night in the old matratzenlager at the height of the busy season cannot but welcome the change as overdue!" During the day it is often very busy since a road from Schladming leads to within an hour and a half's walk of the hut, but it fulfils an important role for wanderers following the Tauernhöhenweg trail.

With several huts along the route to the east the next stage could end either at the Keinprecht, Landwirsee or the Golling hut, depending on fitness, weather, time available and general ambition. We shall assume that the Landwirsee hut suits our purpose, for this allows plenty of time to enjoy some spectacular scenery on the way, as well as a decent refreshment stop at the Keinprecht hut during the morning.

The route from Ignaz-Mattis crosses the Rotmandlscharte at 2340 metres, but on a clear-weather day none should stride over the nearby Rotmandlspitze, which is just over a hundred metres higher, without allowing lots of time to absorb its outlook, for although it's an insignificant peak in appearance, what it offers is a truly magnificent panorama with the Dachstein group to the north looking especially fine, and with the great shark's fin of the Hochgolling skimming over intermediate ridges to the east. Some eight hundred metres below to the left lies the Duisitzsee and another private hut which is not, however, visited on this tour. Instead we descend steeply to the Keinprecht hut via the Krugeckscharte.

The Keinprecht hut is a modest, shingle-walled building formerly used by miners, set in a stony corrie backed by impressive cliffs, and with a junction of trails nearby. One route descends northward to Neualm and Schladming; another crosses the Liegnitzhöhe between Graunock and Rotsandspitze, and heads south to Tamsweg in the Murtal. The Tauernhöhenweg, however, makes a horseshoe curve round the 2396 metre Pietrach and crosses another easy col (the Trockenbrotscharte) to gain the Landwirsee hut above two small tarns.

The next stage across the Gollingscharte (2326m) to the Golling hut is a morning's walk, but from the col an hour's diversion to the summit of Hochgolling by a marked route (moderate scrambling) is strongly recommended, while the fourth stage leads through the amazing Klafferkessel on the way to the Preintaler hut, making what is arguably the finest walk in the district. The Golling hut is one of a trio of such huts in the area owned by the Preintaler mountaineering club (Alpein Gesellschaft Preintaler); others being the Hans-Wödl and Preintaler itself. (Members of the Austrian Alpine Club are awarded the same special rates as at Alpenverein huts.) It stands near the head of the steep-sided Untertal and is dominated by the north face of Hochgolling and the impressive natural amphitheatre of Gollingwinkel - an oasis of green meadows blocked by abrupt, soaring walls of rock. From here to the Preintaler hut involves a steep climb of nearly a thousand metres to the summit of the Greifenberg (2618m), a mountain which provides not only a fine outlook to a series of rugged towering peaks, folding ridges and valleys of the surrounding Schladminger Tauern, but more especially a stunning view of the Klafferkessel, the major landscape feature of the range.

This huge rocky cauldron, formed out of a pair of merging corries, measures nearly two kilometres across, and is up to three hundred metres deep - "but tipped towards the north, as if a gigantic crucible were being emptied into the Untertal far away below." (Cecil Davies) This cauldron contains numerous tarns and pools and jutting towers, and in poor visibility with a coverlet of snow, could be treacherous to manoeuvre a way through. Under normal summer conditions, however, the route should be clearly marked and obvious. The way into the Klafferkessel from the Greifenberg begins with a steep scramble aided by fixed rope, followed by a wild meandering course among curious hills and hollows, round exposed boulders and the mirror-like tarns, until the upright block of the Greifenstein marks an exit to the Preintaler hut, about two kilometres away and some 600 metres below.

The final mountain stage of this tour leads to the Hans-Wödl hut along the Robert Höfer Steig, a well-marked trail constructed by the Preintaler club in order to connect these two huts. The way goes up to the Neualmscharte from where a short detour takes you to the Kleine Wildstelle off to the right (the nearby Hoch Wildstelle is said to reward with better views even than those from the Hochgolling), then northward to the Obersee and views to the Dachstein, and finally down to the shores of the Hüttensee and the Hans-Wödl hut, set amid glorious mountain scenery. All that is needed next day is to wander steeply down to the Bodensee, then follow the Seewigtal out to Aich in the Enns valley east of Schladming.

HUT TO HUT IN THE SCHLADMINGER TAUERN - ROUTE SUMMARY

Day 1: Obertauern/Seekarhaus - Klammlscharte - Ahkarscharte - Znachsattel - Preuneggsattel - Ignaz-Mattis Hut

Day 2: Ignaz-Mattis Hut - Rotmandlscharte - Rotmandlspitze - Keinprecht Hut - Trockenbrotscharte - Landwirsee Hut

Day 3: Landwirsee Hut - Gollingscharte - Hochgolling - Golling Hut

Day 4: Golling Hut - Greifenberg - Klafferkessel - Preintaler Hut

Day 5: Preintaler Hut - Neualmscharte - Hans-Wödl Hut

Day 6: Hans-Wödl Hut - Bodensee - Aich

✳   ✳   ✳

THE GAILTAL & CARNIC ALPS

South of the River Drau which effectively draws a line under the influence of the Hohe Tauern, projecting ridge systems carry outliers of the main Dolomite range trespassing out of Italy. The mountains here are quite different to those of the Hohe Tauern, for the rock is limestone, there are no glaciers nor fields of permanent snow, and an entirely different atmosphere prevails in the warm, sunny valleys.

The Gailtal Alps, including the Lienzer Dolomites

From the important town of Lienz, set in a wide basin where the Isel joins the Drau, a clear view is afforded across the rooftops to the rugged outline of the Lienzer Dolomites whose presence creates a dramatic backdrop to the town. This is the north-western part of the so-called Gailtal Alps, an attractive region wedged between the valleys of the Drau and the Gail, the latter valley forming a divide between the Gailtal Alps and Carnic Alps. Though not high by standards set further west (the highest is the Grosse Sandspitze; 2772m), there's plenty of scope for rock climbers, scramblers and mountain walkers, as well as an attractive and prolific alpine flora to enjoy. For a relatively small area huts are plentiful, one of which is named after E.T. Compton, the London-born artist who went off to live in Austria in the latter half of the nineteenth century and there concentrated his career on mountain painting - his watercolours and drawings were used to illustrate numerous books and articles by the leading climbers of the day.

Perhaps the best and most rewarding of walks in these mountains is the Drei Törl Weg which links the Lienzer Dolomiten, Karlsbader and Hochstadel huts in a short traverse. A strong walker could complete the route in a single day, but better by far is it to give two days to the walk with time to absorb the scenery. The walk begins at the privately-owned Lienzer Dolomiten hut, reached by minibus from Lienz railway station via the popular Tristacher See. The way then follows the Rudl-Eller Weg climbing over the Auerlingköpfl to the base of the 2614 metre Laserzwand. From this point the trail rises steeply with the aid of fixed cables, then a scree slog to the Zellinscharte, from which an exposed traverse leads to the Karlsbader hut, set on a rocky shelf beside the little Laserz tarn, and with Lienz a surprising sixteen hundred metres below.

The first *törl* (gateway) of the route takes its name from the Laserz tarn, and is gained by a two hundred and fifty metre climb from the Karlsbader hut. Through this pass the way then plunges over screes towards the Lavanter Alm, but then climbs once more to reach the Kuhleiten Törl, carpeted with grass amid savage rock walls. Next is the Baumgartentörl, followed by an exposed ridge-walk with an option of continuing to the summit of the Hochstadel which gives a broad panorama and a longer alternative than the standard route down the east side of the peak to the Hochstadel Haus, owned by the Austrian Touring Club (ÖTK). From this hut more choices are available for the descent to the railway halt of Nikolsdorf; the standard trail is longer but considerably easier than the 'sporting' option of the so-called Zabarot Steig, which has a series of wooden ladders to aid the descent.

The Carnic Alps & Karawanken

The Gailtal is a broad, flat-bottomed valley tilted gently towards the south-east. The Gailtal Alps make a wall to the north, the ragged Carnic Alps (Karnische Alpen) to the south. The Carnic Alps rise out of a dark line of forest, their summit crags forming a border with Italy, but at the eastern end that Italian border is exchanged for Slovenia where the Carnic Alps blend into the Karawanken opposite the Julian Alps. Villach guards the valley's eastern end, and it is from here that a branch line eases along the Gailtal via Arnoldstein and Hermagor as far as Kötschach. A single, relatively minor, but good road runs the length of the valley, and at either end joins main routes that cross south out of Austria. West of Arnoldstein two further road passes cross the mountains into Italy: the Plöckenpass (Passo di Monte Croce; 1360m) and the Nassfeldpass (Passo di Pramollo; 1530m).

Hermagor is as good a place as any on which to base a walking holiday, but since public transport is rather sparce walkers would either do better with their own vehicle (if day walks are the plan), or make a hut to hut tour and remain as long as possible along that mountain wall. The Austrian Alpine Club has no less than ten huts dotted along the north slope of the Carnic Alps, while a further half-dozen privately-owned huts or inns extend the opportunities for a walking tour.

The western part of the range above what is known as the Lesachtal is the least frequented, and it is here that the Hohe Warte (2780m), the highest of the region's mountains, makes a large dark block on the frontier crest near the Plöckenpass. The Eduard-Pichl hut nestles below the neighbouring Seekopf and is a convenient base for climbs on this and other nearby peaks, while a trail cuts south from the hut, crosses the ridge and drops on the Italian side to the Marinclli hut. Other trails meander east to the Plöckenpass, and west from one hut to another all the way to the Pustertal which carries the Drau across the far end of the Carnic chain.

Between the Plöckenpass and Nassfeldpass more fine limestone summits punctuate the frontier crest. Reminiscent of the better-known Dolomites, these craggy white peaks burst out of soft, undulating pastures. A few lonely farms dot these pastures; some offer refreshment to passing walkers, or a mattress in an attic for an overnight stay. Several peaks are easily accessible to experienced mountain walkers. From them long views show the Dolomites in one direction, the Julian Alps in the other.

At the Nassfeldpass the small ski resort of Sonnenalpe Nassfeld provides accommodation for walkers in summer (reached by one bus a day from Hermagor). The few ski tows are soon left behind and there are fine ridge-walks to be had in the neighbourhood; peaks to win, pastures to explore, a few tarns to laze by - all in an unfussed setting. Bordering the pass on its eastern side the Gartnerkofel is known for its flora, including the rare, deep-blue bellflower *Wulfenia Carinthiaca*, while below the mountain on the Gailtal flank, the mountainside has been split by the deep shaft of the Garnitzenklamm which spills out at Mödendorf near Hermagor.

The long traverse route of the Karnischer Höhenweg (Carnic High Route) continues to dodge back and forth from one side of the border to the other and winds on as far as St Andrä in the Gallitztal, south-west of Arnoldstein. Beyond this the Carnic Alps blend into the Karawanken which, since 1919, has marked the border between Austria and Slovenia (formerly part of Yugoslavia). Here the mountains fall away steeply towards the Drau on the northern side, but many of the principal peaks offer comparatively easy ways to their summits. The highest is the Hochstuhl at a modest 2238 metres. There are, of course, demanding lines for rock climbers to play on, but for our mountain walker it is the ridge-routes that will appeal most. The Austrian Alpine Club has but two huts, the Berta and Klagenfurter, but these are too far from each other to make a possible linking walk. There are, however, more huts on the Slovenian side of the border for anyone considering an exploration of the south side of the range.

THE EASTERN AUSTRIAN ALPS

Location:
East and south-east of the Zillertal Alps. The Venediger group of the Hohe Tauern continues the main block of the Zillertal Alps and blends with the Granatspitze which forms a linchpin with the Glockner massif. The Niedere Tauern range lies roughly north-east of the Hohe Tauern, while the Gailtal Alps, Carnic Alps and Karawanken follow the southern border of Austria across the head of Italy and Slovenia.

Principal valleys:
The Pinzgau in the north, and the Tauerntal and Mölltal cutting south, are the main valleys of the Hohe Tauern. In the Niedere Tauern these are the Ennstal and Murtal. The Drau and Gail are the principal valleys of the Gailtal and Carnic Alps. The Drau also drains the north flank of the Karawanken.

Principal peaks:
Grossglockner (3798m), Grossvenediger (3674m) and Grosse Muntanitz (3232m) in the Hohe Tauern; Hochgolling (2863m) in the Niedere Tauern; Grosse Sandspitze (2772m) in the Gailtal Alps; Hohe Warte (2780m) in the Carnic Alps; and Hochstuhl (2238m) in the Karawanken.

Centres:
Zell am See, Mittersill, Matrei-in-Osttirol, Kals-am-Grossglockner and Heiligenblut for the Hohe Tauern; Schladming or Radstadt in the Niedere Tauern; Lienz and Hermagor for the Gailtal Alps; Hermagor again for the Carnic Alps.

Huts:
Numerous huts in all regions, mostly (but not exclusively) owned by the Austrian Alpine Club. Plenty of privately-owned huts and mountain inns too.

Access:
Good roads criss-cross the region, including the heavily-used Grossglockner-Hochalpenstrasse. There are main-line and branch-line railways in many areas, and useful bus services also. Zell-am-See is a good place to aim for on the north side of the district, with access routes to most parts.

Maps:
All areas are covered at a scale of 1:50,000 by both Kompass Wanderkarte and Freytag Berndt. The Hohe and Niedere Tauern have no less than seven sheets at 1:25,000 published by the Austrian Alpenverein.

Guidebooks:
Mountain Walking in Austria by Cecil Davies (Cicerone Press) provides details of selected walks in all areas except the Gailtal Alps, Carnic Alps and Karawanken.
Walking Austria's Alps Hut to Hut by Jonathan Hurdle (Cordee/The Mountaineers) describes three multi-day tours in the Hohe Tauern and neighbouring mountains.
Hut Hopping in the Austrian Alps by William E. Reifsnyder (Sierra Club) offers a tour in the Schladminger Tauern.

Other reading:
The Mountains of Europe by Kev Reynolds (Oxford Illustrated Press, 1990). In a chapter on Austria's mountains by Cecil Davies, the Hohe and Niedere Tauern are highlighted.
Walking & Climbing in the Alps by Stefano Ardito (Swan Hill Press, 1995) has a chapter describing an 8-day route across the Hohe Tauern.
The Outdoor Traveler's Guide to the Alps by Marcia R. Lieberman (Stewart, Tabori & Chang, New York) contains some interesting, if brief, information.

The Grutten hut, backed by the walls of Ellmauer Halt

17: THE NORTHERN LIMESTONE ALPS

Austria's numerous mountain groups comprise two roughly parallel chains. Those already described that trace the southern borders and continue to spread through the south-central part of the country are known as the Hochgebirge, while those of the northern chain are the Mittelgebirge - relatively small, saw-tooth peaks of rugged limestone, many of which are shared with Bavaria. These are the fabled Kalkalpen, or Northern Limestone Alps.

With Bludenz in the west and Vienna in the east, the Mittelgebirge form an almost continuous, unbroken chain with but one summit (the Parseierspitze in the Lechtal Alps) topping 3000 metres. The western portion, including the Bavarian Alps, is largely contained in a rectangular block with Munich to the north and the Inn river valley to the south; the eastern section extending south of the Salzburg-Vienna autobahn, with the Enns valley providing an effective buffer against other mountain districts represented within these pages by the Niedere Tauern.

At either end of the chain the mountains are green and wooded, but in between the vast majority bare the hallmarks of other typical limestone ranges; that is, steep cliffs rising to sharply outlined summits linked one with another by airy ridges. There are few permanent snowfields and even fewer glaciers; the flora is rich and varied, lakes and tarns numerous, and huts evenly spaced. Communications are, in general, good, and the whole area is well patronized by local Austrian and German walkers and climbers.

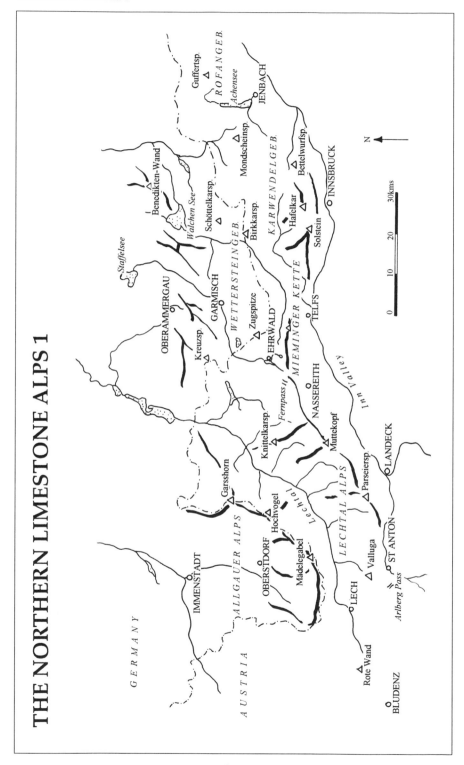

THE NORTHERN LIMESTONE ALPS 1

THE NORTHERN LIMESTONE ALPS 11

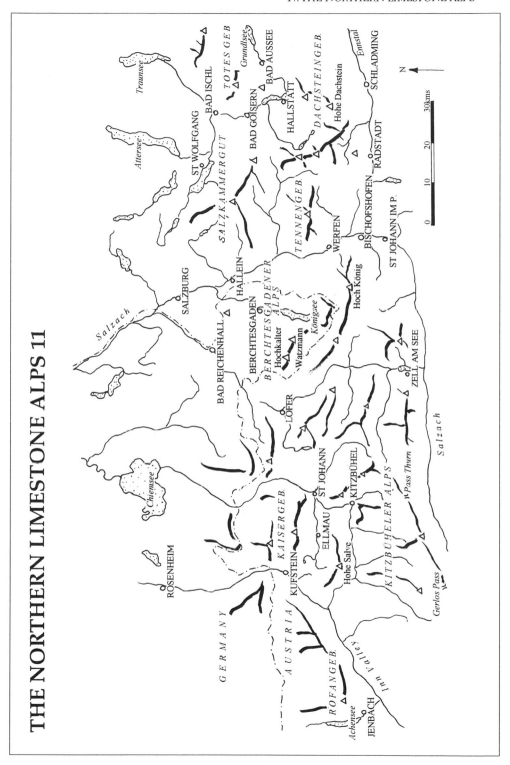

Listing from west to east the Northern Limestone Alps consist of the Allgäuer and Lechtal Alps, the two separated by the long Lechtal valley which gives the latter group its name. Then comes the Wettersteingebirge, followed by the Karwendelgebirge, the last-named rising so dramatically behind Innsbruck as to dominate much of the town's character. The Rofangebirge, also known as the Brandenberger Alps, continues the line north-eastward along the international border as far as the compact Kaisergebirge, which is located entirely within the Austrian Tirol to the east of Kufstein. The Berchtesgadener Alps are next, with the beautiful fjord-like Königsee rippling below the walls of the Steinernes Meer. East of the Salzach river come the Tennengebirge and Dachstein groups, the first soaring over Werfen, the second wedged between the Ennstal and the southern Salzkammergut lake district. Then comes the Totes Gebirge to the east of Bad Ischl, followed by the Ennstaler Alps, Hochschwab and a series of minor ranges less easily defined which blend into one another and change character as heights decrease; the valleys less crowded but still retaining charm, and walking expeditions concentrating now on rolling, vegetated crests and pastoral hillsides - delightful in themselves, though hardly Alpine in nature - until they fade among the hills of the Wienerwald (Vienna Woods).

Among mountaineers the Northern Limestone Alps are known for their climbing and scrambling potential. In some districts a number of routes have been given permanent protection by means of metal ladders, cables and iron pegs - the so-called *klettersteig* (climbing paths) which are the equivalent of the *via ferrata* found in the Italian Dolomites. Many of these routes have been so skilfully protected that even non-climbers are able to venture with a degree of safety on walls that were hitherto the preserve only of those activists capable of climbing grades of III, IV or even V. However, where mention of any *klettersteig* is made in this book, our mountain walker should not be tempted unless he has considerable experience of the Alps, has no trouble with vertigo and is confident of tackling vertical rock faces often with a great deal of breathtaking exposure beneath the heels. The other qualification is that the walker be equipped with, and know how to use, a harness, sling and karabiner as a safeguard against a slip or a fall. *Klettersteig, Scrambles in the Northern Limestone Alps* (an English translation of Paul Werner's German original) is a guidebook detailing forty-four such routes, with an important introductory section that describes methods of self-protection.

Mention of climbing, scrambling and *klettersteig* routes should not, however, be allowed to distract us from the vast potential for mountain walking of every degree of seriousness that exists along this limestone chain. The scope being enormous, and the chain so long and complex, it is only possible here to provide a small sample in order to build a picture - however incomplete that picture might be. As I pick among the offerings I am aware that a lifetime's activity is hardly sufficient to exhaust all that is available here, any more than it would be in almost any other Alpine district. There is, indeed, something for everyone; gentle valley walks, more strenuous routes to accessible summits, and no shortage of hut tours by which to explore individual groups in some detail. Of the many multi-day hut to hut walks, mention should be made right from the start of the three-week epic Kalkalpen Traverse which traces a meandering line between Bödele, south-east of Bregenz, to St Johann in Tirol near Kufstein - in effect exploring a large part of the chain along the Austro-Bavarian border, and including an opportunity to climb to the summit of the Zugspitze, Germany's highest point at 2963 metres. (See *The Kalkalpen Traverse* by Alan Proctor for stage-by-stage details.) There are also two trans-European long-distance routes that encroach on the Northern Limestone Alps: the E4 which extends from the Pyrenees to the low-lying Neusiedlersee on the Austro-Hungarian border, and E5 stretching from Lindau to the Adriatic.

❈ ❈ ❈

ALLGÄUER ALPS

The German Allgäu district pushes south against the Austrian border east of the Bodensee (Lake Constance), the Allgäuer Alps spilling over into the Tirol as far as the Lechtal. Although definitions change, this mountain group is generally considered to be divided by the Walsertal, the upper part of which is politically Austrian but with road access only from Germany. To the west of the Walsertal lie the Allgäuer Voralpen (the Alpine foothills), while to the east rise the Allgäuer Alps proper. Oberstdorf is the principal base for a walking holiday, a ski resort, spa and market town which claims to be (just) the southernmost town in Germany. Several valleys are easily accessible from it; three of these fan out towards the frontier ridge along which entertaining routes are possible. One of these glens leads to the highest mountain in the district, the Grosser Krottenkopf (2657m), rising among others above the huge Kempter hut.

Not only is the Kempter hut a suitable base for climbs on the Grosser Krottenkopf and nearby Muttlerkopf, walkers' routes follow the frontier crest in both directions. One crosses the ridge into Austria on a four-hour linking trail leading to the Hermann-von-Barth hut (named after the Munich lawyer who put up some severe rock climbs in the late nineteenth century), accessible from Elbigenalp in the Lechtal. But perhaps the finest route leading from the Kempter hut is that of the Heilbronner Weg. This airy ridge walk traces a line along the bare and rocky crest heading south-west to the Waltenberger and Rappensee huts, taking in several summits along the way - including the Mädelegabel, Bockkarkopf and Wilder Mann. Much of the route is straightforward, but there are tricky sections and a protected *klettersteig* to add a touch of excitement.

The Allgäuer Alps are exceedingly well stocked with huts, there being no less than twenty-two provided by the Alpenverein, and around twenty more that are either privately-owned, or built by other alpine clubs. It will be seen then, that there is plenty of scope for making hut to hut tours, as well as single day walks from a valley base to a hut or two, then back down again.

❈ ❈ ❈

LECHTAL ALPS

The Allgäuer district is only marginally better off for huts than the neighbouring Lechtal Alps, whose mountains stretch from the Arlberg to the broad furrow of the Fernpass, with the Stanzer Tal and continuing Inn valley to the south, and the

Lechtal itself to the north. Just to the north of the Stanzer Tal's junction with the Paznauntal rises the Parseierspitze (3040m), highest of all the Northern Limestone Alps, with the Memminger hut below its north face and with a little collection of tarns nearby.

The Lechtal range has a south-west to north-east alignment, with a number of tributary glens nibbling into both flanks to give good routes of approach to various huts and mountain inns. The district has almost 500 peaks in excess of 2000 metres, many of which are attainable by non-technical routes. There are a few small glaciers and many high lakes and tarns. There is no one obvious base, and the best way to enjoy the walking potential is to take to the huts and move on day after day. Such hutting tours are enormously popular, of course, and the Lechtal Alps provide lots of opportunities with routes criss-crossing from north to south and from west to east. Some linking routes between huts, such as the partly-protected Augsburger Höhenweg that makes a direct crossing from the Ansbacher to the Augsburger huts, can prove to be demanding and serious undertakings that should not be attempted by Alpine novices. The Kalkalpen Traverse already mentioned works a route through the range, virtually from one end to the other, in eight stages along a noted high trail, and wandering this route would provide as good a means as any to see the best the district has to offer. The following outline tour is based on that high trail, but it also offers suggestions for alternative routes and a few summits, with lovely views, not only of the Lechtal and Allgäuer Alps, but southward too to the Verwall group and more distant Silvretta.

A LECHTAL HIGH ROUTE

The first stage begins either at St Anton am Arlberg, or at the ski resort of Zürs just north of the Flexen Pass. If the former, then follow a trail north-west up to the Ulmer hut which is unfortunately approached through the Valluga ski area, with the second stage heading east on the way to the Leutkircher hut. The alternative starting place of Zürs gives access in only two and a half hours to the Stuttgarter hut, with the Leutkircher hut a further four hours away across the Erlijoch (2430m). It is also possible to reach the Leutkircher hut direct from St Anton without first going to the Ulmer hut. Once at the Leutkircher it would be worth spending a couple of hours on the ascent of the Stanskogel (2757m) which stands above the hut to the north-east and reveals an unforgettable panorama of the country through which the route continues.

The route of our tour now works an easy way across meadows to the Kaiserjochhaus on a pass backed by steep crags, then makes an eastward traverse over grass initially, then into increasingly rocky country with a steep climb over the Hinterseejoch (2484m) which gives views over both the Hintersee and Vordersee tarns. Below the pass the Theodor-Haas Weg is a high route that leads to the broad Alperschonjoch (2301m). A landscape of wild and barren mountains fills one's field of vision from here; another *joch* is crossed (the Flarsch Joch; 2515m) followed by descent to the Ansbacher hut.

Since the next stage leading to the Memminger hut via the Winterjöchl and Griesslscharte takes about five and a half hours, this is the route adopted by most walkers. However, under good summer conditions fit and experienced mountain walkers/scramblers with no record of vertigo and with an extra day to spare, might wish to consider following instead the challenging Augsburger Höhenweg which goes to the magnificently situated Augsburger hut by way of two passes and a summit almost 3000 metres high: Parseierscharte, Dawinscharte and Dawinkopf (2970m), passing close to the Parseierspitze. This is a full-day epic of between eight and twelve hours that should not be tackled lightly, followed next day by a linking five-hour walk along the Spiehlerweg in order to gain the Memminger hut.

The two European long-distance paths, E4 and E5, converge at the Memminger hut, and the onward route to the DAV's Württemberger Haus is shared with these combined classics for the climb to the Seescharte (2599m). Thereafter E4 and E5 part company. We follow the former while the latter descends to the valley. Our route makes a traverse of an extensive scree-slope, climbs the Grossberg Kopf (2612m) and then scrambles (aided by fixed cables) down to the Württemberger Haus.

At least two possibilities exist for the route to the Hanauer hut; the E4 trail (locally numbered 601) goes first by way of the Gebäudjöchl, Rosskarscharte and Steinkarscharte to the Steinsee hut, while a more direct route (path 627) crosses the Bitterscharte and Gufelsee Joch - with an option of climbing the Kogelseespitze (2647m), an easy summit with very fine views - before wandering down to the Hanauer hut.

Two stages remain on our traverse of the Lechtal Alps, the first of which takes in the summit of the Muttekopf on the way to the hut of the same name in about five hours, the second which descends easily to Imst in the Gurgltal. But should you have time and energy for more it would be feasible to extend the tour by crossing the Scharnitzsattel above the Muttekopf hut, then over the Hahntennjoch to spend a night at the Anhalter hut, and next day descend to Nassereith below the Fernpass. As will have been illustrated, the options for hut to hut tours in the Lechtal Alps are almost limitless.

A LECHTAL HIGH ROUTE - SUMMARY

Day 1:   St Anton am Arlberg - Ulmer Hut (then to Leutkircher Hut)

or: St Anton am Arlberg - Leutkircher Hut

or: Zürs - Stuttgarter Hut - Erlijoch - Leutkircher Hut

Day 2:   Leutkircher Hut - Kaiserjochhaus - Hinterseejoch - Alperschonjoch - Flarsch Joch - Ansbacher Hut

Day 3:   Ansbacher Hut - Winterjöchl - Griesslscharte - Memminger Hut

or: Ansbacher Hut - Augsburger Höhenweg - Augsburger Hut (then via Spiehlerweg to Memminger Hut)

Day 4:   Memminger Hut - Seescharte - Grossberg Kopf - Württemberger Haus

Day 5:   Württemberger Haus - Gabäudjöchl - Rosskarscharte - Steinkarscharte - Steinsee Hut - Hanauer Hut

or: Württemberger Haus - Bitterscharte - Gufelsee Joch - Kogelseespitze - Hanauer Hut

Day 6:   Hanauer Hut - Muttekopf - Muttekopf Hut

Day 7:   Muttekopf Hut - Imst

or: Muttekopf Hut - Scharnitzsattel - Hahnennjoch - Anhalter Hut (then to Nassereith)

WETTERSTEINGEBIRGE & MIEMINGER KETTE

Making a buffer between the Lechtal Alps and the Karwendelgebirge, the comparatively small Wetterstein group spills over both sides of the Austro-German border south of Garmisch-Partenkirchen and includes the Zugspitze, which straddles the border itself and is easily reached by cable-car from both sides. It's a compact district neatly outlined by four major roads that effectively contain it in a square block. The mountains are composed of a particularly hard type of limestone known as wettersteinkalk, and are separated by the lovely alpine meadows of the Ehrwalder Alm from the Mieminger Kette, whose highest summit is the Östliche Griesspitze (2759m), but whose best-known peak is the 2661 metre Hohe Munde overlooking the Inn valley above Telfs. The Inn forms part of the district's southern limit. The Fernpass marks its western extent, the Scharnitz Pass the eastern, while Garmisch-Partenkirchen is the obvious springboard from which to approach the mountains on the northern side.

The Wettersteingebirge holds a number of good rock climbs (the fourteen hundred metre north face of the Hochwanner, for example), while several exciting *klettersteig* routes have been created in both the Wetterstein and Mieminger Kette. For such a small area huts are plentiful and access is not at all complicated.

A west to east crossing from Ehrwald to Leutasch can be made in a single day, while a high route which includes the Zugspitze is also possible (but in two days or so), thanks to conveniently located huts. As the highest German summit, the Zugspitze suffers the indignity of over-zealous mechanisation; a cog railway, cableways, restaurants, souvenir and refreshments stands - even a German post office - and a 'hut' (the Münchner Haus) that was built in 1897 on the very summit. The summit panorama, however, is magnificent and extensive. Far off to the north the Bavarian plain stretches beyond the blue-ridged mountains, while southward a jumble of Tirolean peaks is dashed with snow and glinting glacial pockets.

For *klettersteig* enthusiasts the Zugspitze has its own special appeal with two 'climbing paths' to consider. That which ascends from the Höllentalanger hut on the north-east flank is claimed to be the longest continuous artificially protected route in all the Northern Limestone Alps, while the alternative from the Austrian Touring Club's Wiener-Neustädter hut on the west side, takes advantage of a series of near-vertical ladders used by maintenance engineers at work on cableway pylons. The first route is particularly exciting, and has the added interest of ascent of a small crevassed glacier, the Höllentalferner. There is also, of course, the famous ridge route of the Jubiläumsweg that picks a way along the Höllentalgrat connecting the Zugspitze with the Signalgipfel on the Hochblassen; much of it exposed, some of it protected, but not all, and for experienced, equipped scramblers only. But even if the thought of an exposed *klettersteig* fails to appeal, the walk up to the Höllentalanger hut from Hammersbach is certainly worth tackling for the section through a water-cut gorge (translated as 'the gorge of Hell's valley') with tunnels and galleries bored through the rock, and wild thrashing water thundering everywhere.

In the Mieminger group south of the Zugspitze the handsome Hohe Munde attracts walkers and scramblers alike. Summit views are excellent, and there are several small huts in the neighbourhood that give easy access to the mountain. It also has a little-known *klettersteig* linking the south side of the summit ridge with the Niedere Munde, in the midst of surprisingly wild scenery.

✻   ✻   ✻

KARWENDELGEBIRGE

The view north along the Maria-Theresien-Strasse in Innsbruck, backed by a huge wall of mountains, is one of the most easily identifiable of all Austrian scenes, since it appears with such frequency on postcards, calendars and the covers of chocolate boxes, that it has become hackneyed to a marked degree. Yet despite such familiarity it remains a potent symbol for the old provincial capital of Tirol, and few who love mountains could fail to be drawn to it. Those mountains are, of course, part of the Karwendelgebirge.

These rugged, pale grey mountains run west to east in four roughly parallel chains divided by deep valleys, rucked and folded between the Inn valley to the south and the German border to the north, while a fifth, smaller district (the Soiern group) clusters in a horseshoe of peaks beyond that border in Bavaria itself. The western limit is marked by the Scharnitz Pass and the Isar valley, the eastern by the Achenpass above the turquoise Achensee - the largest lake in Tirol.

Heading north away from Innsbruck these four main ridges are the Solsteinkette (locally known as the Nordkette since it dominates the northern aspect of the town), Bettelwurfkette, Hintere Karwendelkette and the Vordere Karwendelkette. The highest of the many peaks is the Birkkarspitze (2749m) which soars above the Karwendelhaus in the Hintere Karwendelkette and is accessible to walkers and scramblers. Much of the rock is brittle, yet the walls of the Karwendelgebirge were adopted as a training ground for young climbers from Munich and Innsbruck especially, and most notably by Hermann von Barth, from the latter years of the nineteenth century on. The tremendous north face of the Laliedererwand (2615m), for example, was climbed by a rope of four in 1911. Next to this the Laliedererspitze rises directly above the Falken hut in a 700 metre thrust of rock, while other notable peaks are (in no particular order) the Lamsenspitze, Grosse Bettelwurf and the Speckkarspitze.

Of the many possible bases for a walking holiday Scharnitz is perhaps the best general centre, but with some thirty or so huts scattered throughout the district, once again it is the ex-centrist who will get the most out of an exploration by wandering from hut to hut and from one valley to the next. Since the mountain ridges are so severe, and the valleys so deep in between, any attempt at a north-south crossing (or vice-versa) will be handicapped from the start. Valley walks however can be very rewarding in this nature reserve once noted for its abundant wildlife, but there are many summits that can be reached without resort to technical aids, while the Karwendel as a whole has a number of challenging *klettersteig* routes too.

Of all the opportunities for walkers in the area to collect summits, one of the best is in the Soiern district where a group of five, two thousand metre peaks containing a deep lake-filled basin, attracts with a first-class circular route that goes over one summit after another. The hut used as a base for this round, the

Soiernhaus, was built in 1867 on the edge of the Soiernkessel as a royal hunting lodge for Ludwig II, King of Bavaria. It now belongs to the Hochland section of the German Alpine Club, who enlarged it in 1968.

In his *Mountain Walking in Austria* Cecil Davies describes a handful of routes accessible from the Bavarian side of the border, including the round of the Soiern horseshoe, and Paul Werner's *Klettersteig* guide has several protected climbing paths outlined for the Karwendel range. But our walker who has ambitions to drift from hut to hut across the district will find at least two traverse routes to choose from. The Kalkalpen Traverse and trans-European E4 trails pass through, and in Jonathan Hurdle's *Walking Austria's Alps Hut to Hut* yet another possible crossing is described.

HUT TO HUT ACROSS THE KARWENDELGEBIRGE

The standard west to east traverse (if it can be so described) takes three days to walk from Scharnitz to the Achensee, but with an optional extra day used to climb the Birkkarspitze. From Scharnitz the first stage leads to the Karwendelhaus in a little under five hours, and gives an opportunity for those with the time next day to climb the Birkkarspitze and the three peaks of the Ödkarspitze linked by a fine ridge and with good views to add to the day's pleasures.

The Karwendelhaus is tucked against cliffs at 1765 metres, the Lamsenjoch hut at the end of the next stage sits almost two hundred metres higher at the top of the lovely Falzturntal with the Lamsenspitze behind it. It's a seven-hour walk from one to the other, passing the Falken hut and alongside the Lalidererspitze after three hours, then over the easy Hochjoch saddle into the Engtal, and finally crossing the Lamsenjoch overlooking the Falzturntal.

For the last stage about five hours will be needed to reach Pertisau on the Achensee. It's an easy valley walk that visits Gramaialm after about two hours and the Falzturn Alm about an hour after that. Because of the proximity of a road through the valley from Pertisau there are likely to be plenty of others wandering there, but it's a pleasant stroll and a remarkably undemanding end to a low-level traverse of the Karwendel mountains. (Steam trains maintain a link between the Achensee and Jenbach in the Inn valley, where main line connections can be made for Innsbruck.)

HUT TO HUT ACROSS THE KARWENDELGEBIRGE - SUMMARY

Day 1: Scharnitz - Karwendelhaus

Day 2: Karwendelhaus-Ödkarspitze-Birkkarspitze-Karwendelhaus (optional)

Day 3: Karwendelhaus - Falken Hut - Hochjoch - Lamsenjoch - Lamsenjoch Hut

Day 4: Lamsenjoch Hut - Gramaialm - Falzturn Alm - Pertisau

✳   ✳   ✳

Left:
The magnetic sight of the Tre Cime from the Forcella di Lavaredo in the Dolomites (Ch 18)

Below: The Tre Cime hut in the Dolomites (Ch 18)

Above:
Golicica and Prisojnik form a dramatic profile from the west (Ch 19)

Centre left:
Maselc in the Trenta valley, Julian Alps (Ch 19)

Bottom left:
Dvojno Jezero, one of the seven Triglav lakes (Ch 19)

ROFANGEBIRGE (BRANDENBERGER ALPS)

This triangular-shaped group is located south of the German border where it spreads east of the Karwendel mountains beyond the Achensee, the point of the triangle being marked by Kufstein, the Inn valley effectively drawing a line along its southern edge, while the valley of the Brandenberger Ache virtually dissects the district in two. The mountains here are of modest dimensions, for not one tops 2300 metres, and several of the summits are easily reached by walkers, including the Sagzahn (2239m) which has a short, fifty metre stretch of *klettersteig* ideal for first-time users of a 'climbing path'.

The Alpenverein's 'green book' lists only three huts of the German Alpine Club (the Bayreuther, Erfurter and Ludwig-Aschenbrenner), but there are half a dozen other privately-owned huts and inns, including the flower-bedecked Kaiserhaus in the very heart of the district in the Brandenberger Ache valley, and the Erzherzhog-Johann-Klause near the head of the same glen which is linked by a cross-country trail with the Aschenbrenner hut. The Erfurter and Bayreuther huts are situated in the bottom south-west corner of the range, the first approached from Maurach by the Achensee, the second from Münster in the Inn valley. A recommended route linking the two huts crosses the Schafsteigsattel (2173m) above the Erfurter hut, then over the Sagzahn to the Vordere Sonnwendjoch (2224m), followed by a zig zag descent on a waymarked path round the Berglkopf to the Bayreuther hut. This route has as its highlight the protected climbing path referred to in the previous paragraph, and because of this safety precautions should be adopted. There is, however, a more straightforward route from one hut to the other, while the Bayreuther provides several opportunities for interesting excursions to be made over green pastures weaving among the steep crags.

A two-day crossing of the range from the Erfurter hut to Hintere Thiersee near Kufstein is part of the Kalkalpen Traverse, this tour being broken with a night spent in the little village of Steinberg am Rofan. It would also be feasible to extend this tour by straying into other valleys that are tributaries of the Brandenberger Ache, and making a circuit or two along the way, using perhaps the Kaiserhaus or Erzherzhog-Johann-Klause for accommodation.

✳   ✳   ✳

KAISERGEBIRGE

Lying east of the Inn valley and north of the Kitzbüheler Alps, the Kaisergebirge offers some of the loveliest mountain scenery in all the Northern Limestone Alps. Although they may be admired from the roads and resorts that encircle this district of sharp peaks and impressive walls, the very best can only be properly seen from the many trails that push into the heartland.

It's a small, compact range built like a capital letter H lying on its side; two parallel groups facing each other across the Kaisertal. The northern sector is the Zahmer (tame) Kaiser, the southern being the celebrated Wilder (wild) Kaiser. The Zahmer Kaiser has no real high mountains, for its most elevated point is only 1999 metres (the Pyramidenspitze), a summit easily reached from the Vorderkaiserfelden hut in less than three hours. The highest of the Wilder Kaiser is nearly 350 metres higher in Ellmauer Halt (2344m), whose three jagged peaks can be climbed from the Grutten hut, or from the Anton-Karg-Haus at Hinterbärenbad in the Kaisertal.

The Kaisertal is something of a sanctuary, a romantic oasis of lush green meadows and woods from which the sheer-sided cliffs burst in fantastic, theatrical shapes. The whole district is protected as a nature reserve and offers an abundance of outings for walkers, scramblers and rock climbers. Not surprisingly there are some exciting *klettersteig* routes too, including the Widauersteig on the 2113 metre Scheffauer which dates from 1911, and the Eggersteig, established in 1903 and reckoned by those in the know to be the most ambitious route open to walkers in the area, but this is said to be dangerous when wet, or if troubled with snow or ice.

This last-named route tackles a cliff-face traverse, a slabby couloir and the high pass of the Ellmauer Tor (1995m), a massive 'gateway' in the mountains east of Ellmauer Halt. A high path, the Höhenweg Hochalm, leads from the Vorderkaiserfelden hut to the Stripsenjoch Haus complex in about three hours. A zig-zag descent then enters a basin below the Stripsenjoch to begin the Eggersteig proper, and makes a dramatic undulating traverse of the north-facing cliffs of the Flieschbank along a narrow ledge safeguarded with cables. Suddenly rounding a corner the Steinerne Rinne, a huge couloir between the Flieschbank and Predigstuhl, draws you up steep slabs with help from fixed ropes on an exhilarating scramble (this is no place to discover you suffer from vertigo) until eventually you emerge at the often snow-carpeted Ellmauer Tor, with its distant views across the Kitzbüheler Alps to the Grossvenediger and other snow peaks of the Hohe Tauern. A diversion of half an hour will take you to the summit of the Hintere Goinger Halt (2195m), then it's a descent either to the Grutten hut or Gaudeamus hut to finish the route - or if you've energy to spare, continue on a further hour's walk from the latter hut down to Ellmau.

This southern side of the range offers plenty of good day walks that nibble at the very edges, as well as a number of summits accessible by challenging trail. But an excellent two-day traverse was created in 1990 between Kirchdorf and Kufstein that makes a very rewarding outing indeed. With the Grutten hut set at the half-way point, the Wilder Kaiser Steig would be worth tackling as a gentle introduction to the countless opportunities that exist for multi-day hut routes in the Eastern Alps.

In the Kaisergebirge huts are plentiful and the whole district is fairly easy of access. Kufstein, overlooked by a grim thirteenth century fortress, makes a reasonable base on its western rim, otherwise there's Söll, Scheffau, Ellmau, St Johann in Tirol, Kirchdorf or even Kitzbühel along the southern edge for walkers with their own transport.

*　　*　　*

BERCHTESGADENER ALPS

To the east of the Kaisergebirge and south of Salzburg, the Berchtesgadener Alps take their name from the popular Bavarian resort town overlooked by the Watzmann massif. At 2713 metres the Watzmann is the highest mountain entirely in Germany (the Zugspitze is, of course, shared with Austria); first climbed in 1801 it's a distinctive mountain with several peaks and towers, it dominates the town and has a stunning east face, said to be the highest in the Eastern Alps, with several hard routes upon it.

A great horseshoe of mountains, open-end towards the north, provides logic for the area to be included within German territory despite the fact that a glance at the map would seem to indicate that it ought to be Austrian. Much of the northern side of the border is protected as a national park, including the Watzmann, nearby Hochkalter (2607m) which contains the last remaining German glacier, and the beautiful Königsee. Towering over this charming lake great slab walls form part of the Steinernes Meer ('Sea of Stone') - Austrian mountains seen as a distant backdrop from Zell am See. Not surprisingly for a limestone district there are scores of caves, the best-known being the Schellenberger Eishöhle; one or two others have been exploited as salt mines.

The German and Austrian Alpenverein has provided a large number of huts in the district and, together with several privately-owned huts and inns the walker has almost forty different lodgings to choose from among these mountains, while Berchtesgaden and Ramsau in Germany, and Lofer, Saalfelden, Werfen and even Bischofshofen in Austria, offer valley based opportunities. Much of the walking is quite demanding, especially above the Königsee and in the high karst country of the Steinernes Meer; many summits are attainable without technical ability, others call for scrambling skills or minimal rock climbing competence, and there are some dramatic *klettersteig* routes too of varying lengths and degrees of seriousness. But there's enough mountain walking of a more sedate nature for those who require it.

Throughout the summer tourist ferries journey along the dark green waters of the Königsee, stopping briefly at the grassy promontory of St Bartholomä on the western shoreline with its little baroque chapel bearing two red onion-topped towers. A trail strikes off from here heading roughly northward, soon climbing among cliffs high above the lake, enters forest and then joins a road leading to the Küroint hut. From here one could either continue on a round to Berchtesgaden, or climb to the Watzmann Haus perched on a shoulder of the Watzmann at 1930 metres. An alternative approach to this hut comes via the Mitterkaser Alm which is reached from the Wimbachklamm bus stop on the Berchtesgaden-Ramsau road.

As its name implies the Watzmann Haus is used as a base for climbs on the Watzmann itself. The standard route leading to the most northerly of the summits (Hocheck; 2653m) provides dramatic views, but is not unduly difficult, while the ridge linking Hocheck with the Mittelspitze (the highest summit) is narrow but protected. This is part of a fine *klettersteig* route that crosses the three main summits and descends to the Wimbachgries hut to achieve a superb traverse of the mountain. It's very exposed in places, but the route has been so well engineered that dangers are few and difficulties no more than climbing Grade I.

On the Austrian side of the mountains the Schönfeldspitze (2653m) in the Steinernes Meer offers another *klettersteig* route in a splendid setting, beginning at the Riemann Haus (approached from either Saalfelden or Maria Alm). Hochkönig (2941m) is the dominant mountain hereabouts, and is the highest in the Berchtesgaden Alps. *Klettersteig* protected paths are to be found here too, not only on the main peak, but on others in the massif; one of the longest and most serious being that which tackles the Hochseiler from the north.

The whole area is full of lonely charm, as is the north-eastern corner known as the Hagengebirge with the Blühnbachtal cutting below. Many years ago when I worked in more crowded mountains further south, I would escape to the Steinernes Meer on the odd day-off and there visit solitary alms, pick my way over ribs of limestone pavement, and photograph the flowers that grew in abundance. And rejoice in hours of solitude. Regrettably there was seldom time to do more, but there is a fine west to east crossing that may be made of the district, setting out from Saalfelden and ending in the Salzach valley at either Werfen or Bischofshofen, where the startlingly white crags of the Tennengebirge soar out of the east flank of the valley.

✳   ✳   ✳

TENNENGEBIRGE

This small block of mountains was once a continuous part of the Hagengebirge until the Salzach managed to breach the wall by making a cut through what is now the defile of the Lueg Pass (562m) between the old market town of Werfen, and Hallein, best known for its salt mine. Seen from the south a majestic wall of pale limestone rears up out of a dark undulating blotch of evergreen forest. From the main road to Salzburg it is a teasing vision. From Werfen a better view is obtained, and at evening time that wall holds on to the alpenglow until shadows from the valley swallow every mountain feature. Best of all, and rightfully too, the true nature of the Tennengebirge is revealed only from close aquaintance. Some may choose to drive the twisting road that climbs the south-west flank and then take a cable-car to the tourist honeypot of the Eisriesenwelt - the world's largest known system of ice caves, forty-five kilometres of which have so far been explored, and whose entrance is near the privately-owned Dr Friedrich-Ödl-Haus. Others will do better to explore a network of trails that winds through the forest and leads to a realm of high pastureland backed by glorious crags riven with gullies.

The highest of its summits is the Raucheck at 2431 metres, but the whole wall maintains a regular altitude of around 2300 metres, broken only by occasional stony saddles, while the pastures and forests that clothe the ankles are rucked and contorted in charming fashion. There are just six huts of the Alpenverein and another half-dozen that either belong to the Austrian Touring Club, or are privately-owned, but the group is so compact that every corner is made readily accessible. To the south lie the western outliers of the Niedere Tauern range, while the better-known Dachstein mountains crowd to the east.

The actual outline of the Tennengebirge is as follows: the western limit is marked by the Salzach river as far south as its confluence with the Fritzbach just outside Bischofshofen. Then eastward along the Fritzbach to Niedernfritz where the St Martinbach flows from the north. The boundary now moves along the St Martinbach to St Martin and Lungötz, then follows the Lammertal on its long north-westerly curve out to the Salzach near Golling, north of the Lueg Pass.

Between Werfen and the Fritzbach valley a road cuts off to the east at

Pfarrwerfen, rising in six kilometres to the small winter sports area of Werfenweng (bus service from Pfarrwerfen), from where a two-hour walk leads to the Dr Heinrich-Hackel hut. This modest-sized refuge serves as a useful base for climbs on the Tauernkogel, Eiskogel and Bleikogel, among others. A trail heads up to the Tauernscharte (2103m) between Tauernkogel and Eiskogel and leads to some scrambling routes in the heart of the range, as well as another route that breaks away to reach the Laufener hut on the Tennalm. Another, more gentle, trail goes east from the Heinrich-Hackel hut, crosses the Jochriedel (1720m) and descends to the Lammertal, while below and to the west of the hut lies the beautiful Wengerau valley, at the head of which is a narrow but magnificent little amphitheatre of rock faces topped by the Vorderes Streitmandl (2378m). On the neighbouring Mittleres Streitmandl is perched the Edelweiss hut, built there by the Edelweiss Club of Salzburg, while yet another, the Leopold-Happisch-Haus, is located in the Pitschenbergtal below the Tiroler Kogel.

A superb, long day's tour of twenty kilometres or more could be made from Werfen itself, heading at first through forest above the motorway tunnel to the Alpengasthaus Mahdegg (beautifully situated below the Raucheck and Fieberhorn, and with lovely views west across the valley to the Hochkönig and surrounding Steinernes Meer), then up to Elmaualm on tilted open pastureland backed by soaring rock walls. One summer's day I came here alone and sprawled in the sun-warmed grass while dozens of horses grazed around me in sheer contentment. When they moved on I had the mountains to myself, even though there's yet another small hut nearby; a peaceful spot with an alternative trail climbing steeply to the Werfener hut at the foot of the Hochthron's south-facing crags. Leaving the Elmaualm the circular tour then descends into the head of the Wengerau valley and follows this south to the few buildings of Wengerau where a series of farm trails leads to Pfarrwerfen and back to Werfen with its crag-topped castle overlooking the town.

There are many footpaths and scrambling routes to be exploited on the south side of the Tennengebirge mountains, and several worthwhile days could be spent here. The range is much less busy than the neighbouring Dachstein; much is accessible from a valley base, but with several huts perched in idyllic locations linking routes prove to be perennially tempting.

✳   ✳   ✳

DACHSTEINGEBIRGE

Honeycombed with impressive caves, crowned by a prominent karst landscape and embedded with glaciers, the Dachstein mountains block the southern edge of the Salzkammergut lake district south-east of Salzburg. Between the main massif itself and the deeply-cut Ennstal to the south, a long precipitous wall plunges steeply to the broad green terrace of Ramsau, while on the northern side above the Hallstätter See will be found the famed Dachstein Caves (Dachsteinhöhlen), Giant Ice Cave (Reiseneishöhle) and the deep Mammoth Cave (Mammuthöhle) all reached by cableway from Obertraun. The jagged western edge of the massif, the six kilometres long Gosaukamm, curves north-west above the Gosautal, and is known locally as the Salzburg Dolomites. In the upper part of the Gosautal the largest of a string of lakes has cableway access to the Gablonzer hut from which a fine network of paths provides plenty of opportunities to explore the Gosaukamm and the delightful alms that surround it.

Walkers with their own transport could nibble at the range from one of a number of comfortable valley bases. On the south-western edge Bischofshofen gives access not only to the Dachstein but to the Tennengebirge also. Schladming in the Ennstal has the Dachstein to the north and the Niedere Tauern to the south. Salzkammergut resorts, notably Bad Ischl and Bad Aussee, enjoy prospects of both Dachstein and Totes Gebirge ranges, while picturesque Halstatt nestles at the very foot of the highest of them all, the 2996 metre Hoher Dachstein which also happens to be the second highest of all the Northern Limestone Alps. As for mountain-based accommodation, the Alpenverein and others have established no less than twenty huts, bivouacs and inns here, thus offering almost unlimited opportunities for the enterprising walker to make tours, circuits and ascents - including one or two *klettersteig* routes - all in a landscape of great charm and beauty.

The Gosaukamm may be approached by road via the straggling village of Gosau on the northern side, Annaberg-im-Lammertal on the west, or from Filzmoos to the south. The most popular way is to drive to the dam at the north-western end of the Vordere Gosausee, for there are very fine views across the water to the Gosau glacier draped down the flank of the Hoher Dachstein; a scene that has been reproduced on countless postcards and calendars. The road continues alongside the lake and goes as far as the Hinterer Gosausee, but is closed to private vehicles. Walkers are not restricted, of course, and from the last lake, which is set in a lovely basin, a trail climbs eastward to the Adamek hut (2196m) at the very foot of the Gosau glacier. From there the Hoher Dachstein may be climbed in about three hours. But before looking at the main Dachstein block we ought to concentrate briefly on the Gosaukamm, and to do so it is necessary to return to the dam at the Vordere Gosausee and follow the lead of Cecil Davies whose guidebook describes a three-day circuit. Although three days are given for the tour, it could be completed in much less time, but a leisurely pace allows plenty of opportunities to divert from the basic route and to 'collect' the odd summit that appeals.

TOUR OF THE GOSAUKAMM

The first hut to reach is the Gablonzer which, as we have already seen, is partly accessible by cable-car from the dam. The walker, however, may decide to ignore this and follow a path instead; a twisting trail that climbs for around 600 metres above the lake before gaining the hut which is very busy in winter on account of the skiing potential of the surrounding area. In summer many of its visitors come up by cable-car just for the day and return to the valley in late afternoon. Should you find the place unacceptably crowded when you arrive, book a place for the night and then visit the nearby Zwieselalmhöhe, a celebrated viewpoint with snowfields of the Hohe Tauern seen in the distance. South of the hut rises the Grosser Donnerkogel (2055m), a mountain whose summit may be reached by a scramble without difficulty in less than two hours.

Next day follow a path up to the Oberer Törlecksattel, followed by the Unterer Törlecksattel at the northern end of the Gosaukamm range, then skirt the western slopes along the Austriaweg unless, that is, you failed to climb the Donnerkogel yesterday and wish to make amends; in which case take the left-hand path. The rustic Theodor-Körner hut, dominated by the 2100 metre Angerstein, is easily reached by the direct Austriaweg, and from it the trail continues roughly south-eastward towards the Bischofsmütze. The route is then forced away in a wide diverting arc before reaching the foot of the Durchgang, a steep but trouble-free gully topped by a significant pass to the west of the Bischofsmütze. Over this views extend to the Niedere Tauern range beyond the unseen Ennstal. The Austriaweg now curves round the southern edge of the Bischofsmütze to gain the popular Hofpürgl hut which, fortunately, has places for more than 150. Most of these places will be needed too, since it is easily reached from the roadhead at the Aualm (accessible from Filzmoos).

The third and final stage of the tour starts with a three hundred metre climb to the Steiglpass. On the way an alternative trail (the Linzer Weg) breaks off to the right towards the Hoher Dachstein and the Adamek hut. Over the pass the Steiglweg entices through a stony trough and down to tree-dotted slopes below a wild collection of grey thrusting pinnacles. The way leads along a natural terrace whose supporting cliffs plunge to the upper Gosautal. This terrace steadily eases down, and the trail eventually returns you to the dam at the far end of the Vordere Gosausee where the tour began.

TOUR OF THE GOSAUKAMM - ROUTE SUMMARY

Day 1: Vordere Gosausee - Gablonzer Hut (Zwieselalmhöhe &/or Grosser Donnerkogel optional)

Day 2: Gablonzer Hut - Theodor-Körner Hut - Durchgang - Hofpürgl Hut

Day 3: Hofpürgl Hut - Steiglpass - Steiglweg - Vordere Gosausee

---

The main Dachstein block is easily gained from the Ramsau terrace above Schladming - there's even a cable-car (the Dachstein-Südwandbahn) swinging up to the Schladming glacier where there is summer skiing. This cable-car makes it possible to tackle an assortment of routes on the Hoher Dachstein and its close neighbours without a long approach march being necessary. And it is, perhaps, better for walkers to enter from the south too, as the following tour suggests.

A DACHSTEIN CIRCUIT

As with most tours described in this book, the circuit proposed here begins with a short first day which assumes weariness after travel from home. In fact it would be possible to take a bus from Schladming most of the way to the Dachstein-Südwand hut (1910m), were conditions so foul as to make walking a misery. In reasonable summer weather, however, it would be advisable to take the bus as far as Ramsau village from where a three-hour walk will lead to the private Dachstein-Südwand hut via the Austria hut. Depending on which route is taken there should be plenty of opportunities to stop for refreshment on the way, for there are several other huts, inns and restaurants dotted around the Ramsau terrace.

Next day follow the Pernerweg westward under the looming Dachstein cliffs on what is normally the route to the Hofpürgl hut on the edge of the Gosaukamm. Instead of going all the way there, though, branch off on the Linzer Weg to cross the main Dachstein ridge at the Reissgangscharte (1954m), and descend to the Adamek hut in a moraine- and glacier-charged landscape.

On day three the route begins by briefly descending westward into the Gosautal, then breaking away to the north over naked rock to gain the 2190 metre Hosswandscharte. Through this the route now swings to the right, tight against the base of crags supporting Hosskogel and Hoher Ochsenkogel ('like some monstrous beehive" is how Cecil Davies described it), then over the Hoher Trog (2355m) to the large Simony hut in time for lunch. Baedeker praised the view from this hut, as have others since, for it gazes out across the Hallstätter glacier to the Hoher Dachstein, whose summit may be reached by way of that glacier in about two and a half hours. From the Simony hut to the Schlicker Haus (also known as the Gjaidalm-Schutzhütte) there's a steady descent across bleached limestone pavement to the Gjaidalm near the head of the cableway from Obertraum.

The final stage crosses back to Ramsau on a waymarked route across the eroded limestone plateau known as Auf dem Stein to the Feisterscharte (2198m), winding among sink-holes and fissures that could create all sorts of difficulties in poor visibility. Then down to Ramsau (Kulm) by way of the Guttenberg Haus sixty metres below the pass; a longish day but in good visibility a very rewarding one.

A DACHSTEIN CIRCUIT

Day 1: Schladming/Ramsau - Austria Hut - Dachstein-Südwand Hut

Day 2: Dachstein-Südwand Hut - Reissgangscharte - Adamek Hut

Day 3: Adamek Hut - Hosswandscharte - Hoher Trog - Simony Hut - Schilcher Haus

Day 4: Schilcher Haus - Feisterscharte - Guttenberg Haus - Ramsau

It would be perfectly feasible to extend this circuit by including the Tour of the Gosaukamm. To do this simply walk from the Dachstein-Südwand hut on day two as far as the Hofpürgl hut, rather than follow the Linzer Weg to the Adamek hut. Then make a two-day tour of the Gosaukamm back to the Hofpürgl hut, and next day cross the Reissgangscharte to the Adamek hut to rejoin the described route.

---

*　　*　　*

TOTES GEBIRGE

The so-called 'dead mountains' rise north-east of the Dachsteingebirge and form the second of the main massifs of the Salzkammergut region. Though not as high as the Dachstein, and completely lacking in glaciers, it is nonetheless an impressive group of mountains with the largest high plateau to be found anywhere in the

Northern Limestone Alps. It is this high plateau that gives the region its name, for it is a veritable desert of stone, a seemingly barren wilderness furrowed by erosion and pocked with sink-holes. Therein lies some of its dangers and some of its charms.

The Totes Gebirge is guarded on most sides by challenging cliffs that offer fine rock routes of all grades. There are dozens of summits in excess of 2000 metres, the highest being the rugged Grosser Priel (2515m) found in the north-eastern corner, from which the whole mass is tilted towards the south-west, while the north face of the massif plummets down to the sombre Almsee, a hauntingly beautiful spot reached from Viechtwang east of Gmunden.

Lakes being a major feature of the Salzkammergut it comes as no surprise to discover several other attractive lakes and tarns, apart from the Almsee, cast about the fringes of the region. The little Offensee to the west of Almsee is designated as a nature reserve; south of that lies the even smaller Wildensee at 1534 metres, while the larger Altausseer See and Grundlsee on the southern edge have shoreside resorts in an open setting, and above them more tarns lie cradled under bare limestone crags. South-east of the main plateau, at a lower elevation, is the Mittendorfer Seenplatte (Mitterndorf Lake Plateau), a secondary terrace-like plateau of alpine meadows and tarns that is transformed into a ski-touring playground in winter.

Clearly there is much that may be achieved here, and with almost thirty huts and inns providing accommodation - in addition to the various outlying resorts - all one needs is sufficient time and energy to go exploring. *Mountain Walking in Austria* gives outline descriptions of three routes worth tackling, one of which is a north-south crossing of the range which begins at the Almtalerhaus (approached from Grünau-im-Almtal) and ends by the Grundlsee by way of the Welser and Pühringer huts. Sections of the route are protected, but the way also makes a traverse of the barren and almost featureless limestone plateau whose guiding waymarks are easily obliterated by unseasonal snowfall. In inclement weather the serious nature of such a route becomes apparent.

✳   ✳   ✳

THE NORTHERN LIMESTONE ALPS

Location:
Extending eastwards along the Austro-German border as far as Salzburg, then continuing in a rough line towards Vienna south of the Salzburg-Vienna autobahn.

Principal valleys:
Every one of the individual groups that comprise the Mittelgebirge chain has its own principal valleys, most of which are named in the preceding pages, but are too numerous to list here.

Principal peaks:
Parseierspitze (3040m), Hoher Dachstein (2996m), Zugspitze (2963m), Hochkönig (2941m), Östliche Griesspitze (2759m), Birkkarspitze (2749m), Watzmann (2713m), Grosser Krottenkopf (2657m), Grosser Priel (2515m), Raucheck (2431m), Ellmauer Halt (2344m), Sagzahn (2239m)

Centres:
The main centres for each group are given in the foregoing text.

Huts:
Literally hundreds of huts, both private and belonging to the German and Austrian Alpenverein, make this one of the best-hutted regions in the whole Alpine chain.

Access:
Since each mountain group is surrounded by roads access is no real problem here. The Austrian rail network can also be valuable in getting from one region to another. International airports are at Zürich (for the far west), Innsbruck, Munich, Salzburg and Vienna.

Maps:
Most areas are covered at a scale of 1:25,000 by the Alpenvereinskarten. Kompass Wanderkarte and Freytag Berndt provide wide coverage at 1:50,000 - with varying degrees of accuracy. Ensure you buy the most up-to-date sheets.

Guidebooks:
No single English-language volume covers all the areas mentioned here. The best is *Mountain Walking in Austria* by Cecil Davies (Cicerone Press) which offers selected routes in most groups.
Klettersteig, Scrambles in the Northern Limestone Alps by Paul Werner (translated by Dieter Pevsner, Cicerone Press) describes 44 of these exhilarating routes covering several areas. The introductory section dealing with methods of self-protection should not be skipped.
Walking Austria's Alps Hut to Hut by Jonathan Hurdle (Cordee/The Mountaineers) outlines multi-day treks in the Lechtal Alps, Karwendelgebirge and Dachstein groups.
The Kalkalpen Traverse by Alan Proctor (Cicerone Press) is a guide to the three-week traverse of the chain from Bödele to St Johann near Kufstein.
Hut Hopping in the Austrian Alps by William E. Reifsnyder (Sierra Club) describes a tour in the Lechtal Alps.

Other reading:
Classic Walks in the Alps by Kev Reynolds (Oxford Illustrated Press, 1991) has a chapter by Cecil Davies dealing with a circuit of the Gosaukamm in the Dachsteingebirge.
Walking & Climbing in the Alps by Stefano Ardito (Swan Hill Press, 1995). One section is devoted to a 9-day route from St Leonhard, near Salzburg, to the Kaisergebirge.
The Mountains of Europe by Kev Reynolds (Oxford Illustrated Press, 1990) contains a good review of all the main mountains in the Austrian and Bavarian Alps written, once again, by Cecil Davies.
The Outdoor Traveler's Guide to the Alps by Marcia R. Lieberman (Stewart, Tabori & Chang, New York) gives basic information about several groups in the Northern Limestone Alps.

*　　*　　*

Monte Cristallo, patterned with cloud, when viewed from Sorapis

18: THE DOLOMITES

This complex range is the most colourful in Europe. Group after group of bizarre mountains, scattered in picturesque confusion, create landscapes of surrealistic imagery. "Keep your eyes level," wrote Janet Adam Smith, "and you see villages, fields, churches, woods, a normal pattern of human life; swivel them up thirty degrees, and you see shocks and freaks of crude pink stone, whose shape, proportion, and colour bear no relation to the valleys from which they spring." (*Mountain Holidays*)

The Dolomites are among the most eccentric peaks of all. By Alpine standards they are not high mountains, and only fifty or so top the 3000 metre mark. But mere altitude measurement counts for little here, for these astonishing limestone pinnacles and towers capture the imagination in other ways.

Picture if you will a country of green hills carpeted with forest and flowery meadow. Set upon these hills in random fashion clusters of rock with precipitous walls and jagged splinters bursting with every conceivable shape and form. Wash them with pastel shades of pink, cream or golden yellow, then introduce the soft blue of cloud-shadow. Fleck the turrets with black, purple or red; add the stain of sunrise or sunset for special effect, and pour bleached-white screes at their ankles and you have, in the words of Leslie Stephen, "the fairyland of the Alps."

It is the light which plays upon the Dolomites that adds a special magic to their fairyland aspect. Take, for example, the great west-facing cliffs of the Catinaccio

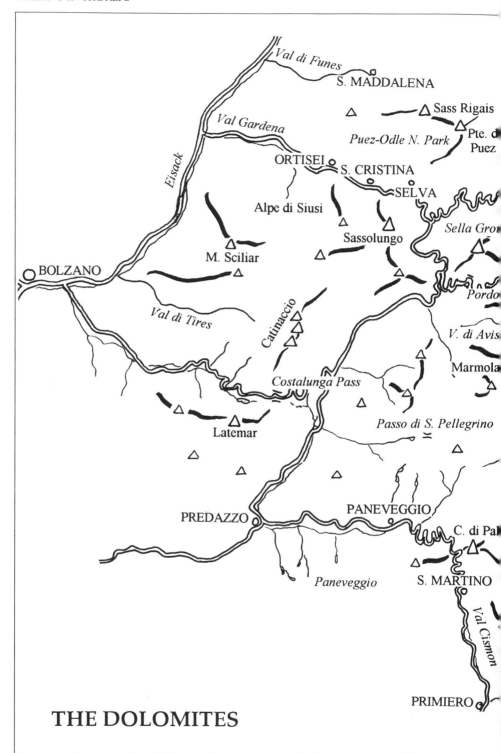

THE DOLOMITES

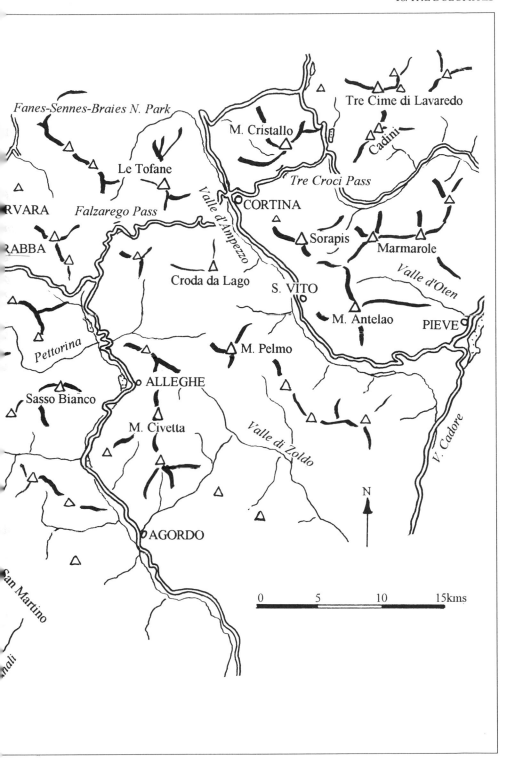

Fanes-Sennes-Braies N. Park

Tre Cime di Lavaredo

M. Cristallo

Cadini

Le Tofane

Tre Croci Pass

RVARA   Falzarego Pass

CORTINA

Valle d'Ampezzo

RABBA

Sorapis   Marmarole

Valle d'Oten

Croda da Lago

S. VITO

PIEVE

M. Antelao

Pettorina

ALLEGHE

M. Pelmo

Sasso Bianco

M. Civetta

Valle di Zoldo

V. Cadore

N

AGORDO

San Martino

0   5   10   15kms

429

(Rosengarten) and Pale massifs. Morning shadow is banished only in the afternoon when the sun casts hues of yellow and pink across their flanks. An intensity of colour deepens until at sunset the peaks seem to burst into flame, scorching the sky. Others, such as Monte Cristallo which faces south, take on the rosy stain of dawn, while the Tre Cima di Lavaredo are as memorably colourful at dusk as they are when flushed with sunrise. Even when the sun is not playing directly upon them, the Dolomites take on colours and tones unique to Nature's palette as witnessed on a day of storm, or under a sky chased with clouds in a fulsome wind. At times these upthrust coral reefs can appear less like mountains than the skeletons of mountains that died long ago. With no streams to murmur in their upper glens, an eery stillness grips the land on a midday in summer. But when studied from a respectable distance, changes occur that are not easy to explain, as Leslie Stephen noted:

> "Never did I see hills change their shape so rapidly, in all varieties of weather...I lay under a chestnut-tree in a lovely meadow at Primiero through a hot summer afternoon, and watched the strange transformation of the cliffs. They would not remain steady for five minutes together. What looked like a chasm suddenly changed into a ridge; plain surfaces of rock suddenly shaped themselves into towering pinnacles; and then the pinnacles melted away and left a ravine or a cavern...and it required a heartless scepticism to believe that the only witchcraft at work was that of the sun, as it threw varying lights and shadows over the intricate labyrinths of the rocks."
>
> (*The Playground of Europe*)

As has been pointed out by many writers, limestone is noted for its boldness of form, but the limestone of which the Dolomites are constructed contains magnesium as well as calcium, is harder than ordinary 'mountain' or carboniferous limestone, and is more liable to crumbling too. Thus it is rather more prone to erosion and the processes of weathering, which has helped create such a startling series of landscapes. Named after the French geologist, the Marquis de Dolomieu, who visited the district in 1789, Italian climbers rightly say that the correct name for their mountains is Dolomiti, but so commonly accepted has it become over the last two centuries, that the Dolomites will continue to be the name used here.

Apart from the Brenta which is divorced from the main range on the 'wrong' side of the Adige, the Gothic assortment of groups that makes up the Dolomite region is concentrated in a rough rectangle east of the Adige which, above Bolzano, has as its main tributary the Eisack, with Val Pusteria to the north, Val Sugana to the south, and the valley of the Piave (the Cadore) as the eastern boundary. Within this rectangle well-engineered roads, many of which were a legacy of military defence work prior to the First World War, traverse the high passes and present the non-walker or climber with some of the finest mountain vistas in all the Alps accessible from a motor vehicle, while the walker is no less generously provided for in a wealth of mountain trails. These roads and passes link the main valleys which divide the Dolomites into their individual groups, as listed below, beginning in the west.

❋　❋　❋

SASSOLUNGO & PUEZ-ODLE GROUPS

Accessible from the busy Brenner highway midway between Bolzano and Bressanone, Val Gardena at first glance seems too green and gentle to offer typical Dolomite scenery. Fragrant meadows clothe the undulating valley bed, with forests dark against the hills. Then you turn a bend and suddenly the Sassolungo (Langkofel; 3181m) springs into the sky; an impressive peak first climbed by Paul Grohmann in 1869. Ortisei (St Ulrich), Santa Cristina and Selva are perhaps the best bases here; to the north rise peaks of the Puez-Odle Nature Park, while the southern side of the valley is marked by the Alpe di Siusi, a high plateau of lush pastureland whose trails provide views south to the Sciliar massif (which towers over Bolzano), and east to the majestic shapes of the Sassolungo. Between Sassolungo and the Sasso Piatto a great hollow leads to a wilderness of scree, at the top of which the narrow Forcella Sassolungo provides a surprise view of the Sella Group which rises just to the east. The summit of Sasso Piatto (2964m) is accessible to walkers via the south flank, while the Oskar-Schuster Way provides an interesting route for *via ferrata* enthusiasts.

The Puez-Odle Group can be reached not only from Val Gardena, but also from Val di Funes which flows roughly parallel with Gardena to the north, as well as from Val Badia to the east. The Puez mountains form a massive block to the south-east of the saw-tooth Odle peaks, their highest summit being Punte del Puez (2918m), while Sass Rigais is the loftiest in the latter group at 3025 metres. Whilst well-known Val Gardena is extremely busy, and its trails invariably stream with walkers in high summer, Val di Funes has a greater sense of remoteness, with Santa Maddalena (bus from Bressanone) near the roadhead being a starting point for many walks. Views from this valley are perhaps the grandest in the Puez-Odle Nature Park, its walking potential being enhanced by prospects of peaceful trails. The Sentiero delle Odle is said to be one of the best; Sentiero dei Signori is another which offers outstanding views of the Odle needles, and the Dolomites high route, Alta Via 2, makes a traverse of the region on its way from Bressanone to Feltre. From Santa Maddalena a local path strikes southward to Rifugio Brogles, nestling at the western foot of Sass Rigais, and this same mountain is also approached via cable-car from Santa Cristina in Val Gardena.

❋ ❋ ❋

CATINACCIO & LATEMAR

Val di Tires and Val d'Ega form a link between Bolzano and Val di Fassa by way of the Costalunga Pass. North of Val di Tires lies the Parco Naturale Sciliar, but at the eastern end of the valley the Catinaccio massif stretches its long line of cliffs in a north-south alignment from the Schlern massif at one end to the vicinity of the Latemar towers at the other. Facing the sunset these mountains are transformed into a world of legend recalled by their original name of Rosengarten - the rose garden. Laurin, king of the dwarves who lived there, turned the roses to stone vowing never to allow them to bloom again by day or night. However, he forgot about the evenings, and now as the sun goes down the alpenglow once more inspires the stone roses to blaze in glory.

Several huts are located along both the west and east flanks of the mountains, with trails and *via ferrata* routes working among them. At the southern, Costalunga Pass, end a relatively new climbing path has been created which, when linked with standard trails, makes for a long day's circuit. The Alberto hut suggests an enticing destination, set as it is beside a small lake below the Santner Pass with the spectacular and elegant Vajolet towers in full view. Three hundred metres or more below Rifugio Alberto stands the Vajolet hut (2243m), from which an hour's walk leads to Rifugio Passo Principe. Cima di Terra Rossa can be climbed from there to gain an excellent view of the northern Catinaccio, while Monte Pez above the hut of the same name is a fine place from which to capture the sunset stain on these delightful mountains.

As for the fluted Latemar towers which rise on the south side of the Costalunga (or Karer) Pass road, these have been a showpiece of the Dolomites for decades, since they're seen reflected in the pine-fringed Lago di Carezza by travellers journeying past on the scenic Bolzano-Cortina road. It is this northern view that shows the mountains at their best, for their inner basin of scree forms a rude contrast, but this cannot be seen from the outside. Gillian Price's guidebook, *Walking in the Dolomites*, describes a loop-trip through the Latemar massif, with an optional overnight being spent in the Torre di Pisa hut on the southern rim of the mountains. This same hut enables a traverse to be made of the group, which includes ascent of the two highest summits. This high route has a section of protected path on it, but otherwise the only 'difficulties' could be found in the amount of exposure that adds a certain buzz to the walker's day.

✳   ✳   ✳

SELLA GROUP

Encircled by roads to the east of the Sassolungo, the Sella Group rises like some gigantic citadel with massive, square-cut blocks supporting a flattish crown topped by the cone-shaped Piz Boè (3152m). There are several scrambling routes onto the summit plateau, and various cableways too that give access to the upper slopes from (among others) the Pordoi Pass on the south side and Corvara at the northeast corner. No less than seventeen rifugios and inns provide accommodation, refreshment or both, and the Alta Via 2 long-distance trail crosses the massif a little to the west of Piz Boè itself. Various *via ferrata* routes explore both the stern outer walls and high projections from it, including the oldest protected path in the Dolomites, the Pössnecker, which ascends the south-west corner from the Sella Pass. The summit plateau is akin to a stone desert, but it's a desert with deep clefts cut into the rock, and with magnificent distant views - north to the Zillertal range on the Austro-Italian border, and south to the heavily glaciated Marmolada.

✳   ✳   ✳

MARMOLADA GROUP

This group begins immediately south of the Passo Pordoi where an extensive ridge running west-east provides one of the finest unbroken views of all to the Marmolada's impressive north face, caked with the only real glacier of worth in all the Dolomites. At 3342 metres the Marmolada is the highest in the range, but appearances suggest it has more in common with traditional Alpine mountains than with its extravagent Dolomite neighbours. Of the two highest peaks, Punta Rocca and Punta Penia, John Ball reached the former in 1860, leaving Paul Grohmann and his guides to make the first true ascent of the main summit four years later. Today the mountain is climbed without great difficulty by its *voie normale*, cableways adorn its north and east flanks, and summer skiing is practised on the Ghiacciaio della Marmolada, but west of the Forcella della Marmolada, and rising as an adjunct to the main massif, are several striking rock peaks dominated by the Gran Vernel at 3210 metres. Paths wander round the massif's surrounding valleys and make a traverse of the southern side, but one of the most scenic trails, and certainly one of the most popular of all, is that which has been adopted by Alta Via 2 from the Pordoi Pass to Lago di Fedaia; the trail known as Viel del Pan.

Soon after leaving Passo Pordoi this well-marked path crosses the low dividing ridge and breaks away eastward on an undulating traverse of steep grass slopes topped with broken crags. An uninterrupted panorama across the depths of the Avisio valley shows the Marmolada in full splendour, with Lago di Fedaia soon coming into view at its foot. It's an extremely busy trail throughout the summer, as I once discovered when caught behind a crocodile of thirty or so walkers where the path was at its narrowest, while dozens more ambled along at their own leisurely pace in small groups or family parties. Rifugio Viel del Pan exploits the view from a small projecting spur and captures plenty of trade; but there's no accommodation to be had there - refreshments only. Just above the hut a narrow cleft in the ridge grants a lovely view north to the Sella Group, and north-west to the distant Sassolungo trinity. Farther along the ridge, beyond the point where the main trail descends towards Lago di Fedaia, Porta Vescovo provides an opportunity to cross back to the north, thereby enabling one to complete a circuit by returning to Passo Pordoi. The Viel del Pan, and Alta Via 2, continue downhill, however, as far as the lake where accommodation is available at both ends of the reservoir.

In order to explore the southern side of the Marmolada, where the massif is buttressed by near-vertical rock walls, one could either follow the main Alta Via trail which stays with the road below the dammed lake as far as Malga Ciapela (cable-car nearby leads almost to the Marmolada's summit), then bears right through Valle di Franzedas where there are alternative options, or take the Alta Via variant up the north face of the mountain to cross Forcella della Marmolada (2910m). By linking these options, and adopting another trail over Passo Ombretta (2704m), a complete circuit could be achieved. Rifugio Falier, located midway between Malga Ombretta and the pass, provides lodging on this south side of the mountain.

Before leaving the Marmolada mention should be made of the numerous *via ferrata* protected routes that exist here, mostly, it must be said, on the southern flank, but others which have been created on the west side of Val di Contrin. Of these, one of the recognised Dolomite classics is Via Ferrata dei Finanzieri on the Collaccio (2715m), a strenuous route of a little over 600 vertical metres.

✳   ✳   ✳

PALE DI SAN MARTINO

This is the most southerly of the major Dolomite groups whose scale and bulk rivals that of the Sella. "The tremendous wall of the Palle di S. Martino, [is] vertical to all appearances if not to the eye of the geologist," wrote Leslie Stephen. "It is scarred and gashed by some of the characteristic gullies of the Dolomite mountains. Some of them may be climbed for a distance, or a path may even lie through their hidden depths to the summit of the mountain, but they appear at any rate to be closed by the most forbidding of rocky walls."

These formidable mountains represent the most dramatic section of the Parco Naturale Paneveggio-Pale di San Martino which stretches south of the Passo di San Pellegrino almost as far as Primiero, and divides at San Martino di Castrozza. East of this division the ragged peaks and karst plateaux form a direct contrast to the vast primeval forest of Paneveggio to the west, a wilderness of silver fir, arolla and mountain pines, larch and Norway spruce from which the Venetian fleet claimed its timber in the seventeenth century. Further west lie the granite ridges of Lagorani, so the Pala is really the last (or the first) of the Dolomites hereabouts. And what Dolomites they are!

If you enter the region from the north and travel down through Val di Fassa from Canazei, the route forks at Predazzo. Turning east now the road follows the Travignolo and rises gently to Paneveggio village (formerly a hospice) before climbing in hairpins to the Passo di Rolle from where the imposing Cimon della Pala (3184m), the so-called 'Matterhorn of the Dolomites' is seen to startling effect like a narrow tapering pinnacle. Below lies Val Cismon and the fashionable resort of San Martino di Castrozza. Originally a monastery, San Martino is beautifully situated in a wooded basin at the foot of tremendous rock walls, while to the south the Vette di Feltre chain seems to block the lower valley beyond Primiero. A chairlift rises to Col Verde from where the Rosetta cableway gives access to the south-west edge of the Pale plateau. A thirty-minute ascent of Cima della Rosetta is recommended for its amazing overview of the surrounding area.

Facing west the long wall of Pale di San Martino rivals the Catinaccio for its reflected alpenglow, which was described long ago by Guido Rey in the following tribute:

"The mountains are aglow with their own light...at the supreme moment the wondrous forms of the ancient towers, palaces and temples appear as if by magic; the dead castles come to life again, the battlements are crowned with shining breastplates...the blind loopholes are endowed with sight and the deep caves reveal their treasures."

The Pale is rich in walking routes, as well as *vie ferratae*. Across the top lies the Altopiano, a high central plateau of stone, once a coral lagoon now dotted with

434

cairns to aid route finding, while to the south lies the Canali glen which flows out to Primiero (Fiera di Primiero to give its full name). A tributary of the Canali is Val Pradidali which flows out behind the Sass Maor and Cima di Ball. This valley was described by Leslie Stephen as "a steep lateral gorge enclosed by precipitous rocks on each side". North of the Pale a minor road branches off the Passo di Rolle, wends its way north then east, passes Rifugio Capanna Cervino and reaches the teeming Baita Segantini hut (refreshments only) with Cimon della Pala looking magnificent to the south. A fine two-day walk leads from here across the Pale di San Martino to Primiero. Several rifugios invite multi-day explorations of the Pale hinterland, which is also traversed by the route of Alta Via 2.

✳   ✳   ✳

CIVETTA & PELMO

First climbed by Tuckett in 1867, Monte Civetta (3220m) presents a seductive face when seen reflected in the green waters of Lago d'Alleghe to the north-west. It's a big, impressive mountain massif whose north-west face is some seven kilometres long and 1200 metres high. It has crusty ridges, chiselled tops, slabs and organ-pipe-like pinnacles; a climber's peak, but one which the modest walker can approach without trepidation along the Alta Via delle Dolomiti 1 which provides such magical views. But the Civetta does not hold a scenic monopoly, for the whole group which takes its name offers a wide spectrum of fine views. Monte Pelmo (3168m) is an outstanding example; overlooking Borca di Cadore its pale rock glows at dawn. Croda da Lago is another, as is Monte Averau, and the curious nobbly spires of the Cinque Torri also capture one's imagination, while long views crowded with white, grey or soft pink peaklets add a lustre to the walker's day.

The Civetta Group is, again, bounded by roads that form an imaginative diamond shape. Place Cortina at the topmost point and follow the road south-west across the Falzarego Pass (the huge pink slab of Le Tofane to the north), then run southward to Alleghe, Agordo and down to Belluno - in so doing here we include the Bellunese Dolomites which have been protected as a national park since 1991 (Parco Nazionale delle Dolomiti Bellunesi e Feltrine). North-east now, then northward along the Piave to Pieve di Cadore where Valle d'Ampezzo sweeps in a clockwise curve back round to Cortina along the base of the Marmarole. Lesser road systems penetrate this diamond block of mountain and forest and, in fact, run between Monte Civetta and Pelmo. Yet it is not roads with which we are concerned here, but trails for walking, and of these there are plenty.

Long distance routes, such as Alta Via 1 and Alta Via 3, describe multi-day tours through these mountains, while numerous 'local' paths visit huts and viewpoints, or link with the longer routes to produce a veritable grid of possibilities, added to which a handful of *vie ferratae* contribute the spice of exposure for those who enjoy such excitement. One of the finest of Dolomite viewpoints is the rocky Nuvolau, on which the Nuvolau hut is located south-east of Monte Averau. From here Le Tofane to the north appears to tower above the stumpy Cinque Torri, while south-eastward Monte Pelmo presents itself as a great wedge of a peak. A circuit of Monte Pelmo is an obvious example of the range of tours available here, with three huts spaced around it providing either accommodation or refreshment on the way; or a loop of this peak followed by a similar loop round part of the Civetta, thereby creating almost a figure of eight trek; although it has to be said that rather too many roads, both made and unmade, plus cableways, tend to fuss the countryside accessible from Alleghe and Selva di Cadore. But crossing the district from west to east, starting say from Alleghe and finishing at either Borca or San Vito di Cadore, provides a consistently high degree of quality views if you choose the way with care, and at the same time teases with prospects of neighbouring districts that cry out for further exploration.

✳︎   ✳︎   ✳︎

SORAPIS & MARMAROLE

North-east of the Civetta, the combined Sorapis and Marmarole Groups overlook a heart-shaped road circuit fed from Cortina. The steep plunging cliffs of Sorapis (3205m) form the east wall of the Ampezzo valley, while the north flank contains a huge amphitheatre that is seen to such good effect from the lake at Misurina - one of the classic Dolomite views that appears on countless postcards, calendars and chocolate boxes. The multi-summited Marmarole spreads east of Sorapis, with the glen of Valle di San Vito nudging between, while south of that, and on the other side of Valle d'Oten, stands the 3263 metre Antelao, from whose crown Monte Pelmo can be seen in full splendour across the depths of the Ampezzo valley. Valle d'Oten flows down to Lago di Cadore where Pieve di Cadore, birthplace of the great sixteenth century painter, Titian, provides a base for exploration of the south and east sides of both Anteleo and Marmarole.

Despite the fact that these mountains consist of bold and seemingly impenetrable fortress-like blocks, there are walkers' routes that exploit those few weaknesses that exist in their defences. In so doing it becomes not only possible to traverse the district from north to south and from east to west, but also to stray onto their ridges, nudge among their inner glens and, by dint of imaginative sections of protected paths, create a high-level circuit of Sorapis, not to mention some exciting routes among the daunting crags of Marmarole with prospects of seeing ibex in their natural habitat.

The ski playgrounds of Cortina stray onto the north-west flank of Sorapis and rather devalue that corner of the mountains for summer visitors, but that still leaves a remarkable wealth of country to explore. The pass of Tre Croci, a grass and tree-crowded saddle at the foot of Monte Cristallo, is as good a place as any to begin, for an easy trail goes through woodland in a south-easterly direction and rises into the Sorapis ampthitheatre where Rifugio Vandelli gazes out to the north, with the 'finger of God' (Dito di Dio) soaring above and behind it from a small tarn. From this point various options present themselves. One trail, a variant of Alta Via 3, climbs west through the cirque to its austere headwall below Punta Nera and then forks. One crosses the ridge heading north, the other goes south, crosses the ridge also and tackles a *via ferrata* before joining a clearer, easier path on a traverse of the south side of Marmarole. This last-mentioned could also link with a traverse of the south-eastern flank before dropping down to Auronzo.

Other options from Rifugio Vandelli include the Via Ferrata A Vandelli across the eastern arm of the amphitheatre, a path adopted by Alta Via 4 on its way from San Candido to Pieve di Cadore, and a more straightforward route crossing of the northern spur at Forcella del Cadin. On the way to this col an amazing long view north-east shows the Tre Cime di Lavaredo at the head of a tree-filled basin, while the nearby Monte Cristallo reveals its great south face to perfection. Turn a corner and out to the south-west shines the Marmolada, and everywhere you look one Dolomite group after another hassles for attention.

❊   ❊   ❊

MONTE CRISTALLO

As we have already seen, this very fine massif stands to the north of Sorapis and is the dominant mountain group above Cortina d'Ampezzo. Once again, as is the norm in the Dolomites, serpentine roads make a complete circle round it, as indeed do a series of trails. Alta Via 3 is one such. This makes a traverse along the east side of the mountain before crossing the Tre Croci Pass onto the Sorapis massif. Monte Cristallo itself rises directly above the pass, and at 3221 metres high, is a handsome, slightly twisted tower that almost looks as though it belongs further west in the Brenta, instead of forming one of the eastern-most Dolomite groups. So closely compacted are the individual turrets, towers and peaklets of the massif when seen from the south, that to all intents and purposes they appear as a solid unit. However the northern side is rather different, for now they become disjointed, cleft by glens that push into the heartland and with a couple of small glaciers wedged in high corries, while the south-western aspect (as seen above Cortina) is graced by open slanting meadows in which the roots of the mountains are firmly planted.

An easy day's stroll returns to Cortina from the Tre Croci (bus from Cortina) by way of Passo Son Forca and the Val Giande, which flows between the Cristallo massif and the Pomagagnon crest, then swings round the northern end of the latter along path 208 on the eastern side of Valle d'Ampezzo. At the other end of the spectrum a short but sometimes tricky protected route may appeal to experienced mountain walkers and scramblers with a good head for heights, for just below the Tre Croci Pass, on the Cortina slope, a cableway ferries visitors to Rifugio Lorenzi at 2932 metres, from where the Marino Bianchi *via ferrata* leads to the Cima di Mezzo (3163m), the central summit of the Cristallo complex - to be attempted in good conditions only. Those two possibilities show the extremes of walking options in the Cristallo area, while between them lie assorted trails offering a wide gamut of experience.

❊   ❊   ❊

DOLOMITI DI SESTO

With the Tre Cime di Lavaredo as its symbol, this group, which is located east and north-east of the Cristallo, contains the best-known and most photographed of all mountains in the Dolomites. Thanks to ease of access by road and an extraordinarily well-maintained system of paths, it will seldom if ever be experienced in solitude. Or at least, not that section of it that pays homage to the Tre Cime. As to the rest, and there's quite a bit of it, the honeypot principle ensures that most of the crowds will be funnelled along specific routes. Let's look at these first.

Cortina being the main centre, most visitors approach by vehicle across the Tre Croci Pass, down and round to Misurina, then by way of an intrusive toll road that ends at a huge terraced car park by Rifugio Auronzo at around 2300 metres. If you can ignore the road, traffic and crowds (and these last are usually confined to the period mid-morning to early evening), this is an impressive spot with the soaring cliffs of the Tre Cime towering above, the Cadini pinnacles clustered to the south, and the deep Vallon di Lavaredo yawning below. A jeep road leads round the base of the Tre Cime to Rifugio Lavaredo, and a broad and easy path continues from there over a bare, windblown saddle (Forcella di Lavaredo; 2457m) which provides a startling view along the north side of the three turrets that are now seen in profile. From this point another hut is seen ahead to the north. This is Rifugio Locatelli, also known as the Tre Cime or Drei Zinnen hut. (Drei Zinnen is a reminder that all these mountains were Austrian before the First World War, and walkers following any one of a number of trails will be conscious of the terrible battles that were fought here, for tunnels, fortifications and other debris of warfare, including coils of barbed wire, have all become part of the landscape.) The Locatelli hut is a sizeable inn from which the Tre Cime may be seen at their individual best. Although the hut is invariably busy, the majority of day visitors leave in time to miss the evening light-show that plays on the mountains round about. Most wander back to the roadhead by the same route by which they arrived at Locatelli, but in order to complete a circuit of the Tre Cime another trail, rougher and not so wide as that which led here, descends into a basin below the north face, then climbs to the Forcella Col di Mezzo (2315m), on the way to which another superb profile view is granted of the Tre Cime to match that enjoyed from the Forcella di Lavaredo.

That circuit is a truly magnificent one, as far as the wild mountain scenery is concerned. But oh how one's experience of it can be affected by the long and loud parties that tackle it day by day throughout the summer! The broad and easy track from Rifugio Auronzo to the Locatelli hut is inviting to all, and the fame of the Tre Cime is such that its popularity is ensured. But the trail from Locatelli over Forcella Col di Mezzo back to the car park is a mountain path pure and simple, and a number of those who tackle it are neither physically capable nor well-enough shod to enjoy it, as I discovered when I came upon an Italian coach party in some distress after an elderly (and overweight) woman wearing town shoes suitable for shopping arcades but not the mountains had slipped on a patch of scree and broken her arm. The freedom of the hills, it appears, exacts a price upon those who are unsure of what to do with that freedom.

Those Tre Cime paths are the busiest of all. Happily that leaves plenty of others. Even a variation of the above circuit will have its rewards, especially if that variation ignores the Forcella di Lavaredo and heads east, then north-east and north round a long ridge extending from Monte Paterno (Paternkofel) where the little Pian di Cengia hut is tucked away on a ridge at 2457 metres. Another trail leads from there to the Zsigmondy-Comici hut in full view of the Elferkofel, Zwölfer and

Einserkofel - so-named because when seen from Sesto (Sexten) in Val di Sesto to the north, the sun is directly above them at eleven, twelve and one o'clock respectively.

Val di Sesto, sometimes claimed to be the prettiest of all Dolomite valleys, marks the start of two long-distance routes, Alta Via 4 (the Grohmann), and Alta Via 5 (the Titian), both of which make a good job of exploring the Sesto (or Sextener) Dolomites before straying to other districts and ending together in Pieve di Cadore. The early stages of those two routes enjoy comparatively empty country, and it is in the tributary glens of Campo di Dentro and Fiscalina that some charming short walks may be had too.

Valle di Landro forms the western boundary of the district, and the view of Monte Cristallo from the shores of Lago di Landro is quite exquisite. Just north of that lake a trail cuts through the feeder glen of Valle di Rienza heading south-east, but as you come to other side glens so alternative paths break away. One or two remain in green pastoral country, while others climb into the stark boneyard of the mountains. One heads roughly northward to Passo Grande dei Rondoi and links up with a variant of Alta Via 4; a second goes south, crosses Forcella dell Aghena then rises up to Forcella Col di Mezzo at the western end of the Tre Cime, while a third follows through Val di Rimbon, at the head of which it climbs to Rifugio Locatelli, thereby confronting the crowds but also gaining access to yet more enticing trails.

One of these, a novel route that adopts paths and tunnels created during the bitter fighting of the First World War, leads to the summit of Monte Paterno (Paternkofel; 2744m) which overlooks the hut from the south-east. This route is dedicated to the memory of Piero de Luca and Sepp Innerkofler, and includes no less than 600 metres of tunnel bored into the heart of the mountain; some windows allow views out to the Tre Cime, but mostly a headtorch will be required. It should be pointed out that the cable protection fitted for use once out of the tunnel is not always in the best of condition and should be checked first before relying on it. Needless to say, the view from the summit to the Tre Cime is a sufficient antedote to the claustrophobic ascent.

South of the Tre Cime, and rising to the east of Misurina, the Cadini Group also offers some adventurous walks, with several *vie ferratae* thrown in for good measure. A circuit could be made beginning at the southern end of Lago di Misurina, heading in a counter-clockwise direction by way of Col del Viro and the Citta di Carpi hut, then sloping down Val d'Onge to its confluence with Valle Marzon, before veering west into the Campedelle glen and over Forcella di Rimbianco which takes you back to the forested valley above Misurina. An alternative path breaks south from the Rimbianco col to reach the Fonda-Savio hut, while north of the col the Via Bonacossa is a protected path leading to the summit of Monte Campedelle (2346m), from which the Tre Cime di Lavaredo look very impressive.

※　※　※

HIGH-LEVEL ROUTES

On a number of occasions in the foregoing paragraphs mention has been made of the various Alta Via long-distance routes that criss-cross the Dolomites, each of which enables the walker to experience the wild nature of these other-worldly mountains, and to gain a true perspective of the region as a whole. These 'high routes' (and there are eight at present) are of assorted length and standard, but most are quite clearly waymarked, although maps of the area are not always as accurate or up to date as one would like. Some routes involve sections of *via ferrata*; all require at some time or another the traverse of fairly remote country, and cross high, exposed ridges where good settled weather conditions are all-important. Huts and occasional village inns provide accommodation along the way, but it should be noted that many huts are extremely busy in the peak summer period, and beds may not always be available at this time unless booked in advance.

The following section describes in very basic terms the route of three of these Alta Via tours. More detailed descriptions will be found in the guidebook *Alta Via - High Level Walks in the Dolomites* (Alta Via 1 & 2 only), while both these and Alta Via 4, are included in the large-format primer, *Walking & Climbing in the Alps*. Of the remaining high routes Alta Via 3, also known as Alta Via dei Camosci, links a number of chamois hunters' trails between Villabassa in Val Pusteria and Longarone in the Piave valley; Alta Via 5 closely follows AV4 between Sesto and Pieve di Cadore, and Alta Via 6 travels through largely peaceful country (hence the name, Alta Via dei Silenzi) on the way from Sappada in the Carnic Alps to Vittorio Veneto south of Belluno

ALTA VIA 1

Making a north-south crossing of the Central Dolomites in a journey lasting nine or ten days, this high route is probably the best-known of all. It is neither as long nor as high as Alta Via 2, nor as remote in places as that of Alta Via 4. But it does have its strenuous stages, and enough challenge to make completion a cause for quiet satisfaction. It begins by Lago di Braies in Val Pusteria north-west of Cortina, and over a distance of about 120 kilometres, the route crosses first the Fanes-Sennes-Braies Nature Park, skirts the Tofane, approaches Monte Pelmo, strays alongside the Civetta and makes a traverse of the Parco Nazionale delle Dolomiti Bellunesi e Feltrine before descending to Belluno on the River Piave. A good head for heights is essential as there are several sections with considerable exposure, but it's an extremely rewarding tour and one that makes the best possible introduction to the Dolomite region.

ALTA VIA 1 - ROUTE SUMMARY

Day 1:   Lagi di Braies - Porta Sora 'l Forn - Rifugio Pederu

Day 2:   Rifugio Pederu - Malga Fanes - Forcella del Lago - Rifugio Monte Lagazuoi

Day 3:   Rifugio Monte Lagazuoi - Rifugio Nuvolau

Day 4:   Rifugio Nuvolau - Forcella Giau - Rifugio Citta di Fiume

Day 5:   Rifugio Citta di Fiume - Lago Coldai - Rifugio Vazzoler

Day 6:   Rifugio Vazzoler - Passo Duran - Rifugio Sommariva

Day 7:   Rifugio Sommariva - Forcella Sud del Val de Citta - Rifugio Bianchet

Day 8:   Rifugio Bianchet - Forcella del Marmol - Rifugio VII Alpini

Day 9:   Rifugio VII Alpini - Belluno

ALTA VIA 2

At the western end of the range Alta Via 2 makes another north-south traverse, this time taking in the Puez-Odle, Sella, Marmolada and Pale Groups before crossing the Vette di Feltre wilderness and descending to Feltre, dominated by its castle to the south-west of AV1's destination of Belluno. The route begins at Bressanone, on the Bolzano-Brenner-Innsbruck highway, an historic town known also as Brixen, which may reached by train from either Bolzano or Innsbruck. The complete walk could be completed in eleven or twelve days, but two clear weeks should be allowed. It's a longer and rather more strenuous route than the better known Alta Via 1, with consistently high terrain, several via ferrata sections, and some remote countryside along the way. Mountain huts provide accommodation throughout.

ALTA VIA 2 - ROUTE SUMMARY

Day 1:   Bressanone - San Andrea - Rifugio Plose *

Day 2:   Rif. Plose - Forcella della Putia - Sass de Putia (optional) - Rifugio Genova

Day 3:   Rif. Genova - Forcella della Roa - Forcella Forces de Sielles - Rifugio Puez

Day 4:   Rifugio Puez - Passo di Crespeina - Passo Gardena - Rifugio Pisciadù

Day 5:   Rifugio Pisciadù - Rifugio Boè - Passo Pordoi - Rifugio Castiglioni

Day 6:   Rifugio Castiglioni - Malga Ciapela - Passo di Forca Rossa - Passo di San Pellegrino - Rifugio Passo Valles

or: Rifugio Castiglioni - Forcella della Marmolada - Rifugio Contrin

then: Rif. Contrin - Passo di Cirelle - Passo di San Pellegrino - Rifugio Passo Valles

Day 7:   Rifugio Passo Valles - Passo di Venegiotta - Rifugio Mulaz

Day 8:   Rifugio Mulaz - Passo delle Farangole - Rifugio Pedrotti - Rifugio Pradidali

Day 9:   Rifugio Pradidali - Passo delle Lede - Rifugio Treviso - Rifugio Cereda

Day 10: Rifugio Cereda - Forcella di Comedon - Rifugio Boz

Day 11: Rifugio Boz - Rifugio Giorgio dal Piaz - Passo di Croce d'Aune - Feltre

* Note: Some walkers choose to avoid the steep uphill section to Rifugio Plose by taking a cable-car from Bressanone, and then going as far as the Genova hut, thereby reducing the overall walk by one day. However, the cable-car only operates in the main summer season. An alternative would be to ride a bus as far as the Val Croce hotel at 2040 metres, and walk from there.

ALTA VIA 4

This short but spectacular route takes about six days to cross the Sesto district, passing the Tre Cime di Lavaredo and Cadini pinnacles, and on to the lovely Sorapis massif where it then curves between the Marmarole Group and Antelao to end at Pieve di Cadore. Parts of the route are shared with Alta Via 5, and others with Alta Via 3. Huts in the Tre Cime region will be very busy, and the trails crowded, but the southern section of the route is likely to be more secluded. It is here, however, that the route takes on a more serious tone with some exposed *vie ferratae* to add zest. All in all a scenically delightful route that begins in San Candido at the junction of Val di Sesto with Val Pusteria just west of the Austrian border. San Candido is served by trains on the Bressanone-Brunico-Lienz railway line, or by bus from Cortina.

ALTA VIA 4 - ROUTE SUMMARY

Day 1:   San Candido - Passo Cavenga (Gwengalpenjoch) - Rifugio Locatelli

Day 2:   Rifugio Locatelli - Forcella Col di Mezzo - Via Bonacossa - Rifugio Fonda-Savio

Day 3:   Rifugio Fonda-Savio - Rifugio Citta di Carpi - Rifugio Vandelli

Day 4:   Rifugio Vandelli - Forcella Alta del Banco - Forcella Grande - Rifugio San Marco

Day 5:   Rifugio San Marco - Forcella Piccolo - Forcella del Ghiacciaio - Rifugio Antelao

Day 6:   Rifugio Antelao - Forcella Antracisa - Pieve di Cadore

---

*   *   *

THE DOLOMITES

Location:

In the South Tirol of north-east Italy; Alto-Adige and Belluno provinces.

Principal valleys:

Naming from west to east, these are Val Gardena, Val di Fassa, Val Badia, Val Cismon, Valle d'Ampezzo, Val Cadore, Valle di Landro and Val di Sesto.

Principal peaks:

Marmolada (3342m), Antelao (3263m), Monte Cristallo (3221m), Civetta (3220m), Cimon della Pala (3184m), Sassolungo (3181m), Monte Pelmo (3168m), Tre Cime di Lavaredo (2999m)

Centres:

Ortisei and Santa Cristina in Val Gardena, San Martino di Castrozza, Cortina d'Ampezzo and Alleghe

Huts:

There are literally dozens of huts throughout the Dolomites. Most are owned by the CAI, although some are in private ownership; a good many are like large mountain inns. Well patronised and, in the more popular districts, likely to be full to capacity throughout the peak season.

Access:
By air to Venice, then by coach to San Martino or Cortina. Also by air to Innsbruck, followed by train via the Brenner Pass to Bressanone and Bolzano. Trains also run along Val Pusteria in the north between Fortezza (north of Bressanone), Brunico and Lienz in Austria. Many private coach companies provide access to major Dolomite centres from such north Italian cities as Milan, Bologna, Verona and Venice. A reasonable local bus service operates throughout the region in summer.

Maps:
Tabacco, Geografica and Kompass all publish maps at a scale of 1:50,000 of use to walkers in the Dolomites. Tabacco also publish 1:25,000 scale for the same area.

Guidebooks:
Walking in the Dolomites by Gillian Price (Cicerone Press) is by far the most useful guide for general walking in these mountains. Thoroughly researched and interestingly written, all the main groups are included.
Alta Via, High Level Walks in the Dolomites by Martin Collins (Cicerone Press) describes the two most popular long distance walks, Alta Via 1 & 2. Nicely illustrated with photographs and line drawings.
Via Ferrata, Scrambles in the Dolomites translated by Cecil Davies from the original German by Höfler and Werner (Cicerone Press). As the title suggests, this guide describes numerous exciting 'protected paths' in each of the main Dolomite districts.
Huts and Hikes in the Dolomites by Ruth Rudner (Sierra Club, San Francisco). This book describes three hut to hut tours (including one in the Brenta); the first in the Tre Cime region, a second in the Catinaccio. Useful, but having been published in 1974, it is a little out of date in places.

Other reading:
Walking & Climbing in the Alps by Stefano Ardito (Swan Hill Press) contains chapters on Alta Vias 1, 2 and 4. Beautifully illustrated, but with rather poor translation from the Italian original.
Classic Walks in the Alps by Kev Reynolds (Oxford Illustrated Press). Alta Via 1 and 2 are described by Martin Collins.
Trekking in Europe by Giancarlo Corbellini (AA Publishing) describes high route Alta Via 1.
The Mountains of Europe by Kev Reynolds (Oxford Illustrated Press) has a chapter by C. Douglas Milner that serves as a good primer for anyone planning a visit to the Dolomites.
Wild Italy by Tim Jepson (Sheldrake Press/Aurum Press); a natural history guide with a good section devoted to the Dolomites.
The Outdoor Traveler's Guide to The Alps by Marcia R. Lieberman (Stewart, Tabori & Chang, New York, 1991) has a few pages devoted to selected districts.
The Dolomites by C. Douglas Milner (Robert Hale, 1951) is a good, if dated, background. Illustrated with 150 b&w photographs.
The Dolomite Mountains by Gilbert & Churchill (Longmans, 1864). This is a classic of mountain travel, beautifully illustrated with line drawings.
The Playground of Europe by Leslie Stephen (Longmans, 1894) contains a chapter entitled 'The Peaks of Primiero' with some fine descriptions of the Pale di San Martino region.

❋   ❋   ❋

Rugged peaks cradle the Kriska stena cirque south of Kranjska Gora

19: THE JULIAN ALPS

C rammed astride the borders of Italy and Slovenia, with the Carnic Alps on the far side of the River Fella forging a tenuous link with the eastern Dolomites, the Julians may be considered the last of the southern spur of Alpine ranges, while the Karawanken continues a short distance to the north along the Austrian frontier. Although the Slovenian Julians have received the lion's share of publicity among western mountaineers, the range is also well represented inside Italian territory. In fact the second highest summit (Jôf di Montasio; 2754m) stands midway between Val Canale and Canale di Raccolane some way west of the Predil Pass.

The Julians are limestone mountains. But the limestone here is not the same as that of the Dolomites, for although they're sometimes compared with those exotic pale mountains the Julian Alps have their own identity, their own specific appeal and their own minstrels to sing their praises. Julius Kugy, for example. Born in Gorizia in 1858, Kugy became the greatest publicist these mountains have ever known and his books proclaim the wild beauty of their stark ridges and lush forested valleys in phrases of romantic erudition. That great Himalayan explorer, Dr Tom Longstaff, was another. This is what he wrote for a book edited by Kugy and published in Graz in 1938:

> "It is a fact that they have become for me, after forty years' devotion to mountain scenery, the most desirable of all mountains. I want to revisit

THE JULIAN ALPS

them more than I desire to see again any other region of the Alps; more than I desire to see again the frosty Caucasus, or Himalaya, or the mountains of Canada and Alaska, or the ineffable primrose light of the low sun on the fantastic peaks of the Arctic. I believe this feeling is greatly due to their surprising quality of mystery." (*Fünf Jarhunderte Triglav*)

That quality of mystery remains, despite the crowds of walkers and climbers who throng there in summer, despite the paint-blazed trails, the threads of cable and iron rungs that adorn rock faces with *vie ferratae*, many of which were constructed a hundred years ago. Despite these things, and the trippers boating on Lake Bled or gathered on the bridge overlooking Lake Bohinj, and the coach parties capturing a vicarious excitement on the twisting road that leads over the pass of Vrsic in the shadow of Prisojnik and Razor - despite all these things, a sense of mystery remains to draw the lover of wild places and then to demand a return.

Limestone frontiers burst with a suddenness unknown among granite mountains, and in this respect the Julians are no exception. Neat fields and orchards that colour the plain of Ljubljana are suddenly interrupted by peaks that thrust from the turf. So it is when approaching from the north on the road west of Jesenice. The valley is broad and flat and green. On one side the wooded hills fold upward to the half-hinted Karawanken, on the other gaunt fenceposts of grey soaring limestone; jagged, ragged, immensely appealing. There is no easing of approach, no gentle transition of chalet-dotted pasture rising in stages to bold snow mountains as in the Western Alps. "The month's approach in the Himalaya is magically traversed in a day," is how Longstaff described it.

It's a small range, neat and compact as to area, and if it were not for the queues of traffic at some of the border crossings in summer, it would be no problem to drive around its outer rim in an easy day, with a short stroll here and there to gather a tease of impressions that could only be satisfied by taking to the trails that score into the heartland. And there are plenty of these. The Slovenes in particular are great lovers of mountains, and they've created a network of paths which, together with a number of well-patronised huts, invite weeks of exploration. There are plenty of day walks of varying degrees of challenge, and multi-day routes that could be created by linking local trails, hut paths and routes to summits. Two European long-distance walks traverse the mountains; the E6 which links the Baltic and Adriatic, and E7 on its journey from the Atlantic to the Black Sea. There are some tough walks, too, with assorted sections of *via ferrata* to enable one to visit peaks and steeply plunging ridges that might otherwise be out of bounds to all but the rock climber.

There are few permanent snowfields among these mountains, and no three thousand metre peaks, but since the valleys are low, the difference in altitude between valley base and mountain summit is similar to that of many regions in the Western Alps, and with cableways being sparse it soon becomes evident that anyone with an eye on summit-bagging will face plenty of exercise. The highest of all, Triglav (2864m), is very much a symbol of Slovene nationalism and a place almost of pilgrimage. In 1981 the Triglav National Park was created with that mountain, naturally, as its focus, and covering an area of almost 85,000 hectares, it embraces nearly all the Julian Alps of Slovenia. It's a haven of alpine flowers, chamois, marmots and a few ibex that have been reintroduced after the native population had been hunted to extinction.

The rugged western Julians of Italy (Alpi Giulie) rise east and south of the Udine to Tarvisio highway, the main valleys being those of the Canale di Raccolana which carries a minor but interesting and useful road into Slovenia via the Val Rio del Lago and the Predil Pass; the U-shaped Canale di Dogna; Val Canale that forms the northern and western limits, and its lovely tributary glen, Valbruna, the head of which is blocked by a huge cirque. Tarvisio stands at a junction of international highways. To the north two roads go side by side through the gap between the Carnic Alps and Karawanken to Arnoldstein in Austria. To the south twists the main Predil Pass road into Slovenia above Bovec, while eastward stretches the highway leading to Passo di Fusine which marks the Slovenian border and the route to Kranjska Gora, Jesenice and Ljubljana. (Just before reaching the pass, a small tarmac road heads south to the two attractive Fusine lakes framed by abrupt mountain walls and with the fourth highest mountain in the Julians, Mangart, rising to the south.) Tarvisio is more than a junction of international highways though, it's also a watershed - of peoples, as well as of rivers. One river flows by way of the Gail and Drava tributaries to the Danube and out to the Black Sea. Another, the Fella, feeds the Tagliamento which flows into the Adriatic. One senses, even in the crowded market of Tarvisio, that one stands at a crossroads, while the mountains gather to them Longstaff's quality of mystery.

East of the frontier the Julians are expressed in dramatic form. These are wild mountains in a very real sense; not wild as in an untrodden wilderness, but wild as to shape and form, their forested lower slopes giving way to a tangle of dwarf pine and shrubbery, then on to open clutters of rock and slab barriers, extensive screes and dry karst plateaux out of which furious pinnacles burst in extravagent fashion. Some of the ridges have huge window-like holes in them through which you gaze on astonishing depths; caves pit the landscape. Wedge peaks and spires head remote glens, their glaring white limestone stark above the lush greenery of the valley bed. Many of the upper valleys are notoriously dry in summer, thanks to the porous nature of limestone. But some of the corries are adorned with small tarns, and in the heart of the district the lovely Seven Lakes Valley (Dolina Triglavskih Jezer) boasts a string of varying size and colour.

Longstaff again:

"It may be that the Triglav complex owes its magic in part to its relatively small scale, making the uninitiated think that he is seeing every secret unveiled at once: a mere delusion; but in a topography so intricate and so difficult, in such a veritable maze, it is a delight to lose oneself, to escape, to be free. Trees, flowers, rocks, snow, all seem to assume some indefinable new quality, some new revelation of beauty. By comparison the Dolomites are obvious. Triglav reigns over a dreamworld, sundered from time, full of unbelievable hidden nooks, of unsuspected passages, of sudden visions of cliffs which cannot be real. Surely there is no other mountain land like this."

✳ ✳ ✳

THE JULIAN ALPS OF SLOVENIA

East of the Fusine Pass the Sava Dolinika valley is a trim furrow separating the Karawanken from the Julians. The road is a busy one for it carries international traffic via a series of crossings into Austria, in addition to that of the Fusine route to Italy. Only four kilometres inside Slovenia at Podkoren, for example, a side road branches north to cross the Karawanken ridge at the Wurzen Pass (Korensko sedlo), with a steep descent to the lower Gailtal; another, of motorway standard, tunnels through the mountains upvalley from Jesenice to link up with the Austrian autobahn system at Villach, while yet a third crossing into Austria leaves the Sava valley below Jesenice and tunnels beneath the Loibl Pass on its way to Klagenfurt. But the Sava Dolinika also provides the major route of access into the Julians from the north by way of feeder valleys carved from the mountains that rise in such attractive and abrupt fashion to the south.

Planica

Counting from the west the first of these glens is the wild-looking Planica with the village of Ratece near its entrance. A minor road cuts into this glen for about six kilometres, and serves the Tamar hut (Planinski dom Tamar), an important base for rock climbers since the valley is flanked by some impressive cliffs and with the international frontier running along the western ridge crest. The major climbing interest in the immediate vicinity of the hut is the splendid eight hundred metres high wall of Mojstrovka (2366m), which extends for some five kilometres as far as Jalovec, and includes the neighbouring Travnik. But walkers have routes of their own to make a visit worthwhile. One strikes away from the Tamar hut, crosses the western ridge into Italy, and descends to the Fusine lakes. Another trail continues upvalley to the stony upper reaches of Mali Kot from where the handsome profile of Jalovec (2643m) effectively blocks the head of the glen. On the northern side of this peak lies a conspicuous saddle, Kotovo sedlo (2138m), by which the Koritnica valley may be reached. There's also a way that leads south of Jalovec into the Trenta valley, and yet another, setting out from the Tamar hut, which crosses the Sleme plateau, rises to the summit of Vratica (1807m), then descends to the Vrsic pass, the scenic road crossing that links the Trenta and Pisnica valleys.

Velika Pisnica

The most important resort, as such, in the Sava Dolinika valley is the village of Kranjska Gora which lies to the east of the Planica glen just off the main road. Kranjska enjoys a favourable position with very fine views south to a cirque of mountains formed by ridges connecting the peaks of Prisojnik, Razor and Skrlatica. These cradle the head of the Velika Pisnica valley, a glen extending south-eastward as Krnica. Kranjska is a ski resort in winter and a honeypot in summer. It's a spruce and welcoming little resort, yet despite its clear attractions, its hotels, shops, bars, restaurants and tourist office, it's a very modest place by comparison with many resorts in the Dolomites or Western Alps, and it barely intrudes into the mountains it serves. A short distance behind the village lies a small lake from which Prisojnik and the tower of Razor look especially fine, with the jagged Skrbina standing between them. Here a tributary glen acts as a south-western offshoot. This is the Mala Pisnica, through which a trail wanders to the north face of Mojstrovka.

From Hotel Erika on the road south of the lake a trail follows the river upstream and continues into the Krnica glen to the Krnici hut. Here the trail forks with one route climbing east then north to the summit of Spik (2472m), a triangular mountain boasting a tremendous north face that is seen to such good effect from Gozd Martuljek in the Sava Dolinika valley. From the summit an alternative descent, by a steep waymarked path, drops westward to rejoin the valley trail by the Velika Pisnica stream.

The other trail which continues from the Krnici hut rises into the cirque of Kriska stena, bounded by the walls of Kriz (2410m), with Razor to the west and Skrlatica, at 2740 metres the second-highest summit in the Julians of Slovenia, rising to the north-east.

The most important north-south road of the eastern Julians leads through the Velika Pisnica valley to provide a scenic traverse of the mountains by way of the Vrsic pass (1611m). This multi-hairpinned route was built along the old border between Italy and the Austro-Hungarian empire by Russian prisoners during the First World War. During the winter of 1915-16 hundreds of these prisoners were buried by an avalanche; a small shingle-walled chapel on the way to the pass was erected in their memory, while their cemetery is on the far side near the village of Trenta. Various paths break away from the road, both on the way to the pass and from the summit itself. Vrsic, in fact, provides access to one of the classic non-technical mountaineering traverses of the eastern Julians, by taking in both Prisojnik (2547m) and Razor (2601m). Although technical climbing skills are not called for, it is a route on which scrambling experience is required, plus a good head for heights and a steady nerve. The route is waymarked and protected with many handrails, rungs and spikes, but there's a nasty loss of more than five hundred metres of height between the two peaks. Exposure, in places, is sensational, with views onto a moonscape of bare rock, with rough outcrops and slabs and a chaos of scree.

The late Dudley Stevens, the professional guide who made a speciality of the Julian Alps throughout the 1960s and early '70s (and whose Alpine memoirs were published in Ljubljana in 1987), claimed that it was his favourite traverse, going from the west of Prisojnik to the Pogacnikov hut in about seven hours. From that hut a steep descent leads to the Zadnjica glen which spills into the Trenta valley, but Stevens suggested a continuation over nearby summits to the Luknja pass and from there either dropping into the Vrata valley, or going up to the Triglav plateau where there are more huts and almost unlimited possibilities.

Martuljek

This little glen consists of a classic and very beautiful cirque created by ridge systems thrown out by Skrlatica, and is dominated by the fierce pyramid of Spik when seen from Gozd Martuljek, three kilometres east of Kranjska Gora. Spik and its neighbouring peaks are climbers' mountains with a wealth of hard routes, as will be evident from first glance, and opportunities for walkers within that cirque are limited. However, it's well worth a day's exploration, for the cirque contains a wild gorge, crashing waterfalls, beechwoods and tumbled boulders fringed with pine. There are screes and crags and towering splinters of rock to feast your eyes upon. And a pair of bivouac huts that overlook scenes of impressive grandeur.

Vrata

Midway between Kransjka Gora and Jesenice stands Mojstrana, an old village at the mouth of the Vrata valley, with the Bistrica river flowing through and the Grancise cliffs looming overhead. A road, partially surfaced, carries traffic (including buses) for twelve kilometres to the Aljazev hut at 1015 metres, a little beyond which stands a huge piton and karabiner monument to partisans killed in the district at the end of the Second World War.

The Vrata is one of the busiest valleys on the northern side of the range, so far as climbers, walkers and general tourists are concerned, because it leads to the tremendous north face of Triglav. However, Triglav is not its only attraction, since Skrlatica, rising north-west of the hut, is impressive too, as are other bullying crags on which climbing routes abound. The Aljazev hut acknowledges this popularity and, being one of the largest in the Julians, can accommodate 180 people. The valley itself is charming, and it's worth taking time to wander through, rather than use a vehicle. The mixed woods open here and there to lush meadows. There are shady glades with hinted views of soaring mountain walls; the Pericnik waterfalls burst with spray after a day of rain; boulders threaten to clog the river bed - and as you draw deeper into the glen, so the limestone cliffs on either side grow in stature until you stand at last beneath Triglav's 1500 metre north face and wonder at the vastness of it all. For here in these mountains of modest altitude is a rock face to stand comparison with almost anything the higher Alps can offer. It's a gem.

Contrary to the initial impression gained on confronting this wall, Triglav is not the sole preserve of expert rock climbers, for a series of routes has been created from all sides, mostly secured with a plethora of artificial aids, which makes it accessible to mountain walkers who have no problems with vertigo. Yet despite an over-abundance of cables, pegs and rungs, despite the huts stationed on its flanks and ridges, the painted waymarks and the gay throng of activists drawn to it in the long days of summer, the mountain has not been stripped either of its character or its challenge. And on gaining the summit rewards are plentiful. Baedeker praised the view as "one of the most sublime among the Alps". But once again let Longstaff have a word to say on this:

> "In 1902 I saw Corsica gleaming marvellously out in the Mediterranean, from the Cima di Mercantour in the Maritime Alps, and until last year this was the most memorable view I had had from any Alpine summit: but the view I got from Triglav over the Slovene country, over the Carso, over Venetia and the Adriatic was as beautiful, and far more mysterious in its suggestions. No mortal ever deserved such an evening as I had up there."

The most popular way of tackling Triglav is to make a traverse of the peak; go up by one route and down by another. The hut system enables this to be achieved without facing over-long days or enforced bivouacs. But for walkers passing through the Vrata valley, there is also the possibility of crossing into neighbouring glens without visiting Triglav's summit. Various passes may be adopted, depending which valley calls. The Luknja (1758m) is one such north-west of Triglav at the head of the Vrata valley, and this gives access by way of a mule trail to the scenic Zadnjica glen on the far side, a tributary of the Trenta. From the Aljazev hut to the Zadnjica roadhead this crossing takes about three and a half hours; a splendid route and a justifiably popular one for it constitutes one of the most important walking routes across the range.

Since this is all Kugy country, and the Vrata played an important role in his long career among these mountains, perhaps before we leave this valley Kugy should have the last word. Writing of a bivouac high above the Vrata, he captures the essence of the place, and the magic that can still be found if you can dodge the crowds and search out the silent, secret corners of the mountains:

> "The cold rouses me, and I hear the gentle murmur of the Bistrica in the depths of the Vrata glen. But instead of breaking the stillness of the night, it seems to deepen it. I look upward, heavy with sleep; black rocks overhanging, and the ghostly sheen of the fretted snow-wall; high over the cleft, the stars pass in slow succession. ...If you have thus dwelt in the secret heart of the mountains, beholding the full glory of their revelation...nothing can efface the memory of such nights." (*Alpine Pilgrimage*)

Krma & Kot

Of the three glacial valleys draining out of the mountains to the Sava Dolinika, Krma is the longest. It lies parallel with the Vrata, is also approached via Mojstrana but also has a much longer and seemingly more devious approach route coming from Bled in the east, by way of the Radovna valley which takes the underground waters of Krma into its own Radovna stream.

The Krma valley is flanked by jagged crests of Rjavina (2632m) on one side, and abrupt walls on the other rising to Tosc (2275m), while the shorter tributary glen of Kot burrows into the mountains between the Vrata and Krma, with the north-east face of Rjavina at its head. All these valleys are heavily wooded, but with bold rock architecture rising above the trees. As was found in the upper Vrata valley, walkers' passes lure trails over the high walling ridges into neighbouring glens. Alongside Tosc, for example, lies the Bohinjska vratca, a 1979 metre col that leads, as its name suggests, to Bohinjska (Bohinj - lake and village) on the south side of the mountains. Just below the col at a junction of several paths on the south-west flank of Tosc, stands the Vodnikov hut; a useful refreshment stop on the popular Triglav trail which attacks the mountain from the south-east.

A second breach in the headwall is the broad saddle known as Konjski preval (2020m), north-west of the other and, like the Bohinjska col, marked by a junction of paths. This is a fine viewpoint, although it can be troublesome in mist, and the trail heading west from it leads in zig-zags to the Planika hut (2401m) en route to Triglav. Below this trail lies the Velska Dolina described as a "typical Tibetan desert; huge rounded slopes and hollow basins leading up to the naked cliffs of a lunar landscape; not a tree; hardly a plant; lifeless." If one were to take the trail, say, from the Konjski saddle to the Planika hut, then descend south-westward on a marked path, a superb traverse could be achieved into the Bohinj basin via the Seven Lakes Valley, spending the night in the hut there. Or, avoiding the climb to the Planika hut, a similar traverse could be made by crossing the Bohinjska col and, passing through the Velska Dolina, also gain the magical lakes valley. But then a glance at the map shows a wealth of possibilities. Just make sure the weather is settled, carry plenty of water, and enjoy the wild and mysterious nature of this Triglav heartland.

Sava Bohinjska

The lakes of Bled (Blejsko Jezero) in the east, and Bohinj (Bohinjsko Jezero) to the south are the only sizeable sheets of water in the Julians, and both add considerable sheen to their valleys. The first is ringed by a road, the second is tree-fringed and, in places, almost fjord-like as mountains rise from the water's edge - Baedeker thought it resembled the lake at Halstatt in the Austrian Salzkammergut region, though that's to stretch the imagination somewhat. Bled, of course, is not exactly unknown, for it has long been regarded as the most famous resort in the country, and in the eighteenth century (when it was known as Veldes) was noted as a favourite watering place with fine hotels and even finer views. A small baroque pilgrimage church adorns an island in the middle of the lake, and a sixteenth century castle stands on a rock promontory above the north-eastern shore.

To reach both Bled and Bohinj from the Sava Dolinika valley, take a well-signed road breaking off the main Jesenice-Ljubljana road in an open flat plain and in four or five kilometres you come to the neat resort of Bled itself. It's also on the Trieste-Munich railway line, with a station to the west of the lake.

Bled lies at the northern end of the Sava Bohinjska valley, a valley that grows wilder and more gorge-like as you head south-west through it. The main block of the Julian Alps stands back, hidden from view, and although there are some barely-veiled sights that lift the spirits, it's not until the valley has twisted westward and opened out near Bohinj (Bohinjska Bistrica) that you begin to sense that the mountains may not be so far away after all. Here the valley becomes a broad, flat-bedded trench. The main Julians can be seen off to the north of the valley, while a secondary range, the Spodnje Bohinjske Gore, forms the southern wall. Barely touching two thousand metres, this secondary range is nonetheless an attractive one that rises in stature towards the west where it curves northward in order to close the valley off. Up there it joins other ridge spurs and confusing plateaux spilling out of the main core of the central Julians.

Several paths cross the ridge south of Bohinj, linking the town with Podbrdo in the Baska Grapa valley on the far side, by way of the Cerna Prst (1844m). Kugy wrote about this section of ridge in rapturous tones, calling it an Alpine botanical garden. Here he describes its special appeal:

> "Usually, we cross the mountain from Podbrdo to the Wochein [Bohinj]. Hay-sheds by our path denote the accustomed halts. The last group but one is a special favourite, by reason of the cheerful halts for breakfast we have here taken. ...Soon the open grassy slopes begin, with a green gully in their midst, where in August stands the purple gentian. But beautiful beyond all is the steep floor of these mountain-meadows in early summer, when the blue gentians are open...On the steep ridge to our right, edelweiss is in flower. Its stars were scattered wide over the sunny slopes when I first visited the Cerna Prst, some fifty years ago. But the malignant stream of

tourists has rooted it up, till it has withdrawn itself to a few, outlying places. ...And now we have come to a saddle. Each time we stand there in awe, for beyond the hollow of the Wochein Lake [Lake Bohinj] the Triglav has suddenly appeared, with all the white peaks of its boulder-seas. ...And so, by flowery paths, we come to the summit of the Cerna Prst; and here we lie by the hour." (*Alpine Pilgrimage*)

Bohinj is a small resort that hasn't quite found the magic touch. There's a tourist office, a few shops and a large campsite, and a railway station that is the closest to the mountains on this side of the range. The lake lies about six kilometres to the west where a cluster of buildings at Ribcev Laz offers more to the visitor than Bohinj itself, while just to the north the delightful village of Stara Fuzina provides limited accommodation amid a jumble of farms, houses, and open-sided barns that express a timeless quality. This eastern end of the lake is a popular starting place for climbs on Triglav, and a statue has been erected to commemorate the four local men who made the first ascent on 26 August 1778. A number of paths strike off to the north and north-west which lead into and onto the Triglav massif, and a good many days of a walking holiday could be spent in linking these trails and the huts they serve.

There's practically no development around Lake Bohinj itself. Trees and grassy banks project to the water's edge, although there's a campsite at the western end near Hotel Zlatorog. Nearby a cable system (cable-car and two chairlifts) operates on the south side of the valley, rising to the Vogel ski area at 1800 metres, from which point an excellent view north shows Triglav and its neighbours across the depths of the valley. A very fine high-level path leads from here round the south side of the upper Bohinj basin to the Komni and Bogatinom huts, and once there other trails could be taken into the Seven Lakes Valley.

West of Lake Bohinj the valley is closed by the rock barrier of Komarca, a scene of forest, crag and mountain. An unmade road bumps through the forest to a parking area at the Savica inn and nearby hut, from which a path (fee charged) leads to the famed Slap Savica, a waterfall that bursts from the mountain wall as the source of the Sava river. The car park also marks the start of a forest path that climbs roughly westward to the large Komni hut (Dom na Komni; 1520m), while another goes north on a direct assault of the Komarca barrier; a very steep path, through beechwoods nearly all the way and aided in places by cables, iron rungs and pegs. Above this a small forest-rimmed tarn (the Crno) is reached, and a more gentle stretch followed before the trail climbs again to enter the Seven Lakes Valley proper. This is a magical glen, spacious in outlook despite the long line of white limestone cliffs that walls it, and the setting for the legend of Zlatorog, the mythical chamois with the golden horns. Clumps of bilberry provide cushions for rocks that seem spaced apart by small larch trees that now replace the pines of the lower valley. And then a wasteland. "A waste, but how beautiful," said Longstaff, "of rolling limestone levels covered with open forest of pine. How could one expect such a bit of western America in Europe?"

The Seven Lakes hut (Koca pri Triglavskih Jezerih; 1685m) overlooks the double tarn known as Dvojno jezero that sometimes becomes a single sheet of water at the end of spring or after prolonged rainfall, and with Mala Ticarica

(2071m) overlooking it from the east. The location of this hut is such that it makes an excellent base from which to tackle a number of outings. Triglav is but one. Ticarica is another; an easily-reached summit that provides a splendid overview of the valley. A good trail also links the hut with the Bogatinom and Komni huts which lie to the south-west on the Komna plateau. Other routes provide opportunities to traverse the range in almost any direction, including a path to the west crossing the walling ridge, and another to the north-west leading into the head of the Trenta valley; one of the longest and most delightful in the Julians.

Trenta

Coming by road from the north over the Vrsic pass one gazes into a great V wedge of a valley carved through the mountains to the south and south-west. This is the valley of the Soca river which, above the village of Soca, is known as the Trenta. The Vrsic road twists down into that valley by a series of well-built hairpins, and just after passing a statue to Julius Kugy (on the left of the road), is joined by a tributary glen flowing from the right. In truth this is no tributary, for it carries the Soca itself, the source of which lies in that glen, the Zadnja Trenta. That glen makes a sweeping curve round a mountain spur, and when entered on foot a track, then footpath, entices the wanderer into a vale of enchantment. One or two tiny hamlets inhabit the glen; a scattering of barns and old cottages half-buried in the soil; a river that loses its way underground, and a cirque at its head topped by Bavski Grintavec (2344m) which is usually ascended from the valley by the north ridge, the summit of which provides a far-reaching panorama - especially fine to the high peaks at the heart of the range.

Just below the Kugy monument the Soca is joined by the Mlinarica, a stream flowing out of a rocky gorge to the left (north-east). This stream drains the southern flank of Prisojnik, but it is the next tributary glen that holds most interest for the walker, for it provides steep access on a mule path to the Pogacnikov hut below Razor; via the Luknja pass to the Vrata valley, and by way of the Cez Dol saddle and Zasavska koca hut to the Seven Lakes Valley. This glen is the Zadnjica, with the village of Trenta (formerly Na Logu) at its entrance. The village houses a National Park Visitor Centre with some fascinating exhibits, displays and audio-visual presentations. There are two or three hotels and, a short distance away, the Alpinetum Juliana botanical gardens.

Soca is the next village downstream. Although it has only limited accommodation it makes a good starting point for several expeditions. The first is an ascent of Bavski Grintavec which rises directly above the village, and via the summit the glens of Zadnja Trenta and Bavsica are both within reach. On the south side of the main Trenta (or Soca) valley routes lead over the Velika Vrata (1924m) to the Seven Lakes Valley, or through the glacier-carved Lepena glen to a pair of tarns north-east of Krn (2245m). This latter summit is also accessible to walkers, and from it a high-level traverse which leads to Kobarid in the lower Soca valley midway between Zaga and Tolmin.

An open fertile plain west of Soca village marks the confluence of the Soca and Koritnica valleys, with Bovec lying below the border with Italy. Bovec is a small town with several hotels, a youth hostel, campsites, bank, shops, bars and tourist office. Rafting trips are arranged on the Soca river, and just outside the town a gondola lift system rises to Prestreljenik (2282m) just below the frontier ridge. Walkers' passes cross the ridge nearby, while the road projecting into the Koritnica valley rises to the Predil Pass (1156m) for vehicular access (including bus) to Italy. Bovec, then, acts a good starting point for journeys, whether by road or on foot, into the western Julians.

* * *

THE JULIAN ALPS OF ITALY

Just below the Predil Pass on the Italian flank of the mountains lies the Lago di Predil with an inn and campsite at its northern end. The road forks here. One branch leads north to Cave del Predel and Tarvisio, the other skirts the lake's west shoreline and climbs through the upper Val Rio del Lago to the Nevea saddle, then descends into the Canale di Raccolana - "grand but shadeless" is how Baedeker described it. Either side of the Nevea saddle trails connect with others to explore ridge systems to both north and south, with modest summits worth collecting as well as distant glens in which to descend. Monte Canin (2587m) on the Italian-Slovenian border displays the largest Julian glacier under its north face; a limestone escarpment that carries the border for a short distance. West of the pass the Raccolana flows down to the Fella which separates the Julian and Carnic Alps, while Val Rio del Lago is fed below Cave del Predel by the tributary Val di Rio Freddo before coming to Tarvisio in Val Canale below the Austrian frontier.

Val Canale flows west and south to act as the range's outer boundary. Into it north of the Raccolana the Canale di Dogna and Valbruna drain the heartland of the Italian Julians. The headwaters of both glens have their sources within a very short distance of each other just to the north of Jof di Montasio. This magnificent peak, much loved by Kugy, is part of a group extending for nearly eight kilometres, with many tops above 2000 metres. Montasio itself appears most impressive from the upper Valbruna glen where the face is noted for its problems of route-finding, while the west face overlooking Canale di Dogna offers a remote and difficult route of ascent. The easiest, and therefore the most popular ascent route on this, the second highest Julian summit, is made from Rifugio Brazza on the Altipiano del Montasio above the Canale di Raccolana.

* * *

THE JULIAN ALPS

Location:
North-east Italy and Slovenia just to the south of the Austrian border.

Principal valleys:
In Italy these are Val Canale, Canale di Raccolana and Val Rio del Lago. On the Slovenian side these are the Trenta, Velika Pisnica, Vrata and Bohinjska.

Principal peaks:
Triglav (2864m), Jof di Montasio (2753m), Skrlatica (2740m), Mangart (2678m), Jalovec (2643m), Razor (2601m), Prisojnik (2547m)

Centres:
Tarvisio and Cave del Predel in Italy; Kranjska Gora, Mojstrana, Bohinj, Trenta and Bovec in Slovenia.

Huts:
About 40 huts and bivouacs give access to walks and climbs on both sides of the border. In the western Julians these are owned by the CAI, in Slovenia by the PZS, the national Alpine Club with an extremely large and active membership.

Access:
By rail the Venice-Tarvisio-Vienna main line is very useful for the Italian side of the mountains. The eastern Julians are served by rail on the Ljubljana-Jesenice and Trieste-Munich lines. International airports are at Venice, Verona, Trieste and Ljubljana. Local buses operate throughout much of the eastern Julians.

Maps:
Tabacco publish a sheet at 1:50,000 entitled *Alpi Giulie* (Sheet no: 8) which covers the Italian side of the mountains. IGM produce two sheets at 1:25,000 for the same district; Sheets 14 and 14a. For the Slovenian mountains PZS have two sheets at 1:50,000, *Julian Alps West* (west of Vrsic pass; includes Italian flank), and *Julian Alps East*. (Not entirely accurate!)

Guidebooks:
Walking in the Julian Alps by Simon Brown (Cicerone Press) describes 31 routes, all except one being single-day outings, based on four Slovenian resorts.

Julian Alps by Robin Collomb with M. Anderson (West Col) is primarily for climbers, but useful also for walkers.

How to Climb Triglav by Stanko Klinar (Planinska Zalozba Slovenije, Ljubljana) is a handy little pocket guide which describes (in a surprisingly good English translation) a number of routes on the highest Julian mountain. Available from tourist offices in the area.

Other reading:
Wild Italy by Tim Jepson (Sheldrake Press/Aurum Press) gives some interesting background to the natural history of the Italian Julians.

Alpine Pilgrimage by Julius Kugy (Murray, 1934). This book reveals Kugy's love affair with the Julians, and makes fascinating reading.

Mountain Paths by H.E.G. Tyndale (Eyre & Spottiswoode, 1948). Tyndale translated Kugy's book, and this collection of his climbing memoirs includes sections devoted to Kugy and the Julian Alps.

This My Voyage by T.G. Longstaff (Murray, 1950). In a book covering many ranges, Longstaff has a chapter entitled 'Eastern Julian Alps' in which he describes a tour made with Kugy from Valbruna to Santa Maria di Trenta.

Beautiful Mountains by Fanny Copeland (Yugoslav Bureau, Split, 1931). The author, a Scot, lived for forty years in Yugoslavia and climbed Triglav for the last time at the age of 86.

The Mountains of Europe by Kev Reynolds (Oxford Illustrated Press) contains a chapter devoted to the Julian Alps by Dudley Stevens.

※　　※　　※

INDEX

Text printed by
WBC Book Manufacturers Ltd., Bridgend, Mid Glamorgan, UK